Agriculture and Rural Development in a Globalizing World

Rapid structural transformation and urbanization are transforming agriculture and food production in rural areas across the world. This textbook provides a comprehensive review and assessment of the multifaceted nature of agriculture and rural development, particularly in the developing world, where the greatest challenges occur.

It is designed around five thematic parts: Agricultural Intensification and Technical Change; Political Economy of Agricultural Policies; Community and Rural Institutions; Agriculture, Nutrition, and Health; and Future Relevance of International Institutions. Each chapter presents a detailed but accessible review of the literature on the specific topic and discusses the frontiers in research and institutional changes needed as societies adapt to the transformation processes. All authors are eminent scholars with international reputations, who have been actively engaged in the contemporary debates around agricultural development and rural transformation.

Prabhu Pingali is a professor in the Charles H. Dyson School of Applied Economics and Management at Cornell University, New York, with a joint appointment in the Division of Nutritional Sciences. He is Founding Director of the Tata–Cornell Institute for Agriculture and Nutrition (TCI).

Gershon Feder is Chair of the Publications Review Committee at the International Food Policy Research Institute (IFPRI), Washington DC. Previously he held various positions at the World Bank, most recently Senior Research Manager at the Development Research Group.

Other books in the Earthscan Food and Agriculture Series

For further details please visit the series page on the Routledge website:
http://www.routledge.com/books/series/ECEFA/

Agriculture and Rural Development in a Globalizing World

Challenges and Opportunities

Edited by
Prabhu Pingali and Gershon Feder

LONDON AND NEW YORK

from Routledge

First published 2017
by Routledge
2 Park Square, Milton Park, Abingdon, Oxon OX14 4RN

and by Routledge
711 Third Avenue, New York, NY 10017

Routledge is an imprint of the Taylor & Francis Group, an informa business

British Library Cataloguing-in-Publication Data
A catalogue record for this book is available from the British Library

Library of Congress Cataloging-in-Publication Data
Names: Pingali, Prabhu L., 1955– editor. | Feder, Gershon, 1947– editor.
Title: Agriculture and rural development in a globalizing world :
    challenges and opportunities / edited by Prabhu Pingali and
    Gershon Feder.
Description: London ; New York : Routledge, 2017. | Series: Earthscan
    food and agriculture | Includes bibliographical references and index.
Identifiers: LCCN 2016052335 | ISBN 9781138231818 (hbk) |
    ISBN 9781138231825 (pbk) | ISBN 9781315314051 (ebk)
Subjects: LCSH: Agriculture—Research—Developing countries. |
    Rural development—Developing countries. | Agricultural innovations—
    Developing countries.
Classification: LCC S495 .A37 2017 | DDC 338.109172/4—dc23
LC record available at https://lccn.loc.gov/2016052335

ISBN: 978-1-138-23181-8 (hbk)
ISBN: 978-1-138-23182-5 (pbk)
ISBN: 978-1-315-31405-1 (ebk)

Typeset in Bembo
by Apex CoVantage, LLC

Contents

Abbreviations

AAEA	Agricultural and Applied Economics Association
AARES	Australian Agricultural and Resource Economics Society
AAWE	American Association of Wine Economists
AET	Agricultural evolution theory
ADB	Asian Development Bank
AfDB	African Development Bank
AFS	Agri-food systems
AGC	Agricultural growth corridor
AGRA	Alliance for a Green Revolution in Africa
AMP	Australian Mutual Provident Society
ANU	Australian National University
APPS	Asia and the Pacific Policy Society
ARD	Agricultural and Rural Development
ARS	USDA Agricultural Research Service
ASA	African Studies Association
ASSA	Academy of the Social Sciences in Australia
BAGC	Beira Agricultural Growth Corridor
BMI	Body mass index
Bt	*Bacillus thuringiensis*
CAADP	Comprehensive Africa Agriculture Development Programme
CADENA	Agricultural Fund for Natural Disasters (Mexico)
CDC	Commonwealth Development Corporation
CDD	Community-driven development
CDD/R	Community-driven development and reconstruction
CEIS	Center of Economic International Studies, University of Rome
CEPR	Center for Economic and Policy Research
CERVO	Community Early Recovery Voucher Scheme
CFS	Committee on World Food Security
CGIAR	Consultative Group on International Agricultural Research (formerly)
CIAT	Centro Internacional de Agricultura Tropical
CIDA	Canadian International Developmental Agency

CIDSS	Comprehensive Integrated Delivery of Social Service
CIFOR	Center for International Forestry Research
CIMMYT	International Maize and Wheat Improvement Center (Centro Internacional de Mejoramiento de Maiz y Trigo)
CIP	International Potato Center
CMA	Centre for Management in Agriculture
CNMI	Combined Normalized Malnutrition Index
CNSM	Comprehensive Nutrition Survey in Maharashtra (India)
COP	Community of practice
CPF	Country Partnership Framework
CPI	Consumer price index
CPIA	Country Policy and Institutional Assessment
CRP	CGIAR Research Program
CRS	Constant returns to scale
CTA	Technical Centre for Agricultural and Rural Cooperation
CV	Coefficient of variation
DAC	Development Assistance Committee
DB	Doing Business indicators (World Bank)
DfID	Department for International Development (UK)
DHS	Demographic and Health Surveys
DMSP	Defense Meteorological Satellite Program
DPF	Development policy financing
DRC	Democratic Republic of the Congo (DRC)
EA	Enumeration area
ECA	Economic Commission for Africa
EPZ	Export processing zone
ERVO	Early recovery voucher
ESPA	Eastern Snake River Plain Aquifer Area
FAO	Food and Agriculture Organization of the United Nations
FCS	Fragile and conflict-affected states
FEWSNET	Famine Early Warning Systems Network
FF	Ford Foundation
FOC	First-order condition
FPI	Food price volatility
FSIN	Food Security Information Network
GATT	General Agreement on Tariffs and Trade (now WTO)
GCARD	Global Conference on Agricultural Research for Development
GCFSI	Global Center for Food Systems Innovation
GDP	Gross domestic product
GGDC	Groningen Growth and Development Centre
GIP	Global Integrating Program
GIZ	Deutsche Gesellschaft für Internationale Zusammenarbeit
GLEE	Global Learning and Evidence Exchange
GMO	Genetically modified organism

GNI	Gross national income
GPFI	Global Partnership for Financial Inclusion
GPG	Global public goods
GSDRC	Government and Social Development Research Centre
GVOAL	Gross Value of Output from Agriculture and Livestock
ha	hectare
HAZ	Height-for-age z-score
HT	Herbicide tolerance
HYV	High-yielding crop variety
IAAE	International Association of Agricultural Economists
IAMO	Institute of Agricultural Development in Central and Eastern Europe
IBI	Index-based insurance
IBLI	Index-Based Livestock Insurance
IBLIP	Index-Based Livestock Insurance Project
IBRD	International Bank for Reconstruction and Development
ICABR	International Consortium on Applied Bioeconomy Research
ICARDA	International Center for Agricultural Research in the Dry Areas
ICDS	Integrated Child Development System (India)
ICRISAT	International Crops Research Institute for the Semi-Arid Tropics
ICT	Information and communications technology
IDA	International Development Association
IDO	Intermediate Development Outcome
IDWR	Idaho Department of Water Resources
IEG	Independent Evaluation Group (World Bank)
IFAD	International Fund for Agricultural Development
IFC	International Finance Corporation
IFPRI	International Food Policy Research Institute
IHDS	Indian Human Development Survey
IIASA	International Institute of Applied Systems Analysis
IIED	International Institute for Environment and Development, London
IITA	International Institute of Tropical Agriculture
ILCA	International Livestock Center for Africa
ILO–GET	International Labor Office–Global Employment Trend
ILRI	International Livestock Research Institute
InSTePP	International Science and Technology Practice and Policy
IP	Intellectual property
IPCC	Intergovernmental Panel on Climate Change
IPF	Investment Project Financing
IR	Insect resistance
IR	Inverse relationship (farm size–productivity relationship)
IRC	International Rescue Center

IRI	International Research Institute for Climate and Society
IRRI	International Rice Research Institute
ISAAA	International Service for the Acquisition of Agri-Biotech Applications
ISNAR	International Service for National Agricultural Research
ISPC	Independent Science and Partnership Council
ISRIC	International Soil Reference and Information Centre
ISSCAS	Institute of Soil Science–Chinese Academy of Sciences
ITC	Internal transaction costs
ITU	International Telecommunication Union
IV	Instrumental variable
IWMI	International Water Management Institute
IYCF	Infant and Young Child Feeding (WHO)
JRC	Joint Research Centre (of the European Commission)
KTDA	Kenyan Tea Development Authority
LAC	Latin America and the Caribbean
LAIS	Land Administration Information System
LAQI	Land Administration Quality Index
LCDD	Local and Community-Driven Development
LEAP	Livelihoods, Early Assessment and Protection
LI-BIRD	Local Initiatives for Biodiversity, Research and Development
LP	Land productivity
LPP	Livelihood Protection Policy
LRM	Linear regression model
LSMS–ISA	Living Standards Measurement Study–Integrated Surveys on Agriculture Initiative
LUSIP	Lower Usuthu Smallholder Irrigation Project
MCC	Millennium Challenge Corporation
MDGs	Millennium Development Goals
MDMS	Mid-Day Meal Scheme (India)
MFP	Multifactor productivity
MFR	Male-to-female sex ratio
MTC	Market transaction costs
MUV	Manufactures Unit Value
NAHEP	National Agricultural Higher Education Project (India)
NAMI	Normalized Adult Malnutrition Index
NARS	National agricultural research system
NASS	National Agricultural Statistics Service
NCMI	Normalized Child Malnutrition Index
NFHS	National Family Health Survey (India)
NGO	Nongovernmental organization
NSP	National Solidarity Program, Afghanistan
ODA	Official Development Assistance
OECD	Organisation for Economic Co-operation and Development
PBA	Performance-based allocation

PCGSDPAA	Per Capita Gross State Domestic Product from Agriculture & Allied Activities
PDS	Public Distribution System (India)
PPR	Portfolio Performance Rating
PSNP	Protective Safety Net Program
PPP	Public–private partnership
QRM	Quantile-regression model
RCT	Randomized controlled trial
REPOA	Research for Poverty Alleviation
RF	Rockefeller Foundation
RIICE	Remote sensing-based Information and Insurance for Crops for Emerging economies
RICE	Research Institute for Compassionate Economics
RNRA	Rwandan National Resource Authority
RSOC	Rapid Survey of Children
SA	South Asia
SADEV	Swedish Agency for Development Evaluation
SAGCOT	Southern Agricultural Growth Corridor of Tanzania
SAT	Semi-arid tropics
sd	Standard deviation
SDC	Swiss Agency for Development and Cooperation
SDGs	Sustainable Development Goals
SFS	Security Farm Supply
SLM	Sector land manager
SLO	System-Level Outcome
SNDP	State Net Domestic Product (SNDP)
SOAS	School of Oriental and African Studies, University of London
SOMECO	Sociedad de Melhoramentos e Colonização
SQUAT	Sanitation, Quality, Use, Access and Trends survey
SRF	Strategy and Results Framework
SSA	Sub-Saharan Africa
ST	Structural transformation
SWMnet	Soil and Water Management Network (Nairobi)
TAC	Technical Advisory Committee
TCI	Tata-Cornell Institute for Agriculture and Nutrition
TFP	Total factor productivity
TSC	Total Sanitation Campaign (India)
UNCTAD	United Nations Conference on Trade and Development
UN DESA	United Nations Department of Economic and Social Affairs
UNDP	United Nations Development Programme
UNEP	United Nations Environmental Programme
UNICEF	United Nations Children's Fund
UNIDO	United Nations Industrial Development Organization
UNOPS	United Nations Office for Project Services
UN SCN	United Nations System Standing Committee on Nutrition

USDA	United States Department of Agriculture
USSP	Uganda Strategy Support Program
VR	Virus-resistant
WAZ	Weight-for-age z-score
WDR	World Development Report
WFP	World Food Programme
WHO	World Health Organization
WHZ	Weight-for-height z-score
WTO	World Trade Organization
ZEF	Center for Development Research, Bonn

Contributors

Kym Anderson is the George Gollin Professor of Economics at the University of Adelaide in Australia, where he has been affiliated since 1984. Previously he was a Research Fellow at the Australian National University's Research School of Pacific and Asian Studies (1977–1983), and in 2012 he rejoined ANU part-time as a Professor of Economics in its Crawford School of Public Policy. He was on extended leave at the Economic Research division of the GATT (now WTO) Secretariat in Geneva during 1990–1992 and at the World Bank's Research Group in Washington, DC, as Lead Economist (Trade Policy) during 2004–2007. He is a Fellow of the Agricultural and Applied Economics Association (AAEA), Australian Agricultural and Resource Economics Society (AARES), American Association of Wine Economists (AAWE), Academy of the Social Sciences in Australia (ASSA), Asia and the Pacific Policy Society (APPS), and the Center for Economic and Policy Research (CEPR). He is also Chair of the Board of Trustees of the Washington, DC–based International Food Policy Research Institute (IFPRI). He has published more than 350 articles and 35 books, including *The Political Economy of Agricultural Protection* (with Yujiro Hayami, 1986), *Disarray in World Food Markets* (with Rod Tyers, 1992), *The World's Wine Markets: Globalization at Work* (2004), *Agricultural Trade Reform and the Doha Development Agenda* (with Will Martin, 2006), and during 2008–2010, a set of four regional and three global books on distortions to agricultural incentives. His publications have received a number of awards from professional associations, including the Australian, European, and American Agricultural and Applied Economics associations. In 2014, he received an honorary Doctor of Economics degree from the University of Adelaide and in 2015, he became a Companion of the Order of Australia (AC).

Derek Byerlee is an Adjunct Professor in the School of Foreign Service, Georgetown University, Washington DC, specializing in land use, agricultural development, and food security. He has held senior positions at Michigan State University, the International Maize and Wheat Improvement Center (CIMMYT) in Mexico and South Asia, and in the World Bank, where he was the lead author of the *2008 World Development Report: Agriculture for*

Development. During his career, he has published widely in several fields of agricultural development and serves on a number of international advisory groups on agricultural science and global food security.

Jacomina de Regt worked for the World Bank for over 30 years in many different sectors and capacities, last as coordinator for Community-Driven Development for the Africa Region. She currently works as an independent consultant on community-driven development with development agencies, as well as for the private sector interested in market chain sustainability. She lived through the civil war and peace process in Mozambique and used this experience as a touchstone while writing *Designing Community-Driven Development Operations in Fragile and Conflict-Affected Situations: Lessons from a Stocktaking*, a 2013 World Bank publication on the issues confronting the design of community development programs in a post-conflict environment. She actively applies development experience to grassroots empowerment work in the region she lives in. Jacomina is a rural sociologist who holds a Master of Science degree from Wageningen University in the Netherlands.

Klaus Deininger is a Lead Economist at the World Bank's Development Research Group. His research focus is on income and asset inequality and its relationship to poverty reduction and growth; and land tenure and land reform and their impact on individual and household welfare, effective land use, and structural change. In addition to more than 70 journal articles, he has authored books, including reports on land policies for growth and poverty reduction and on large-scale land acquisition, that are among the most widely quoted in the agricultural economics literature and with enormous policy influence – the Land Governance Assessment he developed has been applied in more than 40 countries. He launched the Annual World Bank Conference on Land and Poverty and, over 16 years, developed it into the central event for the land community, with participants from more than 120 countries. By helping to improve access to and interoperability of survey, administrative, and remotely sensed data, he has made significant contributions to policy, research, and capacity building. He holds a PhD in applied economics from the University of Minnesota, an MA in agricultural economics from the University of Berlin, and an MA in theology from the University of Bonn.

Gershon Feder is currently the chair of the International Food Policy Research Institute's (IFPRI's) Publications Review Committee. He has contributed to agricultural and development economics as the author of dozens of seminal and widely cited and articles and books. He received a BA (with distinction) in Economics and Development Studies from Tel-Aviv University, and a PhD in Agricultural Economics from the University of California (Berkeley). He undertook various positions at the World Bank, from which he retired in 2008 as Senior Research Manager. He joined IFPRI in 2009. Through his published research, he made contributions in the fields of land policy, extension impact evaluation, the economics of technology diffusion, and farmer behavior under uncertainty. His early works on other development economics topics, such as sovereign debt-servicing capacity and the contribution of exports to economic growth, continue to be cited in recent literature. He served as an associate editor of the *American Journal of Agricultural Economics* (1991–1994) and co-editor of the *World Bank Research Observer* (1998–2008). His achievements were recognized by the agricultural economics profession, with two of his co-authored works receiving the Quality of Research Discovery Award from the American Agricultural Economics Association (AAEA), and two works awarded the Publication of Enduring Quality Award. In 2005, he was inducted as a Fellow of the AAEA.

Sambuddha Goswami has been working with Dr. Uma Lele as a Researcher since 2009 on a variety of papers. After completing his master's degree in Economics from Delhi School of Economics, his work has included data analysis, research support, and co-authoring of papers, presentations, and publications. This has involved assembly and analysis of metadata sets and reviews of a diverse bodies of literature in the areas of structural transformation, productivity growth, food, agriculture, nutrition, water and forest management, poverty, health, gender, energy and the environment, global public goods, external assistance and partnerships. The focus has been on the overall global challenges and the sources of global, regional, and country-level growth in demand for and supply of food and agriculture, and the related changes in the environment. He served as consultant (November 2014–April 2016) at the Agricultural Development Economics Division (ESA) of FAO Statistics Division to support the Technical Working Group on Measuring Food and Nutrition Security of the Food Security Information Network (FSIN) of FAO, WFP and IFPRI, and at the World Bank (December 2015–June 2016) on National Agricultural Higher Education Project (NAHEP) in India. He is currently co-authoring a book, titled *Food for All: International Organizations and the Transformation of Agriculture* (Oxford University Press, forthcoming in 2017).

Peter Hazell trained as an agriculturalist in England before completing his PhD in agricultural economics at Cornell University in 1970. He has held various research positions at the World Bank and the International Food Policy Research Institute (IFPRI), including serving as Director of the Environment and Production Technology Division and the Development Strategy and Governance Division at IFPRI. He later became a Visiting Professor at the Centre for Environmental Policy, Imperial College, London and a Professorial Research Associate at the School of Oriental and African Studies (SOAS), University of London. Peter's extensive and widely cited publications include works on new methods of using mathematical programming to solve farm and agricultural sector planning problems; the impact of technological change on growth and poverty reduction; the appropriate role of agricultural insurance in developing countries; agriculture's growth linkages to the rural nonfarm economy; sustainable development strategies for marginal lands; and the role of agriculture and small farms in economic development. Peter has worked extensively throughout Africa, Asia, the Middle East, and Central America, and is an elected Fellow of the American and African Agricultural Economics Associations. He currently lives in Santa Barbara, California, where he works as an independent researcher.

Ulrich Hess is Senior Advisor at the Deutsche Gesellschaft für Internationale Zusammenarbeit GIZ advising the German Federal Ministry for Economic Cooperation and Development/(BMZ) on agricultural insurance and climate risk insurance. He leads the agricultural component of the Global Initiative for Access to Insurance sector project and leads the direct climate risk insurance implementation component within the Global InsuResilience Project. Prior to joining GIZ, he worked at MicroEnsure, a microinsurance broker, and as Senior Economist at the World Bank Group from 1998 to 2012. He pioneered operational work on weather risk management and index-based insurance at the World Bank Group – for example, assisting successful weather index–based insurance initiatives in India in 2003, Malawi in 2004, Ethiopia in 2005, and in Anhui, China, in 2007. While on secondment to the World Food Programme (WFP) as chief of Disaster Risk Reduction, he pioneered systemic drought risk management with LEAP (Livelihoods, Early Assessment, Protection) in Ethiopia. Prior to joining the World Bank, as a young professional in 1998, Mr. Hess worked in management and development consulting. He is the editor and co-author of *Managing Agricultural Production Risk*, and *Weather-Based Insurance in Southern Africa* at the World Bank, and *Index Insurance and Climate Risk*, published by the International Research Institute for Climate and Society (IRI), as well as numerous publications on risk management, including most recently *Innovations and Emerging Trends in Agricultural Insurance*, published by the Global Partnership for Financial Inclusion (GPFI)/GIZ. Mr. Hess holds a Master in Economics degree from Bocconi University, Milan, and a Master in Political Science degree from Freie Universität, Berlin. He also studied at Institut d'Etudes Politiques de Paris and Yale Law School.

Maros Ivanic, an economist, has worked at the International Finance Corporation and with the Agriculture and Rural Development team of the Development Economics Research Group at the World Bank, Bank, where he analyzed issues related to international trade and poverty. Previously, he worked at the Gulf Organization for Industrial Consulting in Qatar and the Center for Global Trade Analysis at Purdue University. Dr. Ivanic holds a PhD in Agricultural Economics from Purdue University. He is author of several journal articles and book chapters on the topics of international trade liberalization and poverty assessment.

Johann Kirsten is Professor and Director of the Bureau for Economic Research (BER) at the University of Stellenbosch. At the time of the Festschrift conference in August 2015, he was Professor of Agricultural Economics and head of the Department of Agricultural Economics, Extension and Rural Development at the University of Pretoria, a position he occupied for 20 years until his resignation on July 31, 2016. He was born in Cape Town and matriculated from the Hoërskool Jan van Riebeeck in Cape Town in 1979. Subsequently, he enrolled for undergraduate studies at the University of Stellenbosch and completed the BSc Agric degree and a BSc Agric (Hons) degree in Agricultural Economics. He started his career as an agricultural economist in the Department of Agriculture in Pretoria and also enrolled for postgraduate studies at the University of Pretoria. He obtained a master's degree and PhD degree in Agricultural Economics at the University of Pretoria and joined the University of Pretoria as lecturer in 1992. He served as a council member of the National Agricultural Marketing Council in South Africa from 2001 to 2011 and was also appointed by the Minister of Agriculture as Chair of the Food Price Committee during 2003–2004. He also served as the Vice-President of the International Association of Agricultural Economists from 2006 to 2009.

Uma Lele is an independent scholar and development economist, with a PhD from Cornell University and well over four decades of experience in research, operations, management, policy analysis, advisory services, and evaluation. A significant part of her professional work has been carried out at the World Bank, as well as other international organizations, Cornell University, the University of Florida, and the Carter Center. She has published extensively and worked for, advised, or been supported by numerous international agencies (e.g., the CGIAR, FAO, IFAD, UNICEF, and UNDP), and philanthropic organizations (Rockefeller, McArthur, and Bill and Melinda Gates Foundations). She has worked in the areas of food and agriculture, the environment, public health, science and technology, aid and finance, and evaluation. She has served on several boards and advisory committees. She is a Fellow of India's National Academy of Agricultural Sciences, American Applied Economic Association, and was designated Distinguished Alumnus of Cornell University. She was awarded a Lifetime Achievement Award by the Indian Society of Agricultural Economics, and "Honorary Life Membership" by the International Association of Agricultural Economics. In 2017, she was awarded India's prestigious B. P. Pal Award of the National Academy of Agricultural Sciences for "singular outstanding overall contribution to agriculture" and the M. S. Swaminathan Award by the Trust for the Advancement of Agricultural Sciences, for "lifetime achievement in leadership in agriculture." She has established a mentoring program at the American Applied Economic Association and an award for best research in gender at International Agricultural Economic Association. She has written or edited six books, several book-length World Bank reports, and journal articles. Further information on her activities and list of publications is available at http://www.umalele.org.

Man Li is a Research Fellow at the Environment and Production Technology Division, International Food Policy Research Institute. She received her PhD from the Applied Economics Department (AREc) at Oregon State University in 2010. Her research interests include the intersection of land economics, spatial modeling, economic geography, and water economics.

Frikkie Liebenberg was a Senior Lecturer at the Department of Agricultural Economics, Extension and Rural Development, Faculty of Natural and Agricultural Sciences, University of Pretoria, since 2013, focusing on agricultural productivity, research policy, and impact analysis. He was a Research Fellow of the International Science and Technology Practice and Policy (InSTePP) center at the University of Minnesota, and a Theme Coordinator for the database on African Agricultural Censuses under the Harvest Choice program, a collaborative program between InSTePP and IFPRI. A South African citizen, Frikkie earned both his BSc (Agric) and MSc (Agric) in Agricultural Economics at the University of Pretoria and a master's degree in International Agricultural Marketing at the University of Newcastle-Upon-Tyne in Great Britain, followed by his PhD at Pretoria University (with technical leadership from Prof. Phil Pardey of the University of Minnesota). Prior to joining the University of Pretoria as a Research Officer in 2010, he worked as a senior researcher at the Agricultural Research Council (ARC) from 1997 to 2010, engaging in policy analysis and assisting in the implementation of a series of institutional change initiatives implemented by the ARC and the Department of Agriculture. From 2003 to 2008, at the Agricultural Engineering Institute of the ARC, he was involved in research and training on monitoring and evaluation methodologies, some in collaboration with the International Service for National Agricultural Research (ISNAR), and served as an Advisory Committee member of the Agricultural Science and Technology Initiative of IFPRI. Prior to joining ARC, he worked at the Western Cape Department of Agriculture, and earlier, as senior researcher on the Agrifutura Project at Stellenbosch University and an economist at the Directorate of Marketing of the South African Department of Agriculture. Dr. Liebenberg died tragically at his home in Bronkhorstpruit, northeast of Pretoria, South Africa, on March 10, 2017, after being shot through a window by unknown assailants.

Michael Lipton is an economist working on agricultural development, economic demography, poverty analysis, and rural–urban relations. Books include *Why Poor People Stay Poor: Urban Bias in World Development* (1977), *New Seeds and Poor People* (with Richard Longhurst, 1989), and *Land Reform in Developing Countries: Property Rights and Property Wrongs* (2009), plus over 150 papers (see http://www.michaellipton.net). He is currently writing *Malthus in Africa?* He is Emeritus Professor of Economics, Sussex University; Emeritus Fellow, Institute of Development Studies; and a Fellow of the British Academy. He has worked mainly in Bangladesh, Botswana, India, South Africa, and Sri Lanka, and at the International Food Policy Research Institute, the International Fund for Agricultural Development (lead scholar for the *2001 Rural Poverty Report*), and the World Bank.

William J. Martin is Senior Research Fellow at the International Food Policy Research Institute (IFPRI) and President of the International Association of Agricultural Economists (IAAE). His recent research has focused primarily on the impacts of changes in food and trade policies, and food prices on poverty and food security in developing countries. His research has also examined the impact of major trade policy reforms – including the Uruguay Round, the Doha Development Agenda, and China's accession to the WTO – on developing countries, implications of climate change for poor people, and implications of improvements in agricultural productivity in developing countries. He trained in economics and agricultural economics at the University of Queensland, the Australian National University, and Iowa State University and worked at the Australian Bureau of Agricultural Economics, the Australian National University, and the World Bank before joining IFPRI in 2015.

William A. Masters is a Professor in the Friedman School of Nutrition Science and Policy, with a secondary appointment in Tufts University's Department of Economics. From 2011 to 2014, he served as chair of the Friedman School's Department of Food and Nutrition Policy, and before coming to Tufts was a faculty member in Agricultural Economics at Purdue University (1991–2010), and also at the University of Zimbabwe (1989–1990), Harvard's Kennedy School of Government (2000), and Columbia University (2003–2004). He is the co-author of an undergraduate textbook, *Economics of Agricultural Development: World Food Systems and Resource Use* (Routledge, 3rd ed., 2014).

Alex F. McCalla is Professor of Agricultural and Resource Economics, Emeritus, and Professor of Management, Emeritus, at the University of California at Davis. Born in Canada in 1937, he received his first two degrees from the University of Alberta and a PhD in Agricultural Economics from the University of Minnesota in 1966. From 1966–1994, he was a Professor at UC–Davis, where he also served as Dean of the College of Agricultural and Environmental Sciences (1970–75) and Founding Dean, Graduate School of Management (1979–1981). Dr. McCalla is best known for his research in international trade. He has been named a Fellow by three Agricultural Economics Associations – the American in 1988, the Canadian in 2000, and the Western in 2004. He served as the Chair of the Technical Advisory Committee (TAC) of the Consultative Group on International Agricultural Research (CGIAR) from 1988 to 1994. Retiring from UC–Davis in June 1994, he was appointed Director of the Agriculture and Natural Resources, later renamed Rural Development, at the World Bank in Washington, DC, in September 1994. He retired from the World Bank in December 1999. In 1998, he was awarded the Degree of Doctor of Science, *honoris causa*, by McGill University in Montreal, and the Doctor's Degree of Honor by the Georgian State Agrarian University in 2004. In 2014, he was awarded a DSc by the University of Alberta. He served as Chair of the Board of CIMMYT (International Maize and Wheat Improvement Center, a CGIAR Center in Mexico, 2001–2005) and member of the Board of the Danforth Plant Science Center in St. Louis, 1998–2012.

John Murray McIntire is an independent economist, living in Santa Barbara, California. He received his PhD in International Relations from the Fletcher School in 1980. He was an agricultural economist at the International Crops Research Institute for the Semi-Arid Tropics (ICRISAT) for several years in the 1980s, working in Burkina Faso and Niger, where he did some of the first management studies of smallholder agriculture in Francophone Africa. He subsequently was a researcher at the International Livestock Center for Africa (ILCA) in Ethiopia, work that led to the publication of *Crop–Livestock Interactions in Sub-Saharan Africa*, of which he is principal author. He worked for more than 20 years as a staff member and Director at the World Bank, where he managed some of the Bank's largest programs in sub-Saharan Africa. He recently retired as Associate Vice-President for Program Management at the International Fund for Agricultural Development (IFAD). He is currently working on two long-term studies of agriculture in the tropics.

Gianluigi Nico holds a PhD in economics and statistics from the University of Chieti–Pescara (Italy), where he focused his research on a macroeconometric model aimed at assessing policy actions to reduce decent work deficits in Greece during the crisis. He is currently a consultant specializing on rural decent work statistics at the Food and Agriculture Organization of the United Nations. Gianluigi previously worked at the International Labour Office in Geneva, where he carried out analysis on the impact of trade openness on decent work creation.

Prabhu Pingali is a professor in the Charles H. Dyson School of Applied Economics and Management at Cornell University, with a joint appointment in the Division of Nutritional Sciences, and the Founding Director of the Tata-Cornell Institute for Agriculture and Nutrition (TCI). Prior to joining Cornell, he was the Deputy Director of the Agricultural Development Division of the Bill & Melinda Gates Foundation, from 2008 to May 2013. Pingali was elected to the US National Academy of Sciences in 2007. He is also a Fellow of the American Association of Agricultural Economists. He has over three decades of experience working with some of the leading international agricultural development organizations as a research economist, development practitioner, and senior manager. He has written ten books and over 100 refereed journal articles and book chapters on food policy.

Tanvi Rao is a PhD candidate at the Dyson School of Applied Economics and Management at Cornell University and a Research Scholar at the TATA-Cornell Institute for Agriculture and Nutrition (TCI). Her research fields are development economics and applied econometrics, and she works on both education- and health-related research in developing economies. She holds an MS degree from the same department, and prior to coming to Cornell, she obtained a bachelor's degree in economics from Delhi University's Shri Ram College of Commerce.

Daniel S. Robinson is a dual master's degree candidate studying food policy and development economics at Tufts University's Fletcher School of Law & Diplomacy and Friedman School of Nutrition Science & Policy. Daniel worked on agricultural development and food security programs for USAID/ Ethiopia during the summer of 2015 and for Abt Associates during the summer and fall of 2016. Before starting graduate school, Daniel worked as a Corporate Responsibility & Sustainability Associate in the Ghanaian cocoa industry for Olam International, as part of a Princeton in Africa Fellowship.

Mark W. Rosegrant is the Director of the Environment and Production Technology Division, International Food Policy Research Institute (IFPRI). With a PhD in Public Policy from the University of Michigan, he currently directs research on climate change, water resources, sustainable land management, genetic resources and biotechnology, and agriculture and energy. He is the author or editor of 15 books and over 100 papers in refereed journals, on agricultural economics, water resources, and food policy analysis. Rosegrant has won numerous awards and is a Fellow of the American Association for the Advancement of Science, and a Fellow of the Agricultural and Applied Economics Association.

Sara Savastano is Senior Economist at the World Bank for the Development Economics Vice Presidency. She joined Enabling the Business of Agriculture in January 2016, and works as topic leader for land. She is an Assistant Professor in Economics at the University of Rome Tor Vergata, currently on leave. After working from 2001 to 2005 at the Development Research Group of the World Bank, she served as an Economist at the Public Investment Evaluation Unit of the Italian Ministry of Economy and Finance until 2008, when she moved to academia. She is Secretary General of the International Consortium on Applied Bioeconomy Research (ICABR). Her research focuses on land policies and institutions, rural development, agriculture efficiency and productivity, and technology adoption. She has been a consultant to the Food and Agriculture Organization of the United Nations (FAO), World Bank, IFPRI, United Nations Industrial Development Organization (UNIDO); Enam, Ambrosetti s.r.l., Alpetunnel GEIE, and the Italian Ministry of Labor. She holds a PhD in Economics from the University of Rome Tor Vergata.

Pasquale Lucio Scandizzo, who holds a PhD from the University of California at Berkeley, is Professor of Political Economy and Senior Fellow of the Economic Foundation and the Center of Economic International Studies (CEIS) at the University of Rome Tor Vergata. He is President of the Italian Association of Development Economists. He was Senior Economist and Resident Representative with the World Bank, and held several senior positions in government institutions in Italy. He has widely published on topics of development economics and is presently advising the World Bank and other international institutions on the evaluation of policies of sustainable development.

Greg Traxler is a Senior Lecturer in the Evans School of Public Policy and Governance at the University of Washington. Prior to this position, he was Senior Program Officer at the Bill & Melinda Gates Foundation (2008–2014) and Professor in the Department of Agricultural Economics at Auburn University (1990–2008). He was also an Affiliate Scientist in the Economics Program at the International Maize and Wheat Improvement Center (1996–2003). He holds a PhD in Agricultural Economics from Iowa State University, an MS in Agricultural Economics from the University of Minnesota, and a BBA in Economics from the University of Portland. Traxler's research and teaching focus on the economics of science and technology. He has authored studies on the impacts of genetically modified organisms (GMO) – GMO cotton in the United States and Mexico, GMO soybeans in Argentina, and GMO papaya in Thailand. Other studies have looked at the effect of monopoly power and economies of size in technology generation, and on the value of pre-commercial germplasm. At the Gates Foundation, Traxler developed and managed a portfolio of grants to support building the capacity for agricultural policy analysis and implementation in sub-Saharan Africa and South Asia. Traxler served as a member of the National Academies of Sciences Committee, Global Challenges and Directions for Agricultural Biotechnology: Mapping the Course, from 2004 to 2006.

Joachim von Braun is Director of the Center for Development Research (ZEF), Bonn University, and Professor for Economic and Technological Change. His research is on economic development, science and technology policy, poverty reduction, food and nutrition security, resource economics, and trade. He is Chair of the Bioeconomy Council of the Federal German Government. Prof. von Braun is a member of the German Academy of Science and Engineering (Acatech); member of the Pontifical Academy of Sciences of the Vatican; and fellow of African Academy of Science and of American Association for the Advancement of Sciences. He was Director General of the International Food Policy Research Institute (IFPRI), based in Washington, DC, from 2002 to 2009, and President of the International Association of Agricultural Economists (IAAE).

Wenchao Xu is an associate professor in the Economics Department at Xiamen University, with dual appointments from both the School of Economics and Wang Yanan Institute for Studies in Economics (WISE). He received his PhD from the Applied Economics Department (AREc) at Oregon State University in 2010. Prior to joining Xiamen University in September 2015, he was a postdoctoral research associate for Idaho National Science Foundation EPS-CoR program at Boise State University. His research interests are in the areas of agricultural land use, water resources allocation, local water governance, water rights, and sustainable development for rural communities.

Preface

In honor of Hans Binswanger

This book is a Festschrift based on a conference held on August 7, 2015, in Milan, Italy, to honor Hans Binswanger for his incredible contributions to the agricultural and development economics community. Hans's seminal contributions have shaped the thinking and direction of academic research in many of the thematic areas covered in this book. As a senior manager at the World Bank, Hans has shown that high-quality applied research contributes directly to good development practice. Hans Binswanger is a friend, colleague, and mentor to both of us, and we were delighted to organize this Festschrift and to edit it in his honor.

The Festschrift brings together a large number of Hans's long-term colleagues, collaborators, and friends, many of them outstanding luminaries themselves in agricultural and development economics. The Festschrift volume benefits from their insightful contributions. Hans's siblings, daughter, and their families also attended the conference in Milan. Hans's twin brother, Richard Binswanger, gave us a unique perspective on how their rural upbringing instilled in Hans the passion for agricultural economics and rural development.

We would like to thank all our colleagues who attended the conference and wrote the chapters that are in this Festschrift. Richard Binswanger and Ingrid Binswanger (Hans's daughter) helped coordinate the participation of Hans's family at the conference. Mary-Catherine French from Cornell University deserves our gratitude for having spent an extraordinary amount of time managing the logistics of the conference, as well as coordinating the book preparation. Tanvi Rao and Sara Savastano were extremely helpful in managing the conference. Finally, we are grateful to Patricia Mason for her excellent editorial work.

Prabhu Pingali and Gershon Feder

1   Introduction

Prabhu Pingali and Gershon Feder

Over the past 50 years, we have seen tremendous progress in poverty reduction and overall economic development across much of the developing world. The incidence of poverty in nonmember countries of the Organisation for Economic Co-operation and Development (OECD), as measured by the proportion of the population living under $1.25 a day, has dropped from 47 percent in 1990 to 14 percent in 2015 (World Bank 2016). The United Nations reports that developing countries, in aggregate, have achieved the Millennium Development Goal (MDG) poverty reduction target. However, there are significant regional differences, with sub-Saharan Africa and South Asia lagging behind on poverty, hunger, and other welfare indicators.

Several dozen countries in Asia and Latin America have graduated to middle-income status, some well on their way to becoming developed countries. In most of these countries, agricultural growth has played an important role in "jumpstarting" overall economic development and in moving countries along the structural transformation pathway (Timmer 2010). Agricultural growth, often associated with the Green Revolution, focused on enhancing smallholder staple food crop productivity, has been associated with high rates of poverty reduction (Hazell 2010). These emerging economies are well on their way toward agricultural modernization and structural transformation. The challenge for agriculture in the emerging economies is to maintain competitiveness in the face of global integration of food markets and to close the interregional income gap (Pingali 2010).

In the low-income countries of sub-Saharan Africa, continued high levels of food deficits and the reliance on food aid and food imports have reintroduced agriculture as an engine of growth on the policy agenda (Pingali 2012). There is also an increasing awareness of the detrimental impacts of climate change on food security, especially for tropical agriculture systems in low-income countries (Byerlee, de Janvry, and Sadoulet 2009). These countries continue to be plagued by the age-old constraints to enhancing productivity growth, such as the lack of technology, poor market infrastructure, insufficient institutions, and absence of an enabling policy environment (Binswanger and McCalla 2010).

In sub-Saharan Africa, the demand for intensification, and hence the need for land productivity-enhancing Green Revolution technology, was low in the 1960s (Pingali 2012). Also, in the decades of the 1960s and 1970s, agricultural research was not focused on crops important to African smallholders, such as sorghum, millet, cassava, and tropical maize (Evenson and Gollin 2003). In the last decade there has been a significant rise in the introduction and adoption of improved varieties of these crops (Walker and Alwang 2015). At the same time in Asia, lower potential rice lands are witnessing the rapid spread of improved drought- and flood-tolerant varieties (Pandey, Velasco, and Yamano 2015).

In the emerging economies, growing private sector interest in investing in the agricultural sector has created an agricultural renaissance (Pingali 2010). Supermarkets are spreading rapidly across urban areas in emerging economies and are encouraging national and multinational agribusiness investments along the fresh produce value chains in these countries (Reardon and Minten 2011). Consequently, staple crop monoculture systems, popularized by the Green Revolution, are diversifying into high-value horticulture and livestock production. Despite these positive developments, interregional differences in productivity and poverty persist in many emerging economies.

Many of the recently adopted Sustainable Development Goals (SDGs) focus on themes in which agricultural progress plays an important role in bringing the world closer to the internationally agreed-upon objectives. In particular, the goals of eliminating poverty and hunger depend significantly on the ability of agricultural systems to produce affordable food. At the same time, the objectives of improving health, education, gender equality, and access to clean water and sanitation – themes for which rural populations are not as well served as urban populations – are conducive, directly or indirectly, to better agricultural performance.

Guide to the book

This book addresses the challenges of reorienting agriculture and rural development in a world that is going through rapid structural transformation, globalization, and urbanization. It provides a comprehensive assessment with a "state-of-the-art" review of the literature on each of the facets of the transformation process and a policy agenda for tackling the challenges ahead. It is designed around five thematic parts: Agricultural Intensification and Technical Change, Political Economy of Agricultural Policies; Community and Rural Institutions; Agriculture, Nutrition, and Health; and Future Relevance of International Institutions. This book honors Hans Binswanger's outstanding contributions to the agricultural and developmental economics profession. His research work, as well as his hands-on involvement in agricultural development and poverty alleviation programs in the course of his World Bank tenure, contributed enormously to academic research and development practice in all of the thematic areas. The chapters of this book touch on many of the themes that Hans focused on during his distinguished career.

Agricultural intensification and technical change

The first set of chapters deals with agricultural intensification and technical change, with emphasis on the challenges faced by smallholder farmers. In Chapter 2, authors Gershon Feder and Sara Savastano analyze farm-level data from four low-income sub-Saharan African countries to gain insight into possible reasons for the low adoption of modern productivity-enhancing inputs, such as inorganic fertilizers and improved seeds, by Africa's mostly smallholder farmers. The results indicate that distance to markets, illiteracy, and discriminatory policies and practices that disadvantage female farmers are associated with lower adoption of modern inputs. Policies to improve farmers' access to markets, expand rural education, and eliminate discrimination against female farmers should therefore be promoted.

In Chapter 3, authors Pasquale Lucio Scandizzo and Sara Savastano use data from five sub-Saharan African countries to examine the robustness of the negative relation between farm size and productivity that is often observed in empirical studies. The authors conclude that once proper account is taken of the impacts of soil quality, proximity to markets, and other agroecological and climatic factors, the relation between farm size and productivity is nonlinear and not unidirectional. Farms in the lower tail of the land productivity distribution experience an inverse relationship between productivity and farm size only beyond a certain critical size. On the other hand, farms at the upper end of the productivity distribution experience an inverse relationship between size and productivity only below a critical size.

In Chapter 4, authors Derek Byerlee, William A. Masters, and Daniel S. Robinson examine the options for enabling smallholders to gain access to yet unexploited lands, where they will have a potential for high productivity only if the infrastructure (e.g., roads, irrigation, and energy) of such regions is developed. Governments of many low-income countries lack the financial resources needed to undertake such investments on a large scale. The authors show through analyses of historical and current case studies that allowing private, large-scale investors to undertake the infrastructure development for subsequent sale or lease to smallholders, along with appropriate government regulatory supervision to avoid abuses, can yield beneficial results for all involved.

In Chapter 5, the author Michael Lipton points out that subsistence farmers, who satisfy most of their staple food needs from their own production, are efficient given the constraints they face. They should therefore not be viewed as an obstacle to development, as some policymakers and development practitioners tend to do. Accordingly, agricultural policies should be designed so as not to harm their welfare.

Political economy of agricultural policies

The second part of the book focuses on agricultural policies and investments, and how they are related to observed patterns of agricultural and economic development. Chapter 6 examines the sectoral structure of African economies.

The authors Johann Kirsten and Frikkie Liebenberg observe that the evolution of the structure over time does not follow the classical pattern whereby the share of agriculture declines with the growth of per capita income, while the share of manufacturing grows, and eventually the service sector grows while the share of agriculture declines further. Rather, the authors note that there is growth of the service sector with very modest change in manufacturing. They hypothesize that this is the outcome of a failure to significantly raise agricultural productivity through appropriate agricultural policies and investments, and a failure to provide sufficient inducement to private sector investment in manufacturing through adequate public investment in human capital and physical infrastructure.

Chapter 7 reviews the predictions and policy relevance of agricultural evolution theory, a key area of Hans Binswanger's research contributions. This body of theoretical work consists of two strands: (1) the Boserup/Ruthenberg model of agricultural change in response to population growth and market access, focusing on the tropics; and (2) the production relations synthesis that explains rural markets by reference to individual behavior and to the physical characteristics of farming. In this chapter, the author John Murray McIntire demonstrates how the theory's predictions were validated by empirical analyses of themes such as the evolution and adoption of farming techniques, land management, the emergence of land and credit markets, the survival of family farming, and the effects of population and markets on agricultural intensification. He further attributes the design of a number of key policies and agricultural development strategies to the insights gained from agricultural evolution theory. Chief among these is the elimination of the bias against family farming.

In Chapter 8, Klaus Deininger discusses another important focus of Hans Binswanger's research – namely, policies to enhance land tenure security and to improve the efficiency of land markets. He highlights the fact that land policies with potential to enhance efficiency and equity are often not implemented. The chapter then provides examples to show that advances in IT and geospatial technology facilitate the effective implementation of needed policies and public investments by reducing informational imperfections, enhancing benefits from land information and facilitating participation by farmers of all strata.

In Chapter 9, the authors Kym Anderson, William J. Martin, and Maros Ivanic review recent work on governments' policy responses to global food price volatility and efforts at domestic price insulation. The authors point out that countries tended to insulate strongly against shocks to international prices of staple foods. However, within a couple of years, the countries had fully passed the more sustained increases in prices into domestic markets. Further analysis reported in the chapter leads to the conclusion that this is part of a systematic pattern of response by which policymakers resist sharp changes in prices, causing the rate of protection to deviate from its steady-state political equilibrium. Policymakers subsequently reduce this disequilibrium by raising domestic prices to return them closer to their desired rates of protection. The authors argue that while these policies are successful in preventing significantly adverse impacts on poverty rates in the short term, these benefits are eliminated in the aggregate due to the price increases that result from countries collectively insulating their markets.

In Chapter 10, the author Greg Traxler looks at institutional constraints with respect to technology research, development, and dissemination, with specific reference to biotechnology. He assesses the institutional capacity and incentives to deliver GMO technology to farmers, and the metrics that are used to trace the institutional sources of available GMOs. Scientific progress and commercial delivery of GMOs in the United States are compared to that of developing countries, drawing on the experience of the first two decades of what was once called "the biotechnology revolution." The assessment attempts to shed light on the question of whether GMOs are likely to be a significant source of technological progress in developing country agriculture in the future.

Community and rural institutions

The third part of the book assesses the application of the community and rural institutions in agricultural development. Chapter 11 focuses on index-based insurance – an innovation whose utility for smallholder farmers had been questioned by Hans Binswanger in his much cited 2012 article in the *Journal of Development Studies*. The authors Peter Hazell and Ulrich Hess note that while such insurance schemes' coverage has grown in recent years, their uptake is still constrained by weak farmer demand and has been scaled up only with the aid of subsidies. It is argued that governments have been willing to subsidize index-based insurance schemes as part of broader political and social agendas. Indeed, in some cases such programs may be a cost-effective and less distorting way to address social needs. The authors point out that in the case of nature-related calamities, such as droughts, post-disaster assistance programs are already fully funded. Therefore, diverting part of the funds to subsidized index insurance products might lead to better and more cost-effective outcomes.

Chapter 12 assesses the efficiency and productivity of voluntary water trading, as compared to mandatory quotas, in allocating irrigation water resources – the latter being a fairly common approach to assigning water use rights. The authors Mark W. Rosegrant, Man Li, and Wenchao Xu note that, typically, real-life situations entail production uncertainty and information asymmetry between the water agency and individual farmers. The analysis in the chapter demonstrates that for the normally prevailing shape of irrigation water production and cost functions, a voluntary water-trading scheme generates higher benefits than a quota allocation system.

In Chapter 13, the author Jacomina de Regt reviews the experience and lessons learned from the implementation of one of Hans Binswanger's key areas of development practice – the community-driven development approach, whereby communities are allowed to have much greater control over the design and implementation of development activities intended to benefit members of the community. The author notes that the actual record of community-based development schemes is mixed, with some programs encountering problems such as "elite capture" and lack of sustainability. One of the factors hindering successful outcomes is the failure to recognize that just as there are "market failures" and "government failures," there are also "civil society failures" that need to be detected before resources are committed, so that mechanisms to overcome the constraints are built into the design of programs. The chapter then summarizes the key lessons to guide the formulation of successful programs.

Agriculture, nutrition, and health

The fourth part of the book focuses on the interactions between agriculture, nutrition, and health. Chapter 14 highlights the complexity of linkages between agricultural change and health and nutrition, noting that indirect links are underrated, especially the food and agriculture linkages related to water and sanitation. The chapter's author Joachim von Braun emphasizes the importance of recognizing that there are dynamic relationships driven by market volatilities and by a broader set of technical and institutional innovations. He outlines a new framework that focuses on positive linkages and avoidance of adverse linkages between agriculture and health.

In Chapter 15, the authors Prabhu Pingali and Tanvi Rao focus on India's puzzling experience, whereby impressive agricultural and economic development, although leading to a significant decline in the incidence of hunger, has not significantly reduced the high levels of stunting, underweight, and wasting among children. The authors note that significant nutrition deficiency is also widespread among adults. The chapter provides a detailed review of the existing empirical studies on the multidimensional factors that explain malnutrition in India. The review assesses the rigor of the different analyses, so as to throw light on the relative strength of different nutritional determinants and interventions. Furthermore, it also highlights conceptual and methodological gaps in the literature, to set the stage for further research.

Future relevance of international institutions

The last part of the book discusses the developmental impact and future prospects of two important global institutions in which Hans Binswanger spent most of his outstanding career: CGIAR, formerly the Consultative Group for International Agricultural Research, and the World Bank. In Chapter 16, the authors Uma Lele, Sambuddha Goswami, and Gianluigi Nico analyze the record of the structural transformation process of a large set of countries over the past quarter century, noting that economic growth has not always achieved shared prosperity nor led to structural transformation. The authors present evidence on the performance of agriculture, manufacturing, and services, and their roles in transformation. They then review the World Bank's policy concerning "graduation" of countries from receiving highly subsidized credits when they have low per capita income to loans with closer to market interest, once the countries reach middle-income levels. The chapter explores the extent to which the "graduated" member countries and other top recipients of World Bank assistance have achieved transformation, as distinct from simply economic growth. Finally, an attempt is made to assess the contribution of the World Bank to the transformation process. The authors note that while the World Bank's assistance is still needed by many countries, the challenges of climate change, conflict, and violence will not be easy to tackle, and the World Bank will need to devise new ways of operating that would be different from past approaches.

The last chapter of the book, Chapter 17, reviews the evolution of CGIAR since its inception in 1971. Its author, Alex F. McCalla, notes that it was created when there were grave concerns about the ability of global agriculture to feed the world. He describes how the system has grown from a small group of four research centers (two of which had produced Green Revolution semi-dwarf rice and wheat cultivars) to a consortium of 15 centers, spending jointly over US$1 billion annually. The author highlights the shift over time in the CGIAR's agenda away from cutting-edge, applied agricultural research toward more downstream adaptation and implementation, and discusses the relatively frequent donor-induced disruptive changes in its governance and management structure, as well as in its strategic agendas. The author questions the ability of the CGIAR to effectively meet the challenges of feeding 9.7 billion people by 2050 with fairly fixed water and land resources, unless it reduces and restructures its research platforms (centers) and refocuses on high-priority research critical to global food security.

References

Binswanger-Mkhize, H., and A. F. McCalla. 2010. "The Changing Context and Prospects for Agricultural and Rural Development in Africa." In *Handbook of Agricultural Economics*, Vol. 4, edited by P. Pingali and R. Evenson, 3571–712. Amsterdam: North Holland.

Byerlee, D., A. de Janvry, and E. Sadoulet. 2009. "Agriculture for Development: Toward a New Paradigm." *Annual Review of Resource Economics* 1 (1): 15–31.

Evenson, R. E., and D. Gollin. 2003. "Assessing the Impact of the Green Revolution, 1960 to 2000." *Science* 300 (5620): 758–62.

Hazell, P. B. R. 2010. "An Assessment of the Impact of Agricultural Research in South Asia Since the Green Revolution." In *Handbook of Agricultural Economics*, Vol. 4, edited by P. Pingali and R. Evenson, 3469–530. Amsterdam: North Holland.

Pandey, S., M. L. Velasco, and T. Yamano. 2015. "Scientific Strength in Rice Improvement Programmes, Varietal Outputs and Adoption of Improved Varieties in South Asia." In *Sub-Saharan Africa*, edited by T. S. Walker and J. Alwang, 239–64. Wallingford, UK: CABI and CGIAR.

Pingali, P. 2010. "Agriculture Renaissance: Making 'Agriculture for Development' Work in the 21st Century." In *Handbook of Agricultural Economics*, Vol. 4, edited by P. Pingali and R. Evenson, 3867–94. Amsterdam: North Holland.

Pingali, P. 2012. "Green Revolution: Impacts, Limits, and the Path Ahead." *Proceedings of the National Academy of Sciences* 109 (31): 12302–8.

Reardon, T., and B. Minten. 2011. "The Quiet Revolution in India's Food Supply Chains." IFPRI Discussion Paper 01115, International Food Policy Research Institute (IFPRI), New Delhi.

Timmer, C. P. 2010. *A World without Agriculture: The Structural Transformation in Historical Perspective*. Washington, DC: American Enterprise Institute.

Walker, T. S., and J. Alwang, eds. 2015. *Crop Improvement, Adoption, and Impact of Improved Varieties in Food Crops in Sub-Saharan Africa*. Wallingford, UK: CABI and CGIAR.

World Bank. 2016. World Databank. http://databank.worldbank.org/data/home.aspx

Part 1

Agricultural intensification and technical change

2 Modern agricultural technology adoption in sub-Saharan Africa

A four-country analysis

Gershon Feder and Sara Savastano

Introduction

In sub-Saharan Africa (SSA), three-quarters of the population reside in rural areas and rely on agriculture for securing their livelihood, increasing their welfare, accessing food, and fulfilling their basic needs. In recent decades, agricultural productivity (land and labor) has been stagnant in many regions of SSA, and there are concerns regarding the effectiveness of policies aimed at poverty reduction, economic transformation, and growth.

Many of the policy reforms implemented in SSA have attempted to boost agricultural output through increased input use and promotion of the adoption of new yield-enhancing technologies. Despite this effort, and unlike the experience of the Asian Green Revolution of earlier decades that fueled agricultural growth, the uptake of yield-enhancing modern agricultural inputs in SSA has been more limited: for example, cereal yield increased by about 26 percent between 1990 and 2012, but this increase was 10 percent larger in Asia during the same period. Fertilizer consumption in 2012, expressed in kg per hectare of arable land, was 13kg/ha in SSA – far below the levels used in South Asia and East Asia and the Pacific of 174.5 and 381 kg/ha, respectively (World Bank 2016).

There is a wide consensus that African countries should improve the efficiency of agricultural production, and that improvement in agricultural technology is a key vehicle to achieve this goal. The Asian Green Revolution allowed for the doubling of overall food production (Tilman 1999) by introducing improved varieties and increased fertilizer use and irrigation, together with increased use of pesticides. The African context is different in that the agricultural sector is mostly rainfed, characterized by a limited presence of irrigation schemes and high cost of inputs, due to distance from ports and underdeveloped transport infrastructure.[1]

The limited rate of adoption of modern technologies in Africa (improved seed, fertilizers and other agrochemicals, and machinery) is worrisome for policymakers, since those technologies are important for sustaining the fertility of African soils. Adoption of such technologies was expected to enable smallholder farms, which represent the majority of the producers, to take full advantage of the potential gains from improved varieties of staple crops. Many studies have explored the factors underlying the low rate of adoption of modern technologies in SSA. However, the scope for cross-nationally comparable insights on modern input use patterns across sub-Saharan Africa has been limited thus far, partly due to a lack of nationally representative data.

The literature has emphasized the role of poorly functioning input markets in limiting smallholder productivity, by keeping, for example, the price of fertilizer high and limiting its availability. Fertilizer, more than other inputs, is also considered a prerequisite for utilizing some improved technologies. Yet, it is not entirely clear why rates of adoption are so diverse among countries. The literature suggests that poor infrastructure, long distance to market, inadequate access to credit, low crop yield response, and high covariate risks in rainfed areas are among the major constraints to adoption. Some of these constraints are amenable to government remedial action due to their public good nature, and it is of interest to assess the cross-country differences in government provision of public goods, such as rural roads, agricultural research and extension services, and education.

Making use of recent data from the Living Standard Measurement Study–Integrated Surveys on Agriculture Initiative (LSMS–ISA), coordinated by the Development Economics Research Group of the World Bank, our study will try to identify some key factors that are associated with technology adoption among small farmers in four sub-Saharan African countries: Ethiopia, Niger, Nigeria, and Tanzania. The study will use nationally representative and cross-comparable farm and georeferenced data collected between 2010 and 2012 to highlight common patterns, as well as differences across countries. Preliminary evidence suggests that there is a strong heterogeneity in adoption across countries and among types of technology used.

The chapter is organized as follows. The next section reviews the relevant literature underpinning the empirical work. This is followed by the description of the data used. A subsequent section outlines the analytical methodology, followed by the empirical analysis. The last section provides conclusions and policy implications.

Literature review

Our data cover farmers who have long been exposed to information about the use of inorganic fertilizers (for whom these inputs are not an innovation anymore), as well as farmers for whom these inputs are less familiar, and thus viewed as innovations. This implies that the relevant literature underpinning our analysis entails both theoretical and empirical studies on the factors that affect smallholder farmers' performance (input use and output), in general, and the more specific discussions of the determinants of adoption of improved technology. The literature is too voluminous to cover in this chapter, and we confine ourselves to a rather selective discussion that informs the reader of the underlying logic of factors being considered in our analysis as having a bearing on the indicators of farmers' performance. Comprehensive reviews of the early literature on adoption of innovations in agriculture are available in Feder, Just, and Zilberman (1985) and Feder and Umali (1993). A recent review that focused on SSA was provided by Meijer et al. (2015). Because our empirical analysis is obliged to incorporate only the few variables that are contained within our data sets, we focus our select literature review mostly on publications that have included such variables in their discussions.

Human capital has long been perceived by development scholars as a factor that positively affects farmers' performance and inclination to adopt innovations. Although the extent of human capital is not easy to measure, many researchers view formal education as an indicator of such capital (see recent review of the literature by Padhy and Jena [2015]). Among several aspects associated with education, literacy, which is one of the qualities acquired through formal education, enables farmers to access written sources of information. This, in turn, can expand their knowledge regarding production technology and market opportunities, allowing them to make better decisions. The empirical evidence on this hypothesis is mixed, and while many studies find evidence confirming the positive impact of education on farm performance, there are as many studies that fail to substantiate it (e.g., see reviews in Weir [1999] and Reimers and Klasen [2013]). As argued by King and Palmer (2006), the reason for the mixed evidence may be found in the dependence of actual educational outcomes on additional factors within the education system (e.g., the quality of education), as well as factors beyond the education system, such as the social, cultural, economic, and political environments. Another reason for the mixed results is an improper specification of the education variable in empirical studies (Reimers and Klasen 2013).

Agricultural economists often hypothesize that the age of a farmer making decisions affects the farmer's performance and adoption behavior. Adesina and Baidu-Forson (1995) argued that the direction of the impact is an empirical question, as some scholars have maintained that the impact is positive, because age may represent experience; others expect a negative impact due to higher risk aversion among older farmers (and perhaps lower quality of education). Indeed, one can find studies in the empirical literature that indicate a positive relationship between age (or experience) and indicators of farmer performance, such as adoption of improved practices (see Deressa et al. [2009] and several empirical studies cited therein), while others (e.g., Shiferaw and Holden [1998]) report a negative impact of age.

In many farming societies, the gender of the head of the household is of significance in affecting farm performance. There is ample empirical evidence indicating lower productivity on farms managed by female-headed households (see review of 24 studies in Beaman et al. [2013]; Carter, Laajaj, and Yang [2013]; Peterman, Behrman, and Quisumbing [2014]; Deininger, Xia, and Savastano [2015]; Larson et al. [2015]; and the relevant studies cited therein). Much of the evidence on the "gender gap" in agricultural productivity is drawn from SSA and explores socioeconomic aspects, such as social norms: culture-specific gender roles determine the capacity of men and women to allocate labor time across economically productive activities and to respond to economic incentives (Ilahi 2000; Fafchamps 2001; Blackden and Wodon 2006). The explanations provided in the literature for the existence of such a gap are linked to gender-differentiated access to credit and input/output markets, lesser access to extension services, lower security of tenure, differentiated access to off-farm employment, lower stores of human and physical capital, and other informal and institutional constraints (Peterman et al. 2011; Peterman, Behrman, and Quisumbing 2014). These factors in turn lead to lower use of inputs, such as inorganic fertilizer, and a lower rate of adoption of improved practices (Larson et al. 2015).

The distance of the farm from markets for inputs and output is mentioned in the literature as an important determinant of farm performance, as it has a bearing on many aspects of farming. The further a farm is located from markets, the higher is the transport cost, which implies lower farm gate prices for outputs and higher farm gate price for inputs. Easier access to markets often implies better access to information, credit, education, and health facilities. The extensive review of numerous studies of the impacts of roads in Jouanjean (2013) provided ample empirical evidence of the beneficial impacts of roads in reducing farm transportation and transaction costs and promoting trade. The review cites evidence of direct beneficial impacts of roads on farm productivity. For example, the analysis in Stifel and Minten (2008) specifically showed that isolation (measured alternatively as travel time and as cost of transport) causes lower agricultural productivity, in a case study in Ethiopia. Similar results were presented for Kenya by Kiprono and Matsumoto (2014).

Limited access to credit is often mentioned in the literature as a constraint on smallholders' use of cash inputs and a factor limiting adoption of improved practices that require cash outlays. In this context, income from off-farm sources (e.g., transfers from members of the household employed in urban centers) could provide smallholders with the cash needed to finance within-season farm operations. Our data do not have information on credit access (and we note that credit utilization is an endogenous variable), but we do have information on transfers from non-farm sources.

The quality of soil and the general agro-climatic characteristics of the area in which the farm is located certainly affect farm performance. Furthermore, with higher return on input use in environments conducive to farming, the farmer has incentives to use more cash inputs, such as inorganic fertilizer, and to adopt yield-increasing practices, such as use of improved seed.

Estimation strategy

To assess levels and determinants of agricultural performance, as well as to assess cross-correlation between variables of interest, we estimate the following country-specific functional form:

$$Y_i = \beta_0 + \beta_1 X_i + \beta_3 G_i + u_i \tag{2.1}$$

where i indexes households in each country of interest; Y_i is either the logarithm of net income from crop production per unit of land, a dummy equal to 1 if households used fertilizer in the main agricultural season (or actual level of use in Tobit regressions), or a dummy equal to 1 if the household used improved seeds (or the actual level of use in Tobit regressions); X_i is a vector of households characteristics, including operated land area; G_i is a vector of geo-variable controls, including log of household's distance (in km) to the nearest market, soil quality controls, and agro-ecological dummies; and finally, u_i is the i.i.d. error term.

The analysis in this chapter focuses on three measures of agricultural "performance" – namely, the value of crop output per unit of operated land and two key "modern" inputs, inorganic fertilizers and improved seeds.

Factors that are associated with the performance indicators include some clearly exogenous variables (dummy variables for agro-ecological zones, a set of indicators of soil quality), some household characteristics that are most likely exogenous in the context of the current year performance indicators (gender of the household head, age of household head, whether household head is illiterate), and some variables that could potentially be correlated with omitted variables that also affect the performance indicators, or are otherwise endogenous. These variables include the share of household income derived from transfers, the average size of operated farms in the sample from the household's enumeration area (but excluding the respondent's farm), and the farmer's distance from the nearest market (typically a small town). The presence of such potentially endogenous variables, as well as the fact that there may be important omitted variables, may make problematic the interpretation of the estimates as representative of a causal relationship. However, if the extent of endogeneity is small, the relationship we estimate is a highly simplified reduced form, with a focus on the three key variables representing factors that are amenable to government remedial action. First, an estimate of the extent of association between performance and illiteracy could suggest how relevant investment in education is to the improvement of agricultural performance. Second, distance to market represents a key factor in determining farm gate prices faced by farmers, and possibly a determinant in the amount of exposure to information on various farming-related matters.[2] The extent of association between distance and farm performance, if it could be interpreted as a causal relation, could indicate how relevant that government investment in transport infrastructure would be to improved performance (by reducing the "effective distance" to markets, as improved roads shorten travel time and thereby reduce transaction costs). Third, the extent of a "gender gap" in agricultural performance could signify the presence of institutional and cultural factors that limit the ability of female-headed farm households to access input and credit markets and information sources. Such limitations could be ameliorated by targeted programs, such as improved tenure security for female farmers, gender-sensitive extension and credit programs, and targeted group activities. A recent analysis of programs promoting women's self-help groups in Ethiopia, Tanzania, and Mali suggests that such initiatives can overcome constraints in access to credit and market information (Baden 2013).

The estimation strategy we employ entails two steps. First we run a standard OLS on factors associated with net crop income, and then we run a probit regression on a dummy variable that indicates whether households used inorganic fertilizers and improved seeds. As relatively few farmers in our sample used these inputs, the data are characterized by a truncated set of observed actual non-zero values and many zeroes; we complement our estimation strategy with a Tobit regression.

Data and descriptive statistics

We use data from the Living Standards Measurement Study and Integrated Surveys on Agriculture (LSMS–ISA) project, sponsored by the Bill and Melinda Gates Foundation and implemented by the national statistics offices under the supervision of the Development Research Group of the World Bank. We focus on four countries – namely, Ethiopia (2011–2012), Niger (2010–2011), Nigeria (2010–2011), and Tanzania (2010–2011). There are several advantages in using this data set. First, the strong focus on agriculture allows for a comparative analysis of modern technology use across countries to a greater extent than what is feasible from using existing census data.

The surveys contain information on two agricultural seasons (sometimes called the long and short, or rainy and dry). We focus our analysis and construct the outcome variables of interest, drawing from data of the main agriculture season. Our sample includes 10,378 nationally representative households, which account for the large majority of households located in rural areas. The country household samples include 3,013 households in Ethiopia, 2,198 in Niger, 2,884 in Nigeria, and 2,283 in Tanzania.

Table 2.1 depicts general household and farm characteristics, as well as georeferenced information on distance from nearest market. We note that the sample countries are characterized by significant differences in net income from crop production. Two patterns can be identified: on the left side of the distribution are Niger and Tanzania with, respectively, 218 and 297 US$/ha.[3] Farmers in these countries operate relatively large-sized (in the African context) farms (5.2 and 2.28 ha on average, respectively), although differences in average soil quality could make size comparisons less relevant. At the opposite side of the distribution, one observes Ethiopia and Nigeria with net crop income of 996 and 1,189 US$/ha, respectively. Compatible with the results on farm income, cropping intensity is higher in these two countries (1.21 and 1.23 in Ethiopia and Nigeria, respectively, as compared to 1.19 in Niger and 1.07 in in Tanzania). In both countries with higher per-hectare farm income, farmers operate very small farms (1.16 and 0.79 ha on average, respectively). This may explain in part the two distinct patterns of agriculture performance (i.e., smaller farms tend to have higher land productivity due to higher family labor input per unit of land).

As one would expect, inorganic fertilizer use is higher in the two countries with higher crop income (Ethiopia and Nigeria), where about 41 percent of farms utilize some fertilizers, while in the two countries with lower crop income

Table 2.1 Descriptive statistics

	ETH	NER	NGA	TZA
Number of households	**3,013**	**2,198**	**2,884**	**2,283**
Households' characteristics				
Female head	20.83	7.56	11.81	23.26
Age of head	44.12	44.81	50.52	48.93
Head is illiterate (%)	66.61	50.32	39.82	28.43
Household size	5.16	6.84	6.04	5.71
Agricultural income				
Net income from crop production per ha	995.62	218.55	1189.22	297.03
Share of income				
From crop production	68.44	44.34	69.83	53.60
From transfer	2.24	7.22	0.63	6.05
Land operated (ha)	1.16	5.26	0.79	2.28
Dummy use inorganic fertilizer	41.16	18.75	41.13	16.73
Dummy use of improved seeds	17.41	3.53	.	14.89
Cropping intensity	1.21	1.19	1.23	1.07
Geo-variable				
HH distance in (km) to nearest market*	67.60	62.44	71.66	82.57

Source: Authors' estimation based on LSM–ISA Survey.

* Household distance to nearest major market is included in the GEO dataset provided by the LSMS–ISA project. The raw variable has been extracted from FEWSNET, and computes households' distance from the key market centers.

(Niger and Tanzania), less than 19 percent of farms use inorganic fertilizers. We do not have data on improved seed utilization in Nigeria, but this practice is not so present in the other three countries, where adoption is 17 percent in Ethiopia, 15 percent in Tanzania, and less than 4 percent in Niger.

In the four countries, crop production accounts for more than 40 percent of total household income. However, we note that in the countries with higher land productivity (Ethiopia and Nigeria), the share of income from crop production accounts for more the two-thirds of total income. In contrast, in the countries with lower land productivity, the share of crop income in household income is significantly lower, although it is still close to half of total income.

Descriptive statistics also illustrate that the average age of the head of the household is well within middle age – from 44 in Ethiopia to 50 in Nigeria. Sample households are relatively abundant in family labor (six members per household, on average), suggesting the intensive use of family labor in agricultural production.

Levels of illiteracy vary considerably among countries: Nigeria and Tanzania have the lowest share of illiterate household heads (39 and 28 percent, respectively); in Niger and Ethiopia more than half of the household heads are illiterate (50 and 66 percent, respectively).

The share of income from transfers off the farm accounts on average to less than 8 percent of total income (less than 3 percent in Ethiopia and Nigeria). Although these figures are low on average, the variation within the sample may be of significance in the context of the decision-making and performance of individual households. If high shares of transfer income are typical of households with very small land holdings that cannot support consumption needs, they may also be associated with "low" farm performance, as these households may view their agricultural activities as lower priority and tend to direct their labor to off-farm opportunities.

The share of female-headed households differs considerably across countries, with Tanzania and Ethiopia having a relatively large segment of their farm sector (23 and 21 percent, respectively) managed by female farmers, while in Nigeria and Niger the share is considerably lower (12 and 8 percent, respectively).

Results

The regressions of performance indicators show that illiteracy is not necessarily negatively associated with net crop income per hectare (counterintuitive positive signs for Niger and Nigeria), but it tends to be negatively associated with modern input use: three of the four fertilizer use equations indicate that illiterate household heads are significantly associated with lower fertilizer use, and in one country (Tanzania), improved seed utilization is significantly and substantially higher among literate farmers. If the regression is interpreted as a causal relationship (with all due caveats), the magnitude of the coefficient suggests that literate farmers use close to 20 percent more fertilizers than illiterate farmers in Ethiopia and Nigeria, and close to double that amount in Tanzania, as well as accounting for 40 percent more utilization of improved seed. Since education is a key to many aspects of quality of life and economic well-being, one would not base advocacy for improved rural education simply on its contribution to higher modern input use, but it would seem that a non-negligible benefit of enhanced rural education can be reaped when rural schooling coverage is expanded.

The association between distance to market and agricultural performance is even more uniform and pronounced: three of the regressions of net crop income and fertilizer use have significant negative coefficients (at the 10 percent confidence level or better) on the distance variable. Similarly, two of the three improved seed regressions have significantly negative coefficients on the distance variables. If one interprets the regressions as a causal relation (again, with all due caveats), the magnitude of the estimated coefficient suggests that investment in improved transport could have large positive effect on agricultural performance: supposing that distance approximates travel time, then a 10 percent shortening of travel time could be associated with over 60 percent higher per hectare crop income in Ethiopia, and 20 percent and 35 percent increases in Niger and Tanzania, respectively (see Table 2.2).

The fertilizer regressions indicate similar large effects of transportation improvements, if interpreted as causal relationships: a 1 percent reduction in travel time would increase the probability of fertilizer adoption by 1.3 percent in Ethiopia, 2.6 percent in Nigeria, and 0.4 percent in Niger (based on calculations of the marginal effects in the probit equations). The effects are larger for those who already use fertilizer: a 10 percent reduction in effective distance could be associated with 29 percent and 58 percent increases in the quantity of fertilizer used on Ethiopian and Nigerian farms, respectively (Table 2.3).

A similar pattern for the coefficients of the distance variable is observed in the improved seed regressions: a 1 percent reduction in distance is associated with a 0.06–0.08 percent increase in the adoption of improved seed, based on the Ethiopia and Tanzania regressions, while for users of improved seeds a 10 percent reduction in distance to market is associated with an approximately 45 percent higher seed use (Table 2.4).

Table 2.2 OLS regression – net crop income

VARIABLES	(1)	(2)	(3)	(4)
	ETH	NER	NGA	TZA
Head of household is illiterate	−0.08	0.21***	0.36***	−0.04
Log age head	−0.16	−0.17	0.05	−0.21**
Female head	−0.66***	−0.36**	−0.43**	0.05
Log leave out mean operated area at the EA level	0.57***	0.56***	−0.63***	0.38***
Share of income from transfers	−4.52***	−2.11***	0.35	−0.65**
Log distance to nearest market	−6.71***	−2.03*	0.61	−3.50***
Constant	5.92***	3.41***	4.98***	5.39***
Observations	3,013	2,204	2,884	2,283
R-squared	0.09	0.08	0.04	0.04

Source: Authors' estimation based on LSM–ISA Survey.

Note: Dummy variables for agro-ecological zones and soil quality controls estimated, but not reported.

List of soil quality variables used:
• Nutrient availability
• Nutrient retention capacity
• Rooting conditions
• Oxygen availability to roots
• Excess salts
• Toxicity
• Workability (constraining field management)

* Significant at 90% confidence level.
** Significant at 95% confidence level.
*** Significant at 99% confidence level.

Table 2.3 Regressions on inorganic fertilizers

VARIABLES	ETH			NER			NGA			TZA		
	Probit	mfx	Tobit	Probit	mfx	Tobit	Probit	mfx	Tobit	Probit	mfx	Tobit
Head of household is illiterate	**-0.24***		-0.20***	-0.03			-0.17***		-0.15***	-0.73***		-1.01***
Log age head	0.18**		0.16**	-0.10			-0.20***		-0.16**	0.19*		0.26*
Female head	**-0.24***		-0.20***	-0.03			-0.42***		-0.40***	0.05		0.07
Log leave out mean operated area at the EA level	0.89***		0.75***	-0.33***			0.12		0.11	-0.11**		-0.14***
Share of income from transfers	-1.81***	-0.70***	-1.72***	-0.32	-0.08		-0.11	-0.04	-0.08	-0.99***	-0.22***	-1.36***
Log distance to nearest market (km)	**-3.42***	-1.32***	-2.78***	-1.54*	-0.39*		-6.69***	-2.60***	-5.76***	1.09	0.24	1.33
Constant	-0.07		0.07	-0.92*			1.55***		1.39***	-1.08**		-1.48**
Observations	3,013	3,013	3,013	2,198	2,198		2,884	2,884	2,884	2,283	2,283	2,283
Pseudo R-squared	0.0949	0.0949	0.0672	0.0544	0.0544		0.0707	0.0707	0.0485	0.0956	0.0956	0.0735

Source: Authors' estimation based on LSM–ISA Survey.

Note: Dummy variables for agro–ecological zones and soil quality controls estimated but not reported.

List of soil quality variables used:
- Nutrient availability
- Nutrient retention capacity
- Rooting conditions
- Oxygen availability to roots
- Excess salts
- Toxicity
- Workability (constraining field management)

Tobit for NER does not converge.
* Significant at 90% confidence level.
** Significant at 95% confidence level.
*** Significant at 99% confidence level.

Table 2.4 Regressions on improved seeds

VARIABLES	ETH			NER			TZA		
	Probit	mfx	Tobit	Probit	mfx	Tobit	Probit	mfx	Tobit
Head of household is illiterate	**-0.08**		-0.12	-0.02			-0.32***		-0.46***
Log age head	-0.00		-0.01	0.11			-0.15		-0.22
Female head	**-0.13***		-0.17*	0.01			-0.15*		-0.22*
Log leave out mean operated area at the EA level	0.12		0.16	-0.48***			-0.10**		-0.15**
Share of income from transfers	-1.29***	-0.30***	-1.80***	0.16	0.01		-0.89**	-0.19**	-1.32***
Log distance to nearest market (km)	**-3.40***	-0.80***	-4.53***	2.29	0.11		-2.98***	-0.63***	-4.27***
Constant	-0.06		-0.04	-1.67**			0.09		0.13
Observations	3,013	3,013	3,013	2,198	2,198		2,283	2,283	2,283
Pseudo R-squared	0.0820	0.0820	0.0628	0.0512	0.0512		0.0740	0.0740	0.0565

Source: Authors' estimation based on LSM–ISA Survey.

Note: NGA did not collect information on improved seeds. Dummy variables for agro-ecological zones and soil quality controls estimated but not reported.

List of soil quality variables used:
- Nutrient availability
- Nutrient retention capacity
- Rooting conditions
- Oxygen availability to roots
- Excess salts
- Toxicity
- Workability (constraining field management)

Tobit for NER does not converge.
* Significant at 90% confidence level.
** Significant at 95% confidence level.
*** Significant at 99% confidence level.

The results of the regressions confirm the existence of a significant gender gap in the performance of farms, with three of the four net crop income regressions showing a substantially (and statistically significant) lower income per ha on female-managed farms: 66 percent lower in Ethiopia, and 43 percent and 36 percent lower in Nigeria and Tanzania, respectively (the parameter for Niger is not statistically significant). In line with arguments in the literature, two of the fertilizer regressions (Ethiopia and Nigeria) indicate a significantly lower probability of use of inorganic fertilizer in female-managed farms, and even on farms where female farmers use fertilizers, the quantity used is lower than that used by male farmers (lower by 40 percent in Nigeria and 20 percent in Ethiopia). The regressions on improved seed use yield a similar picture: in two countries (Ethiopia and Tanzania), the probability of adoption is significantly lower on female-managed farms, and among farms using improved seed, the quantity used is about 20 percent lower on female-managed farms compared to male-managed farms. The implication is that gender-targeted policies to eliminate direct and indirect biases that limit women's access to markets, information, tenure security, and education could bring about a significant improvement in their farms' performance and their families' welfare. Furthermore, in countries with a high proportion of female-managed farms (e.g., Ethiopia and Tanzania), gender-targeted intervention would have significant impacts on overall agricultural performance.

Conclusions

These results suggest that within the array of interventions considered as potentially conducive to improving agricultural performance, an upgrade and expansion of rural roads should receive serious consideration. Such public investment is less dependent on the quality of large numbers of public employees (as is the case with agricultural extension systems enhancements or other staff-intensive service schemes), and is not as distortionary and subject to leakage as some of the input subsidy schemes. Of course, transport investments have their own implementation challenges: corruption often afflicts the award of large public work contracts, and routine maintenance gets often neglected, leading to periodic costly rehabilitation projects. Remedies to these weaknesses have been developed and experimented with (World Bank 2002). Agricultural development practitioners often focus on more "agricultural" interventions (e.g., research and extension, price policies, rural credit), because infrastructure is organizationally and bureaucratically managed within a different organization (ministry of public works or ministry of transportation). This should not be the case, given the potential agricultural development impact that may be reaped from transport infrastructure investments.

The chapter's results also highlight the merits of investment in rural education, which has been long viewed by development scholars as an important component of developing countries' rural development strategies (Atchoarena and Gasperini 2003). Investments in this area need to consider not only the formal school system and its curriculum's balance between basic education and agricultural education, but also options for adult education and methods to be used when a significant proportion of the farming population is illiterate. With the advent of access to audio and visual mass media, there are more promising options than in the past, with significant cost advantages (Akpomuvie 2010).

Finally, the results of our analysis emphasize the importance of closing the "gender gap" in agricultural productivity. To make progress on this front, a whole array of interventions and proactive programs to empower rural women need to be undertaken, including: (1) improving women's land rights in both formal legislation and actual practice; (2) expanding girls' access to education; (3) introducing targeted microcredit programs; (4) promoting financial literacy among women; (5) supporting the creation of women groups for mutual assistance; and (6) targeting technology development and extension services to address women's conditions (FAO 2011; Baden 2013; World Bank 2015).

Notes

1 Pingali (2012) provides a review of the Green Revolution experience in Asia and Africa.
2 However, the advent of cell phone use by smallholder farmers provides access to price and other relevant farm information that is not dependent on distance (see Nakasone, Torero, and Minten [2014]).
3 For comparability across countries, we use the 2010 average exchange rate provided by the WDI: 16.90 for Ethiopia, 471.87 for Niger, 150.30 for Nigeria, and 1409.27 for Tanzania.

References

Adesina, A., and J. Baidu-Forson. 1995. "Farmers' Perceptions and Adoption of New Agricultural Technology: Evidence from Analysis in Burkina Faso and Guinea, West Africa." *Agricultural Economics* 13 (1): 1–9.

Akpomuvie, O. B. 2010. "Towards Effective Use of ICTS and Traditional Media for Sustainable Rural Transformation in Africa." *Journal of Sustainable Development* 3 (4): 65–170.

Atchoarena, D., and L. Gasperini, eds. 2003. *Education for Rural Development: Towards New Policy Responses*. Rome: Food and Agricultural Organization of the United Nations (FAO) and Paris: United Nations Educational, Scientific and Cultural Organization (UNESCO). http://files.eric.ed.gov/fulltext/ED499625.pdf

Baden, S. 2013. "Women's Collective Action: Unlocking the Potential of Agricultural Markets." Research Report, Oxfam International, Oxford, UK. https://dlc.dlib.indiana.edu/dlc/bitstream/handle/10535/8793/rr-womens-collective-action-unlocking-potential-africa-agriculture-270312-en.pdf?sequence=1

Beaman, L. A., D. Karlan, B. Thuysbaert, and C. R. Udry. 2013. "Profitability of Fertilizer: Experimental Evidence from Female Rice Farmers in Mali." *American Economic Review* 103 (3): 381–6.

Blackden, M. C., and Q. Wodon, eds. 2006. "Gender, Time Use, and Poverty in sub-Saharan Africa." World Bank Working Paper No. 73, World Bank, Washington, DC. http://site resources.worldbank.org/INTAFRREGTOPGENDER/Resources/gender_time_use_pov.pdf

Carter, M. R., R. Laajaj, and D. Yang. 2013. "The Impact of Voucher Coupons on the Uptake of Fertilizer and Improved Seeds: Evidence from a Randomized Trial in Mozambique." *American Journal of Agricultural Economics* 95 (5): 1345–51.

Deininger, K. W., F. Xia, and S. Savastano. 2015. "Smallholders' Land Ownership and Access in Sub-Saharan Africa: A New Landscape?" Policy Research Working Paper WPS7285, World Bank, Washington, DC.

Deressa, T. D., R. M. Hassan, C. Ringler, T. Alemu, and M. Yesuf. 2009. "Determinants of Farmers' Choice of Adaptation Methods to Climate Change Effects in the Nile Basin of Ethiopia." *Global Environmental Change* 19 (2): 248–55.

Fafchamps, M. 2001. "Intrahousehold Access to Land and Sources of Inefficiency: Theory and Concepts." In *Access to Land, Rural Poverty, and Public Action*, edited by A. de Janvry, G. Gordillo, E. Sadoulet, and J.-P. Platteau, 68–96. Oxford: Oxford University Press. doi:10.1093/acprof:oso/9780199242177.003.0003

FAO (Food and Agriculture Organization of the United Nations). 2011. "Closing the Gender Gap in Agriculture and Rural Employment." In *The State of Food and Agriculture 2010–11: Women in Agriculture – Closing the Gender Gap for Development*, 46–60. Rome: Food and Agriculture Organization. http://www.fao.org/docrep/013/i2050e/i2050e05.pdf

Feder, G., R. Just, and D. Zilberman. 1985. "Adoption of Agricultural Innovations in Developing Countries: A Survey." *Economic Development and Cultural Change* 33 (2): 255–98.

Feder, G., and D. Umali. 1993. "The Adoption of Agricultural Innovations: A Review." *Technological Forecasting & Social Change* 43 (3–4): 215–39.

Ilahi, N. 2000. "The Intra-household Allocation of Time and Tasks: What Have We Learnt from the Empirical Literature?" Policy Research Report on Gender and Development, Working Paper Series No. 13, World Bank, Washington, DC. http://siteresources.worldbank.org/INTGENDER/Resources/wp13.pdf

Jouanjean, M.-A. 2013. "Targeting Infrastructure Development to Foster Agricultural Trade and Market Integration in Developing Countries: An Analytical Review." Research Report, Overseas Development Institute, London.

King, K., and R. Palmer. 2006. "Education, Training and Their Enabling Environments: A Review of Research and Policy." Post-Basic Education and Training Working Paper Series – No. 8, Centre of African Studies, University of Edinburgh, Edinburgh, UK.

Kiprono, P., and T. Matsumoto. 2014. "Roads and Farming: The Effect of Infrastructure Improvement on Agricultural Input Use, Farm Productivity and Market Participation in Kenya." Paper presented at CSAE Conference 2014: Economic Development in Africa, University of Oxford, March 23–25, 2014. http://editorialexpress.com/cgi-bin/conference/download.cgi?db_name=CSAE2014&paper_id=293

Larson, D., S. Savastano, S. Murray, and A. Palacios-Lopez. 2015. "Are Women Less Productive Farmers? How Markets and Risk Affect Fertilizer Use, Productivity, and Measured Gender Effects in Uganda." Policy Research Working Paper WPS7241, World Bank, Washington, DC.

Meijer, S., D. Catacutan, O. C. Ajayi, G. W. Sileshi, and M. Nieuwenhuis. 2015. "The Role of Knowledge, Attitudes, and Perceptions in the Uptake of Agricultural and Agroforestry Innovations among Smallholder Farmers in Sub-Saharan Africa." *International Journal of Agricultural Sustainability* 13 (1): 40–54.

Nakasone, E., M. Torero, and B. Minten. 2014. "The Power of Information: The ICT Revolution in Agricultural Development." *Annual Review of Resource Economics* 6 (1): 533–50.

Padhy, C., and B. K. Jena. 2015. "Effect of Agricultural Education on Farmers Efficiency: A Review." *International Journal of Engineering Technology, Management and Applied Sciences* 3 (2): 247–58.

Peterman, A., J. A. Behrman, and A. R. Quisumbing, 2014. "A Review of Empirical Evidence on Gender Differences in Nonland Agricultural Inputs, Technology, and Services in Developing Countries." In *Gender in Agriculture: Closing the Knowledge Gap*, edited by

A. R. Quisumbing, R. Meinzen-Dick, T. L. Raney, A. Croppenstedt, J. A. Behrman, and A. Peterman, 145–86. New York: Springer.

Peterman, A., A. Quisumbing, J. Behrman, and E. Nkonya. 2011. "Understanding the Complexities Surrounding Gender Differences in Agricultural Productivity in Nigeria and Uganda." *Journal of Development Studies* 47 (10): 1482–509.

Pingali, P. 2012. "Green Revolution: Impacts, Limits, and the Path Ahead." *Proceedings of the National Academy of Sciences of the United States of America* 109 (31): 12302–8.

Reimers, M., and S. Klasen. 2013. "Revisiting the Role of Education for Agricultural Productivity." *American Journal of Agricultural Economics* 95 (1): 131–52.

Shiferaw, B., and S. Holden. 1998. "Resource Degradation and Adoption of Land Conservation Technologies in the Ethiopian Highlands: A Case Study in Andit Tid, North Shewa." *Agricultural Economics* 18 (3): 233–47.

Stifel, D., and B. Minten. 2008. "Isolation and Agricultural Productivity." *Agricultural Economics* 39 (1): 1–15.

Tilman, D. 1999. "Global Environmental Impacts of Agricultural Expansion: The Need for Sustainable and Efficient Practices." *Proceedings of the National Academy of Sciences of the United States of America* 96 (11): 5995–6000.

Weir, S. 1999. "The Effects of Education on Farmer Productivity in Rural Ethiopia." Report No. WPS 99–7, Centre for the Study of African Economies, Department of Economics, University of Oxford, Oxford.

World Bank. 2002. Road Financing and Road Funds. http://www.worldbank.org/en/topic/transport

World Bank. 2015. "The Cost of the Gender Gap in Agricultural Productivity in Malawi, Tanzania, and Uganda." Joint Report No. 100234 of UN Women, the United Nations Development Programme–United Nations Environment Programme–Poverty-Environment Initiative (UNDP-UNEP PEI) Africa, and the World Bank, Washington, DC.

World Bank. 2016. Indicators. Agriculture & Rural Development. http://data.worldbank.org/indicator

3 Revisiting the farm size–productivity relationship

New evidence from sub-Saharan African countries

Pasquale Lucio Scandizzo and Sara Savastano

Introduction

The inverse relationship (IR) between land productivity and farm size has emerged as an empirical regularity since the early studies (1950–1960) on Indian agriculture.[1] Although somewhat contrary to expectations, the IR became popular probably because it tended to support peasant farming as a more human and efficient alternative to capitalistic, large-scale agriculture. It also suggested that investing in small, family farms might help solve problems, such as food security and income inequality. In turn, policies to facilitate the redistribution of land from large farms toward the small farms were invoked as beneficial on the grounds of both equity and efficiency.

More recently, since the early 1970s, a large number of empirical studies have reexamined the problem from different angles, using various statistical techniques. As a result of the "Washington Consensus in Agriculture" (Kydd and Dorward 2001), the IR has been perceived as a "stylized fact" of rural development and a guiding principle of the major land reform in the former Soviet Union and the Eastern European countries. The finding, however, remains somewhat ambiguous; many explanations have been given, perhaps too many, that have covered a vast array of hypotheses – in part mutually incompatible and often at odds with parts of the evidence. Although many studies confirm the IR pattern, there are also several cases where alternative findings are reported, often with no productivity–size relationship, once certain factors (land quality, village location, etc.) are controlled for. The ambiguity of the pattern derives also from the apparent independence of the IR from different modes of production, since most studies show an inverse smooth relation across all farm types and not only in correspondence to discontinuous changes in institutional arrangements (e.g., family farms versus plantations).

In this chapter, we investigate several dimensions of the purported relationship between productivity and farm size. We use the Living Standards Measurement Study–Integrated Surveys on Agriculture (LSMS–ISA), nationally representative surveys of five sub-Saharan African countries, which provide standardized location details of sampled communities, allowing the data to be linked to any other georeferenced data. We are thus able to control for many exogenous common and comparative geospatial measures of land quality, infrastructure, access to markets, climate conditions, soil, and topography. This allows us to account for a cross-country comparison perspective, to meet some of the challenges often highlighted by Binswanger in his own research and reflections on the issue (Binswanger and Rosenzweig 1986; Binswanger and McIntire 1987; Binswanger, Deininger, and Feder 1995). We also use an estimation strategy, based on quantile regressions (QRs) at the household level, which allows us to test the IR existence and to verify sign switches across the entire distribution of farm size and between countries located in different agroecological zones.

The contribution of our chapter to the existing literature is threefold:

1   We analyze the existence of the IR in a cross-country context, making use of comparable, nationally representative surveys.
2   We avoid the problems posed by the endogeneity of key farm variables, by using a number of exogenous variables available in the georeferenced data set of the LSMS–ISA project. For example, instead of controlling for soil quality, as self-reported information of farmers, we use exogenous soil quality variables.
3   We control for other omitted variable bias and measurement errors in self-reported areas of farmers by using the GPS information of land area collected by the enumerators.

Our results, using evidence for five countries (Malawi, Niger, Nigeria, Tanzania, and Uganda), suggest the following conclusions:

1   Land quality and its components appear to be significant explanatory variables for land productivity (LP), and so are several other exogenous variables linked to urban and market influence, distance from the roads, temperature, and rainfall.
2   Effects of farm size on average land productivity remain significant across all specifications.
3   However, this relationship is both nonlinear and switches signs across farm size groups.
4   Farms in the lower tail of the land–productivity distribution experience an inverse relationship (IR) between productivity and farm size only once they have reached a critical size. Vice versa, farms at the upper end of the distribution experience a IR only if they are below a critical size, which, in general, tends to be larger (and sometimes much larger) than the critical size of the lower-end farms.
5   Thus, farms in the upper deciles of the LP distribution, in effect, experience the IR for a wider range of farm sizes than farmers of the lower deciles.

The IR literature

The IR, an inverse relationship or inverse productivity hypothesis (Schultz 1964; Hayami and Otsuka 1993; Binswanger, Deininger, and Feder 1995; Vollrath 2007;

Hazell 2011), has long been considered one of the stylized facts of development economics. The finding that land productivity and size of the land operated (both owned and rented) are related negatively originated from studies based on Indian data (see, e.g., for direct evidence and reviews: Mazumdar [1965]; Srinivasan [1972]; Bardhan [1973]; Sen [1975]; Bhalla [1979]; Carter [1984]), and then was confirmed for a variety of other countries (Berry and Cline 1979; Kutcher and Scandizzo 1981; Binswanger, Deininger, and Feder 1995).

The literature has conjured up many different explanations for this empirical regularity:

1   Factor market imperfections in land and other markets, such as credit and modern inputs (Bardhan 1973; Scandizzo and Barbosa 1977; Lund and Hill 1979; Feder 1985; Carter and Wiebe 1990; Dorward 1999);
2   Higher transaction costs for supervision and shirking for larger or non-family farms (Yotopoulos and Lau 1973; Taslim 1989; Frisvold 1994; Binswanger-Mkhize, Bourguignon, and van den Brink 2009; Hazell et al. 2010);
3   Higher technical efficiency of smaller farms (Yotopoulos and Lau 1973; Bravo-Ureta and Pinheiro 1997; Helfand and Levine 2004);
4   A more intensive use of land and higher per-hectare resource inputs on small farms (Barraclough and Collarte 1973; Berry and Cline 1979; Carter 1984; and Cornia 1985);
5   Better information on weather, soil quality, and plants of traditional family farmers, accumulated over generations (Rosenzweig and Wolpin 1985; Byiringiro and Reardon 1996);
6   Omission of soil quality measurements that are inversely correlated with farm or plot size, but positively associated with yields (Benjamin 1995; Bhalla and Roy 1988; Lamb 2003; Assunção and Braido 2007; Barrett, Bellemare, and Hou 2010; Larson et al. 2013);
7   Systematic measurement errors in self-reported area and quantity of crop production (for evidence to the contrary, see Deininger et al. [2012]; Carletto, Savastano, and Zezza [2013]);
8   Risk and uncertainty (Srinivasan 1972; Hazell and Scandizzo 1975; Barrett 1996).
9   Failure to use more adequate performance measures, such as profits (Carter 1984; Rosenzweig and Binswanger 1993; Lamb 2003).

All these explanations and the IR finding itself, however, robust across many studies (Bharadwaj 1974; Carter 1984; Feder 1985), appear somewhat of a puzzle, for several reasons. First, the IR does not emerge from discrete differences between small and large farms, but in most studies, there is a smooth tendency for land productivity to decline with farm size. Second, many explanations seem to reject the equalization of factor prices predicted by market equilibrium theory without, at the same time, fully explaining the nature of the relationship. For example, lower reservation wages are invoked to explain why family farms use more labor per unit of land than do large nonfamily farms, but most of the studies concern essentially small farms (below 10 ha of operated size); and land productivity appears to decline within all ranges of family, as well as nonfamily, farms. This also makes it hard to accept explanations, such as Feder's (1985), based on the lower transaction costs for supervision and higher motivation of family farm managers, as well as on the more intense use of family labor and the fact that supply of working capital is directly related to farm size. All these factors would indeed justify differences between family and nonfamily farms, but not differences within the groups.

Some studies (Bhalla 1979; Bhalla and Roy 1988; Benjamin 1995; Dyer 1997) have suggested an inverse correlation between land quality and farm size, so that ignoring this relation may be the cause of a basic specification error. This implies that if various characteristics of land – such as fertility, water and nutrient availability, soil structure, and composition – are taken into account, the negative correlation between average land productivity and size might be drastically altered or disappear. However, this does not seem to be the case, and the evidence presented is at best ambiguous.

The omission of nonobservable variables, such as transaction costs, weather, and land quality, is an underlying theme of many of the attempts at explaining the IR; and some of the less obvious variables involved may be related to managerial performance and farmers' skills. However, these omitted variables are not necessarily associated with the IR and can, in fact, determine many different patterns of productivity across the distribution of farm sizes. For example, in an insightful study on the impact of the Kenyan extension service, Evenson and Mwabu (2001) conjectured that the complementarity with unobserved farmer ability might account for different impacts of extension programs on productivity. They found the highest productivity effect of agricultural extension for farmers at the extreme ends of distribution of yield residuals. They also found that productivity response to acreage, measured through quantile regression, was not significantly different across quantiles, but displayed a concave shape, first rising and then falling, with the size of the cultivated area.

More persuasive in explaining the findings on the smoothly declining productivity over farm size are the arguments based on risk, since they may imply a more continuous IR, even within family farms. For example, Srinivasan (1972) explained the IR by yield risk, by defining utility over income and imposing restrictions on the coefficients of risk aversion and on how risk enters production, under constant returns. Hazell and Scandizzo (1975) provided a rationale for producers to smoothly reduce planned production in response to the negative correlation between supply and prices, and Barrett (1996) showed that a continuous IR can emerge from price risk if farmers are net buyers of the crop produced, since in this case, risk aversion implies labor overemployment to protect consumption.

As Savastano and Scandizzo (2009) have shown, a continuous relationship between productivity and operated area may also arise because of the investment required by the decision to increase one's farmland. Under dynamic uncertainty, in fact, the amount of land operated by a farmer will depend on the timing of the exercise of the option to invest in land development, and this will vary across the entire size distribution for heterogeneous farmers. With decreasing returns to scale, this implies a non-monotonic relationship between revenue per ha and operated land. If land is available on the market in fixed quantities (i.e., supply of plots for rents or sale, or entire farms of discrete size), and/or investment is lumpy, small farms will exhibit lower revenue thresholds for investment, and thus lower revenues per ha than larger farms. This implies, in particular, that the relationship between productivity and size may exhibit turning points, as farmers switch from one type of investment to another (e.g., from land improvements to irrigation), as their operating land increases as a result of previous investment decisions.

A conceptual framework

On a different front, the IR finding can also be interpreted with reference to the literature on the institutional economic theory of the firm. In this respect, two crucial questions can be raised. First, contrary to reasonable expectations on the division of labor and the role of capital, in most cases the family farm appears to be the dominant form of organization of the productive unit in agriculture. Second, similarly, but more dramatically than for the other types of firms, the existence of profit represents a puzzle for the family farm, since its determination as a residual in a highly competitive market does not follow a clear economic logic. Demsetz (1995), who discussed the issue of the existence of the firm by contrasting Coase's transaction theory with his own, started his treatment by noting that rather than focused on the existence of the firm, the early literature was concerned with a related but separate event – the existence of profit in a perfectly competitive market. Given that profit existed, the institutional theory tried to find a justification in the entrepreneur. In two significant cases, that of Frank Knight (1921) and Ronald Coase (1937), both authors laid the foundation for a productivity theory of the firm, based on the idea that the reason for the firm's existence is to increase productivity by providing managed coordination, thereby reducing risk, in the case of Knight, and reducing transaction costs, according to Coase. Demsetz's own theory is based on two related concepts: specialization and interdependence, in which the development of a business firm is seen as a process of specialization that separates production from consumption, thereby creating interdependence with other firms and households.

For Boserup (1965), Binswanger and Rosenzweig (1986), and Binswanger and McIntire (1987), the process of agricultural development is characterized by population pressure, which brings about the family farm system, chiefly because of hired labor transaction costs that create diseconomies of management. The family farm, in other words, while equally productive in reducing other transaction costs external to the firm (à la Coase), is superior in increasing productivity by internalizing labor supervision costs without increasing transaction costs internal to the firm. According to the family farm theory (Roumasset 1995), in particular, it is the very organization of the farm that is determined by labor transaction costs, rather than by any technical economy of scale. On the other hand, Eastwood, Lipton, and Newell (2010) (henceforth ELN), on the basis of a simple maximization model with homogenous farmers, claimed that development will bring about an increase in family reservation utility and, thus, in equilibrium farm size, but the increasing availability of cheaper capital and technological progress can go either way. Moreover, removal of any of the hypothesis of the simple model (e.g., infinite supply of family farmers, homogeneity of land) tends to open the way for different results, pointing to the impossibility of a unique prediction on the effects of development on farm size. A similar conclusion can be reached for the relationship between efficiency and farm size, with a plurality of possible outcomes, depending on the various components of scale economies and diseconomies, including indivisibilities and transaction costs that may directly and indirectly interest the farm.

While the outcomes of increasing farm size may be many, it seems legitimate to ask whether there is a fundamental tendency, as postulated by Coase (1937), for the farm to grow in response to the need to reduce market transaction costs; and, if not, why or because of which fundamental constraints or countertendencies? This question is dictated by the general issues considered by Coase, but also by the seemingly ubiquitous finding of an inverse relationship (IR) between land productivity and farm size. The answer to the foregoing question, however, requires an answer to a more general question – namely: is the farm, and the family farm in particular, defined by its relationship with transaction costs, within the bigger picture of the relationship between the firm and the market? In this respect, most of the literature cited, with the partial exception of ELN, appears to regard transaction costs as an element of possible scale diseconomies in determining the optimal size of the farm, and not as a constitutive element of the productivity mission of the firm as an institutional agent, as claimed by the institutional economic literature. Rather than asking whether small farms reduce transaction costs, for example, Pingali (2010) focused on the opposite question of whether and how to reduce the transaction costs faced by small farms. On the other hand, ELN noted that there is no theory that predicts optimal farm size to minimize unit transaction costs, because of multiple equilibria, deriving from non-convexities of the transaction cost functions. They claim that these multiple local optima may give rise to sudden jumps from self-cultivation to much larger forms of operations, in effect, because labor transaction costs become less important than capital transaction costs.

These arguments also seem to exclude a tendency toward an optimal farm size, but rely on a particular interpretation that essentially assimilates transaction costs into the costs of accessing factor markets and managing factor usage. A more general interpretation, however, considers transaction costs as all costs related to *ex ante* and *ex post* exchange, including the choice of the trading partners, bargaining, monitoring, and enforcing the related contracts. For Coase (1937), the firm acts as an agent capable of reducing these costs by substituting a structure of command and control for the decentralized structure of the market, and by appropriately standardizing the contracts themselves.

Within this interpretation, as a nexus of contracts, the family farm presents different organizational features from a commercial farm, which may indeed reveal a tendency to settle around an optimal size that, if not reached or once reached, may give rise to scale economies and diseconomies, respectively. The organization of the family farm, in fact, is based on a structure of implicit contracting, grounded in familiarity (in the literal sense); trust and mutual exchange, with community monitoring and enforcement; a strong role for traditional procedures, routines, and rights; and equal importance of utilitarian exchange and ritualized gift giving. As Demsetz (1995) argued, the family farm is also typically organized in a way that promotes a certain degree of self-sufficiency, and thus tends to substitute the contracts between producers and consumers with standard in-house arrangements, which often include family and nonfamily labor.

Family farms may thus be more effective in enhancing productivity than other types of organizations, especially when market transaction costs are high; and they pursue their mission with a panoply of instruments, characteristic of traditional societies, some of which survive within "familistic" cultures, even in more advanced and indeed non-agrarian urban contexts. We should expect their contribution to productivity increases, however, to be uneven and led by different drivers, depending on the features of the environment that they face, their different objectives, and the relative importance that the instruments at their disposal assume. Management ability is certainly a component of a successful performance, but a number of family characteristics may coalesce to determine winners and losers, including the human and nonhuman capital (Sen's renown concept of "capabilities") with which the family is endowed.

Classes of different performances may thus emerge across the spectrum of family farms, depending on the fact that they may have diverse subsistence and marketing goals, and due to characteristics that may be, at the same time, too many and too subtle to observe. Within each class, a tendency to optimize may be present, with several local optima that determine local IRs in different intervals of productivity and farm sizes. In more dynamic terms, the implications of development and transaction costs for the family farm may be rather different from those of the firm. In both cases, an increase in market transaction costs (MTC) may increase the incentives to internalize the production of goods and services, but while this typically means a more vertically integrated enterprise for the firm, it simply tends to enhance the push for self-sufficiency for the family farm, thereby increasing its optimal size. Symmetrically, an increase in internal transaction costs (ITC), such as information and supervision, will reduce the incentive to integrate the value chain for a firm that is already well positioned in the market, while it may reduce optimal farm size by increasing specialization and market dependence for the family farm.

Decisions about family size are also likely to be affected by transaction costs, so that the family farm, unlike the firm, may react to changes in MTCs and ITCs with two instruments – that is, the number of people in the family and the scale of operations. Thus, increases in the ratio between MTCs and ITCs may be expected to encourage larger family sizes, because a higher degree of self-sufficiency requires larger operating sizes, higher diversification, and more general skills, with factors somewhat trapped within the farm or its quasi-market circle of mutual help from extended family systems. Here, we should expect, first, a direct relationship between productivity and farm size and, then, the IR emerging in response to excessive increases led by the forces unleashed by the stronger drive toward self-sufficiency. Alternatively, a decrease in the MTC–ITC ratio will encourage smaller and more specialized enterprises, higher integration with the market, and higher factor mobility, with the IR pushing toward a contraction of farm sizes along these lines. Thus, even though consistent with the Coasian premises, the process of deagrarianization may itself be a cause of the IR. It is, in a sense, the opposite of the process originally described by Coase (1937), with many different types of smaller farm–firms emerging from the rather homogenous population of traditional family farms to exploit the reduction in market transaction costs made possible by development.

Since the family farm has low supervisory costs from higher motivation of its members (Feder 1985), and because of the gratuities that members can experience as parts of an extended family business, the reduction in external transaction costs may be expected to have different effects on differently performing farms. For highly productive family farms that are performing better than their peers because of higher-quality management or other nonobservable farmers' abilities, increases in marketable surplus and development of commercial agriculture may be a chance to be exploited immediately – even before undergoing a transformation to more specialized units, operating exclusively for the market. While increasing farm size may be necessary to exploit the new market opportunities, increasing internal transaction costs (ITC) should be expected to have negative effects on productivity until a certain threshold of successful transformation into commercial farming has been achieved.

For less productive family farms, on the other hand, the opportunities created by lower MTCs may be met with size expansion without major increases in supervision costs, at first, either because of underemployed family labor or because of other benefits from MTC reduction, such as access to modern inputs, extension, and better prices. Beyond a certain threshold of expansion, it is nevertheless reasonable to expect that ITCs will become prevalent again, and that larger farm sizes will be associated with lower productivity.

These considerations also suggest that farmers may operate in different ways, especially in the extreme distribution of farm productivity residuals, due to unobserved cognitive and physical abilities (Evenson and Mwabu 2001), previous experience with investment, or other performance-related characteristics. Thus, for example, at the low extreme of the productivity distribution (or the distribution of its residuals after accounting for the exogenous variables), productivity could increase as farmers take advantage of larger operating areas to overcome other performance disadvantages due to low endowments of skills and knowledge. At the high extreme, on the other end, supervision costs may become more important, and larger sizes may reduce the competitive advantage of abilities and motivation of family farmers (Feder 1985).

If factor productivity is distributed normally, with a constant variance, aside from identification problems, OLS will generally provide an estimate of the relationship based on mean response. In other words, OLS will allow us to estimate a response coefficient that will quantify the average response of the dependent variable (e.g., land productivity) to farm size increases. If the distribution of the response around the mean, estimated accordingly with OLS, is not satisfactorily described by a single variance, however, quantile regression (Koenker and Basset 1978) promises a more robust and appropriate estimate, especially if variance is systematically related to the increase in the response variable (heteroscedasticity). We also conjecture that the relationship between productivity and alternative measures of size (land available, land under cultivation, etc.) may be considerably different for farmers who, for various reasons that cannot be captured by the econometric model, have to operate at low productivity levels, with respect to farmers that operate at high productivity levels.

The estimation problem

Consider the relationship between land productivity and farm size in the stylized form:

$$\frac{y_i}{x_i} = \beta_0 + \beta_1 x_i + \gamma Z_i + \varepsilon_i \tag{3.1}$$

where y_i is some measure of production for the ith farm, x_i is a correspondent measure of farm size (e.g., operated area), Z_i is a set of exogenous variables, and ε_i is a random disturbance. It is important to underline the fact that equation (3.1) is not a production function, but the result of farmers' choices, on the basis, inter alia, of an underlying technology. If we assume that farmers have adjusted production (either through optimization or through any other common behavioral rule) to the circumstances outside their control, including exogenous variables, states of nature, and so forth, the coefficient β_1 in (3.1) should be zero. In other words, all systematic differences in production per acre between farms should be accounted for by differences in the Z_i variables or in the random term ε_i. A β_1 value different from zero, on the other hand, would imply the existence of systematic differences across farmers that are not accounted for in the equation: these differences could be due to different behavioral rules, different abilities in following the same rules, or different levels of information or other omitted variables that are correlated with farm size.

It is also important to note that a non-zero β_1 may be caused by discontinuities in the behavioral function that underlie farmers' adjustments to the exogenous variables. These discontinuities are implied by most of the explanations of the inverse productivity relationship, based on anthropological differences between "family" and "nonfamily," or systematic divergence in behavior between "small" and "large" farms (e.g., Cornia 1985; Feder 1985). However, if the IR is the result of these discontinuities, it should concern the differences only across the two extreme groups of farmers and not within the groups themselves.

In order to test for the existence of an inverse relationship (IR) between land productivity and farm size, we use both the OLS regression model and quantile regressions (Koenker and Bassett 1978). While OLS focuses on modeling the conditional mean of the response variable without accounting for its distribution, the quantile regression model accounts for the full conditional distributional properties of the response variable (or is residual after accounting for the exogenous variables), thereby differing on the assumptions about the error terms of the regression model.

In the case of equation (3.1), the OLS model is based on the assumption that the error term is normally distributed with zero mean and constant variance: $\varepsilon_i \sim$ i.i.d. $N(0, \sigma^2)$.

The consequence of the mean zero assumption of the error term implies that the model fits the conditional mean – namely, $E[y - \gamma Z \mid x] = \beta_0 + \beta_1 x_i$, which can be interpreted as the average value of productivity, after accounting for the effect of the exogenous variables Z, corresponding to a fixed value of the covariate x (i.e., farm size). The linear regression model describes how the conditional distribution behaves by utilizing the mean of a distribution to represent its central tendency, a choice that appears appropriate under the assumption of homoscedasticity – namely, of constant variance for all values of the covariate x.

The quantile-regression model (QRM) estimates the potential differential effect of a covariate (farm size) on various quantiles in the conditional distribution. A conditional quantile is a statistic corresponding to the probability level of a given distribution, according to a function (the quantile function), defined as $q(p) = \{y : \Pr(Y \leq y) = p\}$. By considering the different quantiles, the QRM estimates how the effect of a covariate varies with the distribution of the response variable and accommodates heteroscedasticity. The QRM corresponding to the linear regression model (LRM) in equation (3.1) can be expressed as:

$$y_1 = \beta_0^{(q)} + \beta_1^{(q)} x_i + \gamma^{(q)} Z_i + \varepsilon_1^{(q)} \tag{3.2}$$

The parameter vector, $\left[\beta_0^{(q)} \beta_1^{(q)} \gamma^{(q)}\right]$, is obtained by minimizing the sum of absolute deviations from an arbitrarily chosen quantile of a farm yield across farmers. In the case of equation (3.2), this sum can be expressed as:

$$\text{Minimize: } \Sigma_i \mid y_i^q - [\beta_0^{(q)} + \beta_1^{(q)} x_i + \Sigma_j \gamma_j^q Z_{ij} \mid \tag{3.3}$$

where y_i^q = average productivity for farmer i at quantile q, (i =1, ...n); x_i = farm size; and Z_{ij} = covariate j for farmer i (j = 1, ...K).

The solution to equation (3.3) is found by rewriting the expression as a linear programming problem over the entire sample and solving for the values of the parameters. Both the squared-error and absolute-error loss functions are symmetric, as the sign of the prediction error is not relevant. Although OLS can be inefficient if the errors are highly non-normal, quantile regression is more robust to non-normal errors and outliers. QR also provides a richer characterization of the data, allowing for consideration of the impact of a covariate on the entire distribution of y, not merely its conditional mean.

Figure 3.1 summarizes key aspects of our sample data on land productivity and farm size into a single form. On the horizontal axis, farm size classes are reported by increasing size, while the vertical axis measures average land productivity. The top of the rectangular box shaded in the figure marks the 75th percentile of the data range, while the bottom "hinge" marks the lower 25th percentile. The "whiskers" extend another 1.5 times the interquartile range of the nearest quartile. The horizontal line in the middle of the box marks the median of the data for each group. Intuitively, the range of the box delineates observations that are typical. The whiskers contain values that are somewhat atypical relative to most observations, while the dots mark observations that are extreme, with a large number of suspiciously small values with a tendency toward dispersion, even if we are in the log scale of crop income. The diagram appears to show a clear tendency for productivity to decline with increase in farm size.

This effect is accentuated if we consider the upper and lower tails of the productivity distribution. This crude correlation, however, may be misleading for two reasons: first, it does not consider the effects of the other covariates that are expected to influence farm productivity; second, in the same diagram, dispersion appears to be decreasing with farm size, with a much wider range of values for the smallest size. By characterizing the entire distribution of crop income for each farm class, even for the simple correlation, the plot thus suggests that the

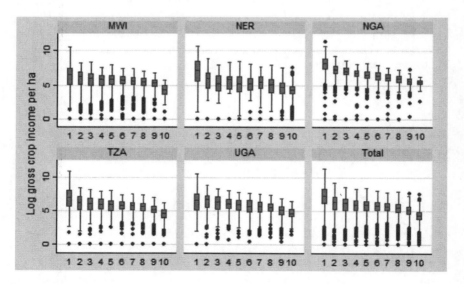

Figure 3.1 Log gross crop income by percentiles of land operated (land productivity)
Source: Authors' computation based on the LSMS–ISA Surveys.

relationship between productivity and farm size may not be the same for different levels of productivity, and that group means or medians do not necessarily represent group behavior.

Data and descriptive statistics

We use data from LSMS–ISA Surveys in Malawi, Niger, Nigeria, Tanzania, and Uganda, all collected between 2010 and 2011. These are large, multipurpose household surveys, nationally representative, with detailed information on agricultural production. Table 3.1 reports some descriptive statistics from the surveys, showing mean values of broadly comparable magnitude across countries,

Table 3.1 Descriptive statistics (averages)

ISO	Malawi	Niger	Nigeria	Tanzania	Uganda	Total
Gross crop income per ha (US$/ha)	507.57	265.2	2229.82	478.52	468.2	733.58
Land operated (owned+ rented in-rented out-fallow) (ha)	0.73	5.21	0.8	2.33	1.45	2.10
Rural population density (pers./sq. km) (2005)	182.5	60.4	218.3	59.9	266.9	157.6
Gross cropped area (ha)	0.74	5.8	1.6	2.03	2.4	2.514
Net crop area (ha)	0.67	4.9	1.3	1.95	1.0	1.964
Crop intensity	1.02	1.19	1.23	1.07	1.89	1.28
Annual precipitation (mm)	1085.54	375.94	1369.17	1089.87	1225.23	1064.8
Annual mean temperature (°C * 10)	218.28	282.03	263.59	227	218.82	233.61
UG: travel time negative exponential, with borders restriction to cities with 500K	142.49	41.36	113.23	49.96	53.59	105.23
HH distance (km) to nearest market	7.96	62.72	71.33	82.67	31.21	35.85
HH distance (km) to nearest major road	9.69	12.92	17.21	21.73	7.31	12.41
Dummy constraints to oxygen availability to roots[1]	0.1	0.15	0.17	0.12	0.28	0.14
Dummy excess salts[1]	0.04	0.09	0.03	0.06	0.04	0.05
Pastoral farming system[2]	0	0.49	0.03	0	0.01	0.06

Source: Authors' computation based on the LSMS–ISA Surveys.

[1] Dummies for oxygen availability and excess salt have been computed from the continuous geospatial variable of the LSMS–ISA. A dummy is equal to 1 for higher constraint to soil fertility. Both raw data are derived from the FAO's Harmonized World Soil Database v.1.2 (soil nutrient availability).

[2] The dummy for pastoral farming system is drawn from the Harvestchoice data set, and follows the classification of the farming systems in sub-Saharan Africa, according to FAO's methodology and based on Dixon et al. (2001).

except for Nigeria, which appears to have a much smaller average operated area, larger yield, and labor intensity than the other countries.

Descriptive statistics for the surveys in our sample provide a number of insights, pointing in particular to a wide distribution of land ownership, but to similar levels of crop intensity, differences in rural population density and market access, large productivity gaps across producers, and sizable variations in infrastructure and agroecological conditions.

In terms of area operated by farmers (defined by area owned, plus area rented, and net of area rented out and under fallow), we note that the average across the five countries is 2.1 ha, with the lowest in Malawi (0.73 ha) and the highest in Niger (5.21 ha). With 267 and 218 persons per sq km, respectively, Uganda and Nigeria are the two countries with the highest rural population density. Somewhat surprisingly, Uganda, with an average rural population density four times the level in Tanzania, has an average operated area quite close to Tanzania's 2.3 ha. Although a larger farm size would be expected to compensate for lower population density, labor constraints prevent farmers from making the necessary investment (mechanization, tractor plowing, or draft animal) to increase farm endowment. In terms of agricultural intensification, we observe that the majority of the countries have reached a stage of permanent agriculture, as the crop intensity (defined as gross cropped area divided by net cropped area) is larger than 1.

The georeferenced structure of the LSMS–ISA data sets allows us to link geo-variables matched by staff at the World Bank to the external data sets of the Harmonized World Soil Database v.1.2 of the Food and Agriculture Organization of the United Nations (FAO) (soil nutrient availability), and use soil quality controls in our regressions. The soil database is the result of collaboration between the FAO with the International Institute of Applied Systems Analysis (IIASA), the International Soil Reference and Information Centre (ISRIC)–World Soil Information, Institute of Soil Science–Chinese Academy of Sciences (ISSCAS), and the Joint Research Centre of the European Commission (JRC).[2] Among all the variables tested, two variables are mostly significant in the regressions to indicate lack of soil quality. They are: (1) a dummy constraint of oxygen availability equal to 1, if the categorical variable "Oxygen availability to roots" is equal to severe and very severe constraints and zero otherwise; and (2) a dummy constraint of excess salt equal to 1, if the categorical variable "Excess salts" is equal to severe and very severe constraints and zero otherwise.

We use urban gravity and distance to the nearest market or the major road as proxies for urbanization and access to infrastructure, respectively. To compute urban gravity, we use light intensity data produced by the Defense Meteorological Satellite Program (DMSP) of the National Geophysical Data Center, and we convert them into urban gravity using the same approach of Binswanger and Savastano (2014). The proxies for market access are taken from the geospatial data set of the LSMS–ISA surveys, which include households' average distances to the nearest market and major road.[3] We note large disparities in terms of market access, with an average household distance to reach the nearest market of 35 km for the five countries, with a minimum of 8 km in Malawi to a maximum of 86 km in Tanzania. Also, as a proxy for urbanization, we note that urban gravity is the largest in Malawi and Nigeria, and the lowest in Niger and Tanzania.

Using both OLS and quantile regression, we estimate the following function at the household level:

$$\ln \frac{y_i}{v_i} = b_o + b_1 \ln x_1 + b_2 \ln Z_1 + u_i \tag{3.4}$$

where $\frac{y_i}{v_i}$ represents an indicator of farm productivity (gross crop income per ha, in which case $x_1 = v_i$, or total labor productivity) for each household i; x_1 is the total area operated; Z_1 denotes a vector of exogenous georeferenced household characteristics, such as variance of precipitation and temperature, urban gravity, distance to the major road or market, soil quality controls; and u_i is an error term.

Table 3.2 presents the main results from the estimation for the pooled sample. The OLS estimates show a significant negative elasticity for the relationship between gross income per ha and land operated, with a value not significantly different from 1 and no significant quadratic response. The first (10 percent) quantile-regression estimates, however, "deconstruct" this result as corresponding to the combination of a positive, more than proportional, linear response and a negative, smaller than unity quadratic response. For the other three quantiles considered (the 25th, the 50th, and the 80th), a similar but reversed sequence of a negative linear and a positive quadratic response is estimated. Moreover, both the quadratic and the linear coefficients increase across the quantiles. The IR hypothesis, therefore, appears to be rejected for all but the very first quantile, where it is reversed, however, after a threshold of operating size is reached. The opposite is found for the other three quantiles – although productivity tends to decrease with the cultivated area, according to the IR hypothesis, this relationship is also reversed, and the threshold of reversal is larger and larger as we move from the 25th to the 80th quantile.

In this regression, the elasticity of productivity, with respect to the urban gravity index, is low and essentially the same (between 0.01 and 0.03) for all quantiles, except the 20th, for which it is not significant. The estimates of the weather impact are somewhat surprising, with a large negative effect of the variance of temperature and a smaller positive effect of rainfall variability, with both effects tending to vanish for the top quantiles. The elasticities, with respect to the distance from the market and the main road, are variable and larger. They follow a quadratic relation with a positive linear (in the logs) and a negative quadratic coefficient. The presence of pastoral farming systems appears to impact negatively on average land productivity, only for the lower half of the quantiles, but appears to have no effect in the quantiles in the top 50 percent. In sum, the results show that performance classes differ significantly in their response to key exogenous variables, and that this response from productivity

Table 3.2 Dependent variable: log gross crop income/ha

VARIABLES	(1)OLS Pooled	(2) Q10	(3) Q25	(4) Q50	(5)Q90
Log land operated	−0.92***	1.25***	−0.86***	−1.72***	−2.70***
Sq. log land operated	0.14***	−0.61***	0.04	0.26***	0.56***
Variance of precipitation		0.56***	0.22***	0.17***	−0.02
Variance of temperature	−3.72***	−15.96***	−4.85***	−1.27***	1.45***
Log UG	−0.02***	−0.03	−0.04***	−0.03***	−0.03***
Log distance to market	0.34***	1.16***	0.30***	0.19***	0.25***
Log distance to market sq.	−0.05***	−0.16***	−0.04***	−0.03***	−0.04***
Log distance to road	0.33***	0.58***	0.46***	0.27***	0.10***
Log distance to road sq.	−0.07***	−0.10**	−0.10***	−0.07***	−0.03***
Dummy constraint oxygen availability to roots	−0.31***	−0.84***	−0.29***	−0.13***	−0.08***
Dummy constraint excess salts	−0.33***	−0.96***	−0.58***	−0.13**	0.21***
Pastoral farming system	−0.24***	−0.27	−0.30***	−0.13**	−0.06
Country dummies					
Malawi	−0.14*	0.39	0.17	−0.12**	−0.28***
Nigeria	1.02***	1.44***	1.11***	0.73***	0.72***
Tanzania	0.04	−0.08	0.08	0.01	0.17***
Uganda	−0.20**	−0.46	−0.24*	−0.18***	0.14**
Constant	4.95***	−1.15*	3.89***	5.72***	8.05***
Observations	18,410	18,410	18,410	18,410	18,410
R–squared	0.18				

Source: Authors' computation based on the LSMS–ISA Surveys.

*** p<0.01
** p<0.05
* p<0.1. NER is the comparison group.

to infrastructure (urban gravity, and road and market distance) tends to be non-monotonic.

Estimates on individual countries confirm the results (see Tables 3.3–3.7), which are summarized in Table 3.8. They suggest distribution dependency of both the form and the intensity of the productivity response to the increases in operating area. We find that productivity effects of acreage increases are different at different levels of productivity and are highest, but with opposite signs, at the extreme ends of the distribution of yield residuals, with very similar patterns of decline for the linear terms, and increase for the quadratic ones over the distribution (see Figures 3.1, 3.2, and 3.3). This may be due to various causes – for example, that unobserved farmer ability acts as a complement for land increases at low levels of yield residuals and as a substitute at higher yield residuals. More generally, it could be because the endowments of critical, unaccounted-for components of human and nonhuman capital are correlated with productivity increases.

Table 3.3 Results for Malawi (MWI)

Y = Log Gross Crop Income/ha

					MALAWI				
	Q10	Q20	Q30	Q40	Q50	Q60	Q70	Q80	Q90
Log land operated	11.22***	1.38**	−0.11	−1.44***	−2.02***	−2.52***	−3.00***	−3.49***	−4.30***
Log land operated sq.	−5.37***	−1.02***	−0.39*	0.15	0.45***	0.68***	0.88***	1.15***	1.52***
Log mean area of land operated by quantile	−7.93***	−0.35	−0.09	1.21*	1.27***	1.60***	1.94***	2.23***	2.90***
Dummy rent in land	−0.11	0.15	0.08	0.08	0.07	0.07	0.06	0.04	0.01
Log UG	−0.33**	−0.28***	−0.28***	−0.20***	−0.15***	−0.11***	−0.10***	−0.08***	−0.07***
Log UG sq.	0.05**	0.04***	0.04***	0.02***	0.02***	0.01***	0.01***	0.01**	0.00
Log distance to road	0.13	0.35**	0.32***	0.30***	0.27***	0.20***	0.21***	0.14***	0.13***
Log distance to road sq.	−0.02	−0.09**	−0.09***	−0.08***	−0.07***	−0.06***	−0.06***	−0.04***	−0.04***
Log distance to market	1.26**	0.44	0.18	0.02	0.07	0.07	0.11	0.10	0.05
Log distance to market sq.	−0.20	−0.06	−0.02	0.01	−0.01	−0.01	−0.02	−0.02	−0.00
Dummy constraint oxygen availability to roots	−2.06***	−1.05***	−0.53***	−0.15**	−0.01	−0.04	−0.01	−0.02	−0.02
Dummy constraint excess salts	−1.93***	−3.39***	−1.51***	−0.96***	−0.58***	−0.31***	−0.09	−0.04	−0.07
Agropastoral/pastoral farming system									
AEZ_TEXT==Tropic – cool/humid	1.01***	0.56***	0.52***	0.45***	0.39***	0.35***	0.36***	0.30***	0.26***
AEZ_TEXT==Tropic – cool/semi-arid	0.59*	0.06	0.04	0.09	0.13**	0.09*	0.10**	0.15***	0.12**
AEZ_TEXT==Tropic – warm/arid	−0.16	−0.13	−0.08	0.01	0.02	0.03	0.02	0.01	−0.01
Constant	12.05***	4.29*	5.36***	3.96***	4.26***	4.13***	3.88***	3.80***	3.17***
Observations	9,157	9,157	9,157	9,157	9,157	9,157	9,157	9,157	9,157

Source: Authors' estimate based on MWI 2010–2011, LSMS–ISA Survey.

* p<0.1
** p<0.05
*** p<0.01

Table 3.4 Results for Niger (NER)

Y = Log Gross Crop Income/ha

					NIGER				
	Q10	Q20	Q30	Q40	Q50	Q60	Q70	Q80	Q90
Log land operated	3.07***	0.76**	−0.27	−0.37*	−0.78***	−1.17***	−1.39***	−1.84***	−2.11***
Log land operated sq.	−0.96***	−0.31***	−0.13*	−0.11*	0.03	0.12**	0.16***	0.26***	0.27***
Log mean area of land operated by quantile	−0.85	−0.48	0.18	0.06	−0.18	−0.06	−0.04	0.18	0.60*
Dummy rent in land	0.50*	0.28	0.14	0.21*	0.18	0.24**	0.20**	0.27**	0.19
Log UG	0.36*	0.18	0.12	−0.03	−0.06	−0.07	−0.07	−0.03	0.03
Log UG sq.	−0.07**	−0.03	−0.02	0.01	0.02	0.02*	0.02*	0.01	0.00
Log distance to road	0.97***	0.77***	0.67***	0.49***	0.45***	0.26***	0.24***	0.22**	0.15
Log distance to road sq.	−0.19***	−0.14*	−0.12***	−0.10***	−0.09***	−0.05**	−0.05**	−0.04	−0.03
Log distance to market	1.51***	1.01***	0.75***	0.72***	0.61***	0.45***	0.46***	0.42***	0.48***
Logdistance to market sq.	−0.26***	−0.18***	−0.13***	−0.11***	−0.10***	−0.07***	−0.07***	−0.07***	−0.08***
Dummy constraint oxygen availability to roots	0.21	0.16	0.15	0.21*	0.18	0.13	0.15	0.23*	0.11
Dummy constraint excess salts	−0.69*	−0.28	−0.24	−0.28*	−0.16	−0.05	−0.01	0.01	0.19
Pastoral farming system	0.58*	0.18	−0.03	−0.12	−0.17	−0.20	−0.21**	−0.31**	−0.49***
Agro-pastoral farming system	0.99***	0.51*	0.14	−0.05	−0.18	−0.20	−0.25**	−0.39***	−0.53***
AEZ_TEXT==Tropic – cool/humid	−0.45*	−0.52**	−0.56***	−0.35***	−0.14	−0.01	0.19**	0.44***	0.78***
Constant	−0.61	2.19*	2.77***	3.72***	5.11***	5.76***	6.16***	6.49***	6.41***
Observations	1,963	1,963	1,963	1,963	1,963	1,963	1,963	1,963	1,963

Source: Authors' estimate based on NER 2010–2011, LSMS–ISA Survey.

* p<0.1
** p<0.05
*** p<0.01

Table 3.5 Results for Nigeria (NGA)

$Y = Log\ Gross\ Crop\ Income/ha$	NIGERIA								
	Q10	Q20	Q30	Q40	Q50	Q60	Q70	Q80	Q90
Log land operated	-3.03***	-4.45***	-4.54***	-4.65***	-5.10***	-5.46***	-5.57***	-5.67***	-5.95***
Log land operated sq.	1.01*	1.48***	1.59***	1.63***	1.84***	1.97***	2.01***	2.08***	2.15***
Log mean area of land operated by quantile	0.43	1.93*	1.33*	1.28**	1.67***	1.99***	1.87***	1.61***	1.98***
Dummy rent in land	-0.06	-0.11	-0.17**	-0.06	-0.04	-0.04	-0.02	-0.02	-0.09
Log UG	-0.26*	-0.16**	-0.13***	-0.08**	-0.06*	-0.06**	-0.06**	-0.07**	-0.04
Log UG sq.	0.01	0.01	0.00	0.00	-0.00	-0.00	0.00	0.00	0.00
Log distance to road	0.25	0.14	-0.01	0.01	0.02	0.03	0.02	0.06	-0.02
Log distance to road sq.	-0.04	-0.02	0.01	0.01	-0.00	-0.01	-0.01	-0.01	0.01
Log distance to market	0.54	0.41	0.31	0.29*	0.21	0.14	0.17	0.07	-0.00
Log distance to market sq.	-0.08	-0.06	-0.05	-0.04*	-0.03	-0.02	-0.02	-0.01	-0.00
Dummy constraint oxygen availability to roots	-0.12	-0.21*	-0.09	-0.02	-0.00	-0.01	-0.03	-0.01	-0.07
Dummy constraint excess salts	0.03	0.02	0.07	0.02	0.01	-0.08	-0.11	-0.03	-0.02
Pastoral farming system	-1.12*	-0.77***	-0.58***	-0.62***	-0.57***	-0.36***	-0.42***	-0.46***	-0.69***
Agro-pastoral farming system	-0.23	-0.21	-0.20**	-0.21***	-0.14*	-0.18**	-0.20***	-0.20***	-0.29***
AEZ_TEXT==Tropic – cool/humid	0.56	0.60	0.33	0.09	0.07	0.10	0.04	-0.14	-0.27
AEZ_TEXT==Tropic – cool/semi-arid	-2.29***	-0.51***	-0.45***	-0.28***	-0.25***	-0.21***	-0.21***	-0.23***	-0.24***
AEZ_TEXT==Tropic – cool/subhumid	-0.11	-0.15	-0.25***	-0.25***	-0.29***	-0.23***	-0.20***	-0.23***	-0.13**
Constant	5.24	3.54*	5.42***	5.69***	5.47***	5.28***	5.66***	6.53***	6.34***
Observations	2,813	2,813	2,813	2,813	2,813	2,813	2,813	2,813	2,813

Source: Authors' estimate based on NGA 2010–2011, LSMS–ISA Survey.

* p<0.1
** p<0.05
*** p<0.01

Table 3.6 Results for Tanzania (TZA)

Y = Log Gross Crop Income/ha

TANZANIA

	Q10	Q20	Q30	Q40	Q50	Q60	Q70	Q80	Q90
Log land operated	7.49***	7.86***	6.35***	2.62***	0.91***	-0.14	-0.78***	-1.27***	-2.11***
Log land operated sq.	-2.17***	-2.25***	-1.80***	-0.79***	-0.38***	-0.14***	-0.01	0.09*	0.31***
Log mean area of land operated by quantile	-4.35***	-4.51***	-4.32***	-2.65***	-1.61***	-0.82***	-0.31	0.07	0.37
Dummy rent in land	0.44**	0.68***	0.53*	0.39	0.37**	0.30**	0.20*	0.23*	0.18
Log UG	0.03	-0.19	-0.57***	-0.44**	-0.36***	-0.21**	-0.21**	-0.06	0.13
Log UG sq.	-0.02	0.02	0.05	0.04	0.04*	0.02	0.02	-0.00	-0.03**
Log distance to road	0.20	0.34**	0.09	0.16	0.16	0.08	0.04	-0.05	0.04
Log distance to road sq.	-0.04	-0.07*	-0.03	-0.04	-0.04	-0.02	-0.01	0.01	-0.01
Log distance to market	0.04	0.34	1.23**	0.93*	0.73**	0.76***	0.79***	0.54**	0.18
Log distance to market sq.	-0.00	-0.05	-0.16**	-0.12	-0.10**	-0.10***	-0.11***	-0.08***	-0.03
Dummy constraint oxygen availability to roots	-0.05	-0.40**	-0.44	-0.37	-0.37**	-0.15	-0.18*	-0.05	0.16
Dummy constraint excess salts	0.01	0.15	0.25	0.37	0.25	0.18	0.26**	0.21	0.08
Pastoral farming system	0.93	0.19	-0.32	-0.63	-0.85	-1.03	-1.41	-1.68	-1.80
Agro-pastoral farming system	0.75	0.97	0.73	0.55	0.41	0.22	0.37	0.19	0.21
AEZ_TEXT==Tropic – cool/humid	1.65***	2.75***	2.72***	1.36**	0.74***	0.57**	0.75***	0.49**	0.21
AEZ_TEXT==Tropic – cool/semi-arid	-0.00	-0.26	-0.31	-0.33	-0.32	-0.20	-0.14	-0.03	-0.01
AEZ_TEXT==Tropic – cool/subhumid	0.01	0.06	0.20	0.14	0.13	0.13*	0.13**	0.15**	0.20***
AEZ_TEXT==Tropic – warm/arid	0.55	1.58***	1.44***	0.92	1.12***	0.86***	0.71***	0.42	0.02
AEZ_TEXT==Tropic – warm/humid	-0.97***	-0.82***	-0.97***	-0.70**	-0.61***	-0.64***	-0.40***	-0.32***	-0.29**
Constant	7.97***	8.10***	7.85***	7.60***	7.19***	6.47***	6.04***	6.37***	7.02***
Observations	1,853	1,853	1,853	1,853	1,853	1,853	1,853	1,853	1,853

Source: Authors' estimate based on TZA 2010–2011, LSMS–ISA Survey.

* p<0.1
** p<0.05
*** p<0.01

Table 3.7 Results for Uganda (UGA)

Y = Log Gross Crop Income/ha

					UGANDA				
	Q10	Q20	Q30	Q40	Q50	Q60	Q70	Q80	Q90
Log land operated	8.31***	3.79***	1.09**	−0.39	−0.79***	−1.37***	−1.70***	−2.18***	−2.37***
Log land operated sq.	−2.67***	−1.39***	−0.51***	−0.14	−0.04	0.11	0.18**	0.36***	0.42***
Log mean area of land operated by quantile	−8.64***	−4.01***	−2.45***	−0.97	−0.56	−0.03	0.42	0.56	0.51
Dummy rent in land	0.80***	0.65***	0.40***	0.22**	0.15*	0.14*	0.15**	0.13**	0.12*
Log UG	0.08	0.07	0.09	0.08	0.11	0.14**	0.07	0.05	0.06
Log UG sq.	−0.03	−0.02	−0.02	−0.02	−0.02*	−0.02**	−0.02*	−0.01	−0.00
Log distance to road	0.18	0.18	0.40*	0.23	0.16	0.16	0.16	0.27***	0.26**
Log distance to road sq.	−0.02	−0.04	−0.11*	−0.06	−0.04	−0.05	−0.05	−0.08***	−0.07**
Log distance to market	0.79	1.42**	1.25***	1.51***	1.42***	1.35***	1.00***	0.88***	0.50***
Log distance to market sq.	−0.14	−0.23**	−0.20***	−0.25***	−0.24***	−0.22***	−0.17***	−0.15***	−0.09***
Dummy constraint oxygen availability to roots	−0.49***	−0.39**	−0.27**	−0.23**	−0.22***	−0.19**	−0.21***	−0.23***	−0.16***
Dummy constraint excess salts	0.76	0.20	0.03	0.01	0.13	0.06	0.21	0.16	−0.02
Pastoral farming system	−0.02	−1.55**	−1.38***	−1.76***	−2.03***	−2.08***	−1.94***	−1.46***	−1.45***
AEZ_TEXT==Tropic – cool/humid	0.51***	0.48**	0.43***	0.42***	0.42***	0.39***	0.37***	0.31***	0.35***
AEZ_TEXT==Tropic – cool/semi-arid	−0.48**	0.20	0.49***	0.72***	0.81***	0.78***	0.69***	0.66***	0.65***
AEZ_TEXT==Tropic – warm/arid	0.54	0.90	0.82**	0.75***	0.71***	0.59***	0.48***	0.30*	0.34*
Constant	15.43***	8.44***	7.23***	5.35***	5.25***	4.78***	4.82***	5.17***	6.15***
Observations	1,976	1,976	1,976	1,976	1,976	1,976	1,976	1,976	1,976

Source: Authors' estimate based on UGA 2010–2011, LSMS–ISA Survey.

* p<0.1

** p<0.05

*** p<0.01

Table 3.8 Summary table for land coefficient: Testing IR by individual countries

		Q10	Q20	Q30	Q40	Q50	Q60	Q70	Q80	Q90
Malawi	Log land operated	11.22***	1.38**	-0.11	-1.44***	-2.02***	-2.52***	-3.00***	-3.49***	-4.30***
	Log land operated sq.	-5.37***	-1.02***	-0.39*	0.15	0.45***	0.68***	0.88***	1.15***	1.52***
Niger	Log land operated	3.07***	0.76**	-0.27	-0.37*	-0.78***	-1.17***	-1.39***	-1.84***	-2.11***
	Log land operated sq.	-0.96***	-0.31***	-0.13*	-0.11*	0.03	0.12**	0.16***	0.26***	0.27***
Nigeria	Log land operated	-3.03***	-4.45***	-4.54***	-4.65***	-5.10***	-5.46***	-5.57***	-5.67***	-5.95***
	Log land operated sq.	1.01*	1.48***	1.59***	1.63***	1.84***	1.97***	2.01***	2.08***	2.15***
Tanzania	Log land operated	7.49***	7.86***	6.35***	2.62***	0.91***	-0.14	-0.78***	-1.27***	-2.11***
	Log land operated sq.	-2.17***	-2.25***	-1.80***	-0.79***	-0.38***	-0.14***	-0.01	0.09*	0.31***
Uganda	Log land operated	8.31***	3.79***	1.09**	-0.39	-0.79***	-1.37***	-1.70***	-2.18***	-2.37***
	Log land operated sq.	-2.67***	-1.39***	-0.51***	-0.14	-0.04	0.11	0.18**	0.36***	0.42***
Pooled	Log land operated	1.42***	-0.62***	-1.12***	-1.50***	-1.74***	-1.94***	-2.15***	-2.39***	-2.67***
	Log land operated sq.	-0.67***	-0.03	0.10***	0.20***	0.26***	0.31***	0.37***	0.45***	0.54***

Source: Authors' computation based on the LSMS–ISA Surveys.

Note: Y = Log Value of Gross Crop Income/ha. The following controls included but not reported: log mean area by quartile of land operated; dummy rent in land; log UG, and square log distance to road; log distance to market; dummy constraint oxygen availability to roots; dummy constraint excess salts; pastoral farming system; AEZ dummies.

* p<0.1
** p<0.05
*** p<0.01

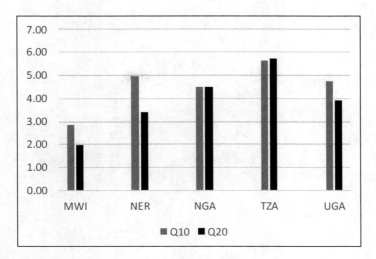

Figure 3.2 Switching values of land size for low performers
Source: Authors' computation based on the LSMS–ISA Surveys.

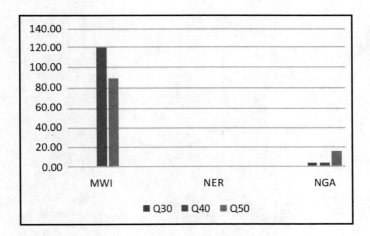

Figure 3.3 Switching values of land size for medium performers
Source: Authors' computation based on the LSMS–ISA Surveys.

Tables 3.9 and 3.10 and Figures 3.2–3.6 show that the disparities in the coefficients estimated for the individual countries correspond to much smaller differences in the ranges over which the IR relationship holds for low performers and correspond to huge differences for medium and high performers. These differences, on the other hand, appear to depend also on the other control variables. In the case of soil quality, for example, differences are especially significant in the

Table 3.9 Summary table for switching land size levels (ha)

	Q10	Q20	Q30	Q40	Q50	Q60	Q70	Q80	Q90	Max. operating area	Average size	SD
Malawi	2.84	1.97	0.87	121.51	9.44	6.38	5.50	4.56	4.11	13.83	0.73	13.8
Niger	4.95	3.41	0.35	0.19	–	130.97	77.00	34.41	49.77	38.25	5.21	38.3
Nigeria	4.48	4.50	4.17	4.16	4.00	4.00	4.00	3.91	3.99	7.35	0.8	7.35
Tanzania	5.62	5.74	5.84	5.25	3.31	0.61	0.00	–	30.06	65.47	2.33	65.5
Uganda	4.74	3.91	2.91	0.25	0.00	–	–	20.65	16.80	13.72	1.45	13.7
Pooled	2.89	0.00	–	42.52	28.39	22.85	18.27	14.23	11.85			

Source: Authors' computation based on the LSMS–ISA Surveys.

Note: The sign – indicates that the switching level is outside the sample range.

Table 3.10 Differences of country regression switching values from pooled regression

	Q10	Q20	Q30	Q40	Q50	Q60	Q70	Q80	Q90
Malawi	−0.04	−0.92	−2.02	118.62	6.55	3.49	2.61	1.67	1.23
Niger	2.06	0.52	−2.53	−2.70	–	128.09	74.11	31.53	46.88
Nigeria	1.60	1.61	1.28	1.28	1.11	1.11	1.11	1.02	1.10
Tanzania	2.73	2.85	2.95	2.36	0.43	−2.28	−2.89	1156.40	27.18
Uganda	1.86	3.91	−267.52	−42.27	−28.39	483.52	94.15	6.42	4.95

Source: Authors' computation based on the LSMS–ISA Surveys.

Note: The sign – indicates that the switching level is outside the sample range.

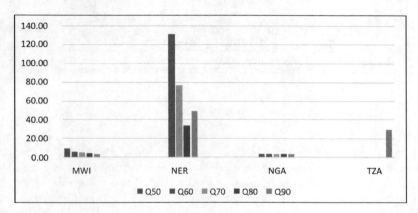

Figure 3.4 Switching values of land size for high performers

Source: Authors' computation based on the LSMS–ISA Surveys.

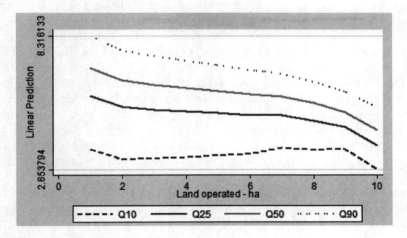

Figure 3.5 Quantile regressions IR land productivity – Pooled regression

Source: Authors' computation based on the LSMS–ISA Surveys.

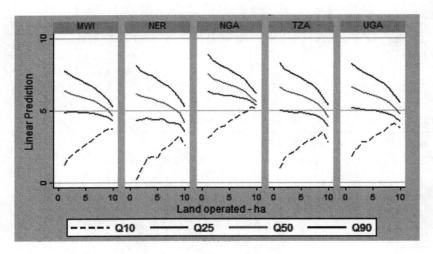

Figure 3.6 Quantile regressions IR land productivity by countries

Source: Authors' computation based on the LSMS–ISA Surveys.

case of the lower performers of Malawi and throughout the quantiles in Uganda. In general, however, for the lower-performing farms of the first two quantiles, the IR appears to take over at about the same level of operating area for values not significantly different from each other and from the pooled sample estimates. This means that land productivity for low performers tends to increase with operating area up to about a level of 2–5 ha and then to decline in accordance with the traditional IR evidence. For the highest performers (farms in the top three deciles of the productivity distribution), the results are the opposite, with productivity declining up to an operating size level of 5 to 80 ha and above, after which increasing returns to scale appear to settle. The much wider range of the switching levels of operating area appears to depend on the range of the operating size variable that is much larger than average for Niger and Tanzania.

The U-shaped pattern at the lower tail of the productivity distribution suggests that a larger operating size may be a positive factor for low performers, but only up to a point, after which the other causes of the IR relation become prevalent (i.e., only if farm size does not become "too large"). For the upper deciles, on the other hand, the IR relationship appears to hold over a much wider range, although in many cases, it appears to reverse itself for moderately large operating areas. As Tables 3.9 and 3.10 and Figures 3.4–3.6 show, the size of the operating area at which the IR relationship prevails for the first two deciles is small, although often above the average, depending on the country. For the upper tail of the distribution, on the other hand, the land size at which the IR relationship reverses itself is only moderately larger, except for a few outliers, so that most large farms essentially do not display any IR.

Conclusions

The inverse relationship (IR) between land productivity and land size has been the object of voluminous literature, raising both objections and explanations. In this study, after a brief review of some of the main arguments, we have presented evidence from five recent farm surveys that, in part, rebut and, in part, confirm the existence of the relationship. The survey data used are from detailed household interviews and contain accurate georeferenced information on farmers' locations, distance from the markets, distance from the main road, and land quality. In order to test the IR hypothesis, we have used a specification that relies entirely on exogenous variables and estimation procedures, according to the quantile-regression model.

The results of our analysis show that for all countries, except Nigeria and for the pooled sample, the IR holds only for the top 6–7 quantiles of the productivity variable (the yield residual once we consider the effect of the exogenous variables), while for the bottom quantiles, a positive relationship tends to hold. These results appear to hold across different specifications, both for the pooled sample and the individual countries. The results suggest that at the two ends of the yield residual distribution, farmers' performance is influenced by land size in a markedly different way. As already noted, although in a different context by Evenson and Mwabu (2001), this may be due to the fact that individual management factors do matter, and that in the two areas of the distribution, different complementary and substitute relations may exist between land sizes and unobserved human capital variables, such as farmers' abilities, skills, and experience.

Our results also suggest the existence of a U-shaped relationship between productivity and farm size. This relationship implies a turning point for the lower quantiles of the yield residual distribution, at which a positive relationship becomes negative, and 1 for the upper quantiles, at which the IR becomes positive. Both turning points are for small- to medium-sized farms, but the ones of the lower quantiles tend to be smaller than those for the upper quantiles. Thus, while there is some significant negative relationship between productivity and operating size for low performers over a relevant range of farm sizes, higher performers tend to display an IR only over a range from small- to medium-sized farms.

In sum, our results confirm that the IR may be a ubiquitous relationship, as found in much of the literature, but indicate that its form, shape, and importance may significantly differ across the spectrum of farm productivity performance. At the low end of the yield distribution, the IR appears to prevail, once a minimum threshold of farm size is reached, while at the higher end, the IR appears only to be mainly a characteristic of farmers with operating sizes not exceeding medium-sized thresholds. The literature on transaction costs and the role of the firm suggest that these differences will require a deeper analysis of some of the critical factors determining the performance of the farm as a "productivity agent" and of the role played by management and capabilities in shaping farmers' choices.

Notes

1 Reviewed by Sen (1975).
2 From the FAO Soils Portal:

> The Harmonized World Soil Database is a 30 arc-second roster database with over 15 000 different soil mapping units that combines existing regional and national updates of soil information worldwide (SOTER, ESD, Soil Map of China, WISE) with the information contained within the 1:5 000 000 scale FAO-UNESCO Soil Map of the World (FAO 1971–1981).
>
> The resulting database consists of 21600 rows and 43200 columns, which are linked to harmonized soil property data. . . . and display . . . the composition in terms of soil units and the characterization of selected soil parameters (organic Carbon, pH, water storage capacity, soil depth, cation exchange capacity of the soil and the clay fraction, total exchangeable nutrients, lime and gypsum contents, sodium exchange percentage, salinity, textural class and granulometry).
>
> (FAO 2016)

   http://www.fao.org/soils-portal/soil-survey/soil-maps-and-databases/harmonized-world-soil-database-v12/en/
3 The source for the variable distance to the main road is OpenStreetMap-Tranroad (http://www.openstreetmap.org), while the source for the distance to the nearest market is USAID–FEWSNET (Famine Early Warning Systems Network) (http://www.fews.net).

References

Assunção, J. J., and L. H. B. Braido. 2007. "Testing Household-Specific Explanations for the Inverse Productivity Relationship." *American Journal of Agricultural Economics* 89 (4): 980–90.

Bardhan, P. 1973. "Size, Productivity, and Returns to Scale: An Analysis of Farm-level Data in Indian Agriculture." *Journal of Political Economy* 81 (6): 1370–86.

Barraclough, S., and J. C. Collarte. 1973. *Agrarian Structure in Latin America.* Lexington, MA: Lexington Books.

Barrett, C. B. 1996. "On Price Risk and the Inverse Farm Size–Productivity Relationship." *Journal of Development Economics* 51 (2): 193–215.

Barrett, C. B., M. F. Bellemare, and J. Y. Hou. 2010. "Reconsidering Conventional Explanations of the Inverse Productivity–Size Relationship." *World Development* 38 (1): 88–97.

Benjamin, D. 1995. "Can Unobserved Land Quality Explain the Inverse Productivity Relationship?" *Journal of Development Economics* 46 (1): 51–84.

Berry, R. A., and W. R. Cline. 1979. *Agrarian Structure and Productivity in Developing Countries: A Study Prepared for the International Labour Office within the Framework of the World Employment Programme.* Baltimore, MD: Johns Hopkins University Press.

Bhalla, S. 1979. "Farm Size, Productivity and Technical Change in Indian Agriculture," Appendix. In *Agrarian Structure and Productivity in Developing Countries*, edited by R. A. Berry and W. R. Cline, 141–93. Baltimore, MD: Johns Hopkins University Press.

Bhalla, S. S., and P. Roy. 1988. "Mis-Specification in Farm Productivity Analysis: The Role of Land Quality." *Oxford Economic Papers* 40 (1): 55–73.

Bharadwaj, K. 1974. *Production Conditions in Indian Agriculture: A Study Based on Farm Management Surveys.* Cambridge, UK: Cambridge University Press.

Binswanger, H. P., K. Deininger, and G. Feder. 1995. "Power Distortions Revolt and Reform in Agricultural Land Relations." In *Handbook of Development Economics*, Vol. III,

Part B, edited by J. Behrman and T. N. Srinivasan, 2659–772. Amsterdam: Elsevier Science B.V.

Binswanger, H. P., and J. McIntire. 1987. "Behavioral and Material Determinants of Production Relations in Land-Abundant Tropical Agriculture." *Economic Development and Cultural Change* 36 (1): 73–99.

Binswanger, H. P., and M. R. Rosenzweig. 1986. "Behavioural and Material Determinants of Production Relations in Agriculture." *Journal of Development Studies* 22 (3): 503–39.

Binswanger-Mkhize, H. P., C. Bourguignon, and R. van den Brink. 2009. *Agricultural Land Redistribution: Toward Greater Consensus*. Washington, DC: World Bank.

Binswanger-Mkhize, H. P., and S. Savastano. 2014. "Agricultural Intensification: The Status in Six African Countries." Policy Research Working Paper No. 7116, World Bank, Washington, DC.

Boserup, E. 1965. *The Conditions of Agricultural Growth: The Economics and Agrarian Change under Population Pressure*. Chicago: Aldine.

Bravo-Ureta, B. E., and A. E. Pinheiro. 1997. "Technical, Economic, and Allocative Efficiency in Peasant Farming: Evidence from the Dominican Republic." *Developing Economies* 35 (1): 48–67.

Byiringiro, F., and T. Reardon. 1996. "Farm Productivity in Rwanda: Effects of Farm Size, Erosion, and Soil Conservation Investments." *Agricultural Economics* 15 (1): 127–36.

Carletto, G., S. Savastano, and A. Zezza. 2013. "Fact or Artifact: The Impact of Measurement Errors on the Farm–Productivity Relationship." *Journal of Development Economics* 103: 254–61, and World Bank Policy Research Working Paper 5908, Washington, DC, December 2011.

Carter, M. 1984. "Identification of the Inverse Relationship between Farm Size and Productivity: An Empirical Analysis of Peasant Agricultural Production." *Oxford Economic Papers* 36 (1): 131–45.

Carter, M. R., and K. D. Wiebe. 1990. "Access to Capital and Its Impact on Agrarian Structure and Productivity in Kenya." *American Journal of Agricultural Economics* 72 (5): 1146–50.

Coase, R. H. 1937. "The Nature of the Firm." *Economica* 4 (16): 386–405.

Cornia, G. A. 1985. "Farm Size, Land Yields and the Agricultural Production Function: An Analysis for Fifteen Developing Countries." *World Development* 13 (4): 513–34.

Deininger, K., G. Carletto, S. Savastano, and J. Muwongue. 2012. "Can Diaries Help in Improving Agricultural Production Statistics? Evidence from Uganda." *Journal of Development Economics* 98 (1): 42–50.

Demsetz, H. 1995. *The Economics of the Business Firm: Seven Critical Commentaries*. Cambridge, UK: Cambridge University Press.

Dixon, J., A. Gulliver, D. Gibbon, and M. Hall. 2001. *Farming Systems and Poverty. Improving Farmers' Livelihoods in a Changing World*. Rome and Washington, DC: Food and Agriculture Organization of the United Nations (FAO) and World Bank.

Dorward, A. 1999. "Farm Size and Productivity in Malawian Smallholder Agriculture." *Journal of Development Studies* 35 (5): 141–61.

Dyer, G. 1997. *Class, State and Agricultural Productivity in Egypt: Study of the Inverse Relationship between Farm Size and Productivity*. London: Frank Cass.

Eastwood, R., M. Lipton, and A. Newell. 2010. "Farm Size." In *Handbook of Agricultural Economics*, Vol. 4, edited by R. Evenson and P. Pingali, 3323–97. Amsterdam: North Holland.

Evenson, R. E., and G. Mwabu. 2001. "The Effects of Agricultural Extension on Farm Yields in Kenya." *African Development Review* 13 (1): 1–23.

FAO (Food and Agriculture Organization of the United Nations). 2016. FAO Soils Portal. Harmonized World Soil Database v 1.2. http://www.fao.org/soils-portal/soil-survey/soil-maps-and-databases/harmonized-world-soil-database-v12/en/

Feder, G. 1985. "The Relation between Farm Size and Farm Productivity: The Role of Family Labor, Supervision and Credit Constraints." *Journal of Development Economics* 18 (2–3): 297–313.

Frisvold, G. B. 1994. "Does Supervision Matter? Some Hypothesis Tests Using Indian Farm-Level Data." *Journal of Development Economics* 43 (2): 217–38.

Hayami, Y., and K. Otsuka. 1993. *The Economics of Contract Choice: An Agrarian Perspective.* New York: Oxford University Press.

Hazell, P. 2011. "Five Big Questions about Five Hundred Million Small Farms." In *Proceedings of the Conference: Conference on New Directions for Smallholder Agriculture 24–25 January 2011, Rome, IFAD HQ*, 65–74. Rome: International Fund for Agricultural Development.

Hazell, P., C. Poulton, S. Wiggins, and A. Dorward. 2010. "The Future of Small Farms: Trajectories and Policy Priorities." *World Development* 38 (10): 1349–61.

Hazell, P. B. R., and P. L. Scandizzo. 1975. "Market Intervention Policies When Production Is Risky." *American Journal of Agricultural Economics* 57 (4): 641–9.

Helfand S. M., and E. S. Levine. 2004. "Farm Size and the Determinants of Productive Efficiency in the Brazilian Center-West." *Agricultural Economics* 31: 241–9.

Knight, F. H. 1921. *Risk, Uncertainty and Profit.* Boston: Houghton Mifflin.

Koenker, R., and G. Bassett, Jr. 1978. "Regression Quantiles." *Econometrica* 46 (1): 33–50.

Kutcher, G. P., and P. L. Scandizzo. 1981. *The Agricultural Economy of Northeast Brazil.* Baltimore: John Hopkins University Press for the World Bank.

Kydd, J., and A. Dorward. 2001. "The Washington Consensus on Poor Country Agriculture: Analysis, Prescription, and Institutional Gaps." *Development Policy Review* 19 (4): 467–78.

Lamb, R. L. 2003. "Inverse Productivity: Land Quality, Labor Markets, and Measurement Error." *Journal of Development Economics* 71 (1): 71–95.

Larson, D. F., K. Otsuka, T. Matsumoto, and T. Kilic. 2013. "Should African Rural Development Strategies Depend on Smallholder Farms? An Exploration of the Inverse Productivity Hypothesis." *Agricultural Economics* 45 (3): 355–67.

Lund, P. J., and P. G. Hill. 1979. "Farm Size, Efficiency and Economies of Size." *Journal of Agricultural Economics* 30 (2): 145–57.

Mazumdar, D. 1965. "Size of Farm and Productivity: A Problem of Indian Peasant Agriculture." *Economica* 32 (126): 161–73.

Pingali, P. 2010. "Agriculture Renaissance, Making 'Agriculture for Development' Work in the 21st Century." In *Handbook of Agricultural Economics*, Vol. 4, edited by R. Evenson and P. Pingali, 3867–94. Amsterdam: North Holland.

Rosenzweig, M. R., and H. P. Binswanger. 1993. "Wealth, Weather Risk and the Composition and Profitability of Agricultural Investments." *Economic Journal* 103 (416): 56–78.

Rosenzweig, M. R., and K. I. Wolpin. 1985. "Specific Experience, Household Structure, and Intergenerational Transfers: Farm Family Land and Labor Arrangements in Developing Countries." *Quarterly Journal of Economics* 100 (5): 961–87.

Roumasset, J. 1995. "The Nature of the Agricultural Firm." *Journal of Economic Behaviour and Organization* 26 (2): 161–77.

Savastano, S., and P. L. Scandizzo. 2009. "Optimal Farm Size in an Uncertain Land Market: The Case of Kyrgyz Republic." *Agricultural Economics* 40 (s1): 745–58.

Scandizzo, P. L., and T. Barbosa. August 1977. "Substitution and Productivity in Northeast Agriculture." *Pesquisa e Planejamento Econômico* 7 (2): 367–404.

Schultz, T. W. 1964. *Transforming Traditional Agriculture.* New Haven, CT: Yale University Press.

Sen, A. K. 1975. *Employment, Technology, and Development.* Oxford, UK: Clarendon Press.

Srinivasan, T. N. 1972. "Farm Size and Productivity: Implications of Choice under Uncertainty." *Sankhyā: The Indian Journal of Statistics.* Series B 34 (2): 409–20.

Taslim, M. A. 1989. "Supervision Problems and the Size–Productivity Relation in Bangladesh Agriculture." *Oxford Bulletin of Economics and Statistics* 51 (1): 55–71.

Vollrath, D. 2007. "Land Distribution and International Agricultural Productivity." *American Journal of Agricultural Economics* 89 (1): 202–16.

Yotopoulos, P. A., and L. J. Lau. 1973. "A Test for Relative Economic Efficiency: Some Further Results." *American Economic Review* 63 (1): 214–23.

4 From land grabs to land development

The past and potential of private investment in frontier agriculture

Derek Byerlee, William A. Masters,
and Daniel S. Robinson

Introduction

Hans Binswanger's work on agrarian relations offers deep insights into the nexus of agrarian structures, property rights, and farm investment. Because agriculture is dominated by family farmers whose capital accumulation comes primarily from retained earnings, financing of capital investments to improve the productivity of farms is an enduring challenge in economic development. In poor countries, farm families typically have much lower levels of capital and earnings per worker than those engaged in nonfarm enterprises, and external investors remain deterred by the difficulty of managing risks, the seasonality of agriculture, transactions costs, information asymmetry, and location-specific management knowledge that make family farming the dominant form of production around the world.

Binswanger and Rozenzweig (1986), in their paper "Behavioural and Material Determinants of Production Relations in Agriculture," noted conditions that may sometimes favor highly capitalized larger farm operations – notably, the so-called classic plantation crops with scale economies in processing or transport that must take place immediately after harvest (tea, sugarcane, oil palm, bananas). Even for these crops, institutional innovations often facilitated by the state, such as contracts and collective action, have, over time, converted most plantation production to family farming (Byerlee 2014). Binswanger, Deininger, and Feder (1995), in their chapter "Power, Distortions, Revolt, and Reform in Agricultural Land Relations," concluded that political economy and policy biases, rather than inherent economies of scale, have historically been the major drivers of the emergence of large-scale farms.

Over the 21st century, it is possible that new technologies from "big data" farming may automate field operations and allow precise field and seasonal management that will allow outside investors and their managers to compete with family farmers. Complying with demanding food safety and sustainability standards is another development that may favor large farms that are vertically integrated with downstream operations (Deininger and Byerlee 2012). These changes could provide new conditions in which company farms become cost-effective, but as of today, crop production remains overwhelmingly in the hands of family farmers, even in the most highly automated precision-farming systems of industrialized countries – reflecting the inherent efficiency advantages of family farms (see Chapter 5, this volume).

This chapter explores an overlooked role of external investors for financing investments in land development to improve agricultural productivity in settings where investors could be repaid with funds earned by renting or selling parcels for family farming, once the land is developed. Recent analyses of outside investments in farmland have emphasized motivations that range from food security in the investor's origin country to commodity booms that have inflated investors' expectations, to land speculation in the face of growing land scarcity. Regardless of investor motivation, the literature has overwhelmingly noted the limited benefits from investor-owned farms to local communities in relation to the high costs borne by those communities, such as land conflicts, loss of grazing and water resources, and tensions from immigrant labor. The idea that companies could invest in land development without necessarily operating the resulting farms offers potential long-term benefits for both investors and communities alike.

We define land development as start-up investment that sufficiently increases the productive potential of land to justify the entry of new farms that transform local farming systems. Notable examples are irrigation and drainage systems, soil amendments, and transportation services and other basic infrastructure that convert low-value areas into productive farmland. Such improvements could be undertaken by self-employed family farmers – sometimes, with the help of contract operators – but in frontier areas there are few farmers that have the requisite skills and access to capital.

Land development efforts in frontier areas often involve significant economies of scale and specialized knowledge that favor large-scale external investors. Operating the resulting farm, however, is not necessarily the most effective way for developers to recoup their investment. Historically, most company-owned large farms introduced during periods of land development have eventually given way to family farms that are more efficient in the operating stage, after the land has been developed. The investor's objective has been to invest in land development as such, and then sell or prefinance sales of the land for family farmers to cultivate.

Historically, too, the costs of land development have often been highly subsidized by state programs, but such programs have fallen out of favor due to cost overruns, frequent failures, and scarcity of resources for public investment (Kinsey and Binswanger 1993). Yet there have been good examples of private companies assuming these costs both in today's high-income countries (e.g., land development in Australia's Ninety Mile Desert) and in tropical areas (e.g., land development companies in Brazil). A closer review of today's investments suggests that some of them could follow a similar model, such as some recent irrigation projects in Africa.

Our review will extend the standard economic framework for understanding drivers of investor-owned, large-scale farms, noting the conditions under which private companies may find it profitable to invest in land development in ways that enhance economic and social welfare. The framework will also note the conditions under which such companies would find it profitable to continue farming, after the initial development costs, versus subdividing and selling or renting the improved farmland to smaller family-operated farms, or to outgrowers around a nucleus farm retained by the company. We then review the success or other outcomes of private initiatives in land development from a historical perspective. In these cases, a variety of policy incentives were used to attract investors to develop land when neither governments nor individual farmers had sufficient means or capabilities to do so. In nearly all of these cases, the end result was an agrarian structure based on family farms, often facilitated by proactive state policies.

This leads us to review contemporary examples of private investment in land development in Latin America and Africa. Many of these could follow the historical example of breaking up into family farms, but much depends on a policy environment conducive for smallholders. Together with the historical experience, our findings allow us to draw lessons (good and bad) for today's investors and governments in Africa. Since investment in land development can often greatly increase productivity, such investments can be transformative, as our historical review demonstrates.

We conclude that conceptually separating the land development phase from the operational phase opens a space for private investors, which has not been sufficiently recognized to date. This allows us to outline promising policy options that, on the one hand, provide incentives for investment in the land development phase, while, on the other hand, open opportunities to in situ smallholders or immigrant settlers to take on the subsequent farming operations.

The roles of private investors in land development

Land development investments may be of several types. A first and most obvious land development activity is an investment that changes the intrinsic physical productivity of the land itself through irrigation and drainage, land clearing and levelling, or soil amendments, such as liming. Some of these investments involve specialized machinery and knowledge with significant economies of scale. For settled areas, in situ farmers can sometimes obtain these services through contracts with custom operators and service providers, or cooperatives. Our focus is on frontier areas, where such investments can create entirely new farming opportunities, which, once developed, can attract additional farmers and workers to expand production.

Beyond physical assets, another type of investment focuses on institutional capital that can improve the value of land by providing secure title, access to capital and markets for inputs or products, and compliance with government regulations or private standards. Establishing these institutional arrangements in areas newly opened to intensive agriculture involves substantial transaction costs and specialized knowledge of surveying, land administration systems, obtaining environmental permits, and so forth. In frontier areas with poorly demarcated land rights, the main challenge may be political legitimacy, attending to complex and sometimes conflicting rights in pursuit of more favorable environmental and social outcomes. Setting up new land use arrangements has high skill requirements, large fixed costs, and risks that may give specialized companies an advantage in the start-up phase, even as the marginal cost of replicating those arrangements falls over time for new entrants.

A third type of investment may not alter land quality per se, but rather provide fixed assets attached to the land, thereby enhancing land productivity. Investments in rural roads and transport logistics are important for bulky products, such as grains in remote areas and oil palm and sugarcane to access mills. And if farm families and workers are to move into a new area, additional investments and organization of schools, health clinics, and other services are needed.

Finally substantial investments and capacity to bear risks may be needed to adapt and experiment in order to bring new crops in new areas to a profitable stage of operation. Large companies, with experience in the same industry in similar environments elsewhere and with established relationships with suppliers and customers, may have a natural comparative advantage in assuming these pioneering risks. In some cases, companies' abilities to bear the risks of land development may come from having a diversified portfolio of assets, including diverse kinds of land in various locations.

Such high, up-front costs of land development in a risky industry like agriculture – especially in frontier areas – provide an advantage to investing companies with access to national or global risk capital. For example, in Sumatra, Indonesia, it may be possible to purchase unimproved land suited for oil palm for less than $1,000 per ha, but at least another $9,000 per ha is required to clear the land, install roads and drainage, obtain required permits, plant the trees, care for the plantation until the first harvest, and install the mill (Byerlee, Falcon, and Naylor 2017). Similarly, in the Cerrado, Brazil, it is reported that unimproved land can be purchased for around $1,000/ha, but another $2,000–$4,000/ha will be needed to convert it into productive farmland (Byerlee, Falcon, and Naylor 2017). States may offer guarantees or pick up part of the costs, especially when the improvements serve local smallholders and resettlement projects, but retrenchment of the state, as well as state failures, has severely curtailed their leadership role (Kinsey and Binswanger 1993).

In this chapter, we seek to differentiate the role of private investors at the farm development stage from the operational stage. Investors in land development may find it more profitable to subdivide parcels and rent out the land or sell it off to family farmers, who are more efficient in the operational phase. In fact, government land concession contracts could explicitly require companies to invest a minimum in land development, as well as provide financing for family farmers to allow them to take over the parcels. During the land development phase, the investor may undertake land surveys, construct roads, provide initial extension advice, and recruit and organize settlement. The transition from large-scale ownership in the developmental phase to family farming in the operational phase takes time, but most investor-owned farms have eventually found it expedient to devolve operations into more efficient family farms. Where land and financial markets are working well, investments will eventually raise land prices and expose the high overheads and transactions costs of investor-operated farms relative to family farms. Further, many costs fall after an industry is established – especially some of the initial technology testing and specialized infrastructure, allowing small farmers to enter at much lower cost.

The distinction between large-scale investments in land development and smallholder operations also occurs spatially. For example, a classic operational structure involves a nucleus estate operated by an investor-owned company, which provides a guaranteed supply of product to a vertically integrated processor, combined with outgrowers who are contractually obligated to sell to the same processor. Operation of a nucleus farm may convey other advantages in terms of allowing experimentation on crops and technology, as well as providing for a demonstration of the productivity of the land that enhances its market value when nearby land is sold or rented to family farmers. In some cases, opportunities for wage labor in company operations offers workers a leg up the tenancy ladder, if the skills and earnings they acquire can be used to access farmland of their own through sharecropping, rental, and eventual ownership.

The temporal and spatial combinations of outside investment and family farming are pictured in Table 4.1. Investors have a potentially large role on the right-hand side, where heavy up-front costs and skills are required to convert land of low productivity to highly productive land, and may have a role in the operational phase, but family farms are usually major players in that phase in all cases.

Table 4.1 Organizational structures for land development and farm operations

		Relative productivity of developed land to undeveloped land	
		Low	*High*
Products suitable for family farms (most crops)	*Land development*	Family farms	Investor
	Farm operations	Family farms	Family farm in situ and immigrant settlers
			Nucleus-outgrower
Products suitable for company farms (plantation crops, high-value products, and some livestock)	*Land development*	NR	Investor
	Farm operations	NR	Investor
			Nucleus-outgrower
			Contract farming

Source: Authors' construction.

Note: NR = not relevant, since land suitable to attract investment in plantation crops and high-value products will require high-value, developed land.

When investments in land development are made over large areas, they can be transformative, in terms of economic development of a region – for example, with irrigation projects in arid areas. The private sector is naturally reluctant to engage in large land development projects unless land markets are well developed and land tenure is secure. Also, investment in land is inherently risky not only because of the usual climatic and market risks of agriculture, but also because such investments are immobile and vulnerable to political disputes, with very low salvage value in the event of failure. Facilitating rapid turnover to family farmers could help investors recoup their funds quickly and limit political, as well as agro-economic, risks. The state may also be able to use guarantees and cost-sharing agreements to attract investors, and also provide local public goods, such as agricultural research stations, extension, schools, and clinics to attract smallholders and workers.

Historically, and even today, the major incentive offered by the state to investors in land development is the provision of large land concessions to investors. Collier and Venables (2012) nicely reviewed state policy alternatives, where investors may seek a large land concession that has a speculative or option value, with future value enhanced by the initial investment operation. Their analysis rationalized a subsidy to investors in the form of cheap land, but they did not explicitly consider the land development phase, or the potential that many such investments may be destined for in situ or settler family farms rather than "mega-farms." The main downside of such concession arrangements is the involvement of the state in allocating large tracts of land, with inherent risks from rent-seeking behavior or weak capacity, to be able to negotiate and monitor investments to enhance social objectives.

A brief history of private investment in land development

Private investment in land development has a long history in the settlement of the Americas and Australia, as well as more limited examples from tropical frontier areas of Africa and Asia. Our review starts in the last part of the 19th century, during what has often been termed the golden period of globalization, when capital (and labor) flowed freely across borders, new land was being opened to settlers, and private investment in land development was often encouraged by cash-strapped states. We exclude cases where the land development was based on state financing, even when the development was outsourced to private companies (e.g., the Gezira Irrigation Scheme in Sudan).

Table 4.2 provides a chronological list of the 16 major examples discussed here. Although the list is not exhaustive, it provides suggestive evidence that the burst of private land development investment in the late 19th century was followed by a long period in which state-led and other forms of finance dominated agricultural expansion. For the entire 20th century, we found only four examples, of which two arose in the 1990s, just before the second burst of private investment in agricultural land occurred after 2000.

Table 4.2 Chronological summary of land development examples

Years	Country/region	Developer	Principal objective	Principal investment
1860s–early 1900s	Thailand – Chao Phraya Delta	Siam Canals Land and Irrigation Company	Private development with "spontaneous" settlement	Irrigation canals
1870s–1890s	United States – Red River Valley	Bonanza farms	Large-scale farming and demonstration of the land value	New technology and strategy
1880s–early 1900s	Argentinian Pampa	Santa Fe Land Company	Organized colonization	Migration and settlement
1880s–early 1900s	Canadian Prairies	Saskatchewan Valley Land Co. and many others	Organized colonization	Migration and settlement
1880s–1890s	United States, Etiwanda, and Ontario, California	Ontario Model Colony	Organized colonization	Irrigation and settlement
1880s–1890s	Australia – Murray River	Mildura Irrigation Co.	Organized colonization	Irrigation and settlement
1930s–1960s	Brazil – Paraná State	Companhia de Terras Norte de Paraná	Organized colonization	Roads and settlement
1940s–1960s	Australia – Ninety Mile Desert	Australian Mutual Provident Society (AMP)	Organized colonization	Land clearing and soil amendment; migration and settlement processes
1990s–present	Sub-Saharan Africa – various countries	Illovo Sugar	Nucleus farm with outgrowers	Irrigation; processing and specialized infrastructure
1990s–present	Uganda	Kakira Sugar	Nucleus farm with outgrowers	Irrigation; processing and specialized infrastructure
2005–present	Nigeria – Benue and Kwara States	Olam Nigeria Ltd.	Contract farming but change of focus to own large farm with outgrowers	Irrigation; processing and specialized infrastructure
2006–present	Brazil – Cerrado	BrasilAgro	Land development and sales	Land clearing and soil amendment; migration and settlement; pioneering technology and strategy

Years	Country/region	Developer	Principal objective	Principal investment
2010–present	Brazil – Cerrado	SLC Landco	Land development and sales	Land clearing and soil amendment; migration and settlement
2009–present	Ghana – Volta Region	GADCO	Nucleus farm working with in situ smallholders	Irrigation; processing and specialized infrastructure
2010–present	Zambia – Kafue District	InfraCo	Nucleus farm with outgrowers	Irrigation; pioneering technology and strategy
2010–present	Sub-Saharan Africa (Ghana, Malawi, Mozambique, Tanzania, Zambia)	AgDevCo	Nucleus farm with outgrowers	Irrigation; pioneering technology and strategy; processing and specialized infrastructure

Sources: Ogilvie (1910); Briggs (1932); Hedges (1934); Edgerley (1953); Bell and Cairns (1958); Drache (1964); Holden (1970); Katzman (1978); Feeny (1979); Fergusson (1984); Wells (1986); Isabirye et al. (2007); Palmer et al. (2010); Sandul (2010); Braga (2012); Johnson, Takeshima, and Gyimah-Brempong (2013); Osei (2013); Rockefeller Foundation (2013); AgDevCo. (2014); BrasilAgro (2014); Chaddad (2014); Kakira Sugar Limited (2015); Larder (2015); Oakland (2015); Illovo (2016); InfraCo (2016).

To describe these 16 case studies, we look first at the earlier historical period and then turn to the contemporary examples, and for each time frame, we divide the examples into three categories corresponding to the distinct agro-ecosystems of rainfed areas, irrigation schemes, and tree crop plantations.

Historical experiences with private investment in land development

Rainfed areas

In the late 19th century, private agricultural colonization companies serving rain-fed areas were common in the Canadian Prairies (e.g., the Saskatchewan Land Company), the US prairies (e.g., the famed bonanza farms), Argentina (e.g., the Santa Fe Land Company), and Australia (e.g., the Australian Mutual Providence Society's scheme to develop the Ninety Mile Desert). Governments usually provided large land concessions to companies that, in return, undertook to build basic infrastructure, especially railways and farm roads, as well as survey, subdivide, and market the land from the concessions. These companies, for their part, raised funds on global capital markets, often from Britain, and agreed to a program of settlement with maximum limits on the land allocated to individuals. Settlers, then, were financed for a few years through a mortgage with the company.

Colonization companies did not usually incur major land development costs beyond the roads and sometimes the clearing of natural vegetation. Nor did they usually operate farms themselves, although they often undertook some experimentation and demonstrations. An extreme and well-known example was the short-lived bonanza farms in the Red River Valley of the Dakotas, where companies applied steam power to operate very large mechanized farms with employee managers, on-site mechanics, and laborers. This proved not to be a profitable mode of farm operation, but did demonstrate the agricultural potential of untried land and enhanced the value of the land that the companies had obtained, as part of the concession to construct a railroad (Drache 1964).

Experiences with colonization companies were highly variable, especially in the early years, when states lacked capacity to conduct due diligence – or worse, engaged in corrupt practices with companies of low repute (Ely 1918). Much has been learned from these early experiences and mistakes that have resulted in some outstanding success stories in the 20th century. One of the largest was the Companhia de Terras Norte de Paraná (North Paraná Land Company in Brazil), owned and financed by British investors. Over a period of 35 years, from 1932 to 1967, the company constructed roads and railways, and surveyed and cleared 1.25 million ha of land area in Paraná State. In the process, the company established 39,000 small farms with secure titles and an average size of 20–40 ha (Box 4.1). A lesser known example is the settlement of the Ninety Mile Desert in southeastern Australia from 1949 to 1964 on an area of 340,000 ha, by clearing low scrubland and adding trace elements and superphosphate that established highly productive farmland in what was previously land of very low productivity used extensively for grazing. In both cases, the investments were transformative – the companies operated profitably over decades and left lasting legacies of family farms with both efficient and equitable distribution of highly productive land.

Irrigation schemes

There were very similar experiences of private development of irrigation schemes starting in the late 19th century. Irrigation, involving canal infrastructure, requires deep pockets and more expertise than settlement in rainfed areas, but the impact on land productivity and land prices in arid zones can be dramatic. Many of the irrigation projects in the western United States were established through private investment in land development and water works, as was the case in Mexico (including the Yaqui Valley of later Green Revolution fame), Brazil, Australia's Murray River, and Thailand's Chao Phraya Delta. As with the colonization projects, the private investment was in the land development phase, after which irrigated and cleared land was made available through medium-term loans to settlers. In the case of Thailand, where such financing for settlers was not available, land was sold to richer urban-based owners, who then leased the land to tenants for operation (Feeny 1979). As with the colonization companies, the record of success is quite variable, although the Murray River Schemes in Australia and the Imperial Valley Scheme in the United States went on to become horticultural food baskets for their nations (Box 4.2).

Box 4.1 Historical examples of land development for rainfed farming

The Paraná Land Company

After costly and very slow progress with state-led settlement, the government of the Brazilian state of Paraná turned to the private sector, the British-owned company Companhia de Terra Norte de Paraná (Paraná Land Company), later sold to the Brazilian-owned Sociedad de Melhoramentos e Colonização (SOMECO) (Nelson 1973; Katzman 1978). The initial interest from Britain was led by Simon Fraser (Lord Lovat), who had previous experience with the colonial Gezira Scheme in Sudan. In agreement with the state, the company purchased 1.25 million ha of extremely sparsely populated area at an average cost of $1.25/ha. From 1932 to 1967, the company built 350 km of rail and 5,000 km of road, as well as undertaking surveys and securing the title to subdivided land. The scheme included surveying of future towns where land sales probably provided the largest returns to the company. Settlers with average sized farms of 20–40 ha were offered four-year mortgages with a 20 percent down payment. Given that the company sustained the investment over 25 years, it appears that the investment was profitable to the company and certainly transformative in terms of the development of the state of Paraná.

The Australian Mutual Provident (AMP) Society

The AMP Society Land Development Scheme in southeastern Australia has some parallels to Paraná, as well as important differences (Bell and Cairns 1958; Holden 1970; Fergusson 1984). The AMP Society, Ltd., was an insurance and real estate company, and provision of mortgage financing to farms was part of its portfolio. Finding itself with surplus capital after the Second World War, one of the company employees who managed its rural portfolio convinced the company to invest in land development in the Ninety Mile Desert, where government scientists had recently discovered that micronutrient deficiencies were the major cause of its extremely low soil fertility. In agreements with the states of South Australia and Victoria, the company took over 340,000 ha of land in 1949 to develop over a 15-year period. Investment in clearing of low scrub, heavy application of superphosphate and micronutrients, and sowing of improved pastures increased the livestock-carrying capacity of the land 40-fold. After five years of land development, lots, each with a house, were allocated at random to interested workers from the development phase on a ten-year mortgage. The company maintained a central farm for demonstration and experimentation of appropriate management practices. The return to the company was estimated at 5 percent in real terms (Holden 1970).

Box 4.2 Historical examples of land development through irrigation

Chaffey Brothers Ltd.

George and William Chaffey, originally from Canada, established two of the early irrigation schemes in California (Etiwanda and Ontario) in the 1880s (Hill 1937; Kershner 1953; Wells 1986; Hamilton-McKenzie 2010). Based on their success in California, Chaffey Brothers, Ltd., was granted up to 100,000 ha in South Australia and 100,000 ha in Victoria in 1887, in an arid zone about 200 km north of the Ninety Mile Desert, as described in Box 4.1, through agreements with the respective state governments.

The Chaffeys were able to raise most of their finance from private sources abroad, with the objective of selling land to establish small family farms of less than 80 acres. In South Australia, the company recruited and provided land to the settlers on a ten-year loan and with a 5 percent down payment. It also established the Renmark Irrigation Company, which owned and managed the irrigation system. Each farmer owned shares in the irrigation company, according to their land area, with the eventual target of full ownership by the settlers. The company was required by the terms of the contract to establish all irrigation and road infrastructure, clear the land, plant the fruit trees, and establish an agricultural college for training farmers. The state government closely supervised the scheme, releasing new land based on a strict program of investment and completion of infrastructure.

The scheme got off to a good start but was hit by the worst financial crisis in Australian history in 1891 that decimated the market for fruits and vegetables, the main products of the scheme, as well cut off investment from abroad. There were also technical issues related to choice of crops and varieties, diseases, and heavy loss of water in transmission. The innovative approach to farmer ownership of the irrigation system ran into problems due to poor communication with settlers expecting free water. At the time, settlers were also unhappy with the rather un-Australian prohibition of alcohol sales in the new colony. The company folded in 1895, and the state had to rescue the scheme financially. However, George Chaffey then returned to California to help establish the Imperial Valley irrigation scheme.

Despite these difficulties, the investments were transformative in the development of sparsely populated areas, although in light of recent prolonged droughts in both Australia and California, some argue that irrigated agriculture had little role in these water-scarce environments (e.g., Hamilton-McKenzie 2010).

Tree crop plantations

Establishment of tree crop plantations may involve land development if roads or rail are required to remove bulky produce (e.g., oil palm, bananas, sugarcane), if there are pioneering risks of new crops in new areas, and if large-scale or specialized processing or shipping infrastructure is needed to handle perishable products. Such development has been generally initiated by investors, with state support through land concessions. In some cases, the developers have devolved farm operations to smallholders or have operated a nucleus estate with outgrowers.

A pioneering case of land development for tree crops is the establishment of rubber cultivation in Southeast Asia. Until around 1900, all rubber was harvested from the wild, but this harvest was not able to keep up with demand, especially after the dawn of the automobile age. A great deal of trial and error took place in Malaysia to select suitable species, planting materials, and tapping methods. Plantation companies led this effort, aided by colonial scientists, and by 1914, over half of the world's rubber came from cultivated trees rather than wild harvests. The success of the plantation companies had immediate spillovers to smallholders who were able to draw on the methods and infrastructure developed by the companies, as well as incorporate rubber into their extensive agroforestry food systems and develop simple processing technologies. Today, Asia produces over 90 percent of the world's rubber, and nearly 90 percent of this supply is produced by smallholders (Byerlee 2014).

Since 1950, the Commonwealth Development Corporation (CDC), a private for-profit company established by the British government, has pioneered efforts to enhance the social impacts of private investments, building on its long colonial experience. About 40 percent of CDC's 179 investments have included an outgrower component or were based entirely on smallholders after the development phase (either in situ smallholders or migrant settlers from other regions). The record is quite varied, with only one-third of the projects reviewed by Tyler and Dixie (2013) showing financial success in their respective project periods, although over the long run, 70 percent eventually showed a positive bottom line. Nucleus-outgrower projects had higher rates of success and also greater development impacts (over 80 percent were rated as successful or moderately successful for development impacts). However, CDC success with smallholders has been confined to crops where the company had a monopoly on processing (e.g., oil palm, tea, and sugarcane) and payments for loans could be subtracted from the mill price. In new areas, the nucleus estate provided the opportunity to experiment and adapt, before adding outgrowers. Some of CDC's successes have been transformative, such as oil palm in Asia and sugarcane and tea in Africa. For example, the Kenya Tea Development Authority, a private smallholder-owned company set up through a CDC loan, has converted Kenya into the world's leading tea exporter based largely on smallholders that now obtain yields close to that of large tea estates (Box 4.3).

**Box 4.3 Historical example of tree crop development
with smallholders**

The Kenya Tea Development Authority (KTDA)

Tea in Kenya is one of Africa's most remarkable export and productivity success stories (Mitchell 2012; Tyler and Dixie 2013). Smallholders have played a central role in this success through ownership of the tea-processing sector. In Kenya, the world's largest tea exporter, smallholders account for a 62 percent share of national tea production. Significantly, the yield gap between smallholders and estates has fallen from 68 percent in 1980 to 18 percent today. The Kenya Tea Development Authority was established with support from the CDC to invest in smallholder tea and tea factories. KTDA was eventually privatized in 2000, under the ownership of smallholder tea producers. KTDA provides inputs and advisory services to 550,000 smallholders with an average of 0.4 hectares, and management services for 63 smallholder-owned factories. KTDA built on the infrastructure, technology, and know-how provided from initial investments in large-scale estate production, while the state provided land with secure title and promoted a business-friendly approach for smallholder tea development.

Lessons learned from the historical case studies

There is a long history of private investment in land development. Our brief and undoubtedly incomplete review reveals that many of the investments have been successful and, in some cases, transformative. There is no way to rigorously compare the effectiveness of the private sector model with the more common state-directed models, but Nelson (1973), in a review of 24 land development schemes in tropical Latin America, found two of the most successful were private sector–led (including the Paraná Land Company, described in Box 4.1). Likewise, in South Australia the private model of land development in the Ninety Mile Desert performed better than the state-led scheme in the same ecological context on Kangaroo Island (Fergusson 1984).

However, it is also clear from the cases reviewed that private land development schemes are risky to investors and participating farmers alike. By definition, these are pioneering ventures with few precedents and no guarantees. For the investors, risks include the technological, climate, and market uncertainties inherent in all new agricultural investments, plus political and institutional challenges in building new governance and contractual relationships. Nearly all of the projects required a considerable period of experimentation, learning, and adjustment to arrive at suitable crops, varieties, irrigation management practices, and machinery design. Land development projects are especially risky since they create an immobile asset that cannot be easily disposed of during economic hard times.

Participating farmers and settlers also experience risks, not just from climatic and market volatility but also from company actions that are unanticipated by farmers or unplanned, such as financial difficulties of the company. In many of the early projects, inexperienced and speculative companies did not bring the expected financial backing or expertise to the investment (Ely 1918). Farmers themselves were also often inexperienced and unsuited to the schemes. The AMP scheme is perhaps unique in that the workers in the land development phase were specifically selected for their future suitability as farmers, and then given additional training and experience during the five-year development phase before they were allocated their farm blocks (Fergusson 1984). Other schemes, such as Siam Canal, Land and Irrigation Company's irrigation investment in Thailand, did not have an explicit objective of creating a class of owner-operated farms, and they experienced high rates of tenancy and inequality (Tanabe 1977; Takaya 1987).

Local communities and, especially, indigenous groups were also often at risk when governments provided land concessions to investors without consideration of the existing land users. The Sonora and Sinaloa Irrigation Company and its successor in northwest Mexico, for example, engaged in a long-running land conflict with indigenous groups, even though they were ostensibly eligible to take up profitable farming of parcels in the newly irrigated land blocks and many did (Hu-Dehart 1974; Radding 1989). Likewise, many of the plantation companies, arising out of land concessions, experienced growing land conflicts, as the local population expanded in part due to immigration attracted by the new industries.[1]

Even if private investors perform better than state-led schemes, an important question is whether there are economies of scale associated with certain types of investments that justify concessions to large investors in the land development phase. From our review, such economies of scale generally follow our foregoing framework – the lumpy and spatial nature of some types of infrastructure, the pioneering technical risks, the specialized knowledge associated with obtaining water and land rights, and the ability of companies to access global capital markets. The Murray River irrigation scheme imported knowledge of irrigation from California that was not available in Australia. The Paraná Land Company often purchased the same piece of land 2–3 times to insure clear title to the land, something beyond the reach of smallholders. In one study, Holden (1970) compared costs of land development for the large AMP scheme to a land development operation one-tenth of the size and found modest cost advantages of the AMP scale, even though the smaller operation started a decade later and built on the AMP experience.

Finally, the historical record reveals how private land development schemes were often closely associated with state actions or regulation. In most cases, the state played important roles in defining the social objectives for the investment (e.g., maximum allowed farm sizes), financing R&D to develop suitable technology, vetting the investors, and monitoring progress. In some cases governments took on roles that they were ill equipped to play, sometimes resulting in collusion between state officials and private investors. The state also generally played an indispensable role in providing the property rights and contract law needed for family farmers to acquire developed land. Where such institutions were not in place, smallholder repayment of long-term loans for the cost of land development was often problematic, as in many of the CDC investments. The exception was where the company had a monopsony on processing that enabled loan repayments when farmers delivered their produce (e.g., sugarcane, oil palm). This type of tied credit, however, risks distorting distribution of benefits away from smallholders through monopsony buying practices.

Modern examples of large-scale private investment in land development

The late 19th- and early 20th-century burst of private investment in land development was halted by the Second World War, and for most of the second half of the 20th century, was supplanted by public financing for rural infrastructure and settlement schemes (Kinsey and Binswanger 1993). Since the 1970s, however, private companies have invested substantially in land improvement in the rainfed Brazilian Cerrado and in irrigation schemes. Private companies, including Brazilian firms, have also invested in land development in Africa through irrigation infrastructure, plantations, and, potentially, in the Africa savannah areas. Here we review those experiences that focus on land development but with significant participation of family farmers in the operational phase.

Rainfed areas

The Brazilian Cerrado is a huge area of over 200 million ha that has been the frontier of agricultural expansion in Brazil and, indeed, globally. It has savannah and woodland ecology, characterized by an undulating topography and reasonable rainfall but infertile acid soils. Research by the Brazilian agricultural research corporation Embrapa provided the technology in the form of soil amendments and adapted varieties to enable conversion of natural areas and low-grade pastures to productive farmland. However, heavy applications of lime, superphosphate, and micronutrients were required, along with significant transaction costs of acquiring land, securing the land title, and complying with a myriad of environmental and other regulations.

After public investment in a major highway across the Cerrado in the 1960s and private investment in processing and port logistics in the 1970s, the Cerrado has become a soy basket for the world. Following the historical success with colonization companies in southern Brazil, more than 35 specialized private enterprises organized more than 104 settlements in the Cerrado. These companies provided many of the initial investments for land development, including facilitating access to credit for soil amendments, securing land titles and extension advice, and constructing some roads and other infrastructure. They made their money by selling the improved land to small family farms facing land shortage in the south of Brazil, including many that had been established one or two generations earlier by the North Paraná Land Development Company (Box 4.1) (Jepson 2006).

A parallel institutional innovation was the emergence of land development cooperatives that were offshoots of cooperatives in the south. These cooperatives reduced transaction costs and pioneering risks of settlement in a new area with a different agro-ecological and institutional base, by providing the same set of services as the private colonization companies (Bickel and Dros 2003; Jepson 2006). One noteworthy example is the Cotrirosa cooperative from Santa Rosa in Rio Grando do Sul state, which settled 60,000 hectares in the Cerrado region and developed a new town called Nova Santa Rosa (Bickel and Dros 2003). Note, however, that both the private companies and the cooperatives depended largely on state credit that was heavily subsidized in the early years.

Although the private colonization companies and cooperatives helped many family-type farmers, the high pioneering costs and risks also gave an advantage to large agribusiness farms. Many of these companies got their start in the settlement of the Cerrado in Mato Grosso state, and although the Brazilian public sector reduced its role, very large agribusiness companies are leading the development of a new frontier in the 21st century – the so-called Mapitoba region, consisting of parts of the states of Maranhão, Tocantins, Piauí, and Bahia. Specifically, as many as 38 large-scale agribusiness companies currently operate farms in the Brazilian Cerrado of at least 30,000 hectares, and seven have farms of 100,000 hectares or greater (Chaddad 2014; Byerlee, Falcon, and Naylor 2017). Two of the biggest companies, BrasilAgro and SLC Landco, focus at least part of their operations on land development, largely by purchasing underdeveloped properties, investing in natural or degraded pastures to convert them into highly productive cropland, and then selling the land on the open market (Box 4.4). SLC Agricola, for example, claims to buy land for $2,000–3,000 per ha and then sell it for $6,000–7,000 per ha, after investing in land development over a two-year period. These are largely market-based transactions that depart from the explicit colonization objective of the earlier companies. The resulting farms are, like their counterparts in the United States and Canada, mostly family-run farms, although larger – averaging over 1,000 ha.

In Africa, there has been much discussion and controversy over a Brazil–Japan–Mozambique initiative, ProSavana, in Mozambique to draw on the Cerrado experience to open up land along the Nacala corridor in the north of the country, again focusing on soybeans. Major investments are required for infrastructure, with some land clearing and soil amendments, and the government of Mozambique initially turned to large investor-owned farms. However, land tensions with smallholder farms, some of whom were successfully producing soybeans, have led to some refocusing of the ProSavana strategy toward nucleus farms as a way to stimulate smallholder production through contract farming. It is unclear that this strategy will work, given the difficulty of providing long-term financing for land development through contract farming, so other forms of smallholder farm finance and product marketing may be needed (Norfolk and Hanlon 2012; Hanlon and Smart 2013; Ekman and Macamo 2014; Tawa, Amameishi, and Noguchi 2014).

Box 4.4 Ongoing investment for the continued development of the Cerrado

BrasilAgro

BrasilAgro was founded in 2006 through an IPO worth 584 million Brazilian Real (approximately US$220 million), with a 40 percent stake owned by a large Argentinian agribusiness company called Cresud. Since 2006, BrasilAgro has expanded its land portfolio to include eight properties in the Brazilian Cerrado, as well as a recently purchased property in Paraguay (Chaddad 2014). Of its total acquisitions of 319,000 ha, 110,000 ha have been developed. BrasilAgro is now one of the largest land development and farming companies in South America, and it stands out for its innovative business model focused specifically on land acquisition, development, operation, and land sales. In order to maximize land productivity, BrasilAgro invests in land clearing, levelling, soil amendments, and land preparation, as well as roads, warehouses, and irrigation systems (Chaddad 2014). Additionally, BrasilAgro's business model focus is on land development rather than farm operations, as it sells off properties after they have been developed (BrasilAgro 2014; Chaddad 2014).

SLC Agricola and Landco

SLC Agricola operates in a similar field to BrasilAgro, but with greater focus on farming than land development. As of 2012, SLC Agricola operated 14 farms throughout Brazil with a total land area of 308,000 hectares. It has focused on land transformation through soil amendments, infrastructure construction, and other means, as well as agricultural production, processing, and storage (SLC Agrícola 2012). Along with its main operations, SLC Agricola created a spin-off company called SLC Landco in 2010, which specifically focuses on land development and is jointly owned by SLC Agricola and Valiance, a British-owned asset management fund (Braga 2012).

The Mozambican experience is particularly relevant to the new generation of agricultural growth corridors (AGCs) in Africa intended to provide access to markets and ports, and to create opportunities for development of commercial agriculture, especially in the savannah areas, where there is still much uncultivated land suited to crop agriculture. To date, there are four active AGCs – the

Beira Agricultural Growth Corridor (BAGC), the Nacala and Zambezi Corridors in Mozambique, and the Southern Agricultural Growth Corridor of Tanzania (SAGCOT), and more are planned. These programs intend to use a variety of public–private partnerships (PPPs) to build infrastructure and provide services, but the specific roles of the public sector and private investors in land development are still quite uncertain (CTA 2012).

Irrigation schemes

After the early experiences with private investment in irrigation in the late 19th and early 20th centuries, the state began to assume the lead role in large-scale irrigation schemes, often assisted by multilateral financial organizations. However, continued high costs and inefficiencies in state-managed schemes led to a revival of interest in private investment in irrigation in the late 20th century. This is most notable in Latin America, where much of the region's new irrigation investment since 1990 has come from the private sector (Ringler, Rosegrant, and Paisner 2000). In many cases, the upsurge in private investment occurred when state-managed irrigation systems were turned over to farmers' groups and cooperatives, largely to bring maintenance up to standards in existing schemes. However, in Brazil, private investment has been responsible for about 95 percent of irrigation expansion in the poor northeast. This area was already densely settled, and some of the investment was made by individual farmers, investing in their own irrigation systems, with loans underwritten by government guarantees (Ringler, Rosegrant, and Paisner 2000). However, other projects, such as the Pontal Irrigation Project, have been developed by private investors who were provided a 25-year concession with returns obtained from selling water and leasing land (Varma, Dhingra, and Raghu Rama Swamy 2012).

Peru also has an excellent track record of private investment in coastal irrigation in greenfield projects, where land without water has zero productivity since it rarely rains. The Peruvians use a novel system of auctioning rights to develop irrigation and require large down payments and well-developed business plans to ensure transparency and avoid speculation (Deininger and Byerlee 2011). In some cases, these investments support smallholders, but this does not seem to be an explicit objective of the schemes.

Finally, an interesting footnote to our historical review is recent private investment in irrigation in northern Australia. A project to develop about 30,000 ha of land in the Ord River area was awarded in 2014 to a Chinese company, through an open bidding process. The project departs sharply from the strong family farm and settler ethos of the earlier private irrigation development initiatives on the Murray River and will operate as a single large-scale unit to produce and process bioethanol feed stocks (sugarcane and sorghum). However, some of the land will be operated by indigenous people (completely ignored in the earlier projects on the Murray River), who now have ownership rights and have negotiated significant compensation of about $50 million for transfer of the land to the private investors (McLean 2013).

There are also several recent examples of large-scale investors developing irrigation and utilizing novel business models in Africa. These are most developed in the sugar industry. Firms such as Illovo Sugar, Ltd., which is the largest sugar producer in Africa and operates in six countries, as well as smaller companies, including Kakira Sugar Limited in Uganda, have made substantial investments in irrigation and processing infrastructure. These investments include large outgrower components that build on the investment in irrigation and have enjoyed reasonable success and little controversy (Box 4.5). They have been effective alternatives for sustainable production, in comparison to companies that have attempted to operate very large farms with little local involvement.

Box 4.5 Ongoing investment for irrigated sugar production in Africa

Kakira Sugar Limited

Kakira Sugar Limited has utilized an innovative outgrower-oriented business model and significant investments in irrigation and processing infrastructure to become an industry leader in Uganda. Kakira Sugar was founded by an Indian businessman in the 1920s and made a substantial irrigation investment early on. Kakira Sugar was acquired by the Madhvani Group in 2000, at which point it commenced substantial expansion efforts, including development of processing infrastructure, power generators, and irrigation systems (Isabirye et al. 2007; Kakira Sugar Limited 2015). Kakira's outgrower model currently includes more than 7,000 farmers, who supply 65 percent of Kakira's total cane output. Additionally, Kakira provides a variety of services to these farmers, including input supplies, agricultural equipment, and training. Furthermore, Kakira has partnered with the Busoga Sugar Cane Growers Association to provide financial services to farmers and organized infrastructure projects, such as road construction (Kakira Sugar Limited 2015).

Illovo Sugar Company

Illovo, a South Africa–based company, expanded from South Africa through purchases and greenfield projects in Malawi, Mozambique, Swaziland, Tanzania, and Zambia. Illovo independently harvests sugarcane on more than 60,000 hectares of land and also purchases sugarcane from outgrowers who operate on an additional 112,000 hectares. In particular, Illovo is currently involved in a public–private partnership in Swaziland called the Lower Usuthu Smallholder Irrigation Project (LUSIP) that has combined public and private funds to build irrigation and electrical infrastructure, which has helped smallholders to develop 2,600 hectares of land for sugarcane production (ABF 2012; Illovo 2016).

Rice is another crop that requires large investments in irrigation, if Africa is to be competitive against rapidly rising imports. Some state-sponsored schemes have been revived with considerable success (e.g., Mali and Senegal) on already existing but poorly managed irrigation projects. However, given meager resources, expansion of irrigation is being driven by private investors. A variety of business models have been attempted. Olam, a large multinational trader, initially focused on contract farming in Nigeria with smallholders but was not able to enforce contracts due to side selling. It has now switched to development of a large-scale farm that it operates with plans to add outgrowers (Box 4.6). In Ghana, GADCO, involving Brazilian expertise, is using a nucleus farm, mill, and supply chain that it owns and manages to support involvement of smallholders as the major suppliers, by offering a premium price for quality rice. As practically the only domestic supplier of quality rice, this model ensures the enforcement of contracts, but it is too soon to claim success. Other rice development projects appear to have focused exclusively on combining land development and farm operations, engendering conflicts with existing land users (Oakland 2015; Larder 2015).

Given the high risks and long-term payoffs to private investment in irrigation development in Africa, a number of public–private partnerships are emerging to improve incentives for private investment, while at the same time ensuring participation of smallholders. The InfraCo design of irrigation for large commercial farms and for smallholders in Zambia, with support from the World Bank, is an example, but needs more time to demonstrate results on the ground (Box 4.6).

Tree crop plantations

Large-scale private investment in tree crop plantations in Africa has accelerated in recent years. The largest such investments are for oil palm in Central and West Africa, its original home, led by Asian investors. These investments may amount to $20 billion, if current plans are realized (Hardman & Co. 2012). One of the largest investors is Sime Derby, the world's biggest oil palm company, based in Malaysia. Sime Darby was provided a concession of over 300,000 ha in Liberia in 2009, in return for an anticipated investment of $3 billion over 20 years – twice the GDP of Liberia at the time. Investments of this magnitude offer the potential for large economic benefits to the country and to the 35,000 employees expected in the Sime Darby operation (Collings and Harrison 2014). However, initial experiences have largely been negative due to conflicts with existing land users within the concession area (as well as the 2015 Ebola outbreak) (Lanier, Mukpo, and Wilhelmsen 2012; Siakor 2012; Chapelle 2014). Other investors in the region, such as Herakles in Cameroon, have drawn fire from local communities and civil society, not only on land rights but also on deforestation in sensitive tropical ecosystems.

What is missing in these recent investments has been a strong state stance on developing smallholders, as part of the concession agreement. The early investments in Indonesia, as well as in West Africa (e.g., Ghana Oil Palm Development Company), required that over half the area of land provided to companies be designated to smallholders in nucleus–outgrower schemes. The Sime Derby investment in Liberia does provide for a relatively small allocation to smallholders (40,000 ha) but does not provide for financing of the smallholder land development, estimated at around $5,000 per ha or a total of $200 million. Private investment in development of in situ smallholder plots does not seem to have been considered as a way to reduce land tensions.

Box 4.6 Ongoing investment for irrigated cereals in Africa

Olam

Olam Nigeria Limited (Olam), a subsidiary of Olam International, organized an innovative scheme for rice production featuring a combination of irrigation programs and contract farming. In partnership with USAID, Olam developed a contract-farming program aimed at increasing farmers' access to credit, technology, and technical assistance, beginning in 2006. This partnership failed due to competition with other rice buyers in the area and was discontinued in 2008 (Johnson, Takeshima, and Gyimah-Brempong 2013). Olam then transitioned to focus on direct rice production on its own farm, through a concession by the government of Nigeria. Olam invested up to US$49.2 million into rice production, including construction of irrigation infrastructure and a milling facility in the Nasarawa State, and research programs related to new rice varieties (Johnson, Takeshima, and Gyimah-Brempong 2013; George 2013). Between the nucleus farm and the outgrowers, Olam seeks to process up to 60,000 tons of rice paddy annually, with 65 percent of the paddy produced on the nucleus farm and the remaining 35 percent purchased via outgrower cooperative agreements with smallholders (Johnson, Takeshima, and Gyimah-Brempong 2013; Rockefeller Foundation 2013).

Chiansi project

The Chiansi Irrigation Infrastructure Project in Zambia stands out as an example of a private firm developing irrigated land for use by smallholders. InfraCo designed the program, using a $3 million investment from the Private Infrastructure Development Group (InfraCo 2016). Some 80 percent of the land utilized for this program has been leased by smallholder farmer cooperatives to commercial farm-operating companies, in exchange for equity interest in the companies and free access to irrigation on the remaining 20 percent of land area. The irrigation program is intended to reach approximately 2,500 hectares of previously undeveloped land and will be managed by an infrastructure services company, co-owned by the Zambian government and a trust managed by farmers and investors (Palmer et al. 2010).

Potential of private land development today in Africa

Successful private initiatives for land development can be found today in Latin America, where land and water markets and financial markets work well. There are large companies in Brazil specializing in land development for subdivision and sale or rental, and also successful examples of concession operations for private irrigation development for family farms, mediated by the state. Private investment in land development has similar potential in Africa, where capital scarcity is acute, the need for land development great, and state capacity is weak. At least two prerequisites are needed to extend the land development model successfully to Africa.

First, both investors in the land development phase and family farmers who take over for the operational phase require secure tenure rights. In the rare case where a local population has secure access to land, local communities could potentially undertake collective action to contract a specialized investor to improve land and water resources in exchange for payments made possible by the resulting productivity gains. The transaction costs involved in negotiating such deals, however, are surely high, and in any case, such arrangements cannot serve areas where land development would need to attract immigrant farmers from other locations. In sparsely populated areas, investments that attract immigrant farmers have historically been important in developing an agrarian structure based on small- and medium-scale family farms. However, transaction costs of three-way negotiations of an equitable deal between in situ communities, immigrant settlers, and investors are high, especially where immigrants are from different ethnic groups.

Second, investors require the ability to enforce contracts with tenant farmers or farmers who are purchasing land with long-term loans provided by the companies. In the absence of strong contract law and its enforcement, the arrangement works for only a few crops, like sugarcane, where the company has a processing monopoly that can enforce loan repayments.

Since the key prerequisites are, for the most part, not in place in Africa, land developers have little choice but to pursue company-owned, large-scale agricultural production after the land is developed. There has been much discussion of public–private partnerships to facilitate smallholder access to land development and reduce the risks to private investors. Although some of these initiatives are being piloted, it is too soon to assess their success. Nonetheless, we believe that the experience in other regions demonstrates the potential of focusing private investment on land development for family farming in Africa. Governments that are giving out large land concessions at bargain rates could be building in stronger requirements for investment in land development, with inclusion of smallholders, to offset the risks and transactions costs inherent in the use of the land development model. In the long run, the transfer of developed land to independent smallholders or outgrowers is likely to be not only more equitable but also more efficient.

Conclusions

Investment in land development in some settings can create a highly productive asset that can be transformative for local economic development. However, many of these investments, such as irrigation, basic infrastructure and roads, and pioneering risks and costs, are associated with significant economies of scale and are beyond the reach of individual family farmers. For much of the 20th century, governments were the major players in land development, but this was not always so: historical examples, mostly from the late 19th and early 20th centuries, reveal that private investors can be attracted to developing farmland, in ways that are somewhat similar to private development of new urban housing areas designed for subdivision to individual owners.

Significant economies of scale and shortage of public resources open space for the private sector to invest in land development, a role that has been overlooked in the burgeoning literature on large-scale land acquisitions in recent years. Our review has shown a plethora of historical examples globally, as well as contemporary examples from Latin America, where the private sector was the major investor in large-scale land development. In the most successful cases, the investor focused on the land development phase and then turned the farm operations over to individual family farms through land sales or rental. The state generally played an important regulatory role in these schemes and made state concessions of large tracts of land conditional on developing a family farm agrarian structure.

We believe that investment in land development is critical in Africa, and that the levels and types of capital needed can be deployed only by attracting private investors. Doing so will require appropriate government policies, including frameworks designed to facilitate transition of newly developed land for rental or sale to smallholders. Considerable experimentation and learning may be needed to develop models appropriate to the African context, but historical precedents exist for governments, investors, and farmers to move beyond the rhetoric of land grabs and recognize the essential role of private land development in many successful family-farming systems.

Note

1 Note that nearly all of the schemes cleared native vegetation, including forests, to make way for farming, although environmental concerns on clearing forests emerged only in the later part of the 20th century (Byerlee and Rueda 2015).

References

ABF (Associated British Foods PLC). 2012. Water, Illovo Sugar, Africa. http://www.abf. co.uk/responsibility/case-studies-archive-2010-2014/water_illovo_sugar_africa

AgDevCo. 2014. AgDevCo's Mission Is to Reduce Poverty and Improve Food Security. http://www.agdevco.com

Bell, H. F., and W. H. Cairns. 1958. "Notes on the A.M.P. Society's Land Development Scheme in South Australia." *Australian Journal of Agricultural and Resource Economics* 2 (2): 104–12.

Bickel, U., and J. M. Dros. 2003. "The Impacts of Soybean Cultivation on Brazilian Eco-systems: Three Case studies." Commissioned by the WWF Forest Conversion Initiative, World Wildlife Fund, Gland, Switzerland.

Binswanger, H. P., K. Deininger, and G. Feder. 1995. "Power, Distortions, Revolt and Reform in Agricultural Land Relations." *Handbook of Development Economics*, Vol. 3B, edited by J. Behrman and T. Srinivasan, 2659–772. Amsterdam: North Holland.

Binswanger, H. P., and M. R. Rosenzweig. 1986. "Behavioural and Material Determinants of Production Relations in Agriculture." *Journal of Development Studies* 22 (3): 503–39.

Braga, D. 2012. "SLC Agrícola Enters Into Partnership for Land Development." SLC Agrícola, Porto Alegre, Brazil, May 31, 2012. http://www.prnewswire.com/news-releases/slc-agricola-enters-into-partnership-for-land-development-156005585.html

BrasilAgro. 2014. "BrasilAgro – Adding Value to the Land." (brochure). BrasilAgro, São Paulo, Brazil.

Briggs, H. E. 1932. "Early Bonanza Farming in the Red River Valley of the North." *Agricultural History* 6 (1): 26–37.

Byerlee, D. 2014. "The Fall and Rise again of Plantations in Tropical Asia: History Repeated?" *Land* 3 (3): 574–97.

Byerlee, D., W. P. Falcon, and R. L. Naylor. 2017. *The Tropical Oil Crop Revolution: Food, Feed, Fuel, and Forests.* New York: Oxford University Press.

Byerlee, D., and X. Rueda. 2015. "A Century of Global Discourse on Tropical Commodities on the Forest Frontier: From Public to Private Standards." *Forests* 6 (4): 1301–24.

Chaddad, F. 2014. "BrasilAgro: Organizational Architecture for a High-Performance Farming Corporation." *American Journal of Agricultural Economics* 96 (2): 578–88.

Chapelle, S. 2014. "Live or Drive: A Choice Has to Be Made. A Case Study of Sime Darby Operations in Liberia." Basta! (http://www.bastamag.net) and Les Amis de la Terre.

Collier, P., and A. J. Venables. 2012. "Land Deals in Africa: Pioneers and Speculators." *Journal of Globalization and Development* 3 (1): 1–22.

Collings, P., and G. Harrison. 2014. "Making FDI Work for Sub-Saharan Africa: Lessons from Liberia." Final Report, Oxford Economics.

CTA (The Technical Centre for Agricultural and Rural Cooperation). 2012. "Agricultural Growth Corridors: New Routes to Opportunity?" *Spore* No. 161, December 2012–January 2013.

Deininger, K. W., and D. Byerlee. 2011. *Rising Global Interest in Farmland: Can It Yield Sustainable and Equitable Benefits?* Washington, DC: World Bank.

Deininger, K., and D. Byerlee. 2012. "The Rise of Large Farms in Land Abundant Countries: Do They Have a Future?" *World Development* 40 (4): 701–14.

Drache, H. M. 1964. *The Day of the Bonanza: A History of Bonanza Farming in the Red River Valley of the North.* Fargo, ND: North Dakota Institute for Regional Studies.

Edgerley, W. F. 1953. "Thoughts on the A.M.P. Land Development Project." *Australian Quarterly* 25 (4): 25–32.

Ekman, S.-M.S., and C. S. Macamo. 2014. "Brazilian Development Cooperation in Agriculture: A Scoping Study on ProSavana in Mozambique, with Implications for Forests." Working Paper 138, Center for International Forestry Research (CIFOR), Bogor Barat, Indonesia.

Ely, R. T. 1918. "Private Colonization of the Land." *American Economic Review* 8 (3): 522–48.

Feeny, D. 1979. "Paddy, Princes, and Productivity: Irrigation and Thai Agricultural Development, 1900–1940." *Explorations in Economic History* 16 (2): 132–50.

Fergusson, J. 1984. *Bush Battalion: The AMP Society's Ninety Mile Desert Development in South Australia.* Sydney: Australian Mutual Provident Society.

George, R. 2013. "Scaling up Rice Production for Local Markets in Nigeria – Olam Experience." Presentation at the Feed the Future Scaling Agricultural Technologies – Gender,

Global Learning and Evidence Exchange (GLEE), Addis Ababa, December 3–5, 2013. http://agrilinks.org/events/feed-future-scaling-agricultural-technologies-glee-africa

Hamilton-McKenzie, J. 2010. "California Dreaming: The Establishment of the Mildura Irrigation Colony." PhD diss., La Trobe University, Melbourne.

Hanlon, J., and T. Smart. 2013. "Small Farmers or Big Investors? The Choice for Mozambique." Research Report 1 (updated): "Soya Boom in Gurué Has Produced a Few Bigger Farmers." http://www.open.ac.uk/technology/mozambique/sites/www.open.ac.uk.technology. mozambique/files/files/Soya_boom_in_Gurue_Hanlon-Smart_updated-2013(1).pdf

Hardman & Co. 2012. "Commercial Viability & Value Creation in West African Palm Oil Production." http://baystreet.ca/articles/research_reports/hardman/Bali_Palm_Oil_ Conference_Presentation.pdf

Hedges, J. B. 1934. *The Federal Railway Land Subsidy Policy of Canada.* Cambridge, MA: Harvard University Press.

Hill, E. 1937. *Water into Gold.* Melbourne: Robertson & Mullens.

Holden, J. S. 1970. "Economies of Scale in Land Development in Australia." *Australian Economic Review* 3 (3): 43–8.

Hu-Dehart, E. 1974. "Development and Rural Rebellion: Pacification of the Yaquis in the Late Porfiriato." *Hispanic American Historical Review* 54 (1): 72–93.

Illovo. 2016. Illovo Sugar Limited Group Overview. https://www.illovosugar.co.za/About-Us/ Group-Overview

InfraCo Africa. 2016. Where We Are Working. http://infracoafrica.com/projects.asp

Isabirye, M., E. Ronsmans, M. K. Magunda, D. Raes, D.V.N. Raju, and J. Deckers. 2007. *Irrigation of Sugar Cane in Mayuge District, Uganda.* Nairobi: Soil and Water Management Network (SWMnet).

Jepson, W. 2006. "Private Agricultural Colonization on a Brazilian Frontier, 1970–1980." *Journal of Historical Geography* 32 (4): 839–63.

Johnson, M., H. Takeshima, and K. Gyimah-Brempong. 2013. "Assessing the Potential and Policy Alternatives for Achieving Rice Competitiveness and Growth in Nigeria." IFPRI Discussion Paper 1301, International Food Policy Research Institute (IFPRI), Washington, DC.

Kakira Sugar Limited. 2015. http://www.kakirasugar.com/

Katzman, M. T. 1978. "Colonization as an Approach to Regional Development: Northern Paraná, Brazil." *Economic Development and Cultural Change* 26 (4): 709–24.

Kershner, F. D. 1953. "George Chaffey and the Irrigation Frontier." *Agricultural History* 27 (4): 115–22.

Kinsey, B. H., and H. P. Binswanger. 1993. "Characteristics and Performance of Resettlement Programs: A Review." *World Development* 21 (9): 1477–94.

Lanier, F., A. Mukpo, and F. Wilhelmsen. 2012. "Smell-No-Taste: The Social Impact of Foreign Direct Investment in Liberia." Center for International Conflict Resolution, Columbia University, New York.

Larder, N. 2015. "Space for Pluralism? Examining the Malibya Land Grab." *Journal of Peasant Studies* 42 (3–4): 839–58.

McLean, J. 2013. "Still Colonising the Ord River, Northern Australia: A Postcolonial Geography of the Spaces between Indigenous People's and Settlers' Interests." *Geographical Journal* 180 (3): 198–210.

Mitchell, D. 2012. "Kenya Smallholder Tea and Coffee: Divergent Trends Following Liberalization." In *African Agricultural Reforms: The Role of Consensus and Institutions*, edited by M. Ataman Askoy, 247–69. Washington, DC: World Bank.

Nelson, M. 1973. *The Development of Tropical Lands: Policy Issues in Latin America.* Baltimore: Published for Resources for the Future by Johns Hopkins University Press.

Norfolk, S., and J. Hanlon. 2012. "Confrontation between Peasant Producers and Investors in Northern Zambézia, Mozambique, in the Context of Profit Pressures on European Investors." Paper presented at the World Bank Conference on Land and Poverty, World Bank, Washington, DC, April 23–26, 2012.

Oakland Institute. 2015. "Irresponsible Investment: Africa's Broken Development Model in Tanzania." Oakland Institute, Oakland, CA; Greenpeace Africa, Johannesburg; and Global Justice Now, London. http://www.oaklandinstitute.org/irresponsible-investment

Ogilvie, C. P., ed. 1910. *Argentina from a British Point of View and Notes on Argentine Life.* London: Wertheimer Lea & Co. https://archive.org/details/argentinafrombri00ogilrich

Osei, R. 2013. "GADCO: A Holistic Approach to Tackling Low Agricultural Incomes." GIM Case Study, United Nations Development Programme (UNDP), New York.

Palmer, K., R. Parry, P. MacSporren, H. Derksen, R. Avery, and P. Cartwright. 2010. "Chiansi Irrigation: Patient Capital in Action." InfraCo Briefing Paper, InfraCo Africa, London. http://www.keithpalmer.org/pdfs/Chiansi_Irrigation_Brifing_Paper.pdf

Radding, C. 1989. "Peasant Resistance on the Yaqui Delta: An Historical Inquiry into the Meaning of Ethnicity." *Journal of the Southwest* 31 (3): 330–61.

Ringler, C., M. W. Rosegrant, and M. S. Paisner. 2000. "Irrigation and Water Resources in Latin America and the Caribbean: Challenges and Strategies." EPTD Discussion Paper No. 64, Environment and Production Technology Division, International Food Policy Research Institute (IFPRI), Washington, DC.

Rockefeller Foundation. 2013. "Rice Nucleus – Olam, Nigeria." Catalytic Innovations in African Agriculture Centennial Series. Rockefeller Foundation. http://b.3cdn.net/rock efeller/ec261fef99375f2ee5_n8m6bksd9.pdf

Sandul, P. J. 2010. "The Agriburb: Recalling the Suburban Side of Ontario, California's Agricultural Colonization." *Agricultural History* 84 (2): 195–223.

Siakor, S. K. 2012. "Uncertain Futures: The Impacts of Sime Darby on Communities in Liberia." World Rainforest Movement, Montevideo, Uruguay. http://www.fern.org/sites/ fern.org/files/uncertain%20futures_baja.pdf

SLC Agrícola. 2012. "SLC Agrícola: Value from Both Farm and Land." SLC Agrícola, Porto Alegre, Brazil. http://www.mzweb.com.br/slcagricola2009/web/arquivos/SLCE3_ PresentationInstitutional_201205_ENG.pdf

Takaya, Y. 1987. *Agricultural Development of a Tropical Delta: A Study of the Chao Phraya Delta.* Honolulu: University of Hawaii Press.

Tanabe, S. 1977. "Historical Geography of the Canal System in the Chao Phraya River Delta." *Journal of the Siam Society* 65 (2): 23–72.

Tawa, M., S. Amameishi, and T. Noguchi. 2014. "Inclusive Development for All: Addressing Land Right Issues in the Nacala Corridor, Northern Mozambique." Paper presented at the 2014 World Bank Conference on Land and Poverty, World Bank, Washington, DC, March 24–27, 2014.

Tyler, G., and G. Dixie. 2013. "Investing in Agribusiness: A Retrospective View of a Development Bank's Investments in Agribusiness in Africa and Southeast Asia and the Pacific." Agriculture and Environmental Services Discussion Paper 01, World Bank, Washington, DC.

Varma, H. K., A. S. Dhingra, and D. T. V. Raghu Rama Swamy. 2012. *Exploring Public–Private Partnership in the Irrigation and Drainage Sector in India.* Mandaluyong City, Philippines: Asian Development Bank.

Wells, S. 1986. *Paddle Steamers to Cornucopia: The Renmark-Mildura Experiment of 1887.* Merbein, Victoria: Welkins.

5 Staples production

Efficient "subsistence" smallholders are key to poverty reduction, development, and trade*

Michael Lipton

Introduction

Globally, about a billion people eat far too much. About another billion eat far too little. Mass death, disease, and misery are caused both by nutrient deficiency and by nutrient excess.[1] Yet, far too little food is transferred from the overfed to the underfed by trade, migration, or financial transfers, as they affect food consumption and/or the use of land and other farm resources. That is the greatest failure of economics in the world today. It is only partly the result of poverty and inequality. It is not substantially the result of "market failure." It is, in part, the result of market *success*, combined with human failure to manage incentives, institutions (including those of control over land), information, and technical progress. In particular, we need much better policies to make incentives, institutions, and public goods, affecting production and trade in food staples, favorable to low-income, family-based smallholders *and, in particular, to "subsistence" farmers.*

Subsistence farmers are smallholders. They usually rely mainly or wholly on family labor. They grow mainly staple foods, in amounts at best sufficient to feed their families – but in most cases less than sufficient (sub-subsistence or *food-deficit farmers*). Food-deficit farm families grow food mainly for home consumption, but need and consume more food than they grow. They buy the difference with income from transfers and selling non-food farm products, hired labor, or products of small, nonfarm enterprises.

"Subsistence farming" has become a term of low abuse. Most writing about farms, especially African farms, assumes (1) a stark contrast between subsistence and commercial farms, (2) inefficiency of subsistence farms, and (3) the need for a rapid shift from subsistence to commercial farms – and sometimes from small to large farms – for successful development. Yet, as almost all agricultural economists (but few macro-economists?) know, the three assumptions are wrong – logically, economically, historically, and in political practice:

- *Logically*, subsistence farms, even deficit farms, can be commercial. They can and do obtain cash in several ways (as discussed later in this chapter), including sale of farm output. They are substantial buyers and users of farm inputs.

- *Economically* – where savings are scarce, and rural labor still plentiful and increasing – such farms are more socially efficient than large farms. That is not because their *production* costs, per unit of output or of land, are very different. Rather, it is because small farms, with small areas and mainly family workers, enjoy lower unit *transaction* costs in managing labor. Thus small subsistence farms, including deficit farms, normally produce more per unit of scarce land and water, with less use of scarce capital, and more employment. And they are no less innovative than big farmers: in many studies, small farms actually use more fertilizer per hectare.

- *Historically*, Asia's takeoff since 1965 into rapid growth with massive poverty reduction is based on a Green Revolution in food staples output, mainly on subsistence and near-subsistence smallholdings. Combining the history and the economics, in a big majority of countries in Asia, Africa, and Latin America with decennial agricultural censuses, it can be seen that proportions of farmland in small farms have risen – reflecting efficiency and ability to innovate.

- *In political practice*, labor forces in sub-Saharan Africa (SSA) and parts of Asia will grow at a rate of over 2 percent/year for decades. These people will not escape poverty without extra demand for labor and/or cheaper locally available food staples. Despite urbanization, neither circumstance will happen without sustained growth of farm output, especially staples, on subsistence smallholdings. The political consequences if that does not happen – mass poverty amid elite takeoff – are cloudy, but bad. Yet Asia's Green Revolution reveals practicable, pro-smallholder, pro-subsistence policies that are efficient, equitable, and sustainable politically, fiscally, and environmentally (see also Lipton [2009]; Eastwood, Lipton, and Newell [2010]).

With such policies, poverty reduction spreads to left-out regions and groups, even in hard economic and climatic conditions. And each "unit" of poverty reduction produces better nutritional outcomes. Such "pro-subsistence" policies, apart from reducing misery, are not anti-trade, but rather steer public and private resources in ways that increase trade. Efficient subsistence farming is the mother of food trade, not its enemy.

I first look at some facts, and some relationships between poverty, nutrition, food staples, and subsistence.

Facts

World trends in poverty, nutrition, and food staples, 1960–2012

There was a fall of over three-quarters – more than in all previous human history – in the proportion of people in extreme poverty (here called the *absolute poor*) – that is, consuming below $1.90 (2015PPP)/person/day. In the early 1960s, these absolute poor were almost certainly over 66 percent of people in developing regions (Asia, SSA, Latin America, and Eastern Europe). In 1981, the proportion was 52 percent; in 2012, 15 percent. Poverty *gaps* – poor people's average shortfall below the $1.25 poverty line – also fell substantially: for example, in India from 23 percent in 1978 to 7 percent in 2010 (World Bank 1990, Table 3.2, 41; Chen and Ravallion 2012a, Table 2, 128; World Bank 2016, 4).[2]

There were similar but slower falls in malnutrition due to *deficiency* (mainly from stunting and wasting due to calorie deficiency and infection, but also micronutrient deficiencies). The incidence of significant underweight (>2SDs below NCHS standards) among children under five in developing regions was well over 40 percent in the early 1960s and fell from 29 percent in 1990 to 19 percent in 2007 (UN SCN 2010, Figure 9, 46, and Table 21, 47).[3] Improvement was rapid in China, slower in India, and almost absent in sub-Saharan Africa (SSA).[4]

Unprecedented increases in staples productivity (especially yield), output, and probably shares of output traded within (but not among) nations, occurred. These three trends were strongest in Asia, above all China, but SSA has largely missed out on all three trends.

A fourth, unwelcome global trend was burgeoning malnutrition due to *excess* (obesity because calorie intake exceeds requirements) – and hence diabetes (also linked to excess sugar), heart disease (also linked to excess fats, especially animal and trans fats), and cancer (with many triggers involving excess nutrients).

Malnutrition depends substantially but not wholly on poverty, via food staples

Undernutrition

The absolute poor devote about half their consumption, by value, to staples (and over 70 percent to all foods). Staples provide 70 to 80 percent of the kilocalories and most micronutrients for the absolute poor; these proportions fall sharply – that is, diets are diversified – as income rises. Most absolute poor work on farms, mainly (except in Latin America) their own, but partly their employers' farms; and over 70 percent of the absolute poor are in rural areas. Poverty is much more responsive to agricultural growth than to growth in other sectors (de Janvry and Sadoulet 2010).[5] And *when staples yields rise, most of the poor* – who are still farmers and farm laborers – *normally get more income from labor and eat more*, unless land is extremely unequal *and* farming inappropriately capital-intensive. *Low staples output and productivity is a major cause of poverty and hunger.* As Sen (1981) implies, that is mainly because low staples output reduces the poor's food entitlements (rather than because too little food is available): low staples output per person means low income for the poor, high local prices, and hence, low food entitlements for the poor, and undernutrition.

Thus, despite the poor's huge concentration of consumption and income on food, poverty causes most undernutrition, measured by wasting and stunting. These are worsened by food–disease interactions: the poor cannot afford enough good food, and live in conditions that increase exposure to malaria and dysentery. As people escape poverty, they reduce exposure to dysentery and food shortage, as best they can. Yet, though poverty has plummeted since 1960, except in SSA, the persistently bad health environment of low-income groups means that undernutrition (outside East Asia) has declined less sharply.

Overnutrition

Overnutrition has also exploded, even in middle- and low-income countries and groups. It is, perhaps surprisingly, also linked to poverty, partly via food staples. Poverty is the main cause of undernutrition of children under 5, and this helps cause *over*nutrition later. Undernutrition selects children who need less food to survive, but keeps them small; and child undernutrition can impair adult immune response. As the nation develops and children reach working age, they often move to urban work, with better income but less movement, more crowding, greater consumption of energy-dense snacks, and displacement of high-fiber staples by animal foods with higher fat content. All this may help explain why early undernutrition is linked to increased risk both of infection in middle age (Prentice's Gambia long series) and of diabetes and heart disease in old age (the Barker hypothesis). In any case, while overnutrition in poor countries starts among the affluent, it soon comes to be associated with poverty (Monteiro et al. 2004). Food staples are implicated since, when incomes rise, staples use shifts from direct human consumption to consumption "filtered" via meat and dairy products. This not only shifts consumption toward less fibrous, fattier foods but also stimulates *over*nutrition, obesity, and disease. Also, farm animals hugely raise demand for staples and, hence, staples prices (mainly because producing 1,000 human kcalories via meat/dairy consumption uses 5–7 times more land than via staples eaten directly as cereals, roots, or tubers). That also cuts entitlements for consumers, increasing *under*nutrition among the poorest.

Thus, while a normal accompaniment of rising income, and a source of dietary diversification and pleasure, the shift of staples toward farm animals, carried to the extent that has been experienced in the past few decades, is a main cause of both undernutrition and overnutrition and the diseases of affluence. The "double *burden*" of low- to mid-income countries, undernutrition and its diseases alongside overnutrition and its diseases, is not a double *problem*: it is a single problem of policy for, or against, staples and subsistence farms.

The extent of subsistence

Of the world's dollar-poor, "the vast majority are small farmers, who rely on a combination of self-provisioning and market sales" (Quan 2007, 2). Yet, amazingly, for most developing areas, there are no estimates of how much total food, staples, or grain output is retained for consumption by the farm household.

In Russia in 2003–2005, 66 percent of families grew for subsistence, producing *over half the farm output by value* (on only 3 percent of the land, mainly because large farms left so much fallow). Eighty-seven percent of these families derived no cash income – that is, farmed only for subsistence. However, except potatoes, most main staples (wheat, barley, oats, rye) were grown on agricultural enterprises, not small farms (Sharashkin 2008).

In Uganda in 2005–2006, 42 percent of total farm output and 54 percent of food output were retained by growers (Kraybill, Bashaasha, and Betz 2012). Tanzania's 2002–2003 National Sample Census of Agriculture estimated that 69 percent of cassava was retained.

In 2003 in rural China, "over 80 percent of grains, beans, and potatoes consumed were self-produced." However, for all food, commercialization (cash purchases) grew by 7.4 percent per year from 1994 to 2003. Consumption of self-produced grain and vegetables fell, even in absolute terms (Gale et al. 2005, 5).[6]

In India, "in the early 1950s, about 30–35 per cent of foodgrains output was marketed, which has increased to more than 70 per cent in recent years" (Sharma and Wardhan 2015, 3). A large household survey of the 3–5 leading states growing rice, maize, wheat, and millet in 2011–12 showed that proportions retained (largely for subsistence consumption) were generally below 20 percent, but were considerably higher among marginal farmers (<1 ha) and small farmers (1–2 ha), who devoted larger proportions of area to each staple, and achieved somewhat higher yields – and also higher in non-"leading" states where markets were less highly developed. In Orissa, in 2007, of the main staple (paddy rice), 35 percent was retained by growers (Reddy 2009; Sharma and Wardhan 2015).

These numbers underestimate production for subsistence, because they measure it as output minus *gross* marketed surplus. Since Narain's (1962) pathbreaking work in India, it has been known that small "subsistence" farms, having sold much of their staple crop after harvest, buy it back steadily until the next harvest. Thus, the proportion of output that a family farm produces for subsistence is significantly higher than the proportion it *retains*. The other side of this story is that when a farm eats most of what it grows, this does not mean that the farm does not sell much after harvest, so it has cash to buy fertilizers and other things. Small subsistence farmers *trade*.

Staples production–trade by subsistence/deficit farmers, "commodification," and malnutrition

Production

Rapid rises in staples productivity almost always reduce undernutrition where they happen, partly by keeping local staples prices down, partly by providing income from work (employment or self-employment) for the rural poor – still a large majority of poor people. Both of these paths – from higher staples productivity to lower poverty and undernutrition – are usually most effective if staples *yields* rise mainly on smallholdings, and by means that generate extra demand for labor rather than equipment.

Trade

While a subsistence buffer has many advantages – and can help, not impede, food trade – for villages to farm *only* a staple, for subsistence, does not promote development. Trade assists specialization and affluence, permits dietary diversification, and helps smooth consumption between times of good and bad harvest. The benefits of a mix of trade and self-provisioning show up in the effects on undernutrition: with similar income, villages specializing almost wholly in *either* staples *or* non-staple cash crops experience significantly more undernutrition than villages with significant plantings of both (Schofield 1979).

"Commodification"

Are poor people, subsistence farmers, staples productivity, and nutrition helped or harmed when food is "commodified?" Many people are unhappy that certain things are "commodified" – turned into items valued only, or almost entirely, for their cash returns when traded or exchanged. Nobody minds if a chess set or a jar of caviar is commodified. However, most people agree that life, for example, should not be treated like that: it is a duty to assist a wounded person if one can, even if there is no reward. So what about commodification of essentials to life: food or health care? There is legitimate controversy about the extent to which profit motives in pharmaceuticals, hospital space, or doctors' services make it more or less likely that care for the sick and wounded will be available, and of high quality, when needed.

On some accounts, food is normally commodified as humans "develop." Human food was originally hunted or (more usually) gathered by each small kin group for its own use. From about 7,500 to 5,000 BC, food was farmed increasingly by settled agriculturists – initially almost everyone, mostly small farmers, feeding themselves; but with development, dwindling numbers of mainly large-farmer specialists trading staples and other farm products to others engaged in industry and services. In this evolutionist approach, subsistence farming does and should evolve into trade by a much smaller group of commercial farm specialists. Quan (2007) cites a standard model of transition from "Rural world 3" ("Farmers . . . primarily self-provisioning") to "Rural world 2" ("Small farmers are primarily local market-oriented, diversified, and adaptable, with . . . some self-provisioning with varying degrees of market engagement"), to the modern "Rural world 1," with commercial farming, but even small farmers "globally competitive, embedded in agribusiness, commodity producers, and processors . . . export driven, adopters of Green Revolution and transgenic technologies . . . highly market-integrated for both staple and higher-value cash crops" (Quan 2007, 5, adapted from Vorley 2002).

So why not squeeze out subsistence?

The model and the mistaken inference

From this model, much development policy derives goals of squeezing out subsistence farming. For instance, Uganda's Poverty Eradication Action Plan, backed by government and main donors, aimed to cut the retained proportion of farm output from 80 percent in 2002–2003 to 30 percent in 2013–14 (Kray-bill, Bashaasha, and Betz 2012). The model sees "subsistence" – families feed-ing themselves – as the enemy of development, and the replacement of small subsistence farmers by large food-selling farmers as evolutionary, normal, and desirable. "Subsistence" farming is seen as an increasingly "inefficient" use of resources, as countries develop. Its reduction is seen as a natural process, to be accelerated by policy.

This is, in crucial respects, completely wrong. What is wrong is not the perception – inherited from Adam Smith – that specialization and trade are keys to "the natural progress of opulence" and the retreat of poverty (Smith 1904 [1776]).[7] What is wrong is to infer that, because trade and specialization are desirable, subsistence farming of staples is the enemy: backward, inefficient, reactionary, to be driven out. This is wrong for five reasons:

1   The account of food commodification/trade/exchange as the rival of food self-consumption or subsistence, bound to drive it out, is empirically false. Often, subsistence is efficient, and then it is the ally of trade and special-ization, even of commercialization – not their enemy. Often, too, subsistence is linked to household food security, and thus the base from which less affluent farm families trade more.
2   Small-scale family farming, including and perhaps especially subsistence farming, slashes the cost of managing the work process. This saving of *transaction costs* makes such farming a more "efficient" use of resources – and of higher land yields – where labor is plentiful and capital scarce.
3   Small, "deficit," and subsistence farms are just as "commercial" as big farms, only smaller.
4   The story of staple foodstuffs – and the gains and losses from shifts between subsistence and trade – is different from the story of other foods, in ways favoring subsistence farming.
5   The global retreat of mass poverty since 1960 – alongside burgeoning inequality since 1980 – has shifted populations into three groups: the ultra-rich 1–5 percent, the adequately well-off, and a dwindling but persistent core of poor people. Only the last group *normally* does not eat quantities and qualities of food needed for a healthy life. Poor populations suffer caloric undernutrition and micronutrient and sugar/fat malnutrition in low-income countries; caloric overnutrition and sugar and fat malnutrition in high-income countries; and both in middle-income countries and in low-income groups, as they become better off. More surprisingly, espe-cially in poor but fast-growing countries, poverty and undernutrition in early life are conducive to the development of diseases of *over*nutrition in later life. All this makes a new case for small-scale subsistence staples farming.

What do these five points tell us about the interplay of staples production, com-modity exchange, and poverty?

Subsistence farms trade!

The standard picture – commercial farming with trade as an alternative to tradeless subsistence farming, destined to drive it out – is wrong. Commercial farming and subsistence farming have three other relationships, based on the fact that most subsistence farms grow fewer staples than their family needs and must fill the gap:

1   In India in 1950–51, many farmers sold most of their grain, soon after harvest, to pay off loans – then bought back the grain over the year, as needed. India has been transformed since 1950–51, but this still happens. Subsistence farmers need loans well before harvest, to buy not only consumer goods but also, increasingly, farm inputs. Far from evolving *from* subsistence to trade and the Green Revolution, hundreds of millions of Asian subsistence farms trade *to obtain* Green Revolution seeds and fertilizers. Indeed, the smaller a farm, the more, normally, is its annual per-hectare fertilizer use – and output. Such grain sales and buybacks bring problems. First, transport is costly and risky. Second, losses of staples in transport, and in large (especially public) grain stores, dwarf the storage losses of staple foods in small farm households – which, contrary to myth, are small, typically below 5 percent.[8] (Indeed, these extra losses are part of the hidden cost of the passage from subsistence, especially if artificially accelerated in advance of provision of efficient storage and other post-harvest arrangements, whether market-driven or state-led.) Third, staples transport and storage costs are paid, plus profit, to food traders by subsistence and deficit farmers – usually poor. Yet such farmers can often finance year-round consumption and purchase key Green Revolution inputs only with loans linked to post-harvest staple crop sales.

2   Households mainly farming staples, but still in staples deficit, enter into trade in other ways. They grow crops like vegetables, cotton, and coffee, selling them to buy staples and farm inputs. They trade by using nonfarm income, typically 30–40 percent of subsistence farm household income (Haggblade, Hazell, and Reardon 2007) (from nonfarm enterprise and off-farm activity, including work on other people's farms, often paid in kind). And they trade by using remittances from relatives, rural as well as urban and international.

3   Deficit farmers, while commercial and trading, are poor, food-insecure, and risk-averse. Higher food production for consumption *raises* their readiness to trade, by reducing their poverty and food insecurity. A bad harvest, health costs, the arrival of twins, sharply dearer food, then mean discomfort instead of disaster. This reduction in "existential risk" – at worst, of starvation; at best, of forced sale of land or animals – makes poor farmers more willing to take other risks: to trade; to seek out markets; to innovate with new techniques; to try new crops, whether staples or others. With more, and more secure, staples production for subsistence, a poor farm family's staples (and other) marketings *rise*. Again the crude, static arithmetic of "more subsistence means less trade and development" fails.

A subtler effect involves price risk. Wealthy staples-farming households, since they sell almost all of their staples output and buy mainly non-staples, are worried about risk of *lower* prices of *sold* staples; this induces them to grow *less* (and buy fewer fertilizers and other inputs) per hectare. Poor, staples-deficit farm households are worried about risk of *higher* prices of *purchased* staples; this induces them to grow *more* and buy more farm inputs, per hectare (Srinivasan 1972; Barrett 1996). Thus, subsistence farms – for example, in maize in Mozambique – may get higher staples yields than big farms.

So "subsistence" and deficit farmers are "commercial" – not only profit-motivated but also engaging in substantial sales, which permit substantial purchases, including farm inputs. The crude arithmetic of "more self-consumption means less trade," so subsistence and staples trade are enemies, is wrong.

Subsistence, family, and smaller farms in poorer countries are efficient, often dynamic

In *capital-intensive, labor-scarce, rural regions*, big commercial farms increasingly rent in, buy, and displace small semi-subsistence farms. In much of North America, Western Europe, and Australia, this is efficient. That is not because big farms have significantly lower unit *production* costs. It is because they have lower *transaction* costs (per hectare and per unit of output) in borrowing, and in managing capital equipment.

The opposite logic works in *labor-intensive, capital-scarce, rural regions*: most of rural SSA and Asia, and much of Latin America and Russia. There, it is small farms that have lower transaction costs (per hectare and per unit of output), due to cheaper search, screening, training, and supervision of their largely family labor. That is why in these areas, successive Censuses of Agriculture – each decade from the 1970 round to the 2010 round – show a market-led drift (sometimes supported by land reform) to *smaller* farm size, alongside small-farm green revolutions in many cases. In such areas, the reversal of this drift to smallness and artificial stimulation of shifts from subsistence to big farms – for example, by land grabs, often nonconsensual, ill-managed, untransparent, or corrupt – make for inefficiency. Such land shifts reduce demand for labor. With workforces increasing at a rate over 2 percent for decades – and nonfarm development having failed to stem unemployment – anti-subsistence is socially harmful too (Lipton 2009; Eastwood, Lipton, and Newell 2010).

As compared with large-scale commercial farms, small-scale family farms, including "deficit" and subsistence farms, slash the cost (per hectare and per unit of output) of managing labor, but raise the cost of acquiring and managing capital. In low-income and many middle-income countries, this means that small-scale, including subsistence and deficit, farms have lower unit transaction costs – they are a more "efficient" use of resources where labor is plentiful and capital scarce. Nor are subsistence farmers sluggards: in many countries, they have enthusiastically adopted irrigation, fertilizers, and radically improved seeds.

There are two caveats. First, as development proceeds, the advantages for labor supervision of small, family, and subsistence farms loom less large, while the advantages for capital management of large farms loom larger. The stronger political position of bigger farms, however, means that such trends will be recognized, probably too soon, in land acquisitions: state support for farm enlargement is seldom indicated, given the power of large units (and the weakness of small and poor farmers) to lobby and to corrupt.

Second, small farms, including subsistence and deficit farms selling post-harvest for later buyback, are often claimed to have major disadvantages in dealing with processors, supermarkets, and export markets, not the least for staple foods. However, bulking up, marketing cooperatives, and intermediation often allow small farms to *produce* competitively for big units that *process and trade*, each with lower unit transaction costs in its own sphere (see Dong et al. [2006]; Reardon et al. [2006]; Haggblade, Hazell, and Reardon [2007]; and Lipton [2009, 87–91]).

Trading plus efficient equals commercial

It is obvious that if subsistence and deficit farms are efficient resource users and enter substantially into trade, they are commercial. The common distinction between "subsistence farmers," to be wound down, and "commercial farmers," to be stimulated, is little more than a lazy group libel on subsistence farmers.

Subsistence and staples

The data for crop mix on subsistence and other farms are scrappy, but in much of SSA most staple food is still grown on subsistence, often food-deficit, farms, including urban farms. However, such farms' competitive advantages are due to labor intensity. So one would expect concentration on high-value horticulture, especially vegetables, where yields can be sharply raised without much capital. There are many cases – from Russia, via Ghana and Kenya, to Indonesia and Sri Lanka – of widespread, competitive vegetable production by tiny farms (often called "home gardens"). Where such farms are in or near big towns, the vegetables are grown mainly for sale; elsewhere, as supplements to nutrition. In either case, even a small home garden is associated with significant nutritional improvements (Gautam, Sthapit, and Shrestha 2006; UN SCN 2010, especially 101–3).[9] A widely implemented homestead food production "package of home gardening, small livestock [poultry/pig] production and nutrition education . . . improves household food production and diet quality" in several cases, notably Bangladesh, compared to control groups without the package (Iannotti, Cunningham, and Ruel 2009, 25). However, the impact is mainly on caloric adequacy and food security, rather than on micronutrient status. Probably, the poorest cannot afford to keep the vegetables and chickens for diversity and nutrients, but sell them to improve caloric adequacy.

"Should" microfarmers grow staples for direct calories, or higher-value vegetables for sale? High vegetable yields from labor power are often found, making tiny holdings highly competitive, given the right technology, seeds, fertilizer or manure, water control, and nearby markets. All of these require-ments, especially markets, are often missing or unreliable in remote rural areas, so the rural subsistence microfarmer often grows mainly staples. Vegetable microfarming is more common in densely populated areas, including towns. There, too, high land values make staples an unlikely long-term land use. Yet, from Kinshasa to Addis and Nairobi, tiny family patches of grains, or even cassava, spring up on almost any patch of unused private, or claimable, land with nearby domestic water or waste. The rural and urban poor are desper-ately concerned with staple food security, especially with rising or gyrating prices. Reducing food insecurity – by agrotechnical progress in staples and by land reform – will greatly reduce poor farmers' aversion to risk. Thus improved prospects to farm subsistence staples raise the share of non-staples in the crop mix.

The absolute poor get 70–80 percent of calories *and most other nutrients* from staples (proportions that fall as poverty recedes). So poor farmers prioritize food "subsistence" in the case of staples, delaying full commodification – farming for pure profit, and so shifting from staples to higher-value products – until food security improves. The very poor and food-insecure seek staples first. As we have seen, this does not impede commercial, efficient, trading behavior, but it limits the spread of such behavior across farm practice. Also agro-economic best practice often dictates *rotating* staples with pure cash crops like cotton, or *mixing* them with crops like beans. Such farmers' good sense influences farm policy, especially on research, much less than it should.

Inequality, nutrition, and the case for expanded subsistence

The final, and most obvious, reason why it is wrong to squeeze subsistence production, and producers, is equity. Such policies probably worsen absolute consumption *poverty* and increase *polarization*.

Though absolute poverty has plummeted since 1960 (except in SSA), in 2012 almost a billion people were absolute poor (Chen and Ravallion 2012b; Sumner 2012; World Bank 2016). Probably over 80 percent of the poor are rural, but deficit sub-subsistence farmers are heavily overrepresented among the rural *and urban* absolute poor. As they get less poor, they diversify away from such farm-ing. However, meanwhile, policies to shrink it – for example, by shifting land into larger farms, or concentrating research upon their priorities – will harm the poor, except on far-fetched assumptions.

Squeezing subsistence farming also increases the vulnerability of the poor, who are much affected by recent uptrends and increased fluctuations in the price of their main food staple. To the extent that they produce for subsistence, they are much less vulnerable. Furthermore, subsistence farming interacts strongly with land equality to benefit the poor: where farmland is very equal, even poor subsistence farmers normally have a surplus for sale, so poverty may actually decline when food prices rise – as in Vietnam (Ivanic and Martin 2011, especially 7; Zaman 2011) and probably China, which have experienced egalitarian reforms of land into small family farms, but not elsewhere.

In many countries, the plummeting of poverty sits alongside a huge rise in the income shares of the richest 10 percent, and especially the top 1 percent. This implies polarization. Middle-income groups are losing out, both to those above and to those below. This reduces the power, and the will, of the "squeezed middle" to relate positively to either the rich or the poor, let alone to mediate politically between them. Thus, polarization increases social distance and damages social coherence. Widespread subsistence farming – middle-income as well as low-income – still exists in China, Russia (Sharashkin 2008), SSA, and parts of South and East Asia, but in many areas is threatened by land grabs (mostly domestic rather than foreign), policies on agricultural research, and – perhaps above all – an ideology that subsistence farming is reactionary and should be squeezed.

Policy

The overriding policy lesson is that in low-income and lower middle-income rural areas, subsistence farming, especially of food staples, should be celebrated and helped, by appropriate policies, to become high-input and scientific – not, as occurs too often, mocked, denigrated, and squeezed out. There are at least six reasons to support subsistence farming. First, subsistence farming is still a main source of nutrition, food security, income stability, employment, and income – for example, in SSA, for over 60 percent of families, and perhaps 75 percent of the absolute poor. Second, subsistence farming cuts post-harvest transaction costs of staples output, mainly by reducing requirements for there-and-back trade (with its associated transport and storage cost and loss, and necessary intermediation). Third, since subsistence production is mostly on small, family farms, such post-harvest economies are *additional* to such farms' generally lower unit transaction costs of labor in production. Fourth, especially with appropriate provision of public goods – above all, those facilitating modern scientific farming methods – improved farming of staples for subsistence is not an enemy of specialization and trade, but a catalyst for them. Fifth, despite considerable land inequality in some cases, much of South and East Asia's Green Revolution in staples production – and much of the subsequent shift to higher-value, traded farm products – started and has been sustained largely on family, subsistence farms; this has induced unprecedented growth and industrialization in the surrounding economies: it can be done. Sixth, the alternative, mainly large-farm development, path amid extreme land inequality, as in most of Latin America, with much higher land inequality, has had much less favorable impact on poverty and on aggregate economic growth: the alternative strategy has seldom worked well. Seventh, binding all this together, is the key issue of employment: rural and urban unemployment has been much more severe and persistent in countries that neglected agriculture or adopted a large-farm strategy, than where green revolutions have been sought mainly via small/subsistence farms.

Which path will SSA governments choose? In the 21st century, many are shifting priorities toward agriculture, which by global standards they had neglected, underfinanced, or even sucked dry. Lead SSA institutions, such as Comprehensive Africa Agriculture Development Programme (CAADP) and Alliance for a Green Revolution in Africa (AGRA), in the light of experience globally, are committed to smallholder-led paths that are based on scientific farming and institutional change. However, initial power holders in many countries oppose that path, instead favoring severe land inequality and even land grab. A powerful tool for such power holders is to present this, however misleadingly, as an economically sound and progressive strategy – and to denigrate "subsistence" farming as a scientifically backward "scratch-a-patch." The reality is that Asia's accelerated development started with policies to increase subsistence farmers' access to farm science, water control, and better seeds and fertilizers; and that the very low availability of these to SSA's subsistence family farmers underpins SSA's still sluggish development.

We know the main requirements of a small/subsistence farm-friendly policy: farm water, fertilizer access, seed research, trade, education, health, rural public goods, and *sometimes* rural financial services, including risk management. We also know the dangers of policies unduly, or for too long, based on subsidy rather than investment. I list five less familiar areas where policy improvement can help subsistence farmers to advance with science and trade.

Improve staples output and employment data, especially for subsistence farms, for better policy for them

To make sensible farm policy, a government needs some idea of *levels and trends of farm output* for main products and regions. Reasonably accurate data have been available for India, Pakistan, and Bangladesh for about 70 years, and much the same applies in China and much of the rest of Asia (though data for minor and mixed crops, so important for many subsistence farms, are weak or absent). However, for some decades, no remotely reliable data for subsistence, small-farm, non-internationally traded staples production – and, to a substantial extent, for smallholder output altogether – have been available, nationally or regionally, for most SSA countries, including, among the largest, DR Congo, Ethiopia, Nigeria, and Sudan (Jerven 2013; Lipton 2013). (Data reported to the Food and Nutrition Organization of the United Nations [FAO] do not, in these cases, rest upon *properly collected and supervised* crop-cutting samples or post-harvest farmers' reports.) Is a policy improving production, locally or nationally? If production levels (let alone trends) are unknown – or, worse, if there is an illusion of knowledge – agriculture-related policies on technology, prices, and institutions cannot be assessed. (Micro studies can help, but cannot replace knowledge of output effects and trends nationally.)

Since the very few available studies suggest that smallholder/subsistence production is 30–70 percent of farm output in much of SSA – and since levels and trends of such production are usually unknown – policy success and need cannot be properly evaluated, so correct policy choice is unlikely. Information, and therefore policy impact on output, is weakest for small subsistence farmers: output of traded cash crops from large farms is usually more reliably known, so policies affecting such output can be evaluated and changed if (and only if) appropriate.

Absent such macro data, micro studies (very seldom random samples) can hint at the *share of output grown for subsistence*, or the gross and net-marketed surplus. Such studies exist only in a few countries, however, and only for some crops, years, and seasons. If policy impacts vary for subsistence and large farms, therefore, the balance of appropriate policies (and their distribution, as well as production impact) cannot be properly assessed. This will shift policies and expenditures away from the unknown – including crops mainly cultivated for subsistence; but that balance is not due to knowledge of what policies work, but to ignorance about subsistence production.

Unfortunately, we cannot usually guess at the size or even direction of bias around the casually reported official numbers for staples output (let alone subsistence share) in most of SSA, though we know that they understate year-to-year fluctuation. Farmers' reports of output are fairly reliable,[10] but *only* if gathered shortly after harvest by properly trained, supervised, and incentivized investigators, using locally calibrated weights and measures.

Policies to strengthen farm output data have long ago largely succeeded in most of the developing world; adequate staff – for data collection, processing, and use – is a prerequisite. However, many fiscally hard-pressed (and often urban-biased) countries of SSA have lacked *national* commitment, whether to agriculture or to statistical information, required to pay, train, and oversee such staff and to embed them into a national statistical system.

Many data in SSA, relevant to policy for subsistence farms, are good or rapidly improving: land use data, as satellite imaging increasingly complements agricultural census; food consumption and poverty data, from the Living Standards Measurement Study (LSMS) and its successors; and demographic and health data, from Demographic and Health Surveys (DHS). However, for the huge subsistence sector, data on inputs – especially nonmarket ones, including family labor – are as weak as for outputs: the Nigerian official estimate of the proportion of the workforce mainly engaged in agriculture around 2007 is 27 percent, but US Department of Agriculture (USDA) and World Bank estimates are double that. "Careful field surveys in 15 SSA countries" give national estimates around 70 percent and "suggest, contrary to received wisdom, that proportions of young workers are even higher" (Lipton 2012, 4, Table 2, 6).

Screen major public decisions for impact on subsistence farms, especially in staples, and act accordingly

Public *investments*, *policy*, and *incentives*, not mainly aimed at subsistence staples farming, can greatly affect it.

For efficiency, possible net "backwash effects" on subsistence farmers, especially in staples, should be evaluated and deducted from benefits when estimating the benefit/cost ratios of public policy or investment. For equity, if such policy or investment causes loss of welfare to subsistence farmers (or smallholders, in general), they should be modified, or else the losers should be compensated, by enacting countervailing policies and investments that benefit them specifically.[11]

Policy

China and many other countries have successfully stimulated exports through export processing zones (EPZs), usually coastal. Such stimuli sometimes, on balance, harm other lines of production – especially non-traded goods, such as subsistence staples – and regions (e.g., the North and West) where they, and their growers, are concentrated. Again, this is not to condemn EPZs, sometimes a very valuable policy tool, but to request pre-assessment of their backwash effect on subsistence farms and compensation, if indicated.

Incentives

After decades of agricultural neglect and exploitation – and mainly subsequent (but overlapping) decades of sometimes undiscriminating war against all agricultural subsidies – SSA is moving toward selective subsidies, designed for "smart" avoidance of misdirection and leakage, and seeking to spread new and promising farm inputs, especially (as in Malawi) fertilizers (Dorward and Chirwa 2011). Given SSA's extremely low fertilizer use,[12] such kick-starting may well be right in some cases, but tends to discriminate against farmers with little cash (or cash crops), water control, or capacity to bear risk. Careful planning can mitigate these dangers; otherwise the programs are not kick-starters, but become permanent support for richer farmers against "subsistence" competitors. In some cases, "costs . . . outweigh benefits" and "at least partial reallocation . . . from fertilizer subsidies to R&D and infrastructure would provide higher returns [in] agricultural growth and poverty reduction," (Jayne and Rashid 2013, 547) but this is contested (Dorward and Chirwa 2014). In India, fertilizer subsidies spread to tiny and subsistence farmers – and accelerated the Green Revolution – but have proved costly and hard to phase out as fertilizer use became widespread and even excessive.

Release some areas likely to be used for subsistence farming

Home gardens

Home gardens are close to home labor, water, and kitchen waste. Small ones, especially, often show very high value-added per hectare. Often, apart from stimulating subsistence farmers to "spread their wings" and trade in local vegetable markets, they significantly raise subsistence staples output. Policy can increase area in home gardens. Governments should be more ready to release superfluous public lands, especially for the poor. Joint villager action can be stimulated to develop cultivable waste, standpipes, and compost pits. Often, such land redistribution has proved feasible where larger-scale land reform has not, reducing poverty and malnutrition (Mitchell and Hanstad 2004).

Much of SSA has the advantage (as did most of South and East Asia) that agriculture is mainly in smallholdings: farmland is not very unequal. This, in part, accounts for the big role of subsistence staples farms. These are the main source, especially for the poor, of employment, calories, and income; and small family farms generate each unit of these with less capital than alternative activities, and with less land than large farms. So governments should refrain from undermining small-farm systems, until adequate and economic alternative sources of food, work, and income are available. "Land grab" should be judged on that criterion: favorably, if fairly negotiated with small subsistence farmers, and enhancing their control over area and productivity – for example, with carefully considered contract farming, nucleus estates, or tenancy-crop purchase arrangements; unfavorably, if new owners destroy informal traditional tenures, not after fair negotiation but through unmandated government action, or replace employment-intensive subsistence farms with capital-intensive large farms.

A few "settler economies" in South and East SSA start with very unequal farms. In such cases – given worldwide evidence of small family farms' major advantages in labor management – careful but substantial redistributive land reform is efficient (Lipton 2009, Chapter 2, 65–123) and equitable, and (as proven worldwide) can be politically feasible. At first, land redistribution raises the proportion of output used for subsistence, cutting transport and storage costs. Must this reduce the flow of staples to the towns? This need not be the case, and sometimes does not happen, because land redistribution normally also increases both output per hectare and the proportion of it comprising staples.

Help smallholders to exploit forward linkages to new(ish) routes to processing and marketing

Some claim that post-harvest advantages of large-scale agriculture – for processing, storage, containerization, meeting national or international "grades and standards," supermarket sales, and export horticulture – increasingly swamp the on-farm advantages of small/subsistence producers. This claim neglects history, theory, and contemporary reality.

Historically, it has long paid large growers to sell post-harvest services to small ones, from milk processing in India to tea-factory processing in Kenya. For centuries, Asian traders, large and small, have bought many million tons of staples every harvest, to resell them (often to the original growers) in the slack seasons.

Theoretically, where microsellers face lower unit *production or transaction* costs but higher unit *sales/processing* costs, even if neither buyers nor microsellers (even cooperatively) find the establishment of market links economically attractive, an intermediary will often find it profitable to provide processing, storage, or other links, as has almost always been the case for crops such as rubber and sugar; the same should apply to bulking up for supermarket transport.

In contemporary reality, there are many successes by microfarmers in selling crops (including staples) according to modern grades and standards, liaising with supermarkets, and exporting horticultural products (as discussed earlier; see Haggblade, Hazell, and Reardon [2007]; and Lipton [2009, 87–91]). There is huge variation among, and even within, countries (and crops) with respect to small/subsistence farmers' success in accessing modern market outlets. State action can help, but may not; for example, India's "regulated markets" have long eased the path of subsistence newcomers into fruit and vegetable marketing in Maharashtra, but not in Orissa. It is worth screening policies on transport, inspection, and regulation for their impact on this entry into the market by largely subsistence farmers.

Consider special policies for the marginal/subsistence/ small-deficit sector

In many respects, what is good for small farms is good for subsistence and deficit farms (e.g., it is larger farms that gain most if seed research seeks to maximize economic yield with no regard to risk). However, it should not be *assumed* that the same policy set benefits these five overlapping types of farming: small, family, subsistence, sub-subsistence, and deficit farmers. This caution applies especially to policies on credit and microfinance.

For several decades, Hans Binswanger's outstanding contributions have analyzed the behavior and impact of smallholder farmers, revealing their potential not only as users of land, water, and infrastructure and as sophisticated managers of risk, but also as contributors to growing agricultural output and national development. Much of his work also illuminates the developmental role of subsistence farming, especially of staples, which is still important in Africa and much of Asia. The older, pathbreaking contributions in comparative statics of Chayanov and Nakajima (Chayanov 1986 [1924]; Nakajima 1969; Nakajima 1986) should be integrated with modern empirical and theoretical advances, many based on Hans's outstanding work. In large part, thanks to Hans's work, it has become a sign of ignorance to dismiss smallholders as comprising a residual, backward, or inefficient sector; rather, they are seen as potential initiators of efficient, equitable, and employment-intensive development. It is time for our approach towards subsistence farmers to follow this path.

Notes

* This is much revised from a version presented orally at United Nations Conference on Trade and Development's (UNCTAD) Global Commodities Forum, Geneva, March 18–19, 2013.
1 In 2008, some 1.5 billion adults were overweight (BMI ≥25 kg/m^2), including 500 million who were obese (BMI ≥30 kg/m^2) (Finucane et al. 2011). In 2011, about 310 million children under 5 were mildly, moderately, or severely stunted, and about 260 million,

plus hundreds of millions over 5, were underweight (Stevens et al. 2012). In 2008–2014, numbers of obese adults rose from 500 million to 640 million (NCD-RisC 2016).

2 Due to relative changes in US and developing world prices, the 2005 $1.25 PPP poverty line is equivalent to $1.90PPP2015. See also http://www.indexmundi.com/facts/india/poverty-gap; http://www.indexmundi.com/facts/india/poverty-headcount-ratio.

3 Other indicators show similar trends.

4 In China, underweight for children aged 0–3 fell from 19 percent to 7 percent in 1987–2002; in India, for children aged 0–5, from only from 44 percent to 42 percent in 1998/99 to 37 percent in 2005. In SSA, falls were negligible: of 42 countries with a post-2000 and an earlier survey of proportion of children underweight, 18 countries show at least a 2 percent fall, 14 at least a 2 percent *rise*, and 10 no change (in Asia, with 25 national repeat surveys, comparable numbers are 14, 1, and 10). Of the 29 African repeat national surveys of child stunting, 12 show improvement, 11 deterioration, and 6 no change (Asia 20 surveys: 13, 1, 6) (UN SCN 2010, 8–9, Tables 21–23, 45, 47–48]). I am grateful to Steve Wiggins for pointing out that more recent surveys (2010–15, not yet collated by UN SCN) show a modest balance of net improvement in Africa.

5 "GDP growth originating in agriculture induces income growth among the 40 percent poorest, . . . [about] three times larger than growth originating . . . [elsewhere]" (de Janvry and Sadoulet 2010, 1).

6 I thank Elaine Liu and Steve Wiggins for this reference.

7 It is less clear that governments should *subsidize* trade – for example, through free roads – in countries with almost no irrigation, or farm capital or research.

8 R. Boxall (2001, 141), in treating all sources of loss, cites nine careful farm studies showing "losses . . . contained at about or below the 5 percent level over the storage season" and explains the huge prevalent overestimates. For confirmation, see Greeley (1978); Boxall, Greeley, and Tyagi (1979).

9 In Lesotho, there was "significant association between the presence of home gardens and lower incidences of wasting and underweight, [but] the nutritional status of children in households with or without home gardens in sampled areas is poor" (Makhotla and Hendriks 2004, 1).

10 In five African countries, they got at least as close to whole-field harvests as did crop-cut samples with similar outlay (Verma, Marchant, and Scott 1988).

11 I am grateful to Gershon Feder for suggesting an accurate formulation of this point.

12 In 2007, 10kg/ha of NPK, below 5 percent of South, Southeast, and East Asia. See http://faostat3.fao.org/download/R/RF/E.

References

Barrett, C. B. 1996. "On Price Risk and the Inverse Size-Productivity Relationship." *Journal of Development Economics* 51 (2): 193–215.

Boxall, R. A. 2001. "Post-harvest Losses to Insects: A World Overview." *International Biodeterioration & Biodegradation* 48 (1–4): 137–52.

Boxall, R. A., M. Greeley, and D. S. Tyagi. 1979. "The Prevention of Farm Level Food Grain Storage Losses in India: A Social Cost Benefit Analysis." *Tropical Stored Products Centre Information* 37: 11–17. ISSN 0564-3325.

Chayanov, A. 1986 [1924]. *Theory of Peasant Economy*. Madison: University of Wisconsin Press.

Chen, S., and M. Ravallion. 2012a. "More Relatively-Poor People in a Less Absolutely-Poor World." Policy Research Working Paper #6114, Development Research Group, World Bank, Washington, DC.

Chen, S., and M. Ravallion. 2012b. "An Update to the World Bank's Estimates of Consumption Poverty in the Developing World." Briefing Note, Development Research Group,

World Bank, Washington, DC. http://siteresources.worldbank.org/INTPOVCALNET/Resources/Global_Poverty_Update_2012_02-29-12.pdf

de Janvry, A., and E. Sadoulet. 2010. "Agricultural Growth and Poverty Reduction: Additional Evidence." *World Bank Research Observer* 25 (1): 1–20.

Dong, X., H. Wang, S. Rozelle, J. Huang, and T. Reardon. 2006. "Small Traders and Small Farmers: The Small Engines Driving China's Giant Boom in Horticulture." Working Paper, Shorenstein Asia-Pacific Research Center (APARC), Stanford University. http://aparc.fsi.stanford.edu/sites/default/files/china_horticulture_working_paper_joswinnen_book_2006.pdf

Dorward, A., and E. Chirwa. 2011. "The Malawi Agricultural Input Subsidy Programme: 2005–6 to 2008–9." *International Journal of Agricultural Sustainability* 9 (1): 232–47.

Dorward, A., and E. Chirwa. 2014. "The Rehabilitation of Agricultural Subsidies?" Working Paper (September), Natural Resources Group, International Institute for Environment and Development (IIED), London. http://pubs.iied.org/pdfs/14633IIED.pdf

Eastwood, R., M. Lipton, and A. Newell. 2010. "Farm Size." In *Handbook of Agricultural Economics*, Vol. 4, edited by P. Pingali and R. Evenson, 3323–94. Amsterdam: North Holland.

Finucane, M. M., G. A. Stevens, M. J. Cowan, G. Danaei, J. K. Lin, C. J. Paciorek, G. M. Singh, H. R. Gutierrez, Y. Lu, A. N. Bahalim, F. Farzadfar, L. M. Riley, and M. Ezzati; Global Burden of Metabolic Risk Factors of Chronic Diseases Collaborating Group (Body Mass Index). 2011. "National, Regional, and Global Trends in Body-mass Index since 1980: Systematic Analysis of Health Examination Surveys and Epidemiological Studies with 960 Country-years and 9.1 Million Participants." *Lancet* 377 (9765): 557–67.

Gale, F., P. Tang, X. Bai, and H. Xu. 2005. "Commercialization of Food Consumption in Rural China." Economic Research Report Number 8, Economic Research Service, US Department of Agriculture, Washington, DC. http://ageconsearch.umn.edu/bitstream/7256/2/er050008.pdf

Gautam, R., B. R. Sthapit, and P. K. Shrestha, eds. 2006. *Home Gardens In Nepal.* In Proceedings of a workshop on "Enhancing the Contribution of Home Garden to On-Farm Management of Plant Genetic Resources and to Improve the Livelihoods of Nepalese Farmers: Lessons Learned and Policy Implications," Local Initiatives for Biodiversity, Research and Development (LI-BIRD), Bioversity International, and Swiss Agency for Development and Cooperation (SDC), Pokhara, Nepal, August 6–7, 2004.

Greeley, M. 1978. "Appropriate Rural Technology: Recent Indian Experience with Farm-level Food Grain Storage Research." *Food Policy* 3 (1): 39–49.

Haggblade, S., P. Hazell, and T. Reardon. 2007. *Transforming the Rural Nonfarm Economy: Opportunities and Threats in the Developing World.* Baltimore: Johns Hopkins University Press for the International Food Policy Research Institute (IFPRI).

Iannotti, L., K. Cunningham, and M. Ruel. 2009. "Improving Diet Quality and Micronutrient Nutrition: Homestead Food Production in Bangladesh." IFPRI Discussion Paper 00928, International Food Policy Research Institute (IFPRI), Washington, DC.

Ivanic, M., and W. Martin. 2011. "Short- and Long-Run Impacts of Food Price Changes on Poverty." Policy Research Working Paper No. WPS 7011, World Bank, Washington, DC.

Jayne, T. S., and S. Rashid. 2013. "Input Subsidies in SSA: A Review of Recent Evidence." *Agricultural Economics* 44 (6): 547–62.

Jerven, M. 2013. *Poor Numbers: How We Are Misled by African Development Statistics and What to Do about It.* Ithaca, NY: Cornell University Press.

Kraybill, D., B. Bashaasha, and M. Betz. 2012. "Production and Marketed Surplus of Crops in Uganda, 1999–2006." USSP Working Paper 08, Uganda Strategy Support Program (USSP), International Food Policy Research Institute (IFPRI), Kampala.

Lipton, M. 2009. *Land Reform in Developing Countries: Property Rights and Property Wrongs.* London: Routledge.

Lipton, M. 2012. "Learning from Others: Increasing Agricultural Productivity for Human Development in Sub-Saharan Africa." Working Paper 2012–007, UNDP Africa Policy Notes, United Nations Development Programme, Regional Bureau for Africa, New York.

Lipton, M. 2013. "Africa's National-accounts Mess." *Journal of Development Studies* 49 (12): 1765–71.

Makhotla, L., and S. Hendriks. 2004. "Do Home Gardens Improve the Nutrition of Rural Pre-schoolers in Lesotho?" *Development in Southern Africa* 21 (3): 575–81.

Mitchell, R. and T. Hanstad. 2004. "Small Home Garden Plots and Sustainable Livelihoods for the Poor." LSP Working Paper 11, Livelihood Support Program, Food and Agriculture Organization of the United Nations (FAO), Rome.

Monteiro, C., E. Moura, W. Conde, and B. Popkin. 2004. "Socioeconomic Status and Obesity in Adult Populations of Developing Countries: A Review." *Bulletin of the World Health Organization* 82 (12): 940–6.

Nakajima, C. 1969. "Subsistence and Commercial Family Farms: Some Theoretical Models of Subjective Equilibrium." In *Subsistence Agriculture & Economic Development*, edited by C. R. Wharton, Jr., 165–85. Chicago: Aldine.

Nakajima, C. 1986. *Subjective Equilibrium Theory of the Farm Household.* Amsterdam: Elsevier.

Narain, N. 1962. *Distribution of Marketed Surplus by Size-level of Holding in India, 1950–1.* Bombay: Asia Publishing House.

NCD-RisC (NCD Risk Factor Collaboration). 2016. "Trends in Adult Body-mass Index in 200 Countries from 1975 to 2014: A Pooled Analysis of 1698 Population-based Measurement Studies with 19.2 Million Participants." *Lancet* 387 (10026): 1377–96.

Quan, J. 2007. "A Future for Small-Scale Farming." Science Review SR25, Foresight Project on Global Food and Farming, Government Office for Science, London.

Reardon, T., J. Berdegue, L. Flores, F. Balsevich, and R. Hernández. 2006. "Supermarkets, Horticultural Supply Chains, and Small Farmers in Central America." Paper for Workshop on "Governance, Coordination, and Distribution along Commodity Value Chains." FAO Commodities and Trade Proceedings, Trade and Markets Division, Food and Agriculture Organization of the United Nations, Rome, April 4–5, 2006.

Reddy, A. A. 2009. "Research Report on Factor Productivity and Marketed Surplus of Major Crops in India: Analysis of Orissa State." Final Report submitted to Planning Commission, Government of India, Administrative Staff College, Bella Vista, Hyderabad, India.

Schofield, S. 1979. *Development and the Problems of Village Nutrition.* London: Croom Helm.

Sen, A. 1981. *Poverty and Famines: An Essay on Entitlement and Deprivation.* Oxford: Clarendon Press.

Sharashkin, L. 2008. "The Socioeconomic and Cultural Significance of Food Gardening in Vladimir Region of Russia." PhD Diss., University of Missouri, Columbia, MO.

Sharma, V., and H. Wardhan. 2015. "Assessment of Marketed and Marketable Surplus of Major Foodgrains in India." Final report, Centre for Management in Agriculture (CMA), Indian Institute of Management, Ahmedabad.

Smith, A. 1904 [1776]. *An Inquiry into the Nature and Causes of the Wealth of Nations.* Edited by E. Cannan. London: Methuen. Library of Economics and Liberty, http://www.econlib. org/library/Smith/smWN.html

Srinivasan, T. N. 1972. "Farm Size and Productivity: Implications of Choice under Uncertainty." *Sankhyā: The Indian Journal of Statistics* 34 (4): 409–20.

Stevens, G. A., M. M. Finucane, C. J. Paciorek, S. R. Flaxman, R. A. White, A. J. Donner, and M. Ezzati; Nutrition Impact Model Study Group (Child Growth). 2012. "Trends in

Mild, Moderate, and Severe Stunting and Underweight, and Progress towards MDG 1 in 141 Developing Countries: A Systematic Analysis of Population Representative Data." *Lancet* 380 (9844): 824–34.

Sumner, A. 2012. "Where Do the World's Poor Live? A New Update." Working Paper 393, Institute of Development Studies, Brighton.

UN SCN (United Nations System Standing Committee on Nutrition). 2010. "Progress in Nutrition." 6th Report on the World Nutrition Situation, UN SCN, Geneva.

Verma, V., T. Marchant, and C. Scott. 1988. "Evaluation of Crop-Cut Methods and Farmers Reports for Estimating Crop Production. Results of a Methodological Study in Five African Countries." Longacre Agricultural Development Centre, London.

Vorley, B. 2002. *Sustaining Agriculture: Policy, Governance, and the Future of Family-based Farming.* London: International Institute for Environment and Development.

World Bank. 1990. *World Development Report 1990: Poverty.* Oxford: Oxford University Press for World Bank.

World Bank. 2016. *Global Monitoring Report 2015/2016. Development Goals in an Era of Demographic Change.* A joint publication of the World Bank Group and the International Monetary Fund. Washington, DC: World Bank.

Zaman, H. 2011. "Estimating the Short-Run Poverty Impacts of the 2010–11 Surge in Food Prices." World Bank Policy Research Working Paper Series 5366.

Part 2

Political economy
of agricultural policies

6 Transforming African economies and the evolving structure of African agriculture

Johann Kirsten and Frikkie Liebenberg

Introduction

The standard view on economic development is that of a process of structural transformation, resulting in a declining share of agriculture in both GDP and the labor force, accompanied by a convergence of labor and total factor productivity toward those of other sectors in the economy. Agriculture's declining share in the GDP does not imply a drop in the absolute size of the sector, and general agricultural output continues to increase throughout the process in absolute terms. Initial studies on the patterns of economic growth and transformation, by Chenery (1960) and Kuznets (1966), have shown important regularities in the structural composition of economic activity. As agricultural economists, we have based our theory on these observed patterns of economic growth and development, as exemplified in the highly cited agricultural economics texts (Johnston and Mellor 1961; Johnston and Kilby 1975; Timmer 1988, 2009). The theory argued that prior to the process of agricultural transformation, agriculture accounts for the bulk of the economic output and employs the major share of the labor force. As industrial growth takes off, industry, and in particular manufacturing, increases its share in the economy and pulls labor out of agriculture more or less rapidly (depending on its particular labor intensity). The services sector eventually starts to increase its share in value-added and in the labor force. By moving workers from lower- to higher-productivity activities, the change in structure accelerates economic growth. During this transformation, productivity in agriculture slowly increases as labor leaves the sector, while food prices and agricultural profitability increase, stimulating technological change and investment. Structural transformation ends in an advanced, modernized, and diversified economy, where the shares of agriculture in output and employment will approximate each other, as will incomes across the sectors. Agriculture will have become just like any other sector of the economy.

Recently Rodrik (2013, 25) challenged some of these views by arguing that "Poor economies are not shrunk versions of rich economies; they are structurally different." He argued that developing countries are characterized by large structural gaps in productivity between traditional and new economic activities. Hence, the essence of development is structural change, which entails moving workers from traditional, low-productivity activities to modern, high-productivity activities that are quite different in terms of location, organization, and technological characteristics.

This paradigm is further supported by McMillan and Rodrik (2011), who argued that the countries that manage to move out of poverty are those that are able to diversify away from agriculture and other traditional products. The speed with which this structural transformation takes place differentiates successful countries from unsuccessful ones. It is often argued that the initial conditions for economic structural transformation today are different than what it was in the 1950s and 1960s, due mainly to globalization. The process of globalization has been largely instrumental in Asia in shaping the transformation process, but McMillan and Rodrik (2011) argued that in Latin America and sub-Saharan Africa, globalization appears to have not fostered the desired kind of structural change. Labor has moved in the wrong direction, from more productive to less productive activities, such as the informal sector.

Hans Binswanger's views about the economic structural transformation process in Africa

The academic debate, in which authors such as McMillan and Rodrik as well as Hans Binswanger have participated, hinges on whether the traditional development models that sought to explain the drivers and processes of structural transformation are still relevant for Africa. With the theoretical foundation and the academic debate on structural transformation in mind, we apply Binswanger's (and his co-authors') assessment of the process of structural transformation in African countries, as prepared for the International Fund for Agricultural Development (IFAD) in 2009, as the basis for this chapter. In the series of working papers, journal articles, and book chapters published in 2009 and 2010, Binswanger and colleagues dealt with various dimensions of economic structural transformation in Africa, following from their analysis of the changing context and prospects for African agriculture. They make a number of important conclusions and present a series of facts that we use to structure this chapter (Binswanger, McCalla, and Patel 2010):

- With both agriculture and the economy at large performing poorly, the classic pattern of economic structural transformation did not take place in Africa.
- The shares in value-added of industry, services, and manufacturing have changed very little: the share of agriculture has declined only from 21 percent to 17 percent, with the corresponding gain in the services sector, rather than in industry.
- The lack of structural transformation is also evident within the structure of agriculture itself: the value-added shares of crops and livestock have remained at around 77 percent and 23 percent, respectively.

- Since there has been little per capita income growth, there has been no increase in consumption of higher-value livestock products, and thus, no increase in the demand for livestock products to drive an increase in the share of livestock in agriculture.
- The growth of agricultural output has not been spurred by technological change and a more intensive use of land and labor; growth was primarily achieved by area expansion and increased labor supply.
- Slow land and labor productivity growth is also explained by the fact that the share of irrigated harvested areas has stagnated for nearly 50 years, at little over 3 percent. In addition, the level of fertilizer use today is still at about the level of 7 kg per ha (the same level as in the 1970s).
- The capital intensity of agriculture in terms of fixed and working capital has not increased. African agriculture remains extremely decapitalized.
- Compared to other regions, total factor productivity growth (a proxy for technological change) in Africa is low.

As a consequence of the failure of agriculture and of structural transformation, poverty and hunger have deepened. This raises two key questions (Binswanger, McCalla, and Patel 2010):

1 Is there any reason to believe that a structural transformation can be revived?
2 If so, what policies would help?

With more detailed studies on African agriculture and more disaggregated statistics available, it will be useful to debate these main points and analyze the structural transformation of African economies to assess whether the points that Hans Binswanger and his colleagues raised still hold.

Acknowledging that Africa is a continent of many different countries with considerable heterogeneity across countries, it would be interesting to see whether a different picture is emerging when using more disaggregated data from Africa. Are the reports and studies showing a rapid demographic transition – higher per capita incomes, increased urbanization, and rapid change in basic diets – describing a universal pattern across the continent, and is this transition really signaling a new impetus for structural transformation? African agriculture is also changing as domestic and foreign investment in agricultural land brings about area expansion, as well as a greater reliance on modern technology (machines, seeds, and fertilizer) to increase agricultural output. At the same time there is "believed" to be evidence of increasing size in land holdings and the emergence of a new class of medium-scale farms (see, e.g., Anseeuw et al. [2016]), with a stronger commercial focus given the access to off-farm capital. There is also evidence of substantial agricultural productivity growth in certain countries, albeit from a low base.

Data from a variety of sources are used to provide a comprehensive picture of economic and agricultural transformation in Africa and to put the stylized facts or myths of transformation in African agriculture in perspective.

Evidence on the patterns of structural transformation in African economies

Recent papers by McMillan and Rodrik (2011), Rodrik (2013), and McMillan and Headey (2014) provide considerable empirical evidence to contextualize this statement: *the classic pattern of structural transformation did not take place in Africa* (Binswanger, McCalla, and Patel 2010, 115).

McMillan and Headey (2014), who probably presented the most up-to-date perspective on the pattern of structural transformation in African countries, acknowledged that prior analyses of structural transformation in developing countries have not substantively dealt with the African question. For that reason, our understanding of the patterns of structural transformation on the African continent remains very sketchy. It is therefore advisable not to generalize the findings about structural transformation in Africa. The papers by Christiaensen and Todo (2014), de Brauw, Mueller, and Lee (2014), and McMillan, Rodrik, and Verduzco-Gallo (2014) go a long way to fill this void and help us understand the nature of structural transformation in Africa over the past few decades.

The papers all seem to confirm the notion that the classic pattern of structural transformation was not followed in Africa. McMillan and Headey (2014) also reminded us again of the finding by McMillan and Rodrik (2011) that in both Latin America and Africa, structural change has made a sizable *negative* contribution to overall growth, while Asia is the only region where the contribution of structural change is positive. They therefore refer to a "curious pattern of growth-reducing structural change" (McMillan and Headey 2014, 3) in African and Latin America. The normal expected flow of labor from traditional to modern parts of the economy as an important driver of growth also did not happen in Africa – despite all the reforms that all African countries have undergone since the late 1980s. The labor flow was on average mainly from high- to low-productivity activities.

McMillan and Headey (2014) further argued that African countries stand to benefit the most from structural transformation, since they are generally the least diversified (see ahead). There is potential for enormous economic gain in African countries from reallocating activity from low- to high-productivity sectors.

The limited analyses of the patterns of structural transformation in Africa warrant a more detailed consideration of the process of transformation, across different countries, that emphasizes the heterogeneity of African countries, as well as the differences in the nature and pace of the process of structural transformation. Unpacking country-level data highlights some commonalities, but also the differences.

The data[1] presented in Figure 6.1 show the relationship in the expected pattern of lower share of value-added in agriculture with higher levels of per capita income for countries in Africa.

The individual country and (within country) sector-specific data reveal interesting differences. Data used by Xinshen Diao[2] (from the Groningen Growth and Development Centre [GGDC] database, 2014 version) revealed a general

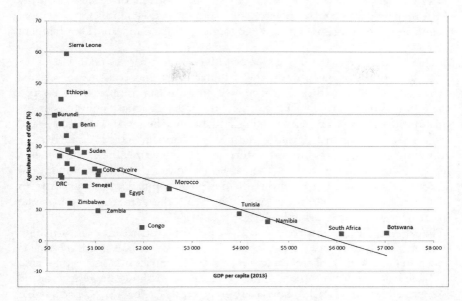

Figure 6.1 Agriculture share of GDP vs. GDP per capita for selected African countries (2013)

Source: Estimated by authors from World Bank development indicators, 2013. World Bank (2016).

view of structural transformation since 1960 for selected countries in Africa (Table A.6.1). Countries with a sharp decline in agriculture's share in GDP include Botswana, Ethiopia, Zambia, and to some extent Ghana and Kenya. Additional analyses, using the World Bank Development Indicator database (World Bank 2016), showed Uganda, Malawi, and Sudan dropping from a 50 percent share in 1960 to below 30 percent in 2010. For other countries, this metric has declined but only marginally and at a very low rate.

What is striking is that the structural decline of agriculture has not resulted from growth in mining (as one would expect in Botswana, Ghana, or South Africa) or manufacturing. If the standard view of structural transformation were true, then there would have been considerable urban industrial growth, with a much greater share in the GDP of the manufacturing sector. Instead, a rather consistently low GDP share of the manufacturing sector was observed, while there was a rapid and substantive increase in the share of the service sectors in GDP of most countries. The decline in the share of agriculture has therefore not been as a result of manufacturing sector growth, but largely as a result of services (trade services, government services, transport services, business services, personal services).

Timmer, de Vries, and de Vries (2014) documented the declining share of total employment in the manufacturing share in Africa since the mid-1970s, with production and employment increasingly originating in the service sector.

They confirm the rather high share of trade and distribution services in many African countries, similar to levels observed in the economies of member countries of the Organisation for Economic Co-operation and Development (OECD).

One would expect the service sector to increase its share of GDP only after, or at least simultaneously, when the manufacturing and construction sectors increased their share in the GDP. In essence, most African countries have skipped the very important structural phase of growth in the secondary industries (manufacturing and construction) by going straight into the services industry – and often only government, transport, and personal services. This is a much more consumption-based economic structure at a very low income level, which is not necessarily going to drive the much-needed growth in the urban industrial sector that can pull labor from the growing rural population in many African countries. It is therefore important to understand the disincentives for private investment in manufacturing in African countries.

Expanding this argument, we review the patterns of structural transformation in many of the larger countries in Asia. The data of sectorial shares of valued-added in GDP and GDP per capita for selected countries in Asia are presented in Table A.6.2 and shown here in Figure 6.2: Panel A shows the results for the Asian countries, and Panel B shows the results for African countries. The notable difference with the data of the African countries is the much larger share of total GDP of the manufacturing sector in Asia. The share of services (not shown here) in the GDP of these countries is also relatively large and similar to that of the African countries. Note the growth in manufacturing in Asia circa 1970 when the share of manufacturing in aggregate GDP started to decline in most African countries. The pattern observed in Asia shows that the share of manufacturing in value-added has remained at about 25 percent of GDP, although shares have also fallen back somewhat since the 1990s (Timmer, de Vries, and de Vries 2014). In contrast, most African countries have "de-industrialized" in terms of a falling share in GDP since the mid-1970s. The data in Tables A.6.1 and A.6.2 also show that for most African countries, the share of manufacturing in GDP and the labor force has never reached levels observed in Asia. Together, these trends suggest that deindustrialization in Africa set in at earlier development stages and without reaching any substantive share of the GDP.

Timmer, de Vries, and de Vries (2014) estimated that in 2010, only 7 percent of the total African workforce was employed in manufacturing, which compared to 15 percent in Asia and 12 percent in Latin America. Workers who moved out of agriculture were mainly absorbed into the (formal and informal) services sector, as mentioned earlier.

Alston and Pardey (2014) argued that, on aggregate, in sub-Saharan Africa, agriculture's share of GDP was much lower than in Asia in 1960. The data presented here suggest a more complex picture. Many of the countries presented here actually had more similar agricultural shares of GDP than in the major Asian countries. There is, however, a general consensus that the share of GDP for agriculture in most countries has fallen relatively slowly, with most countries in

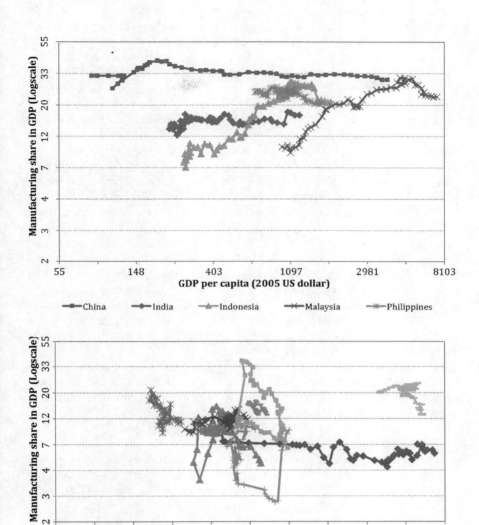

Figure 6.2 Sectorial shares of valued-added in GDP and GDP per capita

Panel A: Selected Asian countries;   Panel B: Selected African countries

Source: Calculated from World Bank (2016).

Africa currently exhibiting much larger shares than that of the major countries in Asia, and for that matter, also larger than in most other regions.

A more detailed analysis of country-level data suggests that – despite the fact that in some countries the classic pattern was followed – it remains true that for the majority of countries we have seen that agriculture's share of the GDP has fallen over the last 50 years, but at a much slower rate, remaining at higher levels than for many other countries. The limited growth in the share in GDP of manufacturing and the dominance of the services sector in most countries also suggest that the classic pattern of structural transformation has indeed not taken place in Africa. It remains an undisputed fact that the slow growth in the urban industrial complex in Africa – probably as a result of the small agricultural surplus and low labor productivity – is considered the main reason for the perceived lack of economic structural transformation in Africa.

Our high-level analysis of the individual country data confirms the drop in the share in value-added of agriculture in GDP, mainly as a result of increases in the share of the services sector. The industrial or manufacturing sector remains very small in most countries and has indeed changed very little, as is contrasted by the Asian experience. We could debate the absolute numbers on the share of value-added in agriculture, with the share declining much more in many countries than what was suggested by Binswanger. In many countries agriculture's share dropped from 50 percent to around 20 percent, but the aggregate picture for 55 African countries indicates a share of agriculture in the 1970s at around 40 percent, declining to 23 percent in 2013.

In essence, we agree with the summary of Anseeuw, Gabas, and Losch (2015) that the countries in Africa have structurally changed little since the 1960s and remain characterized by a heavy focus on its primary sector and the exploitation of its natural resources. As they conclude,

> Agriculture, mining, and the energy sector account for over 50% of GDP for 17 countries, between 40% and 50% for 9 countries and between 30% and 40% for 9 others. The manufacturing sector is extremely limited: only 18 countries have an industrial added value exceeding 10% of GDP and 7 countries reach the threshold of 15%.
>
> (2015, 6)

Most countries in Africa are therefore characterized as economies of urbanization without industrialization. Usually one expects that urbanization will drive industrialization, but the evidence in Africa shows that there has not been significant industrialization in SSA over the last 50 years.

There have been many efforts by African governments in the past to support industrialization. These include initiatives such as industrial free trade zones and certain concessions, but they have produced only mixed results and created few jobs – much less than was anticipated. Many studies reviewed the reasons for the poor industrialization in African economies. It largely boils down to the fact that the various programs and actions by governments failed to create any comparative advantage, resulting in limited investment. The only way this can be turned around is through aggressive investment in infrastructure, training, and various support programs for local industrialists. There is, however, a range of widely quoted additional reasons for the small contribution of manufacturing, which mainly deters investment in manufacturing enterprises. These include the following:

- High levels of corruption
- Red tape and high costs of doing business
- Irregular and unreliable electricity supply
- Poor training of workers and comparatively higher costs of labor
- Incoherent and uncoordinated policies
- Tax regimes that do not favor investment

This is clearly a concern to many countries in Africa and is well articulated in the *2016 Economic Report on Africa*:

> The big opportunity for Africa in 2016, as a latecomer to industrialization, is in adopting alternative economic pathways to industrialization. This requires governments to take on-board the drivers, challenges, and trade-offs in pushing for a greening of industrialization – and to build them into the vision and route-map for action.
>
> (ECA 2016, xx)

There is a lack of structural transformation within the structure of African agriculture itself

To confirm or challenge this statement by Binswanger and colleagues, we need to address a number of points. First, the increased acquisition of agricultural land by large-scale investors across Africa is an important factor that will certainly change the structural dimensions of African agriculture. The size and dimensions of this phenomenon are evident from the statistics of the Land Matrix (2016).

Table 6.1 presents the summary of all land deals in Africa recorded up to June 30, 2015. The global total of 1,042 land deals encompasses over 61.7 million hectares, with 29 million ha (or roughly 50 percent) earmarked for agricultural use. The land investments in Africa include 16 million hectares earmarked for agricultural investments and represent 55 percent of the total global area of agricultural investment deals. The top 10 countries of origin for the investment deals are the United States, Malaysia, Singapore, Arab Emirates, the United Kingdom, Canada, India, Russian Federation, Saudi Arabia, and China (Land Matrix 2016).

Some of the investments in African countries have been implemented by governments and multinational firms, but mainly have been by large investment companies and some large agri-food businesses. Among the latter, South African firms have dominated, participating in 29 of the deals outside South Africa, while

Table 6.1 Number of land investment deals in Africa as of June 30, 2015

Region	Intention	Deal count	Share of global deals (%)
Central Africa	Agri-unspecified, biofuels, food crops, for carbon sequestration/REDD, for wood and fiber, livestock, non-food agricultural commodities, renewable energy, tourism	37	3.55
Eastern Africa	Agri-unspecified, biofuels, conservation, food crops, for carbon sequestration/REDD, for wood and fiber, forest unspecified, industry, livestock, non-food agricultural commodities, renewable energy, tourism	216	20.73
Northern Africa	Biofuels, conservation, food crops, for carbon sequestration/REDD, for wood and fiber, livestock, non-food agricultural commodities, renewable energy, tourism	41	3.93
Southern Africa	Food crops, for wood and fiber	7	0.67
Western Africa	Agri-unspecified, biofuels, food crops, for carbon sequestration/REDD, for wood and fiber, industry, livestock, non-food agricultural commodities, renewable energy	128	12.28
Total number of deals in Africa		429	41.17
Total number of global deals		1042	100

Source: Land Matrix (2016). Accessed July 10, 2015.

in many other countries, such as Tanzania and Zambia, local agribusiness firms are the predominant investors. Clearly, we now have a new set of role players that could rapidly change the structure and composition of African agriculture.

Second, large agribusiness firms are increasingly playing important roles through various initiatives, joint ventures, and investments in processing capacity and controls over the whole value chain. Studies such as those by Kapuya et al. (2015) clearly demonstrate a large structural change in the agricultural and food sector in Africa.

The third dimension of structural change within the agricultural sector relates to the new group of domestic farmers and landowners, the so-called medium-scale farmers. Considered to be an important piece of evidence reflecting structural change in African agriculture – as reported in the study by Jayne et al. (2014b) in Ghana, Kenya, and Zambia, as well as in Malawi (Anseeuw et al. 2016) – is the fact that the land controlled by medium-scale farmers exceeds that of foreign and domestic large-scale holdings. They have also established that holdings between 5 and 100 ha now represent more land in total than land owned by smallholders (0–5 ha). This is an interesting and important change in farm structure in countries in Africa that cannot be ignored. However, the extent of this across all countries on the continent needs to be assessed more comprehensively. Jayne et al. (2014b) presented some disturbing facts that go with this structural change. The structural change has led to a concentration in land holdings, in addition to the fact that 90 percent of the land owned in this 20–100 ha category remains uncultivated.

Despite these three main new trends in the agricultural sector in African countries, the results emanating from the World Bank "Ruralstruc" project (Losch, Fréguin-Gresh, and White 2013) confirm that most regions in Africa continue to lag in their progression to diversify rural areas and to provide decent nonfarm jobs. As a result, most people in rural areas are trapped in structural poverty, which demonstrates the difficulty of rural transformation. Losch, Fréguin-Gresh, and White (2013) established that non-agricultural wage labor is very limited in these areas, with only 15 percent of households participating, mainly in services and informal and poorly paid jobs. This again stresses the importance of household and regional diversification, without which the rural areas in Africa remain untransformed and agriculturally based. This seems to be the prevalent picture, despite the other structural changes reported earlier.

The growth of agricultural output has not been spurred by technological change, but primarily achieved by area expansion and increased labor supply

This argument by Binswanger is also supported by the analysis of Alston and Pardey (2014) and Jayne, Chamberlin, and Headey (2014a) that suggested that most growth in agricultural output in sub-Saharan Africa happened as a result of area expansion – despite many countries investing in fertilizer and other input subsidy programs. Our own analysis (in Figure 6.3) of maize production yields and area expansion in the major regions of the world confirms this assertion. Taking five-year averages of the area harvested, indexed against the average of 1961–1965, and plotting this against the same index for yield per hectare reveals the extent to which the growth in production came about as a result of increases in yield (taken as indicative of technological change) and/or increases in area harvested.

Figure 6.3 shows the performance on this metric for sub-Saharan Africa relative to other continents. The European Union countries, in aggregate, experienced agricultural growth primarily as a result of advances in technology, showing increases in yield per hectare of 2.26 percent per year and an annual increase in area planted in maize of only 0.20 percent per annum. For the Americas, increases in production came as a result of an increase both in area harvested (0.87 percent and 1.36 percent per annum for North and South America, respectively) and in technological improvements (with 1.79 and 2.59 percent increase in yield per annum for North and South America, respectively).

In sub-Saharan Africa, the increased production came predominantly as a result of an expansion in the area harvested, with an annual growth in area of 1.66 percent as opposed to 1.25 percent increase in yield – well below the global average of 2 percent per year. Only five countries in sub-Saharan Africa have shown a decrease in area planted since 1961 – namely, Lesotho, Mauritius,

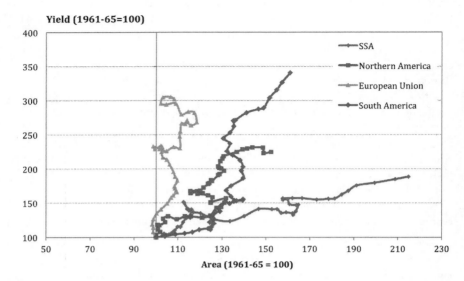

Figure 6.3 Trends in maize yield and area harvested in the major world regions: 1961–2013
Source: Composed by authors using FAOSTAT (2015).

Somalia, South Africa, and Swaziland. Thirty-seven countries in Africa showed an increase in area planted in maize, of which 15 have experienced annual growth rates in the area harvested in excess of 2 percent per year. Six countries have even experienced a decrease in yield per hectare, with another 15 experiencing growth rates less than 1 percent per annum since 1961. These statistics clearly show that most African countries have yet to benefit from the technological advances available.

Is this aggregate pattern identified for sub-Saharan African countries universal for all countries on the African continent? This is discussed next based on an analysis of data of 55 countries in Africa, organized according to the five main regions and considering South Africa and Nigeria (the two largest economies) separately.

Land and labor productivity growth is slow

Figure 6.4 and Table A.6.3 draw on data from the Food and Agriculture Organization of the United Nations (FAO) to place land and labor productivity measures for South Africa and Nigeria separately from the main regions in Africa in context. Here the total land area in agriculture, the economically active population in agriculture (as a proxy for employment in agriculture), and the gross value of agricultural output – valued at 2004–2006 constant international dollars – are used to measure the trends in the partial productivity measures of land and labor used in agriculture.

Figure 6.4 shows the partial productivity metrics of land and labor, using the graphic technique developed by Hayami and Ruttan (1985 [1971]). The South African and Nigerian productivity loci follow paths that are distinctly different from the other regions of sub-Saharan Africa. Both countries had increases in land and, especially, labor productivity at considerably higher rates than the rest of Africa. Moreover, the value of output per unit of labor in 2012 for both countries was also considerably higher than the rest of Africa: $12,289 per worker in the case of South Africa and $3,076 per worker for Nigeria, compared with an average of $943 per worker for Africa. South Africa is the only entry in Figure 6.4 for which the land–labor ratio increased substantially over time (implying more pronounced growth in labor than in land productivity): from 47.89 hectares per worker in 1961 to 83.99 hectares per worker in 2012. In Nigeria, the land–labor ratio (starting from a much smaller

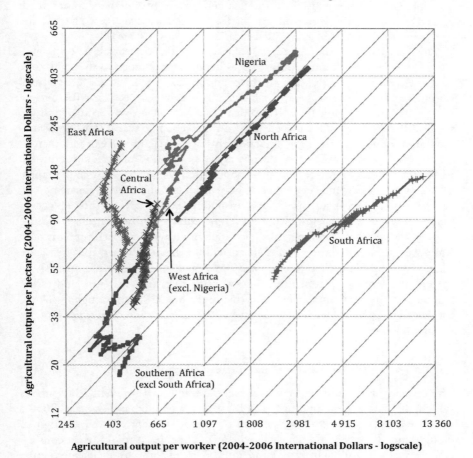

Figure 6.4 Ruttanogram for African regions and South Africa and Nigeria

Source: Calculated by authors using FAOSTAT (2015).

initial value) increased a little: from 4.84 to 5.78 hectares per worker over the comparable period. In almost all the other regions depicted (except northern Africa), real output per worker was low or (in the case of eastern and southern Africa excluding South Africa, actually stagnated), although land productivity in all regions improved over time. Thus the horizontal spans of the productivity loci are smaller than their vertical spans, indicating that land–labor ratios were smaller on average in 2012 than they were half a century earlier.

Northern Africa is an exception to the productivity pattern of the rest of Africa (sub-Saharan Africa, excluding South Africa and Nigeria) in general. This region saw labor productivity grow by 2.78 percent per year from 1961 to 2012 (compared with 2.07 percent per year for South Africa and 2.82 per year for Nigeria). Labor productivity in Eastern Africa barely changed, and in central and southern Africa (excluding South Africa) it increased only marginally. As Liebenberg and Pardey (2012, 29) concluded, "these productivity trends are a dismal record of the poverty and chronic food insecurity that afflict a large share of the population in these parts of Africa."

The performance in labor productivity growth in central, eastern, and southern Africa (excluding South Africa) belies their comparatively rapid rates of growth in total output. These three regions experienced real agricultural output growth in the range of 2.41 to 2.68 percent per year over the period 1961–2012, much faster than the comparative rates of growth in total output for South Africa, which averaged just 1.97 percent per year. However, South African agriculture ended the period with fewer agricultural workers than it had in 1961, whereas the economically active population in agriculture in the rest of the regions of Africa (like their populations, generally) grew in the range of 0.25 to 2.64 percent per year. The poor labor productivity performance of central, eastern, and southern Africa (excluding South Africa) thus reflects a failure of labor to leave agriculture for employment elsewhere in these economies rather than face a comparatively low rate of growth in agricultural output. Moreover, although the land area in agriculture has continued to expand in these parts of Africa, it has done so at a slower pace than the rate of growth in agricultural workers. Given the generally poor rural infrastructure and other market and environmental constraints that limit the transition to higher-valued forms of agricultural output, it is difficult to envisage raising output per worker to substantial levels.

African agriculture remains extremely decapitalized

The decapitalized status of African agriculture, as noted by Hans Binswanger, was corroborated by the findings from Binswanger-Mkhize and Gautam (2010), which showed that in 2007, 89 percent of farmers in Tanzania did not own a plough, and 10 percent did not even own a hand hoe. In contrast, we see considerable increase in capital investment in South African agriculture (at the expense of wage labor), where the latest tractors and modern cropping and harvesting machinery, as well as large-scale livestock operations, have been observed.

We cannot reach, however, any firm conclusion to verify or reject this notion across all countries in the African continent just because the data is nonexistent and what is available is very unreliable. The FAO and many governments do not report any reliable numbers to establish a clear trend on capital investment in African agriculture.

Total factor productivity (TFP) in African agriculture is low

Low agricultural growth is not good for the process of structural transformation. Growth in total factor productivity is an important factor contributing to agricultural growth. We have already shown earlier that productivity growth in African agriculture – at least measured with partial productivity measures – is not impressive and rather low. The notion of "low total factor productivity growth in Africa" emerged from various TFP studies in Africa, nicely summarized by Pardey (2011), as well as the more recent work by Fuglie and Rada (2013). Both sources confirm that agricultural productivity in sub-Saharan Africa (SSA) remains low and is falling further behind other regions of the world. Although agricultural output growth in the region has accelerated since the 1990s, this has been primarily due to resource expansion rather than to higher productivity. Yet there is evidence that agricultural productivity growth has improved in some countries. Fuglie and Rada (2013) showed growth in gross output in the 1960s, stagnation in the 1970s, modest recovery in the 1980s and 1990s, and continued modest growth in the 2000s, the latter somewhat augmented (to 3.25 percent) when favorable price effects are added in. They also confirmed findings of others that growth has recently improved, but productivity growth is not sufficient to lead to a sustained improvement in rural incomes.

Although Pardey (2011) and Fuglie and Rada (2013) presented us with the overall picture of "low productivity growth" in Africa compared to other countries, we do want to caution against the use of these numbers and findings, since we have noted the poor results with multifactor productivity (MFP) or total factor productivity studies in many countries using aggregate data. That we do not have proper estimates on labor numbers, capital accounts, and the true value of production output is a major issue for presenting believable results on TFP/ MFP estimates for most countries in Africa. We, therefore, share Pardey's (2011) view that many of the TFP/MFP estimates are clouded by a fundamental lack of data required to construct meaningful MFP estimates, forcing analysts to rely on incomplete, inconsistent, or proxy measures (especially with respect to agricultural inputs), which have implications for the resulting TFP/MFP estimates that are difficult if not impossible to discern.

We should, therefore, not lend too much weight to these limited "stylized facts" about MFP growth in sub-Saharan Africa. There is a large variation in the reported longer-run average rates of MFP growth for the region, as shown by Pardey (2011), which points to the overall fragility of the estimates. African agriculture is also known for large fluctuations in output levels, as a result of climate, pests, and diseases, which could easily have a large influence on the (end-point) MFP values.

Can economic transformation in Africa be fast-tracked?

Binswanger and colleagues rightfully ask how this non-conventional process of structural transformation can be turned around and whether the pace and nature of structural transformation in Africa can be improved.

In their much-debated paper, Collier and Dercon (2014) showed that the historical experience of most rich economies and the recent experience of developing Asian economies suggest that there are five essential characteristics of successful economic growth and transformation: (1) a vast reduction in the number of people engaged in agriculture; (2) a massive increase in the urban and coastal populations; (3) a vast reduction of the size of the population living in areas relatively far away from urban areas or the coast (as incomes in agriculture can keep up with other incomes only where demand is located or where transport is cheap); (4) a considerable increase in labor productivity in agriculture (as otherwise poverty will have remained high); and (5) a considerable increase in overall agricultural production, especially in those countries and areas relatively inaccessible from coastal areas.

Urbanization and an increase in the African middle class

Although the importance of a massive increase in the urban population is well accepted, latest projections from World Urbanization Prospects (UN DESA 2014) suggest that the rural population in Africa will increase by another 400 million between 2010 and 2050. With the urban areas unlikely to absorb more people, this will further increase the pressure on land and contribute to low agricultural productivity. This is a major constraining factor for structural transformation and can be addressed only via rapid nonfarm employment growth and reduction of the labor intensity of agricultural production. Ideally, this nonfarm employment should happen via value-added processes in the industrial and manufacturing sectors. Although the empirical evidence of the role of nonfarm growth in driving this transformation process still eludes us (Alston and Pardey 2014), growth in the urban areas is an important driver of the structural transformation process and critical for the growth stimulus in agricultural production.

A number of recent studies have presented evidence on the rising middle class, increased urbanization, and dietary changes, as well as evidence of a demographic transition in African countries (see, e.g., Tschirley et al. [2013]; Hollinger and Staatz [2015]). These dimensions are often considered to be the impetus for the much-needed growth in urban demand and an important factor that could stimulate enhanced structural transformation. Although increasing urbanization in African countries is indeed taking place, it is the speed and nature of it that is more of a concern. Jayne, Chamberlin, and Headey (2014a) analyzed the nature of African urbanization and presented a number of facts that challenge the notion of African urbanization as the new growth force and the driver of structural transformation:

- The rising middle class is an important dimension, but all indicators are that it remains small, with 62 percent of the urban population in most African countries living in urban slums;
- Urbanization is more a result of push migration out of rural areas in the hope of finding an alternative livelihood;
- The urban economy consists basically of non-tradable services rather than manufacturing (confirmed in the discussion earlier);
- Africa is only beginning its demographic transition, and the major share of young people will live in rural areas. Currently, 63 percent of all rural people are below 25 years (see also the recent study by Subakanya [2016] in Zambia).

The work by Gollin, Jedwab, and Vollrath (2013) supported the foregoing statements and showed how in many African countries, urbanization has taken place in "consumption cities," where the mix of workers is heavily skewed toward non-tradable services. They presented a useful model to show how African countries in particular have experienced urbanization without structural transformation, thus confirming our evidence and numbers presented earlier. The nature of the urbanization process seems also to be critical, as shown by Christiaensen and Todo (2014). Their empirical findings suggested that migration out of agriculture into rural nonfarm activities and secondary towns was associated with a reduction of poverty, while no statistically significant effect on the rate of poverty reduction was found from agglomeration in megacities. They confirmed the finding of Gollin, Jedwab, and Vollrath (2013) that these megacities are in fact only consumption cities, where one does observe faster income growth, but also higher income inequality, which appears to offset its potential impact on overall poverty.

The elements of a counterargument was presented by Dorosh and Thurlow (2014) showing that urbanization and agglomeration economies are important sources of economic growth and could be drivers of long-term structural transformation in Africa, with the potential to reduce the rural–urban divide. Their simulation study applied data only from Uganda and Ethiopia, which limits the extrapolation to the rest of the continent. However, they did support the argument of Gollin, Jedwab, and Vollrath (2013) that there could easily be an "urbanization of poverty" without supporting investments in urban growth and job creation. Their findings suggest that at least, over the short term, investing in cities is unlikely to adequately address national poverty concerns.

How big is the current urbanization trend in African countries? Potts (2013, 172–3) used recent population census data from a number of countries to show that the rate of urbanization is much lower than the decade just after independence. At the same time, the data showed that the growth in the population in the major towns and capital cities is growing only a little faster than the national population, which supports projections that the majority of the population in Africa will remain rural at least until 2050. Obviously, her argument does not corroborate the majority of studies on African urbanization.

Even with many recent studies, such as Gollin, Jedwab, and Vollrath (2013) and Christiaensen and Todo (2014), trying to understand the role of urbanization on structural transformation, no clear causality can be established. This suggests that we need to more carefully consider the point that urbanization in Africa (especially given that urbanization trends are largely exaggerated)[3] is likely to be an important driver of structural transformation.

The growing middle class, together with rapid urban income growth, in many African countries is also viewed by many authors (Tschirley et al. 2013; AfDB 2011) as an additional factor driving potential structural transformation of African economies. Who is this middle class? Where are they employed? In most cases the middle class originates from the growing government bureaucracy and the growth in the various service industries. Processes of political and economic empowerment and usually large networks of political patronage also play an important part in growing the middle class. The AfDB (2011) study is often referenced to illustrate the growth in the middle class (saying one in three Africans are now middle class), but studies similar to Potts (2013) question these numbers. The issue mainly relates to the definition of the income classes with respect to the middle class, often defined in the $2–$4 per day income bracket. Their social status and living standards are not nearly what one would associate with the typical middle-class household. As a result, the middle class could be much smaller than what is generally assumed.

Alireza Saniei-Pour (2015) presented another interesting perspective on the middle class, which added further caution to the notions around the middle class:

> With wages rising for skilled workers, the stagnation of wages in real terms for unskilled workers acts as a barrier to the exponential growth of the middle class. This is especially true in South Africa, where unlike in OECD countries, income per capita remains low.

The point made by Binswanger that there has been little per capita income growth seems to be confirmed by these authors and their analysis of census data. The perceived urban income growth has changed the food demand structure only in a limited way, and we have not seen the increase in consumption of higher-value livestock products.

Land constraints, land markets, and soil health

Agricultural transformation in the more populous countries in Africa is limited by extreme land constraints and limited available arable land, while households engaged in agriculture have increased threefold (Jayne, Chamberlin, and Headey 2014a, 3). The majority of households in rural Africa cultivate the same small piece of land with limited opportunities for crop rotation and proper fertilization of the soil. As a result, the organic matter and productive potential of the soil in many regions of Africa are depleted. Together, these realities have a constraining effect on structural transformation in African countries.

We are of the opinion that changing land tenure systems and land institutions can play an important role to facilitate agricultural productivity growth. Authors such as Swinnen and Rozelle (2009), Badiane, Ulimwengu, and Badibanga (2012), and Deininger, Xia and Savastano (2015) have already illustrated the benefits of good land institutions and the emergence of land rental markets. As leasing does not require any change in land ownership, land owners will have access to regular income streams in the form of rents, which, if land is transferred to more productive producers and markets are competitive, will be higher than what owners could obtain from self-cultivation (Deininger 2003).

Changes in the land institutions and the tenure systems necessary to unlock the value of land, to enable diversification in the economy and efficiency-enhancing land transfers beyond immediate kin, and for periods longer than a single season assume considerable importance.

Conclusion

We have taken a tour through the literature on structural transformation and agricultural and rural structural change in African countries by using Hans Binswanger's views on these matters as our framework. Hans has made profound statements and usually he is able to do so with authority due to his years of experience and his amazing understanding of Africa and the developing world. It was hard to find fault with many of his arguments and views on structural transformation in Africa. We managed to provide evidence from recent papers and some of our own analysis to confirm his views, but also to highlight some important deviations, which escaped some of his earlier thinking on the structural change in African agriculture. We conclude that the literature is in agreement with his assertion that the classic pattern of structural transformation did not take place in Africa, but that there is considerable disagreement as to whether the growing middle class and increased urbanization are likely to bring about structural transformation. The low share of industry and manufacturing in the GDP value-added of most African countries is the major reason why urbanization is likely to have no real impact on structural transformation, as it only displaces poverty from rural Africa to urban areas. However, many of the views related to capital and productivity growth in agriculture need considerably more work before we will have the evidence that supports Hans's positions on these matters.

Country	Sector	Share of sector employment (%)					Share of sector value-added in GDP				
		1970	1980	1990	2000	2010	1970	1980	1990	2000	2010
Botswana	Agriculture	81.2	59.7	40.2	38.3	38.1	19.1	9.2	4.0	2.5	2.8
	Mining	1.8	4.0	3.3	2.4	2.0	19.4	32.8	40.6	33.2	18.6
	Manufacturing	1.5	1.5	5.8	6.4	6.5	3.6	6.5	6.9	7.4	8.0
	Utilities	0.3	0.8	1.2	0.7	0.6	0.8	1.2	1.3	1.7	1.3
	Construction	2.2	5.2	12.0	9.2	2.7	24.8	12.1	8.8	6.7	7.9
	Services	13.0	28.8	37.5	42.9	50.2	32.3	38.3	38.3	48.5	61.4
Ethiopia	Agriculture	92.5	89.3	89.4	84.9	75.1	73.9	69.3	63.3	49.0	42.4
	Mining	0.0	0.0	0.1	0.2	0.5	0.2	0.1	0.3	0.5	0.6
	Manufacturing	1.9	1.7	1.8	3.1	6.2	3.2	3.9	4.6	5.6	5.2
	Utilities	0.0	0.1	0.1	0.1	0.1	1.0	1.3	2.2	2.1	1.8
	Construction	0.3	0.2	0.3	0.5	2.0	4.4	4.2	3.8	4.1	5.7
	Services	5.3	8.7	8.3	11.1	16.0	17.3	21.2	25.8	38.7	44.4
Ghana	Agriculture	57.0	56.5	53.5	53.6	41.6	37.5	40.2	31.2	32.9	29.5
	Mining	1.0	0.6	0.9	1.8	1.1	5.4	2.7	3.0	2.8	2.9
	Manufacturing	12.1	14.4	12.9	10.6	10.8	18.9	15.0	12.8	11.1	8.8
	Utilities	0.4	0.4	0.4	0.3	0.4	0.7	1.4	2.0	1.8	1.9
	Construction	2.4	2.0	1.6	2.9	3.1	9.9	9.1	5.8	5.4	8.6
	Services	27.1	26.2	30.6	30.7	43.1	27.7	31.6	45.2	45.9	48.2
Kenya	Agriculture	81.0	78.0	71.2	56.1	48.3	38.1	31.8	30.0	28.1	23.8
	Mining	0.1	0.2	0.1	0.5	0.6	0.6	0.7	0.6	0.6	0.6
	Manufacturing	3.8	3.5	5.3	10.0	12.8	7.0	12.6	13.3	12.2	12.1
	Utilities	0.1	0.2	0.3	0.3	0.2	1.7	2.7	2.6	1.9	2.3
	Construction	0.8	1.0	1.4	2.3	2.8	8.7	5.9	5.3	4.7	5.3
	Services	14.1	17.2	21.6	30.8	35.3	43.8	46.2	48.2	52.6	55.9
Malawi	Agriculture	86.7	87.0	86.1	82.3	65.2	33.8	27.5	24.5	38.5	29.9
	Mining	0.2	0.1	0.2	0.0	0.1	1.2	0.8	0.9	0.8	3.1
	Manufacturing	3.1	3.4	3.0	2.7	4.4	11.1	10.4	11.9	9.6	10.4
	Utilities	0.2	0.2	0.2	0.2	0.3	0.9	1.1	1.3	1.7	1.9
	Construction	2.0	2.3	1.5	1.9	4.5	6.2	6.4	4.6	4.2	5.3
	Services	7.8	7.0	9.0	12.8	25.4	46.8	53.8	56.7	45.2	49.3
Mauritius	Agriculture	37.3	23.7	16.7	11.4	7.2	13.1	14.9	12.0	7.4	5.2
	Mining	0.1	0.1	0.2	0.3	0.2	3.0	2.7	2.2	1.7	0.4
	Manufacturing	10.6	21.3	32.2	28.8	19.1	17.5	18.5	25.4	23.7	18.8
	Utilities	1.6	1.9	0.9	0.8	1.0	1.7	1.4	1.5	2.0	1.9
	Construction	7.8	12.1	10.0	9.4	10.0	7.9	6.0	5.8	5.7	7.2
	Services	42.6	40.9	40.1	49.3	62.6	56.8	56.5	53.1	59.5	66.6

Country	Sector	Share of sector employment (%)					Share of sector value-added in GDP				
		1970	1980	1990	2000	2010	1970	1980	1990	2000	2010
Nigeria	Agriculture	64.8	48.3	50.0	63.7	60.7	35.8	18.0	23.2	27.9	37.7
	Mining	0.1	0.5	0.4	0.1	0.2	48.1	63.1	55.9	50.9	29.7
	Manufacturing	7.0	6.6	4.4	3.1	4.2	1.7	3.5	3.8	3.1	3.5
	Utilities	0.1	0.5	0.5	0.3	0.2	0.1	0.1	0.1	0.1	0.1
	Construction	1.0	2.5	1.1	0.7	1.6	1.8	2.8	1.4	1.8	2.2
	Services	26.9	41.6	43.6	32.2	33.1	12.5	12.5	15.6	16.2	26.7
Senegal	Agriculture	73.3	70.3	65.8	58.2	51.4	29.0	22.7	20.9	20.9	17.7
	Mining	0.2	0.1	0.1	0.1	0.2	1.6	1.6	1.5	1.4	1.3
	Manufacturing	5.6	5.4	5.8	8.0	9.9	14.6	15.1	16.6	16.5	14.6
	Utilities	0.3	0.5	0.7	0.2	0.0	2.0	2.1	2.1	2.3	2.7
	Construction	1.3	1.5	1.6	2.8	3.8	1.5	2.2	2.8	4.3	5.2
	Services	19.3	22.2	26.0	30.7	34.6	51.3	56.3	56.2	54.5	58.6
South Africa	Agriculture	34.7	26.0	21.5	18.7	15.0	3.5	3.7	3.7	3.3	2.7
	Mining	8.8	9.4	8.8	3.5	2.1	23.3	14.6	11.6	9.3	6.5
	Manufacturing	13.3	16.5	14.7	13.6	11.9	19.9	23.7	22.3	21.0	18.4
	Utilities	0.6	0.9	1.0	0.5	0.6	1.4	2.0	2.6	2.7	2.2
	Construction	5.8	5.2	5.7	5.0	7.3	4.7	4.4	3.3	2.5	3.8
	Services	36.7	42.0	48.4	58.7	63.1	47.2	51.6	56.5	61.2	66.4
Tanzania	Agriculture	91.4	87.4	86.1	83.5	71.7	36.0	31.3	36.4	38.4	29.9
	Mining	0.1	0.6	0.4	0.5	0.8	1.5	0.9	0.6	2.3	3.3
	Manufacturing	1.7	1.6	1.4	1.7	3.2	11.5	11.6	7.8	8.9	10.2
	Utilities	0.1	0.1	0.1	0.2	0.5	1.2	2.3	2.3	2.6	2.5
	Construction	0.6	0.7	0.8	0.8	1.4	9.9	8.2	11.0	7.6	10.4
	Services	6.1	9.6	11.3	13.3	22.5	39.9	45.7	41.9	40.2	43.7
Zambia	Agriculture	62.7	68.0	75.3	71.6	72.2	15.2	12.3	16.9	23.9	9.4
	Mining	3.9	3.8	2.6	1.3	2.4	28.3	22.7	14.0	4.6	13.5
	Manufacturing	3.1	3.7	4.0	2.8	3.3	12.2	11.8	15.3	11.4	8.7
	Utilities	0.6	0.5	0.4	0.4	0.3	1.1	5.0	3.7	3.3	1.8
	Construction	3.9	2.1	1.5	1.3	1.4	18.7	11.3	7.4	5.2	7.2
	Services	31.4	24.1	19.4	23.6	22.1	24.5	37.0	42.8	51.6	59.4

Source: Adapted from Xinshen Diao's calculation using Groningen Growth and Development Centre (GGDC) data, 2014 version (personal communication, Xinshen Diao; see Endnote #2).

Table A.6.2 Sector share of GDP (value-added at constant 2005 prices) in selected countries in Asia (in percentages)

Industry	Country	1960	1970	1980	1990	2000	2010
Agriculture	Indonesia	51.4	44.9	23.9	19.4	15.6	14.3
	China	23.3	35.2	29.8	26.7	14.7	9.6
	India	42.5	41.9	35.3	29.0	23.0	18.2
	Malaysia	34.3	29.4	22.6	15.2	8.5	10.3
	Philippines	26.9	29.5	25.1	21.9	13.9	12.3
Manufacturing	Indonesia	9	9	16	24	28	26
	China	8	14	21	21	35	37
	India	12	13	14	17	18	18
	Malaysia		11	16	22	29	26
	Philippines		31	30	28	26	23
Services	Indonesia	30	29	31	36	35	42
	China	32	23	26	36	36	40
	India	26	30	35	38	46	53
	Malaysia		24	31	35	40	50
	Philippines	39	39	36	44	48	53

Source: Estimated from GGDC database, 2014. Timmer, de Vries, and de Vries (2014).

Table A.6.3 Growth rates in land and labor productivity in the different African regions (1961–2012, in percentages)

Region	Growth rates (1961–2012)					
	# of Econ Active in Agriculture	Agricultural Land	Agricultural output	Agricultural output per worker	Agricultural output per ha	Agricultural land/worker (ha/worker)
Northern Africa	0.45	0.19	3.26	2.78	3.08	−0.30
Southern Africa (excluding SA)	2.04	0.14	2.41	0.23	2.12	−1.89
Western Africa (excluding Nigeria)	2.13	0.41	3.02	0.94	2.65	−1.71
Central Africa	1.89	0.34	2.49	0.52	2.08	−1.56
Eastern Africa	2.64	0.17	2.68	0.07	2.54	−2.47
Nigeria	0.25	0.59	3.08	2.83	2.48	0.35
South Africa	−1.26	−0.10	1.97	3.17	2.07	1.10

Source: Calculated by authors using FAOSTAT (2015).

Note: *Central Africa* includes Burundi, Cameroon, Central African Republic, Chad, Congo Dem R, Congo Rep, Equatorial Guinea, Rwanda, Sao Tome & Principe, Sudan. *Eastern Africa* includes Comoros, Djibouti, Eritrea, Ethiopia, Kenya, Madagascar, Malawi, Reunion, Seychelles, Somalia, Tanzania, and Uganda. *Western Africa* (excluding Nigeria) includes Benin, Burkina Faso, Cape Verde, Côte d'Ivoire, Gabon, Gambia, Ghana, Guinea, Guinea-Bissau, Liberia, Mali, Mauritania, Niger, Senegal, Sierra Leone, and Togo. *Southern Africa* (excluding South Africa) includes Angola, Botswana, Lesotho, Mauritius, Mozambique, Namibia, Swaziland, Zambia, and Zimbabwe. *Northern Africa* includes Algeria, Egypt, Libya, Morocco, Tunisia, and Western Sahara. Sub-Saharan Africa excludes Nigeria, Northern Africa, and South Africa. See text for data construction and plotting details. The land–labor ratios are constant along each gray diagonal line and values for these ratios are given at the terminus of the respective diagonal line on the top and right axes.

Notes

1 One needs to acknowledge that the problem with GDP estimates in most of these countries is due to the considerable undercount of the informal economy.
2 Personal communication with Xinshen Diao, deputy division director and senior research fellow in the Development and Governance Division of the International Food Policy Research Institute (IFPRI).
3 We remind readers that official data and commercial sources put urbanization in South Africa somewhere between 62 percent and 67 percent, which suggests that the statement cannot be generalized.

References

AfDB (African Development Bank). 2011. "The Middle of the Pyramid: Dynamics of the Middle Class in Africa." Market Brief (April 20), AfDB, Abidjan, Côte d'Ivoire. http://www.afdb.org/fileadmin/uploads/afdb/Documents/Publications/The%20Middle%20of%20the%20Pyramid_The%20Middle%20of%20the%20Pyramid.pdf

Alston, J., and P. Pardey. 2014. "Agriculture in the Global Economy." *Journal of Economic Perspectives* 28 (1): 121–46.

Anseeuw, W., J.-J. Gabas, and B. Losch. 2015. "Africa's Structural Transformation Challenge and the Role of Agriculture: Is China a Player? A Review of Chinese Initiatives in Rural Africa." *World Food Policy* 2 (1): 4–18.

Anseeuw, W., T. Jayne, R. Kachule, and J. Kotsopoulos. 2016. "The Quiet Rise of Medium-Scale Farms in Malawi." *Land* 5 (3): 19. doi:10.3390/land5030019.

Badiane, O., J. Ulimwengu, and T. Badibanga. 2012. "Structural Transformation among African Economies: Patterns and Performance." *Development* 55 (4): 463–76.

Binswanger-Mkhize, H., and M. Gautam. 2010. "Towards an Internationally Competitive Tanzanian Agriculture." A World Bank Draft Report. Paper presented at the 15th Annual Research Conference of the Network for Research for Poverty Alleviation (REPOA), Dar es Salaam, Tanzania, March 19–20, 2010.

Binswanger, H. P., A. F. McCalla, and P. Patel. 2010. "Structural Transformation and African Agriculture." *Global Journal of Emerging Market Economies* 2 (2): 113–52.

Chenery, H. B. 1960. "Patterns of Industrial Growth." *American Economic Review* 50 (4): 624–54.

Christiaensen, L., and Y. Todo. 2014. "Poverty Reduction During the Rural–Urban Transformation – The Role of the Missing Middle." *World Development* 63: 43–58.

Collier, P., and S. Dercon. 2014. "African Agriculture in 50 Years: Smallholders in a Rapidly Changing World?" *World Development* 63: 92–101.

de Brauw, A., V. Mueller, and H. Lee. 2014. "The Role of Rural–Urban Migration in the Structural Transformation of Sub-Saharan Africa." *World Development* 63: 33–42.

Deininger, K. 2003. *Land Policies for Growth and Poverty Reduction.* Washington, DC: World Bank and New York: Oxford University Press.

Deininger, K., F. Xia, and S. Savastano. 2015. "Smallholders' Land Ownership and Access in Sub-Saharan Africa: A New Landscape?" Policy Research Working Paper #7285, World Bank, Washington, DC.

Dorosh, P., and J. Thurlow. 2014. "Can Cities or Towns Drive African Development? Economywide Analysis for Ethiopia and Uganda." *World Development* 63: 113–23.

ECA (Economic Commission for Africa). 2016. *Greening Africa's Industrialization, Economic Report on Africa.* Addis Ababa, Ethiopia: United Nations Economic Commission for Africa (UNECA).

FAOSTAT. 2015. Food and Agriculture Organization of the United Nations. Statistics Division. http://faostat3.fao.org/home/E

Fuglie, K., and N. E. Rada. 2013. "Resources, Policies, and Agricultural Productivity in Sub-Saharan Africa." Economic Research Report ERR-145, Economic Research Service, United States Department of Agriculture (USDA), Washington, DC.

Gollin, D., R. Jedwab, and D. Vollrath. 2013. "Urbanization with and without Structural Transformation." Unpublished Working Paper, George Washington University, Washington, DC.

Hayami, Y., and V. W. Ruttan. 1985 [1971]. *Agricultural Development: An International Perspective*. Baltimore: Johns Hopkins University Press.

Hollinger, F., and J. M. Staatz, eds. 2015. *Agricultural Growth in West Africa: Market and Policy Drivers*. Rome: African Development Bank and the Food and Agriculture Organization of the United Nations.

Jayne, T. S., J. Chamberlin, and D. Headey. 2014a. "Land Pressures, the Evolution of Farming Systems and Development Strategies in Africa: A Synthesis." *Food Policy* 48: 1–17.

Jayne, T. S., A. Chapato, N. Sitko, C. Nkonde, M. Muyunga, and J. Chamberlin. 2014b. "Is the Scramble for Land in Africa Foreclosing a Smallholder Agricultural Expansion Strategy?" *Journal of International Affairs* 67 (2): 35–53.

Johnston, B. F., and P. Kilby. 1975. *Agriculture and Structural Transformation: Economic Strategies in Late Developing Countries*. New York: Oxford University Press.

Johnston, B. F., and J. W. Mellor. 1961. "The Role of Agriculture in Economic Development." *American Economic Review* 51 (4): 566–93.

Kapuya, T., J. F. Kirsten, W. Anseeuw, and F. H. Meyer. 2015. "Agribusiness Corporate Strategies and the Consolidation of the Agro-food System in Africa." Unpublished Working Paper, University of Pretoria.

Kuznets, S. 1966. *Modern Economic Growth*. New Haven, CT: Yale University Press.

Land Matrix. 2016. Online Public Database on Land Deals. http://www.landmatrix.org/en/

Liebenberg, F., and P. G. Pardey. October 2012. "A Long-run View of South African Agricultural Production and Productivity Developments." *African Journal of Agricultural and Resource Economics* 7 (1): 14–38.

Losch, B., S. Fréguin-Gresh, and E. White, eds. 2013. *Structural Transformation and Rural Change Revisited: Challenges for Late Developing Countries in a Globalizing World*. Washington, DC: World Bank and Agence Française de Développement.

McMillan, M. S., and D. Headey. 2014. "Introduction – Understanding Structural Transformation in Africa." *World Development* 63: 1–10.

McMillan, M. S., and D. Rodrik. 2011. "Globalization, Structural Change and Productivity Growth." NBER Working Paper No. 17143, National Bureau of Economic Research, Cambridge, MA. http://www.nber.org/papers/w17143

McMillan, M. S., D. Rodrik, and I. Verduzco-Gallo. 2014. "Globalization, Structural Change, and Productivity Growth, with an Update on Africa." *World Development* 63: 11–32.

Pardey, P. 2011. "African Agricultural Productivity Growth and R&D in a Global Setting." Paper presented at the Stanford Symposium Series on Global Food Policy and Food Security in the 21st Century. Center on Food Security and the Environment, Stanford, CA. October 6.

Potts, D. H. 2013. "Urban Economies, Urban Livelihoods and Natural Resource-based Economic Growth in Sub-Saharan Africa: The Constraints of a Liberalized World Economy." *Local Economy* 28 (2): 170–87.

Rodrik, D. 2013. "The Past, Present, and Future of Economic Growth." Working Paper 1, Global Citizen Foundation, London.

Saniei-Pour, A. 2015. "Inequality in South Africa: A Post-Apartheid Analysis." World Policy Blog, July 7, 2015. http://www.worldpolicy.org/blog/2015/07/07/inequality-south-africa-post-apartheid-analysis

Subakanya, M. 2016. "Changes in the Age and Gender Composition of Agricultural Partici-pation in Zambia: Implications for Economic Policy." Unpublished MSc thesis, University of Pretoria.

Swinnen, J.F.M., and S. Rozelle. 2009. "Governance Structures and Resource Policy Reform: Insights from Agricultural Transition." *Annual Review of Resource Economics* 1: 33–54.

Timmer, M. P., G. J. de Vries, and K. de Vries. 2014. "Patterns of Structural Change in Developing Countries." GGDC Research Memorandum 149, Groningen Growth and Development Centre, University of Groningen, The Netherlands.

Timmer, P. 1988. "The Agricultural Transformation." In *Handbook of Development Economics*, Vol. 1, edited by H. Chenery and T. N. Srinivasan, 275–331. Amsterdam: North Holland.

Timmer, P. 2009. *A World without Agriculture: The Structural Transformation Process in Historical Perspective.* Washington, DC: The American Enterprise Institute Press.

Tschirley, D., T. Reardon, S. Haggblade, and M. Dolislager. 2013. "Megatrend Two: Rapid Urbanization and Food System Transformation." Global Center for Food Systems Innova-tion (GCFSI), Michigan State University, East Lansing.

UN DESA (United Nations Department of Economic and Social Affairs). 2014. "2014 Revision of World Urbanization Prospects." United Nations Department of Economics and Social Affairs, Population Division. https://esa.un.org/unpd/wup/

World Bank. 2016. World DataBank. World Development Indicators. http://databank.worldbank.org/data/reports.aspx?source=world-development-indicators

7 Origins and some empirical tests of theories of agricultural evolution

John Murray McIntire

Introduction

This chapter places agricultural evolution theory in the context of the debate about how to promote agricultural growth. It first reviews the origins of the theory of agricultural evolution and describes its two chief threads, before discussing some of its predictions and studies of those predictions. The discussion evaluates some specific ideas – about technical change, the family farm, and adjustment to shocks – in light of differences in population density, agroclimate, initial physical and historical conditions, emigration from rural areas, and the potential for off-farm employment. The chapter highlights differences among African countries, some countries in Latin America, and others in Asia, in terms of their effects on the success or failure of the theory.

It was long argued that agricultural policy was constrained by the characteristics of peasant agriculture.[1] First was the opinion that peasants were not economically rational and did not respond to incentives. While this bias may have weakened with the demise of the colonial empires in the 1950s and 1960s, it retained currency among analysts and politicians, and hence, influenced development interventions until fairly recently. Second, inequalities of wealth, power, and market access in poor countries caused farmers to be excluded from new opportunities; therefore, it was believed that deep reforms affecting the distributions of assets and market access, especially in land and finance, were necessary for poor farmers to respond to new opportunities. Third, peasant farming was sometimes said to be a transitory phase of development, which would disappear as growth occurred in the urban sectors; and hence, policy attention to small farming was neither necessary nor productive except to provide relief. A fourth feature was that economies of scale in technology and in access to inputs and capital (fertilizer, finance, machinery) gave an innate cost advantage to large farms and would eventually make small farms disappear. A variant of this argument was that family farms were anachronistic, for reasons of scale and managerial quality, and would also disappear under competition from larger farms. A fifth characteristic of poor agriculture was the view that efforts to modernize faced an inherent conflict between productivity and employment; output could grow only through consolidation of large farms into small (the fourth view), with mechanization being a necessary feature of that consolidation, resulting in lower labor intensity, and hence, loss of employment among unskilled workers. The irrationality argument derived from the assumption that farmers strongly preferred leisure to labor; in the case of animal production, there was the related view that herders withheld supply as a form of insurance, or even from the utility of contemplating their wealth on the hoof. This irrationality argument came under attack from many sides:

- From analyses of the behavior of poor farmers, such as Schultz (1964);
- From the meta-analysis of Hayami and Ruttan (1971), showing how knowledge for farm technologies and the technologies themselves evolve from factor proportions;
- From studies of supply response (the dozens of estimates for crops made before 1970, as cited by Askari and Cummings [1976]; for livestock, Jarvis [1974]);
- From studies of agricultural policy bias, notably the landmark work of Michael Lipton (1977) and later, that of Krueger, Schiff, and Valdés (1991);
- From work on Asian rural factor markets, compiled by Binswanger and Rosenzweig (1981), showing the variation and complexity of land and labor contracts across East and South Asia, which demonstrated a strong response to incentives.

General support for the notion of the irrational peasant ultimately collapsed under the weight of such arguments, and it became evident that the Green Revolution could never have happened if the irrationality argument had held.[2]

Despite the theoretical and empirical counterattacks against the stereotype of the irrational peasant, and despite the increases in grain and, later, non-ruminant livestock production in much of the world that resulted from advances in plant breeding and animal health, rural poverty remained deep throughout the tropics – inequalities within rural areas were great, and inequalities between rural and urban areas were also high. Many policy efforts – credit, land reform, public mechanization schemes, public input distribution, resettlement from densely settled areas to virgin lands, large public irrigation projects, programs to improve soil quality, price, and other incentive policies – had failed in the specific sense that individual programs often produced negative returns, and in the general sense that rural incomes either did not grow as rapidly as urban ones, or that per capita agricultural output had grown slowly.

While the "irrational peasant" model was appropriately replaced by one of the rational smallholder, policy failures persisted in part because the rational smallholder model made unrealistic assumptions about factor market operation. Policy failures under different agent models – irrational peasant and rational smallholder – created two needs: (1) to understand how factor markets operated in tropical agriculture – such markets included sharecropping and other forms of tenancy – with market failures, especially in rural credit; the coexistence of a positive wage with high unemployment; and the effects of population growth; and (2) to identify the constraints on poor farmers that prevented them from using better technologies, from growing more rapidly and from defending their incomes and assets against losses to unavoidable external shocks. Among those constraints were: risk aversion; unequal land and labor relations; unfavorable technical conditions; absent markets (especially for financial services and information); and external shocks due to weather, animal disease, or price variability.

Against this mixed background of success and failure of agricultural policies in poor countries, a new theory of agricultural evolution evolved, as an effort to extend the rational smallholder model to better understand rural economies and to propose policies to raise rural living standards. What we are calling the theory of agricultural evolution has two long threads.

The first thread is the Boserup-Ruthenberg (Boserup 1965; Ruthenberg 1980; Boserup 1981) model of agricultural change in response to population growth and market access, which focused largely on tropical agriculture; a widening of that thread is the Hayami-Ruttan (1971) model, in which both technical change in farming and the generation of scientific knowledge are endogenous to factor relations. Much of the empirical focus of the latter model was on a comparison between the United States and Japan.

The second thread is what we refer to here as the production relations synthesis[3] (Binswanger and Rosenzweig 1986; Binswanger and McIntire 1987; Hoff and Stiglitz 1990; Bardhan 1991; Hoff, Braverman, and Stiglitz 1993) that sought to explain the "major features of production relations in rural areas" (Binswanger and Rosenzweig 1986, 505), by reference to a few assumptions about individual behavior and to some inherent characteristics of farming.

The chapter is organized as follows. First, we briefly summarize the two threads. Second, we discuss empirical work on their implications in three areas:

- The evolution of endogenous farm technology and its consequences;
- The persistence of the family farm; and
- Farmers' responses to external shocks.

A final section summarizes some of the achievements of this body of theory, including policy impacts.

Theories of agricultural evolution

The Boserup-Ruthenberg hypotheses

The core Boserup-Ruthenberg hypothesis is that population growth determines the carrying capacity of farmland.[4] Higher population and higher population growth in a given area create greater carrying capacity by stimulating farming practices that yield more output per unit of land and nearly always use more labor. Tests of the hypothesis were carried out by observing farming practices at different population densities and in different farming environments, both temperate and tropical. The set of practices, known collectively as agricultural intensification, include: (1) the evolution of types of hand tools and their eventual replacement by animal-powered or machine-powered implements; (2) the type, length, and location of fallow; (3) the frequency with which a plot of land is cultivated each year; (4) the progressive use of fallow substitutes, such as animal manures and leguminous crops, to maintain soil fertility, with a rise in cultivation frequency; (5) the type and intensity of grazing and their relation to animal mobility and to the use of animal manures as fallow substitutes; (6) the shift from rainfed to irrigated agriculture; (7) the intensity of farm labor, notably the numbers of hours worked and the types of occupations pursued between cropping seasons; and (8) the conversion of common properties (water, forests, grazing, collectible vegetation) into individual property.

The initial book of Boserup (1965) presented the evolutionary theory, while the many papers of Hans Ruthenberg (1968, 1980) confirmed its empirical character in the structure and conduct of farm management in Africa, Latin America, and Asia. These works, and the many others they inspired, identified three universal problems in the long process of agricultural intensification: (1) maintaining soil fertility, which gradually demands rising labor input for falling marginal returns; (2) managing water, which involves solving difficult problems of engineering and of collective action; and (3) controlling weeds, a cost that rises as fallows shorten.[5] The costs of soil fertility maintenance become progressively higher over time, as land becomes scarcer, and as fallow becomes shorter. Rising soil fertility costs create secondary problems of grazing management, of managing risks related to cash fertilizer inputs and their resulting yields, and eventually, of competition for land between crops and animals, which compromise the availability of manure for cropping.

The agricultural production relations synthesis

From the desire to better understand the economic features of agricultural evolution came *the general ambition* of production relations theory – to "analyze the material and behavioral factors which are important determinants of production relations" (Binswanger and Rosenzweig 1986, 503) in an integrated manner, without exogenous assumptions about extreme risk aversion, technologies, or absent markets. *Two specific purposes of the production relations synthesis* were to: (1) explain production relations in an internally consistent manner (Binswanger and Rosenzweig 1986, 503); and (2) "assist in predicting the impact of institutional and legal changes, state interventions and technological change on production relations, productivity and income distribution for any given and technological and institutional environment" (Binswanger and Rosenzweig 1986, 503). Similar purposes were expressed in Bardhan (1991) and in Hoff, Braverman, and Stiglitz (1993).

The *core hypothesis of the production relations synthesis* was that some rural markets were imperfect or absent because of some inherent features of agriculture: (1) asymmetric information, creating moral hazard and adverse selection;

(2) spatial dispersion, creating higher information and other transactions costs; and (3) the importance of high and covariant risks, even where average individual risk aversion is limited. A fourth feature – simple technology that does not require skilled labor or purchased inputs – is characteristic of some types of land-abundant agriculture (Binswanger and McIntire 1987).

The market failures were identified from some assumptions about the behavioral and material conditions of farming. Behavioral assumptions were as follows:

- Individuals are self-interested and derive utility from consumption;
- Individuals have some variable, personal preference for leisure over effort;
- The existence of risk;
- Moderate individual risk aversion and rare extreme risk aversion; and
- Information is costly to acquire and, therefore, valuable.

Added to these behavioral assumptions are the material conditions of agriculture. *Tropical farming is risky*, and many events (e.g., drought or animal disease) are highly *covariant* risks, with their covariance imposing diversification on farmers' activities. The *seasonality of farming* sets basic features of rural financial markets by imposing a lag between payment for inputs (e.g., hiring labor) and sale of products. Seasonality, therefore, determines the cash balances of borrowers and of lenders; seasonality, compounded by the covariance of events, thus makes rural financial markets riskier. The *spatial dispersion of agriculture* raises information costs about factor prices, commodity prices, and individual characteristics. Dispersion's effects on information costs, therefore, aggravate moral hazard in labor and credit markets and make supervision costs more important.

Another material condition is the *fixed costs* of some economic activities, which are higher when enforcement of property rights is weak. The additional fixed costs – of acquiring land or other fixed property, of making loans, of hiring labor, of migrating in search of work – related to weak property rights are, therefore, an impediment to some market transactions. The presence of such additional fixed costs often leads to the absence of markets, especially for credit and insurance, or to the use of linked transactions or intrafamilial transactions as substitutes for market relations.

Policy questions arising from these theories

These two threads of the theory of agricultural evolution have made major contributions to (at least) three areas[6] of rural development policies: (1) theoretical refinement and empirical testing of farm technology choice under population pressure and market access, in both land-scarce and land-abundant environments; (2) explanation of the persistence of family farming (Otsuka, Chuma, and Hayami 1992) in competition with enterprise farming;[7] and (3) the adjustments of rural people to income and asset shocks, and the relation of those adjustments to policy interventions.

How does endogenous farm technology evolve?

Boserup inverted the Malthusian view of technology generation, which began from exogenous technical change and continued to population growth, to one that began from population growth and continued to endogenous technical change. "Endogenous technical change" is henceforth defined as the pattern of shifts in farming practices and productivity as systems evolve under the pressure of population and market density. Boserup's arguments about the evolution of farming systems can be considered as tests of rationality hypotheses of farmers' decisions under the long-term influence of population and markets. Results of such tests, however, depend a great deal on the initial conditions of population density from which population grows and on what we call, broadly, "market access."

Tests of the Boserup-Ruthenberg model

Empirical tests of the Boserup-Ruthenberg model have been hampered by the scarcity of time-series data. Such data are the strongest test of the model because they allow study of temporal and locational effects. That is, analyzing the *evolution of farming practices* – fallowing, controlling weeds, maintaining soil fertility, changing the cropping pattern, managing livestock – *and farming structures* – the scale of owned and operated holdings, landlessness, tenancy, the penetration of formal land sale and rental markets – is best done by comparing evidence from paired sites over a long period.

A more common alternative to time-series work has been to use cross-section tests – for example, by comparing sites of differing population density and market access at roughly equal dates. There are several meta-analyses of the Boserup-Ruthenberg hypotheses beyond those of Boserup (1965); Grigg (1974); and Ruthenberg (1980). Examples are Pingali, Bigot, and Binswanger (1987); McIntire, Bourzat, and Pingali (1992); McCarthy et al. (1999); Wiggins (2000); Dixon, Gulliver, and Gibbon (2001); Baltenweck et al. (2003); and in summaries of many case studies.[8] These analyses cover the principal agricultural systems in the tropics and subtropics and typically allow tests of the main hypotheses *in a cross-section framework*. The focus of this work has been on sub-Saharan Africa (SSA), in response to its general failure of agricultural growth and to its specific failure to match the agricultural performance of South Asia.

A meta-analysis by Turner, Hanham, and Portararo (1977) found a strong positive association between population density and farming intensity, where the latter was measured by frequency of cultivation. Nearly 60 percent of the variation in farming intensity was explained by population density. The basic relation dominated other specifications where only small positive additions to the initial explanatory power were made by staple crop (cereals or roots), livestock production, annual rainfall, and soil type.[9]

A review (Dixon, Gulliver, and Gibbon 2001) covered 70 global farming systems, using data and expert consultations from the 1980s and 1990s. Low- and medium-intensity, food-oriented systems had a population of about 1.3 billion people and sustained about 1.80 persons per cultivated hectare; medium-intensity, market-oriented systems and high-intensity systems had a population of 1.24 billion and sustained about 4.5 persons per cultivated hectare (Dixon, Gulliver, and Gibbon 2001, 316).

A study of 70 mountain sites by Templeton and Scherr (1999, 913) concluded that "most empirical evidence is consistent with, but does not conclusively demonstrate" a U-shaped plot of land productivity as a function of relative land-labor costs. This paper has the virtue of presenting a large sample of regions, countries, agricultural environments, and data types (primary and secondary). Although care must be used in predicting out of sample, the Templeton and Scherr paper does support an important prediction of agricultural evolution theory in samples where the land constraint is imposed both by population and by geography.

An unusually broad paper (Baltenweck et al. 2003) studied intensification at 48 sites in 15 countries (6 in SSA; Thailand, Nepal, Bangladesh, Sri Lanka, and India; plus Bolivia, Colombia, Costa Rica, and Peru). The countries and sites provide enough variability in initial conditions – amount and variability of rainfall, altitude, irrigation, conditions of livestock production, use of animals for power and transport, population density, and market proximity – that they furnish adequate data for non-rigorous tests of the intensification hypotheses. Baltenweck et al. (2003, 1) found "consistent patterns of intensification and crop-livestock interaction, which are generally in line with the predictions of the household model."

Baltenweck et al.'s (2003, 22) specific findings (Table 9) were as follows:

- Two measures of intensification – use of mineral fertilizers and high-yielding crop varieties (HYVs) – were associated with urban proximity and population density.
- These two measures of intensification were positively associated with land rental rates, though not with wage rates. Though the causality problem is intractable with the data set, because of the absence of a time-series panel, the strong association with land rentals and the weak one with wages are consistent with production relations models and with the general finding that intensification does not necessarily induce higher wages, even if it induces more productive land use.
- A measure of extensive land use – fallow land – was significantly negatively associated with population density and with land rental rates, though not with distance to cities (Table 9, 22).
- A measure of intensive land use – joint applications of mineral fertilizers and of manure – was not statistically significant at the 10 percent level.[10]

A more recent paper (Allen 2001) compiled data from 274 agricultural systems in Papua New Guinea, whose agriculture differs considerably from those studied in other meta-analyses. Allen found a strongly positive relationship between population density and the intensity of land use (Allen 2001, Table 1, 241).

He further found a strong positive relationship between specific intensive techniques – short fallowing, fencing, mounding, tillage, and drainage – and the measure of land use intensity (Allen 2001, Table 2, 243).

One criticism of the evolutionary model is said to be its failure to account for initial conditions. Such conditions include: (1) the effects of rapid population growth in initial situations of high or low population density; (2) production environments – tropical or temperate, humid or arid, extent of foreign settlement, availability of introduced technology, the effects of mountains or alluvial soil; and (3) assumptions about the homogeneity of farming populations, especially the distributions of status, effort, risk aversion, and the respective roles of women and men.

Binswanger and McIntire (1987) explicitly accounted for some initial conditions by starting from a stylized farming system with low population density, high risks related to aridity and variable rainfall, and high covariance of production related to monomodal rainfall. Different consequences of initial conditions were then projected in three agricultural environments – the low rainfall semi-arid tropics (SAT), a higher rainfall SAT, and the humid tropics.

Cuffaro (1997) accepted that evolutionary theory has shown, under most conditions, that farming systems adapt to rising population density by shifting to more intensive techniques[11] and by allowing for stronger definitions of property rights. She contended, nonetheless, that the theory is weaker under initial conditions of higher population density and under a weaker "environmental resource base" (Cuffaro 1997, 1159). Though Boserup (1965) explicitly referred to densely populated areas with high rates of population growth as being at the boundaries of her model, there is empirical support for Cuffaro's critique. Mesfin Wolde Mariam (1986) argued that successive famines in Ethiopia were worst under initial conditions of high population density in marginal (short growing season, middle altitude, steep slope) growing areas. Josephson, Ricker-Gilbert, and Florax (2014, 151) studied a high population–density, rainfed farming area of Ethiopia and concluded that "high rural population density creates a situation where farmers are unable to sustainably intensify staple crop production" and that "higher rural population density is associated with a decline in farm income on a per hectare basis."

A compilation of papers on African agriculture (Jayne, Chamberlin, and Headey 2014) in the *Food Policy* edition on "Boserup and Beyond" showed the limits to the intensification of the Boserup-Ruthenberg model. Jayne et al. contended that there is a threshold,[12] beyond about 500 people per square kilometer, at which it is no longer possible to raise yields per unit of land by adding more labor or shortening fallows, since the latter no longer exist.

Muyanga and Jayne (2014) completed a rare analysis using mixed time-series and panel data that allow rigorous tests of the intensification hypotheses over time and across locations. They concluded that the first intensification hypothesis – that measures of intensification are associated with population density – is confirmed up to roughly 500 persons per square kilometer, but the hypothesis is rejected beyond that threshold, and that one even sees "an alarming decline of some intensification measures beyond this intensification threshold" (2014, 98). The unsustainability of intensification is related to the falling efficiency of mineral fertilizers, rising soil acidification, and declining levels of soil carbon, and in very densely cultivated areas, leads to falling crop yields and lower labor productivity.

In areas that have been very densely populated for generations, an "involution" hypothesis can be stated as the point at which intensification fails to maintain per capita productivity. In economic terms, it is the point at which the average productivity of labor approaches zero and even becomes negative. Evidence from South Asia and East Asia tends to confirm that hypothesis – that labor productivity becomes zero or even negative beyond a certain population density in the absence of major emigration or exogenous land-saving technologies. Evidence for involution was found by Geertz (1963) in Indonesia and by Robinson (1970) in Bangladesh (formerly East Pakistan, covering the period 1951–1961). Bilsborrow (1987, 198) noted that intensification responses, while productive, are in some instances "drastically constrained by existing concentration of landholdings." Perkins (2013), on Chinese agriculture over six centuries, found: (1) a positive relation between population growth and intensive production techniques; (2) a shift from lower-yielding dry crops, such as millet and sorghum, to irrigated rice; and (3) varying degrees of involution in the absence of migration, with low productivity and emigration strongest in marginal regions.

Binswanger-Mkhize and Savastano (2014, 17) found "inconsistencies" with the Boserup-Ruthenberg hypothesis, in terms of cropping practice and intensity as functions of population pressure in Malawi and other African countries. They concluded: "agroecological population pressure is so poorly related to population density that rural population density is a poor measure of population pressure on the natural resources." A potential finding in favor of a link from a resource-weighted population to intensification is in Turner, Hanham, and Portararo (1977, 394), who found a significant relation between the length of the dry season (indicating less productive potential) and the measure of farming intensity.

A broader form of the "initial conditions" critique states that farming practices depend on agricultural environments – the amount and timing of rainfall; the cost and form of irrigation; the seasonality of rainfall and its effects on labor demand; and the comparative advantage of cereals, tree crops, and livestock. Such environmental effects have been a major part of the empirical literature that extends Boserup's initial insights (notably, Grigg [1974]; Ruthenberg [1980]; Pingali, Bigot, and Binswanger [1987]; McIntire, Bourzat, and Pingali [1992]). Such work, by incorporating many of the initial physical conditions, tends to broaden the applicability of the core Boserup-Ruthenberg hypothesis.

Tests of the model outside sub-Saharan Africa

Tests[13] of the Boserup-Ruthenberg hypotheses differ by region and agroclimate because of differences in initial conditions and in the costs of irrigation, and, recently, because of changes in Asian urban economies. The endogenous technology model, for example, might be more applicable to SSA because of its physical and historical setting. That setting – with a generally lower population density and denser population in higher, cooler agroclimates; lower production potential; less irrigation; weaker formal land rights; and an implicitly closed economy because of high transport costs – allows empirical tests of a theory that posits technical change in response to shifts from low to high population density, from weak to strong market access, and according to the interactions of climate with population density and market access. Conditions in SSA might be said to be "young," in the sense that they are at the beginning of the transition from extensive to intensive systems, while other continents are "mature" in that the transition is more or less complete, and hence, offer fewer observations of systems to test the Boserup-Ruthenberg hypotheses. Tests of the Boserup-Ruthenberg model outside SSA, where climate, history of irrigation, and rainfed production potential all differ, provide valuable contrast to lessons derived from African conditions.

In South Asia and East Asia, the focus of research after the Second World War was on agricultural involution – the fall of labor productivity to zero as population density becomes very high – and the factors that can prevent or mitigate involution. The factors tending to extreme land use, and related falls in productivity, have not completely disappeared but have become much less important, as economic growth outside agriculture has pulled labor off farms, thereby reducing rural population pressure.

In Latin America, the research focus has been on the productivity effects of inequalities in operational land holdings; on the relations among livestock, crops, and deforestation; and on the sustainability effects of shifts in cropping patterns.[14] The availability of time-series and cross-sectional data is typically greater in South Asia and in Latin America, thus allowing richer empirical tests of the Boserup-Ruthenberg hypotheses about technical change and factor market evolution.

Tests of the Boserup-Ruthenberg hypotheses in Latin America have indeed tended to focus not on young systems but on mature systems of commercial farms, and specifically on:

* Technical choice in the presence of external innovation, such as mechanization and new crops;
* Crop choice where there are many commercial enterprise options, such as coffee, cocoa, livestock, and forest products;
* Environmental problems related to livestock production in forested areas (Kaimowitz and Angelsen 1998); and
* Land-saving versus land-using technologies in Latin American livestock production (Vosti, Witcover, and Carpentier 2002).

Deforestation in the sparsely populated tropics is a special problem for theories of agricultural evolution. The theory (Boserup 1965, 15–18) holds that intensification under low population density develops by shortening fallow and by changing fallow from forest to bush to grass. It does not predict major new cultivation along the extensive margins, because of the labor requirements of such new cultivation; yet that is exactly what occurs with large-scale deforestation. Extensive cultivation in the subhumid and humid tropics involves deforestation, and this has produced a blizzard of papers on the causes of deforestation, its environmental effects, and the potential for eliminating or reducing the causes.[15]

The introduction of new production technologies – machines to clear and harvest land; factories to process timber; higher-value crops, such as soybeans – is understood to induce deforestation by lowering the costs of land clearing and of processing output from newly cleared land. One argument has been that land-saving technologies – those that raise output per unit of land – can prevent deforestation, which is land-using. One proposition from the Boserup-Ruthenberg hypotheses would be that land-saving technologies would not prevent deforestation, unless they yield significantly more than deforestation per unit of the scarcest factor, which would be labor along the forest margins. Kaimowitz and Angelsen (1998) reviewed dozens of studies, including detailed empirical and theoretical models, and could not conclude firmly about the exogenous technology–deforestation relationship. Vosti, Witcover, and Carpentier (2002) found that land-saving technologies accelerate deforestation, because they are more profitable and thereby generate retained earnings that work to relieve credit constraints, which formerly inhibited extensive cattle production.

Effects of market access and of migration opportunities

There are two divides in empirical work on the population–intensification hypothesis. The first is the effect of market access on the uptake of commercial farming. First, market access is bad because of altitude or other factors, even in densely populated areas (two examples are highland Ethiopia and highland Kenya; several others are cited in Templeton and Scherr [1999]). Then population pressure leads to more intensive practices and to higher yields per unit of land but does *not* induce cash cropping, probably because transport, market, and processing infrastructures are unavailable.[16] Where market access is good, for example, after the introduction of roads and new logging technology into the Amazon, intensive practices and cash farming develop quickly despite low population density, because output/input price ratios are high. The evidence from Dixon, Gulliver, and Gibbon (2001, 316) about a small number of medium-intensity, market-oriented systems is that, if market access, including productive technology packages, is good they can develop even where cultivation intensity is low, where rainfed farming dominates irrigated, and where population density per cultivated area is the same as in low-intensity systems. This finding (admittedly from a subsample of six systems in a global sample of 70) suggests that improved market access and a package of more intensive technology can succeed where population pressure is low and can permit some farming systems to "skip" links in the long chain of intensification. The converse, however, does not seem to be true: packages of intensive technologies, such as fertilizer to replace manuring and shortened fallow, and machine power to replace hand tools and animal power, are unlikely to succeed even in densely cultivated areas, unless there is adequate market access for high-profit crops.

A recent paper on Ghana (Nin-Pratt and McBride 2014, 155) incorporated physical conditions to argue that one key link in the intensification chain can be skipped "provided other favorable conditions exist." This link is the shift from longer to shorter fallowing, to animal manures, and to mineral fertilizers as soil amendments. Nin-Pratt and McBride found "no correlation between population density and input intensity," but they did find higher crop yields from mineral fertilizers, even in low population density areas, where natural conditions of soils permit profitable cropping packages.

A second divide concerns the causes and consequences of migration or off-farm work. Boserup argued that "an agrarian surplus population [does not emerge] as the result of population growth" (1965, 104), and hence, she tends to minimize the importance of diminishing returns to intensification. A contrary view is that when diminishing returns to intensification occur, then farmers choose to migrate, to work off-farm, or to devote their farms to permanent crops that require less labor (Schelhas [1996], for the lowlands of Costa Rica). One paper, covering research on four continents, even shows that the intensification movement can reverse as farmers leave and "reduce land-improving investments" (Templeton and Scherr 1999, 911). The recent and comprehensive review of Headey and Jayne (2014) noted the dangers to sustainable intensification posed by lack of off-farm employment as an outlet for falling labor productivity.

Why family farming persists[17]

The industrialization or modernization model of agricultural growth argued that traditional family farming would gradually disappear under the influence of new technologies that were more productive than those used by family farms and under the influence of economies of scale, especially in mechanized farming and in information technology. The policy conclusion from this prediction is that small farms had little role in economic growth, and that, at best, they should be allowed to consolidate into larger ones and, at worst, they should be reorganized as a deliberate policy objective. The counterargument to a policy of neglecting, or eliminating, small farms is that they persist for strong economic and technical reasons and that they have good growth potential (Sourisseau 2015).

The theory of agricultural evolution has contributed importantly to the policy debate about small farms by predicting the persistence of family farming. The theory argues that family farms endure for these reasons:[18]

- Family farming has lower supervision costs than enterprise farming with hired laborers, because family members give more effort per wage than hired workers;

- Because agriculture is site-specific, knowledge of natural resources (land, water, vegetation, grazing) gives a cost advantage to family farming that is not available to enterprise farmers;
- The same logic of a cost advantage accruing to family farms from greater local knowledge of local resources applies to their potential external competitors who lack this knowledge;
- Consolidation of small farms into large ones can be done by families competitively against enterprises, as long as the former have competitive access to land rentals and machinery hiring, though at some point the family labor cost advantage runs into diminishing returns;
- There is another argument against new enterprise farming: such enterprises are unfamiliar with local social and labor conditions, and their incursion may provoke opposition among local farmers;
- Economic growth, of course, reduces the labor force share of farming but, in doing so, creates markets for credit, insurance, and machinery services that were formerly (endogenously) absent from family farms. Growth might, therefore, improve the conditions for the survival of family farms by making new market services available; and
- A final point favoring the survival of family farms is that they can more easily adapt to part-time farming, in which off-farm jobs and agricultural labor coexist.

Land-abundant areas (Binswanger and McIntire 1987) present special conditions that favor family farming more strongly:

- Because land is abundant,[19] self-cultivation dominates because individuals can acquire enough land to meet subsistence needs.
- Where new commodity markets emerge in land-abundant areas, self-cultivators can still take advantage of these opportunities, but seasonal peaks require either exchange or hired labor provided by those (e.g., younger sons, older minor children) who do not yet have the social status or capital needed to have their own plots, or by seasonal migrant labor.
- Higher transport costs and price discovery costs create a wedge between output prices and input costs, which tends to make purchased inputs less profitable and to make specialization less common.

Another factor in favor of family farming is that it is a form of long-term contract in rural areas. Alternative long-term contracts, in the labor or financial markets, are rare unless labor can be compelled by slavery or legal restrictions.[20] Family farming, as a long-term relationship with lenders and input suppliers, may provide a collateral substitute and may allow other means of lowering financing costs that are not available to enterprise farms. Other non–market social relations can act as substitutes for formal long-term contracts. These would include restrictions on land transactions outside the community, requirements to participate in community labor, and social exchanges in times of shocks. Such social relations will tend to disappear with rising wages and land scarcity, which lift the opportunity costs of participating in community work or of alienating lands through sale or rental.

In these conditions – land abundance, self-cultivation, high transport, and price discovery costs – one would expect family farming to continue more strongly than in areas with irrigation, high-value tree crops (some, not all), and greater market density.

One cross-section test of the family farm hypothesis is an analysis of attempts to establish large commercial enterprises where family farmers have been displaced or in low population density areas where family farms are rare. Such attempts, usually justified on the contention that productive land is underused and can be made profitable with investment in large farms, have been made throughout the world. There was a revival of interest in such large enterprises after the food price crisis of 2007–2008.

What does the success or failure of large implantations[21] mean for the family farming hypothesis? The eventual success of large enterprise farms implies that family farms could be widely displaced by policies designed to capture the productivity gap between large and small units.[22] The failure of large units would imply that public support should be withdrawn entirely, diverted to other sectors of the economy, or transferred to smaller farms.

The first issue is where such implantations have been made and with what degree of public support. The review of Deininger and Byerlee (2011), and others, found such a mix of results that it is very difficult to draw policy lessons:

- Some positive examples exist of large industrial farms in Latin America (Argentina and Peru), which seem to be highly leveraged in that land and machines are rented, so the ownership risk to the operator is low.
- Successes of enterprise farming in SSA are rare. The most frequent reasons for failure of large implantations in SSA are: (1) unfamiliarity with local production conditions; (2) the withdrawal of heavy initial subsidies; (3) lack of access to transport, electricity, and water; (4) a bias toward heavy machinery that is not well adapted to local conditions; and (5) bad governance by the foreign operator (harvesting rents) and by the national government (allocating rents). The most successful enterprise farms in SSA were those established by colonial force, and they tended to vanish with the colonial governments.
- The pattern of success and failure of enterprise farming in the transition countries of the former Soviet Union depends so much on specific policies that it is impossible to generalize about the relative advantages of family farming and enterprise farming.
- A recent study (Baumgartner et al. 2015) in western Ethiopia, which benchmarked the site against the assumptions stated in Binswanger and McIntire (1987), found that a foreign implantation was realized on a much smaller scale than planned, created less direct and indirect employment than planned, and used heavily mechanized techniques that were not compatible with local farming systems.

Static exceptions to the advantage of family farming

A static exception occurs under largely unchanged conditions of population density. Examples of static exceptions are those resulting from the introduction of a new enterprise, usually a tree crop, such as oil palm, rubber, or cocoa; a new form of organization into a given situation of population density and population growth;[23] or a history of forced colonization. The chief exception in the tropics is plantation production of export crops, as predicted by Binswanger and Rosenzweig (1986) and as elaborated by Deininger and Byerlee (2012).[24] Plantations succeed because they can successfully manage the coordination problems created by the perishability of such crops as bananas and sugarcane, and because they can exploit economies of scale in collection, shipping, and processing in ways that achieve cost advantages over small farmers. Oil palm in Southeast Asia is a well-known example of successful enterprise farming, though it contrasts with rubber, which has remained a smallholder crop. The chief exceptions in temperate agriculture are specialized monocropping, dairying, and other types of livestock production, where economies of scale (e.g., in hiring private veterinary care or in storing feed) and scope give a cost advantage to enterprise farms.[25]

It is important to distinguish the true cost advantages of enterprise farms from those created by preferential policies. Some advantages of enterprise farming do not occur because of inherent organizational or scale advantages, but because of fiscal or infrastructure incentives provided to large investors or because of legal protection from competition (e.g., family farmers are not allowed to grow certain crops) (Deininger and Binswanger 1995; Binswanger, Deininger, and Feder 1995). Such exceptions do not invalidate the idea that family farms have labor cost advantages.

Dynamic exceptions to family farming advantages

Dynamic exceptions are of two types: (1) those that result from long-term changes in the economy, notably greater market access, the introduction of high-value commercial crops or dairying, and higher labor–land ratios as population density rises; and (2) those resulting from concentration from unequal land ownership; owing to the greater risk assumption and investment capacities of larger farmers, some small farms may be absorbed and disappear as independent units, while others may grow into enterprise types through land rentals and purchases.

In the first exception, higher wages draw labor out of rural areas, making small farms less competitive with a given production function and, by shifting the production function to one that uses more machinery, making small family farms even less competitive because they cannot exploit mechanical economies of scale for lack of finance.[26] The combination of the two trends against small farms – rising wages and lack of access to machinery – would give a cost advantage to larger, mechanized farms and would, hypothetically, reduce the share of family farms in numbers and in area, as their supervision cost advantages weaken and as capital cost advantages accrue to larger farms.

Global evidence is mixed about this first type of dynamic exception. Otsuka (2015) noted a sharp decline in average farm size in Bangladesh, India, Indonesia, the Philippines, and Thailand between the 1970s and the first decade of this century, but this decline has apparently not been accompanied by a commensurate fall in the share of family farms in the total numbers of farms. Von Braun and Lohlein (2003) noted that the breakup of collective farms in the former Soviet Bloc led to the creation of mainly "subsistence" farms, which are presumably family operated. This development would again confirm the cost advantage of family enterprises, even after a radical change in tenure that might have allowed the taking of most farmland by large enterprises. The displacement of small and medium coffee farms by large mechanized soybean enterprises in the south and southeast of Brazil in the 1970s and 1980s (Browder, Pedlowski, and Summers 2004, 204) is an example of this exception, but it is apparently one in which there were strong policy incentives to convert family farming of a traditional crop (coffee) into enterprise farming of soybeans, which was thought to be more profitable.

One long-term economic change affects a base assumption in production relations theory – information is costly to acquire and, hence, may affect the cost advantage of family farms. Without this advantage, many of the theory's predictions about the costs of supervising laborers, diminishing returns to scale in supervision, and cost barriers to financial intermediation become weaker. That costs of information in the goods, inputs, and credit markets have become cheaper is undeniable, even in isolated areas, but we do not have evidence yet that this has weakened the cost advantage of family farming; indeed, lower information costs may strengthen family farms, if lower *fixed* costs of finding information are included.[27]

A second type of dynamic exception involves shifts in the uses of land markets as economies grow. The land market effects of growth include a delinking of farmland unit returns and farmland prices over time in US, European, and even some Asian land markets. This delinking creates an incentive to hold land for tax or for speculative purposes under corporate structures, not for production purposes under family structures. The delinking of land prices from the components of returns could also provide a motive to sell land above its net present value in production and cause the disappearance of family farms. Lastly, because land can be used more easily as collateral in rich countries, then repossession of collateral (especially where farms are heavily mortgaged) creates a new form of land sale and tends to cause further farmland consolidation.

How farmers adjust to shocks

The question of how farmers adjust to income and asset shocks has a long history in theory and empirical work. The major insight of production relations theory on the shock adjustment problem is that credit and insurance markets are incomplete or absent. These incomplete or absent markets shift the burden of adjustment to shocks onto consumption changes or asset disposal as substitutes for insurance and credit.

Binswanger and Rosenzweig (1986, 507–13) summarized why financial markets are incomplete or absent. The reasons are: (1) costly information increases risks to lenders and to providers of credit substitutes, such as insurance; (2) information costs prevent lenders from obtaining full information about borrowers; (3) in some low population density situations, isolation from borrowers raises information costs and sharpens information asymmetries, thereby limiting the potential for loan portfolio diversification; (4) risky and covariant outcomes reduce the risk-adjusted return to lending for productive purposes; and (5) in some farming types, simple technology limits the credit demand or stops it altogether (Binswanger and McIntire 1987). These reasons affect the viability of rural lending and have led to the historic delay in the emergence of rural finance all over the world.

There are also demand-side barriers to financial markets. One important example of demand-side barriers occurs in land-abundant areas. In such areas (e.g., the West African Sahel), landlessness is rare or absent. Farmers typically hire labor only seasonally, because land is available for their own cultivation, making credit less necessary to pay workers.[28] In such areas, without irrigation or introduced cash crops, then farm technology is simple and the demand for purchased inputs is weak, again limiting the demand for credit. The absence of valuable tree crops in drier, sparsely populated areas reduces credit supply by eliminating a class of collateral and, on the demand side, by reducing seasonal labor demands related to harvesting valuable tree products in short periods.

This reasoning leads from absent credit and insurance markets to the hypothesized emergence of credit and insurance substitutes. The major prediction is that, after stocks are exhausted, help from the social network is no longer available, and there are not short-term migration opportunities; asset liquidation becomes the principal substitute for credit and insurance markets when shocks occur. A related prediction follows – as barriers to financial and insurance markets disappear (under population pressure, the extension of cities with associated financial services, and the rise of new financial technologies), then asset sales would become less important for consumption smoothing when more farmers are able to borrow and to hold formal insurance. This "asset sale" prediction would have three chief variants: one of land sales and mortgages in land-scarce areas; a second involving draft animals in land-scarce areas; and a third with livestock sales and mortgages in both land-scarce and land-abundant areas.

The types of assets to liquidate are as follows:

1 *Livestock*: animals are also difficult to liquidate because of covariant risks; moreover, the prices of animals may vary inversely with the price of food crops, so the purchasing power of animal stocks is lowest when most needed;[29]
2 *Draft animals*: draft animals are a unique category of livestock that provides income for years before it is sold and one for which a rental market often exists;
3 *Consumer durables and jewelry*: these are partly liquid assets but, because of quality uncertainty and covariant risks,[30] their collateral value can be very low as a share of their replacement costs; and

4   *Trees*: trees would be difficult to liquidate during covariant shocks though they do have collateral value;[31] and

. 5   *Land*: land is difficult to liquidate because of covariant risks (everyone wants to sell at the same time in case of drought or other causes of low yields).[32]

We categorize these core assumptions as those concerning asset characteristics and management, and as those concerning the comparative advantage of tree crops (Berry 1988; see Table 7.1). The empirical evidence for the assumptions in the Binswanger-Rosenzweig and Binswanger-McIntire models is generally strong. Obviously, if those assumptions had been shown to be empirically wrong or limited to special cases, then tests of their predictions would be correspondingly wrong or limited. The sale of land, because it is not renewable, more often leads to permanent exit from farming or to sharecropping. That

Table 7.1 How animal and tree crop assets evolve as collateral

Assumptions about animal and tree crop assets	*Empirical verification of this assumption*
ANIMALS	
Arid climate promotes animal production.	Successful except where animal traction common
Animal mobility is a cost-effective strategy.	Strong verification except where animal power or dairying dominant
Covariance of animal and crop yields < covariance of crop yields	Partly verified; not as strong as expected; even in drylands, without irrigation
High transport and communication costs raise risks in sparse areas.	Verified in past; lessened over time; now less important
Collateral value is low.	Verified even where animals used for draft power
Slow emergence of land rights in pastoral areas	Partly verified land titles were rare in pastoral areas.
	Many efforts to enforce grazing domains; varying success
	Use rights now common under population pressure and with political empowerment of pastorals
TREE CROPS	
Weak comparative advantage of tree crops in drylands	Formerly verified but changing with new plantings
Faster emergence of land rights in tree crops	Land rights in tree crops typically verified even if land rights in row crops or pastures weak
Collateral value of trees mixed	Sometimes as direct collateral; common as collateral substitute
	Not needed under contract farming; or settler schemes because of other forms of credit

Source: Author's construction.

is, of course, a significant barrier to land sales because permanent exit implies the sacrifice of a long-term income stream in favor of a much more uncertain income stream from labor, combined with the uncertain return on the cash proceeds of land sales.

A practical problem affecting such studies is the skewness of the asset variables, related of course to the skewness of income and wealth.[33] This skewness, when combined with the rare availability of time-series data, makes it much more difficult to estimate temporally reliable relationships, given the high cross-sectional and temporal variability in tropical agriculture. The few studies that have estimated empirical consumption – asset relationships in tropical agricultural settings – have usually done so with cross-sectional data.

Most studies of the relation between livestock transactions and consumption are from SSA or from South Asia. Most work uses cross-sectional data, not time-series. The acceptance or rejection of the livestock sale – the consumption shock hypothesis – varies across study sites, the type of model used, and the scope of the data.

The sale of animals during income shocks[34] is a *major prediction* of Binswanger and Rosenzweig (1986). The prediction is that animal collateral is too risky for lenders, because borrowers may hide the true condition of the animals and, hence, stockholders are forced to sell animals that they might otherwise mortgage. Even for owners of many livestock, it is difficult to mortgage animals because of such risks. The limitations of a mortgage market for animals, due to collateral-specific risks, add to the volume of sales that would occur ordinarily in periods of drought.

Confirmation of a strong draft animal sale response to shocks is provided in the Rosenzweig and Wolpin (1993) model of consumption smoothing of severe credit constraints. The greater sale response of such animals is presumably due to the fact that the services of draft animals sold at times of distress can later be rehired through the rental market. Another factor making such distress sales less costly and, hence, more frequent in land-scarce areas is the existence of land rentals; farmers having sold their draft animals in one year can rent their land in the following year, if they are unable to buy or hire enough draft power to work their own land. These features of land-scarce agriculture – livestock used for draft, a rental market for draft animals, and a rental market for land – are much less common in land-abundant areas.

There are contrary reasons why livestock would *not* be used for consumption smoothing. The obvious one is that many households own few animals or none at all, even in arid and semi-arid areas, where livestock have a comparative advantage. Walker and Ryan (1990), in a ten-year study of six villages in three regions of SAT of India, found that livestock contributed on average only "8 percent to total household wealth" (1990, 56). Livestock (and other asset ownership) was highly skewed in favor of larger operational holdings (1990, 309). A recent report by the World Bank found that livestock ownership in the sub-Saharan African drylands is "highly skewed" (World Bank 2014, 41) in both pastoral and mixed crop–livestock systems. The paper calculated Gini coefficients for crop income and livestock income in 11 African countries where animal production is a major share of agriculture. It found that the Gini for livestock income was higher in each of the 11 countries, and that the (unweighted) average ratio of the Gini for livestock income to the Gini for crop income was 1.65 (World Bank 2014, 9, Table 3).[35] McIntire, Bourzat, and Pingali (1992) observed that most households in a sample of 33 sites across sub-Saharan African households owned few or no livestock at all. Lange and Reimers (2014, 8, Table 1 and 14, Table 2) found that the distributions of live-stock ownership among households in SAT of Burkina Faso are highly skewed. The meta-analysis of Turner, Hanham, and Portararo (1977, 391) found only about half of the groups studied to be engaged in "major livestock produc-tion." Even where farmers do hold animals, the flow of income is too low to constitute significant cash savings (for Africa, World Bank [2014, 41–42]; for SAT of India, Walker and Ryan [1990]).

A second force against livestock transactions to smooth consumption is that sales prices decline during droughts because the costs of fodder and water rise,[36] giving rise to a procyclical valuation of animal assets. The relation between numbers of animal sales and consumption tends to be more significantly negative than does the relation between the value of sales and consumption; this finding (Lange and Reimers 2014) is consistent with a skewed distribution of large and small animal numbers, and with a negative effect of distress sales of livestock and the unit price at which such sales are concluded.

Empirical evidence is mixed about the effect of income shocks on livestock transactions and consumption. Hoogeveen (2001, 15) found a high prevalence of livestock sales during the "serious droughts" in Zimbabwe in 1991 and again in 1992 – 63.1 percent and 60.2 percent of households, respectively, in the two study years, sold livestock, amounting to 39.2 percent and 36.9 percent of the respective annual values of those sales (2001, 15).[37]

The work of Fafchamps, Udry, and Czukas (1998) on Burkina Faso[38] found that livestock transactions accounted for only between 15 and 30 percent of "income shortfalls" related to village income shocks. The weak role of livestock in consumption smoothing – in study sites chosen to have close integration of crop and animal production in the risky semi-arid tropics – is somewhat unexpected. There appears to be two main reasons for the low share of animal transactions in consumption smoothing in this Burkina Faso study. One is that farmers in the study villages receive remittances from relatives working in the cities and coastal economies of West and Central Africa; such remittances make it at least partly unnecessary to sell animals in times of drought. A second reason is that the distributions of livestock holdings are skewed. The median holdings of cattle are much smaller than those of the mean and indeed are sometimes zero; hence, transactions in the largest and most valuable stock, cattle, are unavailable to the median farmer. The ownership of sheep and goats is much less skewed, and it is therefore unsurprising that Fafchamps, Udry, and Czukas (1998) found a stronger negative relationship between income shocks and net sales of sheep and goats (1998, 292, Figure 4).[39]

Zimmerman and Carter (2003, 233) supported the hypothesis that initial differences in wealth, including livestock, lead to bifurcated portfolio strategies. Wealthier agents achieve higher yields and "conventional consumption smoothing," while poorer agents achieve lower yields and follow "asset smoothing." Carter and Lybbert (2012) found a similar divergence in the ability to smooth consumption as a function of wealth; households above a threshold were able to smooth consumption, while those below that threshold could not smooth consumption and, hence, risked falling into a poverty trap (Carter and Lybbert 2012). Lange and Reimers (2014, 28), also for Burkina Faso, using data collected in the drought year of 2004 found that: (1) livestock sales did rise during the drought; (2) household consumption nonetheless fell despite livestock sales and grain stock withdrawals; and (3) the fall of livestock prices during droughts appeared to explain the incomplete consumption-smoothing effect.

In a study of 196 farmers in northern Nigeria, Udry (1995, 1290) rejected the hypothesis that "overall saving" is unaffected by "adverse shocks." With respect to livestock, Udry further found that "livestock saving is not affected by idiosyncratic shocks" (1995, 1292). Udry's finding is perhaps explained by the result for Burkina Faso, reported by Zimmerman and Carter (2003), that livestock are predominantly owned by wealthier households, who can dissave by liquidating grain stocks.

A comparatively new factor in explaining the varying role of livestock sales in consumption smoothing is access to unrequited transfers from family members. Such transfers have grown as the para-pastoral economies have grown, with the numbers of migrants, with the (recent) declining cost of money transfers, and with the availability of food aid and other public safety nets.

Zimmerman and Carter (2003) suggested an additional explanation for the partial absence of asset-based (livestock) consumption smoothing. Poor farmers face such binding subsistence constraints and have such meager savings that they must invest in low risk–low return activities, compared to wealthier farmers who have more savings and a less binding subsistence constraint. Hence, poor farmers both generate low returns on their investments and are more often forced to reduce consumption to preserve. The evidence for this in the Zimmerman-Carter model is the higher foregone rate of consumption in poor households compared to that in richer households, a finding that is empirically consistent with other studies (2003, 248).

McPeak's (2004) work on arid Kenya is the only study to separate asset shocks from income shocks. His findings are partly incompatible with the livestock buffer hypothesis because "liquidation of livestock assets to compensate for a current income deficit comes at the cost of reduced expected future income from livestock production" (2004, 281). A model in which asset shocks are explicitly separated from income shocks would tend to explain why other work (Niger, India, Burkina Faso, Zimbabwe) has found incomplete buffering of income shocks via livestock transactions.

The Binswanger-Rosenzweig and Binswanger-McIntire papers tend to consider such disparities, notably in wealth holdings. Both papers and related work review holdings of livestock by type of agricultural environment, holdings of tree crops, and holdings of consumer durables, including jewelry (Binswanger and Rosenzweig 1981, 511, Table 1; Binswanger and McIntire 1987, 80).

Aggravating the lack of savings instruments is the lack of instruments to monetize certain stocks, which might be largely or even completely illiquid. One example of stocks that cannot be monetized is grain holdings, which are not good collateral because they are perishable. Another example is that while poor people do sell consumer durables, such goods face adverse selection, which makes their markets highly illiquid; moreover, attempts to sell consumer durables face the same covariant risks that attempts to sell livestock face. Tree crops are a store of value but cannot be liquidated unless property rights are firmly established; tree crops, because of their greater density and higher return in humid areas, are less likely to be alternative sale assets compared to livestock in arid zones.

What have theories of agricultural evolution achieved?

Explaining production relations

The literature launched by Boserup successfully inverted the historical model of how population and agriculture interact, thus providing a much deeper understanding of the conditions of rural development. Subsequent empirical work generally confirmed the detailed Boserup-Ruthenberg hypotheses about the development of farming practices in such areas as fallowing, crop rotation, grazing and livestock management, weed control, and soil fertility management. Yet the intensification model had to be completed by an explanation of how rural factor markets emerge and develop. The production relations literature succeeded in completing the intensification model by identifying flaws in earlier models of factor markets, in the sense that they introduced external factors – very high risk aversion among poor farmers, laws and other policies that prevented factor markets from working, the assumption that asset rental and labor-hire markets did not exist, or the impossibility of land sales. The principal addition of the production relations literature to the Boserup-Ruthenberg model of agricultural evolution, therefore, was to define why market failures occur from the behavioral and material conditions of agriculture, to place such failures within the long-term evolution of farming systems, and to analyze the endogenous institutional and individual responses to those market failures.

The enormous volume of research[40] – influenced by the contributions of Ester Boserup, Hans Ruthenberg, Hans Binswanger, Mark Rosenzweig, Karla Hoff, Marcel Fafchamps, Pranab Bardhan, Mukesh Eswaran, and Ashok Kotwal (1985) – is itself confirmation of the importance of these ideas about missing markets, even where there is major disagreement about empirical findings and policy implications. Hypothesis testing, while sometimes not rigorous in a statistical sense, has given strong confirmation of the main ideas about the evolution of farming systems across many systems in the tropical and warm temperate climates, about how financial intermediation develops, about how farm organization changes in response to factor proportions and exogenous technologies, and about how farm and farmer attributes influence response to asset and income shocks. The paper of de Janvry, Fafchamps, and Sadoulet (1991, 1410), showing that missing markets for inputs, factors, and goods explained low supply response in African agriculture better than the "inherent behavior" of African peasants, is a major example of the insights from this body of theory.

The chief empirical shortcomings of agricultural evolution theory are: (1) the difficulty of separating temporal from locational effects, because of the costs of collecting data over many years in a number of places for panel data analysis; and (2) the analytic problems in attributing causality to individual variables that have moved together as systems evolve over time. An example of these problems is seen in two studies of the relation between infrastructure and agricultural development. In one from India, Binswanger, Khandker, and Rosenzweig (1993) deployed a complex set of time-series and cross-sectional data to estimate the separate effects of financial intermediation, irrigation, livestock investment, human capital investment, and fertilizer use on output. Without the Indian data, these estimates would have been impossible, and the resulting policy conclusions on financial intermediation would have been weaker or seriously biased. A study from SSA by Dorosh et al. (2012) estimated the important effects of road transport and market access on crop production, but "lacking time series data" (2012, 1) could not analyze impacts for much of the continent. Related econometric problems afflicted one study of cattle production in western Tanzania (Dercon 1992), and another of financial intermediation in northern Nigeria (Udry 1995), in that the lack of time-series data made it impossible to fully identify the impacts of initial conditions of wealth on production and consumption behavior. The role of livestock in adjusting to shocks is another empirical question that is impossible to answer definitively without time-series data; even with it, the complexities of animal asset ownership and management in different environments are such that wide generalizations are probably impossible.

In some circumstances, as in much of contemporary Africa, adequate data will be available only at high cost, and hence, many important questions have empirical answers that are at best incomplete. Empirical disagreements persist most strongly about: (1) the relation between farm size and productivity; (2) the point at which intensification stops raising yields per unit of land and becomes a process of involution (as in Java, Geertz [1963]; or in some densely cultivated parts of Africa, as estimated by Muyanga and Jayne [2014]); (3) the basic unit of farm organization and its persistence as a family unit, or its evolution into an enterprise unit, as occurs in the industry and service sectors; (4) the extent to which public policy can substitute for missing markets, especially in credit and insurance, and improve welfare above the levels achieved by contractual substitutes for such markets.

A second limitation of agricultural evolution theory, beyond the problem of the substitutability of cross-sectional data for temporal observations, is the implicit assumption that permanent migration is too expensive. That is, permanent migration is not assumed away from the model, but is limited because of the high costs of migration. The absence of permanent migration opportunities forces labor to be used to a point where its marginal productivity becomes zero or even negative – the involution point. The experience of many densely populated areas with respect to their intensification potential – Bangladesh, the highlands of Eastern Africa, Central America – is that migration, or significant off-farm work without migration, occurs to relieve population pressure and allows some shifting of production to less labor-intensive methods and activities. The work of Headey and Jayne (2014) pointed to a significant blockage in the intensification sequence where labor absorption from irrigation and off-farm employment are not available.

A third limitation is the failure to account adequately for exceptional, introduced technical or output price changes. Such changes – oil palm development in Indonesia; livestock production in the Amazon; soybeans in much of Latin America; the availability of high-yielding varieties of rice, wheat, and maize in what had been stagnant cropping systems; the advent of tree crops in what were areas of very low population density in West Africa – fall partly outside the predictions of the intensification framework, because they occur so rapidly and are associated with such large shifts in relative output and land prices. They fall only "partly" outside the framework, however, because the intensification framework still correctly predicts the failure of labor-using innovations in areas of land abundance or where the opportunity cost of labor is high for other reasons.

Influencing policy

The chief practical objective of agricultural evolution theory was to improve policies in such fields as: (1) raising farm productivity through technical change; (2) lowering barriers to efficient factor markets, especially in land and finance; (3) improving the efficiency and equity of public spending; and (4) designing social protection programs for rural areas that are vulnerable to shocks. A review of three major predictions from production relations theory – concerning the evolution of agricultural technology, the persistence of family farming, and the use of insurance substitutes to adjust to shocks – suggests several notable successes in influencing policy.

The most important *policy contribution has been to define constraints to the introduction of markets* where they are thin or entirely absent. The chief example of absent markets, historically, was that for labor-intensive technologies. There were many unsuccessful attempts to introduce such technologies – fertilizer use in low population density areas; resettlement of farmers from densely to sparely populated areas; the replacement of "unproductive" family farms and the introduction of enterprise farming through financial or regulatory incentives; introduction of credit without lending institutions or without an adequate understanding of credit use; provision of social safety nets that compromise the productive livelihoods of farmers. The genesis of agricultural evolution theory in the attempt to understand those failures and the application of its lessons to crafting better policies governing irrigation management, incentives, financial intermediation, land tenure, and administration are major intellectual achievements.

A generally well-confirmed prediction is that *family farms* will remain the dominant type and can become more productive. The policy value of this prediction has been to reduce some of the bias against smallholder agriculture. This prediction does not solve the agricultural duality problem in most developing countries, however. Family farms persist as a high share in the numbers of farm units, but not as a high share of agricultural GDP, notably where new technologies for forestry, livestock, or mechanized arable cropping have been introduced into countries with dualistic farm structures – given that technologies permit physical and financial economies of scale that favor larger businesses. The more rapid growth of enterprise farming deepens the concentration of political power, and of access to public support, among larger farmers. The theory of agricultural evolution has succeeded in explaining why family farms persist and has been valuable in blocking costly efforts to impose enterprise farming where it is unviable without subsidies, but there remains much to do in devising policies that can lessen the inequalities of wealth and income in rural areas and in avoiding more additions to the classes of small, poor, and isolated farmers all over the world.

A major policy problem is *prevention of famine and severe distress* among rural people. In the absence of adequate savings, and of financial instruments to smooth consumption, poor rural people are heavily exposed to income and asset shocks. The identification of this exposure, the explanation of its origins, and the proposal of remedies are components of an outstanding policy result of production relations theory. That theory has given intellectual support to the use of rural employment schemes that can provide employment and income and, hence, prevent extreme deprivation. Such schemes, while they can suffer from management corruption, do not suffer from the larger-scale incentive problems that afflict rural credit schemes, where the latter were once considered as the obvious second-best consumption-smoothing instruments.

Notes

1 "Farming" and "agriculture" are used synonymously throughout and can refer to annual crops, perennial crops, livestock, or trees. "Farmers" is shorthand that also includes herders, fishers, and foresters.

2 We are not saying that there is no controversy about supply response, only that the controversy now tends to be about its aggregate magnitude and about how to estimate it, not about whether it exists at all among peasant farmers.

3 There are many other contributors (notably Dumont [1957], in his chapters on the former Belgian Congo, the African savannas between Lake Chad and Senegal, and Vietnam), but these authors cited here have been the most influential in stimulating research.

4 Chapters 2 to 5 in Boserup (1965) have many examples, as do Chapters 4 through 9 in Ruthenberg (1980). Dixon, Gulliver, and Gibbon (2001) discussed 72 farming systems from four continents.

5 Weeds are more persistent in the tropics where there is no winter, and this adds to the cost of farming there.

6 We do not discuss the productivity–farm size issue or the tenancy-sharecropping issue, given that both have been widely analyzed elsewhere.

7 We understand that family farming is also a type of "enterprise," but in the interest of avoiding the ugly expression "non-family farming," we use "enterprise" in its place.

8 The dozens of case studies cited by Wiggins (2000) nearly always refer to single sites in single African countries without long-term data at the same place. The work of Matlon and Fafchamps (1989) is an exception, in that it presents several years of data for six villages in three agroclimatic zones.

9 The length of the dry season improved the specification a bit more; this finding is discussed later, with reference to Binswanger-Mkhize and Savastano (2014).

10 Work in semi-arid Burkina Faso (Prudencio 1993) found that manure and mineral fertilizers are complementary inputs, not substitutes, because they are used on different land types as functions of cultivation intensity, place in the fallow cycle, distance to the household, and availability of animals for night paddocking.

11 "Intensive" techniques are defined as those having more labor and other variable inputs per unit of land.

12 Jayne, Chamberlin, and Headey (2014, 7) stated, "soil quality decline . . . in high density Africa is our leading hypothesis for why we consistently found a levelling-off of land productivity and intensification beyond a threshold level of population density."

13 "Tests" here include explicit tests using formal methods and implicit ones using more qualitative methods.

14 Caviglia and Andrade (2010) is an example of the latter.

15 Kaimowitz and Angelsen (1998) reviewed more than 100 studies of deforestation from Asia, Latin America, and Africa. The problem of tree crop farm organization is discussed later in the section on family farming.

16 The compendium of Pender, Place, and Ehui (2006) for the East African highlands.

17 Non-operating owners owned 29 percent of US farmland as recently as 2007 (Nickerson et al. 2012).

18 Deininger and Byerlee (2012) reviewed the reasons.

19 Again, slavery is assumed to be effectively banned.

20 One illustrative legal restriction on labor mobility is the *thangata* system in Malawi. *Thangata* began as a form of reciprocal labor obligation and, under colonial rule, evolved into a requirement to work on the estates of settlers (Kandawire 1977).

21 "Implantations" mean large farms allocated to (largely) foreign investors on land that is supposedly underused.

22 Deininger and Byerlee (2012, 82) noted very large gaps between actual and potential yields for maize, oil palm, soybean, and sugarcane in Asia, South America, and sub-Saharan Africa, implying significant potential gains from better agricultural management.

23 We are not referring to forced exit, such as the policies in China to settle pastoralists or Soviet efforts to convert nomads into farmers or settled ranchers (Grigg 1974, 112).

24 Byerlee's paper (2014) on the evolution of Asian plantations is a counterexample. Byerlee found that the long-term decline in the share of plantations, related to the rise of contract farming, was counteracted by the expansion of tree crops (especially oil palm) onto new lands, and revived commodity prices and incentives to large operators. The chief exception for temperate arable farming is specialized monocropping, such as soybeans in Argentina and Brazil, and dairying, as explained by Deininger and Byerlee (2012).

25 A reviewer has pointed out that tax issues may be a reason in temperature agriculture.

26 The availability of land and machine rentals can make up for lack of finance.

27 Evidence from India and Niger produced by Marcel Fafchamps suggests that the output price advantages of lower communications costs are not large (Aker and Fafchamps 2010; Fafchamps and Minten 2012).

28 Other practices reduce the use of cash for seasonal workers. Cash payments to seasonal harvest workers can be substituted by piece rates in kind. Cash payments to seasonal workers at weeding time can be substituted by group labor.

29 Under drought conditions, crop yields fall and crop prices rise; at the same time, pasture yields fall, and herders may then sell animals because they cannot maintain them for lack of feed – hence, animal prices can fall at the same time as crop prices rise.

30 Covariance occurs with jewelry sales because the latter are held by a few groups; this concentration of ownership would lead to price collapses if, for example, many herders sell their jewelry during a widespread drought.

31 There are many examples of tree collateral in which the lender harvests the tree until the loan is repaid.

32 Where land markets emerge in relatively land-abundant areas, it is because customs against selling to outsiders have broken down. For example, Koussoubé (2013) showed in west-central Burkina Faso a rising number and value of land sales, from a very low base, due to urbanization and to the arrival of migrants from other parts of the country, without these changes leading apparently to collateral in land.

33 Udry (1995, 1299) found that the coefficient of variation of overall savings was 5.14 in his sample year, 10.74 in his sample period 1, and 3.29 in his sample period 2. Fafchamps, Udry, and Czukas (1998, Table 2) found that median cattle holdings are from 0 to 15 percent to 30 percent of mean holdings in three subregions of semi-arid Burkina Faso.

34 McPeak (2004) distinguished carefully between income shocks and asset shocks in determining livestock sales.

35 The average crop income Gini coefficient was 0.40 (n=11), and the average livestock Gini was 0.60 (n=11).

36 The cost of water rises because animals must be trekked to water; hence, water scarcity is associated with higher trekking costs and with higher energy expenditure by animals in finding water.

37 Hoogeveen (2001, 15), in Zimbabwe, noted that land sales do not occur, either because they have been forbidden by the Zimbabwean land reform or households do not typically own gold. Baumgartner et al. (2015, 180), in a recent paper on western Ethiopia, observes the assumed conditions of simple technology and absent financial markets.

38 Fafchamps, Udry, and Czukas (1998) made careful reference to southern Niger and northern Nigeria, regions that have much in common with their Burkina Faso study sites, so their results were relevant to more farmers and a larger area.

39 Lange and Reimers (2014) found that the distributions of livestock ownership among households is highly skewed (Table 1), and that more households report selling sheep and goats than cattle (Table 2). A synthesis report by the World Bank (2014, 41) found that livestock ownership in the African drylands is highly skewed.

40 Boserup (1965) has more than 5,700 citations in Google Scholar; Ruthenberg's third edition (1980) has 1,750; Hoff, Braverman, and Stiglitz (1993) on rural institutions have more than 400; Bardhan (1991) has nearly 600. The initial paper of Binswanger and Rosenzweig (1986) has more than 900.

References

Aker, J. C., and M. Fafchamps. 2010. "How Does Mobile Phone Coverage Affect Farm-Gate Prices? Evidence from West Africa." Paper presented at the American Economic Association Annual Meeting, Denver, CO, January 7–9, 2011. https://www.aeaweb.org/conference/2011/meetingpapers.php

Allen, B. J. 2001. "Boserup and Brookfield and the Association between Population Density and Agricultural Intensity in Papua New Guinea." *Asia Pacific Viewpoint* 42 (2/3): 237–54.

Askari, H., and J. T. Cummings. 1976. *Agricultural Supply Response: A Survey of the Econometric Evidence.* New York: Praeger.

Baltenweck, I., S. Staal, M. N. M. Ibrahim, M. Herrero, F. Holmann, M. Jabbar, V. Manyong, B. R. Patil, P. Thornton, T. Williams, M. Waithaka, and T. de Wolff. 2003. "Crop-Livestock

Intensification and Interactions Across Three Continents: Main Report." System-wide Livestock Program (SLP) Project on Transregional Analysis of Crop-Livestock Systems, International Livestock Research Institute (ILRI), Nairobi, Kenya.

Bardhan, P. K., ed. 1991. *The Economic Theory of Agrarian Institutions*. Oxford: Clarendon Press.

Baumgartner, P., J. von Braun, D. Abebaw, and M. Muller. 2015. "Impacts of Large-scale Land Investments on Income, Prices, and Employment: Empirical Analyses in Ethiopia." *World Development* 72: 175–90.

Berry, S. 1988. "Property Rights and Rural Resource Management: The Case of Tree Crops in West Africa." *Cahiers des Sciences Humaines* 24 (1): 3–16.

Bilsborrow, R. E. 1987. "Population Pressures and Agricultural Development in Developing Countries: A Conceptual Framework and Recent Evidence." *World Development* 15 (2): 183–203.

Binswanger, H. P., K. Deininger, and G. Feder. 1995. "Power Distortions Revolt and Reform in Agricultural Land Relations." In *Handbook of Development Economics*, Vol. 3, Part B, edited by J. Behrman and T. N. Srinivasan, 2659–772. Amsterdam: Elsevier Science.

Binswanger, H. P., S. R. Khandker, and M. R. Rosenzweig. 1993. "How Infrastructure and Financial Institutions Affect Agricultural Output and Investment in India." *Journal of Development Economics* 41 (2): 337–66.

Binswanger, H. P., and J. McIntire. 1987. "Behavioral and Material Determinants of Production Relations in Land-Abundant Tropical Agriculture." *Economic Development and Cultural Change* 36 (1): 73–99.

Binswanger, H. P., and M. Rosenzweig. 1981. "Contractual Arrangement, Employment and Rural Wages in Rural Labor Markets: A Critical Review." Agricultural Development Council, New York, and International Crops Research Institute for the Semi-arid Tropics, Andhra Pradesh, India.

Binswanger, H. P., and M. Rosenzweig. 1986. "Behavioural and Material Determinants of Production Relations in Agriculture." *Journal of Development Studies* 22 (3): 503–39.

Binswanger-Mkhize, H. P., and S. Savastano. 2014. "Agricultural Intensification: The Status in Six African Countries." Policy Research Working Paper 7116, Work Bank, Washington, DC.

Boserup, E. 1965. *The Conditions of Agricultural Growth: A Study of Agrarian Change under Population Pressure*. Chicago: Aldine.

Boserup, E. 1981. *Population and Technical Change: A Study of Long-term Trends*. Chicago: University of Chicago Press.

Browder, J. O., M. A. Pedlowski, and P. M. Summers. 2004. "Land Use Patterns in the Brazilian Amazon: Comparative Farm-Level Evidence from Rondônia." *Human Ecology* 32 (2): 197–224.

Byerlee, D. 2014. "The Fall and Rise again of Plantations in Tropical Asia: History Repeated?" *Land* 3 (3): 574–97.

Carter, M. R., and T. J. Lybbert. 2012. "Consumption versus Asset Smoothing: Testing the Implications of Poverty Trap Theory in Burkina Faso." *Journal of Development Economics* 99 (2): 255–64.

Caviglia, O. P., and F. H. Andrade. 2010. "Sustainable Intensification of Agriculture in the Argentinean Pampas: Capture and Use Efficiency of Environmental Resources." *Americas Journal of Plant Science and Biotechnology* 3 (Special Issue 1): 1–8.

Cuffaro, N. 1997. "Population Growth and Agriculture in Poor Countries: A Review of Theoretical Issues and Empirical Evidence." *World Development* 25 (7): 1151–63.

Deininger, K., and H. P. Binswanger. 1995. "Rent Seeking and the Development of Large-Scale Agriculture in Kenya, South Africa, and Zimbabwe." *Economic Development and Cultural Change* 43 (3): 493–522.

Deininger, K., and D. Byerlee. 2012. "The Rise of Large Farms in Land Abundant Countries: Do They Have a Future?" *World Development* 40 (4): 701–14.

Deininger, K., and D. Byerlee, with J. Lindsay, A. Norton, H. Selod, and M. Stickler. 2011. *Rising Global Interest in Farmland: Can It Yield Sustainable and Equitable Benefits?* Washington, DC: World Bank.

de Janvry, A., M. Fafchamps, and E. Sadoulet. 1991. "Peasant Household Behaviour with Missing Markets: Some Paradoxes Explained." *Economic Journal* 101 (409): 1400–17.

Dercon, S. 1992. "The Role of Assets in Coping with Household Income Fluctuations: Some Simulation Results." Centre of the Study of African Economies, University of Oxford, Oxford.

Dixon, J., and A. Gulliver, with D. Gibbon. 2001. *Farming Systems and Poverty: Improving Farmers' Livelihoods in a Changing World*. Rome and Washington, DC: Food and Agricultural Organization of the United Nations (FAO) and World Bank.

Dorosh, P., H. G. Wang, L. You, and E. Schmidt. 2012. "Road Connectivity, Population, and Crop Production in Sub-Saharan Africa." *Agricultural Economics* 43 (1): 89–103.

Dumont, R. 1957. *Types of Rural Economy: Studies in World Agriculture*. London: Methuen and Co.

Eswaran, M., and A. Kotwal. 1985. "A Theory of Contractual Structure in Agriculture." *American Economic Review* 75 (3): 352–67.

Fafchamps, M., and B. Minten. 2012. "Impact of SMS-Based Agricultural Information on Indian Farmers." *World Bank Economic Review* 26 (3): 383–414.

Fafchamps, M., C. Udry, and K. Czukas. 1998. "Drought and Saving in West Africa: Are Livestock a Buffer Stock?" *Journal of Development Economics* 55 (2): 273–305.

Geertz, C. 1963. *Agricultural Involution: The Process of Ecological Change in Indonesia*. Berkeley: University of California Press.

Grigg, D. B. 1974. *The Agricultural Systems of the World: An Evolutionary Approach*. New York: Cambridge University Press.

Hayami, Y., and V. W. Ruttan. 1971. *Agricultural Development: An International Perspective*. Baltimore: Johns Hopkins University Press.

Headey, D. D., and T. S. Jayne. 2014. "Adaptation to Land Constraints: Is Africa Different?" *Food Policy* 48: 18–33.

Hoff, K., A. Braverman, and J. E. Stiglitz. 1993. *The Economics of Rural Organization: Theory, Practice and Policy*. New York: Oxford University Press for the World Bank.

Hoff, K., and J. E. Stiglitz. 1990. "Introduction: Imperfect Information and Rural Credit Markets: Puzzles and Policy Perspectives." *World Bank Economic Review* 4 (3): 235–50.

Hoogeveen, H. 2001. "Evidence on Informal Insurance in Rural Zimbabwe." Discussion Paper TI 2001–001/2, Tinbergen Institute, Amsterdam.

Jarvis, L. S. 1974. "Cattle as Capital Goods and Ranchers as Portfolio Managers: An Application to the Argentine Cattle Sector." *Journal of Political Economy* 82 (3): 489–520.

Jayne, T. S., J. Chamberlin, and D. D. Headey. 2014. "Land Pressures, the Evolution of Farming Systems, and Development." *Food Policy* 48: 1–17.

Josephson, A. L., J. Ricker-Gilbert, and R. J. G. M. Florax. 2014. "How Does Population Density Influence Agricultural Intensification and Productivity? Evidence from Ethiopia." *Food Policy* 48: 142–52.

Kaimowitz, D., and A. Angelsen. 1998. "Economic Models of Tropical Deforestation: A Review." Center for International Forestry Research (CIFOR), Jakarta.

Kandawire, J.A.K. 1977. "Thangata in Pre-Colonial and Colonial Systems of Land Tenure in Southern Malaŵi with Special Reference to Chingale." *Africa: Journal of the International African Institute* 47 (2): 185–91.

Koussoubé, E. 2013. "What Drives Land Sales and Rentals in Rural Africa: Evidence from Western Burkina Faso." Paper prepared for African Studies Association (ASA) Annual Meeting, Baltimore, MD, November 21–24, 2013.

Krueger, A. O., M. Schiff, and A. Valdés, eds. 1991. *The Political Economy of Agricultural Pricing Policy*, Vol. 2. Baltimore: Johns Hopkins University Press for World Bank.

Lange, S., and M. Reimers. 2014. "Livestock as an Imperfect Buffer Stock in Poorly Integrated Markets." Discussion Paper No. 162, Courant Research Center "Poverty, Equity and Growth", Göttingen.

Lipton, M. 1977. *Why Poor People Stay Poor: Urban Bias in World Development*. Cambridge: Harvard University Press.

Mariam, M. W. 1986. *Rural Vulnerability to Famine in Ethiopia: 1958–1977*. London: Intermediate Technology.

Matlon, P. J., and M. Fafchamps. 1989. "Crop Budgets in Three Agro-climatic Zones of Burkina Faso." ICRISAT Progress Report. International Crops Research Institute for the Semi-Arid Tropics, Hyderabad, India.

McCarthy, N., B. Swallow, M. Kirk, and P. Hazell, eds. 1999. *Property Rights, Risk and Livestock Development in Africa*. Washington, DC and Nairobi: International Food Policy Research Institute (IFPRI) and International Livestock Research Institute (ILRI).

McIntire, J., D. Bourzat, and P. Pingali. 1992. "Crop Livestock Interaction in Sub-Saharan Africa." World Bank, Washington, DC.

McPeak, J. 2004. "Contrasting Income Shocks with Asset Shocks: Livestock Sales in Northern Kenya." *Oxford Economic Papers* 56 (2): 263–84.

Muyanga, M., and T. S. Jayne. 2014. "Effects of Rising Rural Population Density on Smallholder Agriculture in Kenya." *Food Policy* 48: 98–113.

Nickerson, C., M. Morehart, T. Kuethe, J. Beckman, J. Ifft, and R. Williams. 2012. "Trends in U.S. Farmland Values and Ownership." Economic Information Bulletin No. 92, Economic Research Service, United States Department of Agriculture (USDA), Washington, DC.

Nin-Pratt, A., and L. McBride. 2014. "Agricultural Intensification in Ghana: Evaluating the Optimist's Case for a Green Revolution." *Food Policy* 48: 153–67.

Otsuka, K. 2015. "Future of Small Farms in Emerging Countries in Asia." National Graduate Institute for Policy Studies, Tokyo, May 30, 2015.

Otsuka, K, H. Chuma, and Y. Hayami. 1992. "Land and Labor Contracts in Agrarian Economies: Theories and Facts." *Journal of Economic Literature* 30 (4): 1965–2018.

Pender, J., F. Place, and S. K. Ehui, eds. 2006. *Strategies for Sustainable Land Management in the East African Highlands*. Washington, DC: International Food Policy Research Institute (IFPRI).

Perkins, D. H. 2013. *Agricultural Development in China: 1368–1968*, Rev. ed. Chicago: Aldine Transaction.

Pingali, P., Y. Bigot, and H. P. Binswanger. 1987. *Agricultural Mechanization and the Evolution of Farming Systems in Sub-Saharan Africa*. Baltimore: Johns Hopkins University Press for the World Bank.

Prudencio, C. Y. 1993. "Ring Management of Soils and Crops in the West African Semi-arid Tropics: The Case of the Mossi Farming System in Burkina Faso." *Agriculture, Ecosystems & Environment* 47 (3): 237–64.

Robinson, W. C. 1970. "Population Change and Agricultural Productivity in East Pakistan, 1951–1961." In *Geography and A Crowding World. A Symposium on Population Pressures upon Physical and Social Resources in the Developing Lands*, edited by W. Zelinsky, L. A. Kosiński, and R. M. Prothero, 467–83. New York: Oxford University Press.

Rosenzweig, M. R., and K. I. Wolpin. 1993. "Credit Market Constraints, Consumption Smoothing, and the Accumulation of Durable Production Assets in Low-income Countries: Investments in Bullocks in India." *Journal of Political Economy* 101 (2): 223–44.

Ruthenberg, H. 1968. *Smallholder Farming and Smallholder Development in Tanzania.* Munich: Weltforum Verlag.

Ruthenberg, H. 1980. *Farming Systems in the Tropics,* 3rd ed. Oxford: Clarendon Press.

Schelhas, J. 1996. "Land Use Choice and Change: Intensification and Diversification in the Lowland Tropics of Costa Rica." *Human Organization* 55 (3): 298–306.

Schultz, T. W. 1964. *Transforming Traditional Agriculture.* New Haven: Yale University Press.

Sourisseau, J.-M., ed. 2015. *Family Farming and the Worlds to Come.* Dordrecht: Springer.

Templeton, S. R., and S. J. Scherr. 1999. "Effects of Demographic and Related Microeconomic Change on Land Quality in Hills and Mountains of Developing Countries." *World Development* 27 (6): 903–18.

Turner, B. L., II, R. Q. Hanham, and A. V. Portararo. 1977. "Population Pressure and Agricultural Intensity." *Annals of the Association of American Geographers* 67 (3): 384–96.

Udry, C. 1995. "Risk and Saving in Northern Nigeria." *American Economic Review* 85 (5): 1287–300.

von Braun, J., and D. Lohlein. 2003. "Policy Options to Overcome Subsistence Agriculture in the CEECs." In *Subsistence Agriculture in Central and Eastern Europe: How to Break the Vicious Circle,* edited by S. Abele and K. Frohberg, 46–70. Halle: Institute of Agricultural Development in Central and Eastern Europe (IAMO).

Vosti, S. A., J. Witcover, and C. L. Carpentier. 2002. "Agricultural Intensification by Smallholders in the Western Brazilian Amazon: From Deforestation to Sustainable Land Use." Research Report 130, International Food Policy Research Institute (IFPRI), Washington, DC.

Walker, T. S., and J. G. Ryan. 1990. *Village and Household Economics in India's Semi-arid Tropics.* Baltimore: Johns Hopkins University Press.

Wiggins, S. 2000. "Interpreting Changes from the 1970s to the 1990s in African Agriculture through Village Studies." *World Development* 28 (4): 631–62.

World Bank. 2014. "Enhancing Resilience in African Drylands: Toward a Shared Development Agenda." Africa Region Flagship Report, World Bank, Washington, DC.

Zimmerman, F. J., and M. R. Carter. 2003. "Asset Smoothing, Consumption Smoothing and the Reproduction of Inequality under Risk and Subsistence Constraints." *Journal of Development Economics* 71 (2): 233–60.

8 Toward more evidence-based decision-making in the land sector

Can it help to close implementation gaps?

Klaus Deininger

Introduction

Few individuals have been as influential and effective as Hans Binswanger in documenting the impact of institutions in governing access to and use of land on socioeconomic development. He broke new ground by demonstrating that benefits from secure land rights and good land governance can be large, pro-poor, and multifaceted for many reasons. First, with land and real estate being one of a household's main assets very nearly everywhere, how ownership and access to land are defined and regulated is an important determinant of equality of opportunity, women's bargaining power, and households' ability to bear risk. Second, secure tenure provides incentives for land-attached investments to enhance productivity of land use and discourage unsustainable practices (e.g., soil mining) that generate negative externalities. Third, having land ownership documented unambiguously provides the basis for efficiency-enhancing land rental transactions to support structural transformation and growth of the rural nonfarm economy. An inverse relationship between farm size and productivity in unmechanized agriculture implies that this is unlikely to have adverse equity effects. Fourth, if land markets are sufficiently liquid and their functioning not impeded by imperfections in other markets, land can serve as collateral to allow access to financial markets for those previously excluded. These benefits are complemented by the advantages that land records provide for managing public land, planning and financing urban expansion and service provision, and guiding private investment in agriculture and beyond.

Yet, a main insight from Hans Binswanger's work is that land institutions were often established to support power structures that serve the interests of a narrow elite, rather than to maximize efficiency and social welfare (Binswanger, Deininger, and Feder 1995). A main reason is informational imperfections, rooted in land's spatial dispersion that has traditionally made creation and maintenance of land records technically complex, time-consuming, and reliant on a large institutional infrastructure. Indeed, associated agency problems have implied that land often has been at the root of the broader political economy of agrarian relations (Binswanger and Deininger 1997).

Even currently, many developing countries' land institutions may fail to harness the sector's potential, as a catalyst for changing the dynamics of gender relations, decentralization, and urbanization, due to gaps between often very progressive legal provisions and their actual implementation. Prima facie, this is due to lack of regulations needed to implement legal provisions by developing realistic implementation plans that can be monitored. Lack of awareness of rapidly expanding possibilities, the benefits they can help realize, and ways to translate these into local reality, however, also plays a part. Of course, lack of progress may be welcomed by vested interests benefiting from the status quo, which may advocate for overengineered solutions that are too complex to make quick progress, or too costly to be sustained, but that involve ample scope for discretion that can potentially be translated into rents.

We argue that recent developments involving enormous improvements in the availability of computing power, connectivity, and high-resolution, remotely sensed imagery have the potential to profoundly change this dynamic and, in doing so, provide opportunities to close implementation gaps via three channels. First, by incorporating user input – for example, having locals operate kiosks to update land information or having local para-surveyors acquire data for first-time land registration using high-resolution imagery – they can reduce the cost of implementing interventions to secure land rights sustainably by an order of magnitude, compared to earlier norms. Second, the ability to easily link land tenure to land use and to data from other domains enhances social and private benefits from land records. Examples include land use planning and land valuation that makes it easier to acquire land and to collect realistic property taxes, but also verification of compliance with private sector certification schemes or provision of location-based services. Finally, increased access to information facilitates more transparent implementation of policies by creating audit trails, allowing for the systematic incorporation of user feedback and for ensuring performance monitoring at all levels. Taken together, this opens up opportunities for more output- and performance-oriented approaches to the land sector that can profoundly change its political dynamics and the nature of programs supporting it.

Global institutions can harness this potential by documenting how new sources of data can inform policy by assessing countries' progress, via research and analytical work; providing technical guidance; building local analytical capacity; and using indicators that combine administrative, survey, and remotely sensed information, to guide design and implementation of land programs they support.

Evidence and implications of the land rights implementation gap

The literature shows that secure property rights are key determinants of equality of opportunity, including by gender; incentives for land-attached investment and higher agricultural productivity; and the operation of factor markets to bring land to its best use. Yet, it also highlights that a failure to account for the desired outcomes of political interests can lead to these political interests preventing desirable outcomes.

Benefits from good land governance and political economy challenges to achieving it

A system of (registered) property rights to land that allows unambiguous low-cost identification of landowners is part of countries' institutional infrastructure. If implemented transparently, efforts to secure land rights encourage investment and effective land use by reducing expropriation risk (Fenske 2011; Lawry et al. 2017) and facilitate market transactions (Besley and Ghatak 2010). This is important as, with economic development, new sources of insecurity, including land loss from urban expansion (Adam 2014), outside investors (Deininger and Byerlee 2011), or urban speculators (Sitko and Jayne 2014) emerge.

Demarcation of land led to higher long-term investment and freed up labor for productive uses in Benin (Goldstein et al. 2015) and increased work away from home after urban land titling in Peru (Field 2007). How land rights are distributed across household members will affect not only the efficiency of land use but also the autonomy of females. Female property rights to land and other assets can affect girls' survival rates (Qian 2008), their anthropometric status (Duflo 2003), their level of schooling (Luke and Munshi 2011; Deininger, Goyal, and Nagarajan 2013), and their ability to use economic opportunities or cope with risks (Deere et al. 2013). Joint land titling is one way to empower women (Newman, Tarp, and van den Broeck 2015) and their children (Menon, van der Meulen Rodgers, and Nguyen 2014), and experimental evidence from Tanzania suggests that spurs to put women on titles could be quite effective (Ali et al. 2016).

Economic development involves specialization and a move of part of the labor force out of the agricultural sector, creating heterogeneity in skills and scope for efficiency-enhancing land transfers. Land rental has long promoted farm pro-ductivity and structural transformation in Africa (Baland et al. 2007; Deininger, Ali, and Alemu 2008), raising land-constrained farm households' income (Jin and Jayne 2013), and allowing labor to move out of agriculture without forsak-ing their assets and the safety net their land provides (Promsopha 2015). A key reason is the inverse relationship between farm size and productivity in unmech-anized agriculture (Ali and Deininger 2015). This relationship may weaken over time, as higher wages and better labor market functioning prompt labor to move out of agriculture, increasing the sector's capital intensity (Deininger et al. 2016). In this process, less supervision-intensive technology (Deininger and Byerlee 2012; Collier and Dercon 2014) may become economically viable, and large farms' advantages in accessing credit or lumpy factors, including management skills, become more relevant.

There is no need for formal documents if land rentals remain short-term and involve only community members. Long-term leases, including with out-siders, offer possibly greater opportunities for increased productivity but may require formal records (Macours 2014), especially if migration is involved. The migration-enhancing impacts of community rights certification in Mexico, which was particularly pronounced for households with weaker initial rights (de Janvry et al. 2015), and evidence of significant and large effects of recording land rights on the rental market operation (Ali et al. 2014) support this possibility.

Full realization of gains from trade in long-term land rights requires that reasonably complete, current, and authoritative information on the assignment of property rights, normally from public registries (Arruñada 2009), be available at low cost to agents with sufficiently diverse skills to allow efficiency-enhancing transactions. Documented land rights allow trade in land and its use as collateral in financial markets. Credit impacts from land titling or registration can be expected, if land markets are sufficiently fluid and third parties, such as mortgage lenders, can access reliable registry information at low cost on a routine basis. In rural or informal settings, where these conditions are unlikely to hold, credit effects of land titling may thus be entirely absent or limited to the better off, as in Paraguay (Carter and Olinto 2003). Institutional change can still have significant effects: in India, land record computerization that reduced costs of registry access, but did not alter the information it contains, increased the number of registered mortgages and volume of credit in urban but not rural areas by 10.5 points (Deininger and Goyal 2012).

Evidence of beneficial effects from efforts to secure land rights raises the question of why interventions to this end are not adopted more broadly. Historically, a key reason is that the main objective for the creation of institutions governing access to and use of land was often not the maximization of economic efficiency but a desire to have these institutions serve the interests of ruling groups (Binswanger, Deininger, and Feder 1995) or their political power (Baland and Robinson 2008). More recently, although countries have adopted laws recognizing traditional rights and gender equality (Boone 2007), progress in putting these into practice has been slow. Important impediments come from (1) regulatory frameworks that reject gradual approaches, offering satisfactory solutions at much lower cost (e.g., demarcating outer boundaries of village or communal land, thereby allowing continued use of traditional processes internally); or (2) new technology (use of unmanned aerial vehicles or drones to acquire high-resolution imagery). This may prevent realization of well-documented benefits (Jacoby and Minten 2007) or development of parallel systems. Overcoming the bureaucratic risk aversion and inertia at the root of this by providing an overarching vision, and by documenting progress toward reaching it, also helps draw in and create awareness among other stakeholders to contribute to overcoming such bottlenecks and avoiding the negative impacts of implementation gaps.

Implications of implementation gaps

While customary institutions can offer high tenure security if population is low (Bruce and Migot-Adholla 1994), they can become less equitable under growing land scarcity (Guirkinger and Platteau 2014), creating scope for appropriation of land by chiefs or high levels of tenure insecurity with negative production and equity effects. For example, in Malawi, 22 percent of smallholders under customary tenure express fear of losing their land, and in addition to reducing investment, this perception is associated with a 10 percent direct reduction in productivity for women but not men (Deininger and Xia 2016a).

The foregoing example highlights that, despite laws mandating gender equality, women may disproportionately suffer from tenure insecurity (Adelman and Peterman 2014) and conflicts (Deininger and Castagnini 2006; Joireman 2008), often related to inheritance (Chapoto, Jayne, and Mason 2011). Legal reforms allowing women to inherit land increased their asset ownership (Deininger, Goyal, and Nagarajan 2013) and benefited their offspring (Deininger et al. 2014), but even the legal basis for women to inherit land often does not exist (Peterman 2012).

Secular urbanization trends have greatly increased (peri-) urban land values. Land and property taxes are progressive and create incentives to put land to productive use. Weak tax maps or an inability to charge meaningful rates, however, implies that land yields only a fraction of its potential value (Franzsen and McCluskey 2016), making it difficult to provide services and increasing dependence on central transfers. Weak property tax systems reduce local governments' incentives to plan land use and provide infrastructure or services proactively rather than reactively. They foster reliance on distortionary and welfare-reducing transfer fees (Dachis, Duranton, and Turner 2012), driving transactions underground or encouraging underreporting of sales prices. Remotely sensed imagery allows for the creation of tax maps to harness this potential, while registry data on sales values allows for the implementation of mass valuation that yields more revenues than alternatives.

Inadequate land information also affects processes of expropriation and compensation. If land records are weak, acquiring land that has been expropriated to "purge" other claims may provide more security than direct acquisition, thus raising demand for the latter, and creating policy challenges (Nath et al. 2013; Ghatak and Mookherjee 2014). Perceived threats of expropriation without proper compensation may imply that productive land with good market access may not be used for production, as in China (Deininger and Xia 2016a) or Nigeria (Deininger, Xia, and Savastano 2015). Similarly, establishment of the institutional infrastructure to improve countries' ability to cope with interest by agricultural investors (Deininger and Byerlee 2011), including the ability to vet investors' business plans, provide advice to affected communities, and independently verify compliance with contract terms, has been slow, increasing reputational risks and compliance costs for potential investors, and possibly jeopardizing large investments, including in contract farming (see more in the subsequent section on documentation of large agricultural investments).

Although land providing public amenities (roads, parks, schools, hospitals) should be held by the state, unclear ways to acquire, manage, or (if unused) divest it create scope for corruption. To avoid such corruption, expropriation should be limited to public purpose and implemented transparently, and with effective appeals mechanisms. Divesting public land no longer needed should be by open tender, publicity of key contractual conditions, and audited. Most importantly, public land needs to be mapped, and encroachment monitored and swiftly dealt with. Doing this with traditional means is costly, but free availability of medium-resolution imagery at high frequencies creates opportunities to monitor land use, which, if combined with maps of public land, could allow major advances in this respect.

New opportunities to bridge implementation gaps

African examples highlight how new technologies can help to overcome traditional implementation gaps. Rwanda's implementation of low-cost and participatory first-time registration illustrates the importance of a stepwise and evidence-based approach with associated investment and empowerment benefits. Experience in Ethiopia, Mozambique, and Malawi illustrates that, even for a topic as emotionally charged as that of large-scale land acquisition, combining different sources of information allows better policy choices to benefit local people.

Low-cost land adjudication

Land tenure regularization in Rwanda illustrates low-cost, "fit for purpose" approaches (Enemark et al. 2014) that make use of new technology and carefully adapt it to local circumstances, with impacts monitored in real time so as to be able to adapt and subsequently upgrade, if needed. With land scarcity and insecure land tenure having been identified as proximate causes of the 1994 genocide (André and Platteau 1998), Rwandan policymakers recognized that addressing land tenure was key for sustainable development, and that there were important gender dimensions. This led to adoption of the 1999 inheritance law to eliminate widespread bias against female land ownership (Daley, Dore-Weeks, and Umuhoza 2010), followed by the 2004 land policy, the 2005 organic land law, and establishment of institutional and administrative structures for land management and administration, consisting of District Land Bureaus, complemented by Sector and Cell Committees, to take responsibility for land administration and planning.

Given the near complete absence of registered land rights, and the lack of examples to be readily drawn on, in 2007–10 a pilot to register some 15,000 parcels was undertaken in four cells reflecting the diversity of the country. A process for systematic, low-cost demarcation and adjudication using aerial photography or high-resolution satellite imagery was designed and implemented via trained local para-surveyors. The latter recorded, in public and with the presence of neighbors and local authorities, agreed-upon plot boundaries on the images, possibly after minor disputes had been resolved by local elders. This led to the issuance of a demarcation slip, generation of a unique parcel ID, registration of a claim, and issuance of a claim receipt to the owner.

Data were then computerized, and results were displayed publicly on office walls at the cell level for a period of at least one month, in which objections could be raised and corrections made as needed. Once satisfactorily completed, titles and lease certificates were issued at the central level and distributed to landowners.

An evaluation of the pilot exercise suggests impacts in three areas: (1) improved land access for legally married women and better recordation of inheritance rights, although women who were not legally married saw diminished property rights, an issue that was corrected before embarking on the national rollout; (2) significant investment impacts – for example, a doubling of the change in investment in soil conservation – that were particularly pronounced for female-headed households in line with the notion that these households had suffered from higher levels of insecurity before; and (3) a marginal reduction in land market activity, rather than a wave of distress sales (Ali, Deininger, and Goldstein 2014).

The fact that the processes had been thoroughly refined, based on review of the pilot experience, allowed rapid scale-up and rollout as a national program. In less than three years, the Rwanda Natural Resource Authority (RNRA) demarcated almost all of the country's estimated 11.5 million land parcels at less than US$6 per parcel (Nkurunziza 2015). A rigorous evaluation, based on 2012 data, suggests that the program improved land rental market functioning and efficiency-enhancing land transfers (Ali et al. 2015), and that tenure security increased for males and females, including those not legally married, implying that modifications to implementation modalities to include women in informal marriages were effective. Administrative data in Table 8.1 show that: (1) 11.42 million parcels (64.3 percent in agricultural, 11.7 percent in residential, 8 percent in forest, 1.5 percent in commercial, and 0.3 percent in administrative use) were registered; (2) 86 percent of the parcels owned by natural persons have a woman either as sole (25 percent) or co-owner (61 percent), with only 14 percent registered exclusively to males – supporting empowerment effects found also elsewhere (Santos, Fletschner, and Daconto 2014); and (3) claimants are not yet recorded for 16 percent of the parcels. Availability of such data in near-real time, at zero marginal cost, and at high levels of granularity allows regular follow-up performance monitoring.

Documenting extent and spillover effects from large agricultural investment

Few topics have been as politically charged as the issue of large-scale land acquisition (Arezki, Deininger, and Selod 2015). To show how data can benefit this debate, Ali, Deininger, and Harris (2015b) reported results from administering an improved questionnaire in Ethiopia's annual census of commercial farms (>10 ha) and analyzing it jointly with more than ten years' data from the country's smallholder survey. Four results stand out. First, since the 1990s, about 1.3 million ha were transferred to 6,612 commercial farms, some 78 percent

Table 8.1 Number and size of registered parcels by type in Rwanda as of December 31, 2015

	Total	Kigali city	Southern	Western	Northern	Eastern
Total no. of parcels						
Total no. of registered parcels	11,420,885	390,788	3,217,847	3,157,232	2,668,212	1,986,806
. . . of which residential	1,341,467	134,203	227,046	419,683	147,693	412,842
. . . of which commercial	169,709	4,369	16,671	117,303	17,272	14,094
. . . of which agricultural	7,344,802	198,262	1,997,104	1,919,423	1,951,886	1,278,127
. . . of which forest	916,359	13,875	262,232	322,117	267,162	50,973
. . . of which admin./ science/social	29,749	1,891	7,503	9,128	4,401	6,826
. . . of which not categorized	1,618,799	38,188	707,291	369,578	279,798	223,944
Parcel size (ha)	0.18	0.18	0.17	0.13	0.11	0.38
. . . for residential land	0.13	0.09	0.15	0.11	0.13	0.16
. . . for agric. land	0.19	0.20	0.17	0.12	0.11	0.42
Share of parcels by claimant type						
Natural person	0.80	0.86	0.72	0.83	0.83	0.81
Non-natural person	0.05	0.02	0.09	0.03	0.03	0.03
Claimant not yet registered	0.16	0.12	0.19	0.14	0.14	0.16
Share of parcels by claimant's gender						
Female only	0.25	0.23	0.26	0.25	0.23	0.24
Male only	0.14	0.17	0.19	0.13	0.10	0.14
Male and female jointly	0.61	0.60	0.55	0.62	0.67	0.62

Source: Rwanda Natural Resource Authority (RNRA), Land Administration Information System (LAIS).

Note: Gender of owners is reported only for parcels registered in the name of natural persons.

of which cultivated more than 50 ha. Even at the peak of the "land rush," the amount of land transferred to commercial agricultural investors, mostly Ethiopians, was much less than claimed in some popular reports (Horne et al. 2011). After 2011, levels of annual land transfers reverted more or less to the levels reached before 2007. Second, largely due to technology and labor constraints, about 55 percent of land transferred remains unutilized. Third, with one permanent job per 20 ha, labor intensity remains low and direct employment generation limited, as are direct benefits to neighboring smallholders: only 36 percent of large farms paid lease fees, investments focused on land clearing and machinery rather than public goods, and less than 20 percent of large farms accessed credit, making them unlikely candidates for expansion of credit to smallholders. Finally, for most crops, commercial farms' yields (on cultivated rather than owned area) peak highest in the 10–20 ha category at about 50 percent above smallholders' yields. If attributable to efficiency rather than more intensive input use or better endowments, this can make positive spillovers from commercial to neighboring smallholder farms plausible.

Study of indirect effects can rely on availability of farm coordinates that allow us to calculate, for every village and year, the distance to the next large farm (or for crop-specific spillovers to the next large farm growing the same crop) and the total area cultivated by large farms (with the same crop) in concentric circles of 0–25, 25–50, and 50–100 km radii around it. Results for Ethiopia in 2004–13 suggest that modest technology spillovers on smallholders in close proximity (<25 km) exist for maize, which is grown by large and small farms using similar technology (Ali, Deininger, and Harris 2015a). A more strategic approach to attracting investors, possibly clustered to facilitate infrastructure access and focus on crops with high labor demand and value-added, may be desirable – a direction indeed chosen by the government.

In Mozambique, analysis of the effects from establishment of large farms in 2012–14 on smallholders' adoption of cultural practices and modern inputs suggests that effects occur in close proximity to new large farms (Table 8.2). Large farm establishment within 25 km is estimated to have led to 7.3 and 6.1 points of increases in crop rotation and intercropping, compared to the base category of a large farm having opened within a 100–250 km radius. For animal traction, the estimated effect is 4.9 points, similar to line sowing (4.9 points) and intercropping (6.2 points), compared to insignificant effects for crop rotation at the distance of 25–50 km. The opening of large farms within 25 km is estimated to have led to 3.3, 1.7, or 2.7 points of increase in the incidence of improved seed, fertilizer, and pesticide use, respectively – an effect that carries over to the 25–50 km radius for fertilizer. Except for intercropping (5.4 points), new large farms at 50–100 km distance have little effect. Although this suggests modestly positive impacts of large farm establishment on factor market operation and agronomic practices, Table 8.2 also implies that, over the time horizon considered here, establishment of large farms did not improve neighboring small farmers' access to off-farm jobs or factor and output markets. No effect on area cultivated is found, possibly because focus is on the short-term effects. At the same time, having seen a new large farm established in the immediate vicinity (< 25 km) is estimated to have resulted in an increase (by 4.2 points) in the likelihood of small farmers' feeling worse off than three years ago previously (Deininger and Xia 2016b).

Although most of the "land grab" debate focuses on allocation of hitherto uncultivated land to investors, investors' failure to use land received in line with contractual stipulations may be more relevant in the long term, especially if land is not transferable and concessions need to be canceled or reassigned by the public sector. Malawi, where about 1 million ha (more than 20 percent of the country's arable land) was transferred to estates, mainly under 21-year leases, in the late 1980s, illustrates the issues and the scope of data to inform policy. As paper-based records made it impossible to assess size and location of unused estate land with expired leases that could potentially be reassigned to other users,

Table 8.2 Estimated impact of proximity to newly formed large farms on smallholders' modern input use, Mozambique

	Agronomic practices			Modern input use			Situation now vs. 3 years ago	
	Rotation	Intercropping	Line sowing	Improved seed	Fertilizer	Pesticide	Better	Worse
Panel A								
Any new large farm <= 25 km	0.073***	0.061**	−0.001	0.033*	0.017*	0.027**	−0.019	0.042**
	(0.027)	(0.024)	(0.029)	(0.018)	(0.009)	(0.011)	(0.026)	(0.021)
Any new large farm 25–50 km	0.009	0.062**	0.049*	0.019	0.024***	0.012	0.021	−0.009
	(0.030)	(0.025)	(0.029)	(0.016)	(0.009)	(0.014)	(0.027)	(0.022)
Any new large farm 50–100 km	0.031	0.054**	−0.013	−0.013	−0.005	−0.001	−0.015	0.034
	(0.032)	(0.026)	(0.031)	(0.014)	(0.009)	(0.014)	(0.027)	(0.022)
Observations	12,202	12,202	12,202	12,202	12,202	12,202	12,202	12,202
R-squared	0.168	0.194	0.295	0.166	0.307	0.251	0.174	0.153
Panel B								
New large farm area <= 25 km	0.012**	0.012***	−0.002	0.003	0.004**	0.003*	−0.006	0.008**
	(0.005)	(0.004)	(0.005)	(0.004)	(0.002)	(0.002)	(0.005)	(0.004)
New large farm area 25–50 km	0.006	0.011***	0.007	0.006**	0.003**	0.003	0.002	0.004
	(0.005)	(0.004)	(0.005)	(0.003)	(0.001)	(0.002)	(0.004)	(0.004)
New large farm area 50–100 km	0.003	0.008*	0.003	0.001	0.001	0.003	0.001	0.002
	(0.005)	(0.004)	(0.004)	(0.002)	(0.001)	(0.002)	(0.004)	(0.003)
Observations	12,202	12,202	12,202	12,202	12,202	12,202	12,202	12,202
R-squared	0.168	0.193	0.295	0.166	0.308	0.251	0.174	0.154

Source: Author's computation based on household survey data.

Note: Other control variables included throughout but not reported are farm size, household composition (number of children, adults, and older people), headship, head's age, highest level of education in the household, a time dummy, and rainfall shocks. Enumeration area (EA) fixed effects are included throughout, and standard errors are clustered by EA.

* p<0.1
** p<0.05
*** p<0.01

Table 8.3 Comparing land tenure and land use, Malawi

	Total	Land use type		Lease status		
		Agric.	Non-agric.	Valid	Expired	Unclear
Characteristics of leases						
Area in ha	23.21	31.21	6.33	22.68	22.57	25.38
Annual rent in $ per ha	6.76	0.79	19.36	20.55	3.46	0.46
Lease status unclear	0.26	0.15	0.47	0.00	0.00	1.00
Length of lease	36.74	23.34	79.77	75.67	20.36	33.52
Signed before 1988	0.17	0.15	0.26	0.10	0.19	0.87
Signed 1988 to 1995	0.19	0.05	0.64	0.66	0.00	0.05
Signed after 1995	0.63	0.81	0.10	0.24	0.81	0.07
Lease still valid	0.22	0.11	0.44	1.00	0.00	0.00
Lease expired	0.52	0.74	0.08	0.00	1.00	0.00
Deed plan exists	0.07	0.01	0.19	0.22	0.02	0.04
Size less than 10 ha	0.37	0.08	0.98	0.74	0.09	0.68
Size between 10 and 30 ha	0.53	0.78	0.01	0.21	0.77	0.27
Size between 30 and 50 ha	0.06	0.08	0.00	0.01	0.09	0.02
Size greater than 50 ha	0.04	0.06	0.01	0.03	0.05	0.04
Land use						
Crops	0.48	0.50	0.40	0.44	0.50	0.47
Pasture	0.16	0.17	0.13	0.14	0.16	0.15
Shrub	0.19	0.21	0.10	0.13	0.22	0.15
Trees	0.09	0.09	0.11	0.09	0.09	0.10
Bare/buildings	0.08	0.03	0.25	0.19	0.03	0.13
No. of observations	18,467	12,322	6,145	4,054	9,627	4,786

Source: Based on interim results from Malawi land use monitoring.

digitization of lease documents and estate boundaries was embarked upon as a first step. This also allows automated land use classification, based on medium-resolution imagery (satellite imagery). Initial results suggest only some 60 percent of estate land is cultivated (Table 8.3), pointing toward scope for policies to improve land use and allowing for pinpointing of relevant areas.

Can good land governance and transparency be self-sustaining?

Consistent reporting on comparable land indicators across countries can address political economy issues by setting into motion competition between countries. The World Bank's "Doing Business" (DB) indicators illustrate how this can create incentives for policy reform. At the national level, the case of Rwanda highlights the usefulness of data for monitoring at all levels and the scope for realizing synergies by linking with administrative data and land use information.

Monitoring at the global level: The Land Administration Quality Index (LAQI)

As access to land has been consistently identified as a key bottleneck for investors, an indicator that measured time, cost, and number of procedures needed to transfer commercial property (a registered and surveyed warehouse outside the main business city) has been part of the standard set of DB indicators since 2005. Recognition that this indicator may fail to cover aspects such as reliability, coverage, and transparency led to the definition of a Land Administration Quality Index (LAQI) covering these aspects.

Key LAQI variables for 189 countries in Table 8.4 highlight a number of issues. First, implementation gaps are nearly universal. High legal scores, with 90 percent of the countries – 94 percent in Latin America and the Caribbean (LAC) and

Table 8.4 Key dimensions of land administration quality globally

	Total	EAP	ECA	LAC	MENA	OECD	SAS	SSA
Land registration infrastructure								
Records fully digital	0.17	0.08	0.36	0.00	0.14	0.52	0.13	0.04
Records scanned	0.43	0.36	0.60	0.59	0.48	0.42	0.13	0.30
Records paper only	0.39	0.52	0.04	0.41	0.38	0.06	0.75	0.66
Electronic database for encumbrances	0.51	0.36	0.92	0.56	0.52	0.90	0.00	0.17
Maps fully digital	0.31	0.24	0.48	0.31	0.14	0.81	0.13	0.04
Maps scanned	0.25	0.28	0.44	0.34	0.33	0.13	0.00	0.15
Maps paper only	0.44	0.48	0.08	0.34	0.52	0.06	0.88	0.81
Maps are stored in electronic database	0.47	0.44	0.76	0.50	0.38	0.94	0.13	0.11
Records and maps in linked databases	0.39	0.28	0.32	0.28	0.71	0.65	0.13	0.30
Records and maps in integrated database	0.11	0.04	0.40	0.03	0.10	0.19	0.00	0.00
Cadastre and registry use a unique ID	0.61	0.64	0.88	0.31	0.81	0.84	0.38	0.45
Transparency and information access								
Records freely accessible	0.15	0.08	0.16	0.22	0.00	0.39	0.00	0.09
Record access at most by intermediaries	0.31	0.32	0.32	0.13	0.62	0.13	0.50	0.38
Records accessible online	0.34	0.12	0.72	0.31	0.14	0.87	0.13	0.04

	Total	EAP	ECA	LAC	MENA	OECD	SAS	SSA
Registration requirements online	0.53	0.48	0.88	0.53	0.57	0.77	0.38	0.23
Registration fee schedule online	0.55	0.44	0.84	0.56	0.43	0.97	0.38	0.26
Registration service standards exist and online	0.25	0.32	0.64	0.22	0.05	0.32	0.13	0.09
Registry complaints mechanism exists	0.09	0.16	0.12	0.13	0.00	0.19	0.00	0.00
Official registry statistics is public	0.26	0.20	0.56	0.09	0.24	0.58	0.13	0.06
Maps freely accessible	0.24	0.12	0.28	0.25	0.19	0.61	0.00	0.09
Map access at most by intermediaries	0.33	0.40	0.20	0.13	0.52	0.03	0.63	0.55
Cadastral fee schedule online	0.42	0.32	0.88	0.41	0.24	0.68	0.00	0.21
Cadastre service standards exist and online	0.14	0.20	0.36	0.13	0.05	0.16	0.13	0.04
Cadastre complaints mechanism exists	0.06	0.12	0.08	0.06	0.00	0.13	0.00	0.00
Geographic coverage								
All private plots in country registered	0.22	0.24	0.32	0.03	0.14	0.68	0.13	0.04
All private plots in main city registered	0.42	0.56	0.56	0.16	0.48	0.90	0.25	0.15
All private plots in country mapped	0.24	0.28	0.40	0.03	0.14	0.71	0.13	0.02
All private plots in main city mapped	0.46	0.52	0.60	0.31	0.48	0.97	0.25	0.13
Dispute resolution and legal reliability								
Law requires registration of transactions	0.90	0.80	1.00	0.94	0.86	0.94	0.88	0.89
Property registration is guaranteed	0.78	0.72	0.88	0.78	0.71	0.97	0.38	0.72
Compensation mechanism is in place	0.29	0.24	0.60	0.31	0.10	0.52	0.00	0.11
Documents checked before registration	0.96	0.84	1.00	0.97	1.00	1.00	1.00	0.96
Parties' ID to be checked at registration	0.98	0.88	1.00	1.00	1.00	1.00	1.00	0.98
Use of national ID database to check	0.46	0.48	0.56	0.56	0.43	0.58	0.25	0.28
Statistics on land disputes available	0.12	0.16	0.36	0.03	0.05	0.19	0.00	0.02
No. of countries reporting	189	25	25	32	21	31	8	47

Source: Author's computation based on 2016 LAQI data.

Note: Data collected in the 2016 round of "Doing Business."

89 percent in sub-Saharan Africa (SSA) – requiring registration, 96 percent check-ing documents, and 78 percent having a state guarantee, contrast with limited coverage: all private plots in the country (or the main city) are registered in 22 per-cent (42 percent) of countries overall; 3 percent (16 percent) in Latin America, 4 percent (15 percent) in SSA, and 68 percent (90 percent) in the countries of the Organisation for Economic Co-operation and Development (OECD).

Second, as land rights are real rights, registration requires not only the owners' name but also a description of agreed-upon property boundaries, normally as a survey or sketch map. The quality of infrastructure to record the textual and spatial elements of land rights varies widely: 39 percent of countries (from 75 percent for South Asia to 4 percent in Eastern Europe and Central Asia) rely exclusively on paper records. Paper maps, which make rational land use plan-ning difficult in the best of circumstances, are still almost exclusively used in regions such as South Asia (88 percent) and SSA (81 percent) that are urbanizing rapidly. Integration of textual and spatial records, a precondition for harnessing the benefits from systematic recording, remains limited; compared to 50 percent of countries globally, only 26 percent, 32 percent, and 41 percent in South Asia, East Asia, and SSA, respectively, have a link between databases. Still, having some developing countries achieve scores well above those of OECD countries high-lights the scope for leapfrogging and for a global indicator to create incentives for improved performance.

Illustrating the opportunities for country-level monitoring

Even if land rights are registered, sustainability may be jeopardized if low perceived benefits and high costs of doing so – due to fees and complex pro-cesses – result in failure to register subsequent transactions, as documented for Africa (Atwood 1990; Pinckney and Kimuyu 1994); Latin America (Barnes and Griffith-Charles 2007; Galiani and Schargrodsky 2011); and Asia (Maurer and Iyer 2008). Rwanda's case shows how administrative data can provide real-time information on sustainability overall and its dimensions (e.g., by gender) at any level of disaggregation, thus allowing targeted follow-up.

Data on transactions, gender of newly registered owners, and mortgages in 2014 and 2015 show much higher levels of registered transfers for residential (0.8 percent and 0.4 percent for sales and others, respectively) than agricultural land (0.1 percent and 0.06 percent for sales and others, respectively). Survey-based evi-dence of much higher transaction volumes in rural areas suggests that many sub-sequent transfers remain informal, requiring policymakers' attention (Table 8.5). Panel C shows that 77 percent of subsequently registered parcels, compared to 86 percent for first registration (Table 8.1), include a woman, so that gender equality may also warrant attention. Panel D, based on direct entries by banks, shows that since 2013 US$2.6 billion of mortgage lending was secured by 49,694 mortgages (65 percent, 30 percent, and 5 percent residential, agricultural, and commercial land/property, respectively). Beyond monitoring land prices, information from the registry can help identify and close tax gaps. Linkage to tax data at the par-cel level suggests that in 2015 only a third of Kigali's residential properties paid

Table 8.5 Characteristics of registered transactions, Rwanda, 2014 and 2015

	Total	Kigali city	Province			
			Southern	*Western*	*Northern*	*Eastern*
Panel A: Transactions involving residential land						
Totals						
All	31,209	16,710	4,234	2,805	2,141	5,319
Sales	21,367	15,145	1,504	1,240	827	2,651
Sale value ($/m²)	30.07	39.38	9.92	14.41	12.41	4.75
Others	10,038	1,665	2,762	1,606	1,319	2,686
Percentage of registered parcels transferred annually						
All	1.16	6.23	0.93	0.33	0.72	0.64
Sales	0.80	5.64	0.33	0.15	0.28	0.32
Others	0.37	0.62	0.61	0.19	0.45	0.33
Panel B: Transactions involving agricultural land						
Total number of transactions						
All	22,850	6,635	3,996	2,390	3,994	5,835
Sales	14,497	6,087	2,178	1,234	1,971	3,027
Others	8,510	609	1,855	1,180	2,033	2,833
Sale value ($/m²)	4.45	6.65	3.70	3.57	3.91	1.47
Percentage of registered parcels transferred annually						
All	0.16	1.67	0.10	0.06	0.10	0.23
Sales	0.10	1.54	0.05	0.03	0.05	0.12
Others	0.06	0.15	0.05	0.03	0.05	0.11
Panel C: Gender of newly registered land owners						
New registrations by gender						
Female only	0.15	0.16	0.16	0.14	0.12	0.15
Male only	0.23	0.22	0.25	0.22	0.19	0.25
Joint	0.62	0.62	0.58	0.64	0.68	0.60
Panel D: Characteristics of registered mortgages						
All mortgages						
Amount (US$ billion)	2.604	1.66	0.173	0.307	0.164	0.3
No. of mortgages	49,694	19,285	7,371	6,682	6,888	9,468
Avg. amount	42,247	86,296	23,488	45,909	23,839	31,705
No. of cells	2148	161	532	538	414	503

Source: Rwanda Natural Resource Authority (RNRA); Land Administration Information System (LAIS).

required fees, implying lost annual revenue of US$4.8 million, a figure that could increase to US$20 million, if actual land prices were used for assessment.

To reduce informality of subsequent transactions, the government placed "sector land managers" (SLMs) in all of the country's 416 sectors, in a phased manner over a period of two years, and conducted awareness campaigns (referred to as "land week") to alert landholders of registration requirements. Results from regressing quarterly numbers of registered market- and non-market transfers for agricultural or residential land on SLMs' presence and characteristics (all from administrative data) and conduct of "land week" events show how administrative data provide a low-cost way to rigorously assess impacts of this intervention (Table 8.6). Using cell fixed effects, SLM appointment is estimated to have

Table 8.6 Determinants of registered transactions at cell level, Rwanda 2014 and 2015

	Agricultural land		Residential land	
	Sale	Inheritance	Sale	Inheritance
Sector land manager appointed	0.594**	−0.081	0.896**	−0.254
	(0.251)	(0.106)	(0.425)	(0.162)
Female sector land manager	−0.074	−0.001	−0.504	0.023
	(0.337)	(0.165)	(0.414)	(0.288)
SLM knowledge	0.383	−0.077	−0.008	0.018
	(0.287)	(0.140)	(0.376)	(0.219)
SLM had taken a refresher training	0.497**	−0.170	0.034	−0.102
	(0.248)	(0.105)	(0.396)	(0.183)
SLM previously worked at the DLO	0.316	−0.084	0.026	0.397
	(0.969)	(0.274)	(1.473)	(0.428)
Sector covered by land week events	−0.071	0.110*	−0.046	0.104
	(0.077)	(0.061)	(0.114)	(0.111)
Sector land manager × land week	−0.038	0.030	−0.065	0.043
	(0.270)	(0.127)	(0.326)	(0.186)
Kigali × 2015	2.120***	0.390***	4.794***	0.534***
	(0.534)	(0.091)	(0.866)	(0.147)
South × 2015	0.524***	−0.302***	0.377*	−0.622***
	(0.162)	(0.112)	(0.208)	(0.168)
West × 2015	0.144	−0.144**	0.262	−0.295**
	(0.111)	(0.056)	(0.178)	(0.135)
North × 2015	0.735***	−0.391***	0.160	−0.213
	(0.157)	(0.122)	(0.185)	(0.171)
East × 2015	1.140***	−0.462***	1.096***	−0.512***
	(0.159)	(0.083)	(0.244)	(0.126)
No. of observations (cell × quarter)	16,776	16,776	16,776	16,776
R^2	0.135	0.024	0.079	0.015

Source: Author's computation based on data from SLM survey combined with LAIS data.

Note: Dependent variable is the number of registered sale or inheritance transactions for each cell and quarter in 2014 and 2015 based on LAIS data. Regressions include cell fixed effects and constant (not reported).

* Significant at 10%
** Significant at 5%
*** Significant at 1%

increased the number of registered sales transactions by 0.89 (0.59) for residential (agricultural) land. While a female SLM dummy is insignificant, SLMs who have taken refresher training are estimated to increase the number of registered sales transactions of agricultural land by 0.5, but have no impact on residential land.

Conclusion and policy implications

If used effectively, new technologies can improve land sector performance by (1) reducing the costs of efforts to secure land rights and calibrating impacts of policy measures; (2) increasing benefits from land registries by realizing synergies from linking land information to other data sources (banks, courts, taxation, land use); and (3) improving accountability and participation through greater transparency of public programs and overall sector strategies. This could narrow implementation gaps and allow for an adoption of an evidence-driven and results-based approach to supporting the land sector.

Harnessing this potential will require action from global institutions in three areas. First, the implementation status of national land policies should be regularly monitored using administrative data on (1) coverage with textual and spatial land records; (2) levels of registered transactions by gender with focus on sales/ mortgages; (3) property taxes; (4) expropriations; and (5) land-related disputes. This can build on advances made in different parts of the world. Second, there is a need to better document benefits derived from improving performance of land sector institutions, and on this basis, identify ways in which those who may lose out from change can be compensated or gain. Well-designed "experimental" approaches can help to rigorously assess impacts in a non-confrontational way and use experience from doing so to prepare regulations to facilitate larger-scale application. Third, routine use of evidence-based and data-driven approaches to design and implement land programs will set proper incentives, support global benchmarking, and strengthen local analytical capacity. Taken together, these actions can help to address deep-rooted political economy issues in the land sector, the importance of which Hans Binswanger's work helped us appreciate.

References

Adam, A. G. 2014. "Land Tenure in the Changing Peri-Urban Areas of Ethiopia: The Case of Bahir Dar City." *International Journal of Urban and Regional Research* 38 (6): 1970–84.

Adelman, S., and A. Peterman. 2014. "Resettlement and Gender Dimensions of Land Rights in Post-Conflict Northern Uganda." *World Development* 64: 583–96.

Ali, D. A., M. Collin, K. Deininger, S. Dercon, J. Sandefur, and A. Zeitlin. 2016. "Small Price Incentives Increase Women's Access to Land Titles in Tanzania." *Journal of Development Economics* 123: 107–122.

Ali, D. A., and K. Deininger. 2015. "Is There a Farm Size-Productivity Relationship in African Agriculture? Evidence from Rwanda." *Land Economics* 91 (2): 317–43.

Ali, D. A., K. Deininger, and M. Goldstein. 2014. "Environmental and Gender Impacts of Land Tenure Regularization in Africa: Pilot Evidence from Rwanda." *Journal of Development Economics* 110: 262–75.

Ali, D. A., K. Deininger, M. Goldstein, and E. La Ferrara. 2015. "Investment and Market Impacts of Land Tenure Regularization in Rwanda." Policy Research Paper, World Bank, Washington, DC.

Ali, D. A., K. Deininger, M. Goldstein, E. La Ferrara, and M. Duponchel. 2014. "Determinants of Participation and Transaction Cost in Rwanda's Land Markets." Case Study, Development Research Group, World Bank, Washington, DC.

Ali, D. A., K. Deininger, and A. Harris. 2015a "Large Farm Establishment, Smallholder Productivity, Labor Market Participation, and Resilience: Evidence from Ethiopia." Policy Research Working Paper No. 7576, World Bank, Washington, DC.

Ali, D. A., K. Deininger, and A. Harris. 2015b. "Using National Statistics to Increase Transparency of Large Land Acquisition: Evidence from Ethiopia." Policy Research Working Paper 7342, World Bank, Washington, DC.

André, C., and J. P. Platteau. 1998. "Land Relations under Unbearable Stress: Rwanda Caught in the Malthusian Trap." *Journal of Economic Behavior & Organization* 34 (1): 1–47.

Arezki, R., K. Deininger, and H. Selod. 2015. "What Drives the Global 'Land Rush'?" *World Bank Economic Review* 29 (2): 207–33.

Arruñada, B. 2009. *Building Market Institutions: Property Rights, Business Formalization, and Economic Development*. Chicago: University of Chicago Press.

Atwood, D. A. 1990. "Land Registration in Africa: The Impact on Agricultural Production." *World Development* 18 (5): 659–71.

Baland, J.-M., F. Gaspart, J. P. Platteau, and F. Place. 2007. "The Distributive Impact of Land Markets in Uganda." *Economic Development and Cultural Change* 55 (2): 283–311.

Baland, J. M., and J. A. Robinson. 2008. "Land and Power: Theory and Evidence from Chile." *American Economic Review* 98 (5): 1737–65.

Barnes, G., and C. Griffith-Charles. 2007. "Assessing the Formal Land Market and Deformalization of Property in St. Lucia." *Land Use Policy* 24 (2): 494–501.

Besley, T., and M. Ghatak. 2010. "Property Rights and Economic Development." In *Handbook of Economic Development*, Vol. 5, edited by D. Rodrik and M. R. Rosenzweig, 4525–95. Amsterdam: North Holland.

Binswanger, H. P., and K. Deininger. 1997. "Explaining Agricultural and Agrarian Policies in Developing Countries." *Journal of Economic Literature* 35 (4): 1958–2005.

Binswanger, H. P., K. Deininger, and G. Feder. 1995. "Power, Distortions, Revolt and Reform in Agricultural Land Relations." In *Handbook of Development Economics*, Vol. 3B, edited by J. Behrman and T. N. Srinivasan, 2659–772. Amsterdam: North Holland.

Boone, C. 2007. "Property and Constitutional Order: Land Tenure Reform and the Future of the African State." *African Affairs* 106 (425): 557–86.

Bruce, J. W., and S. E. Migot-Adholla. 1994. *Searching for Land Tenure Security in Africa*. Dubuque, IA: Kendall/Hunt.

Carter, M. R., and P. Olinto. 2003. "Getting Institutions 'Right' for Whom? Credit Constraints and the Impact of Property Rights on the Quantity and Composition of Investment." *American Journal of Agricultural Economics* 85 (1): 173–86.

Chapoto, A., T. S. Jayne, and N. M. Mason. 2011. "Widows' Land Security in the Era of HIV/AIDS: Panel Survey Evidence from Zambia." *Economic Development and Cultural Change* 59 (3): 511–47.

Collier, P., and S. Dercon. 2014. "African Agriculture in 50 Years: Smallholders in a Rapidly Changing World?" *World Development* 63: 92–101.

Dachis, B., G. Duranton, and M. A. Turner. 2012. "The Effects of Land Transfer Taxes on Real Estate Markets: Evidence from a Natural Experiment in Toronto." *Journal of Economic Geography* 12 (2): 327–54.

Daley, E., R. Dore-Weeks, and C. Umuhoza. 2010. "Ahead of the Game: Land Tenure Reform in Rwanda and the Process of Securing Women's Land Rights." *Journal of Eastern African Studies* 4 (1): 131–52.

Deere, C. D., A. D. Oduro, H. Swaminathan, and C. Doss. 2013. "Property Rights and the Gender Distribution of Wealth in Ecuador, Ghana and India." *Journal of Economic Inequality* 11 (2): 249–65.

Deininger, K., D. A. Ali, and T. Alemu. 2008. "Assessing the Functioning of Land Rental Markets in Ethiopia." *Economic Development and Cultural Change* 57 (1): 67–100.

Deininger, K., and D. Byerlee. 2011. *Rising Global Interest in Farmland: Can It Yield Sustainable and Equitable Benefits?* Washington, DC: World Bank.

Deininger, K., and D. Byerlee. 2012. "The Rise of Large Farms in Land Abundant Countries: Do They Have a Future?" *World Development* 40 (4): 701–14.

Deininger, K., and R. Castagnini. 2006. "Incidence and Impact of Land Conflict in Uganda." *Journal of Economic Behavior & Organization* 60 (3): 321–45.

Deininger, K., X. Fang, S. Jin, and H. K. Nagarajan. 2014. "Inheritance Law Reform, Empowerment, and Human Capital Accumulation: Second-Generation Effects from India." Policy Research Working Paper 7086, World Bank, Washington, DC.

Deininger, K., and A. Goyal. 2012. "Going Digital: Credit Effects of Land Registry Computerization in India." *Journal of Development Economics* 99 (2): 236–43.

Deininger, K., A. Goyal, and H. K. Nagarajan. 2013. "Women's Inheritance Rights and Intergenerational Transmission of Resources in India." *Journal of Human Resources* 48 (1): 114–41.

Deininger, K., S. Jin, Y. Liu, and S. K. Singh. 2016. "Can Labor Market Imperfections Explain Changes of the Inverse Farm Size-Productivity Relationship over Time? Longitudinal Evidence from Rural India." IFPRI Discussion Paper, Markets, Trade and Institutions Division, International Food Policy Research Institute (IFPRI), Washington, DC.

Deininger, K., and F. Xia. 2016a. "Gender-Differentiated Impacts of Tenure Insecurity on Agricultural Productivity in Malawi's Customary Tenure System." Policy Research Working Paper, World Bank, Washington, DC.

Deininger, K., and F. Xia. 2016b. "Quantifying Spillover Effects from Large Farm Establishment: The Case of Mozambique." *World Development* 87: 227–241.

Deininger, K., F. Xia, and S. Savastano. 2015. "Smallholders' Land Ownership and Access in Sub-Saharan Africa: A New Landscape?" Policy Research Working Paper 7285, World Bank, Washington, DC.

de Janvry, A., K. Emerick, M. Gonzalez-Navarro, and E. Sadoulet. 2015. "Delinking Land Rights from Land Use: Certification and Migration in Mexico." *American Economic Review* 105 (10): 3125–49.

Duflo, E. 2003. "Grandmothers and Granddaughters: Old-Age Pensions and Intrahousehold Allocation in South Africa." *World Bank Economic Review* 17 (1): 1–25.

Enemark, S., K. C. Bell, C. Lemmen, and R. McLaren. 2014. "Fit for Purpose Land Administration." A joint publication of the International Federation of Surveyors (FIG) and the World Bank, Copenhagen.

Fenske, J. 2011. "Land Tenure and Investment Incentives: Evidence from West Africa." *Journal of Development Economics* 95 (2): 137–56.

Field, E. 2007. "Entitled to Work: Urban Property Rights and Labor Supply in Peru." *Quarterly Journal of Economics* 122 (4): 1561–602.

Franzsen, R., and W. McCluskey. 2016. "Property Tax in Africa." Lincoln Institute of Land Policy, Cambridge, MA.

Galiani, S., and E. Schargrodsky. 2011. "The Dynamics of Land Titling Regularization and Market Development." WIDER Working Paper 2011/088, UNU-WIDER, Helsinki.

Ghatak, M., and D. Mookherjee. 2014. "Land Acquisition for Industrialization and Compensation of Displaced Farmers." *Journal of Development Economics* 110: 303–12.

Goldstein, M., K. Houngbedji, F. Kondylis, M. O'Sullivan, and H. Selod. 2015. "Formalizing Rural Land Rights in West Africa: Early Evidence from a Randomized Impact Evaluation in Benin." Policy Research Working Paper No. 7435, World Bank, Washington, DC.

Guirkinger, C., and J.-P. Platteau. 2014. "The Effect of Land Scarcity on Farm Structure: Empirical Evidence from Mali." *Economic Development and Cultural Change* 62 (2): 195–238.

Horne, F., F. Mousseau, O. Metho, A. Mittal, and S. Daniel. 2011. "Understanding Land Investment Deals in Africa. Country Report: Ethiopia." Oakland Institute, Oakland, CA.

Jacoby, H. G., and B. Minten. 2007. "Is Land Titling in Sub-Saharan Africa Cost Effective? Evidence from Madagascar." *World Bank Economic Review* 21 (3): 461–85.

Jin, S., and T. S. Jayne. 2013. "Land Rental Markets in Kenya: Implications for Efficiency, Equity, Household Income, and Poverty." *Land Economics* 89 (2): 246–71.

Joireman, S. F. 2008. "The Mystery of Capital Formation in Sub-Saharan Africa: Women, Property Rights and Customary Law." *World Development* 36 (7): 1233–46.

Lawry, S., C. Samii, R. Hall, A. Leopold, D. Hornby, and F. Mtero. 2017. "The Impact of Land Property Rights Interventions on Investment and Agricultural Productivity in Developing Countries: A Systematic Review." *Journal of Development Effectiveness* 9(1): 61–81.

Luke, N., and K. Munshi. 2011. "Women as Agents of Change: Female Income and Mobility in India." *Journal of Development Economics* 94 (1): 1–17.

Macours, K. 2014. "Ethnic Divisions, Contract Choice, and Search Costs in the Guatemalan Land Rental Market." *Journal of Comparative Economics* 42 (1): 1–18.

Maurer, N., and L. Iyer. 2008. "The Cost of Property Rights: Establishing Institutions on the Philippine Frontier under American Rule, 1898–1918." NBER Working Paper No. 14298, National Bureau of Economic Research, Cambridge, MA.

Menon, N., Y. van der Meulen Rodgers, and H. Nguyen. 2014. "Women's Land Rights and Children's Human Capital in Vietnam." *World Development* 54: 18–31.

Nath, A., D. Mookherjee, M. Ghatak, and S. Mitra. 2013. "Land Acquisition and Compensation in Singur: What Really Happened?" *Economic and Political Weekly* 48 (21): 32–44. May 25, 2013. http://www.epw.in/journal/2013/21/special-articles/land-acquisition-and-compensation.html

Newman, C., F. Tarp, and K. van den Broeck. 2015. "Property Rights and Productivity: The Case of Joint Land Titling in Vietnam." *Land Economics* 91 (1): 91–105.

Nkurunziza, E. 2015. "Implementing and Sustaining Land Tenure Regularization in Rwanda." In *How Innovations in Land Administration Reform Improve on Doing Business: Cases from Lithuania, the Republic of Korea, Rwanda, and the United Kingdom*, edited by T. Hilhorst and F. Meunier, 10–19. Washington, DC: World Bank.

Peterman, A. 2012. "Widowhood and Asset Inheritance in Sub-Saharan Africa: Empirical Evidence from 15 Countries." *Development Policy Review* 30 (5): 543–71.

Pinckney, T. C., and P. K. Kimuyu. 1994. "Land Tenure Reform in East Africa: Good, Bad or Unimportant?" *Journal of African Economies* 3 (1): 1–28.

Promsopha, G. 2015. "Land Ownership as Insurance and the Market for Land: A Study in Rural Vietnam." *Land Economics* 91 (3): 460–78.

Qian, N. 2008. "Missing Women and the Price of Tea in China: The Effect of Sex-Specific Earnings on Sex Imbalance." *Quarterly Journal of Economics* 123 (3): 1251–85.

Santos, F., D. Fletschner, and G. Daconto. 2014. "Enhancing Inclusiveness of Rwanda's Land Tenure Regularization Program: Insights from Early Stages of Its Implementation." *World Development* 62: 30–41.

Sitko, N. J., and T. S. Jayne. 2014. "Structural Transformation or Elite Land Capture? The Growth of 'Emergent' Farmers in Zambia." *Food Policy* 48: 194–202.

9   Food price changes, domestic price insulation, and poverty (when all policymakers want to be above average)

Kym Anderson, William J. Martin, and Maros Ivanic

International prices of storable foods tend to be volatile, with occasionally intense but short-lived spikes and relatively long periods of below-average prices. Because movements in the domestic prices of staple foods are politically sensitive – not the least because they may push more households into poverty – many governments intervene to reduce the volatility of these prices by insulating their markets from changes in international prices. While this action can be effective in reducing the volatility of domestic prices in reactive countries, the collective impact of these interventions is to increase the volatility of world prices (Anderson and Nelgen 2012; Martin and Anderson 2012; Jensen and Anderson 2015), thereby increasing domestic price volatility in some more open countries. Thus, the only way that price insulation can be effective in reducing poverty is if the countries that insulate most are those in which the poor are most vulnerable to price spikes, something which Anderson, Ivanic, and Martin (2014) found not to be the case during the food price crisis of 2007–8.

One possible justification of insulating policy responses in developing countries is that it may allow food price volatility to be transferred to high-income countries, which are much better placed to manage this volatility. The industrial countries have, in fact, moved away from using insulating policies themselves, particularly with the abolition of variable import levies in the Uruguay Round (GATT 1994), and with the move to decoupled payments as a means of providing support to farmers. A key challenge for this argument, however, is that the industrial countries have become a much smaller fraction of global food production and trade. The share of global agricultural production covered by countries self-designated as "developed" in the agricultural negotiations has fallen to 24 percent, while the share of trade between industrial countries (and hence, subject to full WTO disciplines) has fallen below 20 percent (Fukase and Martin 2016). For rice, which is particularly politically sensitive in many countries, the share of industrial countries in world production and trade is below 5 percent, leaving almost no opportunity to use industrial country markets to absorb price volatility in this product.

In this chapter, we first review and reorganize some of the findings from our earlier work by looking at the way in which governments intervene to reduce the volatility of domestic food prices. We show that this type of insulation both is widespread and takes the form of seeking to insulate domestic markets from short-term price changes while passing through longer-term changes in world prices (Ivanic and Martin 2014a). We then ask what implications this reaction might have for poor households, taking into account what we have learned in recent years about the impacts of food price changes on poverty.

We then focus on the implications of temporary price insulation for domestic and international prices in the short run, seeking to clarify some concepts that may not have been brought out sufficiently clearly in our earlier work. We show that the widespread practice of price insulation can stabilize domestic prices in countries that insulate to a greater than average degree, but in so doing, it destabilizes domestic prices in those countries that insulate less than the average. Since, by definition, not all countries can insulate by more than the average, price insulation cannot reduce price volatility in all countries. Rather, it merely redistributes volatility from "high-insulator" to "low-insulator" countries.

More specifically, an individual country can avoid importing instability from the international market by insulating its domestic market more than the average country. Since every country has an incentive to insulate to a greater degree than average, however, there is a potential race to the bottom.

Price insulation in developing countries

A comparison of movements in the World Bank's food price index for internationally traded foods with movements in a weighted average of domestic food consumer price indices (CPIs) from the Food and Agriculture Organization of the United Nations (FAO), in the periods 2006–8 and 2010–11, reveals two striking features (Figure 9.1). One is that when international prices increased rapidly, policymakers in developing countries almost fully insulated their domestic markets from that rise. The other notable feature of Figure 9.1 is that the longer-term trends in the two series are almost identical.

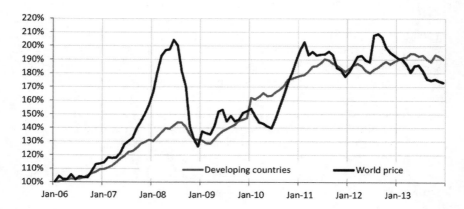

Figure 9.1 Indexes of staple food prices

Source: Based on data from World Bank (2015) and FAO (2015).

The prices of individual staple foods over the same period reveal that this behavior is particularly clear for both rice and wheat (Figures 9.2 and 9.3). By contrast, there is much less insulation of domestic markets for soybeans, which are a major input into livestock feed but a minor item in expenditures by the poor (Figure 9.4). In all cases, however, there appears to be substantial

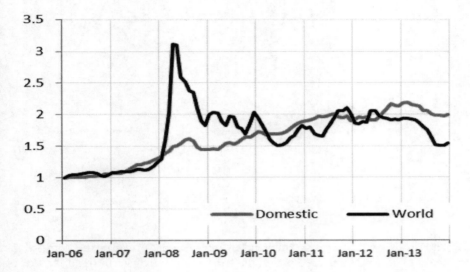

Figure 9.2 Price insulation for rice

Source: Based on data from World Bank (2015) and FAO (2015).

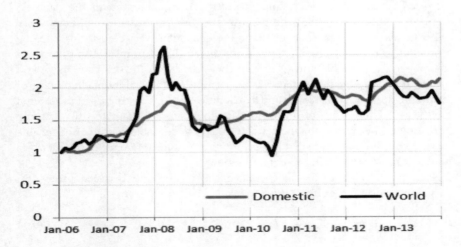

Figure 9.3 Price insulation for wheat

Source: Based on data from World Bank (2015) and FAO (2015).

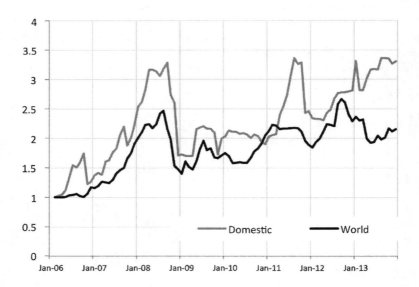

Figure 9.4 Price insulation for soybeans

Source: Based on data from World Bank (2015) and FAO (2015).

transmission of the longer-term trend in international prices to the domestic market. This implies that countries returned to their long-term trend level of taxation of or support for agriculture after the price spike period.

Ivanic and Martin (2014a) used the error–correction mechanism to represent the relationships between international and domestic price levels (or equivalently between international prices and protection rates) observed in the data. As explained by Nickell (1985), this is consistent with the response of policymakers, who are averse both to adjustments in the dependent variable (in this case, the domestic price) and to being away from the equilibrium relationship between the dependent variable and its explanatory variable(s) (in this case, the world price). This specification imposes a very simple and tractable quadratic cost of changing domestic price levels and a quadratic cost of deviating from the desired political-economy level of protection. It allows simple parameters that capture the resulting behavior. This estimator also has the desirable feature of being able to deal with the unfortunate statistical implications for inference of the variables under consideration being integrated series.

Ivanic and Martin (2014a) estimated the relationship between protection levels and world prices using this model:

$$\Delta \tau \;=\; \alpha.(p_t^w - p_{t-1}^w) + \beta.(\tau_{t-1} - \overset{\circ}{\tau}_{t-1}) \tag{9.1}$$

where τ is the log of the rate of protection, defined as $(1+t)$, where t is the tariff equivalent of protection provided at a country's border; p^w is the log of the world price; τ° is the log of the rate of protection desired in the absence of changes in world prices; α is the insulation coefficient, indicating the extent to which protection is used to offset the effects of changes in world prices on protection (and hence, on domestic prices); and β is the error-correction coefficient, indicating the extent to which policymakers adjust protection in response to gaps between protection in the previous year and the desired level of protection. Both α and β should be less than unity in absolute value or the system will be unstable, with any initial deviation causing explosive deviations from equilibrium.

Key findings from the analysis by Ivanic and Martin (2014a) are that: (1) insulation is partial, with average trade-weighted coefficients of insulation all safely less than 1 in absolute value (Table 9.1), and (2) the magnitude of insulation is larger for rice and wheat and for politically sensitive products, such as sugar, than for soybeans, (yellow) maize, and beef.

An important question is why policymakers might respond like this? The inverse relationship between food price levels and protection rates has been long observed (Johnson 1973, 1975), but the tendency for protection rates to return to their long-run level appears not to have received the same degree of attention in the literature. One possible explanation for this behavior is provided by recent work on the implications of changes in food prices for poverty – especially in the context of the price surges that can have such dramatic effects on the poor, because they spend a large fraction of their income on food. This body of work (e.g., Headey 2014; Ivanic and Martin 2014a; Jacoby 2016) shows that unanticipated food price increases can have serious, adverse impacts for poverty (although Headey and Martin [2016] are concerned about the reliability of our evidence on the net purchasing position of poor households), while sustained increases in prices might be helpful once poor farmers' marketable output has a chance to expand and higher food prices are passed through into wage rates. Seen this way, it is clear that the observed policy responses make political sense for each individual country.

Armed with this understanding of policy responses, two important analytical questions arise. The first is whether the policy of insulation is effective in

Table 9.1 Error-correction coefficients, simple averages

	α	β
Rice	−0.50	−0.36
Wheat	−0.52	−0.31
Sugar	−0.53	−0.20
Maize	−0.35	−0.44
Soybeans	−0.40	−0.46
Beef	−0.39	−0.31
Poultry	−0.34	−0.46

Source: Ivanic and Martin (2014a).

dealing with the short-run adverse impact of price shocks on the poor when many countries' governments choose to insulate. The second has to do with the long-run impacts of the equilibrium levels of protection chosen by each country on the welfare of its citizens, and particularly on the poor. The first question was analyzed in Anderson, Ivanic, and Martin (2014), while the second is the subject of ongoing work. To help promote understanding of the Anderson, Ivanic, and Martin (2014) result, we now examine the mechanism by which their result was obtained in more detail than was done in the original paper.

Impacts of price insulation on national and global prices

Do countries' policy responses make any sense when considered collectively? Price insulation of the type observed is widely justified as attempting to protect the poor from the adverse impacts of rapid increases in food prices. Not all policymakers offered this argument, but many did. Many observers, noting that major economies, such as China and India, managed to restrain domestic food price increases in 2006–8 to very low levels, concluded that estimates of the adverse impacts of higher food prices on poverty must have been seriously overstated. Thus, it seems important to assess the net impacts of intervention on prices in each of the countries considered in that poverty analysis.

Analysis of this problem requires taking into account not just the impact of each country's price insulation on its domestic price relative to the world price, but also the collective effects of insulation on international prices. Combining these two estimates allows us to calculate the net impact of the two measures and to assess whether prices in each country would have been higher or lower in the absence of intervention by all countries.

To assess the impacts of price insulation on international and domestic prices, we first calculate the change in protection in each country associated with price insulation between 2006 and 2008. We then estimate the impact of these changes in protection on world prices. A back-of-the-envelope estimate of the impact on world prices is, as discussed in Martin and Anderson (2012) and Anderson, Ivanic, and Martin (2014), an average of the changes in protection rates weighted by shares of global consumption (and production where supply responds to changes in price) and by the elasticities of demand (and supply), where appropriate. Because price insulation is a short-run phenomenon, we consider only the impact on demand, although we showed in Anderson, Ivanic, and Martin (2014) that it makes little difference to the results if we allowed for impacts on supply as well.

Given these (relatively weak) assumptions, the impact of a set of changes in domestic distortions on the international price of a commodity is given by:

$$\hat{p}^{\star} = \frac{\sum_i (-G_i \eta_i) \hat{T}_i}{\sum_i (G_i \eta_i)} \tag{9.2}$$

where $\hat{p}^*$ is the proportional change in the international price; G_i is the share at international prices of country i in global demand; η_i is the uncompensated elasticity of demand in market i; and $\hat{T}_i$ is the proportional change in trade policy from its initial level, where $T=(1+t)$ is the power of the initial *ad valorem* tariff, t. This means that the impact of a set of distortions on world prices is a weighted average of the changes in individual distortions. What this implies for policy is that only those countries that reduce their protection rates by more than the average can lower their domestic prices. Since it is impossible for all countries to lower their protection by more than the average,[1] this result highlights the zero-sum nature of this policy, and the powerful incentives it creates for "beggar-thy-neighbor" policies. Knowing that each country can succeed in reducing the increase in its price only by insulating by more than the average creates a powerful incentive for each country to increase its degree of insulation, a process that results in a higher average degree of insulation, but which leaves all below-average insulators experiencing higher domestic prices than in the absence of insulation.

To compare the domestic price-reducing impacts of reductions in countries' own protection with the price-increasing impacts of higher international food prices, we express both in log-change form, rather than the more familiar percentage-change form used in Anderson, Ivanic, and Martin (2014). Because the log-change in prices is the change in prices divided by the logarithmic average of the before and after prices, the log-change measure has the desirable feature of symmetry in directional price effects, so that a reduction of 20 percent in domestic protection is directly comparable with a 20 percent increase in world prices. If we were to use standard proportional change measures (as in Anderson, Ivanic, and Martin 2014) – defined as the change in prices divided by the initial value – we would need to take into account interaction terms when assessing the impacts of policy changes and changes in world prices on domestic prices.

For simplicity and transparency, we assume that the elasticity of demand in all countries is the same. We recognize that lower-income countries may have lower uncompensated elasticities of demand for staple foods than higher-income countries, but the range of econometric estimates of elasticities is very wide. Also, the introduction of specific estimates for each country would likely introduce spurious precision and distract from the simple message of this chapter – that changes in protection policy can stabilize domestic prices only if they involve above-average changes in protection rates.

Figure 9.5 compares the change in the rate of protection on rice in each country with the average change during 2006–8. It shows that only 11 of the 28 countries, for which we have estimates of changes in protection rates, reduced their own protection by enough to offset the impacts of the higher world prices resulting from reduced worldwide protection. These 11 countries include many with very high poverty rates, such as Rwanda, Nepal, Nigeria, and Bangladesh (Ivanic, Martin, and Zaman 2012), plus others, such as China, in which poverty rates have only recently fallen from high levels. In the other 17 countries, including Egypt, India, Côte d'Ivoire, and the Philippines, the reduction in protection

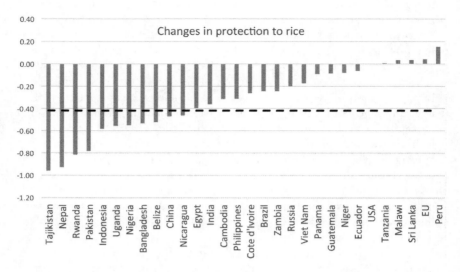

Figure 9.5 Changes in protection to rice, 2006–2008, Δ log

Source: Authors' calculations.

Note: The dashed line shows the weighted average rate of change in protection, which is the negative of the increase in the international price resulting from this intervention.

was insufficient to compensate for the additional increase in the world price brought about by the global average reduction in protection.

In the case of wheat, we find that 13 of the 23 countries, for which we have estimates of the change in protection, were able to reduce their protection by more than the increase in the international price (Figure 9.6). This is possible because two major producers – the EU and the United States – appear to have had no changes in protection policy, thereby helping to stabilize the international price by absorbing shocks. Two other major consumers, Egypt and Russia, appear to have *increased* protection to wheat, thereby directly destabilizing their own domestic prices while contributing to greater stability in international prices.

As for maize, we again find a wide dispersion in the responses of individual countries' protection to the price spike during this period (Figure 9.7). Some major economies – such as Pakistan, Indonesia, and India – appear to have insulated strongly against the price increase during this period, despite the fact that maize is not generally used as a staple food in these economies. Even odder is the increase in apparent protection to maize in three countries – Zambia, Malawi, and Rwanda – where maize is a staple food. This increase appears to have arisen as an unintended consequence of using quantitative restrictions to regulate food trade. In this situation, unexpected reductions in output during the period resulted in increased net demand, which could not immediately be

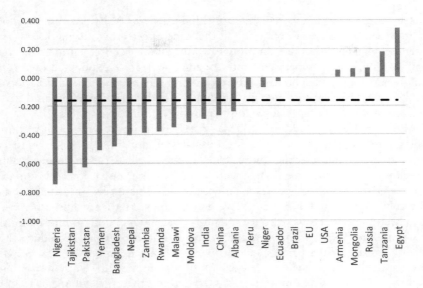

Figure 9.6 Changes in protection to wheat, 2006–2008, Δ log

Source: Authors' calculations.

Note: The dashed line shows the weighted average rate of change in protection, which is the negative of the increase in world prices resulting from this intervention.

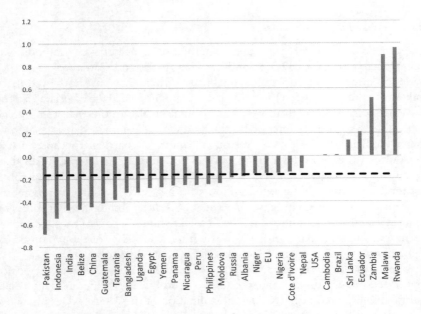

Figure 9.7 Changes in protection for maize, 2006–2008, Δ logs

Source: Authors' calculations.

Note: The dashed line shows the weighted average rate of change in protection, which is the negative of the increase in world prices resulting from this intervention.

met by imports and, hence, resulted in higher prices. Although this was not an intended outcome of policy, it had the same effect on world markets as an intended increase in protection brought about by, for example, an increase in a tariff in an import-competing country, or an increase in an export subsidy in an exporting country. Had buyers in these markets been able to access international markets for the additional quantity needed, this additional demand would have resulted in some additional upward pressure on world market prices.

Anderson, Ivanic, and Martin (2014) examined the impacts of this insulation, taking into account not only the direct impacts of insulation on each country's domestic price but also the cumulative impact of all of the price insulation on the international price. When only the direct impacts of intervention are considered, intervention appears to reduce the adverse impacts on the poor considerably, with 80 million fewer people entering poverty than would otherwise have been the case. However, once the impacts of intervention on international prices are taken into account, it appears price insulation failed to reduce the adverse impact of the price shock on poverty. The insulation itself increased international prices – for simplicity, think of insulation achieved by restricting exports – enough to completely eliminate its otherwise favorable impact on poverty. The collective action problem in this case is strongly analogous to the case where people stand up in a stadium to get a better view of the game: while each person feels the need to act, the actions of the group as a whole are ineffective in improving the view for most.

Implications of food price patterns

The pattern of food prices resulting from their status as storable commodities is one, as characterized by Deaton and Laroque (1992) and Cafiero et al. (2011), by long periods in the doldrums, punctuated by intense but short-lived price spikes. Our results suggest that this pattern is somewhat differentiated at the domestic price level, with those countries that insulate more than the average being able to reduce the intensity of the spikes in their domestic markets. However, a corollary of this is that some other countries – particularly those unable to insulate as much as the average – are subjected to more intense spikes than they would otherwise experience. One such group is clearly the low-income, net food-importing group, who tend to have relatively low rates of protection on food under normal circumstances and, hence, little ability to offset spikes by lowering their initial protection. The limited fiscal resources of most countries in this group also make it difficult to pay import subsidies of the type used by countries such as Egypt and Indonesia in the 2006–8 price spike.

A key concern with this distribution of food prices is that short periods of high prices reduce the real incomes of net food buyers, including many small, subsistence-oriented farmers. The short duration of these spikes does not allow wage rates to fully respond to the increase in food prices that might otherwise have resulted in the food price increase improving the situation of many poor people – potentially resulting in a reversal of an initial, unfavorable impact of higher prices on the poverty rate (Jacoby 2016). Nor does it allow the welfare gains from increases in farm output that Ivanic and Martin (2014b) found to be another important contributor to a long-run reduction in global poverty, when food prices are raised for extended periods. Rather, the outcome is a pessimal one in which sharp increases in food prices have adverse impacts on the poor – likely with many long-lived, adverse impacts – during the relatively short periods in which they occur. By contrast, the low-price periods during which wages and output are depressed and poverty rates increased tend to be much longer.

Conclusions

This brief survey and elaboration of recent work on food price volatility, price insulation, and poverty began by looking at countries' policy responses to world price changes. This revealed that countries have tended to insulate strongly against shocks to international prices of staple foods. However, within a couple of years, they had fully passed the more sustained increases in prices into domestic markets. Further analysis led to the conclusion that this is part of a systematic pattern of response under which policymakers resist sharp changes in prices, which causes the rate of protection to deviate from its steady-state political equilibrium. Policymakers subsequently reduce this disequilibrium by raising domestic prices to return them closer to their desired rates of protection.

A key question is whether the short-run price insulation, which is such a key feature of markets for staple foods, actually achieves the reduction in poverty to which it is, at least partly, directed. If policymakers consider only the direct impacts of their actions between 2006 and 2008, they would have grounds for congratulation: reducing the jump in prices is estimated to have reduced poverty for some 80 million people. However, it is important to keep in mind the collective action problem that is inherent in using price-insulating policies. The higher prices that resulted from countries collectively insulating their markets completely offset the apparent gains when such collective impact is ignored, rendering this approach to policy ineffective in reducing poverty at the global level.

Note

1 A widely cited exception is the mythical village of Lake Wobegon, in which, reportedly, "all the women are strong, all the men are good-looking, and all the children are above average" (https://en.wikipedia.org/wiki/Lake_Wobegon).

References

Anderson, K., M. Ivanic, and W. Martin. 2014. "Food Price Spikes, Price Insulation and Poverty." In *The Economics of Food Price Volatility*, edited by J.-P. Chavas, D. Hummels, and B. Wright, 311–39. Chicago: University of Chicago Press for the National Bureau of Economic Research (NBER).

Anderson, K., and S. Nelgen. 2012. "Agricultural Trade Distortions during the Global Financial Crisis." *Oxford Review of Economic Policy* 28 (2): 235–60.

Cafiero, C., E. Bobenrieth, J. Bobenrieth, and B. Wright. 2011. "The Empirical Relevance of the Competitive Storage Model." *Journal of Econometrics* 62 (1): 44–54.

Deaton, A., and G. Laroque. 1992. "On the Behavior of Commodity Prices." *Review of Economic Studies* 59 (1): 1–23.

FAO (Food and Agriculture Organization of the United Nations). 2015. FAOSTAT. Consumer Price Indices. http://fenix.fao.org/faostat/beta/en/#data/CP

Fukase, E., and W. Martin. 2016. "Who Will Feed China in the 21st Century? Income Growth and Food Demand and Supply in China." *Journal of Agricultural Economics* 67 (1): 3–23. Open access doi:10.1111/1477-9552.12117.

GATT (General Agreement on Tariffs and Trade). 1994. *The Results of the Uruguay Round of Multilateral Trade Negotiations: The Legal Texts.* Geneva: GATT Secretariat.

Headey, D. 2014. "Food Prices and Poverty Reduction in the Long Run." IFPRI Discussion Paper 01331, International Food Policy Research Institute (IFPRI), Washington, DC.

Headey, D., and W. Martin. 2016. "The Impact of Food Prices on Poverty and Food Security." *Annual Review of Resource Economics* 8: 329–51.

Ivanic, M., and W. Martin. 2014a. "Implications of Domestic Price Insulation for Global Food Price Volatility." *Journal of International Money and Finance* 42: 272–88.

Ivanic, M., and W. Martin. 2014b. "Short- and Long-Run Impacts of Food Price Changes on Poverty." Policy Research Working Paper 7011, World Bank, Washington, DC.

Ivanic, M., W. Martin, and H. Zaman. 2012. "Estimating the Short-Run Poverty Impacts of the 2010–11 Surge in Food Prices." *World Development* 40 (11): 2302–17.

Jacoby, H. 2016. "Food Prices, Wages, and Welfare in Rural India." *Economic Inquiry* 54 (1): 159–76.

Jensen, H. G., and K. Anderson. 2015. "Grain Price Spikes and Beggar-Thy-Neighbor Policy Responses: A Global Economywide Analysis." *World Bank Economic Review* 30. doi:10.1093/wber/lhv047

Johnson, D. G. 1973. *World Agriculture in Disarray.* London: Macmillan.

Johnson, D. G. 1975. "World Agriculture, Commodity Policy, and Price Variability." *American Journal of Agricultural Economics* 57 (5): 823–8.

Martin, W., and K. Anderson. 2012. "Export Restrictions and Price Insulation during Commodity Price Booms." *American Journal of Agricultural Economics* 94 (2): 422–7.

Nickell, S. 1985. "Error Correction, Partial Adjustment and All That: An Expository Note." *Oxford Bulletin of Economics and Statistics* 47 (2): 119–29.

World Bank. 2015. Pink Sheets. http://econ.worldbank.org

10 Institutional constraints and options for expanding the biotechnology revolution in developing countries

Greg Traxler

Introduction

The past three decades have witnessed a remarkable series of scientific break-throughs in the application of biotechnology to plant science. The most visible indicator of progress has been the rapid increase in acreage planted with geneti-cally modified crop varieties (GMOs), from no acreage in 1996 to 180 million hectares under cultivation worldwide in 2014 (James 2015). By several mea-sures, progress has been especially impressive in developing countries. In 2014, developing countries accounted for 20 of the 28 countries that planted GMOs, for more than half of the world's GMO-cultivated area and for an estimated 90 percent of all farmers growing GMOs (James 2015).

Just as remarkable as the scientific progress has been the diversity of expecta-tions, claims, and opinions around the impact, applicability, and risks of the use of GMOs in developing countries (Stone 2002; Paarlberg 2010; Gilbert 2013). The polarization of the discussion began even before the introduction of the first GMOs in 1996, and shows little sign of abating. Biotechnology's proponents point to the rapid growth in the use of GMOs worldwide and to the widely shared financial and environmental benefits that have accrued from GMO dif-fusion as reasons to expect important contributions from GMO technology to future world food security (Qaim 2009; Whitty et al. 2013; Klümper and Qaim 2014; James 2015). Other voices argue that GMOs have limited applicability in developing countries and that access should be limited for reasons of safety and equity (Gurian-Sherman 2009; Benbrook 2012). The complexities of the social, ecological, and economic effects of GMOs have resulted in public resistance and lengthy regulatory processes that have slowed the spread of GMOs (Falck-Zepeda and Zambrano 2011; Gleim, Smyth, and Phillips 2015). Qaim (2016) concluded that the core obstacle to the expansion of GM crop technology is "limited public acceptance," and observed that "The prejudices and arguments used against GM technology are still the same as 20 years ago" (Qaim 2016, 10). Both the public and private sectors have been cautious about investing in the development and delivery of new GMO products because of the uncertainty about public acceptance, market potential, and the costs of regulatory compli-ance. The effect of public resistance, fed by civil society, has been felt most acutely in the slow pace of deployment of GMO food crops.

This chapter complements existing reviews by focusing on the institutional structure that has developed around the development and delivery of GMOs. The objective is to assess the institutional capacity and incentives to deliver GMOs for food crops to developing country farmers. It is important to distinguish between the food crops, such as rice, wheat, white maize, cassava, and potatoes, that are consumed directly by humans and the industrial crops that constitute the bulk of GMO use at present. Nearly 99 percent of the global GMO area is cultivated with four animal feed, consumable oil, and fiber crops (yellow maize, soybeans, cotton, and canola). The metrics that are used to trace the institutional sources of available GMOs are discussed below. Scientific progress and commercial delivery of GMOs in the United States are compared to the same indicators in developing countries, drawing on the experience of the first two decades of what was once called the biotechnology revolution. The assessment attempts to shed light on the question of whether GMOs are likely to make a significant contribution to food security in developing countries in the future.

The assessment is conducted through the lens of a very simple model of institutional collaboration in technology generation and diffusion. Institutional capacity builds slowly. The premise of this chapter is that the institutional pedigree of the GMO technologies deployed to date informs the likely pace of evolution in the intermediate future. What institutions have been responsible for delivering GMOs? How has the institutional infrastructure evolved since the first GMOs were adopted? What roles have been played by international, nonprofit, governmental, and private institutions (primarily the multinational life science companies), and what does this evolution suggest for future access to GMO technology and food production in developing countries? I review indicators of the scientific discovery, regulatory approval, and cultivation of GMO varieties that occurred between 1996 and 2015. Data are presented on numbers of distinct GMO varieties that have been entered into biosafety field trials, approved for cultivation, and GMO area by crop. By tracing this pathway from lab to regulated trials, to farm field on a country-by-country basis, the institutional capacity in scientific and commercial delivery realms is defined.

An institutional model of GMO development and delivery

A simple model defining the process for developing and delivering GMOs is represented in Figure 10.1. The model and the data presented later in the chapter break the process for putting GMO technology in the hands of farmers into three stages – discovery R&D, pre-commercialization, and commercialization. The first stage encompasses all upstream research that is required to identify a transgene and transfer it to a viable plant that can survive outside of the greenhouse. The motives for developing a proof-of-concept plant can be purely scientific, or can be with eventual commercialization intent. In the United States, many nonprofit research institutions have placed proof-of-concept GMOs into field trials with no intent to commercialize (Table 10.1). The pre-commercialization

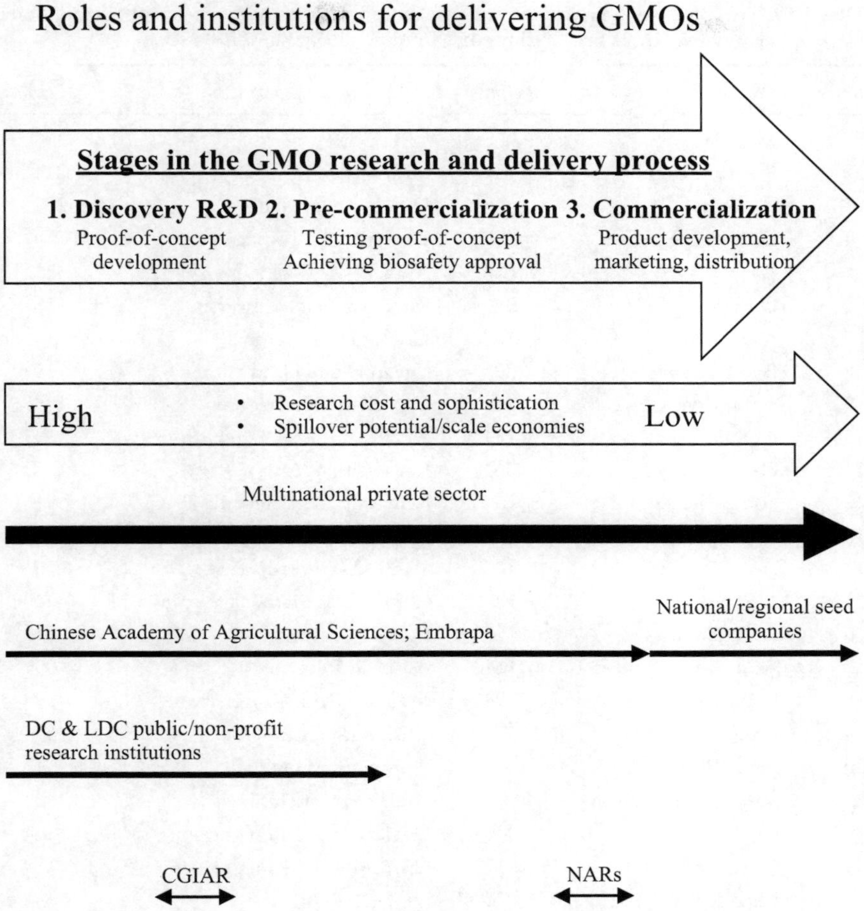

Roles and institutions for delivering GMOs

Stages in the GMO research and delivery process

1. Discovery R&D 2. Pre-commercialization 3. Commercialization

Proof-of-concept   Testing proof-of-concept   Product development,
development   Achieving biosafety approval   marketing, distribution

High
- Research cost and sophistication   Low
- Spillover potential/scale economies

Multinational private sector

National/regional seed
companies

Chinese Academy of Agricultural Sciences; Embrapa

DC & LDC public/non-profit
research institutions

CGIAR   NARs

Figure 10.1 Stages and institutional roles for delivering GMOs to developing countries
Source: Author's construction.

stage begins when developers receive a field trial permit from national biosafety authorities to test the proof-of-concept plant under monitored field conditions. The field trial process takes several years and requires regular reporting of field data to the biosafety authority. During this regulatory phase, adaptive breeding can be done to the proof-of-concept plant to bring in traits or to move its traits closer to those of a commercially appealing variety. Within our model, the commercialization stage begins when the developing institution receives cultivation approval from the biosafety authority. At that point, there is regulatory clearance for the institution to provide seed to farmers for commercial use, and variety development and seed multiplication can begin in earnest.

Table 10.1 The 35 largest private sector and the 35 largest public/nonprofit institutions receiving GMO field trial permits in the United States, 1987–2015

Rank	Private sector	Permits	Public and nonprofit	Permits
1	Monsanto	7,008	USDA/ARS	395
2	Pioneer Hi–Bred	1,159	University of Florida	211
3	Syngenta	619	Iowa State University	202
4	Dow AgroSciences	477	University of Nebraska	144
5	AgrEvo	326	Rutgers University	131
6	Du Pont	320	Michigan State University	118
7	ArborGen	317	University of Kentucky	114
8	Bayer CropScience	292	Oregon State University	112
9	Seminis Vegetable	210	University of Arizona	105
10	DeKalb	181	North Carolina State University	104
11	Calgene	164	University of Idaho	101
12	Forage Genetics Int.	159	University of California/Davis	91
13	Scotts	154	University of Georgia	81
14	BASF Plant Science	127	Stanford University	76
15	J. R. Simplot	125	Cold Spring Harbor Laboratory	72
16	Aventis	122	Purdue University	62
17	Arcadia Biosciences	117	Cornell University	60
18	Betaseed	94	Montana State University	58
19	ProdiGene	89	Washington State University	57
20	DNA Plant Tech	89	University of Illinois	54
21	Stine Biotechnology	86	Louisiana State University	52
22	Northrup King	80	University of Minnesota	50
23	Novartis Seeds	77	University of Tennessee	45
24	M.S. Technologies	76	USDA/APHIS	43
25	Asgrow	75	Texas Tech University	41
26	Upjohn	73	Texas A&M University	38
27	BHN Research	72	University of California/Berkeley	37
28	Biogemma USA	69	University of Missouri	37
29	Cargill	65	University of Wisconsin–Madison	36
30	Targeted Growth Inc.	63	Pennsylvania State University	35
31	Harris Moran	61	Virginia Tech	35
32	Agracetus	60	University of Chicago	34
33	BASF	57	University of Wisconsin	34
34	Frito Lay	54	University of California	34
35	Agritope	53	Max Planck Institute	31

Source: USDA (2016). Retrieved July 1, 2015.

The model suggests that spillover potential, research cost, and scientific sophistication generally decline along the path from basic research to technology delivery. Scale economies and spillover potential have large implications for incentives, and so are important determinants of the role that will be assumed by national and international actors, and of whether those actors reside in the private or in the nonprofit sectors (Pardey and Pingali 2010). Basic research and some strategic research have worldwide applications, while product development research is generally specific to a target market or agroclimatic location. Basic research findings are routinely published in international journals and presented at international conferences, facilitating knowledge spillovers between developed and developing countries. Economists have traditionally considered appropriability to be low for basic research (Pardey and Alston 2010). Historically, scientists at universities and nonprofit research institutes in developed countries have done the bulk of the world's basic research. With changes in the legal ability to protect intellectual property (IP), the private sector has increased the amount of upstream research within agricultural biotechnology over the past 30 years and withholds their findings from public disclosure (Fuglie and Toole 2014). International data on basic research investments in agriculture are not available, but it seems likely that a few developing countries, such as China, India, and Brazil, have significant basic science capacity.

The model highlights the effect of research scale economies and spillover potential of research findings in determining the role of each institution. The international spillover of the herbicide tolerance and insect resistance transgenes discovered in the United States has been a defining characteristic of the global diffusion of GMOs. Because of the ease with which upstream biotechnology research spills over, it is not necessary that each country have such capacity in order to gain GMO access, nor can many countries afford to develop that capacity. Some capacity in either the public or private sector must exist in each country for the other stages in the model. The capacity to regulate biosafety must exist in the national public sector for a country's farmers to have access to GMOs. All other functions can be achieved through spillovers of capacity from multinational private sector actors, as long as an acceptable environment for protecting intellectual property exists. Bolivia and Paraguay are examples of how spillovers can occur with minimal public sector capacity. Farmers in both countries have gained access to soybean and maize GMOs targeted for Argentina and Brazil, even though they have no upstream research capacity and their variety development and delivery systems are weak. China is a unique case where national nonprofit institutions participate in all aspects of GMO development and delivery.

The level of basic and strategic research in crop improvement conducted by the private sector has increased significantly over the past 20 years. Multinational companies, such as Monsanto and DuPont/Pioneer, are now major investors in basic and strategic research, protecting those investments through trade secrecy. The total investment of the multinational firms in genomics dwarfs that of all other players. The mergers among seed and chemical companies have blurred the line between basic and strategic research. What was once considered far upstream genetics now confers a large innovator's head start on product development and has become a justifiable investment for multinational firms. With the acquisition of seed firms in developing countries, the deep financial pockets of the multinational firms now extend all the way from basic research to product delivery – an integration role that no other institution has demonstrated its capacity to achieve.

Achieving regulatory approval for the commercial deployment of GMOs is a critical step in the deployment of GMOs, challenging the scientific, legal/ technical, and financial capacity of developing country institutions. Donors have invested significantly in assisting developing countries to put legislative and regulatory frameworks in place. Successful execution of a biosafety field trial requires that a country have institutions with the necessary scientific and technical capacity. The country must also have a favorable political and legal environment.

The product development and delivery function is highly location-specific and, apart from the multinational corporations, is conducted in institutional partnerships. The CGIAR Centers' main focus is on applied research, and while some Centers have capacity in strategic crop improvement research, none are directly involved in regulatory trials or seed delivery to farmers. The national agricultural research systems (NARSs) focus on downstream product development. Technology delivery is presented in Figure 10.1 to emphasize the importance of institutional development in that area. The overall institutional process is illustrated as a one-way continuum, but clearly there are many feedback loops that are not shown.

Measuring institutional capacity and contribution

Three indicators are used to measure the level and source of GMO capacity in developing countries – discovery R&D capacity is indicated by biosafety field trial permits issued, pre-commercial capacity is indicated by the issuance of cultivation approval, and commercial capacity is indicated by area sown with GMO crops (Table 10.2).

In all countries, GMO regulation occurs in two steps. In the first step, an institution receives a permit to conduct field trials of a genetically modified organism. Receipt of a field trial permit indicates that an institution has the scientific capacity to isolate a gene with an interesting or useful function and transfer that gene to a viable plant. The number of approvals and the number of different institutions receiving approvals indicate the biotechnology scientific capacity of a country. The second permitting step is cultivation approval that grants permission to commercialize a GMO variety for use by farmers. Biosafety regulators require GMO varieties to remain in field trials for a minimum of three years before being granted approval for cultivation, but the trials last much longer in many cases.

These biosafety data tell us three things about a country's institutional capacity. First, they tell us that the government has a functioning biosafety capacity. Second, the field permit data identify the institutions with the upstream research

Table 10.2 Institutional capacity indicators

	Discovery R&D	*Pre-commercialization*	*Commercialization*
Activities	Developing GMO proof-of-concept	Field-testing and adapting model GMO plants	Commercial product development through adaptive plant breeding
	Gene discovery and transfer to field-viable GMO model plant	Biosafety testing	Seed marketing and distribution
Indicator of institutional capacity	Number of field permits issued	Number of cultivation approvals issued	Area planted to GMOs
	Number of distinct institutions	*Identifies institutions with financial might, applied science capacity, and incentive to move to product development.*	*Identifies institutions successful in reaching farmers with a unique GMO*
	Identifies institutions with the scientific capacity to create viable GMO model plant	*Also indicates national biosafety capacity.*	
Categories of institutions involved	Multinationals		Multinationals
	Super NARSs (China, Embrapa)		Medium-size national and regional private seed companies
	DC and LDC public/nonprofit institutions		
	DC and LDC start-up companies		

Source: Author's construction.

Note: DC=developed countries; LDC=less developed countries.

capacity to bring a GMO from lab to field. Bringing a lab product to the field is an important scientific proof-of-concept test, but the sponsoring institution may or may not have long-run intent to commercialize. The vast majority of institutions that bring a GMO variety to field trial never apply for a permit to commercialize. Finally, given the time and expense involved in attaining cultivation approval, those approvals identify the institutions with the threshold financial capacity to consider commercializing a GMO.

Biosafety field trial permits

Data on the first biosafety regulation step, permission to conduct field trials, are available only for the United States, but the US data are informative about institutional roles, in general. Because of the dominance of the United States in the generation and use of GMOs, the US field permit data provide a frame of reference on the roles of the public versus the private sectors. With a total of 18,277 field trial permits issues, the United States has had by far the greatest experience with GMO regulation (USDA 2016). A large number of institutions, 333, have entered at least one event into field trials (Table 10.3). Monsanto is responsible for 38 percent of the trials, 210 other private firms for another 42 percent. The public–nonprofit sector has been an active participant in conducting GMO field trials, with 19 percent of all trials (3,515 trials) conducted by 122 public

Table 10.3 GMO regulatory field trial permits and cultivation approvals, United States, 1987–2015

Type of institution	Field permits			Cultivation approvals		
	Number of permits	% of permits	Number of institutions	Number of permits	% of permits	Number of institutions
Monsanto	7,008	38.3	1	37	33	1
Other private	7,754	42.4	210	71	63	26
Public/nonprofit	3,515	19.2	122	4	4	4
Total	18,277	100	333	112	100	31

Source: USDA (2016). Accessed July 1, 2015.

or nonprofit institutions. There are large differences in scale of the GMO field testing among the large multinational firms, smaller private firms, and public sector institutions. Seventy-five percent of all the private trials were conducted by the ten largest firms, while nearly two-thirds of private firms conducted ten or fewer field trials. No other country has anywhere near the number of institutions with the capacity to develop a proof-of-concept plant that could be entered into a field trial.

Cultivation approvals

Continuing first with an examination of the US data (Table 10.3), the evidence provided by the cultivation approval data in the United States suggests a key difference in the role of the large multinational firms, smaller private firms, and public–nonprofit institutions. The smaller private firms and the nonprofit institutions rarely take the step of obtaining cultivation approval; only 9 percent of institutions conducting a field trial have ever received cultivation approval. Nearly three-quarters of all cultivation approvals were granted to just seven firms, and only four approvals were obtained by public institutions (the USDA Agricultural Research Service [ARS], Cornell University, University of Florida, and University of Saskatchewan). This suggests that the small firms, and especially the public institutions, are conducting field trials out of public goods scientific research interest, rather than as a step in a plan to commercialize a discovery. The Cornell/University of Hawaii virus-resistant (VR) papaya is the only public sector product to be grown commercially. The step of achieving cultivation approval and, especially, of taking a product to market is a very big one, requiring huge financial and scientific might. The institutional scientific capacity to experiment with GMOs and the capacity to make a GMO accessible to farmers are quite distinct.

Worldwide, a total of 699 approvals for GMO cultivation occurred between 1987 and 2016 (Table 10.4). Six developed countries, plus the European Union, and 26 developing countries have had at least one approval. A total of

Table 10.4 Pre-commercial capacity: number of cultivation approvals, all countries, 1996–2016

Developed-countries	Private sector approvals*	Public/nonprofit approvals	Less developed-countries	Private sector approvals*	Public/nonprofit approvals
Japan	133	1	Brazil	48	1
Canada	126	1	Argentina	46	0
US	108	4	Colombia	22	0
Australia	33	0	Paraguay	20	0
Norway	11	0	S. Africa	19	0
EU	10	0	Uruguay	18	0
S. Korea	1	0	Mexico	15	0
			Costa Rica	15	0
			Philippines	13	0
			China	1	12
			Malaysia	8	0
			India	5	1
			Honduras	5	0
			Indonesia	4	0
			Vietnam	4	0
			Chile	3	0
			Pakistan	2	0
			Bangladesh	1	0
			Bolivia	1	0
			Burkina Faso	1	0
			Cuba	1	0
			Egypt	1	0
			Panama	1	0
			Sudan	1	0
			Myanmar	0	1
			Iran	0	1
DC total	422	6	LDC total	255	16

Source: ISAAA (2016). Retrieved June 22, 2016.

* Includes multinational company approvals in all countries.

55 institutions worldwide have had an approval – 40 in the private sector and 15 from the public–nonprofit sector. Multinational companies received 220 of the 255 cultivation approvals granted by developing countries. Some very small countries have approved GMOs for cultivation, suggesting that scientific capacity to regulate may not be a large obstacle when a country has the will to move forward with the use of GMOs (Falck-Zepeda and Zambrano 2011; Chambers et al. 2014). In some small countries, it is likely that civil society opposition is not as well organized as in larger countries, making it less politically costly to

approve a GMO. Vigani and Olper (2013) created an index of GMO standard restrictiveness for 60 countries and found that developing countries, on average, are less restrictive than developed countries. Just 3 percent of cultivation approvals have come from public or nonprofit institutions.

Table 10.5 lists all 17 developing country institutions that have ever received a GMO approval for cultivation. The list includes ten public–nonprofit institutions and seven private sector institutions. Two Chinese universities and one Indonesian company have received three approvals, two other Chinese research institutions have received two approvals, and the remaining institutions have each received one approval. Of these approved events, only the Chinese Academies of Sciences *Bacillus thuringiensis* (Bt) cotton event and the MAHYCO Bt eggplant event have ever been planted commercially. These data are evidence that, 20 years into the GMO era, there is very limited developing country precommercialization capacity, in either the number of institutions or the number of GMO technologies developed.

Table 10.5 Developing country domestic institutions with at least one cultivation approval, by sector, 1987–2015

Public/nonprofit institutions	Country	Crop	Approvals
1. Ag. Biotech Research Inst.	Iran	Rice	1
2. Cotton and Sericulture Dept.	Myanmar	Cotton	1
3. South China Ag. Univ.	China	Papaya	1
4. Chinese Acad. Ag. Sci.	China	Cotton	2
5. Beijing Univ.	China	Pepper, Tomato, Petunia	3
6. Huazhong Ag. Univ.	China	Rice, Tomato	3
7. Institute of Microbiology, CAS	China	Tomato	1
8. Research Institute of Forestry	China	Poplar	2
9. Embrapa	Brazil	Common Bean	1
10. Univ. Ag. Sciences Dharwad	India	Cotton	1
Total public/nonprofit			16

Private sector institutions*	Country	Crop	Approvals
11. JK Agri Genetics	India	Cotton	1
12. MAHYCO	India	Eggplant	1
13. Metahelix Life Sciences	India	Cotton	1
14. Nath Seeds	India	Cotton	1
15. Origin Agritech	China	Maize	1
16. FuturaGene Group	Brazil	Eucalyptus	1
17. PT Perkebunan Nusantara XI	Indonesia	Sugarcane	3
Total private			9

Source: ISAAA (2016). Retrieved June 22, 2016.

* Only domestic private sector, excludes multinational companies.

Area sown with GMOs

The data in this section are taken from James (2015). The rate of growth of GMO area has been rapid, compared to all previous agricultural technologies, including the semi-dwarf varieties of the Green Revolution. GMO area has grown by an average of 10 million hectares (ha) per year for 19 years to achieve 179.7 million ha by 2015 (Table 10.6). More than half of the area and two-thirds

Table 10.6 Global status of commercialized biotech/GM crops: 2015

Rank	Country	Area (m ha)	Cum. % area	GMO crops planted in 2014
1	US	70.9	39	Maize, soybean, cotton, canola, sugar beet, alfalfa, papaya, squash
2	Brazil	42.2	63	Maize, soybean, cotton
3	Argentina	24.5	77	Maize, soybean, cotton
4	India	11.6	83	Cotton
5	Canada	11.0	89	Canola, maize, soybean, sugar beet
6	China	3.7	91	Cotton, papaya, poplar, tomato, sweet pepper
7	Paraguay	3.6	93	Maize, soybean, cotton
8	Pakistan	2.9	95	Cotton
9	S. Africa	2.3	96	Maize, soybean, cotton
10	Uruguay	1.4	96	Maize, soybean
11	Bolivia	1.1	97	Soybean
12	Philippines	0.7	97	Maize
13	Australia	0.7	98	Cotton, canola
14	Burkina Faso	0.4	98	Cotton
15	Myanmar	0.3	98	Cotton
16	Mexico	0.1	99	Soybean, cotton
17	Spain	0.1	99	Maize
18	Colombia	0.1	99	Maize, cotton
19	Sudan	0.1	99	Cotton
20	Honduras	<0.1	100	Maize
21	Chile	<0.1	100	Maize, soybean, canola
22	Portugal	<0.1	100	Maize
23	Cuba	<0.1	100	Maize
24	Czech Rep.	<0.1	100	Maize
25	Romania	<0.1	100	Maize
26	Slovakia	<0.1	100	Maize
27	Costa Rica	<0.1	100	Soybean, cotton
28	Bangladesh	<0.1	100	Eggplant
Total		179.7	100	12 different crops grown in at least one country

Source: James (2015).

of the 28 countries planting GMOs in 2015 were developing countries. Some small countries, including Honduras, Myanmar, Burkina Faso, and Sudan, have commercialized GMOs.

Despite this rapid growth in area, by many measures the use of GMOs has been very narrow, broadening little over time. A total of 12 genetically engineered crops are grown somewhere in the world, but nearly 99 percent of global GMO area is planted with the same four animal feed, consumable oil, and fiber crops (maize, soybeans, cotton, and canola) that ushered in the GMO era in 1996–98 (Table 10.7). Ninety-nine percent of GMO area is under the same two functional traits (herbicide tolerance and insect resistance) that were introduced in 1996. Furthermore, nearly 90 percent of global GMO area is found in just five countries (United States, Brazil, Argentina, India, and Canada), a share that has changed little over the last ten years. The US share of global GMO area has declined slowly from 66 percent in 2001 to 39 percent in 2015.

The impact of GMOs on the global food supply has been overwhelmingly through the planting of GMO soybeans and yellow maize for livestock feed. The direct contribution of the GMO revolution to food security has been negligible, despite the investments that have been made by both the public and private sectors. The only food crop planted to a substantial area is white maize in South Africa and the Philippines, and less than 2 percent of global GMO area is devoted to growing food crops. The concentration of GMO area cultivated by multinational companies is also extreme. The only areas planted with GMO crops not developed by multinationals are VR papaya in the United States and China, Bt cotton in China, and insect-resistant (IR) eggplant in Bangladesh.

Table 10.7 GMO area for crops other than maize, cotton, soybean or canola, all countries, 2015

Crop and country	Area (ha)	Trait	Developer
Eggplant – Bangladesh	12	IR	MAHYCO*
Papaya – US	435	VR	Cornell & Univ. Hawaii*
Alfalfa – US	1,300	HT	Monsanto
Squash – US	2,000	VR	Monsanto
Papaya – China	8,475	VR	S. China U.*
Sugar beet – US and Canada	455,000	HT	Monsanto
Food/feed maize – Philippines	700,000**	IR/HT	Monsanto/Syngenta/DuPont
Food maize – South Africa	1,200,000	IR/HT	Monsanto/Syngenta/DuPont
Total non-big four crop area	2,767,222	(1.5% global GMO area)	
Total food crop area	2,365,922**	(1.3% global GMO area)	

Source: James (2015); Brookes and Barfoot (2016).

Note: HT=herbicide tolerance; IR=insect-resistant; VR=virus-resistant.
* Institution is not a multinational company.
** Distribution between food and feed maize area in the Philippines is not known.

Market size and incentives for GMO delivery to developing countries

With the minor exceptions noted earlier, the GMOs in use at present are feed and fiber crops, developed by multinational companies for farmers in the United States and Canada. These GMOs have spilled over to significant areas in developing countries. How strong is the incentive for a private firm to develop a GMO tailored to the needs of developing country farmers, as compared to the existing focus on adapting an existing GMO so that it spills over to a developing country market? Given that multinationals have been the conduit for nearly all of the GMOs delivered so far, under what conditions does a country represent an attractive market opportunity for a multinational biotechnology or seed firm to invest in products that are not based on products that are already successful in a developed country?

A multinational firm's decision about where and which GMO varieties to introduce can be modeled using a cost function of the variety production and delivery process (Figure 10.2). A firm will enter a market when the expected market price for the new variety (P_{GMO}) exceeds the long-run average cost of delivering the variety to farmers, including discovery R&D, regulatory costs, and distribution costs. To develop a new GMO variety from scratch is very expensive, especially given regulatory costs (Kalaitzandonakes, Alston, and Bradford 2006), and sometimes it is achieved through acquisition of an in-country established seed company that has commercially successful conventional varieties. The lower cost curve in Figure 10.2 represents the market entry decision for a GMO adapted from a crop variety that is already successful in a developed country market. In

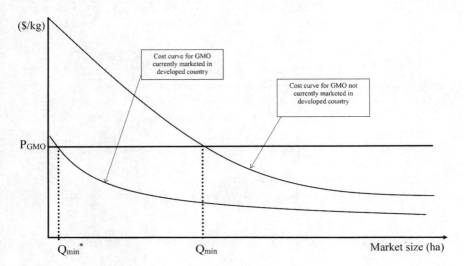

Figure 10.2 Minimum market sizes for GMO varieties that spill in from a developed country and for varieties developed specifically for developing countries

Source: Author's construction.

the case of the adapted variety, a large share of the fixed development costs are sunk, resulting in a much smaller minimum market size ($Q_{min}*$ instead of Q_{min}) requirement for the multinational firm to invest in delivering the GMO to the developing country. Once the sunk cost of gene discovery has been incurred during entry into the US market, GMO development costs are relatively low. The proven gene is simply backcrossed into a successful existing variety whose agronomic properties have already gained acceptance in the target market. Fixed costs are very low for the biotechnology firm, since the firm can partner with a national seed company. In a few instances, multinationals have directly introduced GMO varieties into new countries without any in-country adaptive breeding. Fixed costs are low since no breeding is done. It requires only that seed be multiplied and marketed. Monsanto has used this type of commission agreement with seed distributors in several countries that have agroclimatic conditions similar to the United States, including South Africa, Mexico, and Australia.

The spillover introduction has been the only pathway that has been successful for the private sector to date. It is possible that multinational companies will invest in biotechnology research for some important developing country problems, but the research would need to be for products with both high value to farmers and a large potential area. The potential for spillover to several developing countries would be helpful, so that the firm could amortize the development costs over large geographic areas and across several crops. An important obstacle to this private sector–led approach is the challenge of protecting intellectual property and generating revenue from seed sales in developing countries. Farmers are accustomed to saving seed, and rates of collection of GMO technology fees have been much lower in developing countries than in developed country markets (Traxler 2011). These considerations significantly reduce the incentive for multinationals to enter developing country markets.

Conclusions

The first 20 years of the GMO revolution have demonstrated that multinational corporations can deliver GMOs for animal feed crops, fiber crops, and consumable oil crops to developing countries when the following conditions apply:

1   The crop and trait have already been successfully developed in the United States or Canada;
2   An active seed market already exists; and
3   Intellectual property can be protected through hybrids or enforceable contracts.

In only a handful of instances have GMOs been delivered for food crops or by institutions other than multinational corporations. The challenge of the "GMO Revolution 2.0" is that of delivering GMOs for self-pollinating and clonal food crops that are not important in the United States, when seed markets are absent, and when IP cannot be protected. What does this imply about the potential for GMO technology to make a significant contribution to food security in developing countries in the coming years? What institutional challenges must be faced if the GMO revolution is to be expanded? How will the institutional infrastructure differ from that which has delivered the existing GMOs?

There is little overlap between current GMO crops and the crops that are important for food security in developing countries, and there are fundamental differences between the existing infrastructure for developing and delivering GMOs and the infrastructure for delivering non-GMO improved varieties of food crops. Among the current GMO crops, soybeans, canola, and cotton are not important sources of human food, and the maize GMOs that are currently grown are overwhelmingly hybrid yellow varieties for animal feed markets. The major food crops in developing countries are largely self-pollinating (wheat, rice, white maize, sorghum, millet) and clonal crops (cassava, bananas, potatoes). The CGIAR system and NARSs currently bear primary responsibility for developing and delivering improved varieties of these crops. Commercial seed markets for these food crops in developing countries are generally small, local, or nonexistent, and protection of intellectual property for these crops is difficult. It is unlikely that the multinational corporations that have been responsible for the GMO Revolution 1.0 will be as interested in leading the GMO Revolution 2.0, the food security revolution.

The delivery of food crop GMOs presents a number of new challenges that were not present during the Green Revolution. The scientific and operational span of the institutional infrastructure needed for the GMO Revolution 2.0 is much broader and more complex than that of the Green Revolution. While the CGIAR/NARSs partnership was able to deliver the Green Revolution, neither set of institutions has had a visible role in delivering GMOs to date. The creation of the semi-dwarf varieties was based on applied plant breeding, with little upstream R&D, and no concerns with respect to intellectual property or freedom to operate. Government support for GMO development and delivery is likely to be much lower that it was during the Green Revolution. After brief early resistance, national governments became strong supporters of efforts to deliver modern conventional varieties to their farmers during the Green Revolution. In contrast, the pressure of public resistance suggests that governmental support for the delivery of GMOs is anything but assured. Product liability concerns are also important to both the public and private sectors when GMOs are introduced.

References

Benbrook, C. M. 2012. "Impacts of Genetically Engineered Crops on Pesticide Use in the U.S. – The First Sixteen Years." *Environmental Sciences Europe* 24:24. doi:10.1186/2190-4715-24-24.

Brookes, G., and P. Barfoot. 2016. "Global Income and Production Impacts of Using GM Crop Technology 1996–2014." *GM Crops & Food* 6 (1): 13–46.

Chambers, J. A., P. Zambrano, J. Falck-Zepeda, G. Gruère, D. Sengupta, and K. Hokanson. 2014. "GM Agricultural Technologies for Africa: A State of Affairs." Report of a Study Commissioned by the African Development Bank, International Food Policy Research Institute/African Development Bank, Washington, DC.

Falck-Zepeda, J., and P. Zambrano. 2011. "Socio-economic Considerations in Biosafety and Biotechnology Decision Making: The Cartagena Protocol and National Biosafety Frameworks." *Review of Policy Research* 28 (2): 171–95.

Fuglie, K. O., and A. A. Toole. 2014. "The Evolving Institutional Structure of Public and Private Agricultural Research." *American Journal of Agricultural Economics* 96 (3): 862–83. doi:10.1093/ajae/aat107.

Gilbert, N. 2013. "Case Studies: A Hard Look at GM Crops." *Nature* 497 (7447): 24–6.

Gleim, S., S. Smyth, and P. Phillips. 2015. "Regulatory System Impacts on Global GM Crop Adoption Patterns." Paper prepared for presentation at the 19th International Consortium on Applied Bioeconomy Research (ICABR) Conference "Impacts on the Bioeconomy on Agricultural Sustainability, the Environment, and Human Health," Ravello, Italy, June 16–19, 2015.

Gurian-Sherman, D. 2009. *Failure to Yield Evaluating the Performance of Genetically Engineered Crops.* Cambridge, MA: Union of Concerned Scientists.

International Service for the Acquisition of Agri-Biotech Applications (ISAAA). 2016. GM Approval Database. http://www.Isaaa.Org/gmapprovaldatabase/

James, C. 2015. "20th Anniversary (1996 to 2015) of the Global Commercialization of Biotech Crops and Biotech Crop Highlights in 2015." ISAAA Brief No. 51. International Service for the Acquisition of Agri-Biotech Applications (ISAAA), Ithaca, NY.

Kalaitzandonakes, N., J. M. Alston, and K. J. Bradford. 2006. "Compliance Costs for Regulatory Approval of New Biotech Crops." In *Regulating Agricultural Biotechnology: Economics and Policy,* edited by R. E. Just, D. Zilberman, and J. M. Alston, 37–58. New York: Springer.

Klümper, W., and M. Qaim. 2014. "A Meta-Analysis of the Impacts of Genetically Modified Crops." *PLoS One* 9 (11). http://dx.doi.org/10.1371/journal.pone.0111629

Paarlberg, R. 2010. "GMO Foods and Crops: Africa's Choice." *New Biotechnology* 27 (5): 609–13.

Pardey, P. G., and J. M. Alston. 2010. "U.S. Agricultural Research in a Global Food Security Setting." A Report of the CSIS Task Force on Food Security, January 2010, Center for Strategic International Studies, Washington, DC. http://csis.org/publication/us-agricultural-research-global-food-security-setting

Pardey, P. G., and P. L. Pingali. 2010. "Reassessing International Research for Food and Agriculture." Report prepared for the Global Conference on Agricultural Research for Development (GCARD), Montpellier, France, March 28–31, 2010.

Qaim, M. 2009. "The Economics of Genetically Modified Crops." *Annual Review of Resource Economics* 1: 665–94.

Qaim, M. 2016. *Genetically Modified Crops and Agricultural Development.* Houndmills, Basingstoke, Hampshire, UK: Palgrave Macmillan.

Stone, G. D. 2002. "Both Sides Now: Fallacies in the Genetic-Modification Wars, Implications for Developing Countries, and Anthropological Perspectives." *Current Anthropology* 43 (4): 611–30.

Traxler, G. 2011. "Agricultural Biotechnology in Latin America: Economic Benefits, Regional Capacity and Policy Options." In *Financial Inclusion, Innovation, and Investments: Biotechnology and Capital Markets Working for the Poor,* edited by R. D. Christy and V. L. Bogan, 129–56. Hackensack, NJ: World Scientific.

USDA (United States Department of Agriculture). 2016. Animal and Plant Health Inspection Service Permits and Certifications Database. https://www.aphis.usda.gov/aphis/resources/permits

Vigani, M., and A. Olper. 2013. "GMO Standards, Endogenous Policy and the Market for Information." *Food Policy* 43 (12): 32–43.

Whitty, C. J. M., M. Jones, A. Tollervey, and T. Wheeler. 2013. "Biotechnology: Africa and Asia Need a Rational Debate on GM Crops." (Comment). *Nature* 497 (7447): 31–3.

Part 3

Community and rural institutions

11 Beyond hype

Another look at index-based agricultural insurance

Peter Hazell and Ulrich Hess

Introduction

There is a large literature and body of experience about the challenges of insuring farmers and rural communities, especially from an agricultural development perspective (e.g., Hazell, Pomareda, and Valdés 1986; Hazell 1992; Glauber 2004; Hazell et al. 2010; Mahul and Stutley 2010). Recent years have seen considerable progress in reforming and redesigning agricultural insurance to make it less costly and more attractive to farmers. Of particular note has been a shift away from publicly supported, multiple-peril crop insurance programs to index-based insurance (IBI), and to supplying insurance through various types of public–private partnership arrangements rather than through state-owned institutions (Hess, Hazell, and Kuhn 2016). The use of IBI has removed many of the disincentive problems and high costs that plagued agricultural insurance in the past, while the use of public–private partnerships has helped garner some of the efficiencies of the private sector with targeted public sector financing.

These changes have led to considerable expansion in the number of farmers who are now insured with some kind of IBI product. Based on a recent review of documented index-based agricultural insurance programs in the developing world, Hess, Hazell, and Kuhn (2016) estimated that about 198 million farmers are insured, divided into approximately 650,000 in Africa, 3.3 million in Latin America and the Caribbean, and about 194.2 million in Asia – of which 160 million are in China and 33.2 million in India (Table 11.1). Given that there are about 550 million farms in the developing world (Lowder, Skoet, and Singh 2014), it would seem that about one-third of them now have some kind of agricultural index insurance. Clearly, IBI has now achieved scale.

These are impressive numbers, but there are several reasons for concern. First, most of these programs insure farmers only against losses for specific crops or livestock, or pay to replace purchased inputs, or repay credit when insured losses occur. While useful, this may do little to insure farmers' total income or welfare against severe losses, or to protect them from falling into poverty. When catastrophic (cat) losses from natural disasters occur, many farmers must still depend on public assistance. Second, nearly all the programs are heavily subsidized (Table 11.1), at considerable cost to the public purse. In China, for example, the

Table 11.1 Scale of agricultural index insurance in 2014

	No. of policy holders (millions)	No. of schemes	Weighted average subsidy (%)
Africa	0.65	18	37
India	33.2	4	64
China	160.0	3	77
Other Asia	1.0	7	64
Latin America	3.3	8	91
Developing countries	198.2	40	

Source: Hess, Hazell, and Kuhn (2016).

government now spends about $6 billion annually[1] on its insurance programs, while the Indian government spends about $2.75 billion[2] (Hess, Hazell, and Kuhn 2016). So far, there is little evidence to show that this money is well spent in terms of any social cost-benefit analysis. Third, in nearly every case, the initiative for launching index-based insurance programs has been taken by public sector, civil society, or international development agencies, rather than by private insurers, despite early hopes that index-based insurance would be market-led.

In a thoughtful paper, Hans Binswanger has attributed these problems to an effective demand problem (Binswanger-Mkhize 2012). He argues that there is too much hype about IBI, because few farmers are willing to pay the full costs of providing it: better-off farmers, who can afford to pay, choose not to because they have other more cost-effective ways of managing their risks, while poor farmers, who most need the insurance, either cannot afford it or face severe liquidity constraints that prevent them buying it. Without adequate demand, private insurers will not offer the insurance in the absence of public subsidies. Moreover, to keep the costs of insurance and subsidies down, IBI products must be designed to focus on affordable risks that farmers perceive to be of direct value, and this excludes many of the cat risks to which farmers and rural communities are most vulnerable. In this chapter, we explore these issues more fully, and the conditions under which government subsidies might be justified.

What is holding back index-based insurance?

There have been several recent reviews of the challenges facing agricultural index-based insurance (Hazell et al. 2010; Binswanger-Mkhize 2012; Carter et al. 2014; Greatrex et al. 2015; Hess, Hazell, and Kuhn 2016). These include the problem of weak farmer demand mentioned earlier, but also difficulties in developing appropriate indices and distribution networks, coping with climate change, insufficient public investments in necessary public goods, and first mover problems. We discuss each in turn.

The demand problem

Few IBI schemes for farmers have achieved scale without being heavily sub-sidized and/or the insurance is made compulsory (e.g., for bank borrowers in India). Otherwise, relatively few farmers seem willing to purchase IBI products, in what appears to be a significant demand problem (Binswanger-Mkhize 2012). Several reasons have been suggested for this weak demand:

* Farmers have other ways of managing risk that may be more effective or less costly than insurance. However, better-off farmers probably have more options for managing risk than poor farmers (Binswanger-Mkhize 2012).
* Given that most farm households have developed diversified farming and livelihood strategies, an IBI targeted at severe weather outcomes, correlated with yield losses for specific crops, may correlate only weakly with losses in household income or consumption, and it is these correlations that really matter for rural households (Binswanger-Mkhize 2012).
* Insuring against agricultural risks is expensive. In many countries, cata-strophic events like droughts can occur with sufficient frequency, so that premium rates may need to exceed 10–15 percent just to cover the pure risk cost of the insurance (i.e., the average compensation expected). And such insurance would not even cover the many idiosyncratic risks that farmers face.
* Farmers do not value insurance that might not compensate them, when they have a loss for which they think they are insured. This is the basis risk problem. Worse, if they pay their premium and do not receive a pay-ment when they have a severe loss, they would be worse off that season than if they had not purchased the insurance (Clarke 2011; Binswanger-Mkhize 2012).
* Farmers may not have the liquidity to pay the insurance premium at the beginning of the farming season, particularly poorer farmers.

Estimates of demand elasticity for IBI, based on experimental games played with farmers, fall in the range −0.44 to −1.1, suggesting that the premium rate charged has a moderate impact on demand (De Bock and Gelade 2012). Transactions costs for farmers also matter (De Bock and Gelade 2012). If, for example, there are lengthy forms to be filled out or special journeys to make, then demand is weaker. This highlights the importance of marketing the insurance through existing distribution channels that farmers use and trust, such as microfinance or input suppliers.

Several quasi-experimental studies show that farmers' demand for insurance is negatively related to their degree of risk aversion (De Bock and Gelade 2012; Cole et al. 2013; Hill, Hoddinott, and Kumar 2013). Some studies attribute this to behavioral ambiguity about the insurance (i.e., farmers do not understand or trust the insurance, especially when it is new), which adds to the perceived risk of buying it. This seems to be confirmed by evidence showing that the negative relationship decreases over time as farmers become more familiar with insurance. If trust is the problem, then this again highlights the importance of working through existing distribution channels that farmers use and trust, such as microfinance or input suppliers. Experimental evidence also suggests that training and education do pay off in the case of agricultural IBI products, but results depend on the type of training provided (De Bock and Gelade 2012; Dercon et al. 2014).

Programs vary in how they tackle these problems. Many programs link the insurance to credit, access to modern inputs and better technologies, or to a better market outlet (e.g., contract farming), all of which can make the insurance part of a real value-adding proposition for insured farmers that extends beyond the value of its direct risk-reducing benefits (Hazell et al. 2010). Hess, Hazell, and Kuhn (2016) provide several current examples of these kinds of linkages, such as a PepsiCo scheme in India that provides insurance against potato blight to farmers contracted to sell potatoes of crisping quality to an agroprocessor; the R4 Risk Resilience initiatives in Ethiopia and Senegal that package the insurance with credit and some other risk-reducing interventions; and FreshCo in Kenya and Pioneer in Zambia, which sell insurance against failed plantings along with their improved seeds. In some cases, the IBI products are packaged with other types of insurance that farmers find attractive, such as life or accident insurance. For example, the Security Farm Supply (SFS) program in the Philippines bundles fertilizer insurance with accidental death insurance, and NWK AgriServices in Zambia has built weather and life insurance into its cotton farming contracts, in order to enhance farmers' loyalty and deliveries, and secure them against debt and livelihood problems in case of weather failures. To help make the insurance more affordable to the poor, the R4 Risk Resilience initiative in Ethiopia enables them to pay part (or all) of their premium with labor, working on community-identified projects that help reduce vulnerability to drought (e.g., soil and water conservation projects).

In order to increase the correlation between IBI and household income, there have been attempts to write IBI contracts against total crop or farm revenues rather than yields of individual crops. This approach requires reliable data on cropping patterns, yields, and prices to calculate an appropriate index. It has been adopted in the US agricultural insurance program, but does not seem to have been tried yet in a developing country.

Another factor that may be limiting demand is that index insurance is typically offered only to farmers, and often only to farmers growing particular crops or livestock. IBI has the potential to insure many other types of rural people, who are engaged in nonagricultural activities that are dependent directly or indirectly on local agriculture – for example, agricultural traders and processors, landless workers, and village shopkeepers. One program that reaches out more broadly is the Livelihood Protection Policy (LPP) in the Caribbean, which insures non-salaried income earners against adverse weather events, such as high wind speed and/or excessive rainfall (Hess, Hazell, and Kuhn 2016). The program also gives customers early warnings about adverse weather events, so they can take preventative actions. However, rather than offering the insurance on an unencumbered basis, it is tied to credit and distributed by financial institutions, and this seems to have limited demand.

The index problem

A fundamental requirement for IBI is the availability of an index that correlates highly with the agricultural risk to be insured, and for which there is a suitable and reliable database to perform actuarial calculations and objectively determine when an insured event has occurred. The index also needs sufficient spatial granulation to minimize basis risk. These can be daunting requirements in countries and regions with limited weather stations and variable agroecological conditions, and where the data are unreliable or released too late to be useful for determining payouts.

Technological advances are rapidly reducing the cost of adding secure weather stations, and in some countries private firms now offer weather station services for a fee (e.g., India). Greater problems are that additional weather stations add to the cost of developing and marketing insurance contracts, and new weather stations come without site-specific historical records and, hence, require the calculation of "synthetic" data sets (often based on the triangulation of data from nearby weather stations). The absence of sufficient weather stations in many countries has led to interest in indices that do not require local weather data at all, but which correlate highly with production or asset losses for many farmers. Area-based yield insurance is sometimes a viable alternative, although as an index it suffers because official yield measurements are sometimes unreliable and often reported quite late after the harvest, leading to delays in payment (something that has plagued the India area-yield insurance program NAIS). Mongolia has pioneered a livestock insurance program in which the index is a county-level livestock mortality rate, measured through an annual livestock census (Hellmuth et al. 2009).

There has been a lot of recent innovation in developing indices that can be assessed remotely with satellites, such as cloud cover, vegetative cover, or soil moisture content for a chosen region during critical agricultural periods. Such data is sometimes linked to a biophysical model that relates the remotely sensed data to the agricultural losses to be insured. For example, the Index-Based Livestock Insurance (IBLI) project has developed a remotely sensed vegetation index to insure livestock mortality losses in pastoral areas of Northern Kenya (Mude et al. 2010). In 2007, 10 percent of lower-middle-income countries had IBI schemes that used a satellite-sensed vegetative index (Mahul and Stutley 2010). The European Union's new satellite system Sentinel-2A could also be a game changer for the types of indices that can be developed and monitored around the developing world.[3] The Deutsche Gesellschaft für Internationale Zusammenarbeit (GIZ) Remote sensing-based Information and Insurance for Crops for Emerging economies (RIICE) project has pioneered radar satellite data-based enhancements of area yields for rice in Asia that allow for proper measurement of planted areas and yields in a timely manner.[4]

The distribution problem

There are serious difficulties and costs in marketing index insurance to large numbers of smallholders, and in collecting their premiums and making payments. Few private insurers have the required distribution networks in rural areas in developing countries, so they often work through an intermediary with an existing network of their own (e.g., a microfinance institution, bank, input dealer, agroprocessor, or NGO), or they work with groups of farmers who can be insured as single entities (e.g., farmer associations and mutual funds). For example, FreshCo in Kenya, SFS in the Philippines, and Pioneer and NWK AgriServices in Zambia all use private input dealers to market their insurance (Hess, Hazell, and Kuhn 2016). Examples of users of the aggregator approach are the Zambian National Farmers' Union, which arranges insurance for groups of its members, and Agroasemex in Mexico, which reinsures farmers' self-insurance funds (*fondos*). In China, village committees play the role of aggregator.

To address the problem of collecting premiums and making payouts in a timely and cost-effective manner, some insurers are taking advantage of mobile phone and mobile banking technologies. A good example is the ACRE program in East Africa, which enables farmers to pay their insurance premiums and receive payouts via the M-PESA mobile banking system (Hess, Hazell, and Kuhn 2016).

The climate change problem

Climate change is thought to be increasing both the frequency and severity of extreme weather events, especially in many drought-prone areas, and this is compounded by greater uncertainty about the levels of risk involved. Adapting to these changes may, in some cases, require major changes in farming systems and livelihood strategies, or even relocation for some people. More widely, it is likely to disrupt traditional risk avoidance and coping mechanisms at household- and community-levels, increasing the need for greater public and donor assistance in coping with catastrophic weather events. Under these circumstances, IBI ought to become an even more attractive risk management aid. However, its costs will also increase (IPCC 2014). This is because insurers will need to increase premium rates on a periodic basis to reflect higher payout levels, and they will need to add an additional premium charge to hedge against remaining uncertainties about the changing nature of insured risks. Index insurance can be adapted to climate change (e.g., Collier, Skees, and Barnett 2009). Suggested adaptations include the following:

- Adjusting the types of insurance offered in different regions to reflect changes in growing conditions and risk. Priced correctly, older products may become more expensive for farmers, while new products will be needed as farmers adapt their land use patterns and choice of technologies.
- Adjusting premium rates on a regular basis to reflect changing risks.
- Adapting to more pronounced cyclical weather patterns by, for example, moving toward longer-term (multi-season) contract arrangements.

• Adapting to the emergence of more available and accurate seasonal weather forecast data. This may require establishing earlier sell-by dates or adjusting premium rates to better match the purchase date with the availability of season-specific forecasts.

Public goods and first mover problems

Although private insurers are actively engaged in most of the known IBI programs, they have rarely initiated programs. Instead, governments, multinational agencies, such as the World Bank and World Food Programme (WFP), and international NGOs, like Oxfam, have played crucial initiating roles. This may be partly because insurers perceive a demand problem and are unwilling to move forward without public subsidies. However, there may also be important public roles that need to be met, without which the private insurers face high setup costs and barriers to entry. There is also a first mover problem: the high initial investment costs in research and development of index insurance products might not be recouped, given the ease with which competitors can replicate such products if they prove profitable to sell.

How the public sector can support IBI

The literature suggests a number of ways in which the public sector can promote IBI by creating a more enabling environment for private sector insurers (e.g., Hazell et al. 2010; Carter et al. 2014; Greatrex et al. 2015; Hess, Hazell, and Kuhn 2016). These include the following.

Building weather station infrastructure and data systems

As discussed earlier, weather index insurance requires a reliable weather station infrastructure, and these must be sufficiently dense to avoid excessive basis risk. Beyond the physical presence of weather stations, there is need to collect, maintain, and archive data, and to make it available on a timely basis. Given their multiple uses and public goods nature, these data should be placed in the public domain and made available to all. Much the same goes for making available reliable satellite data that can be used for IBI. It is not necessary that governments themselves collect and provide these data; private firms and research organizations can be contracted for this purpose. However, at least part of their cost will need to be paid by governments or donors if there are to be socially optimal levels of investment.

Supporting agro-meteorological research leading to product design

One of the challenges associated with private sector development of new financial products is the ease with which the products can be replicated by competitors. This free-rider problem discourages private insurers from making initial investments in new product development, especially in underdeveloped markets. Thus, some level of government and/or donor support for product development may be justified. These investments should be targeted at feasibility studies and pilot tests of new products with the involvement of local, private sector partners.

Provide an enabling legal and regulatory environment

Establishing a legal and regulatory environment for enforcing contracts that both buyer and seller can trust is a fundamental prerequisite for index insurance. Additionally, laws and regulations need to be consistent with international standards to improve the chances of insurers gaining access to global markets for risk transfer. Unfortunately, in many countries, regulations are simply not in place to accommodate the development and use of weather insurance products. Human capacity building and technical assistance are essential for preparing the legal and regulatory environment to govern index insurance programs.

Educate farmers about the value of insurance

To increase the likelihood that information is presented in a balanced way, and that sufficient investments are made in a broader educational effort for untested insurance products, public funds from governments and/or donors may be required. While private insurers will invest in marketing their products, they are unlikely to invest at socially optimum levels in educating farmers more generally about the appropriate role of insurance.

Facilitate initial international risk pooling or access to reinsurance

The highly covariate nature of the payouts for IBI poses a challenge to a private insurer. The insurer can hedge part of this risk by diversifying its portfolio to include indices and sites that are not highly and positively correlated, an approach that works best in large countries. Most often it is also necessary to sell part of the risk in the international financial or reinsurance markets. Until a sufficient volume of business is established to attract global reinsurers, extreme losses for the insurance pool may need to be underwritten by government and/ or donors, perhaps through risk pooling or contingent loan arrangements. For example, the World Bank provided a contingent loan arrangement to the Mongolian government as part of the reinsurance arrangements for the Index-Based Livestock Insurance Project (IBLIP), covering around 14,000 herders (Greatrex et al. 2015).

Although these kinds of interventions seem necessary, there is little evidence to suggest that they are sufficient to lead to the successful development of unsubsidized IBI programs. Indeed, if Hans Binswanger-Mkhize is right and the demand problem is as fundamental a constraint as he argues, then substantial subsidies or other forms of public support will nearly always be needed

(Binswanger-Mkhize 2012). Additional support for this argument is provided by Hess, Hazell, and Kuhn (2016); of all the IBI-like programs they review, the only programs with low or no subsidies are for insurance coverage provided within contract-farming arrangements. Most other forms of IBI are subsidized: the average subsidy for input supplier schemes is 37 percent, 40 percent for farmer group schemes, 63 percent for credit-linked schemes, 67 percent for direct insurance, and 80 percent for safety net insurance schemes. However, high levels of subsidy are not sufficient evidence of an effective demand problem because, as we shall discuss ahead, governments often subsidize agricultural insurance for broader political and social purposes, and this may lead to levels of subsidy that are much higher than needed to create an effective demand.

Role of subsidies

Several economic arguments have been made in the literature for temporarily subsidizing IBI programs to correct market failures and externalities (Clarke 2011; Hill, Hoddinott, and Kumar 2013). These include the following:

1   Temporary subsidies to overcome initial setup, first mover, or other market failure problems that can arise when an insurance market is first emerging. These are subsidies that go beyond the need for public investment in basic public services, such as provision of relevant weather and other agroclimatic data;
2   Temporary subsidies might be warranted for some types of farmers if there are positive externalities – for example, the insurance enables them to access game-changing credit and technologies that can lift them out of poverty. To be effective, subsidized insurance for this purpose typically has to be packaged with access to complementary inputs like credit or technology and targeted to the right farmers; and
3   Temporary subsidies might also be warranted as part of a strategy to assist farmers in adapting to climate change, where the subsidy is initially set to cover part or all of the difference in the premium rate between pre- and post-climate change scenarios.

To fulfill their purposes, such temporary subsidies need to be designed carefully, and the literature provides several guidelines for using subsidies in "smart" ways that avoid creating disincentive problems, or becoming a financial burden on the state (Hill, Hoddinott, and Kumar 2014).

•   A smart subsidy should have a clearly stated and well-documented purpose for the policymaker, such as addressing a market failure, equity, or climate change concern.
•   Subsidies should be well targeted to the specific segment of farmers or herders and specific areas that are intended to benefit, so as to minimize leakages to others.

- Subsidies will usually be less distorting if made directly to the insurer to offset administration and development costs rather than subsidizing the premium rates paid by farmers.
- If premium rates are to be subsidized, then it is better to do this on a per farmer basis, rather than on a risk premium proportional basis, in order to benefit smaller and poorer buyers who buy smaller amounts of insurance.
- There should be an explicit exit strategy or strategy for long-term financing.

Governments are rarely constrained by such narrow economic arguments, and often choose to heavily subsidize agricultural insurance for broader political and social purposes. These include using insurance as a means to support farm incomes, to substitute for disaster assistance spending, and to protect agricultural credit programs from bad debt.

If not well designed, these kinds of subsidies can inadvertently create disincentive problems that lead to significant economic costs and inefficiencies. For example, premium subsidies may encourage farmers to grow unsuitable crops in risky environments, leading to net social losses and adding to the future costs of insurance and the size of the subsidy (Siamwalla and Valdés 1986; Hess, Hazell, and Kuhn 2016). One way to reduce this problem is to ensure that the farmer's own premium payments are not less than the pure risk premium, so that on average the farmer pays an amount equal to or greater than the payouts received. Most insurance subsidies are set at levels well in excess of such a guideline, however. Poorly designed insurance subsidies can also reduce due diligence in lending practices by banks when credit is insured and the bank automatically receives the insurance payouts (Hazell, Pomareda, and Valdés 1986; Hazell 1992).

An economic justification for using insurance subsidies to achieve broader political and social purposes might arise, if it can be shown that they are a more cost-effective than alternative government interventions for achieving the same goals – for example, if an insurance subsidy is a more cost-effective way of supporting farm incomes than subsidizing farm inputs like fertilizer, supporting farm gate prices, or paying for environmental services. Analysis of such alternatives should consider the indirect costs of any disincentive problems that might arise from each intervention, and not merely compare their budgetary costs in the form of subsidy or support payments. While some past analysis of these issues has shown crop insurance to be an inferior instrument, this was based on the old model of publicly provided, multiple-peril crop insurance programs. For example, Pomareda (1986) showed that for the Agricultural Development Bank of Panama, a 2 percent increase in the interest rate that it was allowed to charge on farm loans would have been equally as effective as the entire crop credit insurance program in protecting the bank's lending portfolio. Such work needs to be updated to include more recent models of agricultural insurance, such as IBI and new delivery mechanisms like public–private partnerships and digital delivery channels, which may be more cost-effective, better targeted, and less distorting. In the next section, we consider the case of subsidized insurance offered on the grounds that it might be more cost-effective and less distorting in covering cat risks than some existing forms of disaster assistance programs.

Insurance and disaster assistance programs

Disaster assistance programs are driven more by humanitarian than development agendas, and their primary value is in saving lives. Some of them also aim to rebuild assets and livelihoods as part of recovery efforts. They are particularly helpful to the poor, who are generally more exposed to cat risks because of where they live and because they have the least options for coping with losses when they occur. As Carter and Barrett (2006) have shown, periodic cat losses can create poverty traps that suck vulnerable people into poverty and from which it is hard to escape. Disaster assistance programs are fully funded by donors, UN agencies, and governments, and unlike insurance they do not try to recoup any of their costs from the beneficiaries. In effect, beneficiaries receive a 100 percent subsidy, and this begs the question of whether some forms of subsidized insurance might be more cost-effective.

Although most programs achieve their primary objective of saving lives, they vary widely in terms of their cost, efficiency, and protection of assets and livelihoods. Two of the biggest practical challenges facing disaster assistance programs are: (1) the difficulty of targeting assistance to the truly needy under emergency conditions, while at the same time avoiding large leakages to others; and (2) the funding and launching of the assistance in a timely manner – by the time an emergency has been declared and an assistance effort underway, the assistance may arrive too late to relieve the worst suffering and losses.

Approaches to improving disaster assistance

There have been some recent and useful innovations in developing better approaches to overcoming the main challengers of disaster assistance programs, and two involve the application of subsidized IBI. One approach has been to improve the effectiveness of disaster assistance programs and to reduce or regularize their costs by using IBI. Another approach has been to replace part of disaster assistance with new types of subsidized IBI.

In a promising development, some government disaster assistance programs have been able to purchase international reinsurance to cover part of their expected assistance payments. The assured and timely payments received from a reinsurer, when a disaster occurs, can help avoid some of the delays and uncertainties incurred in obtaining emergency funding from government and/or donor sources. Reinsurance can also help smooth out the annual cost of a disaster assistance program to government and/or donors in the form of a predictable and regular annual premium. This kind of reinsurance works because most cat losses caused by natural disasters are relatively easy and transparent to observe, and can be indexed on the basis of existing data series to create an attractive IBI product for the reinsurance market. Moreover, since a disaster assistance agency aggregates losses to regional scales, it is much less troubled by basis risk problems than when index insurance is written for individual communities or households.

A good example is the Agricultural Fund for Natural Disasters (CADENA) in Mexico, which internationally reinsures part of the costs of Mexico's state-managed relief programs (Hess, Hazell, and Kuhn 2016). Several groups of countries have also successfully worked together to pool their risk and access international reinsurance against natural catastrophes. Schemes exist for the Caribbean, the Pacific Island countries, and Africa. Pooling and insuring cat risks in this way are less costly than if each country tries to reinsure independently, but even so, they come at a price. Clarke and Hill (2013) calculated that in a typical sovereign catastrophe risk pool, for every $1 of premium paid to a reinsurer, the members might expect to receive on average between $0.20 and $0.70 in claim payments over the long term. The rest of the premium goes toward administrative costs, capital costs, and profit for the insurance provider. The World Bank sometimes offers contingent loan arrangements that can be a less costly option than international reinsurance.

Another promising development is the linking of disaster relief programs with existing social protection systems, such as safety net and cash transfer programs, as these already have an infrastructure in place for identifying the poor and vulnerable and delivering assistance (Grosh et al. 2008; Alderman and Haque 2010). The objective is to give these social protection schemes the capacity to scale up rapidly after a disaster and increase both the size of the cash payments they make to beneficiaries and the number of beneficiaries they can support. In Ethiopia, for example, the government, the WFP, and the World Bank established the Livelihoods, Early Assessment and Protection (LEAP) mechanism in 2008 (Hess, Hazell, and Kuhn 2016). LEAP is an integrated food security and early response system that combines early warning, capacity building, contingency planning, and contingent finance. Although LEAP is based on donor-provided contingent financing rather than commercial insurance, it uses an index-based approach. LEAP seeks to bridge an "assistance gap" in the case of shocks in the government's Productive Safety Net Program (PSNP), and does this by allowing the immediate scale-up of the PSNP in anticipation of severe droughts.[5]

Another innovative approach is to replace relief with new types of subsidized index insurance. A concept developed at the WFP and GIZ seeks to make relief more assured and effective for the poor through the use of early recovery vouchers (ERVOs) (Hess et al. 2010). ERVOs are index-based insurance contracts targeted to poor households who are identified *ex ante*, based on national poverty lines or by a relevant safety net or cash transfer program. When a disaster occurs, insured households receive a guaranteed and immediate cash payment, preferably though mobile bank accounts. It is hoped that the assurance provided by ERVOs would enable poor households to take on greater risk in their livelihood strategies, increasing their average incomes. Moreover, instead of distributing the vouchers for free, recipient households might be asked to enact certain risk reduction measures, such as participation in training for good agricultural practices or disaster-proofing homes, or by participating in community-organized activities to improve disaster preparedness and mitigation. The index chosen for the insurance should correlate highly (on the downside) with major losses in the income or assets of poor households due to cat events, and should not be limited to farming households. ERVO-like schemes are being piloted in China, Peru, and Mexico's CADENA system, and have been proposed in Paraguay, and their experience bears watching.

Conclusions

Risk remains a serious and growing problem for farmers and rural communities in the developing world, and many governments have long felt the need to intervene through some form of subsidized insurance or disaster assistance program. Many of these past interventions have proven costly and inefficient, often distorting incentives for good risk management in both farming and rural finance. Recent years have seen considerable progress in reforming and redesigning agricultural insurance to make it less costly and more attractive to farmers. Key among these reforms is the growing use of IBI products, which now cover about one-third of all farmers in the developing world.

Although IBI has helped remove many of the perverse incentive problems and high costs that have plagued agricultural insurance in the past, many challenges remain. Without substantial subsidies, IBI is rarely able to scale up to reach many farmers, and tends to be limited to insuring rather narrow risks, like losses for specific crops or livestock, or reimbursing the cost of purchased inputs, or repaying credit when insured losses occur. While useful, this does little to insure farmers' total income or welfare against severe losses, or to protect them from falling into poverty. Nor does it protect them against catastrophic losses from natural disasters, leaving many farmers dependent on government or donor-funded disaster assistance programs.

There are important roles for the public sector in promoting IBI and greater involvement of private insurers. These include creating an enabling regulatory environment, investing in weather stations and agro-meteorological research and data systems, educating farmers about the value of insurance, and facilitating international reinsurance. There may also be a need for smart subsidies to correct initial market failures and externalities that hold back the development of markets for IBI products. Because of a fundamental demand problem (Binswanger-Mkhize 2012), however, these kinds of public interventions seem unlikely to be sufficient for IBI to play a major role in managing many of the more serious risks that plague farmers and rural communities. This leaves a large gap that has to be filled in part by self-insurance mechanisms, which do not work well for the poor, and in part by government- and/or donor-financed disaster assistance programs. This begs the question of whether governments should subsidize IBI at higher levels to enable it to substitute more effectively for these other forms of risk management.

Some governments already heavily subsidize IBI as part of broader political and social agendas, such as supporting farm incomes, substituting for disaster assistance spending, and protecting agricultural credit programs from bad debt. It is possible that use of IBI may be a more cost-effective and less distortionary way of achieving these goals than some other widely used methods of public intervention, though there has been little empirical research of this issue. However, as argued in this chapter, one promising development is the use of subsidized IBI products to improve disaster assistance programs. One approach is to improve the effectiveness of disaster assistance programs and to reduce or regularize their costs by using IBI to insure part of the loss payments they make. Another approach is to replace part of disaster assistance with new types of subsidized IBI products for poor farmers, like early recovery vouchers (ERVOs). In both cases, this might lead to cost savings, as well as more effective disaster assistance. Since disaster assistance programs are already fully funded by governments and donors, diverting part of the funds to subsidized IBI products might lead to better and more cost-effective outcomes.

Notes

1 2014; source: CIRC, Chinese Regulatory Authority.
2 Proposed budget for the new PMFBY scheme, comprehensive agricultural insurance especially for farmers with loans. http://pmjandhanyojana.co.in/pradhan-mantri-fasal-bima-crop-insurance-scheme
3 http://www.cnbc.com/2015/06/25/european-satellite-a-game-changer-for-farmers.html
4 http://www.riice.org
5 https://www.agriskmanagementforum.org/content/ethiopia%E2%80%99s-livelihoods-early-assessment-and-protection-leap-system-improving-climate-risk-ma

References

Alderman, H., and T. Haque. 2010. "Insurance Against Covariate Shocks: The Role of Index-Based Insurance in Social Protection in Low-Income Countries of Africa." World Bank Working Paper No. 95, Africa Human Development Series, World Bank, Washington, DC. http://documents.worldbank.org/curated/en/158791467990329754/pdf/400020PAPER 0Co10082137036701PUBLIC1.pdf

Binswanger-Mkhize, H. P. 2012. "Is There Too Much Hype about Index-based Agricultural Insurance?" *Journal of Development Studies* 48 (2): 187–200.

Carter, M. R., and C. B. Barrett. 2006. "The Economics of Poverty Traps and Persistent Poverty: An Asset-based Approach." *Journal of Development Studies* 42 (2): 178–99.

Carter, M., A. de Janvry, E. Sadoulet, and A. Sarris. 2014. "Index-based Weather Insurance for Developing Countries: A Review of Evidence and a Set of Propositions for Up-scaling." Background Document for the Workshop: "Microfinance Products for Weather Risk Management in Developing Countries: State of the Arts and Perspectives," Paris, June 25, 2014. http://www.afd.fr/webdav/shared/PORTAILS/EVENEMENTS/Ferdi-AFD-working-paper-on-index-insurance.pdf

Clarke, D. J. 2011. "A Theory of Rational Demand for Index Insurance." Discussion Paper No. 572, Department of Economics, University of Oxford. http://www.economics.ox.ac.uk/Department-of-Economics-Discussion-Paper-Series/a-theory-of-rational-demand-for-index-insurance

Clarke, D., and R. V. Hill. 2013. "Insuring Countries against Natural Disasters." IFPRI Policy Brief 22, International Food Policy Research Institute (IFPRI), Washington, DC. http://www.ifpri.org/publication/insuring-countries-against-natural-disasters-pool-rules

Cole, S., X. Giné, J. Tobacman, R. Townsend, P. Topalova, and J. Vickery. 2013. "Barriers to Household Risk Management: Evidence from India." *American Economic Journal: Applied Economics* 5 (1): 104–35.

Collier, B., J. R. Skees, and B. J. Barnett. 2009. "Weather Index Insurance and Climate Change: Opportunities and Challenges in Lower Income Countries." *Geneva Papers on Risk and Insurance* 34 (3): 401–24.

De Bock, O., and W. Gelade. 2012. "The Demand for Microinsurance: A Literature Review." Research Paper No. 26, Microinsurance Innovation Facility, International Labour Office (ILO), Geneva. http://www.ilo.org/public/english/employment/mifacility/download/repaper26.pdf

Dercon, S., R. V. Hill, D. J. Clarke, I. Outes-Leon, and A. S. Taffesse. 2014. "Offering Rainfall Insurance to Informal Insurance Groups: Evidence from a Field Experiment in Ethiopia." *Journal of Development Economics* 106: 132–43.

Glauber, J. 2004. "Crop Insurance Reconsidered." *American Journal of Agricultural Economics* 86 (5): 1179–95.

Greatrex, H., J. Hansen, S. Garvin, R. Diro, S. Blakeley, M. Le Guen, K. Rao, and D. E. Osgood. 2015. "Scaling Up Index Insurance for Smallholder Farmers: Recent Evidence and Insights." CCAFS Report No. 14, CGIAR Research Program on Climate Change, Agriculture and Food Security (CCAFS), Copenhagen. https://cgspace.cgiar.org/bitstream/handle/10568/53101/CCAFS_Report14.pdf

Grosh, M., C. del Ninno, E. Tesliuc, and A. Ouergh. 2008. *For Protection and Promotion: The Design and Implementation of Effective Safety Nets.* Washington DC: The World Bank. http://siteresources.worldbank.org/SPLP/Resources/461653-1207162275268/For_Protection_and_Promotion908.pdf

Hazell, P. 1992. "The Appropriate Role of Agricultural Insurance in Developing Countries." *Journal of International Development* 4 (6): 567–81.

Hazell, P., J. Anderson, N. Balzer, A. H. Clemmensen, U. Hess, and F. Rispoli. 2010. "The Potential for Scale and Sustainability in Weather Index Insurance for Agriculture and Rural Livelihoods." International Fund for Agricultural Development (IFAD) and World Food Programme (WFP), Rome. https://www.ifad.org/documents/10180/32647150-6e8a-41f3-8642-404768cfc99f

Hazell, P., Pomareda, C., and A. Valdés, eds. 1986. *Crop Insurance for Agricultural Development: Issues and Experience.* Baltimore: Johns Hopkins University Press.

Hellmuth, M. E., D. E. Osgood, U. Hess, A. Moorhead, and H. Bhojwani, eds. 2009. *Index Insurance and Climate Risk: Prospects for Development and Disaster Management.* Climate and Society No. 2. International Research Institute for Climate and Society (IRI). New York: Columbia University.

Hess, U., N. Balzer, S. Calmanti, and M. Portegies-Zwart. 2010. "CERVO: Community Early Recovery Voucher Scheme for Catastrophic Weather Disaster Hedging." In *Weather Risk Management: A Guide for Corporations, Hedge Funds and Investors,* edited by K. Tang, 215–30. London: Risk Books.

Hess, U., P. Hazell, and S. Kuhn. 2016. "Innovations and Emerging Trends in Agricultural Insurance." Deutsche Gesellschaft für Internationale Zusammenarbeit (GIZ) GmbH, Bonn and Eschborn, Germany.

Hill, R. V., J. Hoddinott, and N. Kumar. 2013. "Adoption of Weather-index Insurance: Learning from Willingness to Pay among a Panel of Households in Rural Ethiopia." *Agricultural Economics* 44 (4–5): 385–98.

IPCC (Intergovernmental Panel on Climate Change). 2014. *Climate Change 2014: Impacts, Adaptation, and Vulnerability.* IPCC Working Group II Contribution to the Fifth Assessment Report (WGII AR5), edited by C. B. Field, V. R. Barros, D. J. Dokken, K. J. Mach, M. D. Mastrandrea, T. E. Bilir, M. Chatterjee, K. L. Ebi, Y. O. Estrada, R. C. Genova, B. Girma, E. S. Kissel, A. N. Levy, S. MacCracken, P. R. Mastrandrea, and L. L. White. Cambridge, UK: Cambridge University Press.

Lowder, S. K., J. Skoet, and S. Singh. 2014. "What Do We Really Know about the Number and Distribution of Farms and Family Farms Worldwide?" Background paper for *The State of Food and Agriculture 2014.* ESA Working Paper No. 14-02, Agricultural Development Economics Division, Food and Agriculture Organization of the United Nations (FAO), Rome. http://www.fao.org/docrep/019/i3729e/i3729e.pdf

Mahul, O., and C. Stutley. 2010. *Government Support to Agricultural Insurance: Challenges and Options for Developing Countries.* Washington, DC: World Bank.

Mude, A. G., S. Chantarat, C. B. Barrett, M. Carter, M. Ikegami, and J. McPeak. 2010. "Insuring against Drought-related Livestock Mortality: Piloting Index-based Livestock Insurance in Northern Kenya." In *Towards Priority Actions for Market Development for African Farmers: Proceedings of an International Conference.* May 12–15, 2009, Nairobi, Kenya, 175–188. Nairobi: Alliance for a Green Revolution (AGRA) and International Livestock Research Institute (ILRI). https://cgspace.cgiar.org/bitstream/handle/10568/16493/AGRA-ILRI-13-IBLI.pdf?sequence=1

Pomareda, C. 1986. "An Evaluation of the Impact of Credit Insurance on Bank Performance in Panama." In *Crop Insurance for Agricultural Development: Issues and Experience,* edited by P. Hazell, C. Pomareda, and A. Valdés, 101–114. Baltimore: Johns Hopkins University Press, for the International Food Policy Research Institute (IFPRI).

Siamwalla, A., and A. Valdés. 1986. "Should Crop Insurance Be Subsidized?" In *Crop Insurance for Agricultural Development: Issues and Experience,* edited by P. Hazell, C. Pomareda, and A. Valdés, 117–25. Baltimore: Johns Hopkins University for the International Food Policy Research Institute (IFPRI).

12 Beyond water markets

Second-best water allocation policy?

Mark W. Rosegrant,[1] *Man Li, and Wenchao Xu*

Introduction

Rosegrant and Binswanger (1994) made the case that markets in tradable water rights would improve the efficiency and productivity of irrigation in developing countries. A significant literature has further developed this theme (Easter, Rosegrant, and Dinar 1998). Despite the apparent benefits, water markets have developed slowly in developing (and developed) countries (Easter and Huang 2014). The basic argument against markets in tradable water rights is that the transactions and equity costs exceed the social benefits. The transactions costs include not only the changes in physical hardware to convey the traded water but also the analytical, legal, and institutional frameworks to assure both buyer and seller the exact quantities transferred, and to confirm the absence of externalities imposed on third parties due to the trade. It is also argued that equity could worsen within the irrigated sector or across sectors, with richer irrigators and cities dominating markets and marginalizing smaller irrigators. The social benefits include the net income gains generated through water trade and induced efficiency gains, taking account of positive and negative externalities. This chapter examines whether alternative water allocation mechanisms can achieve levels of efficiency and productivity approaching those achievable through formal markets in tradable water rights.

In a seminal paper, Weitzman (1974) pointed out that, in theory, there is nothing to recommend resource allocation through indirect control by prices, compared to direct regulation of quantities. In the context of water allocation to irrigation, there is no fundamental difference between having the water agency assign prices, with farms responding with quantities, and having the agency assign water rights, with the farm revealing marginal costs through its water usage decision. The choice of control mode depends on the relative effectiveness of one over the other. If there is any advantage to choosing price or quantity control modes, it must be due to inadequate or asymmetric information, uncertainty, or unequal sharing of risk among water users (Weitzman 1974; Burness and Quirk 1979, 1980).

Pezzey (1992) discussed the concept of a "charge–subsidy" scheme for control of pollution. He showed symmetry between pollution control through pricing (charge–subsidy) and by quantity, using a marketable permit scheme. Rosegrant, Ringler, and Rodgers (2005) adapted the idea to water allocation, with water rights assigned to farmers based on historical rights, and a price for water assigned by the water agency. Water users are then charged (or paid) at the assigned price for water demand above (or below) the assigned water rights. In a modeling application, Rosegrant, Ringler, and Rodgers (2005) showed that the charge–subsidy approach achieved relatively high economic returns, but they did not establish general grounds for efficiency of this mechanism.

Brill, Hochman, and Zilberman (1997) analyzed "passive" water markets, which are virtually equivalent to the charge–subsidy scheme. Water rights follow historical rights, and the water agency announces a water price that clears aggregate demand and supply in the irrigation system. Farmers determine their water use at that price, pay the marginal price for water use above their historical right, and receive the marginal price for water saved when they use less than the historical right. The passive market is distinguished from formal water markets because the buyer (seller) does not have to pursue a matching seller (buyer). Each farmer determines his or her water use at the price determined by the central management without requiring a unique water market. Brill, Hochman, and Zilberman (1997) showed that passive water markets yield efficient allocation, subject to the water agency knowing aggregate demand and supply in the system.

In this chapter, we examine the efficiency of prices and quantities in the allocation of irrigation water. We extend Brill, Hochman, and Zilberman (1997), by incorporating uncertainty in production and by dropping the assumption that the water agency has perfect knowledge of aggregate supply and demand. Two alternatives to formal water markets are assessed here: voluntary or passive trading, and allocation of quotas.

The remainder of this chapter is organized as follows: the next section models the farmers' and the water agency's decisions under the existing and alternative water allocation systems. Next, we compare the expected net benefits under the alternative systems. Then we undertake an application of the model, using data from Eastern Idaho, and illustrate its major conclusions. The final section provides discussion and conclusions.

The model

We consider the case of a waterway with N farms and a volume of $\overline{W}$ units discharged to agriculture. Compared to the agricultural land resources, water resources are scarce and water constraint is binding in the waterway. All farmers are risk-neutral. They have rights to access water resources for irrigation. Water or water rights are non-tradable.

In particular, we explicitly model farm i's production function of irrigation, $y^i(\alpha w_i, \eta)$, where w_i represents the units of water discharged to farm i, α represents the proportion of received water actually used for agriculture, and η represents a random variable. The rest of water, equivalent to $(1-\alpha)w_i$, returns to the waterway. Uncertainty is introduced into the farm's production since, at any given level of water inputs, outputs are likely to depend on unobserved factors, such as weather. In the context of this study, we use the subscripts of a function to denote the order of partial derivatives of the function. For instance, $y_1^i(\cdot)$ represents the first-order partial derivatives of $y^i(\cdot)$ with respect to (w.r.t.) the first argument αw_i in the function – that is, $y_1^i(\cdot) \equiv \frac{\partial y^i(\alpha w_i, \eta)}{\partial(\alpha w_i)}$ – and $y_2^i(\cdot)$ represents the first-order partial derivatives of $y^i(\cdot)$ w.r.t. the second argument η – that is, $y_2^i(\cdot) \equiv \frac{\partial y^i(\alpha w_i, \eta)}{\partial \eta}$; whereas $y_{11}^i(\cdot)$ represents the second-order partial derivatives of $y^i(\cdot)$ w.r.t. αw_i – that is, $y_{11}^i(\cdot) \equiv \frac{\partial^2 y^i(\alpha w_i, \eta)}{\partial(\alpha w_i)^2}$ – and y_{12}^i represents the second-order mixed partial derivatives of $y^i(\cdot)$ w.r.t. αw_i and η in order – that is, $y_{12}^i \equiv \frac{\partial^2 y^i(\alpha w_i, \eta)}{\partial(\alpha w_i)\partial \eta}$. The production function $y^i(\cdot)$ is assumed to be positive, increasing, and strictly concave in αw_i, and its second derivatives are symmetric. These assumptions imply that $y^i(0, \eta) > 0$, $y_1^i(\cdot) > 0$, $y_{11}^i(\cdot) < 0$, and $y_{12}^i(\cdot) = y_{21}^i(\cdot)$.

For simplicity, the price of outputs is normalized, and a uniform water price p is given. Assuming that water is expensive to transport and water conveyance will cause negative externalities on soil, the associated costs are $\tau d_i w_i$, where τ denotes the unit conveyance cost plus monetized damage caused by water transportation, and d_i is the distance from the water source to farm i. These costs fall on farm i.

Farmer's problem

The farm i's objective is to choose a nonnegative water use level to maximize the profit from irrigation:

$$\max_{w_i} y^i(\alpha w_i, \eta) - \tau d_i w_i - p w_i, \text{ s.t. } w_i \leq \bar{w}_i, \tag{12.1}$$

where $\bar{w}_i$ represents the amount of water that farm i is allowed to use; $\sum_i \bar{w}_i = \bar{W}$ and $\bar{W}$ is the total volume of water discharged for agricultural use. The first-order condition (FOC) of solving (12.1) can be derived as follows:

$$\alpha y_1^i(\alpha w_i^*, \eta) - \tau d_i - p - \lambda_i = 0, \tag{12.2a}$$

$$\lambda_i(\bar{w}_i - w_i^*) = 0, \tag{12.2b}$$

where λ_i is the nonnegative shadow value of farm i's water resource constraint. Based on (12.2a) and (12.2b), one can easily derive farm i's optimal irrigation water inputs:

$$w_i^* = \min\left[h^i(p + \tau d_i, \alpha, \eta), \bar{w}_i\right], \tag{12.3}$$

where $h^i(p + \tau d_i, \alpha, \eta)$ stands for the farm's response function when water constraint is unbounded.

The efficiency of water resource allocation depends on the distribution of water rights, which have often historically been predetermined. The distribution of historical water rights results in inefficient water resource allocation, except when the constraints for all farms happen to be non-binding.

Policy option: Voluntary trading

This section explores whether, or under what conditions, allowing farmers to choose their water use levels voluntarily will lead to an outcome that maximizes social welfare. The voluntary approach has been frequently discussed in the literature of nonpoint pollution control (Segerson 1988; Segerson and Wu 2006). It has the potential to provide greater flexibility than traditional water trading in achieving the first- or second-best solution while lowering transaction costs, especially those of legal obstacles, political and social barriers, and systems of water rights.

Under the concept of voluntary action, a general incentive scheme is introduced:

$$T(w_i, \overline{w}_i) = t(w_i - \overline{w}_i), \tag{12.4}$$

where t is a tax/subsidy payment announced by the water agency. Any given farm i is allowed to "sell" or "purchase" water by the amount that w_i differs from $\overline{w}_i$, although water rights are officially non-tradable. Thus, the individual water constraints no longer bind. More important, a formal water market is not needed. Water conserved by "sellers" will be automatically transferred to "buyers" at little transaction cost, including the cost of obtaining information, finding willing traders, negotiation, effecting and registering trades, enforcing trade contracts, and so forth.

Under this circumstance, farm i revises its objective function by taking into account the potential payment:

$$\max_{w_i} \gamma^i(\alpha w_i, \eta) - \tau d_i w_i - p w_i - t(w_i - \overline{w}_i). \tag{12.5}$$

The FOC is:

$$\alpha \gamma_1^i(\alpha \tilde{w}_i, \eta) - \tau d_i - p - t = 0. \tag{12.6}$$

The farm's response function can be derived accordingly:

$$\tilde{w}_i = h^i \left(p + t + \tau d_i, \alpha, \eta \right). \tag{12.7}$$

Assuming that the water agency knows only farms' aggregate demand for water, given farmers' response functions, the objective of the water agency is to choose a combination of water price p and tax/subsidy payment t to maximize the expected social welfare:

$$\hat{U} \equiv \max_{\{p+t\}} E\left\{\sum_i \left[y^i(\alpha \tilde{w}_i, \eta) - \tau d_i \tilde{w}_i\right] - C(\tilde{W}, \theta)\right\}^2, \tag{12.8}$$

where $\tilde{W} = \sum_i \tilde{w}_i$ and $C(\cdot, \theta)$ represents the cost function; θ is a random variable. $C(\cdot)$ is assumed to be increasing and strictly convex in the total supplied water (i.e., $C_1(\cdot) \equiv \frac{\partial C(W, \theta)}{\partial W} > 0$ and $C_{11}(\cdot) \equiv \frac{\partial^2 C(W, \theta)}{\partial W^2} > 0$). Solving (12.8) and inserting farms' FOC condition (12.6) yields the following:

$$\tilde{p} + \tilde{t} = \frac{E\left[C_1(\tilde{W}, \theta)\left(\sum_i h_1^i\right)\right]}{E\left(\sum_i h_1^i\right)}, \tag{12.9}$$

where $h_1^i \equiv \frac{\partial h^i(p+t+\tau d_i, \alpha, \eta)}{\partial(p+t+\tau d_i)}$. There are numerous combinations of water prices and tax/subsidy payments that satisfy the condition (12.9). In practice, the water agency often sets the price in order to balance the budget:[3]

$$\tilde{p} = \frac{E\left[C(\tilde{W}, \theta)\right]}{E(\tilde{W})}. \tag{12.10}$$

Thus, an average cost-pricing strategy is applied to water price, and the value of $\tilde{t}$ can be derived from (12.9) and (12.10), accordingly.

Policy option: Mandatory quotas

Alternatively, the water agency can choose farm-specific water quotas as an instrument to maximize social welfare. Information about farm-level characteristics is, however, too expensive to be gathered. To simplify the analysis, we make three assumptions about the farm's production function in the region. First, all farms have same technology (production function). Second, the farm's production function is constant returns to scale (CRS), so that it is separable in land and water inputs – that is, $y^i(\alpha w_i, \eta) \equiv l_i f\left(\frac{\alpha w_i}{l_i}, \eta\right)$, where l_i denotes the area of irrigated land and $f(\cdot)$ represents the farm's yield function. Third, the cropping pattern is homogeneous across farms and is stable over time. Under these simplifying assumptions, the water agency can design farm-specific water quotas, according to farm size l_i and the distance from the water source d_i to maximize the expected social welfare:[4]

$$\hat{U} \equiv \max_{\{w_i\}_{i=1}^N} E\left\{\sum_i \left[y^i(\alpha w_i, \eta) - \tau d_i w_i\right] - C\left(\sum_i w_i, \theta\right)\right\}. \tag{12.11}$$

The solution $\{\hat{w}_i\}_{i=1}^N$ must satisfy the FOC:

$$\alpha E\left[y_1^i(\alpha \hat{w}_i, \eta)\right] - \tau d_i = E\left[C_1(\hat{W}, \theta)\right], \quad \forall\, i, \qquad (12.12)$$

where $\hat{W} = \sum_i \hat{w}_i$.

Voluntary trading vs. mandatory quotas

This section compares the expected social welfare benefits under the two policy instruments and investigates the conditions under which one dominates the other. Following Weitzman (1974), we define the comparative advantage of voluntary trading over mandatory quotas as the difference in the expected net benefits under the two instruments: $\Delta \equiv \tilde{U} - \hat{U}$. Voluntary trading will be more efficient if and only if $\Delta > 0$.

To this end, we apply the Taylor series approximation of $y^i(\cdot)$ around $(\alpha\hat{w}_i, 0)$ and $C(\cdot)$ around $(\hat{W}, 0)$ to separate the random terms from the deterministic terms:

$$y^i(\alpha w_i, \eta) = y^i(\alpha \hat{w}_i, \eta) + \alpha(y_1^i + y_{12}^i \eta)(w_i - \hat{w}_i)$$
$$+ \frac{1}{2}\alpha^2 y_{11}^i (w_i - \hat{w}_i)^2, \qquad (12.13)$$

and

$$C(W, \theta) = C(\hat{W}, \theta) + (C_1 + C_{12}\theta)(W - \hat{W}) + \frac{1}{2}C_{11}(W - \hat{W})^2, \qquad (12.14)$$

where y_1^i, y_{11}^i, and y_{12}^i are $y_1^i(\cdot)$, $y_{11}^i(\cdot)$, and $y_{12}^i(\cdot)$, respectively, evaluated at $(\alpha\hat{w}_i, 0)$; likewise, C_1, C_{11}, and C_{12} are $C_1(\cdot)$, $C_{11}(\cdot)$, and $C_{12}(\cdot)$ evaluated at $(\hat{W}, 0)$. Therefore, these partial derivatives are fixed coefficients. The proofs for equations (12.13) and (12.14) are available in the appendix.

Differentiating (12.13) and (12.14) w.r.t. αw_i and W yields:

$$y_1^i(\alpha w_i, \eta) = (y_1^i + y_{12}^i \eta) + y_{11}^i(w_i - \hat{w}_i), \qquad (12.15)$$

and

$$C_1(W, \theta) = (C_1 + C_{12}\theta) + C_{11}(W - \hat{W}). \qquad (12.16)$$

Without loss of generality, we assume that $E(\eta) = E(\theta) = 0$, $E(\eta^2) = \sigma_\eta^2$, and $E(\eta \cdot \theta) = 0$. Combining (12.15)–(12.16) and the FOCs (12.6), (12.9), and (12.12), plugging the resulting values into Δ, and collecting terms, we have the following results.

Proposition 1

The comparative advantage of the voluntary trading over the mandatory quotas in the presence of uncertainty is

$$\Delta = \frac{1}{2}\sigma_\eta^2 \left[(\alpha^2 - 2\alpha)\sum_i \frac{\left(\gamma_{12}^i\right)^2}{\gamma_{11}^i} - C_{11}\left(\sum_i \frac{\gamma_{12}^i}{\gamma_{11}^i}\right)^2 \right]. \tag{12.17}$$

The proof for Proposition 1 is given in the appendix. This comparative advantage is linearly associated with the variance of uncertainty η in the production function – the larger the degree of η, the greater the difference of the expected net benefits between the two instruments.

In comparison, the uncertainty θ in the cost function of water supply does not appear in (12.17), due to the fact that the expected cost function is independent of the variance of θ, as long as the production uncertainty and the cost uncertainty are uncorrelated – that is, $E(\eta \cdot \theta) = 0$ (see Weitzman [1974] and Stavins [1996] for more discussions). To illustrate this argument, let us consider an extreme case in which the marginal product (*MP*) of water is known with certainty (i.e., $\sigma_\eta^2 = 0$), but the marginal cost (*MC*) is uncertain, as shown in Figure 12.1. Let MC_R be the realized marginal cost and MC_E be the water

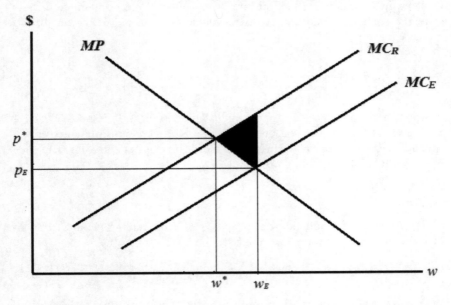

Figure 12.1 Welfare analysis when the marginal cost of water supply is uncertain (trading and quotas are indifferent)

Source: Authors.

agency's expected marginal cost. If the agency chooses voluntary trading, it will set the price of p_E (including tax/subsidy). If the agency chooses mandatory quotas, it will impose a quota of w_E. Both instruments will induce the same level deviation from the optimal level of water use w^*, leading to the same amount of deadweight loss that equals the shaded area. Under this circumstance, trading and quotas are indifferent and $\Delta = 0$.

A simple rule

While Proposition 1 presents the general formula of the comparative advantage of voluntary trading versus mandatory quotas, it is useful to investigate some special cases in order to make the comparison more straightforward. Previously, we have assumed a homogeneous, CRS production function of all farms. This section further simplifies the analysis on the supply side. Specifically, we introduce the farm average cost function of water supply $c(w,\theta) \equiv C(W,\theta)/L$, where $L \equiv \sum_i l_i$ and $w \equiv W/L$, representing the average units of water discharged to each acre.[5] By definition, $c_1(\cdot) = C_1(\cdot)$ and $c_{11}(\cdot) = L \cdot C_{11}(\cdot)$. Under these simplifying assumptions, formula (12.17) can be reduced to (12.18).

Proposition 2

If all farms' production functions are homogeneous and constant returns to scale, the comparative advantage of the voluntary trading over the mandatory quotas equals

$$\Delta = \frac{1}{2} L \sigma_\eta^2 \left(\frac{f_{12}}{f_{11}} \right)^2 \left[(\alpha^2 - 2\alpha) f_{11} - c_{11} \right], \tag{12.18}$$

where f_{11} and f_{12} are $f_{11}(\cdot)$ and $f_{12}(\cdot)$, evaluated at $(\alpha \hat{w}_i / l_i, 0)$, respectively; c_{11} is $c_{11}(\cdot)$, evaluated at $(\frac{W}{L}, 0)$. The proof for expression (12.18) is presented in the appendix. Rearranging the terms in the square brackets of the right-hand side of equation (12.18) implies Corollary 1.

Corollary 1

In the presence of production uncertainty, voluntary trading is more efficient than the mandatory quotas, if and only if

$$c_{11} < (\alpha^2 - 2\alpha) f_{11}. \tag{12.19}$$

Whether the voluntary trading dominates the mandatory quotas depends on the relative curvature of farmers' production functions and the water agency's average cost function, or alternatively speaking, it depends on the relative slope of farmers' marginal product of water (demand curve) and the water agency's marginal cost of water supply (supply curve). When the marginal product of water use is uncertain, voluntary trading is better, if and only if farms' average production function is more sharply curved or the water agency's cost function of providing average water use per farm is closer to being linear.

To illustrate this corollary, let us consider another extreme case in which the marginal cost (MC) of water provision is known with certainty, but the marginal product (MP) of water use is uncertain, as shown in Figures 12.2 and 12.3. Let MP_R be the realized marginal product and MP_E be the water agency's expected marginal product. If the agency chooses voluntary trading, it will set the price of p_E (including tax/subsidy), and the realized water use level is w_R. If the agency chooses mandatory quotas, it will impose a quota of w_E. While both instruments will induce deviation from the optimal level of water use, the amounts of deadweight loss are different because the relative slopes of the MC and MP curves differ. In Figure 12.2, the MP curve is steeper than the MC curve. In this case, a small miscalculation of water quota would induce a large deadweight loss (shaded area in black). In contrast, voluntary trading is superior because it gives farmers flexibility to choose water use level and its social deadweight loss (shaded area in gray) is small. In Figure 12.3, the opposite is true since the MP curve is flatter than the MC curve.

The evidence in the literature supports the case shown in Figure 12.2, with the preponderance of evidence showing that the water demand curve for irrigation is inelastic. Scheierling, Loomis, and Young (2006) undertook a meta-analysis

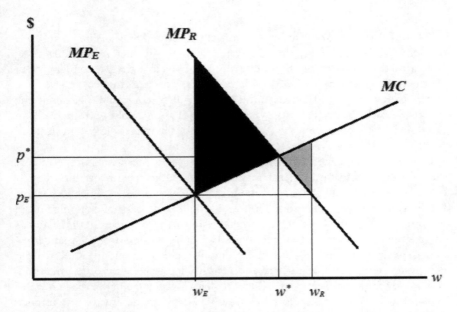

Figure 12.2 Welfare analysis when the marginal product of water use is steeper (trading is better)

Source: Authors.

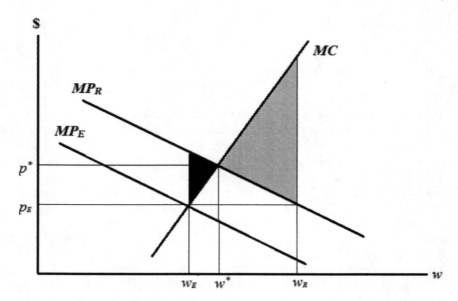

Figure 12.3 Welfare analysis when the marginal cost of water supply is steeper (quotas are better)

Source: Authors.

of 24 studies on irrigation water demand in the United States. The mean price elasticity of demand for irrigation water from the studies reviewed is 0.48, with a median of 0.16 in absolute terms, showing that the preponderance of elasticities is quite low, with a few high outliers. The marginal cost curve for a water agency in an existing irrigation system will, in contrast, be flat since the marginal cost of water delivery will not increase appreciably with increases in water delivery, approaching the design capacity of the irrigation system (English 1990; Qiu and Prato 2012).

One might well expect that farmers are risk-averse, and farmers, especially at the tail ends of irrigation systems, may have some subjective uncertainty regarding whether they will indeed get more than their traditional allocation/rights if they were to plan their production under the expectation of "buying" more water than their historical water allotments. Although this uncertainty is likely to change the comparative advantage of the voluntary trading over the mandatory quotas, we can still demonstrate that trading is superior to quotas, as long as the new water demand curve for irrigation is sufficiently inelastic or the marginal cost curve for a water agency is sufficiently flat. A water agency's expected water demand will always deviate from the realized water demand due to the existence of uncertainty η, independent of whether there is subjective uncertainty about irrigation water supply received by individual farmers with risk aversion. Introducing an additional uncertainty with risk aversion will change farmers' response function (12.7), and the formulas derived in the aforementioned propositions and corollary, but it will not undermine the basic conclusions of this study. A complete derivation is given in the appendix.

In addition to the relative curvature of the production and cost functions, whether trading is superior to quotas is influenced by farmers' water use efficiency (α). This is because water use efficiency is itself a component of farmers' production function. Given one unit increase in water use efficiency, the more sharply curved the production function, the more likely voluntary trading is superior to the mandatory quotas. This result is summarized in Corollary 2.

Corollary 2

The propensity of the voluntary trading dominating the mandatory quotas increases with farmers' water use efficiency (α) if and only if:

$$\frac{\partial \log f_{11}}{\partial \alpha} > \frac{2(1-\alpha)}{\alpha(\alpha-2)}. \tag{12.20}$$

The proof for Corollary 2 follows simply by taking the derivative of $(\alpha^2 - 2\alpha)f_{11}$, w.r.t. α.[6] Because $0 < \alpha < 1$, the right-hand side of expression (12.20) is always negative. It is interesting to look at some special cases of the production function. If water and land inputs are perfect substitutes, for instance, expression (12.20) will always hold, since $\frac{\partial f_{11}}{\partial \alpha} = 0$. Under this condition, increasing water use efficiency will raise the propensity of trading dominating quotas. In contrast, if water and land inputs are perfect complements, expression (12.20) will no longer hold, because $\frac{\partial f_{11}}{\partial \alpha} \to +\infty$ and $\frac{\partial \log f_{11}}{\partial \alpha} \to -\infty$. Under this situation, increasing water use efficiency will reduce the likelihood of trading dominating quotas. If water and land inputs are partly substitutes, whether expression (12.20) holds depends on the elasticity parameters of output w.r.t. water and land inputs. As we will demonstrate in the next section, under the specification of a CRS Cobb–Douglas production function, the propensity of the voluntary trading dominating the mandatory quotas always *decreases* with farmers' water use efficiency.

Empirical analysis

In this section, we use an empirical example to illustrate the major conclusions derived from the model. Data were collected from the Eastern Snake River Plain Aquifer Area (ESPA), one of Idaho's prime agricultural areas. Farmers in the ESPA practice irrigated agriculture. According to the Land Cover and Vegetation for the Eastern Snake River Plain Irrigated Land developed by the Idaho Department of Water Resources (IDWR), approximately 83.1–84.3 percent of farmland was irrigated from 2008 to 2010. Farmers grow a variety of crops, including, predominantly, alfalfa, barley, dry beans, corn, hay pasture, lentil, oat, onion, peas, potato, sugar beet, and wheat (durum/spring/winter). The land that is contributed to these 14 major crops has higher irrigation coverage, ranging from 92.0 percent to 94.2 percent.

To calculate the average crop yield, we first identified crop varieties at the field level using the Cropland Data Layer that is published annually by Cropscope through the United States Department of Agriculture–National Agricultural Statistics Service (USDA–NASS). We integrated the field varieties with the average crop yield, referenced at the state level and reported through the Quick Stats of Crops and Vegetables Price Received and Yield (for 2003–2007) for Idaho by the USDA–NASS. The crop reference yield, composition, and irrigation status data are combined to calculate average crop yield in each farm. We distinguished crop yields under irrigation and non-irrigation status and focus only on the average yield under irrigation status, which is consistent with the setups of the theoretical model. The average crop yield of irrigated major crops reaches 12,296–13,125 pounds per acre. We noted, however, that adding yields in a multi-cropping environment requires stable crop mixing patterns, which generally applies in the ESPA region, where relative shares of each crops do not demonstrate significant changes over time.

Irrigation application or diversion data in the region are subject to strict data access restrictions due to privacy concerns and are generally unavailable at the micro level. The information on irrigation application rate was retrieved in two steps. We integrated the field varieties with the average evapotranspiration, the reference level of crop water use intensity reported by the weather station network, AgriMet (Bureau of Reclamation, US Department of Interior). The average crop water use intensity was calculated for farms, representing water necessary for crop physiological needs and thus highly relevant to crop productivity. The calculation indicates that farm-level crop water use intensity for irrigated major crops is approximately 32.26–32.74 acre-inches (or 2.68–2.73 acre-feet) per acre per annum. Next, we introduced a loss factor to the crop water use intensity to approximate actual irrigation application rate. The loss factor was assembled using factors related to dissipation, evaporation, leakage, and transport loss based on distances to major water bodies and the ratio of irrigated land to total farmland.

Parameterization

The parameter values used in this illustration are reported in Table 12.1. The actual irrigation application efficiency (α) in the field is not available. Howell (2003) provided a range of typical farm and field irrigation application efficiencies. Considering the relatively higher percentage of land using sprinkler irrigation (Kenny et al. 2009) and the existence of other irrigation technologies, such as gravity and central pivot irrigation, we set the value of α at 0.75 and choose a range of (0.65, 0.85) for the purpose of a robustness test.

On the production side, the yield elasticity of farm water use (adjusted) is estimated at 0.1598, which is consistent with the inelastic yield response to water application in the existing literature (Moor, Gollehon, and Negri 1993; Frisvold and Konyar 2012; Frija et al. 2014). The estimated variance for the random term associated with the production function (σ_η^2) is 0.0981. The value was obtained

Table 12.1 Parameter values used in this illustration for equation (12.18)

Parameters	Symbols	Value
Irrigation application efficiency	α	0.75
Yield elasticity of farm water use	β	0.1598
Variance of uncertainty in crop production function	σ_η^2	0.0981
Slope of marginal yield of irrigation	f_{11}	−9.19
Derivative of marginal yield of irrigation, w.r.t. production uncertainty	f_{12}	32.4
Slope of marginal cost of irrigation	c_{11}	0.1–15.1
Total irrigated major cropland area (million acres)	L	1.82
Farm water use intensity (acre-feet/acre)	w	3.99
Comparative advantage of trading over quotas (million US$)	Δ	9.556–(7.450)
Per acre comparative advantage of trading over quotas (US$/acre)	Δ/L	5.245–(5.089)
Threshold for c_{11} (no difference between trading and quotas)		8.53

Source: Authors.

Note: Farm water use intensity is the total water diverted to farm divided by irrigated land area. Taking into account the loss in the diversion process, the water use intensity will reduce to approximately 2.73 feet per acre. Parentheses in the column of value represent a minus sign.

from the estimated variance–covariance matrix for the random effects associated with the crop yield per acre water use as the sole input.

On the cost side, the slope of marginal cost function of irrigation is insufficiently addressed in the literature. The literature uses the linear form of cost, in general (see, e.g., English [1990]; Qui and Prato [2012]), implying that the value of c_{11} is small. Therefore, it is assumed that c_{11} takes the value of 0.10, at which inequality (12.19) holds. All parameters are calculated based on the formulas provided in the appendix. We use an average price index of $0.059 per pound to adjust f_{11} and f_{12} to be consistent with the dimension of c_{11}.

When α equals 0.75 and c_{11} takes the value of 0.10, compared to mandatory quotas, employing voluntary trading would reduce the deadweight loss by approximately 5.245 USD per acre. This figure is large. It is equivalent to 9.556 million USD in the whole study area. Even when the value of c_{11} increases due to the capacity constraints in water supplies, trading is still superior to quotas, as long as the value of c_{11} is less than 8.53. Once c_{11} passes the threshold of 8.53, quotas become more efficient. Given that the cost function is expected to be relatively flat, voluntary trading dominates quotas over the likely range.

As a robustness check, we considered alternative levels of water use efficiency by assuming α equals 0.65, 0.85, and 1, respectively. We compared the results with the reference level and illustrate the comparison in Figure 12.4. Three points emerge from this sensitivity analysis. First, the increased irrigation application

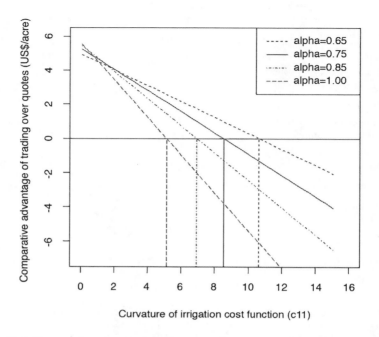

Figure 12.4 Comparative advantage of voluntary trading over mandatory quotas under various assumptions of c_{11} and α (water use efficiency)

Source: Authors.

efficiency decreases the threshold value for c_{11}, all else being equal. Intuitively, if farmers are using water more efficiently, the need to trade is reduced. This result is consistent with our previous discussion of Corollary 2. That is, if the production function is of the Cobb-Douglas type and exhibits CRS, the voluntary trading is less likely to dominate the mandatory quotas as farmers' water use efficiency increases. Second, in an extreme case of zero return flows (i.e., $\alpha = 1$), trading dominates over quotas as long as the value of c_{11} is less than 5.12. This finding is important. In ESPA, voluntary trading could be safely employed if the marginal cost curve for the local water agency is relatively flat. Third, the more efficient the irrigation application, the more sensitive the comparative advantage of trading over quotas to changes in c_{11}. This observation indicates that while the improvement of irrigation application efficiency is widely promoted, the water agency should carefully evaluate the marginal cost of irrigation water supply to avoid big miscalculations of the relative benefits of trading versus quotas.

Conclusions

We have shown theoretically, and in an empirical example, that for the normally prevailing shape of irrigation water production and cost functions, a voluntary water-trading scheme generates higher benefits than a quota allocation system. The greater the uncertainty in production, the larger the benefit advantage for trading, which is an important finding, given the likelihood of increased production uncertainty under climate change (Rosegrant et al. 2013). A third important finding is that the more efficient the farmers' water management, the lower the relative benefits generated by voluntary trading. An intuitive explanation of this finding is that the more efficient usage of the diverted water for each farmer in the system increases the value of water use and production and, therefore, reduces the need and benefits for trade. Water trading is in effect a partial substitute for farm-level water use efficiency. Moreover, the voluntary trading system has significantly lower transaction costs than formal markets in water rights. Under the voluntary system, water conserved by "sellers" will be automatically transferred to "buyers" at little transaction cost, avoiding the cost of obtaining information, finding willing traders, negotiation, effecting and registering trades, and enforcing trade contracts. Voluntary trading also appears to be a politically feasible approach. Historical water rights are recognized, and the marginal efficiency prices (charge–subsidies) apply only to marginal water use, so voluntary trading introduces nonpunitive incentives compared to other water pricing schemes.

Appendix

Proof of equations (12.13) and (12.14)

We applied the Taylor series approximation of $\gamma^i(\cdot)$ around $(\alpha\hat{w}_i, 0)$ and $C(\cdot)$ around $(\hat{W}, 0)$. We considered the Taylor series approximation only up to the second order throughout the following discussion in order to be simple and consistent.

$$
\begin{aligned}
\gamma^i\left(\alpha w_i, \eta\right) &\approx \gamma^i\left(\alpha\hat{w}_i, 0\right) + \gamma_1^i \alpha\left(w_i - \hat{w}_i\right) + \gamma_2^i \eta \\
&\quad + \frac{1}{2}\gamma_{11}^i \alpha^2 \left(w_i - \hat{w}_i\right)^2 + \frac{1}{2}\gamma_{22}^i \eta^2 + \gamma_{12}^i \eta\alpha\left(w_i - \hat{w}_i\right),
\end{aligned}
\tag{A.12.1}
$$

where γ_1^i, γ_2^i, γ_{11}^i, γ_{22}^i, and γ_{12}^i are $\gamma_1^i(\cdot)$, $\gamma_2^i(\cdot)$, $\gamma_{11}^i(\cdot)$, $\gamma_{22}^i(\cdot)$, and $\gamma_{12}^i(\cdot)$, respectively, evaluated at $(\alpha\hat{w}_i, 0)$. By definition,

$$
\gamma^i\left(\alpha\hat{w}_i, \eta\right) \approx \gamma^i\left(\alpha\hat{w}_i, 0\right) + \gamma_2^i \eta + \frac{1}{2}\gamma_{22}^i \eta^2.
\tag{A.12.2}
$$

Combining (A.12.1) and (A.12.2) gives:

$$
\begin{aligned}
\gamma^i\left(\alpha w_i, \eta\right) &\approx \gamma^i\left(\alpha\hat{w}_i, \eta\right) + \alpha\left(\gamma_1^i + \gamma_{12}^i \eta\right)\left(w_i - \hat{w}_i\right) \\
&\quad + \frac{1}{2}\alpha^2 \gamma_{11}^i \left(w_i - \hat{w}_i\right)^2.
\end{aligned}
\tag{A.12.3}
$$

Likewise, the cost function can be approximated as:

$$
\begin{aligned}
C\left(W, \theta\right) &\approx C(\hat{W}, 0) + C_1(W - \hat{W}) + C_2\theta + \frac{1}{2}C_{11}(W - \hat{W})^2 \\
&\quad + \frac{1}{2}C_{22}\theta^2 + C_{12}\theta(W - \hat{W}),
\end{aligned}
\tag{A.12.4}
$$

where C_1, C_2, C_{11}, C_{22}, and C_{12} are $C_1(\cdot)$, $C_2(\cdot)$, $C_{11}(\cdot)$, $C_{22}(\cdot)$, and $C_{12}(\cdot)$, respectively, evaluated at $(\hat{W}, 0)$. By definition,

$$
C(\hat{W}, \theta) \approx C(\hat{W}, 0) + C_2\theta + \frac{1}{2}C_{22}\theta^2.
\tag{A.12.5}
$$

Combining (A.12.4) and (A.12.5) gives:

$$C(W,\theta) \approx C(\hat{W},\theta) + (C_1 + C_{12}\theta)(W - \hat{W}) + \frac{1}{2}C_{11}(W - \hat{W})^2. \quad \text{(A.12.6)}$$

Proof of Proposition 1

Substitute $w_i = \hat{w}_i$ into (12.15) and $W = \hat{W}$ into (12.16), then taking the expected value of $y_1^i(\alpha\hat{w}_i, \eta)$ and $C_1(\hat{W}, \theta)$ gives:

$$E\left[y_1^i\left(\alpha\hat{w}_i, \eta\right)\right] = y_1^i, \quad \text{(A.12.7)}$$

and

$$E\left[C_1(\hat{W}, \theta)\right] = C_1. \quad \text{(A.12.8)}$$

Substituting from (A.12.7) and (A.12.8) into (12.12):

$$\alpha y_1^i - \tau d_i = C_1. \quad \text{(A.12.9)}$$

Substituting from (12.15) into (12.6) and rearranging the equation yields:

$$\tilde{w}_i = h^i(\tilde{p} + \tilde{t} + \tau d_i, \alpha, \eta) = \hat{w}_i + \frac{(\tilde{p} + \tilde{t} + \tau d_i) - \alpha(y_1^i + y_{12}^i\eta)}{\alpha y_{11}^i}, \quad \text{(A.12.10)}$$

implying,

$$h_1^i = \frac{1}{\alpha y_{11}^i}. \quad \text{(A.12.11)}$$

Substituting from (A.12.11) into (12.9) and canceling $\sum_i \frac{1}{\alpha y_{11}^i}$ yields:

$$\tilde{p} + \tilde{t} = E\left[C_1(\tilde{W}, \theta)\right]. \quad \text{(A.12.12)}$$

Replacing W ($W = \sum_i w_i$) in (12.16) by the expression for $\tilde{w}_i$ from (A.12.10) and plugging into (A.12.12), we have:

$$\tilde{p} + \tilde{t} = C_1. \quad \text{(A.12.13)}$$

Combining (A.12.9) and (A.12.13), (A.12.10) is reduced to:

$$\tilde{w}_i = \hat{w}_i - \frac{y_{12}^i}{y_{11}^i}\eta, \quad \text{(A.12.14)}$$

Alternately, substitute $w_i = \hat{w}_i$ and $w_i = \tilde{w}_i$ from (A.12.14) into (12.13) and (12.14) and collecting terms, we have equation (12.17).

Proof of Proposition 2

By definition, $f_1(\cdot) = \gamma_1^i(\cdot), f_{11}(\cdot) = l_i\,\gamma_{11}^i(\cdot)$, and $f_{12}(\cdot) = \gamma_{12}^i(\cdot)$. Replacing the production $\gamma^i(\cdot)$ with the yield function $f(\cdot)$ in (12.17) and collecting terms,

$$\Delta = \frac{1}{2}\sigma_\eta^2\left(\frac{f_{12}}{f_{11}}\right)^2\left[(\alpha^2 - 2\alpha)f_{11}\sum_i l_i - C_{11}\left(\sum_i l_i\right)^2\right], \tag{A.12.15}$$

where f_{11} and f_{12} are $f_{11}(\cdot)$ and $f_{12}(\cdot)$ evaluated at $(\alpha\hat{w}_i/l_i, 0)$.

Let $L \equiv \sum_i l_i$, representing the total land area in the waterway. Then, $c(w,\theta) \equiv C(W,\theta)/L$ implies that $c_{11} = L \cdot C_{11}$, where c_{11} is $c_{11}(\cdot)$, evaluated at $(\frac{W}{L}, 0)$. Inserting γ_{11} and c_{11} into (A.12.15) yields equation (12.18).

Superiority of voluntary trading under water supply uncertainty and risk aversion

This appendix presents a more rigorous discussion regarding the superiority of the voluntary trading modality under the assumptions of uncertainty in individual irrigation water supply and risk-averse farmers.

Let us assume that all farmers are risk-averse with a concave utility function. There exists uncertainty ξ, in addition to η and θ, in individual irrigation water supply when "voluntary trading" is implemented. Let γ be a vector of moments of the random variable ξ. Each farmer maximizes his/her expected utility with respect to water demand at a given water price. At equilibrium, farmer i's demand for water $\tilde{w}_i'$ will deviate from the original optimal water demand $\tilde{w}_i$, as shown in equation (12.7) in the text. This deviation also changes farmers' aggregate demand for water. Without loss of generality, we write $\tilde{w}_i'$ as $\tilde{w}_i' = g^i(p + t + \tau d_i, \alpha, \eta, \gamma)$.

The water agency, however, cannot observe farmers' utility functions or the farmers' concerns about water supply uncertainty. Therefore, the water agency's problem remains unchanged – that is, the agency still chooses a combination of price and tax/subsidy payment to solve the FOC (12.9) in the text.

The effect of uncertainty ξ on Δ will depend on how the new realized aggregate water demand for irrigation deviates from the previous realized aggregate water demand for irrigation. In general, we can still demonstrate that voluntary trading is better, as long as the new farms' average production function with uncertainty is more sharply curved or the water agency's cost function of providing average water use per farm is closer to being linear.

To illustrate this statement, let us consider two cases. In the first case, the existence of ξ increases risk-averse farmers' individual and aggregate water demand, as shown in Figure A.12.1. This situation is likely to happen when farmers' marginal product of water is a convex function – that is, the marginal product of water decreases at a decreasing rate. The intuition of the increase is that increasing water use above the amount that is needed on average imposes less

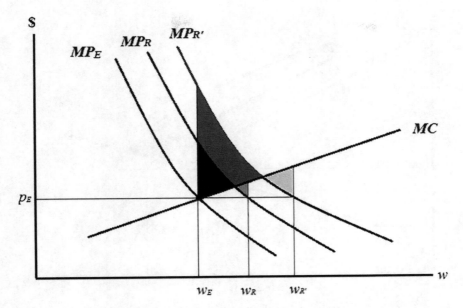

Figure A.12.1 Welfare analysis when the marginal product of water use is a convex function
Source: Authors.

loss when water is abundant than the gain when water is deficient. Thus, it pays for a *risk-neutral* farmer to use more water than would be needed if the irrigation water supply is known with certainty.[7] The separate effect of risk aversion can be demonstrated by solving the risk-averse farmer's problem—the expected marginal product of water at the optimal solution is less than the risk-neutral solution, implying that a risk-averse farmer's demand for water is greater than a risk-neutral farmer's water demand. This effect, together with the effect of a convex marginal product of water, leads to an increase in farmers' individual and aggregate water demand.

Let MP_E be the water agency's expected marginal product; MP_R, the previous realized marginal product (without ξ); and $MP_{R'}$ the new realized marginal product (including ξ and risk aversion). The MP_R and $MP_{R'}$ curves are steeper than the MC curve. In this case, the existence of ξ increases the deadweight loss induced by voluntary trading from the shaded area in medium gray to the shaded area in light gray; it also increases the deadweight loss induced by mandatory quotas from the shaded area in black to the shaded area in black and dark gray. Trading is still superior to quotas because it has a small deadweight loss.

In the second case, the existence of ξ reduces risk-averse farmers' individual and aggregate water demand, as shown in Figure A.12.2. This situation is likely to happen when farmers' marginal product of water is a concave function (i.e., the marginal product of water decreases at an increasing rate), which causes a

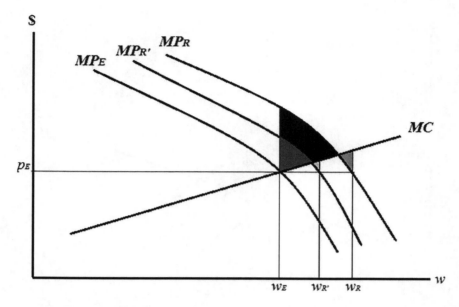

Figure A.12.2 Welfare analysis when the new marginal product of water use is a concave
function and the effect of the concavity outweighs the effect of risk aversion

Source: Authors.

reduction in farmers' demand for water with uncertainty. In addition, the negative effect of a concave marginal product function on water demand outweighs
the positive effect of risk aversion. As a result, the realized marginal product
shifts to the left. Under this situation, the deadweight loss induced by mandatory
quotas decreases from the shaded area in black and dark gray to the shaded area
in dark gray, and the deadweight loss induced by voluntary trading decreases
from the shaded area in medium gray to the shaded area in light gray. In this
case, trading is better. It is easy to show that this conclusion is still valid if the
positive effect of risk aversion on water demand outweighs the negative effect
of a concave marginal product function.

Estimating the farm's production function

Using farm-level measures of crop water use intensity and crop yield, we estimated the farmer's production function. We assume that the production func-
tion takes the Cobb–Douglas functional form $f\left(\frac{\alpha w_i}{l_i}, \eta\right) = A e^{\eta} \left(\frac{\alpha w_i}{l_i}\right)^{\beta} =: e^{\mu} \left(\frac{w_i}{l_i}\right)^{\beta}$,
where A is a non-stochastic term representing technology, η is a random variable
with mean zero and variance σ_{η}^2, and β stands for the elasticity of output w.r.t.
irrigation water. We define $\mu \equiv \log A + \eta + \beta \log \alpha$. As shown in the latter
specification, μ and β are unknown parameters to be estimated directly from

the data sample, and σ_η^2 can be derived indirectly from the estimated variance–covariance matrix.

Taking the logarithm of the yield function and using the random effects model to estimate the equation gives the estimates of unknown parameters.

$$\widehat{\log f} = 9.024 + .1598 \times \log\left(\frac{w}{l}\right). \tag{A.12.16}$$

By definition, $\hat\sigma_\eta^2 = \hat\sigma_\mu^2 + \hat\sigma_\beta^2 (\log\alpha)^2 - 2\hat\sigma_{\mu\beta} \log\alpha$.

$$\hat{f}_{12} = \hat{f}_1 = \hat\beta\alpha^{-1}e^{\hat\mu}\left(\frac{w}{l}\right)^{\hat\beta-1}, \text{ and}$$

$$\hat{f}_{11} = \hat\beta(\hat\beta-1)\alpha^{-2}e^{\hat\mu}\left(\frac{w}{l}\right)^{\hat\beta-2}.$$

Data on 14 major crops

Table A.12.1 Reference levels of yield and water use, percentage on irrigated land, and yield elasticities for 14 major crops surveyed by the USDA–NASS in Idaho

Crops	Average yield per acre			Average crop water use-ET (inches)	Farm-level crop percentage on irrigated land	Yield elasticity to water (with reference)
	Irrigated	Non-irrigated	Units			
Alfalfa	4.72	1.43	ton	41.5	37.3	0.1382 (Moore et al. 1993)
Barley	98.26	43.36	bu	26.9	13.4	0.0201 (Moore et al. 1993)
Corn (sweet & field)	139.40	36.40	bu	26.7	8.8	0.0641–0.0856 (Moore et al. 1993)
Dry beans	23.28	19.40	cwt	20.5	2.1	0.0257 (Moore et al. 1993)
Hay pasture	1.81	0.93	ton	33.0	2.3	0.0779 (Moore et al. 1993)
Lentil*	10.60	–	cwt	20.5	–	–
Oat	80.00	31.30	bu	26.9	0.7	–
Onion*	660.00	–	cwt	28.7	0.0	0.0509–0.0511 (Just et al. 1983)
Peas*	15.00	–	cwt	15.6	0.4	–
Potato*	368.60	–	cwt	27.5	10.3	0.1145 (Moore et al. 1993)

(Continued)

Table A.12.1 (Continued)

Crops	Average yield per acre			Average crop water use-ET (inches)	Farm-level crop percentage on irrigated land	Yield elasticity to water (with reference)
	Irrigated	Non-irrigated	Units			
Sugar beet*	30.22	–	ton	33.9	4.7	0.0549 (Moore et al. 1993)
Wheat (durum)	95.27	24.33	bu	26.9	19.9	0.0410 (Antle and Hachett 1986)
Wheat (spring)	91.32	40.46	bu	26.9		0.0833 (Moore et al. 1993)
Wheat (winter)	112.94	62.76	bu	24.7		0.1510 (Frija et al. 2014)

Source: *Yield*: the US Department of Agriculture, National Agricultural Statistics Service, Stats of Crops and Vegetables Price Received and Yield for 2003–2007; the yield data on corn and hay are unavailable for Idaho, and thus the average value from neighboring states of Wyoming and Montana is used. *ET*: the US Department of Interior, Bureau of Reclamation, Pacific Northwest Region, AgriMet, Crop Water Use Information. *Crop percentage*: Idaho Department of Water Resources, Land Cover and Vegetation, Eastern Snake River Plain Irrigated Land; Idaho Department of Water Resources, Water Rights Layers; the US Department of Agriculture, National Agricultural Statistics Services, Cropscope, Cropland Data Layer.

Note: Corn is assigned a bushel weight of 56 pounds; soybeans and wheat are assigned bushel weights of 60 pounds; barley is assigned a bushel weight of 48 pounds; and oat is assigned a bushel weight of 32 pounds.

* Crops are grown only under irrigation status.

Notes

1　Senior authorship is shared.
2　Note that the term $\sum_i t(\tilde{w}_i - \bar{w}_i)$ is canceled, because the aggregate water constraint is binding – that is, $\tilde{W} = \bar{W}$.
3　Marginal price in a water market should reflect parity between the marginal willingness to pay of all consumers in the market (i.e., the marginal social demand) and the marginal social cost of provision (that accounts for private costs, externalities to third parties, storage and conveyance costs, and resource scarcity). Practically, however, water is often administratively priced by management institutions, which are reluctant to raise prices to reflect water scarcity.
4　Cautions must be exercised to use mandatory quotas. First, their use must be accompanied by some type of compensation/penalty scheme, according to the historical water rights that farms have possessed. While the amount of payment will not affect the optimal social welfare, a proper compensation scheme to senior rights holders helps to reduce barriers to operation. Second, this instrument might lead to monopoly as the water quota is designated positively associated with farm size.
5　This simplification is equivalent to imposing the CRS assumption on the agency's water provision function, which allows the cost function to be homogenous of degree 1 in output W, and therefore transforms the cost function to $C(W,\theta) = L \cdot C(W/L,\theta)$.
6　Define $\delta \equiv (\alpha^2 - 2\alpha) f_{11}$. Taking the derivative of δ w.r.t. α gives $\frac{\partial \delta}{\partial \alpha} = 2(\alpha - 1) f_{11} + \alpha(\alpha - 2)\frac{\partial f_{11}}{\partial \alpha}$. $\frac{\partial \delta}{\partial \alpha} > 0$, if and only if expression (12.20) holds.
7　If the function of the marginal product is linear, then increasing uncertainty about irrigation water supply would have no effect on optimal water use for a risk-neutral farmer.

References

Antle, J. M., and S. Hatchett. 1986. "Dynamic Input Decisions in Econometric Production Models." *American Journal of Agricultural Economics* 68 (4): 939–49.

Brill, E., E. Hochman, and D. Zilberman. 1997. "Allocation and Pricing at the Water District Level." *American Journal of Agricultural Economics* 79 (3): 952–63.

Burness, S. H., and J. P. Quirk. 1979. "Appropriative Water Rights and the Efficient Allocation of Resources." *American Economic Review* 69 (1): 25–37.

Burness, S. H., and J. P. Quirk. 1980. "Water Law, Water Transfers, and Economic Efficiency: The Colorado River." *Journal of Law and Economics* 23 (1): 111–34.

Easter, K. W., and Q. Huang, eds. 2014. *Water Markets for the 21st Century: What Have We Learned?* Global Issues in Water Policy, 11. Dordrecht: Springer.

Easter, K. W., M. W. Rosegrant, and A. Dinar, eds. 1998. *Markets for Water: Potential and Performance*. Boston: Kluwer Academic.

English, M. J. 1990. "Deficit Irrigation. I: Analytical Framework." *Journal of Irrigation and Drainage Engineering* 116 (3): 399–412.

Frija, I., A. Frija, A. Chebil, H. C. M'Hamed, S. Speelman, and M. Makhlouf. 2014. "Marginal Water Productivity of Irrigated Durum Wheat in Semi-Arid Tunisia." *Journal of Agricultural Science* 6 (10): 84–95.

Frisvold, G. B., and K. Konyar. 2012. "Less Water: How Will Agriculture in Southern Mountain States Adapt?" *Water Resources Research* 48 (5). W05534. doi:10.1029/2011WR011057.

Howell, T. A. 2003. "Irrigation Efficiency." In *Encyclopedia of Water Science*, edited by B. A. Steward and T. A. Howell, 467–72. New York: Marcel-Dekker, Inc.

Just, R. E., D. Zilberman, and E. Hochman. 1983. "Estimation of Multicrop Production Functions." *American Journal of Agricultural Economics* 65 (4): 770–80.

Kenny, J. F., N. L. Barber, S. S. Hutson, K. S. Linsey, J. K. Lovelace, and M. A. Maupin. 2009. *Estimated Use of Water in the United States in 2005*. Reston, VA: US Department of the Interior, US Geological Survey.

Moore, M. R., N. R. Gollehon, and D. H. Negri. 1993. "Alternative Forms for Production Functions of Irrigated Crops." *Journal of Agricultural Economics Research* 44 (3): 16–32.

Pezzey, J. 1992. "The Symmetry between Controlling Pollution by Price and Controlling It by Quantity." *Canadian Journal of Economics* 25 (4): 983–91.

Qiu, Z., and T. Prato. 2012. "Economic Feasibility of Adapting Crop Enterprises to Future Climate Change: A Case Study of Flexible Scheduling and Irrigation for Representative Farms in Flathead Valley, Montana, USA." *Mitigation and Adaptation Strategies for Global Change* 17 (3): 223–42.

Rosegrant, M. W., and H. P. Binswanger. 1994. "Markets in Tradable Water Rights: Potential for Efficiency Gains in Developing Country Water Resource Allocation." *World Development* 22 (11): 1613–25.

Rosegrant, M. W., C. Ringler, and C. Rodgers. 2005. "The Water Brokerage Mechanism – Efficient Solution for the Irrigation Sector." Conference Proceedings, XII World Water Congress: "Water for Sustainable Development – Towards Innovative Solutions," November 22–25, 2005, New Delhi, India.

Rosegrant, M. W., C. Ringler, T. Zhu, S. Tokgoz, and P. Bhandary. 2013. "Water and Food in the Bioeconomy: Challenges and Opportunities for Development." *Agricultural Economics* 44 (s1): 139–50.

Scheierling, S., J. Loomis, and R. Young. 2006. "Irrigation Water Demand: A Meta-analysis of Price Elasticities." *Water Resources Research* 42: 1–9. W01411 doi:10.1029/2005WR004009.

Segerson, K. 1988. "Uncertainty and Incentives for Nonpoint Pollution Control." *Journal of Environmental Economics and Management* 15 (1): 87–98.

Segerson, K., and J. Wu. 2006. "Nonpoint Pollution Control: Inducing First-Best Outcomes through the Use of Threats." *Journal of Environmental Economics and Management* 51 (2): 165–84.

Stavins, R. N. 1996. "Correlated Uncertainty and Policy Instrument Choice." *Journal of Environmental Economics and Management* 30 (2): 218–32.

Weitzman, M. L. 1974. "Prices vs. Quantities." *Review of Economic Studies* 41 (4): 477–91.

13 Reflections on community-driven development

Jacomina de Regt

Introduction

This chapter attempts to assess what has happened in the last 15 years with community-driven development (CDD). Has it spread beyond the World Bank, its biggest financier? Have governments, sectors, and donors embraced this visionary approach to development? What are the lessons learned along the way? What have impact evaluations shown? And what is the way forward?

Much has been written on the CDD approach since Hans Binswanger and Deepa Narayan coined the term "community-driven development" in 1995 to denote an integration of participatory approaches with decentralization and direct community empowerment. Many pilot projects, multi-phased projects, and programs have been financed, implemented, and, to some extent, evaluated. Guidance papers have been written. A growing community of practice (COP) exists, of which I have been an active member from 2001 to 2006 as CDD coordinator for the Africa Region of the World Bank, and afterwards in a private capacity.

In this time, many critical voices have been heard, culminating in Mansuri and Rao's seminal literature review (2013) on participatory approaches and their efficacy. The August 2015 occasion of the Festschrift for Hans Binswanger in Milan accorded the opportunity for reflection on where the COP stands in comparison with the critics, and in comparison with Binswanger's original conceptual thinking.

Though Binswanger built on the work of many worldwide practitioners, researchers, and academics, he was able to mold this body of work into a vision. The World Bank, as a large development organization, could then rally around and develop this vision into a set of practices for large-scale lending. Binswanger's international standing as an economist surely contributed to the serious reaction he was able to elicit, but his deeply held and sincerely expressed beliefs and values about the dignity and rights of people in communities were equally important to advancing his conceptual vision.

Binswanger's (2000) paper "Community-Driven Development in Africa: A Vision of Poverty Reduction through Empowerment" defined the concepts. The Africa Region of the World Bank first embraced this set of concepts, as did the rest of the World Bank (Binswanger and Aiyer 2009).

Binswanger always maintained that CDD needed to invest in rigorous monitoring and evaluation research to show that it was more efficient and effective than the counterfactual (development through top-down sector programs) in achieving the multiple objectives of poverty alleviation, good governance, and inclusion. Given the poor results of the counterfactual, he passionately believed that research and practice would show that CDD would be an effective approach.

Critics of CDD are equally passionate about the need for more evidence that participatory programs like CDD work better than the counterfactual, before financiers embark on wide-scale investment programs.

My conclusion is that the recommendations for moving forward from the critics and from the COP are remarkably similar, which is surprising given the acrimony that has been expressed between the two camps. Furthermore, the recommendations for the future are close to Binswanger's original conceptual framework and vision for what constitutes CDD and how to scale it.

Rather than continuing to wrangle over whether community-driven development is or isn't "the answer" to development and poverty reduction, I believe that the real challenge now is to continue to embed community development in larger development strategies that can expand on CDD's principles for achieving tangible results in poor people's welfare, and to subsequently measure them meaningfully so that we can keep on learning and improving.

What is community-driven development?

This section presents the definitions of CDD used by the World Bank and other institutions.

CDD is not new and best practices in the development field cycle between decentralizing and re-centralizing power. The definitions of community development have changed since the 1950s; the historical approaches are shown in Figure 13.1.

World Bank definition

The first articulation of the World Bank's CDD vision was produced by the CDD Working Group of the Africa Region (Binswanger 2000).[1] It defined five pillars of CDD, as well as four core features, set out in Box 13.1. This definition was also used in the 2001 Bank-wide source book for poverty reduction strategies (Dongier et al. 2002).

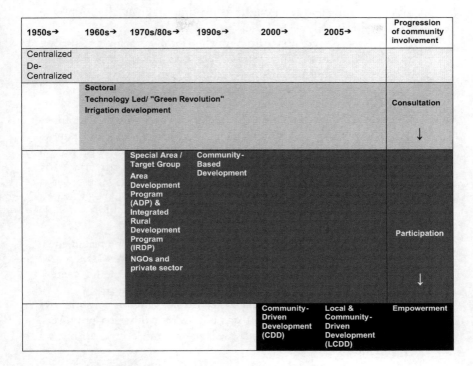

1950s→	1960s→	1970s/80s→	1990s→	2000→	2005→	Progression of community involvement
Centralized De-Centralized						
	Sectoral Technology Led/ "Green Revolution" Irrigation development					Consultation ↓
		Special Area / Target Group Area Development Program (ADP) & Integrated Rural Development Program (IRDP) NGOs and private sector	Community-Based Development			Participation ↓
				Community-Driven Development (CDD)	Local & Community-Driven Development (LCDD)	Empowerment

Figure 13.1 Timeline of approaches to local and community-driven development

Source: Binswanger, de Regt, and Spector (2010, Figure 1.2, 8), a World Bank publication; reprinted here under license CC BY 3.0 IGO license.

Box 13.1 Elements of community-driven development (CDD)

Core expected outcomes of local and community-driven development (LCDD)

Real participation and linkage by stakeholders
Improved accountability
Technical soundness
Sustainability

Pillars for success in an integrated LCDD approach:

1 *Empower communities.* Empowering communities involves assigning functions, duties, and corresponding authority to them; providing an institutional framework in which they elect their officials and

make decisions; and assigning revenues and other fiscal resources to communities.

2   *Empower local governments.* Empowering local government involves assigning functions, duties, and corresponding authority to them; providing an institutional framework in which they elect their officials and make decisions; and assigning revenues and other fiscal resources to local governments (decentralization).

3   *Realign the center.* Realigning the center involves distributing functions and powers from central agencies and sectors to communities and local governments, a process that involves both deconcentration and devolution, and shifting the mix of activities performed by central institutions, so that the local communities and local governments are more involved in direct service delivery and the central government is more involved in policy setting and support functions.

4   *Improve accountability.* Accountability systems need to be realigned so that accountability is to citizens and users of services (not just upward accountability from citizens and service providers to the center), adapted to the new context and improved all around.

5   *Build capacity.* Capacity building is needed not only for communities and local development participants but also for other co-producers, the technical sectors, the private sector, and nongovernmental organizations.

In essence, CDD was understood to be an approach that gives control of development decisions and resources to community groups and representative local governments. Poor communities would receive funds, decide on their use, plan and execute the chosen local projects, and monitor the provision of services that result from it (Binswanger, de Regt, and Spector 2010, 6). Success requires a deep transformation of political and administrative structures to ensure that communities' and local governments' control of their own development is embedded in a sustainable and supportive government structure.

CDD had the explicit objective of reversing power relations in a manner that creates agency and voice for poor people and gives them more control over development assistance. It also strengthened their capacity to undertake and manage self-initiated development activities.

Guggenheim and Wong (2015) discussed the three original hypotheses underlying CDD as an approach to the role that information, choice, and programs can play in improving local level service delivery:

1   "The first core argument for community-driven development is a belief that if given financial resources and a structure for negotiation, poor communities can plan, negotiate, and manage a broad range of local-level development programs more effectively than what can be done through alternative methods" (2015, 2). In that sense, CDD programs follow the standard economic principles that more information, more choice and direct negotiations are key instruments for achieving optimal outcomes under given circumstances of knowledge and resources: the standard public choice theory applied. "This is because communities will have the most knowledge about local conditions and, as long as the technologies involved are not especially complicated, they can obtain most of the resources needed from local suppliers and sources of expertise. Communities will also have, at least potentially, the greatest incentives to use funds properly, as well as the greatest ability to monitor their use" (2015, 2–3). Giving communities the money and some simple engineering support can also be an efficient way to finish off the infrastructure network connections and within-village distribution systems for large infrastructure investments and provide that last, tertiary network.

2   "The second argument for community development programs is that mobilizing communities to be the active agents of development programs rather than just their 'targets' or 'beneficiaries' reduces the burden on government institutions, freeing them up to concentrate on larger, technically and financially more challenging investments. . . . Community-driven development projects are institutionally light. . . . By treating the primary obligation of the government as the delivery of a grant to each participating village, community-driven projects can cover very large areas as long as they have their transfer systems under control, even if other parts of government such as engineering departments, audit bodies, or contract managers are not yet functioning. This makes community-driven development projects particularly useful for governments trying to cope with conflict or disaster recovery, when government services are particularly weak and vulnerable to disruption" (2015, 3–4). It also creates the beginning of a partnership model in governance, which can be expected to "increase trust in government, increase poor people's negotiating power in their dealings with other primary providers, and increase their stock of social capital, as they learn to negotiate agreements over how best to invest public funds in local development" (2015, 4–5).

3   "A third argument for community-driven development is that providing resources to sustain and enrich a community's associational life will provide a way to smooth the disruptions caused by urbanization and the breakdown of traditional social institutions. The 'strong' version of this argument is undoubtedly a highly romanticized picture of a stable, conservative village that has never actually existed, but the more pragmatic version that working *with* rather than *around* local institutions is a better way to ensure legitimacy, avoid conflict,

and provide a forum and the means for people to question, discuss, and adapt. Strengthening community institutions by giving them statutory recognition and providing them with bureaucratic legitimacy also improves the quality of their engagement with higher level parts of government, reducing poor people's alienation from state institutions and providing the foundation for a more democratized development than what would emerge from a strict regime of individualized market transactions" (2015, 5).

Other development institutions' definitions

Other development institutions, such as bilateral donors and many NGOs, also incorporated or continued to use participatory approaches, community empowerment, and/or decentralization approaches after 2000, and some embraced the term CDD. About 2003, the International Fund for Agricultural Development (IFAD) defined CDD as:

a way to design and implement development policy and projects that facilitates access to social, human and physical capital assets for the rural poor by creating conditions for

- transforming rural development agents from top-down planners into client-oriented service providers;
- empowering rural communities to take initiative for their own socio-economic development (i.e. building on community assets);
- enabling community-level organizations – especially those of the rural poor – to play a role in designing and implementing policies and programmes that affect their livelihoods;
- enhancing the impact of public expenditure on the local economy at the community level.

(IFAD 2009, 10)

More recently, in the context of the Sustainable Development Goals (SDGs), Goal 16 (UN 2016) calls for "building participatory, effective and accountable institutions at all levels," including at the community level where basic needs are met. The SDGs also call for integrated solutions – especially critical for nutrition, women's economic empowerment, and resilience – and this integration must happen at the community level. In response, in 2015, the Movement for Community-Led Development was launched by 32 international NGOs, committed to taking community empowerment to a transformative scale, as a key to achieving the SDGs. It sees CDD or community-led development as a means to sustainable development, as well an end in itself – namely, the human right of self-determination.

The Millennium Challenge Corporation in its latest Strategic Plan (2016–2021) also champions community-led development to concentrate program ownership and accountability at the local level (MCC 2015).

However, most of these institutions have not quantified their investment or aid portfolios with exactly the same definitions, because most development institutions classify by sector, while CDD is seen as an approach. The quantification of CDD lending in the World Bank has always been a painstaking exercise.

Furthermore, there are considerable variation and confusion, as the definitions of CDD vary over time and by institution, sector, country, and financing and/or implementing agency. The fundamental difference between many participatory community-based programs and projects and CDD is whether the community is the key decision-maker on the use of resources and/or manages these financial resources directly and is accountable. This considerable variation in the implementation of CDD approaches is the source of many of the criticisms of the CDD approach. Some quantification of the extent to which the CDD approach has been adopted and applied is given in the appendix.

Demonstrated impact of CDD

The demonstrated impact of CDD is hotly contested.

What is the evidence that CDD has worked over the last 15 years?

Jean-Paul Faguet, professor of the Political Economy of Development at the London School of Economics and Political Science, in a 2015 lecture, "Identifying the Gaps between Citizens and Government," summarized the debate about the impact of CDD:

> The degree to which local governments are both efficient and responsive to local needs can vary greatly within a country. Optimists claim local governments are more responsive to citizens than centralized government institutions, arguing that they increase citizen participation and governmental accountability, while improving allocative efficiency and generating greater equity in service distribution.
>
> Pessimists dispute this, arguing that local governments are too susceptible to elite capture – that is, the process by which powerful individuals divert state resources to their own ends. They also argue that government at the local level normally lacks the technical, human, and financial resources needed to provide public services that are both efficient and responsive to local demand. So far, neither side has been able to win this debate with convincing empirical evidence.
>
> (Faguet [2015], based on Faguet and Pöschl [2015])

The picture that Faguet painted in 2015 – a lack of convincing empirical evidence allowing both optimists and pessimists to continue to debate the merits of decentralization and capacity of local governments – is a familiar one to practitioners of CDD, because similar arguments exist around community capacity and impact of community empowerment programs and projects. Many mid-term and final evaluation studies have been done of CDD programs, but few studies with robust experimental designs have been carried out by independent researchers.

This section will present a summary of the evidence from CDD programs, a summary of the questions posed by critics of CDD, and further answers, looking toward the future, provided by the COP in response to those questions. This debate has raged over the last 15 years.

What do CDD impact evaluations tell us?

Wong (2012) pulled together the evidence from 17 robust impact evaluations (based on experimental or quasi-experimental design) of CDD programs from 2003 onwards. Her review answers six questions:

1   What is the *poverty or socioeconomic welfare impact* of CDD/social fund programs?
2   *Who benefits* from these program interventions (poorest quintiles, women, ethnic groups)? Do they reach poor areas and poor households?
3   Do the programs *improve access to and use of basic services*?
4   Do they *improve social capital* (using the standard proxy measurements for social capital – trust, collective action, association, groups, and networks)?
5   Do they *improve local governance* (participation in local meetings, satisfaction, and increased confidence with government officials, awareness of program activities, etc.)?
6   In conflict-affected areas, do CDD operations have any *impact on violent conflict?*

This review found generally positive evidence for poverty welfare reduction (income and consumption), poverty targeting (reaching more poor than non-poor households), increased access to services (education, health, and drinking water), and provision of tertiary infrastructure and services. As most of the project objectives and financial resources focused on improving access and service delivery, these projects achieved their stated aims. Evidence is limited and mixed, however, on governance, social capital spillovers, and conflict impacts. CDD operations were effective in delivering services quickly in post-conflict settings.

Wong's research also looked at issues related to cost-effectiveness and rates of return, and generally found positive results when compared to other modes of service delivery. Many of these programs showed between 13 and 40 percent lower costs for equivalent works, and better construction quality and maintenance. These cost savings come primarily from factoring in community contribution of labor and materials and/or eliminating the middleman or contractor overhead.

Beath, Christia, and Enikolopov (2015) summarized similar positive and negative findings for one of the largest CDD programs in the world in a conflict situation: the National Solidarity Program (NSP) in Afghanistan. It financed over 64,000 projects between mid-2003 and early 2013, at a combined cost of US$1.01 billion.[2] Using a randomized controlled trial across 500 villages, the evaluation found that the National Solidarity Program:

- had a positive effect on access to drinking water and electricity;
- increased the acceptance of democratic processes;
- improved the perceptions of economic well-being; and
- lessened constraints on the participation of women in public affairs.

However, positive effects on perceptions of local and national government performance faded quickly following the completion of NSP-funded projects. Perceptions of local governance quality among male respondents were negatively affected, and the composition and behavior of the customary village leadership appears to have been unaffected by the intervention. Material economic outcomes were also more limited and short-lived.

The study suggested that the limited impact of NSP on economic welfare is potentially explained by the apparent ineffectiveness of infrastructure projects in inducing changes in agricultural productivity and access to markets and by the fact that more successful types of projects (e.g., water and electricity) are not designed to induce changes in local economic activity in the near term. However, the sustained positive impact on female economic perceptions demonstrates the broader improvements brought to women's lives by female participation in Community Development Councils' activities and by NSP-funded drinking water projects.

Questions posed by the critics of CDD

There are several serious efforts ongoing to fine-tune what works and does not work in the CDD approach and to measure which interventions produce consistent outcomes and impacts. There is an abundance of very legitimate criticism. In this section, I select four critical assessments that merit further reflection by the COP:

- the in-depth review by Mansuri and Rao (2013) on whether participation works;
- the ongoing in-depth review of women's empowerment and participation in CDD;
- the questions being asked about whether facilitation, a hallmark of CDD methodology, is making a contribution in all circumstances; and
- the in-depth review of lasting impact of CDD programs in conflict situations by the International Rescue Committee.

Literature review on participation

Mansuri and Rao (2013) reviewed the literature on induced participatory projects, including CDD projects, but also other types of participatory projects.[3]

They noted that jumping into participatory projects as an answer to market and government failures could be a mistake, because those projects are based on many assumptions about civil society's capacity to organize itself in a strong, coordinated fashion. This ignores the fact that in each community, groups that live in geographical proximity do not necessarily have the capacity to act collectively to reach a feasible and preferable outcome. They came to these cautionary conclusions:

- Participation by the poor: "On balance, the review of the literature finds that participants in civic activities tend to be wealthier, more educated, of higher social status (by caste and ethnicity), male, and more politically connected than nonparticipants. This picture may partly reflect the higher opportunity cost of participation for the poor . . . . 'Capture' also tends to be greater in communities that have high economic inequality, are remote from centers of power; have low literacy; are poor; or have significant caste, race, or gender disparities" (Mansuri and Rao 2013, 5). Yet, there is evidence that participation has intrinsic value, the value of being heard.
- Social capital: Disparate groups may participate for the duration of the project, but there are no lasting social capital gains and spillovers unless the program lasts a long time. The role of the facilitators is a crucial but poorly understood one.
- Decentralization and/or top-down oversight: In both cases, putting in place strong downward accountability mechanisms can improve outcomes, in targeting, participation, and sustainability.
- "On balance, greater community involvement seems to modestly improve resource sustainability and infrastructure quality" (Mansuri and Rao 2013, 6), but with the caveats on capture noted here.
- Outside of CDD projects, there is evidence that mandated participation by disadvantaged groups, over time, will create changes in perceptions and norms.
- Local development is context-driven; and for each situation, the intersection of market and government, but also of civil society failures, will need to be analyzed before local participation programs are designed. Civil society may not have the capacity to counteract the failures of the market and/or government.

(Mansuri and Rao 2013)

They concluded that "local participation tends to work well when it has teeth and when projects are based on well-thought-out and tested designs, facilitated by a responsive center, adequately and sustainably funded, and conditioned by a culture of learning by doing" (Mansuri and Rao 2013, 14).

Review of gender in CDD

The World Bank's Independent Evaluation Group's (IEG) evaluation of the gender dimensions of CDD/rural livelihood projects, approved between FY03 and FY11, should provide further information on gender impacts (forthcoming). IEG is conducting this review, because earlier literature has suggested mixed outcomes.

IEG cites the *Gender in Agriculture Sourcebook* (World Bank, FAO, and IFAD 2009, 55), which states that there is limited availability of evidence on CDD's impacts for rural women and calls for an increased attention to gender in the monitoring and evaluation of these types of projects to ensure the intended impact on inclusive poverty reduction. IEG also notes that the experiences of East and South Asia suggest that CDD interventions in the livelihood projects and "self-help groups" that pay particular attention to gender impacts have the potential to achieve better results on the ground and become a vehicle of women's empowerment. Browne (2014) reaches very similar conclusions: only the explicit integration of a gender strategy in CDD, aimed at generating women's participation in community meetings and activities, can produce positive results for women.

IEG summarized guidance offered in the *Sourcebook*, noting these points: CDD projects should explicitly take into account gender-specific needs, constraints, and opportunities and should be designed in such a way to ensure equal participation of men and women in deciding about community priorities, implementing projects, managing funds, and monitoring and evaluating community projects, as untargeted CDD projects often bypass women and the poor. Moreover, more female participation in CDD projects does not necessarily translate into active participation and equal benefits for women (World Bank, FAO, and IFAD 2009).

Questions about facilitation efficacy and costs

There is also criticism about CDD's ubiquitous use of community facilitation to promote democratic decision-making, participation of socially marginalized groups, and transparent budgeting and management practices. Facilitators are on the frontline and are paid to induce social change at the community level. Mansuri and Rao (2013, 97–8) describe these least-paid staff as "street-level bureaucrats." Some research points to their influence on the decision-making processes and preferences, their identification with elites, and the enormous problem of aligning incentives of an organization that looks for results with the messy business of social change, which does not work on a fixed timetable. Casey, Glennerster, and Miguel (2012) also questioned the need for facilitators in a society – Sierra Leone, in this case – where there is a high level of cohesion, and they considered it money not well spent.

Questions about CDD being implemented in conflict-affected areas

The International Rescue Committee (IRC), financier of many CDD programs in conflict-affected areas, reviewed the results of its rigorous evaluation studies and focused on developing theories of change for the least effective CDD interventions. The results of its evaluation studies include the following:

- Although community-driven development and reconstructions (CDD/R) "is context-driven, it is generally implemented as a standard model.
- According to rigorous impact evaluations from programmes in Afghanistan, Democratic Republic of Congo (DRC), Aceh (Indonesia), Liberia and Sierra Leone, and interviews with practitioners, policymakers and academics, the record of CDD/R in conflict-affected contexts is mixed and, overall, disappointing in terms of reaching the ambitious goals set out.
- As currently designed, implemented, and evaluated, CDD/R is better at generating the more tangible economic outcomes than it is at generating social changes related to governance and social cohesion, although even the economic effects are found in just a few studies. Moreover, CDD/R programming is better at producing outcomes directly associated with the project rather than broader changes in routine life.
- CDD/R has been plagued by a panacea-type approach to goals and a generalised theory of change that is, as interviewees characterised it, 'lofty', 'unrealistic', 'inherently flawed' and even 'ridiculous'.
- A variety of issues related to programme design merit rethinking: the relatively short timeline of CDD/R projects, the small size of block grants, the limited reach of the projects, the menu restrictions on CDD/R programming, the limitations of social infrastructure, the quality and intensity of social facilitation, the manner in which communities are conceptualised and thus often not meaningful to participants, and how community institutions build on existing institutions and relate to the state."

(King 2013, 3)

Building on this evaluation review and many other recent works referenced before, such as Mansuri and Rao (2013) and Beath, Christia, and Enikolopov (2015), the IRC set out to develop a better theory of change to manage expectations and inform policy, practice, and learning. This is especially important for the goals of governance and social cohesion, which have poor results, rather than for the more successful goal of CDD, as a means to deliver a product of greater welfare outcomes to people (Bennett and D'Onofrio 2015).

Their paper suggests developing explicit theories of change for CDD interventions by objective (deliver outputs, change processes and behavior, improve efficiency, fill a gap or transform institutions). It recommends: defining specific objectives; examining the context; thinking through the core processes (community definition, information dissemination, convening, deliberation, preference articulation, commitment and performance) and ways to facilitate these processes; then drawing up theories to develop plausible change pathways and their corresponding assumptions; and finally beginning to parse out design options.

The authors concede that the focus on theory might feel like a step back, but that it will be useful to have "more theoretically grounded motivations and expectations for what we do and how we do it," because it "will get us closer to understanding what 'works', what doesn't, why, and what we should do differently" (Bennett and D'Onofrio 2015, 31), and it will help us understand why we observe some trends and not others in the evidence on the effectiveness of CDD.

Community of practice (COP) lessons

Guggenheim and Wong (2015) posited that the CDD community of practice (COP) has learned several lessons beyond those cited in the Wong (2012) review, as well as in response to the Mansuri and Rao (2013) criticisms and from a review of lessons from CDD in conflict situations (de Regt, Majumdar, and Singh 2013). These lessons will be useful going forward.

A first lesson is that one-off, small, CDD programs with low per-capita project allocations have little or no impact on living standards. Programs which touch a community only once may provide for a quick provision of infrastructure, but cannot be expected to have any lasting impact on the social structure and power relationships.

A second lesson is that the model is replicable and can be scaled up, always allowing for regional and local variation and "franchising." Adaptation to the local context, the community demand, especially of poor people, should always be at the center of program design. Mansuri and Rao (2013) argued that the requirement to adapt to the local context and its specific civil society, government, and market failures is key to understanding why it is so difficult to implement CDD with any consistent, predictable results.

A third lesson is that the programs are popular with national and local governments, because they allow governments to deliver tangible and visible public goods and services to citizens quickly and transparently. Therefore, governments scale them up nationally. However, the expected local governance and social capital spillovers beyond the project period do not materialize, because the COP underestimates the time needed to build trust between the citizens and the state. This could occur because CDD interventions remain isolated in vertical programs of specific line ministries, or multisectoral CDD programs encounter opposition from line ministries. In either case, government norms create the barrier to spillover, and Guggenheim and Wong (2015) posited that a push from below, as well as from above, to integrate participatory planning through national programs and laws could be the next logical step and would go a long way toward solving this problem. However, bureaucratic and human resistance to change is not easily overcome; communities, too, are resistant to change if they do not trust that the program will last. Trust-building is a very long-term process.

The fourth lesson is the logical extension of this lack of coordination. It has been difficult to coordinate and/or mandate that there be a handshake between the supply side and community demand, hence the lack of service or quality of service once infrastructure is built. How CDD programs tackle this hurdle of lack of incentives for line ministries and local governments to provide services, technical inputs, and operations/maintenance funds to communities is an open question, which will require further experimentation.

The fifth observation of the COP is that it remains important to have longitudinal program evaluations to shed light on whether program impacts on welfare, social capital, and governance attenuate or change.

A sixth observation is that the COP does not truly understand how decisions are being made at the community level and local government level, and how the dynamics of this interaction evolve. Community heterogeneity, the roles of elites, and the evolving roles of marginalized groups in the larger society all play a role in decision-making. How does one reach marginalized groups successfully? Does the introduction of funds into communities, let alone in fragile and post-conflict situations, lead to more conflict, crime, and strife in the communities? The research being done by the Social Observatory in India is shedding light on the local civil society factors and local social change processes that play into such decision-making when an intervention like a CDD project enters into the community dynamics.[4] Their first publications show the importance of truly understanding the very local dynamics (Sanyal, Rao, and Majumdar 2015; Sanyal, Rao, and Prabhakar 2015).

A seventh observation is that we do not know how to translate short-term employment creation and business development under the CDD program into long-term economic growth. Microcredit, while it has assisted millions of mostly poor women, is only one tool. More experimentation with value chain development, as in South Asia and Latin America, and inclusive economic models will be needed for both urban and rural areas. In addition, experimentation with skill enhancement might lead to larger economic gains.

CDD remains an underutilized toolbox and conceptual framework for the rapidly urbanizing world. There, heterogeneous communities are the norm, and trust-building tools will need to be developed. A recent review of urban CDD projects concludes the following:

- The role local governments need to play vis-a-vis communities may be larger, given the size of urban infrastructure investments.
- Beneficiary targeting may need to go beyond spatial boundaries – for example, target high-poverty pockets.
- Mobilizing urban communities requires more time and effort due to constraints in people's availability, physical space, and trust.

(Arnold 2015)

Clearly, CDD is not the "be-all and end-all" answer to poverty reduction and service delivery.

Conclusion

CDD going forward is likely to look much more like the elements of CDD, as described by Binswanger in the early 2000s (see Box 13.1), putting into practice his vision that scaled-up CDD programs would be fully embedded in poverty reduction strategies and programs. Successful nationally scaled-up CDD programs, managed by national governments, are increasingly integrating all five elements recommended by Binswanger: empowered communities, empowered local governments, realigned central sectors, downward accountability, and capacity building of all stakeholders. This is an exciting future.

All stakeholders, proponents, and critics alike emphasize the critical importance of good research and continuous learning.

Appendix

Community-driven development has been scaled up

CDD has been scaled up within the World Bank and in other development institutions, including NGOs, such as the International Rescue Committee, and multilateral and bilateral aid organizations. CDD is being used in and by all sectors. Countries have also integrated CDD in their own poverty alleviation and development programs, as well as their laws and budget processes.

Scaling up by the World Bank and other development institutions

In the last 15 years, the World Bank has financed more CDD projects than any other institution. In 2015 the Bank supported 182 active CDD projects valued at USD 16 billion in 77 countries around the world (see Figure 13.2). Over the past 10 years, the Bank has lent an average of USD 2.6 billion annually to CDD programs, representing 5 to 10 percent of overall Bank lending each year. Nor is this wave showing any sign of cresting.

Within the World Bank portfolio, the CDD approach is especially popular for fragile and conflict-affected states (FCS) because of its ability to deliver rural infrastructure to populations in deprivation. More than a third of the countries implementing CDD are FCS.

Multilateral institutions, such as the Asian, Inter-American and African Development Banks, as well as IFAD, also finance CDD operations. Bilateral donors, such as the Nordic countries and the Swiss government, have long been strong supporters of participatory approaches and good governance, both aspects of the CDD approach. Both the Department for International Development (DfID, UK) and the Canadian International Developmental Agency (CIDA) use CDD-type approaches, as part of sustainable livelihoods and basic needs development assistance.

For instance, the Asian Development Bank (ADB) reported in 2008 that it had funded 57 projects worth about US$2.5 billion between 2001 and 2007 that included CDD approaches – constituting 14 percent of the total loans during that period.

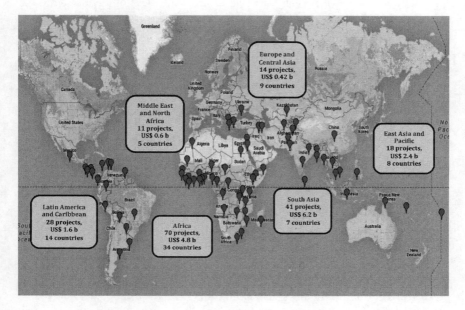

Figure 13.2 World Bank–supported CDD programs as of March 2015 – Global coverage
Source: Adapted from World Bank CDD Projects Database.

Scaling up by governments

Countries have scaled up by integrating funding for CDD programs into national budgets and national laws and regulations. For example, Indonesia now funds a national CDD program covering its entire territory. What started in 1998 as the Kecamatan Development Program, a US$273 million, four-year program financed through a US$225 million World Bank loan (i.e., 82 percent of total funding), had become, by 2012, a US$1.5 billion annual program, with 90 percent of its funding coming from national and local governments. By 2015, it expanded to become a national Village Law program, with a budget of approximately US$4.4 billion, providing for annual community transfers to its 73,000 villages in its recurrent budget.

Post-conflict and post-disaster countries have embraced CDD projects, with the National Solidarity Project in Afghanistan accounting for as much as 30 percent of the government's budget from the Afghanistan Reconstruction Trust Fund to reach all 30,000-plus of the country's villages; Myanmar is similarly planning to scale up its first-generation program.

In the Philippines, the Kalahi–CIDSS (Comprehensive Integrated Delivery of Social Service) program has matured from a US$182 million, seven-year project in 2002 with a 45 percent government contribution to being a US$3 billion operation that further supports other sectoral programs to adopt a CDD approach. Morocco's National Initiative for Human Development Program II is a US$2.1 billion program (2011–2016), with 70 percent cofinancing by the national government.

Scaling up by national governments through institutionalization of CDD approaches

The World Bank CDD Global Solutions Group collected case studies on the institutionalization of CDD approaches through governments' formulation of key legislation or procedures that institutionalize community-based participatory approaches. Examples include the following:

- Indonesia's new Village Law (Law No.6/2014) from January 2014. The law provides a stronger legal status for villages and strengthens the delegation of authority and decision-making power to individual villages. It incorporates key CDD principles, including participatory village planning, community implementation of village-level projects, intervillage collaboration, and improved accountability mechanisms.
- Cambodia's Organic Laws of 2001 and 2008, and the Strategic Framework for Decentralization and Deconcentration Reforms in 2005.
- Mongolia's 2013 Integrated Budget Law.
- Afghanistan's 2013 Policy for Improving Governance and Development in Districts and Villages. This policy gives official recognition to the Community Development Councils created under the National Solidarity Program. It encourages the use of these community councils as the primary vehicle for development and governance at the district and village levels until formal District Councils and Village Councils are elected, as mandated by the Constitution.

CDD programs have been used to add meaning to laws "on the books" that were not being implemented – for instance, citizen engagement in the Philippines Local Government Code of 1991, Vietnam's Grassroots Democracy Decree of 1998 and 2003, and Ghana's 2010 Decentralization Policy Framework.

Notes

1 The statement was written by Swaminathan Aiyer. In 2001, the Africa Region followed with a *Sourcebook on Community-Driven Development in sub-Saharan Africa* (Aiyar 2001).
2 Hogg et al. (2013). Seventy-three percent of NSP funding is allocated to block grants, 18 percent to facilitation costs, and 9 percent to administration.
3 Guggenheim and Wong (2015) cautioned that the Mansuri and Rao (2013) review "took the eclectic approach and combined as broad a range as possible by trying to analyze any project making a claim about popular participation. Their sample included community development projects that ranged from one-time, small-scale projects launched and managed by international and national nongovernmental organizations, to large-scale, long-term, nationally financed and managed programs that extend over a country's entire national territory."

4 The Social Observatory is a collaborative effort of researchers and national and World Bank staff who are responsible for implementing livelihood projects, a complex and participatory intervention with US$2 billion in World Bank financing. This innovative adaptive research is described in Rao (2014).

References

Aiyar, S. S. 2001. *Sourcebook for Community-Driven Development in Sub-Saharan Africa*. Washington, DC: World Bank.

Arnold, M. 2015. "Participatory and Community Driven Development in Urban Areas." World Bank, Washington, DC. http://documents.worldbank.org/curated/en/423581468127795248/World-Participatory-and-community-driven-development-in-urban-areas

Beath, A., F. Christia, and R. Enikolopov. 2015. "The National Solidarity Program: Assessing the Effects of Community-Driven Development in Afghanistan." Policy Research Working Paper 7415, World Bank, Washington, DC.

Bennett, S., and A. D'Onofrio, 2015. "Community-Driven? Concepts, Clarity and Choices for Community-Driven Development in Conflict-Affected Countries." International Rescue Committee, New York.

Binswanger, H. P. 2000. "Community-Driven Development in Africa: A Vision of Poverty Reduction through Empowerment." World Bank, Africa Region, Washington, DC.

Binswanger, H. P., and S. S. Anklesaria Aiyer. 2009. "Historical Roots of Community-Driven Development: The Evolution of Development Theory and Practice at the World Bank." In *Scaling Up Local & Community Driven Development (LCDD): A Real World Guide to Its Theory and Practice*, edited by H. P. Binswanger-Mkhize, J. P. de Regt, and S. Spector, Chapter 2, 18–44. Washington, DC: World Bank. (Chapter 2 updates "Historical Roots of Community-Driven Development: Evolution of Development Theory and Practice at the World Bank", 2003, rev. 2006).

Binswanger, H. P., J. P. de Regt, and S. Spector, eds. 2010. *Local and Community-Driven Development: Moving to Scale in Theory and Practice*. Washington, DC: World Bank.

Browne, E. 2014. "Gender in Community Driven Development." GSDRC Helpdesk Research Report 1079, Government and Social Development Research Centre (GSDRC), University of Birmingham, UK. http://www.gsdrc.org/docs/open/hdq1079.pdf

Casey, K., R. Glennerster, and E. Miguel. 2012. "Healing the Wounds: Learning from Sierra Leone's Post-War Institutional Reforms." NBER Working Paper No. 18368, National Bureau of Economic Research, Cambridge, MA.

de Regt, J., S. Majumdar, and J. Singh. 2013. "Designing Community-Driven Development Operations in Fragile and Conflict-Affected Situations: Lessons from a Stocktaking." Social Development Department, World Bank, Washington, DC. http://documents.worldbank.org/curated/en/115121468327411033/pdf/830220WP0P12560Box0379879B00PUBLIC0.pdf

Dongier, P., J. Van Domelen, E. Ostrom, A. Rizvi, W. Wakeman, A. Bebbington, S. Alkire, T. Esmail, and M. Polski. 2002. "Community Driven Development." In *A Sourcebook for Poverty Reduction Strategies*, edited by J. Klugman, Chapter 9, 301–31. Washington, DC: World Bank.

Faguet, J.-P. 2015. "Identifying the Gaps Between Citizens and Government." Lecture (video transcript), April 2015, for "Engaging Citizens: A Game Changer" MOOC (Massive Online Open Course). http://blogs.worldbank.org/governance/engaging-citizens-game-changer-development

Faguet, J.-P., and C. Pöschl, eds. 2015. *Is Decentralization Good for Development? Perspectives from Academics and Policy Makers.* Oxford: Oxford University Press.

Guggenheim, S., and S. Wong. 2015. "Community-Driven Development: What Is It, What Do We Know about It and What Is It Good For?" Draft Discussion Paper, April 2015, World Bank, Washington, DC.

Hogg, R., C. Nassif, C. G. Osorio, W. Byrd, and A. Beath. 2013. *Afghanistan in Transition: Looking Beyond 2014.* Washington, DC: World Bank.

IFAD (International Fund for Agricultural Development). 2009. "Community-Driven Development Decision Tools for Rural Development Programmes." IFAD, Rome.

King, E. 2013. "A Critical Review of Community-Driven Development Programmes in Conflict-Affected Contexts." International Rescue Committee, New York.

Mansuri, Ghazal, and Vijayendra Rao. 2013. *Localizing Development: Does Participation Work?* Washington, DC: World Bank. https://openknowledge.worldbank.org/handle/10986/11859

MCC (Millennium Challenge Corporation). 2015. Strategic Sustainability Performance Plan, FY 2016. December 22, 2015. https://www.mcc.gov/resources/doc/plan-strategic-sustainability-performance-plan-fy-2016

Rao, V. 2014. "Are Impact Evaluations Enough? The Social Observatory Approach to Doing-by-Learning." World Bank Development Impact Blog, June 16, 2014. http://blogs.worldbank.org/impactevaluations/are-impact-evaluations-enough-social-observatory-approach-doing-learning

Sanyal, P., V. Rao, and S. Majumdar. 2015. "Recasting Culture to Undo Gender: A Sociological Analysis of Jeevika in Rural Bihar, India." Policy Research Working Paper No. 7411. World Bank, Washington, DC. https://openknowledge.worldbank.org/handle/10986/22667

Sanyal, P., V. Rao, and U. Prabhakar. 2015. "Oral Democracy and Women's Oratory Competency in Indian Village Assemblies: A Qualitative Analysis." Policy Research Working Paper No. 7416, World Bank, Washington, DC. http://documents.worldbank.org/curated/en/525821467998531383/Oral-democracy-and-women-s-oratory-competency-in-Indian-village-assemblies-a-qualitative-analysis

United Nations. 2016. Sustainable Development Goals. Goal 16: Promote Just, Peaceful and Inclusive Societies. http://www.un.org/sustainabledevelopment/peace-justice/

Wong, S. 2012. "What Have Been the Impacts of World Bank Community-Driven Development Programs? CDD Impact Evaluation Review and Operational and Research Implications." Social Development Department, World Bank, Washington, DC.

World Bank, FAO, and IFAD (World Bank, Food and Agriculture Organization of the United Nations, and International Fund for Agricultural Development). 2009. *Gender in Agriculture Sourcebook.* Washington, DC: World Bank. http://siteresources.worldbank.org/INTGENAGRLIVSOUBOOK/Resources/CompleteBook.pdf

Part 4

Agriculture, nutrition, and health

14 Agricultural change and health and nutrition in emerging economies

Joachim von Braun[1]

Introduction

In many developing countries, agriculture is still the main source of labor and a significant contributor to GDP. It is well understood by now that agriculture has multiple functions for economy, ecology, and people's livelihoods. For a long time, production for food supply and income and forward and backward growth linkages in the economy were the main areas of attention, whereas linkages to health were neglected. Starting slowly in the 1990s, the more specific linkages between agriculture, health, and nutrition have received more attention (e.g., von Braun and Kennedy [1994]; Fogel [1999]; Fan and Pandya-Lorch [2012]; von Braun, Ruel, and Gillespie [2012]; Jaenicke and Virchow [2013]; Dubé et al. [2014]), including in international research programs (e.g., Hawkes and Ruel [2006]; McDermott et al. [2013]; WHO [2013]). Important early research drew attention to health effects of agriculture, such as pesticide use (Pingali, Marquez, and Palis 1994), and later on HIV/AIDS' agriculture and food linkages (Binswanger 2006). More research is needed as agriculture's complex linkages with health become better understood and change in the context of urbanization, behavioral change, and rural market integration (Balter 2010; Ruddiman et al. 2015). The linkages, for instance, with nutrition are not easy to quantify (Masset et al. 2012), but that does not mean they are weak (Webb and Kennedy 2014).

This chapter reviews the nature and evidence of agriculture–health/nutrition[2] linkages with the aim of identifying opportunities for positive impacts of investments in institutional and technological change. Investments for enhanced health improvement through agriculture may target agriculture directly, such as nutrition-sensitive agriculture, or may aim at enhancing synergies or reducing transaction costs in markets and services, or may actually be outside agriculture to complement agriculture's health effects, such as water and sanitation systems.

A brief assessment of prevailing frameworks of agriculture–health links

Currently, there are two conceptual frameworks that dominate the research discourse about food and nutrition security, where agriculture and health and nutrition links are implicitly involved. In the framework provided by the Food and Nutrition Organization of the United Nations (FAO), food and nutrition security depends upon the availability of food through production and trade, access to food due to purchasing power or self-production, the utilization of food for nutrition, and the stability of the food system, especially of related markets and prices (FAO, IFAD, and WFP 2014). This framework is helpful, but pays little attention to health and nutrition, as it focuses on food security. To be fair, the framework did not originally consider health and nutrition. The other framework, developed by the United Nations Children's Fund (UNICEF) and applied in the *Lancet* nutrition series (Black et al. 2008), identifies the basic and immediate causes of maternal and child undernutrition. This framework does add value by more explicitly including health, but the linkages to economic and political contexts and to agriculture are exogenous aggregates and not defined. We thus have two frameworks where one has a strong emphasis on agriculture, but little emphasis on health, and one where consideration of health is strong, but the roles of agriculture are neglected. Disciplinary biases may result in priorities for programs and policies from this dichotomy of frameworks, and synergy potentials are missed. A more detailed assessment of the current frameworks points to four limitations.

Lack of causality depiction

The food security framework lacks linkages between drivers and impacts on health outcomes. Empiric analyses demonstrate the relations of the prevalence of nutritional conditions and associated risk factors (Black et al. 2008; Black et al. 2013). More comprehensive frameworks of sustainable diets (Burlingame and Dernini 2012; Johnston, Fanzo, and Cogill 2014) and resilient food systems (e.g., Fan, Pandya-Lorch, and Yosef [2014]; Tendall et al. [2015]) draw on multidisciplinary findings, and thereby disclose causal deficits of the traditional food security framework. Of critical importance is the distinction between drivers that are inside versus outside the food system (Pangaribowo, Gerber, and Torero 2013). Here is where clarity of system boundaries and causalities will have to be defined, through complex feedbacks, such as urbanization; rural and agricultural growth linkages; and consumption and behavioral change. At a more micro level, detailed food and nutrition security concepts have been developed, depicting the food, health, and care aspects as drivers. While certainly helpful at the household level to understand causalities, it is necessary to connect these concepts with a broader contextual framework.

Lack of depiction of synergies

The impacts of technology enhancing production have consequences for stability and income (access to food). Moreover, productivity (important for availability of food) and access are partly endogenous to human capabilities (determined partly by health and nutrition). Ignoring such synergistic linkages has led to the compartmentalization of food and nutrition security initiatives. This can lead to unproductive singular emphasis on food availability, versus food access, versus nutrition actions (Pinstrup-Andersen 2010; CFS 2012). A useful way out of this deficiency may be a well-defined health and nutrition value chain concept, especially because the existing frameworks rely on assumed trickle-down effects to improve nutrient uptake (e.g., through increasing yields from a purely agricultural perspective). As Herforth, Jones, and Pinstrup-Andersen (2012) and Webb (2013) depicted, only when considering the synergies and interlinkages in systems and value chains can nutrition improvements be well targeted. Synergies could be enhanced among complementary sectors, such as agriculture, health, water and sanitation, and early child education, explicitly taking their nexus into account (Ruel and Alderman 2013). Assessments of the nutrition sensitivity of food systems would call for inclusion of such linkages (Pinstrup-Andersen 2013).

Ignoring dynamics

Neither of the frameworks has established time subscripts of their respective building blocks. Impacts of agricultural change can appear in the short or long term, and can result from abrupt shocks or more continuous drivers of change (von Braun 2015b; Kalkuhl, von Braun, and Torero 2016). Changes of food availability due to agricultural seasonality, intensified by climate change, have tremendous impacts on nutrition outcomes, such as body weight and stunting (Ferro-Luzzi and Branca 1993; Lokshin and Radyakin 2012; IFPRI 2015). Economic variabilities have indirect impacts on nutrition through livelihoods (Devereux et al. 2011). Larger societal trends (e.g., urbanization) or environmental trends (e.g., land degradation) foster new challenges for food production and consumption and, hence, for food and nutrition security. Missing out on these dynamics can limit the explanatory power of frameworks. However, the choice of indicators to capture links is critical here (de Haen, Klasen, and Qaim 2011; Pangaribowo, Gerber, and Torero 2013). Stunting is typically used as a long-term indicator of undernutrition and malnutrition. It can be the result of seasonal food and nutrition insecurity over a sustained period of time or the result of structural constraints. Caloric and nutrient deficiencies, as well as weight loss, are medium-term (months) indicators of food and nutrition insecurity. Short-term food and nutrition shortages (weeks or days), especially in early childhood, are often the result of shocks. Further, the periodicity of the drivers and their impacts (seasonal and recurrent versus continuous and lasting) cannot be ignored. Finally, impacts can be irreversible and intergenerational. For instance, sustained undernourishment over a period of time can lead to stunting, which cannot be fully compensated subsequently by improved nourishment. Mothers' *in utero* malnutrition may impact the next generation's level of schooling (Kim et al. 2014). Thus, cognitive and physical development in support of an individual's full capability can be assured only if sufficient levels of nutrients are continuously available (Kar, Rao, and Chandramouli 2008).

Ignoring the broader political and ecology context

Capturing political economy determinants of health and nutrition requires special consideration (Pinstrup-Andersen 2013). Furthermore, structural issues, such as discrimination, marginalization, and conflicts, would require a broader framework to capture complex causes of nutrition and health deficiencies (von Braun and Gatzweiler 2014). Such problems are deeply rooted in institutional and governance deficiencies, affecting agriculture and health sector performances. In certain contexts, it seems hardly feasible to achieve improved health and nutrition without addressing these deficiencies. This concerns international arrangements, as well as national- and local-level nutrition-sensitive, intersectoral policies and their implementation (IFPRI 2015). Where relevant, these political dimensions need to be taken into account explicitly, rather than treating them as distant framework conditions, as done in both frameworks mentioned earlier.

Toward a new framework design to account for deficiencies

Either framework could in principle be augmented and redesigned to address the deficiencies mentioned earlier. This would entail building a new and much more complex framework for agriculture, food, and health/nutrition security in an economic and ecological systems context. This, however, is not proposed here, as either high levels of aggregation would be dissatisfactory in many instances or high disaggregation would easily lead to a lack of focus in certain contexts. With agriculture–health/nutrition linkages, we are confronted with an evolving and adaptive complex system, and therefore should borrow from complexity sciences (Axelrod and Cohen 2012) – that is, the scientific study of complex systems with many parts that interact to produce change that cannot be explained in terms of the interactions between the individual constituent elements, such as with IT networks or ecosystems. It embraces concepts of agents, strategies, interactions, and co-evolution. Frameworks should be purpose-driven; thus many agriculture/health/nutrition frameworks are called for, not one mega-framework. As long as limitations of frameworks and their boundary conditions are taken into account, and the intellectual framework of complexity science is considered for benchmarking, some research progress may be expected in a well-defined context, where agriculture, health, and nutrition interact (Jha et al. 2014).

Conceptual relationships of agriculture and health

Keeping the aforementioned limitations of prevailing frameworks in mind, a rather aggregated conceptual framework is put forward here. The concept takes a broad perspective on agriculture, comprising crops, animal production, and connected value chains, as well as the natural resource base and the technological foundations of agriculture. Institutions, information, and behavior are crosscutting issues that influence linkages in all of the domains that describe the framework. The linkages of agriculture with health can be broadly grouped into six domains as depicted in Figure 14.1.

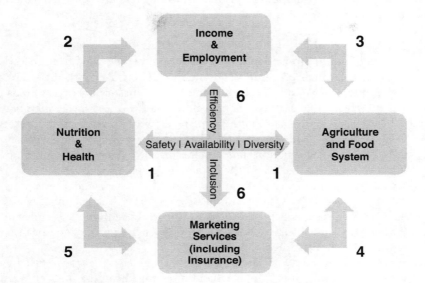

Figure 14.1 Agriculture–health/nutrition linkages
Source: Author's design.

Link 1: Agricultural production- and processing-related health linkages are central, especially in the long run (see middle of Figure 14.1). They entail, for example, nutrition and health-sensitive agriculture, paying attention to food supply and access to nutrients with diverse diets, quality and safety of foods, and production conditions. Technology is critical for these links.

Link 2: Income and employment-related health and nutrition linkages greatly determine access to nutrition and health, especially by farm households and agricultural laborers.

Link 3: Agriculture and income and employment links are fundamental for onward linkages to nutrition.

Link 4: Agriculture linkages with markets and services drive nutrition and health via income, but also directly via price formation and forward and backward linkages.

Link 5: Markets and services are critical for delivering affordable nutritious food, as well as nutrition and health-related services.

Link 6: The efficiency of markets and inclusive services, including insurance mechanisms, is a key force behind income and employment generation and households' capacity to deal with risks and shocks. This in turn drives many aforementioned linkages. To the extent that home production of food serves as a substitute for unavailable insurance markets, the links here can be understood as via self-insurance.

Like any framework, simplifications and abstractions are implicitly introduced, in order to focus on key causal linkages. These need to be highlighted as well:

- The six principal sets of linkages include various *feedbacks among them*, such as from health to production through labor productivity, and from markets to income through prices and consumption effects. Actually, all six linkages depict two-way relationships. Some of these are strongly two-way, such as between income and nutrition/health, whereas others are less strongly two-way, such as from agriculture to markets (where the link from markets to agriculture is certainly strong). This indicates a fundamental problem of causality identification in nutrition/health and agriculture relationships, with which econometric approaches have to grapple.
- Overarching, and sort of surrounding Figure 14.1, are *agricultural and environmental as well as macroeconomic framework conditions*. Related linkages exist on a large or even global scale, such as related to greenhouse gas emissions through land use change, and on a local scale, such as water and sanitation in the context of irrigated agriculture.
- All the links operate with *diverse dynamics under short- or long-term time lags*, which require attention in policies and programs. Even the links between production and health can be rather short-term – for example, with acute food safety problems. Production–income links can be rather long-term, if production resources, such as soils, are enhanced or degraded.
- The dimensions of the agriculture–health linkages need to consider structural problems, such as access to markets and resources, as well as risks that affect the resilience of poor people and low-income countries – problems that often erode societal cohesion.

Strategies of enhanced roles of agriculture for health and nutrition need to take note of a fundamental change that repositions food and nutrition in the global and national economies. Food and agriculture are now embraced by the larger bioeconomy (von Braun 2015a), and this entails that a lot more drivers from outside agriculture shape the nature of agriculture–health linkages in positive or risky ways – for example, bioenergy systems, biomass-based raw material uses in industries, financial markets integrated with food commodity markets, novel non-land-based foods, and so forth.

The following sections of the chapter address selected key components of the framework in which agriculture and health/nutrition linkages are operating, and may need more attention in emerging economies.

Agricultural production links with health and nutrition

Agricultural production-related health linkages are direct and via income-related poverty reduction. Dangour et al. (2012) pointed out that low- and middle-income countries, especially, are significantly influenced by the linkages between agriculture and health, as their economies often highly depend on agriculture as a major provider of employment and national income. Direct agricultural production–health linkages need to take account of the large population of small farms that are homes to the majority of the poor in the world. There are about 450 million farms worldwide; the majority is in China and India (von Braun and Mirzabaev 2015). Improving the productivity and incomes of small farmers can help significantly to reduce poverty. There are several ways this can be achieved, and they have been researched extensively (Holden and Binswanger 1998). First, commercialization and technological innovations among small farmers can help reduce poverty (Binswanger and von Braun 1991; von Braun and Kennedy 1994). Diversification from solely staple crop production to the production of commercially high-value crops is another avenue for reducing poverty among small farmers. Diversification typically may also involve specialization at the farm level, with growing varieties of production and processing at the regional level. Efficient storage and food processing plants are as important as improving agricultural systems to being able to provide a diverse and safe diet (Keding, Schneider, and Jordan 2013).

Obviously, not all small farms are economically viable, especially in the context of increasing opportunity costs of labor due to higher wage growth rates in nonfarm sectors. Already, many small farmers are engaged in rural, multiple-income-generating activities. Presently, about 50 percent of earnings of rural households in Asia come from the nonfarm sector (Haggblade, Hazell, and Reardon 2010). Brookfield (2008) suggested that pluriactivity is a strategy to increase incomes due to lower labor requirements in the farm, and not merely a survival strategy for small farmers. In any case, improving access to nonfarm jobs is another critical aspect of poverty reduction among small farmers.

Exploiting the positive linkages between agricultural production and health is particularly constrained by intersectoral and disciplinary bias that impedes collaboration (von Braun, Ruel, and Gillespie 2012). Interdisciplinary training of researchers and professionals in this field is limited. Also the lack of communication between institutions (e.g., the World Health Organization [WHO] and FAO at the global level and, similarly, of respective ministries at national levels) restrains stakeholders in their perspectives of the issues. Intersectoral collaboration is enhanced when there are inclusive programming and jointly agreed-upon and compatible monitoring and evaluation systems in place (IFPRI 2015).

Agricultural practices can also be the source of health hazards through the use of toxic substances, such as pesticides and fertilizers. Mycotoxins are another case in point, which evolve, for example, due to improper crop handling or use of inferior seeds (Smith, Stoltzfus, and Prendergast 2012). In addition, there are several foodborne diseases that can occur through the mishandling of agricultural products. For this reason, effective food safety schemes are just as important for health as are policies to reduce food insecurity. A large and possibly growing issue of agriculture–health linkages is the risk of virus infections related to livestock, such as SARS and H1N1 (Mackey and Liang 2012; Castillo-Chavez et al. 2015). The economics of these require more attention by agricultural economists.

Nutrition-sensitive agriculture

In recent years more attention has been paid to nutrition-sensitive agriculture. Nutrition-sensitive agriculture focuses on the causes of malnutrition and is more long-term oriented (Jaenicke and Virchow 2013; Balz, Heil, and Jordan 2015). The approach encourages production and consumption of a variety of foods, recognizes and emphasizes the nutritional value of food, and considers the significance of food production for the agricultural sector, as well as for rural livelihoods (Thompson and Amoroso 2014). Existing food systems are altered by strengthening – for example, the gender dimension, nutrition education, agricultural value chains, and marketing (FAO 2015). Public policy may consider two strategic options: (1) to introduce policies that change the behavior of farmers, food processors, and, in the end, consumers; or (2) to implement health and nutrition-specific interventions, which compensate for nutritional damages that are partly a consequence of food system failures (on the latter, see Pinstrup-Andersen 2013); or (3) to pursue both options. Pinstrup-Andersen (2013) in that context draws attention to the "fixation of the health and nutrition community on randomized controlled trials (RCTs) as the only legitimate source of evidence" (Pinstrup-Andersen 2013, 376). RCTs are not ideal tools to deal with improvements in complex food systems, as they are often not comprehensively capturing synergies, such as health benefits of cultivating fruit and vegetables, including related market and income effects.

Biofortification

The important evolution of biofortification of staple foods through plant breeding is a specific class of nutrition-sensitive agriculture (Bouis et al. 2013). Biofortification is seen as one major contributor to eliminate micronutrient deficiencies, though there are challenges regarding the willingness of consumers to accept biofortified products (Chowdhury et al. 2011). The provision of information for consumers is essential to the success of these kinds of interventions. Generally speaking, biofortification seems to be cost-effective in most countries (Meenakshi et al. 2010). Most studies on biofortification have considered one biofortified crop. However, a diet normally consists of several crops that can potentially be biofortified. The interactions between multiples of biofortified crops (or industrially fortified foods) and the interaction with other plant-based or animal-sourced food items should be taken into consideration.

Income, health, and nutrition linkages

Increasing per capita GDP is seen by most national governments as a proxy for development, and with that, greater purchasing power, so that, hopefully, there is improved health and nutrition. Obviously, the links are complex, and much depends on distributional effects and the employment content of growth. Grouping a set of developing countries (selected by availability of the respective

Table 14.1 Growth and health and nutrition in developing countries

Nutrition and health outcomes	GDP per capita (2010)[a]					
	Group 1 (low)[b]		Group 2 (middle)[b]		Group 3 (high)[b]	
	High growth	Low growth	High growth	Low growth	High growth	Low growth
Average change in stunting* (%) (1989–2014)	−1.7	−1.5	−0.3	−1.1	−2.2	−1.5
Average change in child mortality (%) (1990–2010)	−4.2	−2.9	−3.3	−2.6	−4.3	−4.0

[a] Countries included: Bangladesh, Benin, Bolivia, Burkina Faso, Burundi, Cameroon, Democratic Republic of Congo, Arab Republic of Egypt, El Salvador, Guatemala, Guinea, Honduras, India, Indonesia, Kenya, Lao People's Democratic Republic, Madagascar, Malawi, Mali, Morocco, Mozambique, Nepal, Nigeria, Pakistan, Philippines, Rwanda, Senegal, Sierra Leone, Sri Lanka, Sudan, Tanzania, Togo, Uganda, Zambia, and Zimbabwe.

[b] Number of observations (n): Group 1 n=12; Group 2 n=12; Group 3 n=11.

* Source: World Bank data; author's own calculation. Data on stunting are approximated to the periods of observations, as there are no annual nutrition data.

data) by three classes of per capita GDP levels (low, middle, and high), and within each of these, two subclasses of high and low growth suggests that high growth is good for health and nutrition in all three groups, with only the middle group being an outlier for the stunting indicator. Large gains from growth for health (child mortality) and nutrition (stunting) are obtained in both the low- and high-income groups (see Table 14.1).

To the extent agriculture contributes to overall growth, the effect would be part of the drivers leading to the finding in Table 14.1. Actually, given the prevalence of low-income households in agriculture, growth in agriculture could be expected to have an over and above impact on health and nutrition. A respective regression exercise for the countries captured in Table 14.1 (not reported here) does indicate this is so, but the parameter for agricultural growth is not significant.

Ruel and Alderman (2013) have shown that an increase in GDP has a stronger effect on the reduction of child underweight than on stunting. The regression analysis in Table 14.2 does not lend significant support to that. Webb and Kennedy (2014) pointed out that anthropometric measures may not effectively capture long-term effects on nutrition.

Vollmer et al. (2014) found that there is not necessarily a direct association between an increase of per capita GDP and reduction of childhood undernutrition. There are several reasons for this, including unequal distribution of income. Studies dealing with the linkages between economic growth and child undernutrition have clear limitations due to lack of data; however, Demographic and Health Surveys as well as Food and Nutrition Surveillance Programs offer future opportunities to revise the studies with better and consistent data (Headey and Ecker 2013). Over the long term, child undernutrition can also be a direct cause for poor economic performance. For this reason, direct intervention programs to improve nutrition and health are called for (Vollmer et al. 2014).

Gulati et al. (2012) investigated whether there is a possible interplay between agricultural performance and malnutrition in Indian states that achieve higher agricultural performance. They used different nutrition indicators to develop a Combined Normalized Malnutrition Index (CNMI). In their model, the CNMI is used as the dependent variable, and agricultural performance and income measures are two of the considered explanatory variables in a linear regression. They found that the higher the agricultural performance the lower is the CNMI, whereas the gross land productivity demonstrated low significance. India's overall strong economic growth levels do not necessarily translate into similar improvements in health; and among Indian states that show strong performance in growth are several that show below-average performance in the progress of health and nutrition (UNICEF and Government of India 2015).

Ruel and Alderman (2013) argued that an effective agricultural intervention program that targets nutritional status should include women's empowerment activities. To the extent that women's lack of empowerment is determined by lack of land rights or lack of access to agricultural product and credit markets, this nutrition and health link is also an agricultural link. Ruel and Alderman (2013) concluded that investment in health and nutrition has a direct effect on the nutritional outcome, while investments in early childhood nutrition can have an added effect that may result in higher future development outcomes.

Agricultural market linkages with nutrition and health

Functioning agricultural markets are important for access to food and services, and thereby also for income and health (Kalkuhl et al. 2013). However, volatility in prices, even in efficiently functioning markets, may adversely impact consumption capabilities and health. Price volatility is not a new phenomenon, though some causes are. Several studies (Abbott, Hurt, and Tyner 2009; Gilbert 2010; Roache 2010; Abbott, Hurt, and Tyner 2011) have identified the drivers of price upsurges, such as biofuel demand, speculation on commodity futures markets, public stockholding, trade restrictions, macroeconomic shocks to money supply, exchange rates, and economic growth. Tadesse et al. (2014) argued that a food crisis is more related to extreme price spikes, whereas long-term volatility is more aligned to general price risks. In 2007–2008, the prices for almost all food commodities increased significantly, inducing negative effects, especially for low-income countries and the part of their population who spend the majority of their income on staple foods (Tadesse et al. 2014).

Different policy measures were used to cope with the effects, though some might have aggravated the whole situation, as some countries used export bans

Table 14.2 Volatility: a risk for children's nutritional status

	Underweight (in percent)	Stunting (in percent)
Log GDP per capita (PPP)	−4.408*	−6.292*
	(2.605)	(3.238)
Improved sanitation (%)	−0.327***	−0.375***
	(0.109)	(0.114)
Food price volatility (CV of FPI)[a]	9.904***	3.894**
	(1.490)	(1.619)
Female/male school enrollment	−0.156***	−0.213*
	(0.071)	(0.108)
N	300	291
R-squared	0.430	0.392
Number of countries	93	92

Source: Data from Kalkuhl et al. (2013), World Bank development indicators: GDP; WHO: Sanitation, Stunting, Underweight; ILO: Food price indices 1990–2012.

Note: Cluster robust standard errors in parentheses. A panel regression for low- and middle-income countries; country fixed effects included.

* $p < 0.01$
** $p < 0.05$
*** $p < 0.01$
[a] Coefficient of variation of food price volatility.

to protect their domestic market (Kalkuhl et al. 2013). Countries with per capita income below US$2,000 (PPP) exhibit higher volatility than countries with per capita income above US$10,000 (PPP), which may suggest that health and nutrition are more affected by volatility in poor countries. Kalkuhl et al. (2013), using country panel data, found a significant effect of price volatility for indicators of child undernutrition (Table 14.2). The short-term effect of price increases for households can be split into two effects: first, the increase of food prices results in lower available real income, referring to the income effect, and second, spending patterns might be adjusted – that is, the substitution effect (Kalkuhl et al. 2013).

Ziegelhöfer (2014), using Demographic and Health Survey (DHS) data, also found that an increase of the indicator for month-to-month volatility negatively impacts child health status. However, it should be kept in mind that households are not a homogenous group, and different households can deal with price shocks, using various coping measures. For this reason, price shocks do not necessarily translate into worsened child health in every case. Ziegelhöfer (2014) concluded that volatility, short-term price changes, and permanent shocks have a negative effect on child health. Interestingly, price decreases were not found to have significant beneficial impact on child health.

Ecology, water, and sanitation links with agriculture

A particularly complex set of agriculture–health linkages is within the broader ecological and public health context of farming communities. An important subset of these is the environmental health linkages of partly agriculture-related water quality and quantity problems, interacting with farm populations' sanitation and hygiene behaviors. Figure 14.2 provides a sketch of the complex ecological context in which agriculture is embedded, with related water and sanitation systems under multiuse water systems that are common for the habitat of millions of farming households.

The importance of water quality for health is well known (Bradley 1977; Moe and Rheingans 2006). The impact of agriculture on both the water quality and quantity with respect to health issues is not well researched. The health costs of sanitation and water problems are large (Prüss et al. 2002). In addition, in peri–urban settings, farmers often have neither a choice other than using wastewater for irrigation nor the knowledge of the potential risks related to that resource (Qadir et al. 2010; Tsegai, McBain, and Tischbein 2015) – including harm for human health and the environment through introduction of pathogens or contamination with chemical substances. Still, if handled appropriately,

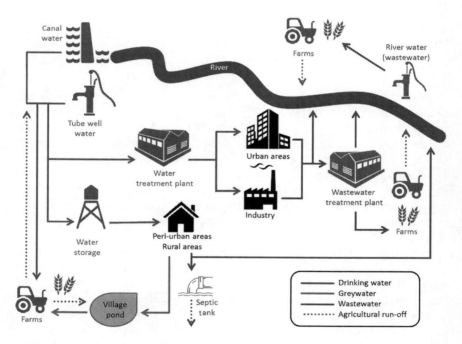

Figure 14.2 Agriculture in multiuse water systems and sanitation problems

Source: (Usman, Gerber, and von Braun (2016); Vangani et al. (2016); and Malek et al. (2016). Icon elements generated by flaticon.com under CC BY. Picture credit: icons made by Freepik, OCHA from www.flaticon.com.

wastewater can be regarded as a valuable resource, as reusing water means cost savings, and using wastewater for irrigation translates into additional value for society through the crops produced (Qadir et al. 2010). While urban food production makes up 15 percent of all food production, in most countries there are no policies in place that pay attention to the beneficial role or adverse health effects of (peri-) urban agriculture for society (Mara and Sleigh 2010; Gerster-Bentaya 2013).

Water quality at the level of consumption is partly related to sanitation behavior.[3] Water quality can be associated with health issues, such as the prevalence of diarrhea (Usman, Gerber, and von Braun 2016; Vangani et al. 2016; Malek et.al. 2016). Studies have shown that improvements in water and sanitation are major contributors to the reduction of stunting. The so-called Asian Enigma that children in India are shorter than even poorer children in Africa can be linked to the prevalence of open defecation (Spears and Haddad 2015). The prevalence of open defecation and the prevalence of underweight children show a strong correlation in India, according to the Rapid Survey on Children in India (UNICEF and Government of India 2015).

There is also a clear linkage between these health, environmental, and behavioral issues and nutritional status and farming (Usman, Gerber, and von Braun 2016; Vangani et al. 2016; Malek et.al. 2016). As a result of chronic diarrhea, the human body is not able to store essential nutrients, causing long-term negative effects, especially when children are affected (WHO and UNICEF 2013).

Conclusions

The Sustainable Development Goal of ending hunger and malnutrition of all forms calls for a sound framework, covering the main relationships between agriculture and health/nutrition. The prevailing concepts about agriculture and health/nutrition links need to be revisited and augmented, in view of new insights, and in order to provide appropriate guidance for policy. In order to effectively tap opportunities and to avoid adverse effects of agricultural change for health and nutrition, a suitable conceptual framework is needed. Such framework must give due consideration to the complexity of the evolving and adapting food and agricultural system, yet it also needs to be simple and transparent enough to be acceptable for policymakers.

The key linkages identified in the proposed framework include four blocks (nutrition/health, agriculture, markets, income) interlinked with each other, which makes for six linkages: (1) agricultural production- and processing-related health linkages; technology is critical for these links; (2) income and employment-related health and nutrition linkages are equally important; (3) agriculture and income and employment links; and (4) agriculture linkages with markets and services, driving nutrition and health via income but also directly via price formation, are of probably growing importance; (5) markets and services are critical for delivering affordable nutritious food, as well as nutrition and health-related services; and (6) lastly, efficiency of markets and inclusive services, including insurance mechanisms, are key forces behind income and employment generation and households' capacity to deal with risks and shocks.

A major challenge for research is that all these linkages are actually two–way linkages – that is, mutually endogenous – making exceedingly difficult the narrowly defined causality identification using econometric tools. The linkages also have different time lags of impact. Moreover, agriculture–health/nutrition linkages are often context-specific. Especially, the water–sanitation and hygiene linkages with farming are not well understood as yet. The appropriate depiction of the linkages requires interdisciplinary research of agronomists, economists, public health experts, and hydrologists, among others. A focus on nutrition and health, working backwards to the identified linkages with agriculture and the intermediate forces of markets and income, may be most practical.

Notes

1   This chapter was prepared for the Festschrift in honor of Hans Binswanger-Mkhize. Valuable research assistance for this chapter by Till Ludwig, ZEF junior researcher, and Kristina Mensah, research assistant at ZEF, is gratefully acknowledged.
2   In the following, nutrition is understood as being included in health and, therefore, mostly not mentioned separately, unless explicitly stated.
3   Source: http://www.who.int/topics/sanitation/en.

References

Abbott, P. C., C. Hurt, and W. E. Tyner. 2009. "What's Driving Food Prices? March 2009 Update." Issue Report, March 2009, Farm Foundation NFP, Oak Brook, IL. http://ageconsearch.umn.edu/bitstream/48495/2/FINAL 3-10-09–Food Prices Update.pdf

Abbott, P. C., C. Hurt, and W. E. Tyner. 2011. "What's Driving Food Prices in 2011?" Issue Report, July 2011, Farm Foundation, NFP, Oak Brook, IL. http://farmfoundation.org/news/articlefiles/1742-FoodPrices_web.pdf

Axelrod, R., and M. D. Cohen. 2012. *Harnessing Complexity: Organizational Implications of a Scientific Frontier.* New York: Basic Books.

Balter, M., 2010. "The Tangled Roots of Agriculture." *Science* 327 (5964): 40406. http://www.sciencemag.org/cgi/doi/10.1126/science.327.5964.404

Balz, A. G., E. A. Heil, and I. Jordan. 2015. "Nutrition-sensitive Agriculture: New Term or New Concept?" *Agriculture & Food Security* 4 (1): 6. http://www.agricultureandfoodsecurity.com/content/4/1/6

Binswanger, H. P. 2006. "Food and Agricultural Policy to Mitigate the Impact of HIV/AIDS." Invited paper for the AAEA session on "Agriculture, Nutrition, and Health in High- and Low-Income Countries: Policy Issues" at the International Association of Agricultural Economists (IAAE) Conference in Brisbane, Australia, August 13–18, 2006.

Binswanger, H. P., and J. von Braun. 1991. "Technological Change and Commercialization in Agriculture: The Effect on the Poor." *World Bank Research Observer* 6 (1): 57–80.

Black, R. E., L. H. Allen, Z. A. Bhutta, L. E. Caulfield, M. de Onis, M. Ezzati, C. Mathers, and J. Rivera; for the Maternal and Child Undernutrition Study Group. 2008. "Maternal and Child Undernutrition: Global and Regional Exposures and Health Consequences." *Lancet* 371 (9608): 243–60. http://linkinghub.elsevier.com/retrieve/pii/S0140673607616900

Black, R. E., C. G. Victora, S. P. Walker, Z. A. Bhutta, P. Christian, M. de Onis, M. Ezzati, S. Grantham-McGregor, J. Katz, R. Martorell, and R. Uauy; the Maternal and Child Nutrition Study Group. 2013. "Maternal and Child Undernutrition and Overweight in Low-income and Middle-income Countries." *Lancet* 382 (9890): 427–51.

Bouis, H. E., J. Low, M. McEwan, and S. Tanumihardjo. 2013. "Biofortification: Evidence and Lessons Learned Linking Agriculture and Nutrition." Food and Agriculture Organization of the United Nations (FAO) and the World Health Organization (WHO), Rome. http://www.fao.org/fileadmin/user_upload/agn/pdf/Biofortification_paper.pdf

Bradley, D. 1977. "Health Aspects of Water Supplies in Tropical Countries." In *Wastes and Health in Hot Climates*, edited by R. Feachem, M. McGarry, and D. Mara, 3–17. Chichester: John Wiley and Sons.

Brookfield, H., 2008. "Family Farms Are Still Around: Time to Invert the Old Agrarian Question." *Geography Compass* 2 (1): 108–26. http://doi.wiley.com/10.1111/j.1749-8198.2007.00078.x

Burlingame, B., and S. Dernini, eds. 2012. *Sustainable Diets and Biodiversity. Directions and Solutions for Policy, Research and Action*. Rome: Food and Agriculture Organization of the United Nations (FAO).

Castillo-Chavez, C. R., Curtiss, P. Daszak, S. A Levin, O. Patterson-Lomba, C. Perrings, G. Poste, and S. Towers. 2015. "Beyond Ebola: Lessons to Mitigate Future Pandemics." *Lancet Global Health* 3 (7): e354–e355. http://www.thelancet.com/journals/langlo/article/PIIS2214-109X(15)00068-6/fulltext?rss=yes

CFS (Committee on World Food Security). 2012. "Coming to Terms with Terminology: Food Security, Nutrition Security, Food Security and Nutrition, Food and Nutrition Security." 39th Session, Rome, October 15–20, 2012. http://www.fao.org/docrep/meeting/026/MD776E.pdf

Chowdhury, S., J. V. Meenakshi, K. I. Tomlins, and C. Owori. 2011. "Are Consumers in Developing Countries Willing to Pay More for Micronutrient-Dense Biofortified Foods? Evidence from a Field Experiment in Uganda." *American Journal of Agricultural Economics* 93 (1): 83–97.

Dangour, A. D., R. Green, B. Häsler, J. Rushton, B. Shankar, and J. Waage. 2012. "Linking Agriculture and Health in Low- and Middle-income Countries: An Interdisciplinary Research Agenda." *Proceedings of the Nutrition Society* 71 (2): 222–8. http://www.journals.cambridge.org/abstract_S0029665112000213

de Haen, H., S. Klasen, and M. Qaim. 2011. "What Do We Really Know? Metrics for Food Insecurity and Undernutrition." *Food Policy* 36 (6): 760–9.

Devereux, S., R. Chambers, R. Longhurst, and R. Sabates-Wheeler, eds. 2011. *Seasonality, Rural Livelihoods and Development*. London: Routledge. http://www.tandfebooks.com/isbn/9780203139820

Dubé, L., P. Webb, N. K. Arora, and P. Pingali. 2014. "Agriculture, Health, and Wealth Convergence: Bridging Traditional Food Systems and Modern Agribusiness Solutions." *Annals of the New York Academy of Sciences* 1331 (1): 1–14. http://doi.wiley.com/10.1111/nyas.12602

Fan, S., and R. Pandya-Lorch. 2012. *Reshaping Agriculture for Nutrition and Health*. An IFPRI 2020 Book. Washington, DC: International Food Policy Research Institute (IFPRI). http://ebrary.ifpri.org/cdm/ref/collection/p15738coll2/id/126825

Fan, S., R. Pandya-Lorch, and S. Yosef. 2014. *Resilience for Food and Nutrition Security*. Washington, DC: International Food Policy Research Institute (IFPRI). http://www.ifpri.org/sites/default/files/publications/oc79.pdf#page=108

FAO (Food and Agriculture Organization of the United Nations). 2015. "Designing Nutrition-sensitive Agriculture Investments. Checklist and Guidance for Programme Formulation." Food and Agriculture Organization of the United Nations (FAO), Rome. http://www.fao.org/documents/card/en/c/6cd87835-ab0c-46d7-97ba-394d620e9f38/

FAO, IFAD, and WFP (Food and Agriculture Organization of the United Nations, International Fund for Agricultural Development, and World Food Programme). 2014. *The State of Food Insecurity in the World 2014. Strengthening the Enabling Environment for Food Security and Nutrition.* Rome: FAO.

Ferro-Luzzi, A., and F. Branca. 1993. "Nutritional Seasonality: The Dimensions of the Problem." In *Seasonality and Human Ecology*, edited by S. J. Ulijaszek, and S. S. Strickland, 149–65. Cambridge: Cambridge University Press. http://ebooks.cambridge.org/ref/id/CBO9780511600517A019

Fogel, R. W. 1999. "Catching Up with the Economy." *American Economic Review* 89 (1): 1–21. http://pubs.aeaweb.org/doi/abs/10.1257/aer.89.1.1

Gerster-Bentaya, M. 2013. "Nutrition-sensitive Urban Agriculture." *Food Security* 5 (5): 723–37. http://link.springer.com/10.1007/s12571-013-0295-3

Gilbert, C. L. 2010. "How to Understand High Food Prices." *Journal of Agricultural Economics* 61 (2): 398–425.

Gulati, A., A. G. Kumar, G. Shreedhar, and T. Nandakumar. 2012. "Agriculture and Malnutrition in India." *Food and Nutrition Bulletin* 33 (1): 74–86. http://fnb.sagepub.com/lookup/doi/10.1177/156482651203300108

Haggblade, S., P. Hazell, and T. Reardon. 2010. "The Rural Non-farm Economy: Prospects for Growth and Poverty Reduction." *World Development* 38 (10): 1429–41.

Hawkes, C., and M. T. Ruel, eds. 2006. *Understanding the Links between Agriculture and Health.* Washington, DC: International Food Policy Research Institute (IFPRI). http://www.ifpri.org/2020/focus/focus13.asp

Headey, D., and O. Ecker. 2013. "Rethinking the Measurement of Food Security: From First Principles to Best Practice." *Food Security* 5 (3): 327–43.

Herforth, A., A. Jones, and P. Pinstrup-Andersen. 2012. "Prioritizing Nutrition in Agriculture and Rural Development: Guiding Principles for Operational Investments." Health, Nutrition and Population (HNP) Discussion Paper, World Bank, Washington, DC.

Holden, S. T., and H. P. Binswanger. 1998. "Small Farmers, Market Imperfections, and Natural Resource Management." In *Agriculture and the Environment: Perspectives on Sustainable Rural Development*, edited by E. Lutz, H. Binswanger, P. Hazel, and A. McCalla, 50–69. Washington, DC: World Bank.

IFPRI (International Food Policy Research Institute). 2015. *Global Nutrition Report 2015: Actions and Accountability to Advance Nutrition and Sustainable Development.* Washington, DC: IFPRI. http://ebrary.ifpri.org/cdm/ref/collection/p15738coll2/id/129443

Jaenicke, H., and D. Virchow. 2013. "Entry Points into a Nutrition-sensitive Agriculture." *Food Security* 5 (5): 679–92. http://link.springer.com/10.1007/s12571-013-0293-5

Jha, S. K., J. McDermott, G. Bacon, C. Lannon, P. K. Joshi, and L. Dubé. 2014. "Convergent Innovation for Affordable Nutrition, Health, and Health Care: The Global Pulse Roadmap." *Annals of the New York Academy of Sciences* 1331 (1): 142–56. http://doi.wiley.com/10.1111/nyas.12543

Johnston, J. L., J. C. Fanzo, and B. Cogill. 2014. "Understanding Sustainable Diets: A Descriptive Analysis of the Determinants and Processes that Influence Diets and Their Impact on Health, Food Security, and Environmental Sustainability." *Advances in Nutrition* 5 (4): 418–29.

Kalkuhl, M., L. Kornher, M. Kozicka, P. Boulanger, and M. Torero. 2013. "Conceptual Framework on Price Volatility and Its Impact on Food and Nutrition Security in the Short

Term." FOODSECURE Working Paper No. 15, LEI Research Institute, Wageningen University, The Hague. http://www.foodsecure.eu/PublicationDetail.aspx?id=43

Kalkuhl, M., J. von Braun, and M. Torero, eds. 2016. *Food Price Volatility and Its Implications for Food Security and Policy*. Cham: Springer International. http://link.springer.com/10.1007/978-3-319-28201-5

Kar, B. R., S. L. Rao, and B. A. Chandramouli. 2008. "Cognitive Development in Children with Chronic Protein Energy Malnutrition." *Behavioral and Brain Functions* 4 (1):31. http://behavioralandbrainfunctions.biomedcentral.com/articles/10.1186/1744-9081-4-31

Keding, G. B., K. Schneider, and I. Jordan. 2013. "Production and Processing of Foods as Core Aspects of Nutrition-sensitive Agriculture and Sustainable Diets." *Food Security* 5 (6): 825–46. http://link.springer.com/10.1007/s12571-013-0312-6

Kim, S., Q. Deng, B. M. Fleisher, and S. Li. 2014. "The Lasting Impact of Parental Early Life Malnutrition on Their Offspring: Evidence from the China Great Leap Forward Famine." *World Development* 54: 232–42.

Lokshin, M., and S. Radyakin. 2012. "Month of Birth and Children's Health in India." *Journal of Human Resources* 47 (1): 174–203.

Mackey, T. K., and B. A. Liang. 2012. "Lessons from SARS and H1N1/A: Employing a WHO–WTO Forum to Promote Optimal Economic–Public Health Pandemic Response." *Journal of Public Health Policy* 33 (1): 119–30.

Malek, M.A., T. N. Khan, N. Gerber, R. Saha, and I. Mohammad. 2016. "Can a Specially Designed Information Intervention around the WASH-Agriculture Linkages Make Any Difference? Experimental Evidence of Behavioral Changes and Health Impacts." ZEF Discussion Papers on Development Policy No. 213, Center for Development Research (ZEF), University of Bonn. http://www.zef.de/uploads/tx_zefportal/Publications/zef_dp_213.pdf

Mara, D., and A. Sleigh. 2010. "Estimation of Norovirus and *Ascaris* Infection Risks to Urban Farmers in Developing Countries Using Wastewater for Crop Irrigation." *Journal of Water and Health* 8 (3): 572–6. http://jwh.iwaponline.com/cgi/doi/10.2166/wh.2010.097

Masset, E., L. Haddad, A. Cornelius, and J. Isaza-Castro. 2012. "Effectiveness of Agricultural Interventions that Aim to Improve Nutritional Status of Children: Systematic Review." *BMJ* 344 (d8222). http://www.bmj.com/cgi/doi/10.1136/bmj.d8222

McDermott, J., M. Aït-Aïssa, J. Morel, and N. Rapando. 2013. "Agriculture and Household Nutrition Security – Development Practice and Research Needs." *Food Security* 5 (5): 667–78. http://link.springer.com/article/10.1007/s12571-013-0292-6

Meenakshi, J. V., N. L. Johnson, V. M. Manyong, H. DeGroote, J. Javelosa, D. R. Yanggen, F. Naher, C. Gonzalez, J. García, and E. Meng. 2010. "How Cost-Effective Is Biofortification in Combating Micronutrient Malnutrition? An *Ex ante* Assessment." *World Development* 38 (1): 64–75.

Moe, C. L., and R. D. Rheingans. 2006. "Global Challenges in Water, Sanitation and Health." *Journal of Water and Health* 4 (Suppl. 1): 41–58.

Pangaribowo, E. H., N. Gerber, and M. Torero. 2013. Food and Nutrition Security Indicators: A Review." ZEF Working Paper No. 108, Center for Development Research, University of Bonn.

Pingali, P. L., C. B. Marquez, and F. G. Palis. 1994. "Pesticides and Philippine Rice Farmer Health: A Medical and Economic Analysis." *American Journal of Agricultural Economics* 76 (3): 587–92.

Pinstrup-Andersen, P., ed. 2010. *The African Food System and Its Interactions with Human Health and Nutrition*. Ithaca, NY: Cornell University Press in cooperation with the United Nations University.

Pinstrup-Andersen, P. 2013. "Nutrition-sensitive Food Systems: From Rhetoric to Action." *Lancet* 382 (9890): 375–6. http://linkinghub.elsevier.com/retrieve/pii/S0140673613610533

Prüss, A., D. Kay, L. Fewtrell, and J. Bartram. 2002. "Estimating the Burden of Disease from Water, Sanitation, and Hygiene at a Global Level." *Environmental Health Perspectives* 110 (5): 537–42. http://www.ncbi.nlm.nih.gov/pmc/articles/PMC1240845/pdf/ehp0110-000537.pdf

Qadir, M., D. Wichelns, L. Raschid-Sally, P .G. McCornick, P. Drechsel, A. Bahri, and P. S. Minhas. 2010. "The Challenges of Wastewater Irrigation in Developing Countries." *Agricultural Water Management* 97 (4): 561–8. http://linkinghub.elsevier.com/retrieve/pii/S0378377408002989

Roache, S. K. 2010. "What Explains the Rise in Food Price Volatility?" IMF Working Paper WP/10/129, International Monetary Fund, Washington, DC. https://www.imf.org/external/pubs/ft/wp/2010/wp10129.pdf

Ruddiman, W. F., E. C. Ellis, J. O. Kaplan, and D. Q. Fuller. 2015. "Defining the Epoch We Live In." *Science* 348 (6230): 38–9.

Ruel, M. T., and H. Alderman. 2013. "Nutrition-sensitive Interventions and Programmes: How Can They Help to Accelerate Progress in Improving Maternal and Child Nutrition?" *Lancet* 382 (9891): 536–51. http://www.thelancet.com/pdfs/journals/lancet/PIIS0140-6736(13)60843-0.pdf

Smith, L. E., R. J. Stoltzfus, and A. Prendergast. 2012. "Food Chain Mycotoxin Exposure, Gut Health, and Impaired Growth: A Conceptual Framework." *Advances in Nutrition* 3 (4): 526–31. http://advances.nutrition.org/cgi/doi/10.3945/an.112.002188

Spears, D., and L. Haddad. 2015. "The Power of WASH: Why Sanitation Matters for Nutrition." In *Global Food Policy Report 2014–2015*, 19–23. Washington, DC: International Food Policy Research Institute (IFPRI). http://ebrary.ifpri.org/cdm/ref/collection/p15738coll2/id/129074

Tadesse, G., B. Algieri, M. Kahkuhl, and J. von Braun. 2014. "Drivers and Triggers of International Food Price Spikes and Volatility." *Food Policy* 47: 117–28. http://linkinghub.elsevier.com/retrieve/pii/S0306919213001188

Tendall, D. M., J. Joerin, B. Kopainsky, P. Edwards, A. Shreck, Q. B. Le, P. Kruetli, M. Grant, and J. Six. 2015. "Food System Resilience: Defining the Concept." *Global Food Security* 6: 17–23.

Thompson, B., and L. Amoroso, eds. 2014. *Improving Diets and Nutrition: Food-based Approaches.* Rome: Food and Agriculture Organization of the United Nations (FAO) and CAB International. http://www.fao.org/3/a-i3030e.pdf

Tsegai, D. W., F. McBain, and B. Tischbein. 2015. "Water, Sanitation and Hygiene: The Missing Link with Agriculture." ZEF Working Paper No. 147912, Center for Development Research, University of Bonn.

UNICEF (United Nations Children's Fund) and Government of India. 2015. "Rapid Survey on Children in India 2013/14." *The Economist*, July 2, 2015. http://www.economist.com/blogs/graphicdetail/2015/07/daily-chart-0

Usman, M.A, N. Gerber, and J. von Braun. 2016. "The Impact of Drinking Water Quality and Sanitation on Child Health: Evidence from Rural Ethiopia." ZEF Discussion Papers on Development Policy No. 221, Center for Development Research (ZEF), University of Bonn. http://www.zef.de/uploads/tx_zefportal/Publications/zef_dp_221.pdf

Vangani, R., D. Saxena, N. Gerber, D. Mavalankar, and J. von Braun. 2016. "Impact of Different Irrigation Systems on Water Quality in Peri-Urban Areas of Gujarat, India." ZEF Discussion Papers on Development Policy No. 219, Center for Development Research (ZEF), University of Bonn. http://www.zef.de/uploads/tx_zefportal/Publications/ZEF_dp_219.pdf

Vollmer, S., K. Harttgen, M. A. Subramanyam, J. Finlay, S. Klasen, and S. V. Subramanian. 2014. "Association between Economic Growth and Early Childhood Undernutrition: Evidence from 121 Demographic and Health Surveys from 36 Low-income and Middle-income Countries." *Lancet Global Health* 2 (4): e225–e234. http://www.thelancet.com/article/S2214109X14700257/fulltext

von Braun, J. 2015a. "Bioeconomy: Science and Technology Policy to Harmonize Biologization of Economies with Food Security." In *The Fight against Hunger and Malnutrition: The Role of Food, Agriculture and Targeted Policies*, edited by D. E. Sahn, 240–62. Oxford: Oxford University Press.

von Braun, J. 2015b. "Food and Nutrition Security: The Concept and Its Realization." In *Bread and Brain, Education and Poverty*, edited by A. M. Battro, I. Potrykus, and M. Sanchez Sorondo, 69–85. Vatican City: Pontifical Academy of Sciences, Scripta Varia 125.

von Braun, J., and F. W. Gatzweiler, eds. 2014. *Marginality: Addressing the Nexus of Poverty, Exclusion and Ecology*. Dordrecht: Springer Netherlands. http://link.springer.com/10.1007/978-94-007-7061-4

von Braun, J., and E. Kennedy, eds. 1994. *Agricultural Commercialization, Economic Development, and Nutrition*. Baltimore: Johns Hopkins University Press for the International Food Policy Research Institute (IFPRI).

von Braun, J., and A. Mirzabaev. 2015. "Small Farms: Changing Structures and Roles in Economic Development." ZEF-Discussion Papers on Development Policy No. 204, Center for Development Research (ZEF), University of Bonn.

von Braun, J., M. T. Ruel, and S. Gillespie. 2012. "Bridging the Gap between the Agriculture and Health Sectors." In *Reshaping Agriculture for Nutrition and Health*. An IFPRI 2020 Book, edited by S. Fan and R. Pandya-Lorch, 183–90. Washington, DC: International Food Policy Research Institute (IFPRI).

Webb, P. 2013. "Impact Pathways from Agricultural Research to Improved Nutrition and Health: Literature Analysis and Research Priorities." Food and Agriculture Organization of the United Nations (FAO) and World Health Organization (WHO), Rome.

Webb, P., and E. Kennedy. 2014. "Impacts of Agriculture on Nutrition: Nature of the Evidence and Research Gaps." *Food and Nutrition Bulletin* 35 (1): 126–32.

WHO (World Health Organization). 2013. *Research Priorities for the Environment, Agriculture and Infectious Diseases of Poverty*. Technical Report of the TDR Thematic Reference Group on Environment, Agriculture and Infectious Diseases of Poverty. Geneva: WHO. http://apps.who.int/iris/bitstream/10665/78129/1/WHO_TRS_976_eng.pdf

WHO and UNICEF (World Health Organization and United Nations Children's Fund). 2013. "Progress on Sanitation and Drinking-Water 2013 Update." WHO, Geneva.

Ziegelhöfer, Z. M. 2014. "Use What You've Got: Three Essays in Development Economics Using Real World Data." Graduate Institute of International and Development Studies, Geneva. http://repository.graduateinstitute.ch/record/289611/

15 Understanding the multidimensional nature of the malnutrition problem in India

Prabhu Pingali and Tanvi Rao

Introduction

India's high rates of malnutrition have been an object of enigma[1] in academic and policy circles for over two decades now. India's slow progress in combating its malnutrition problem was highlighted most starkly when a comparison between its rates of poverty and malnutrition decline between the mid–1990s and mid–2000s was brought to the fore, with the release of the National Family Health Survey (NFHS-3) in 2005. Despite a robust decline in overall poverty during the period, by approximately 7.8 percentage points (Smith 2015), the proportion of underweight children showed a dismal decline of less than 1 percentage point between the two NFHS surveys spanning the period (Deaton and Drèze 2009; Pathak and Singh 2011). The prevalence of overweight and obesity had increased slightly over the last two NFHS rounds, but the rising trends are more pronounced in urban and high-income populations (Wang et al. 2009).

That complex interactions among various factors are at play in determining nutritional outcomes is amply evident when the Indian experience is viewed both internationally and intranationally. The Indian case has often been compared to sub-Saharan Africa, which has had lower malnutrition levels than India, despite greater poverty and civil unrest. More recently, countries in India's own neighborhood have been shown to outperform it, despite having much lower levels of per capita income. For instance, Bangladesh's successes in scaling up health-related efforts, like gains in immunization coverage or vitamin A supplementation, have been attributed to women-centered and highly focused health programs and a wide network of community health workers (Chowdhury et al. 2013). Holding wealth constant, it has also been documented that children in West Bengal are one-tenth of a height-for-age z-score (HAZ) standard deviation (sd) shorter than children in Bangladesh, and these findings have been correlated with differences in open defecation between the two genetically similar populations (Ghosh, Gupta, and Spears 2014). Between 1990 and 2009, India's rank, in comparison to its five South Asian neighbors – Sri Lanka, Bangladesh, Bhutan, Nepal, and Pakistan – improved in terms of GNI per capita, while its rank in the proportion of underweight children slipped to the last spot (Drèze and Sen 2011).

State-level malnutrition in the country also offers a diverse picture. In 2005, across 15 major Indian states, stunting prevalence among children under five ranged from 25 percent in Kerala to 57 percent in Uttar Pradesh, and the prevalence of underweight from 23 percent (Kerala) to 60 percent (Madhya Pradesh) (Kanjilal et al. 2010). While, on average, State Net Domestic Product (SNDP) is positively associated with HAZ, Indian states that have experienced more economic growth saw less of an increase in HAZ between 1998–99 and 2005–06. Moreover, the cross-sectional relationship between SNDP and HAZ was stronger in 1998–99 than in 2005–06 (Coffey, Chattopadhyay, and Gupt 2014). How then can India make progress in tackling its persistently high levels of malnutrition? Much of the academic discourse around Indian malnutrition today relies on NFHS-3 data that are over a decade old. Undoubtedly, crucial pieces in the Indian puzzle will remain out of place, until more up-to-date and nationally representative anthropometric data are disseminated and used. Recent health and nutrition data releases[2] by the Indian government will undoubtedly spur research to help foster a deeper understanding of what has or has not worked in the past decade to combat malnutrition in the Indian context. Already, numbers emerging[3] from UNICEF's Rapid Survey of Children (RSOC), in July 2015, indicate unprecedented changes in India's nutrition profile. Reported figures show substantive overall drops, in comparison to the 2005 data, in all three child undernutrition measures, although state-level figures remain varied. While progress is seen in both economically prosperous states, such as Maharashtra (decline in underweight prevalence of 12 percentage points), and laggard states, such as Madhya Pradesh and Bihar (drops in underweight prevalence of 24 and 19 percentage points, respectively), states such as Uttar Pradesh and Gujarat seem to provide a less favorable contrast. Moreover, reports based on the RSOC reveal much less progress in reducing the proportion of underweight adolescent girls, with only four Indian states succeeding in doing so in the past decade.

In this chapter, we bring together several strands of research on malnutrition in India in a comprehensive narrative synthesis of the existing literature. By focusing exclusively on comparable anthropometric outcomes, we throw light on the relative strength of different nutrition determinants and interventions. We also differentiate rigorous studies from ones with poor internal validity, to highlight gaps in the literature. With this, we hope to set the stage for further research with up-to-date anthropometrics, relevant to the new and changed environment around nutrition in India. We do not restrict our review to a particular type of nutrition intervention, but instead cover a breadth of nutritional determinants and interventions to populate evidence along each of the four interlocking pathways shown in Figure 15.1, which are generally thought to improve child and adult nutrition. A detailed description of Figure 15.1 can be found in Pingali, Ricketts, and Sahn (2015).

Readers may also want to draw parallels between the framework presented here and UNICEF's (1990) framework, which has commonly been the de facto choice for conceptualizing the multiple drivers of undernutrition. Our framework explicitly accounts for household-level and intrahousehold determinants

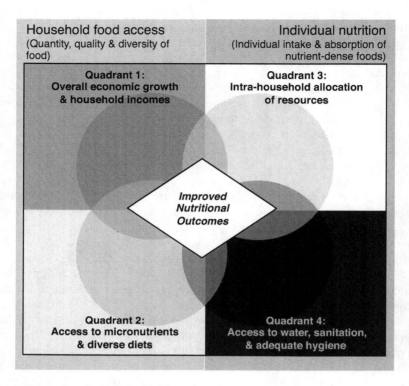

Figure 15.1 Multisectoral pathways for improved nutritional outcomes
Source: Adapted from Pingali and Ricketts (2014, 251, Figure 1).

of individual nutrition outcomes. It provides a clearer representation of the drivers of household access to food (in terms of quantity, quality, and diversity), as well as the factors that determine individual intake and absorption of nutrients.[4]

In general, macroeconomic growth, accompanied by an augmentation of household incomes (Quadrant 1), is necessary for a household to be able to afford a sufficient diet in terms of both quantity and quality of food. In India, where a predominant fraction of the malnourished is rural and belongs to agricultural households, income is determined in significant part by agricultural output and is subject to seasonality. Moreover, households are often unable to smooth consumption, facing high transaction costs and missing markets for nutritious foods, and also suffer from substantial information and knowledge gaps that may hinder the consumption of a diverse and micronutrient-rich diet and the practice of proper child-feeding practices. Therefore, to address adverse anthropometric outcomes, especially among young children, it is necessary to ensure access to a micronutrient-rich diet (Quadrant 2). Potentially delivered via supplementary feeding, food fortification, or crop diversity, such diets need to be actively promoted. Government interventions and food-based safety nets to address malnutrition are relevant here.

The intrahousehold allocation of resources (Quadrant 3) is a crucial determinant of how household-level food access translates into individual-level nutrition outcomes. When household incomes/resources are not pooled, the identity of the individual with access to resources (e.g., fathers versus mothers) can have a considerable effect on outcomes of vulnerable groups, like children and women. Joint familial relations and a pronounced preference for sons heighten the role of such factors in the Indian context. Finally, it is crucial that nutrient intake translates into nutrient absorption, which can be greatly inhibited by gastric and parasitic infections and diarrheal disease. Access to proper sanitation and adequate hygiene (Quadrant 4) are essential to ensure nutritional improvements via this pathway.

Methodology

As discussed in the previous section, this review cuts across different types of nutrition determinants and interventions, but focuses solely on either studies that explain child stunting, underweight, or wasting in terms of prevalence or z-scores,[5] or studies that explain analogous adult underweight (low body mass index [BMI]) outcomes. Primarily, our focus is on young children because stunting/underweight/wasting classifications follow international reference standards that are applicable, at a country-level, only for young children, typically under five years of age (de Onis and WHO Multicentre Growth Reference Study Group 2006). Studies for the review were screened using a combination of methods. First, we started with a list of widely cited studies relevant to each quadrant, which met our inclusion criteria, and then searched for other relevant and related studies by a method of "forward" and "backward" snowballing of reference searches (Hagen-Zanker and Mallet 2013). Then we searched three economics databases – RePec, AgEcon Search, and Econlit – and one biomedical database – MEDLINE – with a keyword search using a combination of keywords related to "India" and "malnutrition." Any study not previously found during snowballing was screened for inclusion, and then either retained or discarded. While we concentrate this review primarily around articles published in academic, peer-reviewed journals, some well-cited working papers from the last five years have also been included in the review, for completeness.

The main inclusion criteria during screening for studies retrieved via the aforementioned search methods were that the studies should (1) have a population focus on young children and adults in India; and (2) conduct econometric/statistical analysis with anthropometric measures as the outcome of interest. In addition, we include only studies published between 1990 and 2015,[6] as this is the period wherein national tracking of anthropometrics in India was commenced and during which time an explicit recognition of India's lack of progress in tackling malnutrition was made. Finally, only articles published in English language journals and those that could be digitally retrieved were included.

More than half of the studies that we review are based on one of three rounds (1992–93, 1998–99, and 2005–06) of the NFHS data. This is not surprising, given that NFHS is the only nationally representative anthropometric data, comparable across years, that are available for India. Another survey used, which is also nationally representative and collects a different set of complementary data along with anthropometrics, is the Indian Human Development Survey (IHDS), released in 2005. Although IHDS data used by nutrition researchers, to date, have been cross-sectional, a subsequent round of the data set, pertaining to the years 2011–12, was released in August 2015 and makes available the opportunity for panel data analysis in the future. Regionally focused and smaller-scale surveys, like the Young Lives Survey and the HUNGaMA[7] data set, have also been used by researchers to draw specific insights on the nature and causes of malnutrition. A substantial and informative body of evidence is also available on the determinants of nutrition outcomes, based on randomized evaluations and case-control studies.

A subset of papers included in our narrative synthesis is organized by quadrant, effect size, and extent of control of confounding effects, in Table A.15.1a (children) and Table A.15.2a (adults). Both tables are accompanied by additional details regarding the included predictor variables – that is, the precise variable definition and unit of measurement of the variable, which are presented in Tables A.15.1b and A.15.2b. Papers discussed in the narrative synthesis but not included in Tables A.15.1a and A.15.2a were excluded for the sake of comparability. The main reason for exclusion was nonstandard measurement of malnutrition. Some medically focused studies and some non-rigorous studies with extremely large effect sizes were also excluded. We also distinguish between statistical significance and effect size in the two tables – all studies, irrespective of effect size, are placed in column 1 of Tables A.15.1a and A.15.2a if the effects found are not statistically significant.

Since we do not restrict our analysis to studies that employ a particular type of analytical method (e.g., randomized controlled trials, or RCTs), the reviewed studies vary greatly in terms of the analytical models they employ and the extent to which they account for confounders in establishing cause and effect. To help readers discern between the quality of included studies, purely on account of established causality and internal validity of the study, the studies were classified into three groups – low (L), medium (M), and high (H) – to signify the extent to which they control for confounding effects.

Studies classified as being low control (L) use cross-sectional data, include few controls, or omit important controls while estimating the relationship of interest. Findings of these studies are not to be interpreted as causal. Studies with medium control (M) also mainly use cross-sectional data, but include a comprehensive set of relevant control variables, or use other causal techniques, such as instrumental variables or matching methods. High control (H) studies include randomized control trials (RCTs), panel data with appropriate fixed effects, or multiple methods that yield consistent results.

Crosscutting findings

Looking across Tables A.15.1a and A.15.2a, it is at first obvious that a lot more research informs pathways for addressing child malnutrition in India (31 distinct studies) as compared to adult malnutrition (6 distinct studies). Moreover, around half of the studies focused on adult outcomes are of low quality, compared to a quarter of such studies that look at child malnutrition. Given that better maternal nutrition has important contemporaneous and intergenerational implications for health and productivity, thinness among adults, especially women, is an important avenue for future research.

Out of the 31 distinct studies included in Table A.15.1a, 8 are low-quality, 15 are medium-quality, and 8 are high-quality. Out of the six distinct studies in Table A.15.2a, three are low-quality, two are medium-quality, and only one is high-quality. In Table A.15.1a, Quadrants 2 and 3, which deal with access to a good-quality diet and the intrahousehold allocation of resources, respectively, have the highest concentration of research. While all four quadrants in Table A.15.2a are sparse, the foci of Quadrant 2 (diets) and Quadrant 4 (sanitation, water, and hygiene) are particularly understudied.

Focusing exclusively on high-quality studies, what does the current literature tell us? First, daily supplementation under India's Integrated Child Development System (ICDS) has more recently proven to be an effective strategy for producing appreciable effects in reducing child malnutrition for young children under two (Jain 2015). If we are particularly interested in child nutrition as an outcome, then the government's ICDS program has a better track record than its Public Distribution System (PDS) (Tarozzi 2005). Secondly, two features of Indian families have demonstrably serious implications for children's and women's health – the birth order of the child (Jayachandran and Pande 2013) and the rank of the daughter-in-law in joint families (Coffey, Spears, and Khera 2013). Both these features are tied to elder son preference in India, with children born later having worse nutrition outcomes if the firstborn is a son, and with wives of the eldest sons enjoying greater decision-making autonomy in a household, as compared to wives of younger sons. Thirdly, although the association between open defecation and child anthropometrics (specifically stunting) is strong, randomized evaluations of toilet construction programs in India (Clasen et al. 2014; Patil et al. 2014) have failed to show statistically significant effects on malnutrition. This is likely due to poor usage of the current pit latrine toilets being promoted in rural areas, lack of awareness around toilet usage, and norms among Hindus regarding defecating at home and handling fecal matter (Coffey et al. 2014).

The rest of the chapter follows with a narrative synthesis pertaining to each quadrant in the next four sections. Each section summarizes quadrant-specific findings in its last paragraph. We conclude in the final section by highlighting avenues for future nutrition research. The tables are in the appendix.

Detailed synthesis by quadrant

Economic growth and household incomes

At the country level, it is clear that at least until 2005, India's progress in tackling malnutrition has been discordant with its pace of economic growth and poverty decline. As can be seen in Quadrant 1 of Table A.15.1a, there is some evidence to suggest that macro-level changes in economic performance at the state level might also bear little association with improvements in metrics of child malnutrition (Subramanyam et al. 2011). On the other hand, although increases in income at the household level seem to have an appreciable effect in reducing child malnutrition (Kanjilal et al. 2010; Pathak and Singh 2011; Bhagowalia, Headey, and Kadiyala 2012), it is important to note that *large* increases in household income are required to achieve this end. Nevertheless, studies that examined the nutrition consequences of wealth inequality in India (Joe, Mishra, and Navaneetham 2009; Kanjilal et al. 2010; Pathak and Singh 2011; Chalasani 2012) repeatedly have found poor nutritional outcomes to be disproportionately concentrated among the poor, suggesting that household income and factors influencing access to good health are indeed intimately tied. Additionally, Quadrant 1 of Table A.15.2a discusses the effect of the nature of work on nutrition outcomes for adults. While the BMI penalty of manual labor work for adults is evident, the precise size of the effect is not robust, due to the low level of confounder control employed by the studies that have examined this relationship (Subramanian and Smith 2006; Headey, Chiu, and Kadiyala 2012).

What do empirical investigations of economic growth at the state level find? Is the existing analysis of the link between state-level economic growth and malnutrition persuasive? In general, the findings have been mixed, and have been found to depend on the level at which the relationship is modeled, as well as on the selection of control variables. Moreover, limited variation in economic growth across states, because of a small number of states and few time periods of data, is undoubtedly a major limitation to current research. Using three rounds of NFHS data and modeling individual-level child stunting, underweight, and wasting as functions of SNDP per capita growth, with child- and mother-level controls, Subramanyam et al. (2011) found no statistically significant associations of SNDP per capita growth for either outcome, in their preferred specifications. The authors found a unit increase in SNDP per capita (in 5,000 rupee terms) to be associated with a 0–3 percentage point reduction in the likelihood of the individual being undernourished. A 5,000 rupee increase in per capita SNDP growth is roughly one-third of the mean per capita SNDP increase that has taken place in the country between 1993 and 2005. Their estimates suggest that if Bihar grew exactly the way it did between 1993 and 2005, undernutrition in the state would fall by less than 0–5 percentage points.

Findings of two other papers (Radhakrishna and Ravi 2004; Coffey, Chattopadhyay, and Gupt 2014), which used similar data but modeled both economic progress and the prevalence of undernutrition at the state level, found an inverse and statistically significant relationship between the two, albeit one that has weakened over time. It is striking that in 1998, a difference of 5,000 rupees in SNDP per capita was associated with a 7 percentage point difference in stunting prevalence and more than a quarter of a standard deviation difference in average HAZ scores. However, in 2005, a 5,000-rupee difference in SNDP per capita was found to be associated with a 3 percentage point difference in stunting prevalence and a smaller difference in average HAZ scores to the magnitude of 0.13 sd (Coffey, Chattopadhyay, and Gupt 2014). As a caveat, it is important to keep in mind that both Radhakrishna and Ravi (2004) and Coffey, Chattopadhyay, and Gupt (2014) modeled state-level variables cross-sectionally and presented bivariate associations with the intention of drawing attention to trends.

Another pathway through which macroeconomic conditions can influence nutrition outcomes is through food prices. Children's consumption of different food groups in India dropped considerably, as food prices spiked during the global food crisis of 2007–08. Vellakkal et al. (2015) documented that the change in average daily rice intake of children between 2006 and 2009 was around 33 grams/day, which was associated with a 0.165 sd decline in child weight-for-height z-scores (WHZ).

Trends in economic inequalities with regards to malnutrition, which refers to the degree to which malnutrition rates differ between the poor and the rich, support the notion that overall improvements in state-level malnutrition might mask the slow progress/stagnation of the economically disadvantaged on this front (Joe, Mishra, and Navaneetham 2009; Kanjilal et al. 2010). States like Punjab and Tamil Nadu that achieved higher declines in child underweight during 1992–2006 (with relative change in prevalence being more than 20 percent) also registered higher increases in economic-based malnutrition inequalities, implying a larger concentration of the poor in the malnourished category (Pathak and Singh 2011). Similarly, a regression-based inequality decomposition by Chalasani (2012) found that the largest contributions to wealth-based malnutrition inequality come from inequalities in maternal education, followed by birth order.

Insights from two separate nationally representative data sets reveal that only large income increases make a difference (Kanjilal et al. 2010; Pathak and Singh 2011; Bhagowalia, Headey, and Kadiyala 2012). For instance, Bhagowalia, Headey, and Kadiyala (2012) used IHDS–2005 data and found the effects of increases in household income to be very modest. They found no statistically significant differences in HAZ scores of children between the 1st and 4th income quintiles; however, compared to children in the 1st quintile, those in the 5th quintile had 0.43 sd higher HAZ scores. Similarly, they found no statistically significant differences in the WHZ scores of children in the 1st–3rd quintiles, but compared to children in the 1st quintile, children in the 4th and 5th quintiles had WHZ scores that were statistically significantly higher.

Is malnutrition more responsive to income in nonagricultural or agricultural households? Several studies, including Babu, Thirumaran, and Mohanam (1993) and Bhagowalia, Headey, and Kadiyala (2012), suggested that malnutrition in nonagricultural households and urban areas is more responsive to income. Although specific features of the agricultural system have great potential for improving malnutrition (see Pingali, Ricketts, and Sahn [2015] for a detailed review), overall differences in agricultural productivity at the state level have not been shown to be associated with large differences in malnutrition outcomes in India. For instance, a 1,000-rupee increase in the gross value of output from agriculture and livestock per hectare of gross cropped area (GVOAL/Ha), an increase amounting to 3.33 percent of the mean GVOAL/Ha, was found to be associated with a 0.007-point reduction in an author-constructed Normalized Adult Malnutrition Index (which varies between 0 and 1); and a 1,000-rupee increase in per capita gross state domestic product from agriculture and allied activities (PCGSDPAA), an increase amounting to 12.5 percent of the mean PCGSDPAA, was found to be associated with a 0.032-point reduction in an author-constructed Normalized Child Malnutrition Index (NCMI)[8] (Gulati et al. 2012).

Effects of seasonality in agriculture are also stark. A study collecting data from villages near Pune City in Maharashtra found that, after controlling for the sex of the child, parity of the mother, gestation, prepregnancy weight, maternal caloric intake at eighteenth week, and maternal activity at the twenty-eighth week, one week of *in utero* exposure to the winter season (harvest season) was associated with an increase of 5.6 grams in birthweight. Thus, babies born to women who are exposed while pregnant to the entire harvest season of 16 weeks are likely to have birthweights higher by 90 grams (Rao et al. 2009). The nature of work, in particular calorie expenditure based on physical labor, is also purported to affect adult BMI. While controlling for wealth, health, education, and location, in comparing the BMI of adults in different occupational groups, agricultural workers were found to have the lowest average BMI among both women and men (Headey, Chiu, and Kadiyala 2012). More generally, there exists a BMI penalty for manual work occupations. With the same set of controls, Headey, Chiu, and Kadiyala (2012) also established that, compared to the reference category of those who do not work, those in manual work have lower average BMI by 0.46 points. Subramanian and Smith (2006) found a lower likelihood of 6 percentage points for having low BMI if an adult is engaged in manual work, with the same reference category as earlier, but they could not establish this effect as statistically significant.

In summary and with reference to Table A.15.1a, the effects of macro-growth on child malnutrition outcomes are small (Subramanyam et al. 2011; Coffey, Chattopadhyay, and Gupt 2014). On the whole, this debate is currently taking place in a data vacuum in the Indian context. Moreover, malnutrition inequalities on account of economic inequalities are pronounced, and only very large increases in household incomes seem to produce appreciable results (Kanjilal et al. 2010; Pathak and Singh 2011; Bhagowalia, Headey, and Kadiyala 2012). Additionally, in Table A.15.2a, the effects of adult employment on adult nutrition are inconclusive and are to be treated with caution, owing to the low level of confounder control (Subramanian and Smith 2006; Headey, Chiu, and

Kadiyala 2012). The limited impact of economic growth on nutrition in India can be attributed to the multidimensional nature of the problem. Unlike in other countries, income growth has not translated into women's empowerment and the consequent improvement in intrahousehold equity with respect to access to micronutrient-rich food. Also, India has lagged far behind countries of similar economic status in terms of investments in clean drinking water and access to toilets. The adverse consequences of poor sanitary conditions for nutrition are discussed in a later section.

Access to micronutrients and diverse diets

High levels of hidden hunger in India are evident, and of grave concern, with markers such as stunting, iron deficiency anemia, and vitamin A deficiency all being concurrent and highly prevalent. Elsewhere in the developing world, as in Latin America, low levels of hidden hunger have been achieved with the simultaneous deployment of micronutrient interventions, nutrition education, and basic health services (von Grebmer et al. 2014). Income growth alone may not be enough to address hidden hunger at the household level because critical nutrition inputs – such as the consumption of a balanced, nutritious diet and proper child-feeding practices – suffer because of information and knowledge gaps (Malhotra 2013).

The Indian government's single largest machinery to combat malnutrition is the Integrated Child Development System (ICDS), which is a village-level institution manned by an *"anganwadi* worker" responsible for the supplementary feeding of children aged 0–6 years and pregnant and lactating mothers.[9] Earlier evaluations of the ICDS program, based on NFHS 1 and NFHS 2 data, failed to find significant effects of the program (Lokshin et al. 2005). Partly, this could be due to lower coverage of the program at the time, larger inefficiencies in the working of the program early on, and a focus on only the "presence of an ICDS center" as the exposure measure. More recent evaluations of the program and of other specific interventions that aim to increase the efficiency of the program in some way have found appreciable effects on child malnutrition, indicating that the program may have improved in its later years.

One study that uses NFHS-3 data and controls for endogenous program placement by matching individuals on the basis of propensity scores, which are estimated using individual characteristics, village population, and other community-level indicators, found relatively small effects of the presence of an ICDS center in a village, to the magnitude of 0.10 HAZ sd for boys and 0.07 HAZ sd for girls. While the effects are relatively small, they are statistically significant, and the same model yielded no statistically significant effects of the ICDS program when estimated with earlier data (Kandpal 2011). A separate study, also using the most recent NFHS data, compared anthropometric outcomes of children in the 0–2 years age group who received daily supplementation from the ICDS with those of children who did not, matching on the basis of a relatively exhaustive set of controls and state fixed effects, and found daily supplementation to be associated with a 0.4 sd increase in HAZ – a relatively large effect (Jain 2015).

There is also some research that indicates that alterations in the working of the ICDS can yield favorable results, as opposed to the "business-as-usual" working of the program. A controlled experiment in the urban slums of Chandigarh in Punjab revealed that combining a performance-for-pay incentive treatment[10] for *anganwadi* workers who were giving mothers information, in the form of recipe books with nutritious recipes for complementary feeding of young children, can positively affect child underweight status (Singh 2015). The author found that while compared to the control group, individually, each of these treatments did not have an impact, but the combined treatment increased WAZ scores by approximately 0.10 sd and also reduced the prevalence of wasting. The complementarity is suggested to be driven by better mother–worker communication and by mothers feeding more calorific food at home. Programmatic evidence allows us to study the effects of intensifying ICDS outreach by having village volunteers aid an *anganwadi* worker in providing services, in the context of Jharkhand's *Dular* program (Dubowitz et al. 2007). Comparing underweight outcomes of children in villages with and without the program, and with some controls in place, the authors found that the average WAZ score in the program villages was higher by 1.29 WAZ sd, which is a very large effect, though undoubtedly biased due to nonrandom placement of the program.

Another governmental program which has the potential to appreciably impact the nutritional status of children attending school is the Mid-Day Meal Scheme (MDMS). Using the calendar year of birth as an instrument for MDMS participation, Singh, Park, and Dercon (2012) provided evidence that access to MDMS in school can result in catch-up growth for children adversely affected by drought during the critical ages of growth. They found that children with access to MDMS had higher WAZ (0.62 sd) and HAZ (0.98 sd) than children without access, with both sets of children having been exposed to drought when they were less than two years old.

India's national vitamin A program is characterized by low coverage with only around 20 percent of Indian children between 1–5 years having received vitamin A supplementation according to NFHS-3 data. With a few child, parent, and household-level controls in place, it is estimated that children receiving vitamin A supplementation had lower malnutrition prevalence, modest in magnitude, with stunting and underweight being approximately 7 percentage points lower and with no effects observed on wasting (Semba et al. 2010). However, as is apparent in Table A.15.1a, more rigorous studies are required to examine the efficacy of vitamin A supplementation in the Indian context. One study, with poor internal validity, examined the effect of iodized salt on child WAZ, finding it to be associated with a 0.08 sd increase in child WAZ (Kumar and Berkman 2015). Even food fortification studies of an experimental nature present mixed findings. While Bhandari et al. (2001) did not find significant effects of fortified milk cereal (along with nutritional counseling) on the proportion of wasted or stunted children, another separate milk fortification[11] RCT found moderately high and statistically significant impacts across all three child undernutrition metrics for children between 1–4 years (Sazawal et al. 2010).

Even though dietary diversity and the production of food crops are hypothesized to have favorable effects on nutrition outcomes, in the Indian context with current data sets and methods utilized, the evidence is mixed. Using two measures of dietary diversity – a dietary diversity score (a count of the number of food groups consumed) and the budget share spent on different food groups – Bhagowalia, Headey, and Kadiyala (2012) established that there were favorable income effects on dietary diversity. However, controlling for household income, they did not find that either dietary diversity measure had significantly impacted child stunting or wasting. However, Menon et al. (2015) focused on child-feeding practices of exclusively young children (<24 months) and found that, out of the eight recommended WHO Infant and Young Child-Feeding (IYCF) practices, an indicator of diet diversity (continuous indicator) was most strongly associated with reducing malnutrition. They found a 1 point increase in the dietary diversity score increased HAZ by 0.09 sd, WAZ by 0.06 sd, and WHZ by 0.02 sd. WHO indicators related to appropriate breastfeeding timing and timely introduction of semi-solid food were not found to be statistically associated with increases in HAZ/WAZ/WHZ. Controlling for household income and socioeconomic status, the fraction of food consumed from one's own farm was not found to statistically impact child stunting, underweight, or wasting, nor stunting and wasting of adolescents and adults (Parasuraman and Rajaretnam 2011).

A set of well-identified and rigorous studies has failed to find that food price subsidies in India and elsewhere[12] improve nutrition outcomes. In a prominent study on the nutrition effects of India's Public Distribution System (PDS) for food grain, Tarozzi (2005) used the staggered rollout of the NFHS 1 survey, in the state of Andhra Pradesh, which collected data on child weight-for-age between April and July 1992. In January 1992, the price of PDS rice in Andhra Pradesh saw a marked increase. Modeling child weight as a function of child age, the number of months spent by a child in the high price regime, and other controls, the study found statistically insignificant effects of an additional month spent by a child in the high food price regime on his/her WAZ, and the author concluded that the program may not have been acting as an effective food safety net from the outset. Using three rounds of the NSS data between 1993 and 2005 and instrumental variable (IV) methods to model nutritional intake, as a function of the extent of PDS subsidy enjoyed by a household, Kaushal and Muchomba (2015) also failed to find significant effects of the subsidy on nutrient intake and found that the subsidy might have altered the source of nutrient intake from coarser grains to sugar and sugar products. Here, some evidence is also provided to show that the subsidy led to a modest reduction in total food expenditure (which is expected in the case of a food subsidy, if households do not divert expenditure to unsubsidized foods) and a concomitant increase in expenditure on non-food items.

However, it is important to note that both the working of the PDS and the context in which it functions vary greatly from state to state in India. For instance, in Chhattisgarh, where immediately after its formation in 2000, the government instituted unprecedented reforms in procurement and distribution of PDS rations, Krishnamurthy, Pathania, and Tandon (2014) found favorable impacts of the program on consumption of pulses and animal-based proteins, which can have favorable impacts on anthropometric outcomes, though these outcomes have not be directly measured. Moreover, for subsistence farmers, the PDS could also have beneficial crop diversification effects – an angle that is yet to be explored extensively in the literature.

Table A.15.1a summarizes the relative efficacy of the government's food and micronutrient interventions, as well as dietary diversity at the household level. As can be seen, a rigorous evaluation of the ICDS program showed large impacts of the program on child anthropometrics (Jain 2015), while a relatively less rigorous exercise showed smaller effects (Kandpal 2011). However, the two studies used different measures of the program. The effect of the PDS on child anthropometrics is insignificant (Tarozzi 2005). Across both tables, the bulk of the studies that looked at food supplementation and dietary diversity found small effects – though a lot can be done to address these channels more rigorously.

Intrahousehold allocation of resources

The intrahousehold status of individuals is widely acknowledged as a determinant of individual nutrient and food intake and an important link between household food availability and individual nutritional status. Several indicators of women's status in the literature consistently rank women in the countries of South Asia as lower in comparison to their counterparts in Asia, Africa, Latin America, and the Caribbean (Haddad 1999). Low intrahousehold status has been shown to impact not just a woman's health and nutrition but also that of her child, both *in utero* and otherwise, because of a woman's compromised capacity to care for her child in the latter case.

Most of the existing literature that explores aspects of intrahousehold distribution in India measures women's status by levels of education, freedom of mobility, autonomy in decision-making, incidence of domestic violence, or intrahousehold rank. Gender and birth order of children have also been shown to be an important determinant of their nutritional status. Much of the work in this line of research relies on survey data (predominantly, the NFHS data) and survey responses with respect to mobility, autonomy, and violence questions, which are most certainly endogenous to unobserved women's characteristics. On the other hand, education, employment status, and intrahousehold rank are more objective measures of a woman's status.

As can be seen in Table A.15.1a, two studies (Bose 2011; Imai et al. 2014), which explored the effects of a woman's education on her child's anthropometrics, did not find large effects of the woman's education. Partly, this can be explained by the fact that the studies were non-experimental and thus unable to capture useful independent variation in women's education, after controlling for factors like household standard of living. Both studies used NFHS data and estimated cross-sectional OLS models with controls. Imai et al. (2014) used the

2005 round of NFHS data to look at the effect of the ratio of maternal education relative to paternal education on child malnutrition, after controlling for the total years of education of the father and the mother. They found relatively small effects to the magnitude of 0.02 and 0.06 HAZ sd for the categories of stunted and severely stunted children, respectively. They found no effects on WAZ or WHZ. Bose (2011) also used the NFHS-3 dataset but operationalized the education variable in the form of a continuous measure of the years of completed schooling and found that an additional year of schooling was associated, on average, with 4 percentage points lower underweight probability for children. Another study (Subramanian and Smith 2006) compared women's underweight status across different education categories, using NFHS-2 data, and found that compared to women with more than 15 years of education, women with 6–8 years of education have 28 percentage points higher underweight probability. If these results are to be extrapolated to draw inference for the marginal effect of one year of education, the effects are similar to the findings in Bose (2011). However, these estimates are not to be interpreted as causal. Bose (2011) also looked at the impact of maternal employment in a model similar to the one employed for education status to document that the children of working mothers have 15 percentage points *higher* underweight probability, compared to children of mothers who are not employed. However, again, these effect sizes are only correlations, as the study controls for limited confounders in its analysis.

NFHS surveys measure autonomy as freedom of mobility (answers to questions such as whether the woman needs permission to go to the market) and independence of decision-making (e.g., whether she can set aside money to use as she wills). In NFHS-3 data, Imai et al. (2014) found that freedom of mobility of mothers is associated with an increase of 0.09 HAZ sd of their children. Using NFHS-2 data from Andhra Pradesh, Shroff et al. (2009) estimated cross-sectional logistic regressions to estimate that mothers having financial autonomy and mobility reduce the probability of their children's stunting by ~27 and ~41 percentage points, respectively. However, even within the same data sets, estimates of the autonomy variables are not robust and are sensitive to employed controls, as is seen not only in the differing estimates of Imai et al. (2014) and Shroff et al. (2009) but also in Bose (2011), who did not find any significant effects of women's autonomy on child underweight using NFHS-3 data.

Similarly, evidence on the effects of domestic violence on child and adult malnutrition is mixed, and also sensitive to the measure of violence used. A dummy variable for "whether or not a wife thinks that a husband is justified in beating his wife when she is unfaithful to him," as a measure of domestic violence, was not found to be statistically significantly associated with child anthropometrics (Imai et al. 2014). On the other hand, using a categorical measure of self-reported (by women) domestic violence in NFHS-2 data, authors estimated a multinomial, logistic framework, and reported that, compared to the reference category of "never been abused," women who faced abuse by a family member more than once in the last 12 months had children who were more likely to be stunted and wasted by 14 and 18 percentage points, respectively, and the women themselves more likely to be underweight by 21 percentage points. (Ackerson and Subramanian 2008).

Robust effects of family composition on the intrahousehold allocation of resources, translating into adverse nutrition outcomes, have been estimated by Jayachandran and Pande (2013) and Coffey, Spears, and Khera (2013). By carefully controlling for covariate confounders and using more objective measures of intrahousehold status, these studies were able to circumvent some of the between-household unobserved factors that could likely bias the aforementioned studies.

Using Demographic and Health Surveys (DHS) from around 25 countries, Jayachandran and Pande (2013) studied birth order effects in the India–Africa child height gap. They established that firstborn Indian children are taller than their African counterparts, but second- and third-born children and those born subsequently are statistically significantly shorter. Because the focus is on controlling for covariates that may disproportionately affect later-born children in India versus Africa, factors such as access to services (like health or sanitation), which do not vary much by birth order, are not found to confound the established birth order gradient. The authors accounted for India–Africa differences in mother's age, child's age, mortality selection among later-born children, mother's predetermined health, and high fertility households, to establish that Indian second-born or third- and later-born children are shorter by 0.17 and 0.35 HAZ sd, respectively. Overarching explanations for the phenomena focus on cultural norms, such as an elder son preference, with the authors finding worse outcomes for later-born children if the first child is a son.

Coffey, Spears, and Khera (2013) used NFHS-3 data to compare nutritional outcomes of family members of differing rank, in a model that used only within-family variation in ranks. They found that, after controlling for a child's gender, age in months, and the interaction of sex and age-in-month dummies, there is a negative and statistically significant effect of a mother's rank on her child's height – children of lower-ranked daughters-in-law are,[13] on average, approximately 0.422 HAZ sd shorter than children of higher-ranked daughters-in-law. The authors complement their results by showing that lower-ranked daughters-in-law have lower status: controlling for age, lower-ranked daughters-in-law are significantly less likely than higher-ranked ones to report having a final say for decisions related to health, daily purchases, and spending money. Robust to relevant controls, lower-ranked daughters-in-law are about 0.4 BMI points lighter than higher-ranked daughters-in-law. Griffiths, Matthews, and Hinde (2002) did not find significant differences in the WAZ scores of children in households in which mothers-in-law and daughters-in-law reside together, when compared to households in which they do not; but compared with Coffey, Spears, and Khera (2013), their study unsatisfactorily accounts for between-household differences due to other factors.

Strong preference for sons in India also manifests in a positive association between male–female sex-ratios (MFR) and reductions in undernutrition for surviving girls. Likely mechanisms that explain this are girls being born into families with weaker preference for sons and smaller families. Hu and Schlosser (2015) estimated that a 1 sd increase in state-level MFR is associated with a 3–4 percentage point reduction in the proportion of underweight and wasted girls. For Punjab, a state which saw the highest increase in MFR between 1992 and 2005, this effect size implies a 10 percentage point reduction in underweight girls.

Tables A.15.1a and A.15.2a clearly bring out the main comparisons of the pathways relevant to this quadrant. For child anthropometrics in Table A.15.1a, effects of maternal education (Imai et al. 2014) and (Bose 2011) do not appear to be strong, but these studies also employ a low level of confounder control. The same can be said of the effect of a woman's education on her own health (Subramanian and Smith 2006) in Table A.15.2a. The impact of maternal autonomy was measured in a nonrobust manner (Shroff et al. 2009; Bose 2011; Imai et al. 2014) with regards to child nutritional status, and the evidence is scarce for adults. However, mostly, the effects of family composition due to intrahousehold rank both are measured robustly and are in the highest effect size bracket (Coffey, Spears, and Khera 2013; Jayachandran and Pande 2013). Interestingly, MFR at the state level is positively associated with a reduction in proportion of underweight girls (Hu and Schlosser 2015). As seen in Table A.15.2a, lower-ranked daughters-in-law have lower BMI (Coffey, Spears, and Khera 2013), but one study, Sabarwal et al. (2012), looked at the impact of husbands' preferences for sons and the sex composition of the children in a household, but did not find statistically significant effects on the mother's BMI status. However, a low level of confounder control is employed in this study (Table A.15.2a).

Water, sanitation, and adequate hygiene

Access to clean drinking water, the availability of toilets and sanitation, and the practice of good hygiene are deemed to be critical for nutrient absorption and utilization. Nutrient intake can translate into improved nutrition metrics only if the concerned population is not fraught with a high incidence of diarrheal disease, soil-transmitted helminth infection, and other gastrointestinal disorders.

Sanitation in India is a particular public health concern because over half of the population defecates in the open. About 60 percent of the approximately 1 billion people in the world who defecate in the open live in India (Spears 2012b). The link between open defecation and child stunting is well established. Using repeated cross-sections of DHS data on 65 countries, Spears (2013) estimated that changing the fraction of the population defecating in the open from 0 to 1 at the country level is associated with a linear decrease of 1.24 sd in HAZ. This result is robust to controlling for country fixed effects and time-varying factors, such as a country's GDP, female literacy, immunization, and electrification. The density of open defecation – the number of people defecating in the open per square kilometer – is critical, too. In the same study, it is also established that the India–Africa child height gap would close by 30 percent if one controls for open defecation and by 83 percent if one controls for the density of open defecation. Exploiting variation in open defecation within India, cross-sectional data from 112 Indian districts, part of the HUNGaMA survey, are used. Here, too, a 10 percent increase in open defecation is found to be associated with a 0.7 percentage point increase in stunting (Spears, Ghosh, and Cumming 2013).

While the association between open defecation and child anthropometrics (specifically stunting) is strong, randomized evaluations of toilet construction programs in India have failed to show statistically significant effects on malnutrition. For instance, a randomized control trial in Madhya Pradesh was run to assess the impact of subsidizing toilet construction and mobilizing communities to build toilets, under the framework of the Indian government's "Total Sanitation Campaign (TSC)" (Patil et al. 2014). The study found no statistically significant differences either in child anthropometric outcomes or in diarrheal and other diseases between treatment and control villages. Reductions in men, women, and children defecating in the open were found to be small compared to increases in latrine availability. Another very similar experiment in Orissa also yielded similar results (Clasen et al. 2014). These authors also followed the framework of the government's TSC and found no statistical differences in child anthropometrics in the villages "treated" by the toilet construction program. The only study that found favorable effects of the TSC is Spears (2012b), in which variation in the intensity of toilet construction at the district level is exploited, with district fixed effects and other controls in place. The study found that at its mean intensity, toilet construction under the program was associated with an increase of 0.2 HAZ sd. Rah et al. (2015) also found that having a toilet facility at home was associated with a lower likelihood of 16 percentage points for stunting among children, but the study analyzed a cross-section (NFHS-3) and included controls unlikely to fully account for selection into toilet ownership.

Why has toilet construction failed to show impacts on malnutrition despite such a strong relationship between open defecation and stunting? One reason could be that randomized evaluations with follow-up periods of 1.5–2 years are not long enough to detect changes in anthropometrics. While this is plausible, both of the RCTs under question also failed to find statistical reductions in diarrheal and other diseases, an outcome which should be observable within such a time frame. A more plausible explanation relates to the findings of the Sanitation Quality, Use, Access and Trends (SQUAT) survey, as summarized in Coffey et al. (2014), which argues that, for various cultural and religious reasons,[14] there is a revealed preference for open defecation in India, and a large fraction of Indians defecate in the open despite having a working toilet at home. Moreover, the type of simple and affordable latrine that has been used to eliminate open defecation elsewhere in the world and the type which falls under the budget allocation of the Indian government's TSC are not acceptable to most Indians. The features that SQUAT survey respondents describe in a sanitation system that they would use are about ten times the current budget allocation per toilet. While an important component of the TSC is community mobilization and inducing demand for toilets by discussing the ills of open defecation, on the ground Boisson et al. (2014) documented that implementation in the region of their evaluation

(Orissa) was well short of the goals, and none of the tools that have proved effective in community-led total sanitation programs were being employed. Therefore, in the Indian context, it is clear that toilet construction, at least of the pit latrine kind, is not the inverse of open defecation, and a better understanding of incentivizing toilet use is critical to the success of a policy of this type.

The effects of access to water and hygiene practices on malnutrition outcomes are under study in the Indian context. One notable study here used three cross-sectional data sets – NFHS 3, the HUNGaMA data set, and the Comprehensive Nutrition Survey in Maharashtra (CNSM) (Rah et al. 2015). In the analysis of all three surveys, household access to improved drinking water or piped water was not found to be a predictor of child stunting, and the authors did not observe any significant interactive effects between household access to improved water and sanitation on stunting. Effects of personal hygiene on child stunting were investigated in the HUNGaMA survey. Caregivers reported that the practice of washing hands with soap after defecation was associated with a 14 percentage point lower likelihood of stunting, and washing hands before eating food was associated with a 15 percentage point lower likelihood of stunting. Effects of personal hygiene on child stunting were found to be stronger in households with access to piped water and in households with access to a toilet facility.

Water quality, as measured by the presence of fertilizer agrochemicals in water, also bears a statistically significant, but small, association with child HAZ in the country. Using variations resulting from a combination of month of conception and across-state variation in planting seasons, it has been estimated that a 10 percent increase in the level of agrochemical toxins in water leads to a 0.014 sd reduction in HAZ (Brainerd and Menon 2014).

Table A.15.1a reiterates by way of its "Quadrant 4" papers that the most rigorous evaluations of toilet construction programs in India (Clasen et al. 2014; Coffey et al. 2014) have not found an effect on child malnutrition, and the effects of water and hygiene practices remain to be properly examined (Rah et al. 2015). Water quality is also associated with child malnutrition, and findings warrant future research on the topic (Brainerd and Menon 2014). As is evident in Table A.15.2a, none of the reviewed studies examined the impact of water, sanitation, or hygiene on adult malnutrition.

Agenda for future research

We include studies of varying quality in our review with the specific purpose of highlighting topic-wise gaps in the current state of the literature. Important avenues for future research emerge from our synthesis of the literature.

Overall, there is a lack of high-quality evidence to support the efficacy of pathways relevant to Quadrant 1, especially with regard to understanding better the connection between economic growth and malnutrition in India. Given the availability of at least some district-level anthropometric data from the DLHS surveys, it will be interesting to study the association between district-level growth and malnutrition. It is hard to measure district-level economic growth in India, though some new types of data, like satellite imagery and night lights data, might provide interesting solutions. Among Quadrant 2 papers, while there is some programmatic evidence regarding specific government programs that aid nutrition, in the Indian context, we have a poorer understanding of the general effects of food supplementation, dietary diversity, and own production of food. In studying the intrahousehold allocation of resources in Quadrant 3, only the effects of features of family composition, such as birth order and daughter-in-law rank, on malnutrition have been studied robustly. Much more can be done to leverage the women's autonomy and domestic violence modules of the NFHS datasets to yield more causal estimates of the relationship between women's empowerment and child and maternal nutrition. This includes the possibility of quasi-experimental variation in women's autonomy with respect to changes in India's female inheritance laws and legislation on domestic violence. Lastly, a more detailed understanding of what works to create behavioral change around the usage of toilets in India will be critical to address a major roadblock to improving nutritional outcomes of Indians.

Appendix

Table A.15.1a The role of different pathways in the reduction of child stunting, underweight, and wasting in India: a summary of select effect sizes from the literature

	Effect size		
Change in likelihood	*<10 pp.*	*10–30 pp.*	*> 30 pp.*
Change in z-scores	*<0.10 sd.*	*0.10–0.30 sd.*	*> 0.30 sd.*
Statistical significance	*No/Yes*	*Yes*	*Yes*
	(1)	*(2)*	*(3)*
Quadrant 1 papers			
State-level economic growth	Subramanyam et al. (2011)[L]		
	Coffey, Chattopadhyay, and Gupt (2014)*[L]		
Food prices		Vellakkal et al. (2015)**[M]	
Household income			Kanjilal et al. (2010)***[M]
			Bhagowalia, Headey, and Kadiyala (2012)***[M]
			Pathak and Singh (2011)***[M]
Quadrant 2 papers			
ICDS+ICDS treatments	Lokshin et al. (2005)[M]	Kandpal (2011)***[M]	Jain (2015)***[H]
		Singh (2015)**[H]	Dubowitz et al. (2007)***[L]

(*Continued*)

	(1)	*(2)*	*(3)*
Quadrant 2 papers continued			
Supplementation and fortification	Semba et al. (2010)***[L]	Sazawal et al. (2010)***[H]	
	Kumar and Berkman (2015)***[L]		
	Bhandari et al. (2001)[H]		
Diet diversity and self-production	Bhagowalia, Headey, and Kadiyala (2012)[M]	Menon et al. (2015)**[M]	
	Parasuraman and Rajaretnam (2011)[M]		
PDS	Tarozzi (2005)[H]		
Quadrant 3 papers			
Mother's education	Bose (2011)***[L]		
	Imai et al. (2014)***[M]		
Mother's employment		Bose (2011)***[L]	
Mother's autonomy	Imai et al. (2014)**[M]		Shroff et al. (2009)**[L]
	Bose (2011)***[L]		
Domestic violence	Imai et al. (2014)[M]	Ackerson and Subramanian (2008)**[M]	
Family composition	Griffiths, Matthews, and Hinde (2002)[L]		Jayachandran and Pande (2013)***[H]
			Coffey, Spears, and Khera (2013)***[H]
State MFR	Hu and Schlosser (2015)**[M]		
Quadrant 4 papers			
Household has toilet	Clasen et al. (2014)[H]	Rah et al. (2015)**[M]	
	Patil et al. (2014)[H]	Spears (2012b)**[M]	
Household has water	Rah et al. (2015)[M]		

	(1)	(2)	(3)

Quadrant 4 papers continued

Water quality	Brainerd and Menon (2014)*[M]		
Hygiene		Rah et al. (2015)**[M]	

Source: Authors' construction.

Note: The superscripts are L for low, M for medium, and H for high level of confounder control.

***, **, and * represent significance at the 10, 5, and 1 level, respectively.

Table A.15.1b Units of measurement of predictor variables of interest in studies listed in Table A.15.1a

	Reference	*Predictor variable*	*Unit*
Quadrant 1 papers			
State-level economic growth	Subramanyam et al. (2011); Coffey, Chattopadhyay, and Gupt (2014)★	SNDP per capita	Continuous (5000 rupees)
Food prices	Vellakkal et al. (2015)	Change in rice consumption instrumented for with rice price increase	Grams/day
Household (HH) income	Bhagowalia, Headey, and Kadiyala (2012); Kanjilal et al. (2010); Pathak and Singh (2011)	1st vs. 5th quintile of HH income	Categorical
Quadrant 2 papers			
ICDS	Lokshin et al. (2005); Kandpal (2011)	Presence of ICDS center in a village	Binary
ICDS	Singh (2015)	"Treatment" ICDS centers	Binary
ICDS	Jain (2015)	Receipt of daily ICDS supplementation	Binary
ICDS	Dubowitz et al. (2007)	Presence of *Dular* program in a village	Binary
Vitamin A supplementation	Semba et al. (2010)	Receipt of vitamin A supplementation	Binary

(Continued)

	Reference	*Predictor variable*	*Unit*
Quadrant 2 papers continued			
Iodized salt	Kumar and Berkman (2015)	Usage of iodized salt	Binary
Cereal and suppl.+nut counseling	Bhandari et al. (2001)	"Treatment" infants	Binary
Fortified milk	Sazawal et al. (2010)	"Treatment" children	Binary
Dietary diversity	Bhagowalia, Headey, and Kadiyala (2012); Menon et al. (2015)	Dietary div. score/ budget share of FGs	Continuous
Consumption from self-production	Parasuraman and Rajaretnam (2011)	Proportion of food consumption from own production	Continuous
PDS	Tarozzi (2005)	No. of months spent with lower subsidy	Continuous
Quadrant 3 papers			
Maternal education	Imai et al. (2014)	Ratio of maternal to paternal education	Continuous
Maternal education	Bose (2011)	Years of education	Continuous
Maternal employment	Bose (2011)	Employment status: employed	Binary
Maternal autonomy	Shroff et al. (2009); Imai et al. (2014)	Needs permission to go to market	Binary
Maternal autonomy	Shroff et al. (2009)	Can set aside money w/o permission	Binary
Maternal autonomy	Bose (2011)	Autonomy Index	Continuous
Domestic violence	Ackerson and Subramanian (2008)	Multiple instances of violence in past year	Binary
Domestic violence	Imai et al. (2014)	Wife believes domestic violence justified	Binary
Family composition	Jayachandran and Pande (2013)	Country by birth order interaction	Binary
Family composition	Coffey, Spears, and Khera (2013)	Low-ranking daughter-in-law	Binary
Family composition	Griffiths, Matthews, and Hinde (2002)	Households in which mother and daughters-in-law co-reside	Binary
Family composition	Hu and Schlosser (2015)	MFR interacted with female dummy	Continuous

	Reference	Predictor variable	Unit
Quadrant 4 papers			
HH has toilets	Clasen et al. (2014); Patil et al. (2014)	"Treatment" TSC villages	Binary
HH has toilets	Rah et al. (2015)	HH has toilet	Binary
HH has toilets	Spears (2012b)	TSC toilets per capita[1]	Continuous
HH has water	Rah et al. (2015)	HH has improved/ piped water source	Binary
Water quality	Brainerd and Menon (2014)	Presence of fertilizer agrochemicals	Continuous
Hygiene	Rah et al. (2015)	Caregiver washes hands	Binary

Source: Authors' construction.

Note: Unless otherwise specified, for the binary variables, the reference group is the negation of the predictor variable mentioned in the table.

[1] However, the effect reported is the coefficient times the mean intensity of TSC toilets per district.

Table A.15.2a The role of different pathways in the reduction of adult underweight (low BMI) in India: a summary of select effect sizes from the literature

	Effect size		
Change in z-scores	<10 pp. <0.10 points	10–30 pp. 0.10–0.30 points	> 30 pp. > 0.30 points
Statistical Significance	No/Yes	Yes	Yes
	(1)	(2)	(3)
Quadrant 1 papers			
Nature of employment	Subramanian and Smith (2006)[L]		Headey, Chiu, and Kadiyala (2012)***[L]
Quadrant 2 papers			
Consumption from self-production	Parasuraman and Rajaretnam (2011)[M]		
Quadrant 3 papers			
Education	Subramanian and Smith (2006)[L]		
Domestic violence		Ackerson and Subramanian (2008)**[M]	
Family composition	Sabarwal et al. (2012)[L]		Coffey, Spears and Khera (2013)*[H]

Source: Authors' construction.

Note: The superscripts are L for low, M for medium, and H for high level of confounder control.

***, **, and * represent significance at the 10, 5, and 1 level, respectively.

Table A.15.2b Units of measurement of predictor variables of interest in studies listed in Table A.15.2a

	Reference	*Predictor Variable*	*Unit*
Quadrant 1 papers			
Nature of employment	Headey, Chiu, and Kadiyala (2012)	Involves manual work	Binary
Nature of employment	Subramanian and Smith (2006)	Involves manual work	Binary
Quadrant 2 papers			
Consumption from self-production	Parasuraman and Rajaretnam (2011)	Proportion of food consumption from own production	Continuous
Quadrant 3 papers			
Woman's education	Subramanian and Smith (2006)	Woman has 6–8 years of education (effect size in 2A for 1 year of education)	Binary (reference category >15 years of education)
Domestic violence	Ackerson and Subramanian (2008)	Multiple instances of violence in past year	Binary
Family composition	Coffey, Spears, and Khera (2013)	Rank of daughter-in-law	Binary
Family composition	Sabarwal et al. (2012)	Couple has only girl children	Binary (couple has only boy children)

Source: Authors' construction.

Notes

1 The "Asian Enigma," when first flagged, highlighted high rates of child malnutrition in South Asia, as compared to sub-Saharan Africa, despite comparable purchasing powers at the time in the both regions (Ramalingaswami, Jonsson, and Rohde 1996).

2 The fourth round of the District Level Household and Facility Survey (DLHS-4) was made available recently at http://iipsindia.org/dlhs4.htm, and reports from the National Family and Health Survey (NFHS-4) on state-level aggregates for Phase 1 states were also released in the third week of January 2016.

3 UNICEF's RSOC, which measured and weighed 90,000 children and 28,000 teenage girls, was conducted in 29 states and union territories in 2013 and 2014. While the data and report have not yet been formally released, media reports based on the data (*Economist* 2015; Rowlatt 2015; Rukimini S 2015) have come into focus since early July 2016.

4 The Lancet Nutrition Series Framework (Black et al. 2013) extends the UNICEF framework by providing a conceptual mapping of the programmatic and policy interventions for achieving improved nutrition. It is an operational guide rather than a behavioral representation of the determinants of nutrition outcomes.

5 Hereafter, HAZ=height-for-age z-scores, WAZ=weight-for-age z-scores, and WHZ= weight-for-height z-scores. Stunting, underweight, and wasting prevalence refers to the fraction of children under -2 sd of HAZ, WAZ, and WHZ, respectively.
6 We also include only those studies that utilize data collected in this period.
7 http://www.hungamaforchange.org.
8 For constructing the Normalized Child Malnutrition Index (NCMI), three indicators of child malnutrition – that is, the fraction stunted, wasted, and underweight – in a state were taken and normalized according to the formula

$$Normalized\ indicator = \frac{actual\ values - minimum\ value}{maximum\ value - minimum\ value},$$

and then combined using a simple average of the normalized indicators. The Normalized Adult Malnutrition Index (NAMI) was constructed similarly, using the fraction of "thin" (BMI<18.5) men and women.
9 Children aged 3–6 are generally fed at the center, and younger children receive take-home rations that last anywhere between a week and a month. ICDS centers are supposed to provide food for 25 days a month, and figures from the NFHS show that the program provides approximately 300 calories and 8–10 grams of protein to children aged 0–72 months on a daily basis (Chalasani 2012).
10 The treatment involves a payment of 100 rupees for each child whose weight-for-age grade improved, minus the number for whom it declined within a three-month period.
11 The treatment group received milk fortified with essential micronutrients (zinc and iron), and the control group received equal doses of regular milk.
12 See Jensen and Miller (2011) for analysis of the nutrition effects of food price subsidies in China.
13 Daughters-in-law married to younger brothers in a joint family setup.
14 Authors suggest that the reluctance of Indians to defecate in toilets in or close to their homes, especially when emptying of pit latrines is involved, is perhaps related to concepts of purity and pollution, uniquely tied to the Hindu caste system in India.

References

Ackerson, L. K., and S. V. Subramanian. 2008. "Domestic Violence and Chronic Malnutrition among Women and Children in India." *American Journal of Epidemiology* 167 (10): 1188–96.

Babu, S. C., S. Thirumaran, and T. C. Mohanam. 1993. "Agricultural Productivity, Seasonality and Gender Bias in Rural Nutrition: Empirical Evidence from South India." *Social Science and Medicine* 37 (11): 1313–19.

Bhagowalia, P., D. Headey, and S. Kadiyala. 2012. "Agriculture, Income, and Nutrition Linkages in India. Insights from a Nationally Representative Survey." IFPRI Discussion Paper 01195, International Food Policy Research Institute (IFPRI), Washington, DC.

Bhandari, N., R. Bahl, B. Nayyar, P. Khokhar, J. E. Rohde, and M. K. Bhan. 2001. "Food Supplementation with Encouragement to Feed It to Infants from 4 to 12 Months of Age Has a Small Impact on Weight Gain." *Journal of Nutrition* 131 (7): 1946–51.

Black, R. E., C. G. Victora, S. P. Walker, Z. A. Bhutta, P. Christian, M. de Onis, M. Ezzati, S. Grantham-McGregor, J. Katz, R. Martorell, and R. Uauy the Maternal Study Group. 2013. "Maternal and Child Undernutrition and Overweight in Low-income and Middle-income Countries." *Lancet* 382 (9890): 427–51.

Boisson, S., P. Sosai, S. Ray, P. Routray, B. Torondel, W.-P. Schmidt, B. Bhanja, and T. Clasen. 2014. "Promoting Latrine Construction and Use in Rural Villages Practicing Open Defecation: Process Evaluation in Connection with a Randomised Controlled Trial in Orissa, India." *BMC Research Notes* 7: 486.

Bose, S. 2011. "The Effect of Women's Status and Community on the Gender Differential in Children's Nutrition in India." *Journal of Biosocial Science* 43 (5): 513–33.

Brainerd, E., and N. Menon. 2014. "Seasonal Effects of Water Quality: The Hidden Costs of the Green Revolution to Infant and Child Health in India." *Journal of Development Economics* 107: 49–64.

Chalasani, S. 2012. "Understanding Wealth-based Inequalities in Child Health in India: A Decomposition Approach." *Social Science and Medicine* 75 (12): 2160–9.

Chowdhury, A. M. R., A. Bhuiya, M. E. Chowdhury, S. Rasheed, Z. Hussain, and L. C. Chen. 2013. "The Bangladesh Paradox: Exceptional Health Achievement Despite Economic Poverty." *Lancet* 382 (9906): 1734–45.

Clasen, T., S. Boisson, P. Routray, B. Torondel, M. Bell, O. Cumming, J. Ensink, M. Freeman, M. Jenkins, M. Odagiri, S. Ray, A. Sinha, M. Suar, and W.-P. Schmidt. 2014. "Effectiveness of a Rural Sanitation Programme on Diarrhoea, Soil-transmitted Helminth Infection, and Child Malnutrition in Odisha, India: A Cluster-randomised Trial." *Lancet Global Health* 2 (11): e645–e653.

Coffey, D., A. Chattopadhyay, and R. Gupt. 2014. "Wealth and Health of Children in India." *Economic and Political Weekly* 49 (15): 65.

Coffey, D., A. Gupta, P. Hathi, N. Khurana, D. Spears, N. Srivastav, and S. Vyas. 2014. "Revealed Preference for Open Defecation." *Economic and Political Weekly* 49 (38): 43.

Coffey, D., D. Spears, and R. Khera. 2013. "Women's Status and Children's Height in India: Evidence from Joint Rural Households." Research Institute for Compassionate Economics (RICE) Institute. http://riceinstitute.org/research/womens-status-and-childrens-height-in-india-evidence-from-joint-rural-households/

Deaton, A., and J. Drèze. 2009. "Food and Nutrition in India: Facts and Interpretations." *Economic and Political Weekly* 44 (7): 42–65.

de Onis, M., and WHO Multicentre Growth Reference Study Group. 2006. *WHO Child Growth Standards: Length/Height-for-Age, Weight-for-Age, Weight-for-Height and Body Mass Index-for-Age.* Geneva: World Health Organization (WHO).

Drèze, J., and A. Sen. 2011. "Putting Growth in Its Place." *Outlook India*, November 14, 2011. http://www.outlookindia.com/magazine/story/putting-growth-in-its-place/278843

Dubowitz, T., D. Levinson, J. N. Peterman, G. Verma, S. Jacob, and W. Schultink. 2007. "Intensifying Efforts to Reduce Child Malnutrition in India: An Evaluation of the Dular Program in Jharkhand, India." *Food and Nutrition Bulletin* 28 (3): 266–73.

The Economist. 2015. "Of Secrecy and Stunting." Nutrition in India. July 4, 2015. http://www.economist.com/news/asia/21656709-government-withholds-report-nutrition-contains-valuable-lessons-secrecy-and

Ghosh, A., A. Gupta, and D. Spears. 2014. "Are Children in West Bengal Shorter Than Children in Bangladesh?" *Economic and Political Weekly* 49 (8): 21–4.

Griffiths, P., Z. Matthews, and A. Hinde. 2002. "Gender, Family, and the Nutritional Status of Children in Three Culturally Contrasting States of India." *Social Science and Medicine* 55 (5): 775–90.

Gulati, A., A. Ganesh-Kumar, G. Shreedhar, and T. Nandakumar. 2012. "Agriculture and Malnutrition in India." *Food and Nutrition Bulletin* 33 (1): 74–86.

Haddad, L. 1999. "Women's Status: Levels, Determinants, Consequences for Malnutrition, Interventions, and Policy." *Asian Development Review* 17 (1–2): 96–131.

Hagen-Zanker, J., and R. Mallet. 2013. "How to do a Rigorous, Evidence-Focused Literature Review in International Development." A Guidance Note, Overseas Development Institute, London.

Headey, D., A. Chiu, and S. Kadiyala. 2012. "Agriculture's Role in the Indian Enigma: Help or Hindrance to the Crisis of Undernutrition?" *Food Security* 4 (1): 87–102.

Hu, L., and A. Schlosser. 2015. "Prenatal Sex Selection and Girls' Well-Being: Evidence from India." *Economic Journal* 125 (587): 1227–61.

Imai, K. S., S. K. Annim, V. S. Kulkarni, and R. Gaiha. 2014. "Women's Empowerment and Prevalence of Stunted and Underweight Children in Rural India." *World Development* 62: 88–105.

Jain, M. 2015. "India's Struggle Against Malnutrition – Is the ICDS Program the Answer?" *World Development* 67: 72–89.

Jayachandran, S., and R. Pande. 2013. "Why Are Indian Children Shorter than African Children?" Unpublished draft, Harvard University. http://scholar.harvard.edu/files/rpande/files/why_are_indian_children_shorter_than_african_children.pdf

Jensen, R. T., and N. H. Miller. 2011. "Do Consumer Price Subsidies Really Improve Nutrition?" *Review of Economics and Statistics* 93 (4): 1205–23.

Joe, W., U. S. Mishra, and K. Navaneetham. 2009. "Inequalities in Childhood Malnutrition in India: Some Evidence on Group Disparities." *Journal of Human Development and Capabilities* 10 (3): 417–39.

Kandpal, E. 2011. "Beyond Average Treatment Effects: Distribution of Child Nutrition Outcomes and Program Placement in India's ICDS." *World Development* 39 (8): 1410–21.

Kanjilal, B., P. G. Mazumdar, M. Mukherjee, and M. H. Rahman. 2010. "Nutritional Status of Children in India: Household Socio-economic Condition as the Contextual Determinant." *International Journal for Equity in Health* 9: 19. http://www.ncbi.nlm.nih.gov/pmc/articles/PMC2931515/

Kaushal, N., and F. M. Muchomba. 2015. "How Consumer Price Subsidies Affect Nutrition." *World Development* 74: 25–42.

Krishnamurthy, P., V. S. Pathania, and S. Tandon. 2014. "Food Price Subsidies and Nutrition: Evidence from State Reforms to India's Public Distribution System." UC Berkeley Public Law Research Paper No. 2345675, University of California, Berkeley.

Kumar, S., and L. F. Berkman. 2015. "Association of Inadequately Iodized Salt Use with Underweight among Young Children in India." *Asia Pacific Journal of Public Health* 27 (2): 185–94.

Lokshin, M., M. Das Gupta, M. Gragnolati, and O. Ivaschenko. 2005. "Improving Child Nutrition? The Integrated Child Development Services in India." *Development and Change* 36 (4): 613–40.

Malhotra, N. 2013. "Inadequate Feeding of Infant and Young Children in India: Lack of Nutritional Information or Food Affordability?" *Public Health Nutrition* 16 (10): 1723–31.

Menon, P., A. Bamezai, A. Subandoro, M. A. Ayoya, and V. Aguayo. 2015. "Age-Appropriate Infant and Young Child Feeding Practices Are Associated with Child Nutrition in India: Insights from Nationally Representative Data." *Maternal & Child Nutrition* 11 (1): 73–87.

Parasuraman, S., and T. Rajaretnam. 2011. "Agriculture, Food Security and Nutrition in Vidarbha: A Household Level Analysis." *Economic and Political Weekly* 46 (19): 43.

Pathak, P. K., and A. Singh. 2011. "Trends in Malnutrition among Children in India: Growing Inequalities across Different Economic Groups." *Social Science and Medicine* 73 (4): 576–85.

Patil, S. R., B. F. Arnold, A. L. Salvatore, B. Briceno, S. Ganguly, J. M. Colford, Jr., and P. J. Gertler. 2014. "The Effect of India's Total Sanitation Campaign on Defecation Behaviors and Child Health in Rural Madhya Pradesh: A Cluster Randomized Controlled Trial." *PLoS Medicine* 11 (8): e1001709. http://journals.plos.org/plosmedicine/article/asset?id=10.1371%2Fjournal.pmed.1001709.pdf

Pingali, P., and K. Ricketts. 2014. "Mainstreaming Nutrition Metrics in Household Surveys – Toward a Multidisciplinary Convergence of Data Systems." *Annals of the New York Academy of Sciences* 1331: 249–57.

Pingali, P., K. Ricketts, and D. E. Sahn. 2015. "Agriculture for Nutrition: Getting Policies Right." In *The Fight Against Hunger Malnutrition: The Role of Food, Agriculture, and Targeted Policies*, edited by D. E. Sahn, 165–91. Oxford: Oxford University Press.

Radhakrishna, R., and C. Ravi. 2004. "Malnutrition in India: Trends and Determinants." *Economic and Political Weekly* 39 (7): 671–6.

Rah, J. H., A. A. Cronin, B. Badgaiyan, V. M. Aguayo, S. Coates, and S. Ahmed. 2015. "Household Sanitation and Personal Hygiene Practices Are Associated with Child Stunting in Rural India: A Cross-sectional Analysis of Surveys." *BMJ Open* 5: e005180.

Ramalingaswami, V., U. Jonsson, and J. Rohde. 1996. "Commentary: The Asian Enigma." In *The Progress of Nations Report 1996*, 11–17. New York: UNICEF.

Rao, S., A. N. Kanade, C. S. Yajnik, and C. H. Fall. 2009. "Seasonality in Maternal Intake and Activity Influence Offspring's Birth Size among Rural Indian Mothers – Pune Maternal Nutrition Study." *International Journal of Epidemiology* 38 (4): 1094–103.

Rowlatt, J. 2015. "Mystery Surrounds India Health Survey." *BBC News*, July 3, 2015. http://www.bbc.com/news/world-asia-33369710

S, Rukimini. 2015. "Over 50% of Children Under Five Stunted in UP." *The Hindu*, July 6, 2015. http://www.thehindu.com/news/national/unicef-rapid-survey-on-children-over-50-of-children-under-five-stunted-in-up/article7389926.ece

Sabarwal, S., S. V. Subramanian, M. C. McCormick, and J. G. Silverman. 2012. "Husband's Preference for a Son and Women's Nutrition: Examining the Role of Actual and Desired Family Composition on Women's Anaemia and Body Mass Index in India." *Paediatric and Perinatal Epidemiology* 26 (1): 77–88.

Sazawal, S., U. Dhingra, P. Dhingra, G. Hiremath, A. Sarkar, A. Dutta, V. P. Menon, and R. E. Black. 2010. "Micronutrient Fortified Milk Improves Iron Status, Anemia and Growth among Children 1–4 Years: A Double Masked, Randomized, Controlled Trial." *PLoS One* 5 (8): e12167.

Semba, R. D., S. de Pee, K. Sun, M. W. Bloem, and V. K. Raju. 2010. "The Role of Expanded Coverage of the National Vitamin a Program in Preventing Morbidity and Mortality among Preschool Children in India." *Journal of Nutrition* 140 (1): 208S–12S.

Shroff, M., P. Griffiths, L. Adair, C. Suchindran, and M. Bentley. 2009. "Maternal Autonomy Is Inversely Related to Child Stunting in Andhra Pradesh, India." *Maternal and Child Nutrition* 5 (1): 64–74.

Singh, A., A. Park, and S. Dercon. 2012. "School Meals as a Safety Net: An Evaluation of the Midday Meal Scheme in India." *Economic Development and Cultural Change* 75 (2): 275–306.

Singh, P. 2015. "Performance Pay and Information: Reducing Child Undernutrition in India." *Journal of Economic Behavior & Organization* 112: 141–63.

Smith, L. C. 2015. "The Great Indian Calorie Debate: Explaining Rising Undernourishment during India's Rapid Economic Growth." *Food Policy* 50: 53–67.

Spears, D. 2012a. "Policy Lessons from Implementing India's Total Sanitation Campaign." Paper prepared for India Policy Forum, New Delhi, July 17–18, 2012.

Spears, D. 2012b. "Effects of Rural Sanitation on Infant Mortality and Human Capital: Evidence from India's Total Sanitation Campaign." Research Institute for Compassionate Economics (RICE).

Spears, D. 2013. "How Much International Variation in Child Height Can Sanitation Explain?" Policy Research Working Paper 6351, World Bank, Washington, DC.

Spears, D., A. Ghosh, and O. Cumming. 2013. "Open Defecation and Childhood Stunting in India: An Ecological Analysis of New Data from 112 Districts." *PLoS One* 8 (9): e73784.

Subramanian, S. V., and G. D. Smith. 2006. "Patterns, Distribution, and Determinants of Under- and Overnutrition: A Population-based Study of Women in India." *American Journal of Clinical Nutrition* 84 (3): 633–40.

Subramanyam, M. A., I. Kawachi, L. F. Berkman, and S. V. Subramanian. 2011. "Is Economic Growth Associated with Reduction in Child Undernutrition in India?" *PLoS Medicine* 8 (3): e1000424.

Tarozzi, A. 2005. "The Indian Public Distribution System as Provider of Food Security: Evidence from Child Nutrition in Andhra Pradesh." *European Economic Review* 49 (5): 1305–30.

UNICEF (United Nations Children's Fund). 1990. "Strategy for Improved Nutrition of Children and Women in Developing Countries." UNICEF, New York.

Vellakkal, S., J. Fledderjohann, S. Basu, S. Agrawal, S. Ebrahim, O. Campbell, P. Doyle, and D. Stuckler. 2015. "Food Price Spikes Are Associated with Increased Malnutrition among Children in Andhra Pradesh, India." *Journal of Nutrition* 145 (8): 1942–9.

von Grebmer, K., A. Saltzman, E. Birol, D. Wiesmann, N. Prasai, S. Yin, Y. Yohannes, and P. Menon. 2014. "Global Hunger Index 2014: The Challenge of Hidden Hunger." International Food Policy Research Institute (IFPRI), Washington, DC.

Wang, Y., H. Chen, S. Shaikh, and P. Mathur. 2009. "Is Obesity Becoming a Public Health Problem in India? Examine the Shift from Under- to Overnutrition Problems Over Time." *Obesity Reviews* 10 (4): 456–74.

Part 5

Future relevance of international institutions

16 Structural transformation and the transition from concessional assistance to commercial flows

The past and possible future contributions of the World Bank[1]

Uma Lele, Sambuddha Goswami, and Gianluigi Nico

Introduction

Two overarching debates, each with a positive and a normative bend, have reemerged among development economists, particularly in the case of sub-Saharan Africa (SSA), but also applicable to South Asia (SA) and other countries lagging behind in the process of structural transformation (ST): what has been – and what should be – the appropriate role of agriculture, vis-à-vis other sectors of the economy, in the transformation of countries, particularly those countries at early stages of development? Typically, the bulk of their populations make their living from low-productivity agriculture (World Bank 2007). Even the traditional champions of smallholder agriculture worry that in the age of accelerated globalization, except for a few smallholders with market access, most cannot compete in world markets. And even if agriculturally led strategies are followed, what has been the role of international assistance to agriculture, and what should it be, relative to other sectors of the economy – for example, in education, skill development, and infrastructure – going forward to promote transformation? Additional considerations leading to these debates include a concern about jobless growth and the need to increase productive employment, the need to meet a rapidly growing urban demand for increased and more diversified food, and the non-viability of a great deal of smallholder farming in the face of growing population pressure on the land.

Future outcomes will clearly depend on a better understanding of the ST process and the role of international assistance in agriculture to date. In this chapter, we address several questions:

1 How has agriculture performed relative to other sectors, among a large number of developed and developing countries, and contributed to structural transformation?

2 Which countries have "graduated" from low- to higher-income countries, according to the International Development Association (IDA) and the International Bank for Reconstruction and Development (IBRD) lending criteria? How have the "graduated countries" and other large recipients

of World Bank loans and credits performed, as assessed using some specific criteria of transformation – that is, changes in labor productivity in agriculture relative to other sectors, decline in the share of employment in agriculture, and changes in the employment shares in service and industry – rather than simply gross domestic product (GDP) growth?

3   How has the World Bank contributed to the structural transformation of countries? How has the World Bank portfolio performed in "graduated" and "non-graduated" countries, relative to the groups of low-, lower-middle-, and upper-middle-income countries; to politically fragile countries and those experiencing conflict; and to countries in different regions? What advice did the Bank give to its borrowers? And how much of it was adopted and with what outcomes?

There is a long history of the Bank's involvement in many countries dating back to the 1960s and 1970s, with a few exceptions. China joined the Bank in 1980, and the former Soviet Bloc countries joined in the early 1990s. This short chapter can do little more than provide an overview of this long history with 188 member countries. Further details are in the forthcoming book *Food for All: International Organizations and the Transformation of Agriculture* (Lele et al., forthcoming 2017, Oxford University Press). The purpose of this chapter is to identify some key issues for future strategies of countries and donors, including, in particular, the role of the World Bank, in a changed world. The Bank's IDA 18 replenishment process has five theme papers, which all stress the importance of agriculture in the new priorities: climate change, jobs and economic transformation, conflict and violence, gender and development, and governance and institutions. The "Demand for IDA 18 Resources" (World Bank 2016a) stresses the importance of agriculture, mentioning it 20 times, and the IDA 18 Special Theme: Climate Change paper (World Bank 2016b) mentions agriculture 30 times. The IDA 18 Overarching Theme paper (World Bank 2016c) includes attention to global value chains, spatial data analysis tools, small and medium enterprise impact analysis, jobs measurement tools, and private sector investment, all with potentially rich agendas. In the IDA Special Theme: Governance and Institutions report (World Bank 2016d), the focus is on public administration and corruption, with health and education singled out as special sectors for improving service delivery, but the word "agriculture" is mentioned only once when analysis on governance and institutions should have been encouraged in all sectors. Evidence shows that good project performance critically depends on good policies, and the Bank's analytical work makes a difference, particularly in countries with limited internal capacity (Denizer, Kaufmann, and Kraay 2013).

Evidence base

The analysis here is an extension of our earlier work on structural transformation, which explored agricultural growth and equity, food security, total factor productivity, productivity of land and labor, and sustainability of productivity.

This more focused analysis is based on the newly available panel data on sectoral breakdown of employment for 139 developed and developing countries over the 1991–2014 period, from the International Labor Organization–Global Employment Trend (ILO–GET), as compared to the data from the Food and Agriculture Organization of the United Nations (FAO), which we, like other scholars, have used (Timmer and Akkus 2008; Timmer 2009; Fuglie, Wang, and Ball 2012; Timmer 2015). For more detail on all data used here, the reader is directed to the book by Lele et al. (forthcoming 2017) noted earlier.

The chapter first presents results using ILO data on the process of ST for the 1991–2014 period of rapid growth and food and financial crisis. This is followed by a review of the World Bank's overall assistance, the graduation of countries using IDA eligibility criteria including changes therein, measures of the structural transformation of the "graduated" countries and other large-scale recipients of IDA credits and loans, and examination of the performance of the World Bank's investment lending to the Agriculture and the Rural Development sector (ARD), since the inception of the IBRD and IDA. The World Bank data also permit comparisons of the performance of investment lending in agriculture relative to other sectors, and review of its analytical work and policy advice, thereby enabling the possibility of exploring the World Bank's contribution to the process of structural transformation. The highlights of this latest analysis are presented in this chapter. The larger history and implications will be included in Lele et al. (forthcoming).

Why multilateral aid?

There is much skepticism about aid and its effectiveness, leading to widespread aid fatigue. The member countries of the Organisation for Economic Co-operation and Development (OECD) have been the principal donors of Official Development Assistance (ODA), but they have been facing slow growth, growing fiscal woes, and a huge influx of refugees – the largest since the Second World War. These developments have contributed to the fateful referendum on June 23, 2016, in support of Brexit, raising concerns about the likely impacts on British and European aid (Lele 2016). Yet continued international cooperation is needed, because despite rapid progress in developing countries, growth has slowed and inequalities have increased. Most of the remaining poverty now is found in lower-middle-income and low-income countries, although even upper-middle-income countries contain some poverty – leading to a "poor countries or poor people" debate. Poor households and poor countries have low saving and investment capacity. Substantially greater investment is needed, targeted at poor countries and the poor populations in the middle-income countries (Kanbur 2016). Even after 70 years of Bretton Woods institutions, created to fill the capital market failures and assure monetary stability, capital markets today still face problems of uninsured risk and risk of another crisis (Ravallion 2016). Despite substantial accumulated savings in the world, with perceived risks, the private sector tends to be reluctant to lend to poor countries (World Bank 2013) and to poor populations in middle-income countries. Multilateral lending helps directly to fill this gap, and thereby assists in creating the enabling conditions for private sector investments (Ravallion 2016). Multilateral lending provides positive signals to the private sector and generates the necessary macroeconomic and sectoral information on an objective basis, which can help private actors make informed decisions.

There is growing consensus that international assistance should provide global public goods (GPG). Such assistance, for example, can slow climate change, control communicable diseases (Birdsall et al. 2010; Deaton 2013), and contain conflicts. All three are priorities of IDA 18. Developing countries have, however, argued that GPG financing should not come at the cost of development assistance at the country level.

Equally important, multilateral lending is less politicized, more efficient, more equitable and transparent, more selective, and preferred by clients over bilateral aid. Furthermore, multilateral aid is less fragmented (Rondinelli 1993; Kharas 2007, 2008, 2009; Birdsall et al. 2010; Custer et al. 2015).

Multilateral institutions are able to generate knowledge, which is a public good. Supporters of aid (Rodrik 1996; Kanbur 2004; Kharas 2007, 2008, 2009; Birdsall et al. 2010; Isenman and Shakow 2010; Isenman 2011, 2012; Kanbur and Sumner 2012) have argued that the World Bank is a source of the "soft power" of knowledge, citing examples in the areas of agriculture, education and health, social safety nets, trade, and fiscal policies in which the bank's analytical capacity has made a difference (Rodrik 1996; Clemens, Radelet, and Bhavnani 2004; Radelet 2006; Isenman 2012; Clemens and Kremer 2016). It contains the world's largest collection of expertise in development economics. There are economies of scale in generating large-scale information. It requires substantial initial capital, which international organizations have invested over the years by establishing decades of record, trust, and experience. Their near universal membership gives them legitimacy and access to governments. The private sector, on the other hand, has little interest, breadth, or depth of reach, or incentive to collect such information, and analyze and share that information. Not only can multilateral institutions play a more effective role in providing global public goods of information and knowledge, norms, and standards, and achieve international consensus and agreements, but also they can help contain regional public "bads," such as pandemics, involuntary migration, and climate change – which have cross-border spillovers and contribute to poverty.

There are also many critics of aid (Lal 2006; Easterly and Pfutze 2008; Easterly and Williamson 2011; Deaton 2013; Easterly and Pfutze 2013). Easterly (2006) argued that billions of dollars spent on aid in developing countries have had very little impact. Deaton (2013) asserted that aid has had little impact in Africa because governments receive too large a share of their expenditures as aid. That makes them more accountable to donors and less accountable to their poor constituents. In contrast, he argued, aid to China and India has been successful – that is, poverty has declined and social indicators have improved. This is because aid has been a small share of GDP, and governments have not spent most of their time being accountable to donors rather than to their own people (Easterly 2006). We test these hypotheses in the case of the World Bank support to agriculture and rural development.

Principal findings of the structural transformation analysis

On average, for all 139 countries, the service sector enjoys the largest share of the employment (47 percent), bigger than agriculture's average 35 percent share of the total employed population. The greatest variation tends to be in the shares of agriculture across countries than in other sectors, ranging from 0.2 percent in Singapore to 92 percent in Burundi. According to the *World Development Report* (WDR) *2008* (World Bank 2007), agriculturally based countries had lower GDP per capita, greater shares of GDP in agriculture, greater rate of rural poverty, and slower non-agricultural GDP growth than transforming countries. There was no difference in the share of rural population in the agriculturally based and transforming countries according to WDR 2008 classification (World Bank 2007). In a similar vein, we note a difference between IDA-only countries, IDA-graduated countries, and middle-income countries that have never qualified to receive IDA credits. But we are getting ahead of the story.

On average, the share of value-added is the lowest in agriculture at only 17 percent of the total GDP, followed by industry (30 percent), and the service sector (53 percent), with the highest share. Again, on average for 139 countries, labor productivity, defined as value-added per worker employed, tends to be higher in industry and services than in agriculture (Table 16.1). On average, workers in the industrial sector tend to produce three times more value, and for those in the service sector, twice the value produced by workers in the agricultural sectors. Yet there are major differences among countries with regard to the level of per worker productivity in the service sector – that is, the extent to which per worker service sector value-added is closer to the level of the industrial or agricultural value-added per worker. Large variation is noticeable in labor productivity across countries. Industry has the highest standard deviation, followed by service and agriculture sectors.

Main findings: developed and developing countries

The relationships discussed ahead are correlations and not causalities. There are several different ways to interpret these correlations from a development perspective. Hence, analysis of what lies behind the correlations is important. There is a very clear difference in the way productivity of labor among agriculture, industry, and the service sectors behaves among regions, in relation to each other, over time, and in developing and developed countries, each as a group. These outcomes are a function of several independent variables, including changes in per capita income.

For all (139 developed and developing) countries, shown in Figure 16.1a, the share of agricultural value-added in total GDP declines as per capita income increases. But the behavior of developing and developed countries (not shown

Table 16.1 Key characteristics of 139 countries

	Obs.	Mean	St. Dev.	Min	Max
$\dfrac{VAagr_{i,t}}{GDP_{i,t}}$	3,336	0.17	0.15	0.00	0.94
$\dfrac{VAind_{i,t}}{GDP_{i,t}}$	3,336	0.30	0.13	0.01	0.97
$\dfrac{VAser_{i,t}}{GDP_{i,t}}$	3,336	0.53	0.14	0.02	0.87
$\dfrac{EMPagr_{i,t}}{totEMP_{i,t}}$	3,336	0.35	0.26	0.002	0.92
$\dfrac{EMPind_{i,t}}{totEMP_{i,t}}$	3,336	0.18	0.09	0.02	0.43
$\dfrac{EMPser_{i,t}}{totEMP_{i,t}}$	3,336	0.47	0.20	0.06	0.85
VA_agr_US$	3,336	9.93E+09	2.86E+10	3.08E+07	3.87E+11
VA_ind_US$	3,336	8.10E+10	2.71E+11	2196362	2.83E+12
VA_ser_US$	3,336	1.91E+11	8.05E+11	4831997	1.06E+13
VA_agr_per_worker_US$	3,336	9492.82	18597.54	37.43	276990.2
VA_ind_per_worker_US$	3,336	27723.45	44642.77	107.28	458601.7
VA_ser_per_worker_US$	3,336	17594.04	24407.1	28.5	101376.7
$\dfrac{VAagr_{i,t}}{GDP_{i,t}} - \dfrac{EMPagr_{i,t}}{totEMP_{i,t}}$	3,336	−18.20	16.50	−70.54	31.94
$\dfrac{VAind_{i,t}}{GDP_{i,t}} - \dfrac{EMPind_{i,t}}{totEMP_{i,t}}$	3,336	12.25	12.68	−16.06	82.79
$\dfrac{VAser_{i,t}}{GDP_{i,t}} - \dfrac{EMPser_{i,t}}{totEMP_{i,t}}$	3,336	5.80	16.85	−81.94	51.29
GDPpc_US$	3,336	8632.09	13431.94	69.58	69094.75
Pop*1000	3,336	43.03	145.65	0.19	1364.27
A_{def_I}	3,336	1.15	0.47	0.19	6.39
A_{def_s}	3,336	1.15	0.42	0.22	5.53

Source: Authors' calculations based on data used in the analysis.

in figures) varies. With the rise in per capita income, the share of value-added in agriculture in developing countries declines at a faster rate than in developed countries and is accompanied by a rise in the share of value-added in both industry and services. As the development process advances in developing countries, the share of agriculture value-added in total GDP decreases at an increasing rate, as confirmed by the positive coefficient of the quadratic term of per capita GDP.

In developed countries, changes in per capita income are associated with little and non-significant effects on the share of agricultural valued-added in total GDP. This is in part because agriculture's share in GDP is already low; the share of value-added in the industrial sector in total GDP increases with the change in per capita income, but at a declining rate. In the industrial sector, however, changes in shares and rates of change are much faster in developed than in developing countries. This explains the inverted U-curve trend in the share of industrial value-added for all (developing and developed) economies with changes in per capita income (Figure 16.1a). This means that as countries mature in their

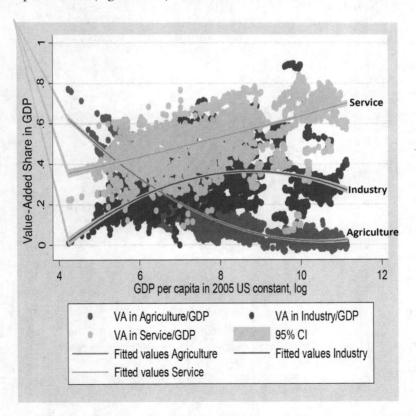

Figure 16.1a Relation between share of value-added in agriculture, industry, and service sectors (in total GDP) with respect to per capita income in 139 developed and developing countries (1991–2014)

Source: Authors' calculations based on data used in the analysis.

economic growth process, share of industry in GDP declines with growth in per capita income. Finally, in developed countries' advanced economies, the share of value-added in the service sector in total GDP increases with growth in per capita GDP, but only after the turning point has been reached at the level of GDP per capita of about US$12,000. Below that level, GDP per capita growth does not seem to have any positive effect on changes in the value-added share of the service sector (in total GDP). The dynamics in developing countries are very different. The share of value-added in the service sector in total GDP is positively associated with the rise in per capita GDP in developing countries first, but then starts to decline after a threshold of per capita GDP of US$3,000 is reached and at a very slow pace. In short, the scenario described earlier reflects the stylized facts behind the process of development of a given economy.

Changes in per capita income are associated with decreasing share of employment (with increasing rate) in the agriculture sector, whereas the share of employment in industry increases (with decreasing rate) in both developing and developed countries (Figure 16.1b). The employment share in agriculture,

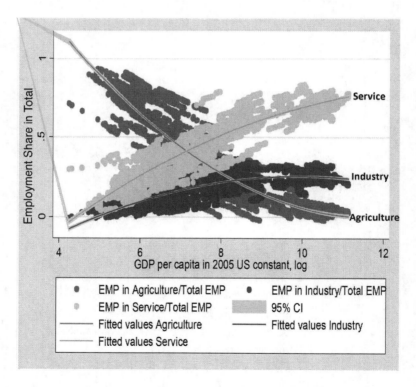

Figure 16.1b Relation between share of employment in agriculture, industry, and service sectors (in total employment) with respect to per capita income in 139 developed and developing countries (1991–2014)

Source: Authors' calculations based on data used in the analysis.

however, declines at double the pace in developing countries compared to developed countries with changes in per capita GDP; and changes in per capita GDP tend to be associated with an increase in the share of employment in the industrial sector, up to a per capita income level of $6,634 (in constant 2005 US dollars). This reflects the deindustrialization process thereafter, and the change in employment share in the industrial sector, which is almost double the magnitude in developed countries compared to developing ones. The rate of decline in the developed countries, however, is higher than in developing ones. In the service sector, employment share declines more in developed countries than developing countries first, but after a given threshold of per capita GDP, employment share in the service sector starts to increase at double speed in developed countries, compared to developing countries with per capita GDP growth. An important question in the transformation process is about the sectors to which labor shifts when the share of employment in agriculture declines. We discuss this ahead in the case of IDA recipients and IDA-graduated and never-IDA countries.

The gap between the value-added in agriculture and the share of employment in agriculture reflects the differences between per worker productivity in the agricultural and non-agricultural sectors and is important for the process of convergence in incomes between the two sectors. The turning point is reached when labor productivities in the two sectors begin to converge. For this to occur, agricultural (including labor) productivity needs to increase rapidly. The share of agricultural employment in total employment declines at a rate slower than the share of value-added in agriculture in total value-added in developing regions at early stages of development. We show ahead in the case of 27 countries that agricultural value-added share in GDP is declining in all developing countries, and so is the share of agricultural employment in total employment, except in Zimbabwe, where the share of agricultural employment in total employment is typically not declining as rapidly, which means that most of the poverty still remains in the rural sector and calls for more investments. At very low levels of per capita income, labor productivity in agriculture starts at levels far below levels for the non-agriculture (industry and service) sectors. It then gradually runs parallel, if not rapidly increasing, and then converges with the other sectors in the development process in the context of the successfully transforming countries. For example, in East Asia, agriculture productivity growth converges with the service sector.

The results for all 139 countries suggest that the elasticity of labor productivity, with respect to changes in per capita income, is highest in agriculture, followed by the services and industry sectors. This outcome could be a result of increased investment in agriculture, but it could also be explained by the rapid withdrawal of labor from agriculture to the industrial or the service sector. Indeed, both phenomena are necessary for transformation to occur. The responsiveness of agricultural labor productivity to a percentage change in per capita income is 1.1, whereas in the services and the industrial sectors, the elasticity is lower – that is, 0.945 and 0.202, respectively. In developing countries, elasticity of labor productivity is higher in services (1.010) than agriculture (0.735), and the elasticity in the industry sector is not statistically significant.

Empirical evidence at the regional level suggests that an increase in per capita income is positively and significantly associated with agricultural labor productivity mainly in the SA and SSA regions, the two lagging regions, because of the very low levels of per worker value-added in those regions in the agriculture sector. However, changes in agricultural labor productivity per worker are much higher in SA than in SSA, with the estimated coefficients statistically significant at the 95 percent confidence level. SSA countries appear to have a relatively disproportionate lower growth rate of agricultural labor productivity, when compared to SA. On average, for a 1 percentage point change in per capita income, elasticity of agriculture labor productivity in SA tends to be three times higher than agricultural labor productivity in SSA; and the situation in SSA turns out to be worse when we exclude upper-middle-income countries like South Africa from SSA. In South Africa, like Brazil, for example, large-scale agriculture has achieved rapid productivity growth but created little growth in employment. In both SA and SSA regions, only in agriculture are changes in per capita income associated with changes in labor productivity; this is not the case in the industrial sector, where changes in per capita income are at a statistically insignificant level. In the case of South Asia, the service sector labor productivity shows a statistically significant relationship to per capita income.

These estimates suggest that investments in agriculture and the service sector are likely to have a large payoff, particularly for countries at an early stage of development. These results are confirmed ahead in the case of a number of IDA recipients and those that have graduated from IDA.

Role of the World Bank Group in structural transformation

History of IDA and graduation

Since its establishment in 1945, the World Bank has lent well over a trillion US dollars to developing countries, 68 percent of it on IBRD terms and 32 percent on IDA terms (Table 16.2). More than 70 percent was investment lending; slightly more than a quarter was policy-based lending. The Agriculture and the

Table 16.2 IBRD–IDA total commitment by lending instrument type, 1947–2015 (in nominal USD billion)

Lending instrument type	Lending instrument	IBRD commitment	IDA commitment	Total commitment	Grant
Adjustment (AD)	Debt and debt service reduction loan	2.71	0.09	2.80	0.0002
	Development policy lending	**108.66**	**26.37**	**135.02**	**0.62**
	Poverty reduction support credit	0.00	3.12	3.12	0.05

Lending instrument type	Lending instrument	IBRD commitment	IDA commitment	Total commitment	Grant
	Programmatic structural adjustment loan	11.27	0.55	11.82	0.02
	Rehabilitation loan	2.43	0.48	2.91	0.00
	Sector adjustment loan	42.98	10.37	53.35	0.01
	Special structural adjustment loan	0.25	0.00	0.25	0.00
	Structural adjustment loan	46.09	18.39	64.48	0.01
	Total adjustment lending	**214.39**	**59.36**	**273.75**	**0.71**
Investment (IN)	Adaptable program loan	19.92	17.81	37.73	0.95
	Emergency recovery loan	7.88	13.62	21.50	2.82
	Financial intermediary loan	42.77	7.72	50.48	0.13
	Investment project financing	**47.64**	**37.92**	**85.56**	**5.09**
	Learning and innovation loan	0.22	0.39	0.60	0.06
	Sector investment and maintenance loan	50.73	19.67	70.40	0.11
	Specific investment loan	312.47	166.23	478.70	12.47
	Technical assistance loan	5.08	6.35	11.44	1.99
	Total investment lending	**486.71**	**269.71**	**756.42**	**23.63**
PR	**Program-for-Results**	**5.51**	**4.56**	**10.08**	**0.01**
Unidentified	**Xx**	**0.08**	**0.00**	**0.08**	**0.04**
Grand total		**706.69**	**333.64**	**1040.33**	**24.39**

Source: Authors' calculations based on data from World Bank (2016e), http://www.worldbank.org/projects?lang=en.

Note: Program-for-Results started in 2012.

Development policy financing (DPF) provides rapidly disbursing financing to help a borrower address actual or anticipated development financing requirements and is determined in the context of the Country Partnership Framework (CPF).

Investment project financing (IPF) is used in all sectors, with a concentration in the infrastructure, human development, agriculture, and public administration sectors. IPF is focused on the long term (5–10 year horizon) and supports a wide range of activities, including capital-intensive investments, agricultural development, service delivery, credit and grant delivery (including microcredit), community-based development, and institution building.

Unlike commercial lending, Bank IPF also serves as a vehicle for sustained, global knowledge transfer and technical assistance. This includes support to analytical and design work in the conceptual stages of project preparation, technical support, and expertise (including in the areas of project management and fiduciary and safeguards activities) during implementation, and institution building throughout the project.

Program-for-Results, a new instrument introduced in 2012, links disbursement of funds directly to the delivery of defined results, helping countries improve the design and implementation of their own development programs and achieve lasting results by strengthening institutions and building capacity.

Rural Development Sector received 37 percent of lending at the peak of lending to the ARD sector in 1977–78, but has since diminished to 6 to 7 percent in the latest post 2007–2008 period. Most of it has been investment lending. Therefore, the legacy of the past lending and its impacts are important in assessing the Bank's contribution. Figure 16.2 shows how the Bank has tended to assess its performance, starting from the project level and going to the corporate level.

IDA is one of the largest sources of assistance for the world's 77 poorest countries, 39 of which are in Africa. IDA is also perhaps the single largest source of donor funds for basic services in these countries. Among 59 IDA-only countries, 29 countries were in the low-income category, 26 countries in the lower-middle-income category, and 4 countries in upper-middle-income category but heavily indebted. An estimated 1.3 billion people lived in IDA-only countries in 2015. Of the 77 countries eligible to receive IDA resources in 2016, 59 were IDA-only, and 18 were blend countries (eligible to receive IDA and IBRD). In addition, India, the largest recipient of IDA since its establishment, is receiving transitional support since having graduated from IDA in 2014. Ahead we explore the relationship between IDA recipients and structural transformation.

In the recent period, total shares committed by the World Bank to Agricultural and Rural Development declined significantly. IBRD shares have declined more sharply than IDA shares. The latter reached an all-time low in 2005, but have recovered to 10 percent (Figures 16.3a and 16.3b). The increase may be

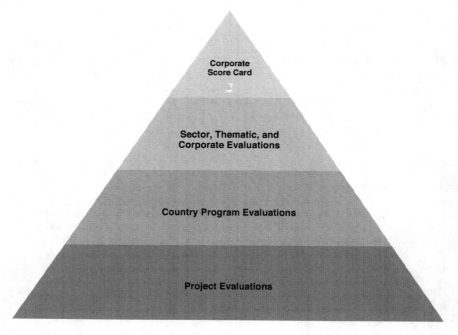

Figure 16.2 Evaluation framework of financing organizations: a "pyramid"
Source: Lele et al. (forthcoming 2017), adapted from Gray (2014).

Panel A

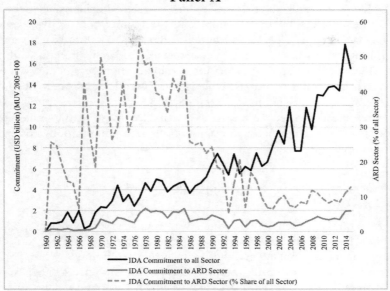

Panel B

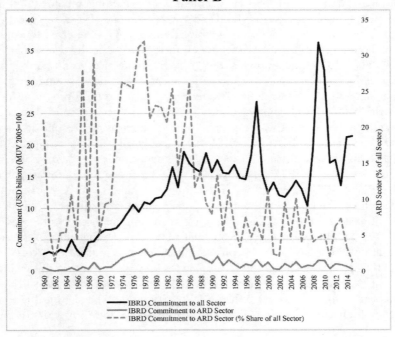

Figure 16.3 Commitment to all sectors and ARD sector and ARD sector share as percentage of total commitment (1960–2015) Manufactures Unit Value (MUV Index 2005=100) for a) IDA and b) IBRD

Source: Lele et al. (forthcoming 2017) based on data from World Bank (2016e), http://www.worldbank.org/projects?lang=en.

explained by the 2007–2008 crisis, leading to a broad acknowledgment that agriculture's neglect by the development community for nearly a quarter century had, at least in part, contributed to the 2007–2008 food crisis and to the ensuing price volatility. In theory, as the share of agriculture in GDP and employment declines and per capita income increases in developing countries, and as countries graduate from IDA, demand for World Bank loans to the public sector support for agriculture and rural development to generate public goods should be expected to decline, relative to demand for investments in other "public goods," such as infrastructure for transportation, communications, power, and telecommunications.

IDA's changing goalposts and eligibility with increased scarcity of IDA resources

IDA has complemented IBRD, which was envisaged to function as a self-sustaining business. IBRD provides loans and advice to middle-income and creditworthy poor countries, and the income generated from interest and repayments contributes to the Bank's administrative expenses. Since 1960, IDA, with three-year replenishments and a large grant element, has supported development work in 112 countries. Eligibility for IDA support has depended first and foremost on a country's relative poverty, defined as gross national income (GNI) per capita below an established threshold and updated annually ($1,215 in fiscal year 2016). The threshold value of gross national income (GNI, referred to as gross national product [GNP] at the time) per capita for IDA eligibility was initially set at US$250 in 1964 (now known as the "historical cutoff") (World Bank 2012). By the early 1980s, rising costs and a series of economic crises around the globe meant that available IDA resources were not adequate to fund programs for all countries below this eligibility ceiling. As a result, IDA ceased to lend to countries at the upper end of this per capita income scale, creating a second and lower "operational cutoff." IDA donors formally recognized the operational cutoff in IDA 8 and have reaffirmed it in each subsequent replenishment round. The operational cutoff in the financial year (FY) 1989 was equivalent to 18 percent of the global GNI per capita; in FY 2013 it was estimated to be equivalent to 13 percent. If the operational cutoff had maintained its relative value since FY 1982, in relation to the global GNI per capita, its nominal value would now be US$1,722, or 44 percent above the current value. Operational cutoff has clearly been set lower and lower when considering countries' "graduation" from IDA. Many IDA graduates would still be eligible for IDA were it not for this changed goalpost. Kanbur and others have argued that the developed world still needs to support countries with large shares of poverty on moral and ethical grounds, but such high ground seems to have eroded its appeal in recent years (Kanbur and Sumner 2012).

IDA allocation to countries is determined by each country's performance, as measured by the Country Policy and Institutional Assessment (CPIA) and Portfolio Performance Rating (PPR). In addition to country performance, country needs are also taken into account through population size and GNI per capita. Fifty percent of IDA goes to sub-Saharan Africa. Increasingly, IDA has been under pressure to take up other considerations. And five have merited exceptions: (1) capping of allocations to blend countries with large populations and with access to IBRD resources to less than their Performance-Based Allocation (PBA), due to their broader financing options; (2) providing additional resources to countries emerging from severe conflict, or after prolonged disengagement with IDA; (3) support for arrears clearance operations for eligible IDA countries; (4) a special provision for funding selected regional integration projects; and (5) providing some additional resources in the aftermath of natural disasters (World Bank 2010).

Thus, countries such as Vietnam and Pakistan are IDA-eligible, based on per capita income levels, and are also creditworthy for some IBRD borrowing as blend countries. IDA also supports some countries, including several small island countries, that are above the operational cutoff but lack the creditworthiness needed to borrow from IBRD. IBRD and IDA share the same staff and headquarters and evaluate projects using the same standards.

Since 1960, IDA has supported development work in 112 countries; 41 countries have graduated since then. Twenty-eight countries had graduated before 1990, and 13 countries after 1990. Among those 28 countries, 11 graduates reentered IDA due to drops in per capita income, and 3 of the 11 countries "reverse-graduated," IDA terminology that means the countries fell back into the status of being IDA-eligible after 1990. Thus, a total 16 countries graduated after 1990.[2] The reasons for countries reentering IDA included a combination of poor macroeconomic management; external shocks to their commodity exports; and weak, less diversified economies than those which graduated earlier in the 1970s.

IDA and IBRD in the context of multilateral aid

Total use of multilateral organizations (core contributions/multilateral ODA + noncore contributions/earmarked/multi–bilateral funding) now constitutes 42 percent of the Development Assistance Committee (DAC) member countries' total gross Official Development Assistance (ODA), $149 billion, constant 2013 USD in 2014. Core contributions/multilateral ODA represented only 29 percent and noncore contributions/earmarked/multi–bilateral funding represented the remaining 13 percent in the form of development assistance. Of the core contributions, 23 percent, and of the noncore contributions, 19 percent, were IDA lending, respectively (OECD 2015).

ODA does not include IBRD lending. Overall capital flows to developing countries have increased from a variety of sources, and thus, the World Bank's relative share and clout have declined. The new sources include foreign direct investment, sovereign bonds, remittances, philanthropic organizations, South–South cooperation, emerging countries' assistance from newly set-up multilateral organizations, such as the New Development Bank and the Asian Infrastructure

Development Bank, increased financing from regional banks, and, of course, bilateral assistance.

Assessing transformation of IDA and IBRD countries in the post-1990 period

Ahead we analyze the performance of 27 countries (18 of 24 IDA-graduated and reentered or "reverse-graduated" countries[3] and 6 of the top 15 recipient countries[4] of World Bank lending to ARD sector – that is, China, Egypt, India, Indonesia, Nigeria, and Philippines) (Table A.16.1a).

Their performance is interesting to understand because robust growth in developing countries was not uniformly shared. Extreme poverty declined most rapidly in China and to a lesser extent in India and Indonesia, and is increasingly concentrated in challenging environments even in those countries. A high number of those that escaped extreme poverty remain vulnerable to relapsing into it. Large differences in country growth performance are apparent in per capita income growth, and while some African countries, such as Ethiopia, have joined the ranks of high-growth countries, several other African countries are experiencing negative growth. IDA 18 documents note this challenge, especially among a number of fragile and conflict states, where resurgence of conflict and fast population growth have hindered poverty reduction. Meanwhile, financial flows to IDA countries have expanded, as a number of them have gained access to more diverse financing options, with several issuing bonds in the international capital markets. However, for the majority of IDA countries, concessional resources are an important source of external financing, as they do not have access to market-based financing at affordable rates. Concerns remain over sustainability, selectivity, coordination among the sources of financing, and the vulnerable debt outlook in a number of countries.

It is not surprising, therefore, that the demand for resources in IDA 18 is at an all-time high. IDA's six regions have submitted requests for approximately US$ 90 billion over the IDA 18 period for programmable resources, much higher than the demand for US$52 billion at the beginning of the IDA 17 Replenishment (World Bank 2016c). IDA 18 proposes replenishments of $75 billion, with the significantly increased financing package accompanied by reducing the ratio of every dollar of partner contributions to total mobilized resources from 1:2 in IDA 17 to 1:3 in IDA 18 (World Bank 2016a). IDA 18 proposals also envisage providing more concessionality through more efficient use of IDA reflows and partner contributions, using these not simply to fund IDA programs but also to buy down market-price debt to concessional terms, in a sustainable manner without depleting IDA's ability to serve its clients in the future through innovative solutions to unlock, multiply, and catalyze flows across all sources of financing – public, private, domestic, and international. The themes of IDA 18 replenishments focus on: climate change; fragility, conflict and violence, jobs and economic transformation, governance and institution building, and gender and development. Many of these areas are not ones with proven track records (IEG

2011; World Bank 2014). Moreover, for IDA graduates, their access to concessional funds from bilateral donors and multilateral funds becomes limited as IDA graduation criteria have become a de facto standard for eligibility to concessional funds from other sources.

Structural transformation: Performance of 27 countries

We explored the extent of structural transformation in the 27 selected countries using the following criteria: growth rates of GDP per capita, and growth rates of value-added per worker in agriculture, industry, and services, each as important indicators of development. We also explored levels of per worker productivity and changes in it over time in each sector, and productivity in agriculture relative to industry and services.

Typically, in less developed, slow-growing countries, per worker labor productivity in the service sector is close to per worker agricultural productivity, but in more rapidly advancing developing countries, per worker service sector productivity is close to that of industry. This list includes China, Bangladesh, India, Pakistan, and Ethiopia. Ethiopia's GDP composition and growth make it clear that, beyond its impressive agricultural performance in recent years showing the importance of the policy environment, Addis Ababa not only is the seat of the government but also has benefited from housing a large array of international and African regional cooperation institutions – that is, United Nations (UN) Offices: UN Human Rights Organizations, UN Conference on Trade and Development (UNCTAD), UN Office for Project Services (UNOPS), Economic Commission of Africa, UN Environment Programme (UNEP), UN Women, UN Development Programme (UNDP), International Telecommunication Union (ITU), World Health Organization (WHO), FAO, and ILO – with international meetings and conferences, and a thriving hotel and a tourism industry. This near equivalence of service and industry sectors in labor productivity seems to be a result of a combination of investment in skill levels, domestic and foreign direct investment, and international trade in services, as compared to countries that have not had similar investments. It also suggests that countries that are not able to industrialize as rapidly as their earlier industrializing counterparts may be better off actively promoting productivity growth in their service sector – for example, developing a cutting-edge software industry or interpreting legal and medical documents remotely. The latter may pay more than waiting on tables or working at Wal-Mart cash registers. India is an outlier in the software industry, relative to its per capita income, because of investment in human capital. It is also the level of difference in human capital which Wood argued explains the difference in the greater value-added in primary commodity-based industries in Latin America, as compared to Africa (Wood 2003).

We next looked at (1) growth rates in employment shares with respect to changes in GDP per capita and (2) total value-added shares in GDP with respect to GDP per capita in the three sectors, as indicators of structural transformation. Table A.16.1a shows these results for IBRD and IDA countries. Overall, IDA graduates have done well on transformation, and IDA has certainly helped in that process.

China ranks at the top in GDP growth and changes in value-added per worker (an indicator of labor productivity), with respect to change in per capita income that also increased very rapidly in all sectors. In China, industry and service sector labor productivity is moving almost in parallel. Azerbaijan and Armenia follow next in rapid per capita GDP growth with ranks in growth of per worker productivity in all three sectors consistent with that of overall growth. In Azerbaijan, it was a result of solid economic growth fueled by gas and oil, combined with socially oriented expenditures. Armenia's economy, too, has undergone a profound transformation since its independence in 1991. Sustained growth, ambitious first-generation transition reforms, and inflows of capital and remittances have created a market-oriented environment there. However, the global financial crisis of 2008–2009 had a significant negative impact on the country and eroded some of the welfare gains. Ethiopia and Albania stood fourth and fifth, respectively, in GDP growth and growth of value-added per worker in all three sectors, followed by India, although their relative rankings in growth in value-added per worker in the three sectors do not always coincide fully with ranking on per capita GDP growth. India, for example, stood sixth in per capita GDP growth, but fourth in per worker value-added growth in industry and fifth in per worker value-added growth in service. In Ethiopia, Albania, and India, labor productivity in the service sector is higher than in industry. Albania has made a remarkable transition from controlled to market-based reforms under IMF and World Bank, with annual remittances of $600 million. Both in Ethiopia and India, industry and service sector labor productivity have been moving almost in parallel, whereas in Albania, industry and service sector labor productivity initially converged and now are diverging.

The least well-performing countries were Papua New Guinea, Republic of Congo, Côte d'Ivoire, and Zimbabwe. Their per worker sectoral productivity growth rates were commensurate with their overall performance (Table A.16.1a).

The fastest-growing countries also experienced the most rapid decline in the share of agricultural employment, but their rankings in the changes in the shares in industrial and service sectors differed somewhat. For example, Ethiopia, Tanzania, India, and Bangladesh, in that order, experienced the most rapid rate of growth in the share of industrial employment ahead of China, albeit from a small base in the case of the early industrializers, whereas Ethiopia, Albania, China, Tanzania, India, and Bangladesh experienced the most rapid growth in the service sectors (Table 15A.1a). The slowest-performing countries, Papua New Guinea and Côte d'Ivoire, also experienced slow changes in sectorial shares. Latin American countries like Mexico and Brazil lagged in employment share changes in agriculture and industry, as well as in the service sector, in part because they are more mature economies. In addition, several recent studies have shown that it has been difficult for developing countries to grow their manufacturing sectors, which have become concentrated in a few large countries in East and Southeast Asia. That is explained, in part, by the spread of labor-saving technical change. Latin American countries have been particularly adversely affected by this nonindustrialization or deindustrialization phenomenon (Felipe, Mehta, and Rhee 2016; Gollin, Jedwab, and Vollrath 2016; Haraguchi, Cheng, and Smeets 2016; Rodrik 2016).

As is to be expected, according to theory, the agricultural value-added share in total GDP has declined in all countries. Zimbabwe is the only exception.

Contribution of World Bank assistance to the structural transformation of 27 countries

Over the entire period, 1960–2015, during which the World Bank has been active in most of these countries, excluding China, which joined in 1980, and Eastern Europe, which joined in 1990, smaller countries typically received a higher share of GDP as World Bank loans and credits (1.4 percent in constant 2005 dollars in Honduras and Tanzania each), compared to mega countries – 0.14 percent in China, 0.25 percent in Brazil, and 0.54 percent in India. On a per capita basis, too, China, India, Nigeria, Bangladesh, and Ethiopia ranked lower than middle-income countries, like Turkey and Mexico. Lending to large countries was more stable than small countries – that is, the standard deviation of year-to-year commitments as a share of GDP was only 0.2 in China, compared to 2.6 in Tanzania. Armenia, and Republic of Congo at the high end of the variability in World Bank assistance, compared to China, Brazil, Mexico, and India (Table A.1.b). This variability was even greater on a per capita basis in small countries than in large countries. Large countries offer more investment opportunities than small countries, but it is also apparent that many low-income and small countries, such as Tanzania, Republic of Congo, Ethiopia, and Côte d'Ivoire, have also had much more unstable macroeconomic and/or political environments over the last 50 years, as compared to countries like China and India. Turkey, Brazil, and Mexico fall in the middle of the pack. And this shows up in the absence of lending activity over long stretches in countries with macroeconomic or political problems.

Independent Evaluation Group (IEG)–assigned project performance ratings for the 1,186 ARD sector projects, which exited between FY 1972 to 2015 in 27 countries, provide additional insights. However, there is a great range in the number of projects rated by the IEG in countries, as shown in Table A.16.1b. Countries with large numbers of rated projects provide a more reliable barometer of country performance over time and space than do countries with few such ratings.

There is a huge range in the performance of satisfactory projects over the entire period. Armenia had 100 percent of the IEG-rated projects in the satisfactory range, albeit from a small portfolio, followed by China and Azerbaijan at 92.6 percent each, and 92.3 percent in Armenia. In China, however, as many as 94 projects were evaluated by the IEG, compared to 18 projects in Albania and 13 in Azerbaijan. Brazil, India, Pakistan, and Bangladesh each had large portfolios and had ratings of satisfactory in the case of about 70 percent of the projects; the least well-performing projects were in African countries: Ethiopia, Tanzania, Cameroon, Republic of Congo, and Côte d'Ivoire. This is consistent with the findings of our larger review of the 11,212 projects evaluated by IEG in all sectors[5] exiting in project exit financial year period 1964–2015 for other sectors, and 2,475 ARD sector projects exiting from exit financial year 1972–2015. On the whole, agricultural projects have performed less well than the World Bank's overall project portfolio, but they have also performed differently in different regions. East Asia was on top in overall project performance, and Eastern Europe's and South Asia's agricultural performance was on par with each region's overall portfolio performance, although in each case, the performances were less than East Asia's. Upper-income countries, classified by World Bank criteria, had higher performance ratings of about 73 percent in agriculture, with lower-middle-income countries having about 67 percent, followed by low-income countries of about 53 percent. The same phenomenon is noted in the International Finance Corporation's (IFC) lending performance of its agricultural portfolio. It performed least well in sub-Saharan Africa, and performance was weaker in agriculture than in other sectors in Africa. Other sectors (4 percent of total) had higher shares of "highly satisfactory" projects than did the ARD sector (2 percent of total).

Fragile country borrowers perform less well than others

The IEG of the World Bank rated 702 ARD sector projects in 44 of the 55 fragile countries, containing 20 percent of the world's population. Fifty-eight percent were rated satisfactory and above, compared to the Bank-wide average for all countries of 67 percent satisfactory and above. Yet, fragile countries are going to need much more and better-quality investment on a continuous, long-term basis by the international community as a whole than has been accorded so far, while keeping expectations of good outcomes modest and focusing on institutions and capacity building.

World Bank's and IDA's contribution to transformation

Some of the Bank's biggest contributions to agriculture have been through IDA financing, and those have been in South and Southeast Asia: the Green Revolution, Dairy Development in India, and China's impressive rural poverty reduction. Preconditions in Asia were very different than those in sub-Saharan Africa. Countries were larger with greater population densities, better rainfall, and soils with huge irrigation potential, more institutional human and administrative capacity, and stronger political resolve on the part of the policymakers to achieve food security (energy security), in part because of greater incidence of hunger. Yet two-thirds of the global poverty and hunger is still in Asia.

Among the donors there was strong resolve to help reach food security (filling the calorie gap) in Asia for larger geopolitical reasons. There was longer-term, relatively more predictable support, availability of agricultural technology, focus on policy dialogue, institution building and investments, and active championship and support for strong public sector interventions dictated by donors, all leading to the IDA/World Bank contribution to productivity growth, poverty reduction, and employment generation. The Bank also provided support during macroeconomic crises to India and Indonesia.

China has certainly excelled in its economic performance, as well as in the implementation of the World Bank's portfolio. China has also been more open to advice, which is relevant to addressing its challenges, an example of a good borrower. Some small middle-income countries, such as Armenia and Azerbaijan, have also performed well. The Bank's portfolio in these countries has performed better than in countries with unstable political and economic environments. How much credit the Bank gets for these achievements relative to client countries is difficult to say. They both share in the success.

Now second-generation, seemingly intractable problems of environment and poverty have become daunting in Asia. These include unsustainable groundwater exploitation and soil depletion in India, rapid deforestation in Indonesia contributing to climate change, resource conflicts, under- and overnutrition, insufficient outreach to marginal populations, and generally, a more limited record of influence on government policies as the Bank's clout has diminished.

In Africa, in the 1960s and 1970s almost the opposite was true. Constraints included low population densities, limited infrastructure, rainfed agriculture, small countries, limited market integration, and limited technologies for rainfed agriculture, weak institutions, and human capital. The Bank promoted public sector interventions but then lost faith in the ability of governments to deliver services in the case of absent or weak markets, leading to the abolition of public interventions and liberalization of markets on a scale grander than accomplished in Asia. In each of these cases, the use of the counterfactual would have produced robust results of the Bank's initial substantial contribution to agricultural service delivery and to the subsequent creation of markets for products and services. The Bank has had a more stable and regular presence in countries with stable political environments and macroeconomic management; lending programs have been unstable in countries with political and macroeconomic challenges.

Going forward, challenges of climate change, conflict, and violence will not be easy to tackle. In short, the future will be very different than the past, and the Bank will need new ways of operating – going beyond projects and countries to bring knowledge from the South to tackle challenges of the Global South. Countries able to cope with the external shocks and domestic political and economic factors have performed better. That calls for strong institutions and internal capacity. The Bank, too, has performed better in those countries. Countries need not only more and more predictable access to capital but also support to build their institutions and capacity. The Bank has an important role, not only to mobilize capital but also to provide the skills needed to address these new challenges by helping to build global consensus.

Appendix

Table A.16.1a. Key indicators of structural transformation

Classification	Country	Rate of change (predicted values based on the 139 countries regression equation) (1991–2014) (%)									Gap between rate of change
		Agriculture value-added per worker, log	Industry value-added per worker, log	Services value-added per worker, log	Share of agricultural value-added in GDP	Share of industry value-added in GDP	Share of services value-added in GDP	Share of agricultural employment in total employment	Share of industry employment in total employment	Share of services employment in total employment	Share of agricultural value-added in GDP – share of agricultural employment in total employment
Middle-income/never-IDA	Brazil	0.26	0.20	0.09	−6.64	−0.58	0.94	−1.31	−0.47	0.64	−5.34
	Mexico	0.15	0.09	0.05	−4.72	0.25	0.22	−1.06	−0.42	0.51	−3.65
	Romania	0.47	0.38	0.22	−6.03	−1.16	2.24	−1.09	−0.35	1.37	−4.94
IDA-graduated	Albania	0.77	0.62	0.35	−4.11	−2.22	6.79	−1.11	−0.13	2.46	−3.00
	Angola	0.46	0.34	0.29	−8.10	0.40	1.50	−1.32	0.44	1.27	−6.77
	Armenia	0.74	0.56	0.62	−3.30	0.52	2.28	−1.75	0.93	1.38	−1.55
	Azerbaijan	0.84	0.44	0.66	−8.55	2.91	−0.34	−1.96	0.88	1.33	−6.59
	China	0.88	0.80	0.77	−4.56	0.38	1.22	−2.04	1.06	2.31	−2.52
	Georgia	0.67	0.46	0.48	−3.03	−0.10	1.44	−1.13	0.82	1.15	−1.90
	India*	0.61	0.50	0.47	−2.02	0.99	0.34	−1.19	1.15	1.78	−0.84
	Morocco	0.29	0.23	0.19	−2.27	0.21	0.55	−0.85	−0.05	1.06	−1.42
	Turkey	0.21	0.23	0.13	−1.65	−0.61	0.67	−0.89	−0.41	0.94	−0.76

Re-graduated	Egypt	0.27	0.22	0.20	-2.06	0.45	0.29	-1.24	0.12	0.77	-0.82
	Indonesia	0.33	0.24	0.25	-1.72	0.32	0.31	-0.90	0.18	0.91	-0.82
	Philippines	0.31	0.22	0.16	-2.72	0.17	0.72	-0.99	-0.01	0.80	-1.73
IDA-graduated but reverse graduation	Cameroon#	0.10	0.02	0.01	-1.09	1.03	-0.09	-0.35	-0.58	1.14	-0.74
	Congo, Republic of#	0.10	-0.12	0.02	-8.17	2.20	-2.35	-0.50	-0.44	0.63	-7.67
	Côte d'Ivoire$	0.02	-0.03	-0.14	-1.01	-0.94	0.97	-0.19	-1.70	0.73	-0.82
	Honduras	0.17	0.11	0.07	-2.20	0.13	0.61	-0.82	-0.20	0.81	-1.38
	Nicaragua	0.19	0.13	0.14	-1.32	0.62	0.20	-0.91	0.00	0.68	-0.42
	Nigeria#	0.45	0.32	0.30	-2.23	0.68	1.38	-1.21	0.78	1.06	-1.02
	Papua New Guinea#$	0.02	0.01	-0.03	-0.36	-0.20	0.71	-0.30	-1.50	1.20	-0.06
	Zimbabwe#$	-0.38	-0.30	-0.30	2.97	-0.72	-0.50	0.37	-2.52	0.14	2.60
IDA-eligible, not yet graduated	Bangladesh	0.54	0.36	0.31	-2.76	0.12	1.02	-0.92	1.08	1.43	-1.84
	Ethiopia	0.58	0.38	0.38	-1.14	3.44	0.51	-0.83	4.98	3.42	-0.31
	Pakistan#	0.22	0.22	0.12	-0.65	-0.85	0.68	-0.73	0.10	0.90	0.08
	Tanzania	0.38	0.23	0.17	-1.38	0.74	0.86	-0.60	1.92	2.31	-0.79

Source: Authors' calculations based on the data used in the analysis.

Note: Pakistan and Bangladesh may soon graduate if their per capita incomes increase.

* IDA deputies agreed to provide temporary transitional support to India on special terms during IDA 17.

Countries are blend countries as of July 2016, World Bank List of Economies.

$ Countries are in the World Bank Harmonized List of Fragile Situations for FY 17.

Table A.16.1b Key indicators of IEG project performance outcome and World Bank lending

Classification	Country	Per capita World Bank (IBRD+IDA) lending to all sectors (USD) (MUV 2005=100) (1960–2015)		IEG project performance ratings of ARD sector (exit FY 1972–2015)(total 1186 projects in 27 countries)	
		Mean	Standard deviation	Number of IEG-rated ARD projects	Share of outcomes in the satisfactory range (%)
Middle-income/ never-IDA	Brazil	7.82	5.33	94	70.21
	Mexico	12.80	9.05	59	71.19
	Romania	11.27	15.32	34	64.71
IDA-graduated	Albania	11.42	21.78	18	88.89
	Angola	1.44	3.69	0	NA
	Armenia	12.57	19.43	13	92.31
	Azerbaijan	7.04	18.14	8	100.00
	China	0.83	0.82	95	92.63
	Georgia	10.47	19.29	7	57.14
	India*	2.47	1.14	186	75.27
	Morocco	12.52	9.52	47	80.85
	Turkey	13.35	10.20	36	86.11
Re-graduated	Egypt	5.24	5.75	34	76.47
	Indonesia	5.25	3.80	111	69.37
	Philippines	6.25	5.07	66	75.76
IDA-graduated but reverse graduation	Cameroon#	6.85	6.88	32	50.00
	Congo, Republic of#	8.65	17.10	2	50.00
	Côte d'Ivoire$	12.15	12.32	29	68.97
	Honduras	13.62	11.94	12	91.67
	Nicaragua	10.86	13.01	8	87.50
	Nigeria#	3.62	3.44	54	57.41
	Papua New Guinea#$	7.24	8.83	15	46.67
	Zimbabwe#$	3.42	7.07	9	77.78
IDA-eligible, not yet graduated	Bangladesh	3.91	2.79	67	76.12
	Ethiopia	4.02	4.04	42	50.00
	Pakistan#	5.31	2.95	61	81.97
	Tanzania	7.15	5.43	47	44.68

Source: Authors' calculations based on IEG Project Performance Ratings data: World Bank (2016f), http://data.worldbank.org/data-catalog/IEG, and World Bank Projects & Operations data: World Bank (2016e), http://www.worldbank.org/projects?lang=en.

Note: Pakistan and Bangladesh may soon graduate if their per capita income increases.

* IDA deputies agreed to provide temporary transitional support to India on special terms during IDA 17.
# Countries are blend countries as of July 2016, World Bank List of Economies.
$ Countries are in the World Bank Harmonized List of Fragile Situations for FY 17.

Notes

1 We have benefited from comments on earlier drafts by Balu Bumb, Javier Ekboir, Gershon Feder, Douglas Gollin, William Hurlbut, Ravi Kanbur, Richard Manning, Prabhu Pingali, Stephen O'Brien, Pasquale Lucio Scandizzo, and Adrian Wood. We alone are responsible for any deficiencies that remain.

2 They are the Philippines, St. Kitts, China, Egypt, Equatorial Guinea, Macedonia FYR (Former Yugoslav Republic), Albania, Montenegro, Serbia, Indonesia, Azerbaijan, Angola, Armenia, Bosnia and Herzegovina, Georgia, and India. Eight countries graduated before 1990, but reentered IDA again. They are Nigeria, Côte d'Ivoire, Honduras, Cameroon, Nicaragua, Republic of the Congo, Papua New Guinea, and Zimbabwe.

3 We excluded 6 countries of 24 IDA-graduated and reentered or "reverse graduated" countries from our analysis for lack of continuous data. They are: Bosnia and Herzegovina, Equatorial Guinea, Macedonia FYR, Montenegro, Serbia, and St. Kitts.

4 They are India, Mexico, China, Brazil, Indonesia, Pakistan, Turkey, Nigeria, Morocco, Philippines, Egypt, Bangladesh, Romania, Ethiopia, and Tanzania.

5 Other sectors (except ARD sector) include: Economic Policy; Education; Energy and Mining; Environment; Financial and Private Sector Development; Financial Management; Financial Sector; Financial Systems Practice; Gender and Development; Global Information/Communications Technology; Health, Nutrition and Population; Investment Climate Practice; Poverty Reduction; Private Sector Development; Public Sector Governance; Sector Board not Applicable; Social Development; Social Protection; Transport; Urban Development; and Water.

References

Birdsall, N., H. Kharas, A. Mahgoub, and R. Perakis. 2010. *Quality of Official Development Assistance Assessment*. Washington, DC: Center for Global Development.

Clemens, M. A., and M. Kremer. 2016. "The New Role for the World Bank." *Journal of Economic Perspectives* 30 (1): 53–76.

Clemens, M. A., S. Radelet, and R. Bhavnani. 2004. "Counting Chickens When They Hatch: The Short-Term Effect of Aid on Growth." CGD Working Paper No. 44, Center for Global Development, Washington, DC.

Custer, S., Z. Rice, T. Masake, R. Latourell, and B. Parks. 2015. "Listening to Leaders: Which Development Partners do they Prefer and Why?" AidData, Williamsburg, VA. http://aiddata.org/listening-to-leaders

Deaton, A. 2013. *The Great Escape: Health, Wealth, and the Origins of Inequality*. Princeton, NJ: Princeton University Press.

Denizer, C., D. Kaufmann, and A. Kraay. 2013. "Good Countries or Good Projects? Macro and Micro Correlates of World Bank Project Performance." *Journal of Development Economics* 105: 288–302.

Easterly, W. 2006. "Why Doesn't Aid Work?" *Cato Unbound*, April 2, 2006. http://www.cato-unbound.org/2006/04/02/william-easterly/why-doesnt-aid-work

Easterly, W., and T. Pfutze. 2008. "Where Does the Money Go? Best and Worst Practices in Foreign Aid." *Journal of Economic Perspectives* 22 (2): 29–52.

Easterly, W., and T. Pfutze. 2013. "Comment: Response from William Easterly and Tobias Pfutze." *Journal of Economic Perspectives* 23 (1): 243–6.

Easterly, W., and C. R. Williamson. 2011. "Rhetoric versus Reality: The Best and Worst of Aid Agency Practices." *World Development* 39 (11): 1930–49.

Felipe, J., A. Mehta, and C. Rhee. 2016. "Manufacturing Matters. . . but It's the Jobs that Count." Draft. (Extends the November 2014 Asian Development Bank Economics Working Paper No. 420, of the same name).

Fuglie, K., S. Wang, and V. Ball, eds. 2012. *Productivity Growth in Agriculture: An International Perspective*. Wallingford, UK: CAB International.

Gollin, D., R. Jedwab, and D. Vollrath. 2016. "Urbanization with and without Industrialization." *Journal of Economic Growth* 21 (1): 35–70.

Gray, C. 2014. "Finding Out What Works: Tracking Results in the Inter-American Development Bank." *Journal of Development Effectiveness* 6 (4): 480–9.

Haraguchi, N., C. F. C. Cheng, and E. Smeets. 2016. "The Importance of Manufacturing in Economic Development: Has this Changed?" Inclusive and Sustainable Industrial Development Working Paper Series/WP 1, United Nations Industrial Development Organization (UNIDO), Vienna.

IEG (Independent Evaluation Group). 2011. "World Bank Country-Level Engagement on Governance and Anticorruption: An Evaluation of the 2007 Strategy and Implementation Plan." Independent Evaluation Group, World Bank, Washington, DC.

Isenman, P. 2011. "Architecture, Allocations, Effectiveness and Governance: Lessons from Global Funds." ODI Meeting on Climate Change, Overseas Development Institute, London.

Isenman, P. 2012. "Learning from Assessments of Overall Effectiveness of Multilateral Organisations." Paper submitted to the Swedish Agency for Development Evaluation (SADEV), Stockholm.

Isenman, P., and A. Shakow. 2010. "Donor Schizophrenia and Aid Effectiveness: The Role of Global Funds." IDS Practice Paper No. 5, Institute of Development Studies at the University of Sussex, Brighton, UK.

Kanbur, R. 2004. "Cross-Border Externalities and International Public Goods: Implications for Aid Agencies." In *Global Tensions: Challenges and Opportunities in the World Economy*, edited by L. Benería and S. Bisnath, 54–64. London: Routledge.

Kanbur, R. 2016. "Can a Country be a Donor and a Recipient of Aid?" In *Development in India: Micro and Macro Perspectives*, edited by S. M. Dev and P. G. Babu, 71–81. India Studies in Business and Economics, New Delhi: Springer.

Kanbur, R., and A. Sumner. 2012. "Poor Countries or Poor People? Development Assistance and the New Geography of Global Poverty." *Journal of International Development* 24 (6): 686–95.

Kharas, H. 2007. "Trends and Issues in Development Aid." Wolfensohn Center for Development Working Paper 1, Brookings Institution, Washington, DC.

Kharas, H. 2008. "Measuring the Cost of Aid Volatility." Wolfensohn Center for Development Working Paper 3, Brookings Institution, Washington, DC.

Kharas, H. 2009. "Action on Aid: Steps toward Making Aid More Effective." Brookings Institution, Washington, DC.

Lal, D. 2006. "Reply to Easterly: There Is No Fix for Aid." *Cato Unbound*, April 3, 2006. http://www.cato-unbound.org/2006/04/06/deepak-lal/there-no-fix-aid

Lele, U. 2016. "Exit, Voice, and Loyalty: Lessons from Brexit for Global Governance." Brookings Institution. July 7, 2016. https://www.brookings.edu/blog/future-development/2016/07/07/exit-voice-and-loyalty-lessons-from-brexit-for-global-governance/.

Lele, U., M. Agarwal, S. Goswami, with K. White and E. Ramborger. 2017. *Food for All: International Organizations and the Transformation of Agriculture*. Oxford: Oxford University Press, forthcoming.

OECD (Organisation for Economic Co-operation and Development). 2015. OECD Statistics: Multilateral Aid. http://www.oecd.org/dac/aid-architecture/multilateralaid.htm

Radelet, S. 2006. "A Primer on Foreign Aid." CGD Working Paper Number 92, Center for Global Development, Washington, DC. http://www.cgdev.org/files/8846_file_WP92.pdf

Ravallion, M. 2016. "The World Bank: Why It Is Still Needed and Why It Still Disappoints." *Journal of Economic Perspectives* 30 (1): 77–94.

Rodrik, D. 1996. "Why Is There Multilateral Lending?" In *Annual World Bank Conference on Development Economics 1995*, edited by M. Bruno and B. Pleksovic, 167–205. Washington, DC: IBRD.

Rodrik, D. 2016. Premature Deindustrialization. *Journal of Economic Growth* 21: 1–33.

Rondinelli, D. A. 1993. *Development Projects as Policy Experiments: An Adaptive Approach to Development Administration.* New York: Routledge.

Timmer, C. P. 2009. *A World without Agriculture: The Structural Transformation in Historical Perspective.* Washington, DC: AEI Press.

Timmer, C. P. 2015. *Food Security and Scarcity: Why Ending Hunger Is So Hard.* Philadelphia: University of Pennsylvania Press.

Timmer, C. P., and S. Akkus. 2008. "The Structural Transformation as a Pathway out of Poverty: Analytics, Empirics and Politics." Working Papers 150, Center for Global Development, Washington, DC.

Wood, A. 2003. "Could Africa Be like America?" In *Annual Bank Conference on Development Economics 2003*, edited by B. Pleskovic and N. Stern, 163–200. Washington, DC and New York: World Bank and Oxford University Press.

World Bank. 2007. *World Development Report 2008: Agriculture for Development.* Washington, DC: World Bank.

World Bank. 2010. "IDA's Performance Based Allocation System: Review of the Current System and Key Issues for IDA16." IDA16, World Bank, Washington, DC. http://documents. worldbank.org/curated/en/814051468159604047/IDAs-performance-based-allocation-system-review-of-the-current-system-and-key-issues-for-IDA16

World Bank. 2012. "IDA 16: Review of IDA's Graduation Policy." IDA Resource Mobilization Department Concessional Finance and Global Partnerships. World Bank, Washington, DC. http://documents.worldbank.org/curated/en/833691468338981825/Review-of-IDAs-graduation-policy

World Bank. 2013. *Capital for the Future: Saving and Investment in an Interdependent World.* Global Development Horizons (GDH) series. Washington, DC: World Bank. http:// documents.worldbank.org/curated/en/2013/05/17723744/global-development-horizons-capital-future-saving-investment-interdependent-world.

World Bank. 2014. *World Bank Group Assistance to Low-Income Fragile and Conflict-Affected States: An Independent Evaluation.* Independent Evaluation Group, World Bank, Washington, DC.

World Bank. 2016a. "IDA 18: The Demand for IDA18 Resources and the Strategy for their Effective Use." IDA Resource Mobilization Department (DFiRM). World Bank, Washington, DC. http://documents.worldbank.org/curated/en/160171468191361245/IDA18-the-demand-for-IDA18-resources-and-the-strategy-for-their-effective-use

World Bank. 2016b. "International Development Association (IDA) 18: Special Theme – Climate Change." IDA Resource Mobilization Department (DFiRM). World Bank, Washington, DC. http://documents.worldbank.org/curated/en/661931467989537070/International-Development-Association-IDA-18-special-theme-climate-change

World Bank. 2016c. "IDA18 Overarching Theme – Towards 2030: Investing in Growth, Resilience and Opportunity." IDA Resource Mobilization Department (DFiRM). World Bank, Washington, DC. http://documents.worldbank.org/curated/en/471761467993490105/IDA18-IDA18-overarching-theme-towards-2030-investing-in-growth-resilience-and-opportunity

World Bank. 2016d. "IDA 18: Special Theme – Governance and Institutions." IDA Resource Mobilization Department (DFiRM). World Bank, Washington, DC. http://documents. worldbank.org/curated/en/368341467989536274/International-Development-Association-IDA-18-special-theme-governance-and-institutions

World Bank. 2016e. Projects & Operations Data. http://www.worldbank.org/projects? lang=en

World Bank. 2016f. World Bank/IEG Project Performance Ratings Data. http://data. worldbank.org/data-catalog/IEG

17 The relevance of the CGIAR in a modernizing world

Or has it been reformed *ad infinitum* into dysfunctionality?

Alex F. McCalla

Introduction

The Consultative Group on International Agricultural Research (CGIAR) was created in 1971, in a time of grave concerns about feeding the world. It was crafted as an informal, decentralized mechanism to let scientists, rather than aid bureaucrats, set the research agenda. It has been judged to be a very successful organization, yet it has been subjected to constant reform efforts for the last 20 years. Is it better off for all of this fiddling? This chapter addresses that question by first, for those unfamiliar with its origins, reviewing its unique characteristics and its early scope. We then fast-forward to 2016 to review the global food security challenges today, and then forward to 2050 to ask how the CGIAR will have responded to those changes. Some would argue not so well – we address how well the CGIAR responded. The chapter closes with some thoughts about how the CGIAR would be better off restructuring from the bottom up, rather than fiddling endlessly with successive layers of management and governance superstructure – leaving the basic building blocks, the centers, unchanged.

Origins, initial challenges, and unique characteristics of the CGIAR

The CGIAR, formally established in 1971, had its origins in a unique partnership between the Rockefeller Foundation (RF) and the Ford Foundation (FF). In the 1960s, the two foundations had established four international agricultural research centers – IRRI (the International Rice Research Institute), 1960; CIMMYT (Centro Internacional de Mejoramiento de Maiz y Trigo), 1966; IITA (International Institute of Tropical Agriculture), 1967; and CIAT (Centro Internacional de Agricultura Tropical), 1967. They were formed to meet – what was considered to be, in the 1960s – a serious likelihood of widespread famine. The concerns were fanned by two bad monsoons in 1965 and 1966, which reduced grain production in South Asia and underlined the fragility of the global food production capacity.

Recall this was the decade of the Paddock brothers' *Famine 1975! America's Decision: Who Will Survive?* (Paddock and Paddock 1967) and Paul Ehrlich's *Population*

Bomb (1968), which talked about the need for global triage to decide who would starve. It led Caltech's early molecular biology star, James Bonner, in his review of *Famine 1975!* (in *Science*), to state, "All serious students of the plight of the under-developed nations agree that famine among the peoples of the underdeveloped nations *is inevitable*" (Bonner 1967, 914). The names of Norman Borlaug and M. S. Swaminathan were not yet on the global radar screen. The price spike of 1973–74 caused fears to soar again, and Ehrlich (1974) was at it again, publishing *The End of Affluence*, in which he declared that India was doomed.

The financial challenge of creating an international agricultural research system, however, exceeded the Foundation's financial resources, especially after the US reform of rules for charitable foundations hit the Ford Foundation especially hard, causing a halving of its outlays. An appeal to the World Bank for funding helped to bring the newly appointed World Bank president Robert McNamara into the picture. McNamara bought the concept of an informal international research network and worked hard to create a way bilateral and multilateral aid donors could support what the RF and FF had started. He did not want what became the CGIAR to fall into the clutches of aid bureaucrats who had, in his view, short-term, quick-fix mentalities and, moreover, did not understand agriculture or research.

The result was a unique organization – a *virtual* entity – which was, in reality, nothing more than an informal forum facilitated by the World Bank – where *three* independent pillars of the system could meet: (1) *independent centers* with their own Boards of Trustees; (2) *independent donors*, who could give directly to their center of choice (no pooling of funds); and (3) *independent technical advice* from a Technical Advisory Committee (TAC) made up of global scientific experts. The TAC advised on what new areas needed to be addressed in periodic priority papers. Each year centers made detailed presentations of their proposed research programs to donors, which were followed by pledging sessions in which donors pledged money to support centers of their choice. The World Bank, serving as the donor of last resort, made the program coherent by bringing underfunded centers up to agreed-upon priority funding levels.

The name "Consultative Group" came from a long-standing World Bank procedure of convening all donors to a particular country to determine if all were on the same page. The CGIAR was not a legal entity; it had no funds of its own. It was highly informal with decisions depending on rulings of consensus, as determined by the chairman. The World Bank provided the secretariat and the chair, who was always a Bank vice president with agriculture in his or her portfolio.

By the time the CGIAR was formally approved in 1971, it was already a blazing success as IRRI and CIMMYT both had produced high-yielding, semi-dwarf rice and wheat cultivars, which were credited with staving off a famine in South Asia in the latter part of the 1960s. The second two centers were not conceived as commodity centers like IRRI and CIMMYT, but rather were focused on complex tropical farming systems in Africa (IITA) and Latin America (CIAT).

All four had clear and simple missions – increase the productivity of the targeted production system – commodity or tropical farming system.

The CGIAR was at the outset a small, informal operation – four centers, 11 donors, and a budget of $US15 million – but there were many other proposed or existing centers at the gates, waiting to get in. By 1976, there were 11 centers and 26 donors, and the budget had quadrupled to $US63 million. Fast-forward to 2016: when the CGIAR was, in at least one year (2013), a billion dollar operation, with a much broader agenda, a multilayered superstructure, *but an unchanged first-level structure of 15 independent, primarily commodity-focused research centers*. The question asked here is, how well is it positioned to meet today's and tomorrow's challenges?

Global challenges today and forward to 2050

Population growth, income growth, and urbanization

When the IRRI was established in 1960, the world population had just reached 3 billion people; by 1999, in just 39 years, it had doubled to 6 billion people, and today, it exceeds 7.4 billion. It is forecast to be 9.7 billion in 2050 – more than tripling in 90 years. All growth going forward will be in currently developing countries, and the population on average will be richer and two-thirds will live in urban areas, most in megacities in the now developing world. The Food and Agriculture Organization of the United Nations (FAO) estimated in 2010 that the quantities of food needed would rise by an estimated 70 percent (this was before the UN median population projection was increased from 9.2 to 9.7 billion) (FAO 2010). Food demand will be more varied and complex, and to get the food from farm gate to the dining table will require a much more sophisticated and longer delivery system.

No more land, less water, and adjusting to global warming

The production system that will have to produce the additional food, including nearly doubling supplies of livestock products and fruits and vegetables, will have to do it by increasing productivity on the existing land base and with less water, while adjusting to global warming.

FAO's most recent report, *Climate Change and Food Systems*, uses very strong language: "The growing threat of climate change to the global food supply, and the challenges it poses for food security and nutrition, requires urgent concerted policy responses," wrote Maria Helena Semedo, FAO Deputy Director-General of Natural Resources, in her foreword to the volume (FAO 2015, xi).

The book's editor, Aziz Elbehri, of FAO's Trade and Markets Division, stated, "climate change is likely to exacerbate growing *global inequality* as the brunt of the negative climate effects is expected to fall on those countries that are least developed and most vulnerable" (FAO 2015, 10).

Less certain sources of energy

Petroleum will eventually reach its limits, and renewable sources will have to expand rapidly. These clearly will include biomass, which will compete with the food supply system for land and water.

Global political system more complex and unstable

The end of the Cold War and the bipolar standoff have led to increased regional and national conflicts and increased geopolitical instability. Food and refugee crises are on the increase. These are always accompanied by hunger and disease.

Global economic performance since the 2008 recession seems to be mixed and more unstable, leading to growing income disparities

Expanded international trade in resources, goods, and services plus access to the Internet and instantaneous forms of communication has made the world more interdependent and more prone to international instability.

Molecular biology revolution is not yet fully played out

The scientific revolution in biology has fundamentally changed the nature of agricultural research in many ways. It has greatly enhanced our understanding of how plants and animals function and transmit traits. We can now map genomes and better understand how organisms grow, manage stress, and try to protect themselves from disease and insect attacks. We have learned how to make interspecies genetic transfers, which has both opened vast new possibilities for genetic improvements and ignited debate about the desirability of GMOs (genetically modified organisms) – a debate that threatens future positive possibilities.

Intellectual property rights and the expansion of private sector investment

The increased understanding of how organisms work and the possibilities of interspecies transfer of traits, coupled with changes in the management of intellectual property rights, has encouraged growing private sector investments in agricultural research, while the costs and scale of doing modern molecular biology research have made it a much more expensive proposition. Large-scale and long-term investment requirements mean that the ability of research programs to survive merely on annual aid funding is becoming more challenging and potentially insecure.

Sir Gordon Conway has written a powerful and comprehensive analysis of the challenges ahead in meeting future food needs. Provocatively titled *One Billion Hungry: Can We Feed the World?* Conway presents, in my view, the best, most comprehensive analysis of the challenge. It is buttressed by an incredible exposition of the complex scientific challenges and an extensive review of the literature. Conway characterizes the problem as an *acute and chronic crisis* caused by a complex set of interactions between physical, biological, economic, social, and political forces far more complicated and serious than the challenges of the 1960s and early 1970s. A repeat of the Green Revolution in not enough, he says. What is needed is a "Doubly Green Revolution" – a revolution that substantially and sustainably increases the productivity of a wide range of agricultural commodities and species grown in an immense spectrum of complex farming systems, large and small.

At the core is sustainable intensification of farming systems, particularly of small-scale farming systems operated by hundreds of millions of small farmers producing both crops and livestock. This will require appropriate technology, access to markets, capitalizing on farmers as innovators, integrated pest management, better conservation management of soils, more efficient use of less available amounts of water, and dealing with climate change. It is a tall order. At the core is reducing rural poverty by increasing the productivity of small subsistence farmers and finding markets for their surplus production. If this happens, it has the triple benefit of increasing food supplies, improving incomes of the rural poor, and better managing precious natural resources.

Conway's last chapter asks, can it be done? Conway notes that he is an optimist, saying, *it can be done if . . .* and then proceeds to list 24 "ifs." Among them are that, globally, everybody must be on the same page, substantially increasing investments in science and technology; reducing policy distortions, especially in trade; using the best science has to offer ("*we accept that biotechnology is an essential tool in attaining food security*" [Conway 2012, 304]); and developing partnerships among nations and between the public and private sectors. The book is a difficult read, is loaded with complex science, uses a complicated truly general equilibrium approach, and is a tersely written analysis, but it is the best I have found. Interestingly, the CGIAR gets very little mention as part of the solution.

How has the CGIAR responded to radical global changes and resulting challenges?

By 2015–16, the CGIAR had grown in: size (15 instead of the original 4 centers); number of scientists; and budget ($1 billion in 2013). In the 44 years of its existence, the world's population has more than doubled and will triple by 2050. Global agricultural research priorities have changed radically from the simple goal of "doubling the pile of rice" to building environmentally sustainable production systems, toward the goals of food security and poverty reduction. The molecular biology revolution has greatly enhanced possible scientific breakthroughs. Computer and modeling developments have opened the potential for better natural resources management, policy analysis, and projections. The global economy has grown rapidly and become much more interdependent and unstable. Global warming, desertification, and the loss of biodiversity have all emerged as critical global issues with significant potential impact on the world's capacity to feed itself.

And how has the CGIAR responded?

It has fiddled with its administrative bureaucratic superstructure, but left its research platforms – the centers – basically unchanged. Over the same 44 years, innumerable committees, study teams, ministerial consultations, task forces, change design and management teams, steering groups, independent reviews, transition management teams, and restructuring consultants have sought to reform the CGIAR. Its organizational simplicity and focus have been repeatedly attacked and pushed in the direction of becoming a centralized corporate structure with top-down management.

So much talk, analysis, and study and yet *little fundamental change* has happened in the *basic building blocks* of the CGIAR System – "a loose federation of independent Centers" (McCalla 2014, 8). Many *system governance mechanisms* have been added: committees galore – executive, steering, oversight, finance, and on relations with the private sector and the NGO community; and since 2010, two new global entities: a *CGIAR Consortium* with a Board, a CEO, and an office; and a *CGIAR Fund*, with a Fund Council and Fund Office. An attempt to illustrate the "New CGIAR" graphically is presented in Figure 17.1, which shows instead a complicated set of boxes and arrows, defying simple explanations.

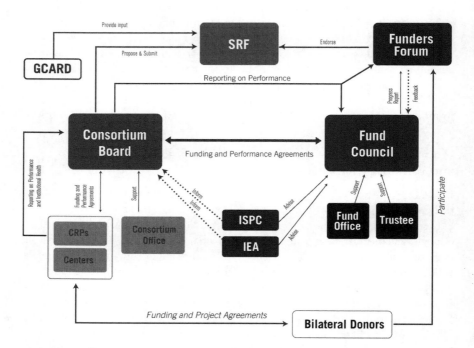

Figure 17.1 The "New CGIAR" as depicted by Selçuk Özgediz in *The CGIAR at 40*
Source: Reprinted from Özgediz (2012, 88).

To try to address the fact that the world has changed, as has the research and development agenda, the CGIAR has also implemented successive overlays of programmatic superstructures: *Ecoregional* and *Systemwide Programs* in the 1990s; *Challenge Programs* in the early 2000s; and in 2008–2010, 16 *CGIAR Research Programs (CRPs)*. Over the last 20 years, the system has added in excess of 20 Inter-Center Initiatives, Systemwide and Ecoregional Programs (of which some remain on the books), five Challenge Programs (CPs), and now the 16 CRPs. Each CRP quickly developed its own management structures and advisory panels. As noted in the *Final Report of the Mid-Term Review Panel of the CGIAR Reform,*

> The joint submission from the Centers states that "each CRP has a program management committee with an average size of roughly 10 members thus engaging 150 people (15 CRP X 10 members) at the management level with statutory meeting roughly four times per year. In addition, each CRP has an advisory committee/panel/board of roughly 10 people each, thus engaging about another 150 people at the advisory/governance level, meeting on average twice per year."
>
> (CGIAR 2014, 24)

Putting this additional management and governance bureaucracy on top of long-standing and already existing similar management structures for each of the 15 CGIAR Centers has obviously more than doubled the management super-structure overload. The Technical Advisory Committee (TAC), the one original committee, has been reorganized and renamed at least four times. Much also has been added in terms of subject matter: 20 more food commodities, forestry, fisheries, water management, policy, and capacity building. But it is still the same 15 centers that house CGIAR scientists and provide the research platform to manage the work (see McCalla [2014] for details on reform attempts).

By 2014, issues of excessive bureaucracy, high transaction costs, Centers feeling left out and not being on the same page as the Consortium Board and CEO, and lack of communication between the now two governing boards emerged. All of this and more was exacerbated by drops in funding levels and led to the commissioning of a Mid-Term Review Panel of the CGIAR Reform. Their final report in late 2014 contains a comprehensive and critical review of CGIAR's lack of a strategy, lack of efficiency, rising transaction costs, and general lack of clarity of who was responsible for what. It also contains a hard-hitting pathology of many bureaucratic governance problems that were not solved, and in many cases made worse, by the 2008–2010 "creation" of the "New CGIAR" (CGIAR 2014).

So the system in 2015 was again trying to reform itself. It finally produced a comprehensive *CGIAR Strategy and Results Framework 2016–2030*, which was approved by the Consortium Board and the Fund Council in May 2015 (CGIAR Consortium 2015). It contains a global vision of "*a world free of poverty, hunger, and environmental degradation*" (2015, 1); a mission statement so micro that it could be for a village-level rural development project; 3 goals (System Level Outcomes, or SLOs), and each SLO has 2–4 targets for two future years, 2022 and 2030, for a total of 20 targets; 10 Intermediate Development Outcomes (IDOs), and 30 sublevel IDOs; and 4 crosscutting themes – climate change, gender and youth, policies and institutions, and capacity development. The complexity of how all these dimensions fit together is attempted in something called the *CGIAR Results Framework.* But there is more – there are also eight research priorities listed to help the CGIAR reach its targets. The documents claim the CGIAR will develop a "theory of change" (2015, 4) to make sure that research outcomes have impact. The result is a complex maze of overlapping objectives, which are almost incomprehensible.

The *Independent Science and Partnership Council (ISPC)* will provide guidance "through an appropriate qualitative prioritization for the next generation of CRP's" (CGIAR Consortium 2015, 6). The only quantitative guideline in the whole document is that the system will spend over 50 percent of its investments in Africa, about 30 percent in Asia, and about 20 percent on poverty hot spots in Latin America. And as if it is not already complicated enough, they "will develop Site Integration Plans to bring together the work of CGIAR Centers and programs in key countries" (2015, 6).

How this multifaceted, multilayered set of SLOs, IDOs, sub-IDOs, targets, research priorities, and crosscutting issues will be translated into the CGIAR's research program is not clear. As it is written, it is so all-inclusive that almost any research or development project could be a priority. The Mid-Term Review Panel reached the same conclusion: "The Mission reflected in the SLOs . . . is remarkably broad. It would not be too difficult to justify almost any research and development proposal as fitting this mission" (CGIAR 2014, 23).

Perhaps the expectation was that it would come together as the Centers prepared the next round of CRPs. The call asked for pre-proposals for the CRP II Portfolio, which would contain 13 CRPs, down from the current 16 CRPs. CRP II will be "structured around two interlinked clusters of challenge-led research" (Rijsberman 2016) (Cluster 1 is about innovation in Agri-food Systems (AFS) and contains eight CRPs with very familiar names: Rice; Wheat; Maize; Dryland Cereals and Legumes; Roots, Tubers, and Bananas; Livestock; Fish; and Forestry and Agroforestry. Cluster 2 is made up of Global Integrating Programs (GIPs): Gene Banks; Nutrition and Health; Water, Land, and Ecosystems; Climate Change; and Policies, Institutions, and Markets. In addition, the call asked for Expressions of Interest by Centers in coordinating one of four crosscutting platforms addressing gender, capacity development, genetic resources policy, or big data and ICT (information and communications technology).

While the Strategy and Results Framework (SRF), commissioned by the CGIAR Consortium, was going through its multiple revisions, the Fund Council commissioned a paper titled "Options for CGIAR Structures and Decision-Making" to propose options for improving systems governance mechanisms following the report of the Mid-Term Review Panel of the CGIAR Reform in 2014. The report is 50+ pages of detailed discussions about administrative structure, lines of authority, and page upon page of tedious discussion about how to enforce fiduciary responsibility. However, little is said about how all of this relates to the research mission. After reviewing six "comparable international entities" the Options report presented four options for improving CGIAR governance (CGIAR Fund 2015).

They recommended the most comprehensive, "radical" Option 4, which was accepted at the Fund Council Meeting, April 28–29, 2015, in Bogor, Indonesia. Option 4 proposed to restructure and broaden the Consortium Board into a System Council and abolish the Fund Council, shifting its responsibilities to the new System Council. The option proposed combining the two system-wide offices into one CGIAR System Office and appointing a CGIAR System CEO. The location of the CGIAR System Office would be Montpelier, France. So, yet another round of reform begins, the third in the last eight years. This proposal, if finally implemented, will create a top-down, centralized corporate bureaucracy, the very antithesis of what the original founders created. One could say the CGIAR, as a conceptual model is gone, and only the name remains.

How much these proposed changes will help to reduce the multiple layers of bureaucracy and improve CGIAR efficiency is questionable, given that the new CGIAR Council will have no more authority over the independent centers than did the Consortium Board. And whether it moves the CGIAR back to a focused, strategic agricultural research outfit is unclear.

A positive element did come out of the Bogor meeting. The Fund Council agreed to move toward a stable, multiyear, replenishment-style funding system, with a targeted, quantitative resource mobilization strategy. Any movement toward longer-term, more stable funding has to be seen as a positive step.

A final comment on the Bogor decisions seems appropriate. The World Bank has always played a special leadership role in the CGIAR: leading its early development (Robert McNamara); being a stable, large, unrestricted core donor, and in early years the donor of last resort; serving as a cosponsor; providing the CGIAR/Fund Council Secretariat; and always providing the chair. If all of these linkages are broken, the Bank may cut its funding even more than it already has (US$30 million, down from US$50 million), as many within the Bank want it to, and drift away. This would surely have a destabilizing, if not lethal, impact on the CGIAR.

Has this constant fiddling with system governance mechanisms and programmatic management structures better positioned the CGIAR to respond to a changed world? Some would argue the opposite and charge that the CGIAR has lost its focus, is no longer on the cutting edge in terms of science, can no longer attract the best and the brightest scientists, and is smothered in bureaucracy that constantly escalates transaction costs and detracts scientists from doing science. It is no longer a focused, applied agricultural research organization, because it is being asked to do a wide variety of tasks, many of which better fit the definition of development assistance than research. Alas, it is said, the aid and World Bank bureaucrats have finally taken over the show.

Some estimate that strategic applied research now gets less than 30 percent of the budget. The system seems to have lost its coherence, with mega centers fighting each other for bigger budgets, as direct donor support to Centers still is about equal to unrestricted core support to CGIAR system priorities (CRPs), each getting about 40 percent of the funds. But these numbers do not include direct support to bilateral projects within Centers. In fact, the Mid-Term Review states that "centers raise about 65 percent of total CGIAR funding" (CGIAR 2015, 30), as Center-specific support or bilateral project support – this, despite the avowed intent of trying to channel all funds through CRPs, and not Centers.

Knowledgeable veterans of the CGIAR say that they feel that the CGIAR may not exist in ten years, even though the food supply challenges as we approach a world of 10 billion people are, according to Sir Gordon Conway (2012), much greater than they were in the 1960s and 1970s. How valid are these concerns? Can the proposed new version of the CGIAR help meet the challenge? The remainder of the chapter focuses on these questions.

How well has the CGIAR responded to a changing world?

Changes in science

The rapid advances in molecular biology, and in computer and information sciences, in recent decades have been breathtaking. In biology, the advances in our understanding of how sexually reproduced organisms – especially plants and animals – function continue to create tantalizing opportunities for productivity improvement, using upstream advances in molecular biology. Modern molecular biology, however, requires large-scale, sophisticated, and expensive facilities and with big teams of scientific talent that are leaders in their fields. One molecular biology company, Monsanto, has spent more on fundamental and applied agricultural research each year since 2009 (US$1 billion+) than the CGIAR spent in its best year, 2013. Monsanto's R&D budget in 2014 was US$1.725 billion. And Monsanto is only one of four or five major private sector companies investing in basically proprietary agricultural research. Team research across commodities in large-scale, modern facilities is the order of the day.

The CGIAR's budget is spread across 16 CRPs being operated by 15 independent Centers. Centers have complex and expensive management and governance systems, and CRPs, as noted earlier, are similarly accumulating large and expensive separate management and advisory systems. The largest CGIAR Center budget in the best year (2013) was CIMMYT at US$150 million, followed by the International Food Policy Research Institute (IFPRI) at US$108 million, IRRI at US$78 million, IITA at US$72 million, and ILRI at US$71 million; five centers have budgets less than US$50 million, and the smallest is AfricaRice at under US$30 million.

The CGIAR's talent in molecular biology is scattered across at least eight Centers and probably is below critical minimum mass in most, if not all of them. This means that the CGIAR has basically missed the molecular biology train. It should be in the lead, especially as it relates to regionally, but not globally, important food crops. It could partially offset this deficiency with partnerships with the private sector, but there is little evidence of this being done on a comprehensive and coherent scale. The CGIAR is further constrained by some donors, particularly European, who are negative toward biotechnology and GMOs.

The CGIAR continues to resist adjusting its fragmented system of small, individual commodity-focused centers to the new scientific realities, meaning that, in the eyes of some, the CGIAR now has only a limited ability to take advantage of new scientific opportunities. Further, it has made it more difficult to attract the best young scientists and provide them with first-class, expensive facilities. Thus, one of the critical roles historically played by the CGIAR – that is, a link between advanced institutions, public and private, and developing countries' national programs is eroding.

Changes in the global research agenda

As time passed, the global research agenda necessarily became more complex and interdisciplinary, as issues of the environment, natural resource management, ecosystem sustainability, poverty, nutrition, climate change, water, aquatic resources, and so forth have come on board. The CGIAR's donors have pushed for a broadened agenda. As the CGIAR is a creature of its donors, who basically come from the development world, they have insisted that the CGIAR cover the spectrum from strategic research all the way to the delivery mechanisms. In the development game, it's called mission creep. Thus, it became harder to keep focused on a clearly defined, selective research agenda. Further, the early success of the CGIAR in wheat and rice improvement attracted donors who wanted to use this apparently successful mechanism to address their other different or pet priorities. Periodic slowdowns in traditional CGIAR funding led successive CGIAR chairs to seek new funding sources, necessitating, of course, the expansion of the mandate, as happened first in forestry in 1988–89.

These changes might have been manageable if the original informal concept of the CGAIR had been sustained – independent centers, independent donors, and independent scientific advice; unrestricted core funding; limited periodic reviews; and the World Bank as donor of last resort to link scientific priorities to funding. When Chairman Ismail Serageldin (seventh chair, from 1993–2000) broke the link between system priorities and resource allocation and brought bilaterally funded special projects into the system, the only mechanism for system coherence disappeared. The result of Centers having the freedom to adjust their activities to induce donor support was the loss of a coherent CGIAR system research program. What remains is the summation of individual Center and CRP funding, which is unlikely to add up to the total budget because of overlap and competition.

The CGIAR has become a development organization

In search of funding, the CGIAR has often gone downstream, focusing on multiple interdisciplinary, decentralized partnerships – paying more attention to theories of change and potential impact pathways than to cutting-edge research. A quote from the newest CGIAR Results and Strategy Framework 2016–2030 is disturbing (emphasis added):

> To make sure our research outputs have impact, we will build on earlier GCARD [Global Conference on Agricultural Research for Development] consultation processes and put in place a *theory of change*: This will identify the expected changes and benefits for the next users of these outputs, and what needs to occur for these outputs to be translated into outcomes among targeted groups.
>
> (CGIAR Consortium 2015, 4, 6)

This does not describe research; it is development rhetoric. Research is about discovering things that we do not know the answers to, adding to knowledge, discovering new facts, and verifying hypotheses. The foregoing statement encapsulates why the CGIAR has lost its standing as a frontier-level research organization.

In the development business, the CGIAR has many more competitors: International Fund for Agricultural Development (IFAD), FAO, World and Regional Development Banks, 100+ bilateral aid agencies, and thousands of nongovernmental organizations (NGOs) doing agricultural development work, some with budgets bigger than the CGIAR (e.g., World Vision). The CGIAR played an almost unique role as an applied research organization focused on international public goods relevant to expanding sustainable food supplies, improving nutrition, and indirectly reducing poverty by making small farms potentially profitable. That unique quality, however, is greatly diminished because the further the CGIAR goes downstream toward the delivery end, the lesser its comparative advantage. Although this work could be done, in principle, by partners, the CGIAR, in practice, is involved all over the map.

Yes, partnerships and team research, both disciplinary and interdisciplinary, are critical to addressing the complex challenges that Sir Gordon Conway so clearly spelled out and in which the CGIAR should be engaged. It should be at necessary scale, highly focused, and using the best minds and cutting-edge science. The CGIAR should be positioning itself between basic and upstream, applied research done by advanced institutions – public and private – and national program partners. It must focus on exploring how new fundamental developments can be applied to a focused set of problems, identified as critical priorities for the vision and mission of the CGIAR. It should be a working partner of national programs that face serious food security issues with limited resources. Its Strategy and Results Framework is a broad tent, under which almost anything would qualify as a CGIAR priority. Belatedly asking the Science and Partnership

Council to reengage in priority setting shows how far away the CGIAR has drifted from linking priorities to funding.

Adding layers of bureaucratic superstructure has done little to adjust what was the premier international agricultural research organization to the realities of the 21st century. Instead, it has taken science out of priority setting and let the aid agenda dictate the research and development agenda. Even the price spikes of 2007–08 and 2010–11 and the potentially devastating impacts of global warming have not refocused the development community on the long-term, difficult research problems of sustainable agriculture and improved food security. The CGIAR has succumbed to development speak instead – impact pathways, outcomes rather than output, and developing theories of change – and is getting further out of step with the challenges that are facing it (if it had read the Conway [2012] treatise).

Some thoughts about how the CGIAR could be revitalized

The foregoing may seem unduly negative and suggesting that the obvious conclusion is that within a decade or so the CGIAR might well collapse under the weight of its own bureaucracy and management ineptitude, disappearing from the global scene as yet another failed international organization. If that were to happen, it would be such a great pity, because there is still much to do that could be best done by an international research organization focused on international public goods, as the CGIAR was set up to be.

Can it be saved? The answer could be a qualified yes – but only if the CGIAR undertakes a restructuring from the bottom up rather than from the top down – its current inclination. It needs to rediscover what made the CGIAR so successful in its early years. The concepts of independence of centers, donors, and scientific advice, organized in an informal consortium of centers, are still valid. In a rapidly changing world, however, that does not mean that the same static numbers and mandates of the current Centers must persist. Every research organization must have a research platform on which to build and manage research programs. That platform needs long-term, core, unrestricted funding to provide first-class facilities, which will provide a stable research base for cutting-edge scientists. The nature of the facilities and the qualifications of scientists, however, must change over time to meet a changing agenda.

So the first question should be: are there still truly global public goods crucial to global food security, which would be underfunded or ignored by even the largest of countries? The CGIAR identified them in the beginning, reaffirmed them in the 1990s, and they are still valid: *genetic resources*; *cross-boundary natural resource management issues* – oceans, the atmosphere/climate change, river basins, forests and plains; erosion and desertification; and global water conservation, to name a few; *international policy challenges* – trade, exchange rate and capital flows, intellectual property rights, externalities of national policies, and access to the Internet; and *information on a global scale crucial to long-term food security*. Loss of attention to these critical global public goods that the CGIAR could provide would be devastating.

The second question is how best to determine scientific priorities for research relevant to the mission. As before, it has to be done by drawing upon the best scientific minds – public and private; the leading thinkers in the international development community; the forward thinkers from the private sector, all along the global supply chain; forecasts of future research needs as seen by the CGIAR's beneficiaries/clients and by NGOs; and by scholars and practitioners who study and implement national food security policies, as part of macro development policy. Ultimately, it will require a relatively large committee of the world's best thinkers, supported by a competent staff. It is critical that the CGIAR develop a clear set of goals and objectives and prioritized strategy for accomplishing them.

The third question is how best to organize the CGIAR, given the current state of science and future global food security priorities. To begin the analysis, let us assume the current CGIAR Strategic Results Framework (SRF) document generally contains the broad landscape of most of the critical elements, even though they may be too fragmented and not prioritized.

Therefore, let us critically look at the proposed 13 CRPs. Start with *Cluster I: Agri-food System Programs* – rice; wheat; maize; dryland cereals and legumes; roots, tubers, and bananas; livestock; fish; and forestry and agroforestry. Are individual commodity research programs still the best way to organize research? Modern molecular biology strongly suggests working across like commodities, which have great similarities in their genetic makeup. Therefore, why not combine the cereals and other annual crops into one Crops CRP – including rice, wheat, maize, millet, sorghum, and annual legumes. A second program could include root, tuber, and perennial food crops – for example, potatoes, sweet potatoes, yams, cassava, bananas, and plantains. A third could focus on the land use continuum from intensive agriculture to virgin boreal, temperate, and tropical forests. And a fourth one could focus on animal products/protein of fish and animals. So you could have four Agri-Food Systems programs, one of which, crops, would be very large. This would be an advantage, because it would be large enough to be of the necessary scale for engaging in modern molecular biology.

In the second cluster of Global Integrating Programs, one could also have four components: Nutrition and Health; Climate Change combined with Water, Land, and Ecosystems; Policies and Institutions; and Genetic Resources, making sure to put the totality of CGIAR genetic resources in one program.

Thus, you would have a total of eight major research programs and could then ask how best to restructure the CGIAR research platforms to deliver these programs, getting from where CGIAR is now to what is needed. It is not that complicated.

Starting with existing CGIAR Centers, one could first merge CIMMYT, IRRI, AfricaRice, ICRISAT, the International Center for Agricultural Research in the Dry Areas (ICARDA), and the cereals programs of IITA and CIAT into one decentralized Center – a *Global Cereals and Annual Legume Center* (GCALC) – and leave it to the new entity to decide what parts of existing infrastructure should be retained and be managed. Second, one could combine the International Potato Center (CIP), the cassava programs of CIAT and IITA, banana and plantain work from IITA, and Bioversity International into a Center using IITA and CIAT/CIP facilities. This would be the *Root, Tuber, Banana, and Perennial Crops Institute (RTBPI)*. Third, you would obviously merge the Center for International Forestry Research (CIFOR) and World AgroForestry into an *International Center for Forestry and Land Management (ICF&LM)*, and finally, merge International Livestock Research Institute (ILRI) and WorldFish into *a World Livestock and Fish Institute (WLFI)* to take care of the animal side of the business. These new entities could take up the research programs of Cluster I (AFS); thus, the formal structures of CRPs would be redundant and could be abolished. The Centers would be responsible for the research programs and the maintenance of the research platform. This approach would reduce Center numbers from 12 to 4, and oversight could be provided by a single Agri-Food System Board.

Organizing for the Global Integrating Cluster II is more complicated. Bioversity, with help from the four Global Commodity Centers, could manage *Genetic Resources*. The International Water Management Institute (IWMI) is the obvious lead center for *Climate Change, and Water, Land, and Ecosystems*, and IFRPI for *Policies and Institutions*. IFPRI could be the lead center in the case of *Nutrition and Health*, because of its cross-programmatic character, but draw scientific talent from other centers and partners, with the program overseen by a scientific advisory committee. For this cluster, you could have two boards, one focused exclusively on *Genetic Resources* collection, conservation, improvement, and preservation, both ex situ and in situ, with significant budget resources to work in partnership with the AFS centers. A second board could provide oversight and governance for the remainder of the *Global Public Good Programs*.

Some possible conclusions about how the CGIAR might remain relevant

In total, you could have seven research platforms (Centers) and three Boards of Trustees. There would be a need to greatly strengthen the Independent Science and Partnership Council, giving it responsibility for clearly articulated system priorities, proposed resource allocations, and authority to approve Center/CRP budgets. Best practice suggests continuing with an independent evaluation mechanism, as that now seems to be the international norm. The CGIAR could continue to participate in GCARD, but it should return to an Annual CGIAR meeting of substance, which would highlight the Centers' current research and future aspirations and involve all donors in the general meeting. Given the large number of donors, one would probably need a Donor Council. Clearly, the idea of a centralized corporate structure with a high-level board, an expensive CEO, and top-down management should disappear.

There would need to be a core, unrestricted multiyear fund to implement system priorities. It might be necessary to put bilateral projects back outside the core and return to periodic comprehensive program and management reviews.

Policies would be needed to restrict individual donor annual reviews of bilateral projects and to insure that these projects pay for full overhead and indirect costs.

To achieve this revitalized "old CGIAR" would require willingness by all players to recommit to meeting future needs, rather than protecting old turf. Donors would need to lead by agreeing to provide multiyear commitments of unrestricted funds to system priorities and refrain from funding pet bilateral projects on the side. Centers, and particularly their directors general and boards, would have to voluntarily give up long-standing mandates and independence to move via consolidation to build new platforms. It has been done before with the development of the ILRI. Multilateral entities, such as the World Bank, FAO, IFAD, World Health Organization (WHO), and World Trade Organization (WTO), need to lend political and financial support. There is no question that World Bank leadership would be critical. Emerging middle-income developing countries, especially those currently hosting Centers, have a special role to play, as both financial and intellectual donors. Multinational private sector firms should also be engaged intellectually and financially. Finally, private foundations should play a critical leadership role, as they did in the beginning of the CGIAR. The Gates Foundation, now the CGIAR's largest donor, could be the necessary hegemonic leader. Everybody needs to rise to the new challenges ahead.

The result would be a greatly simplified system with half the number of Centers and seven major programs. All of the costly overhead of CRPs competing with Centers, and all the costly inter-Center superstructure with two global boards, two system offices, and two competing CEOs, would disappear. And the CGIAR could go back to doing cutting-edge applied research relevant to feeding the world in 2050 and contributing to global food security.

Given population projections to 2050 (9.7 billion) and 2100 (11.2 billion) and the specter of global warming, some international entity will need to be producing critical international public goods. With redirection and commitment, it could be the CGIAR, with a budget headed for US$2 billion and beyond, spending at least 20 percent of its budget on its global comparative advantage in genetic resources and their application. Given population projections to 2100, at least 50 percent of its budget would be focused on Africa, which by 2100 will have over 4 billion people – over 40 percent of the global population. It should also be focused on and target programs for the poorest counties – Nigeria, Kenya, Ghana, and Uganda, for example, should be contributing to, not drawing from the CGIAR. Likewise, of course, middle-income countries, like India, China, and Brazil, should be contributing substantially, both intellectually and financially. The remainder of the budget could be targeted as follows: 10 percent to global, cross-country policy and natural resource management issues; 15 percent to poor countries and regions outside of Africa; and 5 percent to strategic linkage and translational research in partnership with advanced institutions and the private sector.

The CGIAR needs to be remodeled from the bottom up. Twenty years of fiddling with its bureaucratic superstructure have not worked. Left to continue in its current direction, the doomsayers could be proven correct, and that would be a major global loss.

References

Bonner, J. 1967. "Book Review: *Famine – 1975! America's Decision: Who Will Survive?*" *Science* 157 (3791): 914–15.

CGIAR. 2014. "Final Report from the Mid-Term Review Panel of the CGIAR Reform." https://library.cgiar.org/handle/10947/3368

CGIAR Consortium. 2015. "CGIAR Strategy and Results Framework 2016–2030: Redefining How CGIAR Does Business until 2030." Approved by the Consortium Board May 11, 2015 and approved by the CGIAR Fund Council May 18, 2015. CGIAR, Montpellier, France.

CGIAR Fund. 2015. "Options for CGIAR Governing Structures and Decision-Making." Working Document submitted to Fund Council 13th Meeting (FC13), Bogor, Indonesia, April 28–29, 2015.

Conway, G. 2012. *One Billion Hungry: Can We Feed the World?* New York: Cornell University Press.

Ehrlich, P. 1968. *The Population Bomb.* San Francisco: Sierra Club/Ballantine Books.

Ehrlich, P. 1974. *The End of Affluence: A Blueprint for Your Future.* New York: Ballantine Books.

FAO (Food and Agriculture Organization of the United Nations). 2010. "How to Feed the World in 2050." FAO, Rome.

FAO (Food and Agriculture Organization of the United Nations). 2015. *Climate Change and Food Systems: Global Assessments and Implications for Food Security and Trade.* Rome: FAO.

McCalla, A. 2014. "CGIAR Reform – Why So Difficult?" Giannini Foundation of Agricultural Economics Working Paper No. 14-001, Department of Agricultural and Resource Economics, University of California, Davis.

Özgediz, Selçuk. 2012. *The CGIAR at 40: Institutional Evolution of the World's Premier Agricultural Research Network.* Washington, DC: CGIAR Fund Office. https://library.cgiar.org/handle/10947/2761

Paddock, W., and P. Paddock. 1967. *Famine 1975! America's Decision: Who Will Survive?* Boston: Little, Brown and Co.

Rijsberman, F. 2016. "CGIAR Research Program and Platform Full Proposals Submitted for Review." CGIAR, April 11, 2016. http://www.cgiar.org/consortium-news/cgiar-research-program-platform-full-proposals-submitted-for-review/

Index

Note: Page numbers in *italics* denote references to Figures and Tables.